STAFFORD CLIFF

THE WAY WE LIVE

Making Homes / Creating Lifestyles

WITH 1162 COLOUR PHOTOGRAPHS BY

GILLES DE CHABANEIX

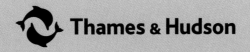

Thames & Hudson

THE WAY WE LIVE | *CHAPTER ONE*

INTRODUCTION

Homes and lifestyles

LOCATION

BUILDING

DESIGN

DECORATION

DETAIL

LIVING

ON THE VERY FIRST PAGE OF THIS BOOK there is an oddly mysterious picture of a man, apparently standing before half-open windows. The surreal quality of the image is due to its being, in fact, a *trompe-l'œil* feature on a façade in Rome. Yet, there is much in the image that fascinates us. Why is he there? What is he looking at? And can we see it, too? In a larger sense, this is a visual metaphor of the contents of this book, an account of how artifice is employed to make our environment a pleasanter place to live in – we design; we build; we decorate and embellish; and, hopefully, we have the freedom to take delight in what we have created. The windows behind the figure of the man are half-open, hinting at the interior on the other side; and, effectively, much of the subject-matter of the chapters which follow is perceived from the position of a person on the outside looking in. But the man is also looking out to a wider perspective, just as this remarkable photographic archive draws its material from homes and lifestyles around the world.

This is a book about living in the broadest and narrowest of senses; thus, it ranges from the bigger picture of humanity placing its imprint on the planet to the illustration of intimate details of decoration and design, to the day-to-day enjoyment and celebration of our homes and their surroundings. In their evocation of so many different and varied styles of living, these photographs constitute a unique body of detailed design inspiration, a record of how we live that is also a guide to where we might live in our various environments: by water, on the land, in villages, towns and cities around the world.

For the first time, we can observe here the solutions that individuals, families and whole communities have found to major concerns: choice of location; siting and building; decoration of interiors; cultivation of the areas around the home. Given the enormous range of places and dwellings illustrated on the pages of this book, it is striking and perhaps reassuring to see patterns emerging in the way people do things in very different habitats. At every stage in the broad processes of building, embellishing, refining and enjoying the final result, the

MOROCCO   SCOTLAND

connections and parallels between myriad national, regional and historical styles are almost more evident than the predictable

differences. The same attention to detail can clearly inform the arrangement of a dining-room in a modest Mexican home as it does in an exclusive club in Buenos Aires. Here, humble settings and structures, artefacts and designs commingle with the grandiose, elaborate and exclusive, sometimes revealing surprising similarities: an impoverished New York tenement interior, restored for historical purposes, finds echoes in fashionable London and Paris kitchens whose owners have a taste for the utensils of the pre-plastic age; a narrow street in Katmandu, essence of urban intensity, has its counterparts in Rome and Stockholm. Yet all these places are treated with the same sympathetic eye; the shack

BALI   MEXICO

or cottage interior, cheaply furnished, may yield as much decorative inspiration as the grandest of *palazzi* or the most exclusive of metropolitan apartments.

If there is a bias in this book, perhaps it is towards environments coated with the patinas of time and occupation, places and settings that have evolved and tell a story rather than those that have just emerged fresh from the interior designer's computer. This is really a book about what people make of their environment in their own way, with their own possessions, many or few, in their instinctive use of colours and

14

materials, in the way they inhabit the spaces they have made their own. Old and new, man-made and man-found co-exist happily; the textures, patinas and accretions of use and age are the visible expressions of our will to live as we wish.

Inevitably, much of the imagery in the chapters which follow (apart from the final chapter) is of the inanimate – buildings, architectural detail, interior spaces and individual objects. Even so, there is something in the way the camera has been directed that emphasizes the human scale in everything photographed. Arrangements of objects, the disposition of furniture in a room, the detailing on a façade, all look peculiarly enticing, lived-in, and full of promise and inspiration. We are led down narrow streets – some orderly, others chaotic – through doorways, alleys, passages and entrances, always looking out for the prospect of something

NEPAL   PHILIPPINES

delightful beyond. That 'beyond' may be a sunlit square vibrant with neighbourhood life, a seafront lined with fishing vessels, a market full of fresh produce, or a gorgeously and extravagantly appointed room, magnificently framed through an arch or open door. Staircases and other transitional spaces, like passages or landings, are given due importance as they connect different spaces within the same home,

leading us on from room to room, placing the particular in the context of the general.

Through the sequence of chapters and their sub-sections, we encounter the whole gamut of lifestyle options; the first concerns are with location: natural sites, buildings both in groups and individual, markets, shops, bars, cafés and churches. The textures of outward appearance are illustrated in profusion: surfaces, patterns, arrangements, signs, decoration, presentation, and national, regional and historical styles. Inside the home, there are examples of rooms where we meet, where we relax and where we work, and all the details within them: doors, windows, lighting, colour, texture, displays of objects and works of art. Finally, there are the themes of living, of celebration, of making the most of what we have, grand or humble, of being part in some measure of the whole human achievement. A village in the Philippines celebrates its harvest festival with streets full of glowing arrangements of local produce; a Moroccan house coolly mixes the modern and

CHILOÉ   MEXICO

traditional in elegant interiors; an arrangement of shells looks dramatically decorative on a table top in Mauritius; two children in the dress of their region smile at the camera in a Mexican town; flowers are strewn across the bare floorboards for a Christmas feast in Sweden; and women in a Romanian village move their cooking utensils outdoors to prepare for a community wedding.

The plan of the book follows a simple progression: how we build in the community in different habitats; how we add to and refine to create our own lifestyle; and how we then inhabit what we have with the possessions we have gathered around us. As such, this is a sourcebook of thousands of possibilities: as we bring our finds home from flea-markets and yard sales, so what we see in other contexts, other cultures, can also affect our own lives. Choosing where we live is a starting-point: a beach house in Chile or on the west coast of France, or a loft space in Paris or New York? In what kind of terrain do we feel most at ease and in what kind of building? We may find the answer to our own questions in very different places: on a waterfront, by a lake, by a river, on an island, in hill villages, or in the midst of plantations or farmland. There are the urban alternatives: New York 'brownstones' and their near-cousins, English townhouses; converted industrial spaces

BALI   SUMBAWA

and high-rise apartment blocks; courtyard compounds in south-east Asia; and complexes of houses around the Mediterranean and in Africa

where each habitation seems organically connected to its neighbour.

From the larger issues of location and the making of the human imprint, we move to the more personal ones of self-projection within the home: interiors, decoration, arrangement and presentation. Here, within this Aladdin's Cave of choices and inspirations, are the contrasts of stark simplicity and sumptuous embellishment, minimal modernism and Baroque splendour, the self-consciously urbane and the authentically rustic, the classical and romantic, the rough and the smooth, the uniform and the eclectic. There are national, regional and historical styles: English Georgian and French Neoclassicism;

SALZBURG   GOA

Oriental minimalism and high ornament; colonial crossovers, where western tastes have mingled with the indigenous traditions; very personal looks and formal arrangements. All the schemes and arrangements illustrated are unique and many are very individual, yet how striking the underlying similarities in, say, the treatment of doors, staircases, windows, the arrangement of furniture, the choice of colour and material. Scandinavian and Oriental approaches commingle to produce a modernist interior in London; colonial furniture sits happily in a drawing-room in Versailles; a discreetly decorated bed-sitting-room in Morocco could easily inspire a home-maker in northern Europe.

And within whole interiors are revealed the details. In the fourth chapter are the minutiae of design and decoration: arrangements of objects on walls, in cupboards and on shelves; the placing of pictures or free-standing ornaments; the treatment of those awkward transitional spaces in the home, like staircases, corridors, entrance-halls and landings. Often there is some quirkiness in what we see, a lack of contrivance. Perhaps the colours are slightly faded, the materials showing wear and tear, the alignment not quite straight, condition not quite perfect. Wall displays, the disposition of ornaments, the little vignettes of personal memorabilia, all indicate 'living' rather than 'contrivance'. Usually, too, there is an implied meaning in what the camera has picked out – a personal history, a

QUEBEC   NICE

family tradition, an artist's concern for materials and textures, a respect for the vernacular.

Finally, the doorway from the home leads again to the outside; it is now the chance for interior life to mingle with the larger community. We leave the house for the loggia, the veranda, the patio, the courtyard, and the garden. Sometimes these moments of transition can be defined by nothing more than a table and

chairs set up almost at random in some agreeable spot; in other circumstances, custom and practice have dictated the making of something more like a fully furnished outside room.

Beyond the garden gate or front door lies the street, artery of communication and exchange, deserted at times, animated at others in small and large communities alike. Places of colour and creativity, real, living streets, squares and markets repay in abundance close attention to their details: shop fronts in their original state; mountains of produce; household goods, all displayed and presented with instinctive care. There is a joy in many of these places, a kind of celebration of the way humanity manages to remain positive about its future, in spite of vicissitudes and catastrophes. Fitting, then, that the book should close with the final ingredient, people going about their business, some self-conscious, some indifferent, but all making their contribution to the human achievement – the making of homes in a thousand different ways. We end our journey with a glorious burst of colour by the villagers of an island in the Philippines, ingeniously transforming their

IRELAND   ROME

homes in celebration of their harvest festival!

THE WAY WE LIVE | *CHAPTER TWO*

WHERE WE LIVE

Dwellings around the world

BY THE WATER

ON THE LAND

IN TOWN AND CITY

WINDOWS ON THE WORLD

THE DEVELOPMENT OF THE URGE TO BUILD shelter for ourselves and to create the necessary tools for construction must rank among the most important of mankind's great leaps forward: the transition from dwelling in caves or holes in the ground to assembling the wherewithal to create an entirely new edifice, to put, literally, roofs over our heads, is a cultural shift of seismic proportions. But however basic the human instinct to create habitations for the individual, the group or the community at large, the forms and styles of the final result are largely dictated by local conditions, the availability of wood, stone, clay, metal, and by the subsequent craftsmanship that brings the materials together.

Coastal hamlet to city centre: these two extremes represent only a fraction of the varied locations in which we can choose to live and create our individual lifestyles. Where we spend the major part of our lives is, of course, rarely entirely a matter of free choice; necessity, accident, and occasionally catastrophe can all play a part. But, in the locations illustrated on the pages which follow, much will engage our dreams and fantasies as we look upon man's remarkable ingenuity in finding solutions to living in very different environments.

Whether taking over a house previously occupied, with the patinas and characteristics of long occupation still somehow present, or building to our own tastes and imagination, there is a peculiar satisfaction in occupying an enclosed space in which our own order prevails against the unpredictability of the outside world. Some of these houses really do give the impression of having been set down on their sites almost in defiance of surrounding nature. Others lie easily in the folds of the landscape, their contours and materials configuring those of the earth from which they seem to spring. And whole towns and villages may look thus, as though they had burgeoned and grown together as living organisms, which indeed they have.

In contrast, some large conurbations can seem almost entirely divorced from the terrain on which they have been founded and over which they have gradually spread. The land beneath is seemingly compressed out of existence by the enormous layers of masonry and steel, marvellously evoked in Gilles de Chabaneix's photographs of large cities.

Yet within those towering walls lie imaginative and exciting living spaces: townhouses, apartments, lofts, penthouses, just as satisfying to their owners as the most stately plantation house to a rural landowner. Nor are all high concentrations of human habitation cut off from their immediate natural surroundings: the towers and battlements of the Berber dwellings of the Dra valley in Morocco reflect the colours and textures of the earth itself. Whatever the location, though, those illustrated in this chapter are all interesting and many are very beautiful.

Those of us who choose to live by water may reflect on the suitability of lake, river or the sea for the development of our lifestyles. Many of the waterside homes that form the subject of the first part of this chapter are clearly conceived as havens of peace by their owners. Isolated cottages, villas with verandas and terraces looking out to sea, or even apartments in sea-front towns represent a tempting alternative to city life. Then there is the special quality of the light and air that comes off the water, luminous and refreshing, a direct tonic after the grime and noise of a large city. Even the interiors in waterside locations can seem more intensely illuminated than their inland counter-parts.

The types of dwelling in waterside locations are so varied as to represent a lifetime of choices in themselves. Even within the relatively constricted space devoted to this kind of living in these pages, there is sufficient variety to correspond to most of the moods and temperaments at play when we try to answer that all-important question: where shall I or we live? On the west coast of Ireland, amid the fells and lakes of Connemara, someone has clearly found the ideal home, if isolation is a primary need. The sense of being apart from the bustling crowds of town and city is

ÎLE DE RÉ

hugely increased by a location in a natural habitat of beauty and power, dominated by the watery stretches of the lake.

Other options, mentioned above and illustrated on the

following pages, extend the ideal of living by water to locations around the world, all of them attractive, yet very different. There is, for instance, a very special quality to life on an island – a concept in itself that immediately evokes strong feelings of apartness, yet also of being in touch with the larger forces of nature, of which the background sound of the sea provides a constant reminder.

Water as an ornamental adjunct to the house has long excited both conventional architects and their landscape counterparts. Ornamental ponds, rills, waterfalls, cascades, fountains, canals, even whole lakes, have long graced the grounds of the great houses of Europe. But we can also see that water around or within the house is universally recognized as bringing an extra dimension to the domestic environment – in the Islamic courtyard and in the

PARIS

compound arrangements of Balinese architecture, where the presence of water, bubbling, running or just standing still, brings an element of peace to buildings and gardens.

Houses, especially those built in relative isolation, have very different relationships to the land around them, cultivated or wild. Some seem to have been simply thrust up with a disregard for their appropriateness in the landscape; others look down from hills and mounds in domination; others hide discreetly behind trees, somehow settled in park or plantation, surrounded perhaps by a garden which is in itself a transition from the land around; others have so many elements of locally available material in their con-struction that they are scarcely distinguishable from the local terrain. In effect, the successful single house must express, at least in some measure, the spirit of the place in which it stands. Without this, any building outside the larger communities seems curiously at odds with its location and therefore with itself.

Outside the European tradition, houses in Latin America, Africa, south-east Asia and, notably, Mauritius, seem to blend successfully with their location as long as their form and use of materials has been sensitively handled. Long, low houses, with plenty of shade in the form of loggias and verandas, provide a satisfactory respite from days of heat and humidity. Low building, too, has more chance of blending with the landscape, of sheltering behind screens of vegetation; interestingly, our two very grand examples from Goa and Sri Lanka respectively, lie spread across their sites without any of the height of elevation associated with status in temperate climes. Indeed, reflection of local and indigenous cultures and conditions in colour and materials characterizes many of the houses illustrated and helps to give them an air of completeness. Even a low-level habitation in Los Angeles may appropriately symbolize that city's commitment to the modernist design aesthetics of the

GRENOBLE

twentieth century. And a new hotel in Kenya derives its charm and effectiveness from its composition as a series of 'houses' built in the traditional manner with local materials.

What is true of the single house, modest or grand, is also true of the larger communities – village, town and city. Many older concentrations of people and housing presumably grew up largely for defensive or mutually supportive purposes: an enclosure was built for security so that the people of a group could survive and flourish. And

once there was a group of habitations, then all the attendant substructures of services, utilities, governance would fall into place. But even such well-established communities share an inherent contradiction and tension with their newer, planned counterparts: how to balance the privacy of the individual with the intensely public nature of mass building, transport, and commerce?

Many of the illustrations in this chapter of private urban architecture, and town and city living in general, express in some degree the attempts to find an answer to the private/public problem. Streets like those of Bath, Stockholm, parts of London and New York are given a sense of order by a classically-based domestic architecture, behind whose pilasters and architraves the middle classes of the city could retreat to privacy. The high-rise block, born of steel and concrete technology, provides another solution to the housing of large numbers of people in circumstances that guarantee that a reasonable amount of human dignity and individuality can be preserved.

We began the book with a window, albeit a symbolic one. Windows as architectural features can dictate the whole look of a street or square – its line, scale, its feeling of openness or of closure and claustrophobia – as the many examples at the end of the chapter show. At the same time, windows (like doors) are the means by which we can both satisfy our need for privacy, and observe the world outside. Is it raining or sunny? Dawn or dusk? Whether we like it or not, the greyness of a day or the sight of a patch of sunlight on the wall may influence our lives as much as the number of bathrooms, the choice of furniture or the colour of walls.

NICE

21

Very few places on the earth's surface are totally devoid of indications of the human imprint. On the plains or in the mountains, there are almost always signs that man has made some attempt to impose himself on the environment, however inhospitable. Other landscapes – that of Tuscany, for example (*p. 27*) – seem to plead for human habitation in their richness and variety; almost any view in that land will take in villages clustered around some hill, rising above vineyards punctuated by the tall forms of cypresses.

Choosing a place to live is frequently a means of expressing how we wish to live, both in work and leisure. This house near Cape Town (*top left*) stands amid its owner's vineyards; a fishing lodge is the very symbol of isolation on the shores of a Scottish loch (*below left*).

The classic landscape of Tuscany and its classic habitation: a hill-top farmhouse surrounded by cypress trees (*top right*); this is a vision which somehow seems to spring from a Renaissance painting, one of those happy instances where man has created houses, villages and towns at one with the natural surroundings. Access to leisure facilities and opportunities may also dictate choice of lifestyle; these alpine chalets offer easy access to the ski slopes of Haute-Savoie, eastern France (*below right*).

CORSICA

CUBA

CHILOË

SCOTLAND

BURUNDI

CHILE

TANGIER

MASSACHUSETTS

CANADA

MEXICO

MASSACHUSETTS

ROMANIA

The places – communities and single habitations – in which we choose to live sit differently in the landscape (*opposite*). Some look so at ease with their immediate topography as seemingly to have grown out of it, like the village in Burundi or the hillside town on the island of Corsica. Others, like the Scottish shooting lodge or the Massachusetts farmhouse, while still using local materials, appear more the result of deliberate building, of an effort to dominate the land around. Farming and husbandry, of course, are foremost in man's effort to make sense of the natural environment; and so in this Welsh agricultural community (*right*), the local herd is moved along the lanes which are in themselves another way of inhabiting nature.

BY THE WATER

Dwellings at the water's edge – by the sea or on the banks of lake or river – hark back to a primitive stage of human occupation of the land. Water provided immediate and abundant food, a means of transport and, in some cases, of defence, although this simple lakeside cottage in Connemara, western Ireland, looks lost and vulnerable against the masses of water and land.

These examples of waterside living and construction (*overleaf*) all have something in common, despite their very different forms and locations: the presence of water dramatizes and enlivens their position on lake, river or sea. Whole towns and cities, such as Venice and Stockholm, are illuminated by the special light which attends closeness to the sea; single houses gain an extra dimension on natural or man-made stretches of water.

SRI LANKA

VENICE LAGOON

CHILOË

MARSEILLES

SANTORINI

IRELAND

BORA-BORA

BURGUNDY

ÎLE DE RÉ

STOCKHOLM

NORWAY

BALI

Light from the sea is unlike light over land: it is more luminous, more vibrant and somehow more pure. The very ordinary architecture of these two communities – one bathed in the colder light of the Scottish coast (*top left*), the other very much under southern skies on the island of Chiloë at the tip of Chile (*below left*) – is transformed into something attractive and engaging.

From the inside looking out; again, the presence of water enlivens and lightens interiors. This terrace of a summer residence in southern Chile (*top right*) gives the illusion of being immediately over the water. Smaller islands, too, are charged with special excitement by the encircling presence of the sea; on the loggia of this villa in Mauritius (*below right*) there is a sense that water is not far away.

A house by the sea or on an island is one solution to the need to escape increasingly crowded and cramped urban centres, to find space and light and also establish a pleasant domestic environment. The owners of this house (*top* and *below left*) on the Île de Ré, off the west coast of France, have sought simplicity in these bright interiors, which clearly benefit from the fresh island light. On another French island, Corsica, the owner of this house (*opposite*) constructs fantastic furniture-sculpture with driftwood.

ON THE LAND

All the houses illustrated here (*these pages* and *overleaf*) have been built in their particular locations as the result of very conscious decisions. Although their siting varies, topographically and climatologically, they all have the air of having been deliberately raised in their individual settings.

Some, indeed, look positively assertive, pitched roofs thrusting upwards, announcing their domination of the land around them. Each one, though, is undeniably stylish in its own way: high ornamental in Sri Lanka (*top left*); suburban villa in Quebec (*below left*); modern minimalist in Belgium (*opposite top*); and Gustavian classicism in Sweden (*opposite below*).

Overleaf
Many of these dwellings are essentially estate houses, homes of the owners of the land immediately around them and possibly of that much farther afield. All are a combination of historical, geographical and social factors, from a broadly based European classicism in France and Sweden to Islamic forms in Andalucia, to decorative elaboration in Thailand.

CHILE

SWEDEN

BURGUNDY

CHILOË

MAURITIUS

HAUTE-SAVOIE

CANADA

MAURITIUS

BURGUNDY

BANGKOK

LOT

ANDALUCIA

DORDOGNE

CANADA

LUCCA

SCOTLAND

CANADA

SRI LANKA

Grand houses, whether in the town or the country, have traditionally provided security and comfort. As the need for the former declined, so the attention paid to the latter increased, finding one of its finest expressions in the decoration of the great Italian palaces of the Renaissance and Baroque periods: here, all the accoutrements of gracious living in the summer palace of the Chigi family, Rome (*right*).

The estate houses in former European colonies frequently show interesting mixtures of styles: Indo-Portuguese in Goa (*top left*), and English Suburban in Sri Lanka (*below left*). In its elaborately styled façades, embellished with multiple balconies, this privately owned Goan palace has a grandeur which is entirely Iberian, a reflection of the sumptuous lifestyle of the family for whom it was built in the eighteenth century.

Inside the Bragança Palace in Goa (*top* and *below right*) gallery leads to gallery via open-work doors of carved wood. The magnificent ballroom, seen here, was redecorated during the nineteenth century; its floor is covered in Italian marble, reflecting the light from the Belgian chandeliers. More light floods through the arched windows of the whole *piano nobile*.

When natural building materials are immediately available and plentiful, local housing really does seem to take on the forms and colours of the surrounding vegetation and of the land from which it grows. In Tahiti, paradise island of Gauguin, this waterside house (*top left*) is scarcely distinguishable from the dense plant life that surrounds it. A compound in Kenya (*below left*) has the same quality of seeming to grow from the ground it stands on, the roof forming a canopy like that of trees in a forest. New building regulations for such locations stipulate that houses should be no higher than a palm tree.

In recognition, perhaps, of the common-sense of building in local materials, a number of hotel chains around the world have begun to make this a feature of new constructions. Such developments are also a recognition that local and indigenous cultures are important and to be respected. This hotel (*top* and *below right*), at Kurayu in Kenya, close to that country's northern border with Somalia, is made up of twenty separate 'houses', thus granting independence to the guests but still retaining the luxury of hotel services. Each separate residential entity is built from woven palm leaves in the traditional manner of the region. Inside, the local themes are continued in the furnishing, but with a distinctly luxurious interpretation.

Overleaf

An entirely private residence built in local materials is this house on the Indonesian island of Sumbawa, east of Bali and Lombok. As the contents of this splendid space suggest, it belongs to an artist who works principally in wood, sculpting marvellous and strange articles of furniture. In this, he has taken up the traditions of the local community, makers of dugout canoes out of solid wood.

SAN FRANCISCO

CARIBBEAN

CHILOË

MAURITIUS

NEPAL

CAIRO

FLORIDA

SCOTLAND

BANGKOK

SLOVAKIA

LOS ANGELES

BURUNDI

SALZBURG

MAURITIUS

SAN FRANCISCO

MAURITIUS

MAURITIUS

IRELAND

CANADA

MAURITIUS

THAILAND

CHILE

BALI

CHILOË

Preceding pages

Modernist one-storey in Los Angeles, Normandy-style villa in Mauritius, or Islamic enclosure in Cairo, all these houses suggest life on the edge of towns, somewhere at the point where the rural meets the urban. They are, effectively, in their very different ways, examples of the villa, neither country estate house nor yet townhouse.

Even though many of the houses illustrated here (*opposite*) are effectively in towns – for instance, the 1894 villas of the San Francisco hills ('painted ladies') or elegant Irish Georgian – most still retain a certain sense of scale; they do not yet suggest the intensity of the city life of apartments and narrow-fronted townhouses. Paradoxically, however, the façade of this house in the Massachusetts model village of Sturbridge does have a distinct look of its antecedents in English and Dutch towns (*top right*), while having the same proportions as a very urban block in Luxor, Egypt (*below right*).

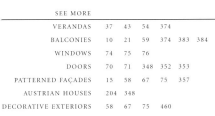

STOCKHOLM

MANHATTAN

STOCKHOLM

NICE

BATH

MANHATTAN

IN TOWN AND CITY

One practical and elegant solution to the problems of living with privacy in large conurbations is the townhouse (*opposite*). The 'brownstones' of Manhattan, with their characteristic sandstone façades and 'stoops', and their cousins in England, Ireland and northern Europe, provided comfortable urban living for the burgeoning middle and merchant classes of the nineteenth century. However, pressure of demand for accommodation has led to the conversion of the majority of them into apartment houses to provide the same kind of living as the high-rise blocks of larger European and American cities.

The 'main street' is repeated endlessly in different forms all over the world, from Brazil (*top right*) to Ireland (*below right*): the one street in town or in the neighbourhood where people meet, shop, gossip, sit in bars. In northern climates actual street life tends to be less vigorously pursued than in southern climates with Latin traditions. Sadly, these centres of community life are now under threat as activity transfers to edge-of-town malls.

The form of the tower has become
the modern city's answer to the
problem of masses of people
congregating in cities to live and
work. While the post-office
(*opposite*) at Trivandrum, Kerala,
India may not be compared in
function to a modern apartment
block in Cairo (*right*), the juxtaposition does emphasize the way in
which cityscapes the world over have
become very much more vertical at
the expense of the lateral, a
verticality largely made possible by
the advent of reinforced concrete.

Concentrations of population demand to be housed. Where communities grow up without planning, their habitations, too, seem to cling together in some strange organic fashion, like this cluster of houses and churches on the Greek island of Santorini (*top left*). Classical order and planning, in contrast, are guiding principles in the city of Bath, a place of stylish terraces and townhouses (*below left*).

Like the Santorini hill villages, the homes of the mountain Berbers in the Dra valley of Morocco (*top right*) seem simply to have grown into place and look entirely at one with the local rock. They also show that large numbers of humans had found it possible to live together long before the flat roofs of the apartment blocks and industrial buildings of Manhattan (*below right*) were raised to their lofty position.

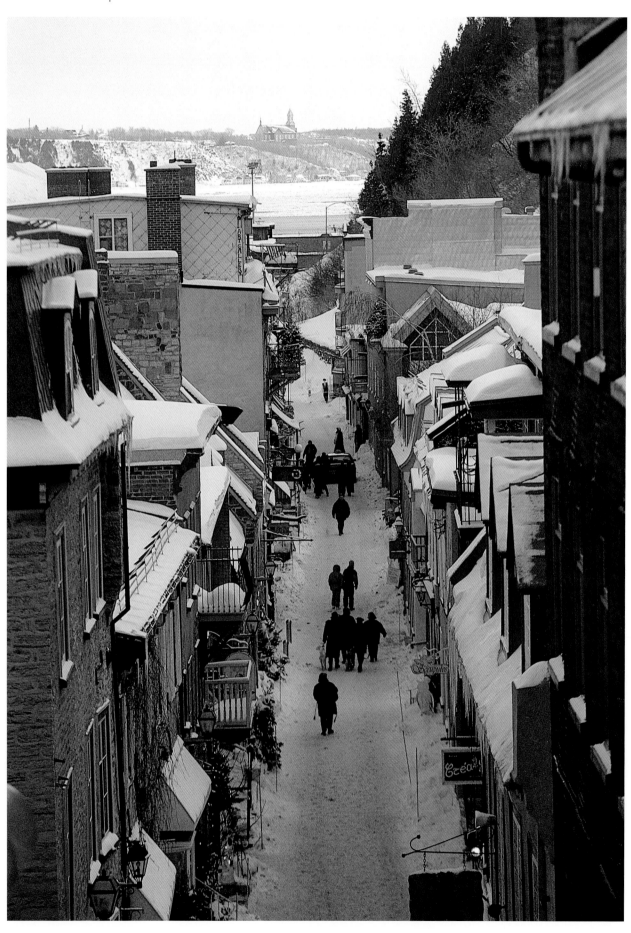

A snow-bound street in Quebec looks all the friendlier for the relative absence of motorized traffic (*left*). The closeness of the housing expresses a sense of community, reinforced by the sight of pedestrians in the street.

The presence of large numbers of pedestrians enlivens the urban environment. What happens spontaneously and naturally in a town of colour and celebration like Lucban on the island of Luzon in the Philippines (*right*) is now part of local government legislation in many towns and cities of the Western world: the introduction of pedestrianized zones.

An essential part of any community's life, providing havens of peace and places for reflection, are its chapels, churches and temples. Their interiors, too, are usually immediately expressive of how a community approaches its engagement with religious practice and belief, of how it worships. A small church in Atacama, southern Chile, is still full of imagery and decorative elements (*top left*). A spartan Methodist chapel in a Welsh village (*below left*) has a simplicity in keeping with the underlying puritanism of that particular inter-pretation of Christianity.

Whatever belief or creed a community subscribes to, buildings devoted to worship provide relief from the material, sometimes painful concerns of the world without. The styles in which they are decorated are a means of celebration for their congregations, whose own homes may be in strict contrast to the opulence of the altars and chapels illustrated here: in Chile (*top* and *below left*) and in a Goan palace (*below right*).

Overleaf
The public face of churches and temples usually confirms their status as being among the most important buildings in village, town and city, demanding lavish attention and care, dominating surrounding dwellings by their height and architectural magnificence.

COCHIN

SANTORINI

MEXICO

CHILOË

MEXICO

CHILOË

ROMANIA

MANILA

COCHIN

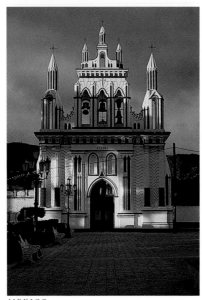

MEXICO

ST. PETERSBURG

MEXICO   GUATEMALA >

SHANGHAI

CHILE

MEXICO

SCOTLAND

TUNIS

COPENHAGEN

MAURITIUS

IRELAND

CHILE

CHILOÉ

CHILOÉ

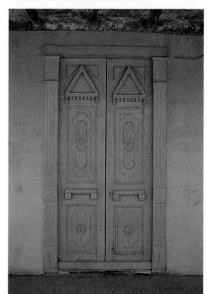

CHILE

Urban planning in the West reached a kind of perfection in the development and refinement of the townhouse. There are few sights more satisfying to the lover of order in the city than that of a row of New York 'brownstones', or of nineteenth-century English or Dutch terraces. In the case of the 'brownstones', the door – always an important feature – is given enhanced importance by the massive 'stoop' leading to it from the pavement.

As the means of transition from the public world of the street to the privacy of the interior the outside door of access has been recognized by most cultures as worthy of intense design attention and decoration (*these pages*). From the public statements of good proportions and order in Irish Georgian to the suggestion of secret things within the enclosure guarded by a massive portal in Tunis, all these doors tell us something about the building for which they are the means of entry.

ST. PETERSBURG

HELSINKI

HELSINKI

NORWAY

SALZBURG

LUXOR

CANADA

IRELAND

CHILE

SANTIAGO

NICE

BUDAPEST

NICE

SEVILLE

UMBRIA

NAPLES

SHANGHAI

SALVADOR DI BAHIA

CHILOË

SWEDEN

LUXOR

ROME

PORTO

HAUTE-SAVOIE

CHILOË

MANHATTAN

PORTO

NEPAL

BANGKOK

PROVENCE

BOMBAY

ISTANBUL

ISTANBUL

BATH

NAPLES

CHILE

NEPAL

PORTO

NICE

MAURITIUS

VIENNA

CHILOË

MARRAKESH

BUDAPEST

PALERMO

NEPAL >

GOA

GOA

NICE

MEXICO

ARGENTINA

PARIS

WINDOWS ON THE WORLD

Like doors, windows are agents of transition between public and private. Looking out from them, we can observe our surroundings from a vantage point; in turn, they allow the outside into our living and working spaces in the form of light and air. Again, like doors, they are important details in the overall design of buildings, set within elaborate surrounds or taking surprising shapes. Sometimes their forms are strictly utilitarian, like those in these traditional dwellings in Bangkok (*pp. 72–73*), set amid materials of such rough texture that the structures themselves suggest the very activity of building, or the window in a Nepalese house, surrounded by drying maize (*p. 77*).

On the inside looking out, windows may be major features in any interior decoration scheme (*these pages*), enhanced by curtains or elaborately patterned blinds and shutters, partly veiled or open to reveal some pleasing vista, or providing the ideal position for a favourite chair.

IBIZA

Windows always act as framing devices, as we look out to the great beyond or to the other side of a city courtyard: agricultural peace in Wales (*left*), or a secret corner of Havana (*opposite*). In both cases, we seem to have been given access to other, mysterious worlds.

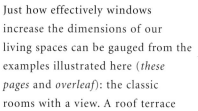

Just how effectively windows increase the dimensions of our living spaces can be gauged from the examples illustrated here (*these pages* and *overleaf*): the classic rooms with a view. A roof terrace provides a further extension to a French window in a Corsican house (*above left*); from the windows of the main house on a Massachusetts model farm the working buildings can be observed (*above right*).

This long balconied window of a Paris apartment gives on to the sumptuous architecture of the Place des Vosges beyond (*above left*); beyond an open door lie the varied colours of an English cottage garden at Charleston in Sussex (*above right*). In both cases, the division of the door-windows into smaller panes of glass emphasizes the sense of the inside looking on the outside.

BANGKOK

SHANGHAI

ÎLE DE RÉ

CORSICA

PARIS

CORSICA

BANGKOK

PROVENCE

PROVENCE

PROVENCE

IRELAND

PARIS

THE WAY WE LIVE | *CHAPTER THREE*

DESIGNING FOR LIVING

Inside the home

IN A MODERNIST STYLE

TRADITIONAL SIMPLICITY

COLONIAL INFLUENCES

IN GRACIOUS AND GRAND STYLES

STYLES FOR COMFORT

INDIVIDUAL TOUCHES

INHERITED TEXTURES

A NEW ECLECTICISM

SURVEYING THE DEVASTATION and destruction visited on Italy by the events of the Second World War, the scholar and art critic Mario Praz wrote, 'The houses will rise again, and men will furnish houses as long as there is breath in them. Just as our primitive ancestor built a shapeless chair with hastily-chopped branches, so the last man will save from the rubble a stool or a tree stump on which to rest from his labours; and if his spirit is freed for a while from his woes, he will linger another moment and decorate his room'. Praz's own interest in interior decoration eventually led him to assemble a remarkable collection of original paintings of interiors of all ages, which he eventually published as *An Illustrated History of Interior Decoration*. His sentiments about man's need to embellish the interiors of his habitat will find many echoes in the pages which follow, for all the domestic and some of the public spaces illustrated here are very much direct extensions of the lives of the people who designed them and who, in many cases, still live in them.

This sequence of illustrations is not historical, nor do they relate in any way to strictly defined styles. In fact, what is especially engaging about many of the rooms here is the eclecticism in arrangement and furnishing that informs their appearance, sometimes to the extent of making a positive virtue out of clutter and the deliberate juxtaposition of apparently incongruous artefacts. Yet, in the larger sense, humble or grand, they are all stylish, whether coated with the patinas of long occupation or the fresh expression of the home-maker's latest vision. If any central theme emerges from the images, it is that of addition and accretion; we begin with relatively spare, purist designs and then progress by various degrees of more or less self-conscious embellishment, to the straightforward search for comfort, and end with rooms where pure, formal arrangement of apparently disparate elements is the guiding principle.

A modernist aesthetic can be applied in various circumstances; it doesn't necessarily emerge only in contemporary or near-contemporary buildings and designs. A way of arranging furniture can be modernist, even though it is in the context of a seventeenth-century apartment, where it can be even more effective. One of the more uncompromisingly pure modern interiors illustrated is in fact in a converted London Victorian house. Another development of such an aesthetic is a relative lack of free-standing furniture, thus obliging us to take more notice of surfaces – walls and floors – and of interconnecting devices like staircases. There is still an eclectic excitement here, however, notably in the cross-fertilization of styles; thus, Oriental and Scandinavian influences come together in a contemporary English interior. In the United States, especially in Los Angeles and Chicago, many of the theories and practices of design developed at the Bauhaus and loosely grouped under the term 'International Modernism' found their most complete expression, often in the work of European *émigrés*.

The spare elegance of the modernist interior can easily inform more traditional settings, especially when the furniture and decor are of very fine quality. The period and the style of the interiors may vary, but there is a kind of traditional good taste that surmounts national, regional and

NEW YORK

cultural differences. We may find the same spirit in the pared-down reserve of a Manhattan apartment, in the cool interiors of a Marrakesh house, or even behind the restored vaulted stone walls of Mediterranean dwellings in Provence and Mallorca.

There is usually a certain homogeneity in the furnishings and decors of such homes. From this point onward, however, we begin to look at eclecticism in the interior, first from a personal aspect and then from the point of view of intermingling cultures. We now see the use of furniture of varying styles, perhaps mixing inexpensive but classic items from furniture chain stores with older, rustic pieces. Personal objects begin to take on prominence, reflecting sporting or cultural interests. Kitchens and the other working rooms of the house provide valuable opportunities

for mixing utensils as well as more conventional ornament; there is now a recognition that the equipment of the kitchen can be attractive in its own right and therefore worthy of display. Studies and book-rooms, too, can become highly personalized spaces for the arrangement of objects, squeezed between books or placed in front of them, which might look out of place in the formality of a drawing-room or dining-room.

Influences from other cultures make for especially exciting possibilities. We have included many examples of Oriental styles, minimalist and highly decorative; both extremes are instructive for the home decorator. Minimalism in the handling of the volume and scale of some of the interiors has contributed to western modernism, as witness some of the schemes illustrated in the early part of this chapter. Decorative furniture – cabinets, chests in lacquer-work – can look effective anywhere in the world; they can also strike a marvellously exotic note in apartments in, say, London, Paris and New York. We respond to the messages they bring and the history and cultures they evoke – particularly when seen outside their own context.

FINLAND

What we have termed 'Colonial Influences' covers a number of strikingly beautiful interiors that derive much of their interest from the meeting of distinct cultures: Hispanic with Latin American and Filipino, English with Sri Lankan and, in one remarkable Goan palace that has been in the possession of the same family for nearly three hundred years, Portuguese and Indian.

Some of the interiors illustrated in these pages are very

grand indeed, notably those within *palazzi* in Rome and Sicily, where the decorators of the Baroque and Rococo periods indulged their wildest fantasies in the creation of sumptuously painted rooms and voluptuously curving plasterwork. Of course, such places were exclusively the domain of the aristocracy and rich merchant classes. When the burgeoning middle classes of western Europe and North America wished to give outward expression to their growing financial power, they too wanted a version of traditional luxury, with the trappings of wealth – libraries, paintings, trophies; hence, we have the heavily furnished, heavily patterned interiors of the Victorian era, which can be found

PARIS

as far apart as Sicily and Quebec. Cultural and geographical differences, however, can be quite distinctive; there is, for instance, an entirely northern economy and restraint in the many Scandinavian and Scottish interiors illustrated here. But there is one remarkable example of cultural crossover in a Finnish country house decorated in varying interpretations of southern Baroque and Rococo.

Comfort is classless; each person searches for it according to his or her means. It is warmth and shelter; it is the accommodation of the family, sometimes extended; it is flexibility – allowing for winter and summer, for heat and cold, for children to grow up; it is also the freedom to enjoy the company of friends, of prized and loved possessions, to project an atmosphere of one's own making within the walls of the home. From the humble miner's cottage, from log cabin (both examples now preserved as folk-museums, now an important source for our knowledge of the past domestic environment) to metropolitan apartments stuffed with the

books, paintings and ornaments of vigorously cultural urban lives, the search for a welcoming, personalized environment is a powerful force indeed. This projection of the individual through decor can take many forms: the display of personal effects, of collections (ranging from ceramics to sumptuous fabrics), the theming of rooms, or even the adoption of a *laissez-faire* attitude towards decoration, entailing minimum intervention in what is already there. Thus, walls may be left untreated, floor boards unpolished and plasterwork and painting incomplete.

Collecting can be seen as another stage in the process of creating a specific atmosphere; the formal arrangements and displays illustrated in the final pages of this chapter are the visible statements of a wish on the part of the home-makers to live in a very particular and individual way. But although there is a unifying spirit of formality in the cabinets, kitchens, sitting-rooms and bedrooms in places as diverse as Provence, Paris, New York and Milan, not one of the

SAN FRANCISCO

arrangements has the dead air of a museum; all of them still resonate with the spirit of the person or persons who created them.

Finally, we concur, with Mario Praz, on the fascination these varied expressions of the decorative impulse hold for us, '…beautiful were the richly-decorated salons of your palaces, the calm rooms of your old bourgeois houses, the rustic kitchens of your simple dwellings in the mountains; beautiful also was your furniture with its time-stained patina, your objects lovingly worked by generations of cabinet-makers, potters and goldsmiths!'.

IN A MODERNIST STYLE

These two apartments (*preceding pages* and *these pages*) express an essentially modernist aesthetic by careful juxtaposition of setting and objects. In the first, the generous spaces of a seventeenth-century Paris apartment have been stripped to their essentials to house a collection of twentieth-century furniture classics. The chairs and tables, though of very different date from that of the huge sitting-room, do not in any way seem at odds with it; but, then, the lines of the pieces by Jean Prouvé, Charlotte Perriand and Harry Bertoia are also expressive of a new classicism.

In contrast, the apartment illustrated here (*these pages*), which belongs to a Parisian interior designer, has an entirely contemporary feel to its rooms, but the artefacts it contains are self-consciously decorative: an elaborately branched chandelier, looking-glasses within Rococo frames, and a button-back settee. Storage shelves are concealed by the voluminous curtains which are drawn by means of long bamboo poles.

Behind the traditional façade of a London house lies this interior (*above*), cool and minimalist, seemingly Scandinavian and Oriental in inspiration. The orderly lines of the design start, literally, at floor level with wide boards of Oregon pine. All the decorative elements of the original Victorian interior have been suppressed and the interior walls removed; only two vestiges remain in the form of the open fireplaces, given horizontal proportions to accentuate the length of the room and simplified to their bare, functional essentials. All the clutter which could detract from the strength of the rectilinear design is safely concealed in capacious floor-to-ceiling cupboards.

One gesture towards a more
flamboyant approach to decoration
in this otherwise simple Mallorcan
interior (*above*) is the Ottoman star
form of the ceiling lights.
Otherwise, everything is simplifica-
tion itself, from the director chairs
to the ingenious creation of a
fireplace by inserting a second wall
to form the chimney-breast.

The disposition of furniture in this San Francisco apartment (*top* and *below left*) makes a feature of the windows as points of focus. Such a loose and fluid use of space is entirely appropriate to contemporary apartment living, where rooms have often been stripped of all traditional features.

The effect of total, stripped-down modernism is very similar in both these houses. Their difference lies in the fact that one (*top right*) is a masterly, transforming conversion within the shell of a traditional London Victorian house, while the other is part of a totally conceived and realized modernist construction by Richard Neutra in Los Angeles (*below right*). Indeed, Neutra's own brand of International Modernism very much shaped the design vision of that city from the 1930s to the 1960s in its promotion of cool, logically managed environments – the Californian interpretation of the European work of Gropius and Le Corbusier.

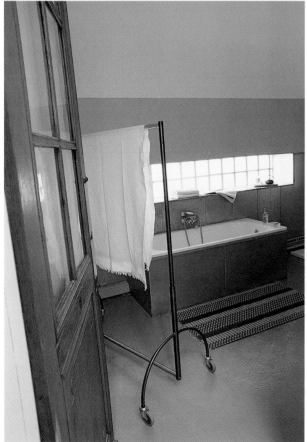

The successful management of space is the key to making most modernist interiors work. A relative absence of free-standing furniture concentrates attention on walls, floors and connecting elements like staircases and openings. Within the converted London house (*p. 97*) the kitchen area and bedrooms connect with other parts of the house by open square arches (*top far left* and *below right*). The influence of Japanese minimalism is plainly evident in the bedroom arrangement. Ingenious and dramatic use of adjoining spaces characterize this Brussels interior: a staircase leading to a light, uncluttered bedroom which, in turn, gives on to a roof terrace covered in teak decking (*top right*).

Living in converted industrial premises is often associated with New York and the fashion of loft dwelling; however, this converted print factory is in Paris (*below far left* and *opposite*). In keeping with the building's origins, the bathroom makes use of industrial elements – a clothes rack for towels and heavy-duty glass blocks concealing a light source. White cotton drapes soften the lines of the mezzanine reading area (*opposite*); a further counter to the straight lines of the main layout is provided by the curvilinear organic-modernist 'Butterfly' chair, originally designed in the late 1930s, and the splendid sweeping form of 'La Chaise', by Charles Eames, a prototype in 1948.

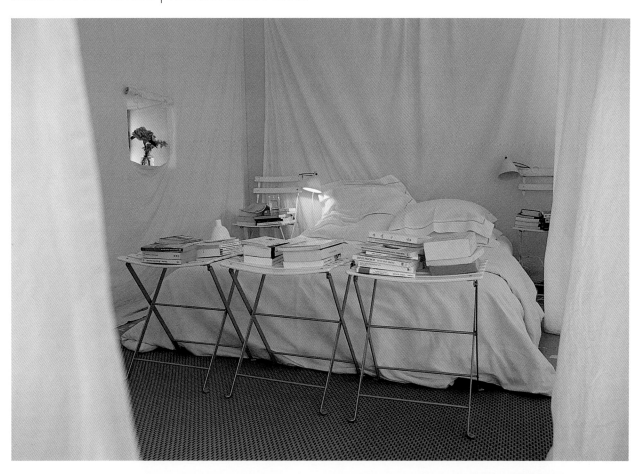

The strict lines and colour schemes of modernist interiors can be successfully countered and also enhanced by the introduction of softer forms and materials into the decorative scheme. The interiors illustrated here (*top* and *below left*), in Paris and London, have the rigour of contemporary minimalism, yet both of them are made more attractive by the presence of textiles and other isolated elements: voluminous bed coverings; the contours of a large duvet; a vase of flowers. In the Paris apartment the whole room has a 'soft' quality much enhanced by the tent-like hanging of white cotton drapes.

In these two interiors – in Paris (*top right*) and Mallorca (*below right*) – a number of elements have been introduced which mitigate what would otherwise be a very spartan effect. A large artwork, with strong graphic motifs, dominates this mezzanine area. The Mallorcan summer house, the home of a rug and carpet designer, though of relatively recent construction, still manages to reflect tradition in exposed beams and sloping ceilings. Strongly shaped free-standing objects and flowers provide other points of focus.

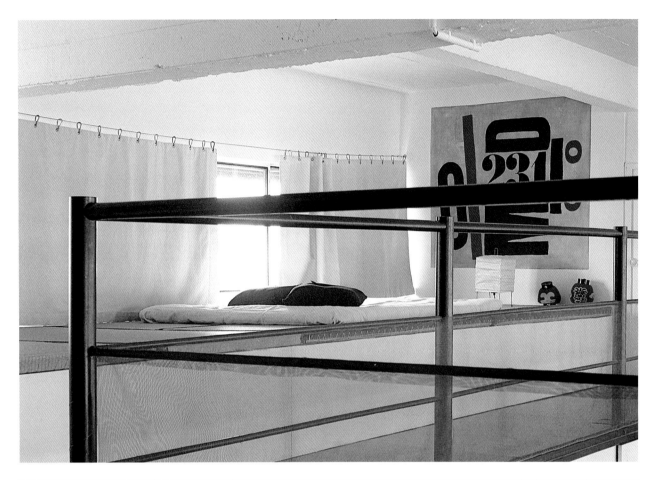

DEVON

All the bathrooms illustrated here are utilitarian (*these pages*); they are also beautiful and exciting spaces, a reflection of this room's modern status as a place for serious design focus. Though eschewing all additional decoration, the quality of the materials and the style of the fittings make these spaces ones in which to linger. Again, the presence of a folded towel, wall photograph or vase of flowers sets off hard surfaces of zinc, stainless steel and white ceramic.

CARPENTRAS

PARIS

CARPENTRAS

LONDON

PARIS

MALLORCA

PARIS

A modernist aesthetic does not necessarily mean that design should be dull. The shapes of the fittings in a London house (*above*) are intriguing in themselves, though they have the clean lines of a purist approach to decoration. The baths are interpretations of traditional Japanese forms; the shower room is a complete, integrated environment, where water simply drains away through outlets in the floor.

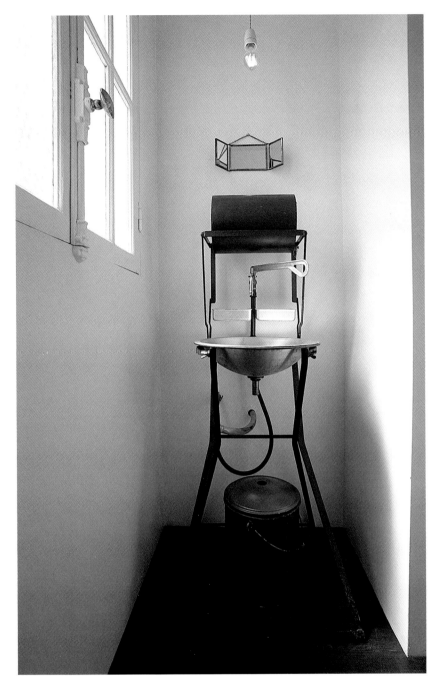

Taking a somewhat different
approach to introducing fantasy into
otherwise very simply conceived
bathrooms, the owners of these two
Paris interiors (*above*) have chosen
to enliven small spaces by installing

highly decorative fittings. These
look all the more dramatic for being
in all-white settings, and have a
truly surreal look, arising from the
juxtaposition of disparate objects
and their apparent incongruity here.

Though still clearly contemporary in colour and form, the bathrooms illustrated here are distinctly places of pleasure. Materials and decorative additions announce them as environments in which the senses are to be satisfied. Carefully placed ornaments provide an elegant distraction in Marrakesh (*top left*). And one certain way to lend notes of interest to any bathroom is to make a small display of bottles of scent and waters (*below left*).

An even greater sense of sybaritic
luxury pervades this Italian
bathroom (*top right*), with walls
hung with framed engravings. In
this Moorish bathroom (*below right*)
walls and bath are coated in a
traditional chalk-based plaster.

Modernist kitchens can sometimes have a distinctly industrial look; this example in a Brussels apartment, for instance, is dominated by neat linear units and an extractor vent (*opposite*). This somewhat spartan effect can be softened by the open display of kitchen utensils in all their variety of form and colour. The number of objects and equipment displayed in this Paris kitchen (*top right*) indicates that this is a place devoted to serious food preparation. Another Paris apartment (*below right*) uses open semi-industrial units for storage, but achieves a distinctly lived-in effect through the visible accumulations of crockery and utensils.

Finding ways of linking eating areas with other parts of the house, either kitchens or sitting-rooms, calls for some design ingenuity. The introduction of open storage units can sometimes provide the solution. This striking blue dresser in a Sicilian kitchen immediately extends the room's decorative possibilities (*above left*). In this Paris apartment (*below left*), two metal support pillars have been inserted to open up the wall between the sitting-room and the dining area, thus fully displaying the immense 'Trapèze' table and the 'Standard' chairs designed by Jean Prouvé. As a fashion, Hi-Tech moved to the centre of the decorative arts and interior design in the 1970s; it was characterized by the use of heavy-duty industrial artefacts and equipment in domestic contexts. This dining area of a Provençal house picks up resonances of the style with mass-produced steel chairs and an industrial refrigerator unit mounted on wheels (*opposite*).

Simple lines and simple shapes are just as effective as displays of opulence in creating attractive living quarters. Indeed, the elegance of the finest Oriental design has often been the inspiration for western modernist architects and designers. However, the creator of the house (*above left*) in Tokyo, the potter Shoji Hamada, was influenced in his work by a westerner, the Englishman Bernard Leach, another advocate of uncluttered, earthy form in the decorative arts. The rooms in this Carpentras house (*above right*) are connected by archways with open-work screens of Japanese inspiration.

These two interiors, one in New York (*above left*) and one in Paris (*above right*) exude elegant modernism in their distribution of furniture in simple, tidy groupings. Yet, the forms of the chairs and sofa also suggest a more old-fashioned concern with comfort. The elegant chic of the Paris interior is entirely in keeping with the spirit and ideals of the organization to which it belongs, the house of Chanel.

It would be reasonable to expect an apartment in Manhattan to exhibit some of the qualities of New York's devotion to change and progress in the nineteenth and twentieth centuries. And there is indeed a straightforwardness and modernity in the arrangement of furniture in these two rooms (*these pages*). Effects of lightness and spaciousness are enhanced by the presence of the large mirrors above the fireplaces and two sumptuous Fortuny lights.

The furniture is largely early-nineteenth-century; one particularly interesting piece is an Empire Style day-bed, with characteristic scroll ends. American furniture of the period was much influenced by French fashions, several French firms of cabinet-makers having established themselves in New York during the period as an escape from the political instability of Europe.

TRADITIONAL SIMPLICITY

Traditional vaulted ceilings, especially if quite low, create a sense of intimacy and containment, ideal for a dining area or place where people can engage in intimate conversation. The roughly hewn stonework of an Apulian house provides an ideal setting, giving on to a courtyard, for eating outside (*above left*). The more formal interior dining-room in the same house (*above right*) takes up the shape again in a much more finished form, although it was in fact converted from a former stable.

In the same Italian house (*above right*) a more relaxed sitting area occupies the interesting spaces created by the relationship of several arches and a vaulted ceiling. As an architectural form the arch is of great significance in the Islamic world, since it suggests the prayer alcove, the mihrab, repeated on every traditional prayer rug. This

example, a conversation corner (used also as the winter dining-room) in a Marrakesh house (*above left*), is decorated with finely detailed polychrome decoration. The walls are covered to mid-height with padded canvas, decorated with motifs taken from desert Arab tents. The design of the chairs is derived from traditional Moroccan forms.

In the old stone houses of the whole Mediterranean region the rounded arch and vaulted ceiling are traditional forms, usually built in rugged local stone which, when cleaned, is a decorative element in itself. Underneath the majestic curving vault of this former stable of a house in Mallorca (*above*) the owners have installed a bath-house. One of the only features to have been completely renewed is the floor, now a mosaic of blue *pâte-de-verre*.

A vaulted room in this Provençal *mas*, home to a French interior designer, makes a light and airy bedroom (*above*). The rough-cast wall surface has been cleaned but still lends a rugged charm to the whole ensemble. The floor is composed of traditional Provençal terracotta tiles. The arch is echoed in the forms of door and window, but the angled bed form has been chosen to contrast with it.

Overleaf
Again, the vaulted form is visible in the dining area of the house in Mallorca, where more recent additions have the material strength and forthrightness of the original structure. A chimney has been created on one side of the area to provide a vent for the table-height grill; beneath it is a rectangular cavity for storing logs.

All the bedrooms illustrated here demonstrate one fundamental design principle: how the strong traditional lines of an original building and its interiors can be set off by the judicious arrangement of interesting personal objects and soft furnishings. An arch provides a convenient niche for the bed-head (*top far left*) in this Paris apartment and an opportunity to hang part of the owner's collection of paintings and photographs by contemporary artists. More personal clutter is stacked on the bedside chest of drawers. In this Marrakesh bedroom (*top left*) the bed and the matching armchair are strong decorative elements in themselves. Light textiles, either in hanging form or as bed linen, enliven these two bedrooms – one, French (*below far left*), and one, Sicilian (*below left*). Even this somewhat monkish, cell-like guest bedroom in a Provençal house (*opposite*) has been personalized by the addition of traditional terracotta jars to serve both utilitarian and ornamental purposes.

Simplicity of structure and decoration are somehow utterly appropriate in houses in warmer climates. Both this bedroom (*above*) and this children's dormitory (*opposite*) are in a Provençal house.

Both exhibit a straightforward
attitude to construction and
decoration. But the addition of any
decorative element, such as an
Oriental rug, has an instantly
dramatic effect.

Inviting, with the promise of easy, intimate conversation, yet also relaxing in its combination of whites and greys, this bed-sitting-room in a Marrakesh *riad* beautifully combines the traditional and the new. The simple, direct forms of the chairs and fireplace are a perfect foil for the rich textures of the heavy curtains (protection from the sunlight during the day and from the cold at night) and, on the floor, a traditional Tuareg rug in woven straw and leather. Invisible here is another feature: the ceiling is in the form of an upturned boat.

The interiors illustrated on the pages that follow have been chosen because they incorporate very distinctive and often very personal elements in their decorative schemes, but often from very different sources. Emphasis here is very much on the contents of rooms, sometimes simple, sometimes complex, sometimes exotic, sometimes eclectic, but always fascinating and inspirational. Multiple shifts in wall and ceiling surfaces make this Marrakesh bedroom (*above*) a place of subtle complexities – a suitable setting for furniture whose sturdiness is countered by the delicate decorative touch of the three hanging lamps in a traditional Moroccan design.

This room in a Provençal house (*above*), the holiday home of a fashion designer, painted plainly in white, with exposed beams, is made warm and inviting by the addition of a number of carefully chosen articles of low-level furniture, including two North African *tabourets*, used as occasional tables. Splashes of dramatic colour enliven but never overwhelm the whole setting; large floor candles provide alternative points of focus to the briskly ascending flames of the fire.

These two interior spaces (*top left* and *below left*) in the same house in Carpentras, Provence, show how an eclectic approach to acquiring furniture and objects can result in an entirely pleasing yet workmanlike domestic environment. Much of the furniture has been made to the owner's designs in relatively inexpensive materials. Other items have either been recovered from salvage shops, like the 1940s architect's lamp, or bought from household goods chain-stores.

The house in Marrakesh, already illustrated (*pp. 126–128*), contains several rooms on a smaller scale that the owners have brought to life by the careful positioning of small objects, including traditional hats, and single items of furniture (*top right* and *top far right* and *below right*). One feature common to all is the use of traditional hanging lamps, with their distinctive lines and strong graphic patterning. In a Corsican house, potentially 'dead' space (*below far right*) has been saved by decorative ingenuity in the placing there of two huge flexible baskets and the continuation of the lower wall colour on to the window frame.

Overleaf
A similar attention to detail is evident in all the interior spaces illustrated here. Sometimes it is the transitional space – the stairwell, the corridor, the landing – which requires the most attention in terms of ornament or colour, rather than the grander proportions of principal rooms. But even in the latter it is often important to create corners of interest away from the main axis of attention. These spaces all use pale background colour punctuated by bursts of deeper, brighter hues.

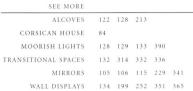

PROVENCE

IBIZA

IBIZA

SICILY

SICILY

PARIS

PROVENCE

MANHATTAN

TUNISIA

NICE

MARRAKESH

PARIS

CÉVENNES

ITALY

NAPLES

CORSICA

PARIS

BALI

PROVENCE

PARIS

MARRAKESH

IRELAND

SAIGON

TUNISIA

Successful decorative effects are not always achieved by the display of intrinsically interesting objects or items of furniture. Personal whimsy can often be turned to effective ornamental use; in this house on the Île de Ré, western France, the owner's sporting interests have delivered him a ready-made wall frieze. The furniture is an eclectic mixture of the formal and the casual, though the placement is very deliberate.

ÎLE DE RÉ

For the creation of a homely yet functional eating area, classic furniture bought from popular stores, such as Habitat and Ikea, can be as effective as more expensive items. Mixed with older pieces, still to be found relatively cheaply in bric-à-brac emporiums, it can create the feeling of warmth and informality which the kitchen-dining-rooms illustrated on these pages exude. Only the minimalist Parisian dining-room (*opposite below far right*) attracts by the sculptural form of a single article of furniture.

ÎLE DE RÉ

ÎLE DE RÉ

SEVILLE

MALLORCA

SICILY

PROVENCE

PARIS

The circumstances of modern urban living often re-emphasize the central role of the kitchen in our culture; for reasons of space, this is the place where many of us choose to eat and where food can be served directly from the utensils of its preparation. There is, then, good reason to make sure that the kitchen is made attractive by displays of crockery, fruit or flowers, as in this example in San Francisco (*top left*), and in a more rustic version in Mallorca (*below left*).

We expect to be looked after in the kitchen; the combination of heat and sustenance there recalls a distant ancestor, the communal cooking fire. It is associated with stir, bustle, warmth, richness and ripeness. It is the one room which drives the apartment or house in which it is located. So, this very friendliness makes it an ideal place for self-indulgence in decorative detail, in the display of objects of interesting shape but of no particular value, like this arrangement of bowls and teapots in an Irish kitchen (*below right*); even the refrigerator offers opportunities for embellishment. Kitchen utensils themselves, especially polished pans and baskets, combined with herbs or fruit, can make very engaging displays – here, in a kitchen of a house on the island of Ibiza (*top right*).

This magnificent kitchen in a house in Santiago, Chile, is clearly intended as a serious temple of the culinary arts (*opposite* and *top right* and *far right*). All the actual cooking facilities are located centrally under the powerful and sculptural abstract form of the extractor vent. It is worth noting, though, that the table also occupies a position of prominence, reminding us of the importance of this flat surface in the kitchen environment, as an area for food preparation and for eating. After all, who needs a dining-room if the kitchen table is large and accommodating? It draws groups and families together and associates them with both the preparation and consumption of food. Both these examples (*below right* and *far right*) – one in Buenos Aires, and the other the kitchen-like corner of a *salon* in a house on the Île de Ré, western France – are attractive enough; the latter's decoration includes kitchen items and objects reflecting the owner's nautical interests.

COLONIAL INFLUENCES

The quality of light flooding through the windows of these two interiors – a New York loft (*top left*) and a palace bedroom in Goa (*below left*) – gives both of them a look of being elevated above the more earthly concerns of ground-floor living. The apartment in New York is in fact in the city's SoHo district, where an abundance of warehouse and light industrial premises became available for conversion in the 1970s, as businesses relocated to the suburbs, thus initiating the fashion for loft living. Of quite different provenance, the grand scale of this palace in Goa (*below left*) was intended to reflect the lavish lifestyle of one of the grand families of the former Portuguese colony. The same opulence is abundantly expressed in the furniture of the palace – like this four-poster bed hung with lacework – a strange cross of Iberian and Goan styles.

This first-floor sitting-room of a
house in Versailles (*right*) is also
furnished largely in a mixture of
European and Indian styles and
materials. Around a black lacquer
table, on which is displayed a
collection of 1930s bronzes by
Christofle, are grouped a number of
Anglo-Indian armchairs in carved
ebony, a chest of similar provenance
in mahogany and ivory and a
seventeenth-century cabinet in
ebony. The whole grouping is
illuminated by the special quality of
light that floods through the first-
floor windows.

The Spanish and Portuguese taste for lavishly carved furniture reappears in houses in many parts of the world: a *salon* in Havana (*above left*); rooms in the Bragança Palace, Goa (*above right* and *opposite*). Carved in rosewood by local craftsmen, the design of the chairs and tables in the palace is eighteenth-century Portuguese.

Although very clear decorative impulses have been brought to bear on the rooms of this Sri Lankan house (*left*) in the form of carved doorways and furniture, the overall effect is one of graceful simplicity. Also decorative, but with the clutter and memorabilia, the accretions of continuous occupancy by generations of the same family since the eighteenth century, the galleries of the Bragança Palace in Goa are a treasure house of Indo-European design (*opposite*).

The generously proportioned galleries of the Closenberg Hotel, an old-style colonial building in Galle, Sri Lanka (*these pages*), are made luminous by the natural light filtered by huge arched windows. Disposed throughout all the rooms is a magnificent assembly of antique furniture made by local craftsmen, ranging from the sobriety of traditional planters' chairs to highly ornate re-interpretations of indigenous and European styles.

Domestic architecture of the far Orient has much to teach the West in the use and articulation of spatial volumes. Low roofs and ceilings limit the amount of bright light entering the extensive sitting areas in a house in Manila (*top left*) and in this Balinese residence (*below left*). Low furniture, often made of local hardwoods, is distributed evenly around the floor space so that no one area is the main focus of attention.

In the more personal and private rooms of this house in Bali (*top* and *below right*) there is still the same obvious need to filter light by means of shutters. Arrangement of furniture, though, is more intense, more European, than in the public rooms, and highly personal ornaments and decorative elements add to the impression of intimacy.

Simple yet ingenious, naïve yet sophisticated, these inside/outside spaces in Kenya (*these pages*) use local and immediately available materials to create spaces in which all normal domestic requirements are met, though still retaining clear evidence of their origin in the land surrounding them.

An open place for people to gather and socialize is essential to the success of public places like hotels, clubs and bars. Both these rooms (*above* and *opposite*), in hotels in Jaipur and Udaipur respectively, former palaces, have exactly the right combinations of low-level seating and filtered light to induce pleasant, subdued social contact while, at the same time, successfully assimilating more exuberant elements into their decoration.

Overleaf
Elegance and refinement characterize this extended and tranquil space
in a Manila house, providing a
marvellous sanctuary in the midst of
the vigorous vegetation that
surrounds it. Enormous low day-
beds dominate the floor-space,
adding to the feeling of peace and
relaxation.

Although there is still a basic simplicity underlying these Oriental interiors, there are distinct notes of high ornament. From an interior decorator's point of view, it is instructive to contemplate how some of these elaborate pieces would translate to, let us say, an all-white minimalist interior of the kind illustrated in the early pages of this chapter. Here, however, they are entirely at one with the decor: a house in Manila (*top far left* and *left*); a museum-house in Bangkok (*below far left* and *left*).

More personal, in a way more ordinary, are the artefacts in these interiors: a garden seat, planters' chairs, a carved chest, figurines. Although the room settings here are drawn from various parts of the East, they still have a common feeling, a constant tension between the utmost simplicity of construction and very complex forms of decoration: houses in Bangkok and Manila (*top right* and *far right*) and, finally, a house in Bali (*below right* and *far right*).

Not surprisingly, the influence of Iberian Baroque is very apparent in the great houses of Manila. Yet in this setting in a nineteenth-century house, the Casa Manila, now preserved as a museum (*left* and *opposite*), the overall effect is really quite uncluttered, mainly because the highly wrought and ornate furniture is allowed sufficient space in which to make its effect.

Overleaf
On the walls of the dining-room of the Casa Manila hang the kind of family portraits associated with the interiors of the European aristocracy or merchant classes.

One of the great houses of Manila, the Casa Manila, is now a museum devoted to evoking life during the Spanish colonial era. Every room has been carefully restored to its period style, expressed in furniture, chandeliers, lamps, paintings, ceramics and general bric-à-brac. The ceilings are painted (*top left*) and often have additional ornament in the shape of elaborately carved wooden friezes (*below left*).

One of the unifying elements in the decor of the Casa Manila is the presence in every room of polished hardwood floors, which beautifully set off the ornate furniture. All the bedrooms have been fully restored (*top right* and *far right*), but the true glories of the place are in the public rooms, where the Spanish colonial furniture, derived from French models, sits beneath ceiling ornament in traditional Filipino styles (*below right* and *far right*).

The combination of an overall simplicity punctuated by ornate and complex detailing in the form of screens, arches and friezes, which characterizes much Oriental design, is especially effective in the layout of rooms for public encounter and conversation. In a private residence, the sitting-room fulfills this function; in public places, like bars and hotels, seating areas must make discreet conversation possible for guests and members – as does this supremely elegant lounge (*above*) in the Temple Club, Shanghai.

Elaborately carved and exotically shaped furniture always looks more pleasing in a very simple context. These two wonderfully organic-looking examples were found, respectively, in Shanghai (*above left*) and Havana (*above right*).

A deep sense of calm after the vicissitudes of war seems to pervade this coolly elegant sitting-room in a large, French-owned private house in a suburb of Saigon (*above*). The orderly arrangement of substantial items of furniture, even the poses of the figures on the wall-hangings, all bespeak a world where quiet and tranquillity are now at a premium.

Even though international tourism has invaded Bali, any visitor will still be able to attest to the skill in woodcarving of the island's craftsmen. Hardly surprising, then, that the grander houses there should have chosen this aspect of local art to embellish their interiors; note the intricate carving of the doors and chairs in this *salon* (*above*). The pictures hang at an angle to avoid reflecting the strong daylight.

Throughout the capitals of Latin America can be found the influence of Iberian Baroque. This dining-room in the Military Circle club in Buenos Aires (*left*) could easily have been copied exactly from an example in a Spanish royal palace.

Modest, yet exploiting every possible decorative opportunity in colour and in the arrangement of a few locally made artefacts, this small dining-room in a house in Zihuatanejo, Mexico, still manages to look inviting (*right*). How effective and dominant in the whole scheme of things is the vase of flowers in the centre of the table – a dramatic note against the green of the dresser.

The success of the arrangement of the *piano nobile* of this house-turned-museum in Manila, the Casa Manila, depends pretty well entirely on the magnificent proportions of the furniture and wall embellishments. A massive table dominates the room from the centre and looks all the more imposing for standing on the bare polished boards of the floor, exactly beneath a fine crystal chandelier. Between the windows two immense wall mirrors hugely increase the sense of space and light in a room where the overall tones are sombre.

IN GRACIOUS AND GRAND STYLES

Places of food preparation and consumption, especially when this is done communally, are of especial importance to the well-being of any house or apartment. There are few more pleasing domestic sights than that of a well-laid table, whatever the extent or complexity of the meal to come. In this Buenos Aires dining-room (*left*), fine white table linen provides the perfect foil to family silver, glass and tableware.

A similar use of furnishing elements, a similar feeling of careful and stylish preparation, attends tea in this Paris apartment (*right*). It is this sense of self-conscious stylishness in the way we live and conduct domestic matters that forms the subject-matter of the pages to come.

A sense of family life, still strong in Mediterranean Europe, pervades this table setting in a Sicilian household (*above*). The ritual of eating together is one of the great bonding ties in the life of families; here, taking care over details is clearly considered worthwhile.

Details of preparation for dinner seem to be on the mind of the person assuring the cleanliness of the glasses in this private house in Mauritius (*above*). Through open French windows those who will be seated at the table can also enjoy the close proximity of the long veranda.

The impulse to decorate and embellish our immediate living quarters does not always demand the purchase of additional furniture or ornament. This apartment on the banks of the Nile in Cairo (*above*) has many interesting pieces and features, including a fetching mural on the fireplace wall of the main sitting-room.

Much of the charm of this same apartment is derived from the arrangement of highly personal memorabilia and photographs in carefully ordered display devoted to one of Egypt's most famous singers, Farid el-Atrach (*top left* and *right*). Another Cairo apartment, however, relies heavily for its charm on traditional Arab furnishing and decoration (*above left* and *right*). The seating is made up largely of low-level carved chairs, while open-work screens and window decorations conceal more than they reveal. A frieze of Arabic script completes the upper part of the wall decoration.

The burgeoning economic and social importance of the middle-classes throughout the latter years of the nineteenth century was accompanied by a taste for opulence and ostentatious comfort in decoration, wonderfully exemplified in the interiors of the Castello

Falconara in Sicily. Individual lamps and candelabra (*above left*) are so highly decorated that it is easy to forget that their original function was to illuminate. Button-back sofas and armchairs (*above right*) are unashamedly the expression of a society at ease with itself.

Wallpapers are heavily patterned; curtains and other hangings are thick and voluminous; furniture promotes ease at the expense of line; and other features are covered in complex detailing. Even the wooden articles of furniture are elaborately carved versions of a mixture of past styles (*above*).

In one sense, the 'bourgeois' interior was only a more popular re-interpretation of a vision of gracious living that had been traditionally the preserve of the European aristocracy and wealthy merchant families. Nowhere was the vision so elaborately expressed as in the building and decoration of the great houses of the Italian cities of Venice, Rome and Florence. In Venice, whether standing on the Grand Canal or facing on to some secluded square, the city's *palazzi* have always had the finest craftsmanship lavished upon them – in this instance, stuccowork of the mid eighteenth century (*these pages*).

Overleaf
Family portraits gaze upon a scene of faded opulence in the billiard room of the summer palace of the Chigi family, Ariccia, Rome.

The Palazzo Biscari in Catania, Sicily, in 1787 received a visit from Johann Wolfgang von Goethe; although fascinated by the number of antiquities in its apartments, it is doubtful whether the classicism of Germany's foremost writer would have permitted him to enjoy the building itself. The palace (*top left*) is, effectively, a Rococo gem, from the design of the public rooms to the detailing of the furniture. Another curious example of high decoration in the Italian manner is the Farmacia Santa Maria Novella in Florence (*below left*).

The centrepiece of the Biscari palace is the magnificent Salone da Ballo (*this page*), finished in 1772, complete with a frescoed vaulted ceiling around a cupola, fireplaces in the corner niches, and console tables and mirrors. One especial treasure is the exquisite staircase which leads to the orchestra gallery (*top far right*), embellished with more frescoes and stuccowork showing the influence of *rocaille* design, a mainstay of French Rococo.

Built to impress and amaze, filled with antique sculptures, exotic birds, slaves and Moors, the Villa Medici in Rome was the inspiration of Cardinal Giovanni Ricci of Montepulciano. On his death in 1574 it passed into the hands of Cardinal Ferdinando de'Medici, fifth son of Grand Duke Cosimo I of Tuscany. The improvement of the villa and its gardens then became the responsibility of Bartolomeo Ammanati, official architect to the Medici. But, most interestingly, beyond the grandiose effects of the main rooms and gardens lie quiet corners of elegance and interest – small, instructive vignettes (*left* and *opposite*).

There is almost a behind-the-scenes look about these two room settings in the Villa Medici (*above left* and *right*), as though a family may suddenly take up residence within them. It is such settings, and not necessarily those in great public rooms, which can prove most inspirational for more modern decorative schemes.

Simple, yet with an underlying note of opulence, are these two settings, one in Umbria (*above left*) and one in a house on the island of Madeira (*above right*). Note especially how relatively plain spaces can immediately acquire a distinctive feeling of luxury by the use of richly coloured paint schemes.

In the bedroom, a taste for gracious living can be satisfied by close attention to detail – arrangements and objects, perhaps very personal, which are pleasing and distinctive and give importance to an environment in which we spend more time than we realize.

One notable feature of all these bedrooms in Sicilian houses and apartments (apart from one in the Palazzo Chigi, Ariccia, *top right*) is the ornateness of the beds themselves, often the dominant decorative element in the room.

Decoration and the conferring of engaging qualities on any room, especially a bathroom, does not have to be complicated or structural. A simple shower assembly, coupled with a few pieces of elegant furniture, make this bathroom in a Mauritian house (*above*) a place to be enjoyed at leisure.

The fittings themselves are such powerful features in this bathroom (*above*) that very little else is needed to complete its decoration. Once the villa of the princely Odescalchi family and eventually one of the residences of John-Paul Getty, La Posta Vecchia, on the Tyrrhenian Sea at Ladispoli, is now a luxury hotel, but still retains much of the decor of its chequered past, including this bathroom of relatively recent date.

Certainly not grand in scale but entirely pleasing are these two bathrooms which make extensive use of decorative qualities of simple materials. A Chilean bathroom (*above left*) is entirely covered with a kind of crazy paving. In a Marrakesh house a modern Moorish bathroom (*above right*) is enlivened by the use of rose-coloured brick to outline the shower and windows and to form a central floor panel. An antique hanging lamp and terracotta pots provide other decoration.

Both these bathrooms – one Italian (*above left*) and one American (*above right*) – have fittings of the utmost simplicity in retro styles.

In both cases, however, a powerful decorative element is provided by the colour, patterns and form of the floor tiles.

These two Sicilian kitchens (*above left* and *right*) have all the air of welcome that kitchens should have; crockery, ornaments and bottles provide an array of interesting shapes. Kitchen tables provide important surfaces, either for food preparation or as additional eating areas, a function for which the traditional refectory table is ideal.

In an age where the 'dream kitchen' inevitably means something pre-designed and carefully fitted in every aspect, there is something refreshing about cooking and eating areas that seem to have grown up piecemeal, using individual elements of varying age and style, as in this Florida house (*above left*). The presence of wood is always sympathetic to the eye and, here combined with traditional terracotta tiles, looks doubly appealing in this Tuscan farmhouse (*above right*).

The decorative properties of collections of books, objects or paintings are powerful indeed, especially if displayed together. Serried rows of family portraits cover the wall of one room (*opposite* and *below right*) – a kind of cabinet of curiosities – in the summer palace of the Chigi family in Rome, a medieval original transformed into a seventeenth-century Baroque gem (used by Luchino Visconti for the filming of *The Leopard* in 1963). Although much less cluttered, the library of a Swedish manor house (*top right*), now preserved in a folk-museum, makes a powerful decorative effect with undertones of accumulated knowledge and culture.

Books certainly furnish a room and few more splendidly than in the library of the Chigi summer palace; a sense of calm and learning pervades a space already replete with material comforts. The rooms of this palace are decorated in a variety of styles and filled with furniture of all periods – the accretions of time and custom that come with the occupancy of a single family for several centuries. Variously decorated with wall coverings of Cordovan leather, naturalist frescoes, birds both painted and as hanging mobiles, and *trompe-l'œil* paintings, they seem curiously frozen in time. At no point, however does luxury spill over into vulgarity; everywhere there is the happiest kind of opulence and good taste. Similar qualities are abundantly evident in another example of Italian interior decoration in the grand manner – a house in Umbria (*top right*).

At the heart of every thinking-person's house should lie a well-stocked library or book-room, a repository of the intellectual adventures of the owners. These are rooms where the arrangement of the books on shelves imposes its own kind of decorative order, sometimes immaculate, as in this Austrian reading-room in Salzburg (*top left*), sometimes more lived-in, as in this very much used study in a Paris apartment (*below left*). This latter room is also full of objects and furniture that reflect the eclectic tastes of the owners. The actual shelves were made simply from rough planks.

This library-study in a distinguished old Provençal house (*top right*) still retains its original eighteenth-century panelling. The contents of the room, however, are engagingly eclectic and of all periods; the arrangement of the books seems almost deliberately casual. Furniture includes a 1940s cane armchair and, in the foreground, a split chaise-longue of the type known as a 'duchesse'.

In this Paris apartment (*below right*) the library is contained effectively within the *salon* in carefully ordered, enclosed bookcases: a reader's library and music room, perhaps, rather than a study.

This book-room was created by simply lining the two long walls of the room with shelves. Its pleasant atmosphere of friendly vitality springs from the fact that it is both a workspace and an additional sitting-room, full of unlikely objects. The two plaster caryatids, for example, were inherited from an architect great-uncle of the owner; they were the original models for the decoration of an Art Nouveau building façade. A generally homely atmosphere is further enhanced by the rough tiles that form the floor.

The remarkable interiors illustrated here are the result of meetings of northern and southern European styles at various levels. Drawing inspiration from Italian Baroque palaces in the seventeenth century, then later receiving the attentions of eighteenth-century decorators inspired by French *trompe-l'œil* motifs, the owners of Louhisaari, near Turku, Finland, brought a very special blend of interior decoration to this Palladian villa, originally built in the style known

as 'Baltic Renaissance'. The furniture is a
bewildering mixture: Baroque, Rococo, Empire,
Biedermeier, and mainly the work of local Finnish
craftsmen working from pattern books. Yet
everything seems to have its place beneath the
beautifully frescoed interior walls. The house is
also notable for having been the childhood home
of Carl Gustaf Mannerheim, leader of the Finnish
people during their struggle for independence
from Russia, and their President in 1944.

Although both the decoration and furniture of Louhisaari are eclecticism run riot, there still remains an underlying sense of Scandinavian and Baltic good taste; there is a restraint in the use of the more exuberant elements taken from design cultures further south. This may be partly due to the use of lighter, pastel colours – greys, pale yellows or blues. Within this context there seems no incongruity between a *trompe-l'œil* panel in mid-eighteenth-century French style and a classically proportioned long-case clock of Swedish design.

The influence of northern European furniture and interior design began to make itself felt in the Baltic countries and in Scandinavia during the late seventeenth century, reaching a peak in the eighteenth century. Trade with the German states, the Netherlands and, especially, England in timber produced a return flow of goods made in wood, so that local designers became familiar with the taste in furniture of those countries. Most of the pieces visible here, including a fine long-case clock, were probably copied from English models, but there is again a lightness about this arrangement, as a delicate pale blue picks up the rays of northern light.

In decorating an interior and arranging objects within it, it is often the transitional spaces – corridors, landings, mezzanines – which present the greatest problems. One solution is to turn them, effectively, into miniature galleries, where collections of objects can be displayed. In the Castello Falconara in Sicily, a long gallery (*above left* and *right*) has become a place of interest and pleasure, with fine furniture and wall arrangements. Above, a line of ornamental hanging lamps lends another, practical focus of interest to the space.

Virtually bereft of all other forms of decoration, apart from fanlights and a tiled floor, this hall in a Burgundy house (*above*) is the ideal setting for a dramatic arrangement of deer heads and antlers. So dramatic is the impact of their pointed, branched forms, that the inclusion here of any further wall decoration or furniture would have seemed superfluous.

This Swedish bedchamber of the
Gustavian period (*above*), recreated
in the folk-museum of Skansen,
Stockholm, may also have been used
as a sitting-room, since the bed is
arranged along the wall and
embellished with drapes swept back
from the crowning tester. The chair
looks like a copy of a traditional
English carver, with a checked linen
loose cover in traditional style. A
child's chair, bureau and a cot
complete the furniture. In the
eighteenth century the walls would
have been covered in canvas painted
to create a panel effect.

If any lesson in interior design is to be learnt from these simple eighteenth-century bedrooms, now preserved in folk-museums, it must be how to create a feeling of comfort with simple means. Hanging curtains from a central tester give the bed space a warm and inviting quality, especially in contrast to the cold surround of bare floorboards. The Swedish example (*above left*) would probably have been considered a fairly extravagant piece in a culture traditionally given to restraint in all matters of style. Restraint is certainly present in this bedroom (*above right*), preserved in the model village of Sturbridge, Massachusetts, a reconstituted rural community, reflecting New England life between 1790 and 1840.

A coolly reticent northern classicism sets the tone of this Swedish dining-room (*above*), now preserved as a museum exhibit; the panelled walls, relieved by large portrait ovals, are painted a characteristic light grey, with highlights in gold. The table, attractively set for a forthcoming Christmas repast, heralded by the sprinkling of flowerets over the floor, is surrounded by chairs which look like simple reinterpretations of mid-eighteenth-century English styles. A classical bust by the window and a chandelier with multiple crystal drops provide two decorative additions to the overall sobriety.

Still focused around an imposing table, but in strict contrast to the retiring quality of the nordic dining-room (*opposite*), is this Tuscan arrangement (*above*) whose lineage might be safely described as Southern Baroque. The curves and complications of ornate cornices and wall mouldings are repeated in the heavy frames of mirrors and paintings – the chairs around the banqueting table, however, reveal an English influence in their simple lines. The enormous Oriental jars make effective but easily removable ornaments. Just visible in the huge mirror on the chimney-breast is the vaulted and decorated ceiling.

The effect is one of direct honesty, sturdiness of construction and suitability for purpose in this traditional Swedish kitchen, preserved in the manor of Tureholm. And, yet, an urge to decorate has been clearly present in the subtle application of the deeper blue to panels, ceiling and door, then extended to the free-standing cabinet. Simple chairs form a contrast to the elaborate wall sconce, while casually arranged blue-and-white crockery makes a pleasing display.

There are few sights more impressive in a domestic context than the shelves of a traditional dresser fully stacked with blue-and-white plates (*left*), an indicator of family wealth. More formal than the display illustrated on the preceding pages, this arrangement in a room in the manor of Tureholm, Sweden, nevertheless retains the restrained homely quality that characterizes so much Scandinavian design. Presumably the presence of the folding table and the simple, decorated dining chairs indicates that this room was also used as a dining-room.

The late Georgian period saw the highest achievements in Irish architecture and design. This wall display of a dinner service above the neo-classical lines of a late-eighteenth-century sideboard with pedestal cupboards (*opposite*) amply conveys the sense of refinement and order of those times. The elegant tapering legs of the furniture suggest that this piece may have been made after designs published in the pattern books of George Hepplewhite and Thomas Sheraton.

Strongly patterned tiling, black-and-white check especially, makes a wonderful space filler in rooms with a utilitarian purpose. The pattern of the floor visually dominates this saddle-room in a Scottish country house (*top left*). A more restrained version provides a decorative backdrop to the brilliantly polished copper pans in this magnificently preserved big-house kitchen in Wales (*below left*).

The careful preservation of this traditional kitchen in a large Scottish house (*right*) does make a point of some relevance to the owners and decorators of more contemporary examples: that the forms, materials and usefulness of the utensils of the past often make them stunning additions to the kitchen, contrasting with modern equipment. The drawback of some of them, like copper saucepans, is that they require a lot of time-consuming maintenance. But others, illustrated here, have the warmth and patina of long-established use: a mortar and pestle, earthenware bowls, wooden trays, a set of scales with weights, and a huge wall clock.

FRANCE

WALES

MASSACHUSETTS

MASSACHUSETTS

SCOTLAND

SCOTLAND

The kitchens illustrated on these pages (*right* and *opposite*) are, in one sense, museum pieces, in that they are all in houses that have been restored to illustrate and commemorate the life of bygone times. In another sense, they are immediately contemporary, in that they contain features which are constantly being applied to present-day, working kitchens. All of them emphasize the importance of a good-sized kitchen table, which can be used as an area for food preparation as well as for food consumption. How attractive, too, are the patterns and colours created by dresser-like arrangements of pots and pans on shelves and by large tiled surfaces, especially floors.

MASSACHUSETTS

A sense of spaciousness and light pervades the whole of this fashion designer's holiday home in Saint-Rémy-de-Provence (*above* and *opposite*). What could have been the darkening effect of low ceilings and their supporting beams has been nullified by the overall white colour scheme. Two long kitchen tables, placed together, create a substantial dining surface for family and guests, while the metal chairs can easily be used for other purposes – eating outdoors, for instance. One touch of elegance, though, are the two tall silver candelabra.

In the same house, the kitchen retains the overall white colour scheme of the other rooms, but with subtle additions and variations. The actual units are painted a light shade of grey, while a pleasant splash of colour is introduced in the form of the tiles lining the wall behind the main work units. Bottles, jars and containers in open display provide both practical and ornamental elements.

The beauty of simple things is an ideal well worth bearing in mind in the furnishing of kitchens. Although this Scottish kitchen (*above left* and *right*) has been preserved as a historic example, many of its elements still have immediate relevance today. How impressive is the traditional cupboard, topped by a huge burnished brass dish. The stove, too, has a powerful and welcoming presence and is not so different in form from gas-fired and wood-burning models today.

A kind of grand simplicity marks both traditional Scottish and Scandinavian design – the signature of a specifically northern sensibility, perhaps. Both these arrangements – somewhere between the sphere of the kitchen and that of the dining-room – are in museum settings: Scotland (*above left*) and Sweden (*above right*). The corner of the room in the folk-museum of Skansen, Stockholm, evokes all the classicism of the Gustavian period, marvellously expressed in the form of a console table with characteristic tapering legs.

As befitting a country subject to long, harsh and very dark winters, a Swedish sitting-room was traditionally dominated by its stove. This example (*above*), in a room preserved in Skansen, is of particularly simple design; often, the stove would have been covered in elaborately patterned faïence, further emphasizing its importance as a comfort to the family and an expression of its prosperity. This room setting is completed by simple rustic furniture, with two sophisticated Neoclassical looking-glasses.

In addition to the warmth from the stove, the traditional Swedish interior was often enlivened by brightly painted furniture: here, in the form of a long-case clock (*above*), which would no doubt have figured among a family's most treasured possessions. In this arrangement of rooms at Skansen, a classic cylindrical Swedish faïence stove is visible through the doorway.

Overleaf
The wall decoration in this traditional Swedish interior may have been intended to imitate marbling, but the use of a quick-dry distemper probably left the painter very little time to achieve subtle effects. The result, however, is one of great graphic boldness and originality, oddly suggestive of massive cell structures.

STYLES FOR COMFORT

The interiors illustrated here and on following pages are a very far cry from the purist minimalism with which we opened this chapter. Their principal aim has been the creation of a warm, protected, comfortable environment, although many of them apply very simple, unsophisticated means to achieve this. In three interiors (*this page*), all in reconstituted Welsh miners' houses, an immediate sense of well-being is induced by the presence of an open fire, a pleasure that can no longer be enjoyed in many contemporary interiors. These fires were also the means for heating food and other items in the small side ovens. Furniture is simple and wooden, but there is plenty of it, including a very fine wheel-back Windsor chair (*top far left*). A third layer of comfort is applied by the plentiful display of what would have been cherished objects: plates, vases, mugs, polished brasses and clocks. The family crockery for special occasions is proudly displayed in a glass-fronted corner cupboard. In a similarly unsophisticated traditional Canadian interior (*below left*) it is a stove that provides that focal point of warmth and energy around which the family would have gathered.

This simple colonial-era dwelling is preserved as a folk-museum near Quebec. The substantial timbers used in its construction and the simple wooden cupboards suggest indeed a land where timber is plentiful and the winters cold. In spite of the massive presence of the elaborately decorated stove, there is an overall severity about the place, a reminder perhaps that Canada, too, has strong connections with that northern aesthetic so forcefully expressed in Scottish and Scandinavian interiors.

More examples of traditional Swedish decoration in the folk-museum of Skansen; but these interiors (*above left* and *right*) are of a very different order from the Gustavian Neoclassicism of the houses of the great families of Stockholm. These are family environments where everything precious is on display, from the few plates on the racks of the dresser to treasured articles of painted furniture. The table and chairs are rough and rustic, but in a corner stands an elaborately decorated cupboard, the most important piece on view, often a wedding present or the receptacle for the bride's trousseau.

One striking aspect about the wooden furniture in this Canadian interior (*above left*) is how graceful it is in all its simplicity. The chairs, table and double-bodied cupboard have an extraordinary refinement that comes from simple lines and a fitness for purpose. A much more self-conscious attempt to introduce strong decorative elements into a simple interior has been made in this Swedish dining-room (*above right*). There are several examples here of rustic painted furniture, with by far the most elaborate decoration being applied to the most precious objects: the long-case clock and the corner cupboard.

There is a sympathetic quality to wood and to its use in the kitchen in preference to metal, plastic or ceramic surfaces. Here, a wooden dresser and shelving (*above left*) provides an entirely appropriate background to a collection of country pottery in this house in Haute-Savoie, France. Even in a strictly urban environment, the warm tones of a distinctively coloured hardwood can be an agreeable relief from the sense of being surrounded by stone, brick and concrete. This small Parisian kitchen (*above right*) is a veritable haven of delights, all framed in the glow of the surrounding wood, in a modern interpretation of traditional rustic elements.

Wood in the bedroom provides a sympathetic background to the soft furniture usually present. In this house in Haute-Savoie (*above left*), the chalet-like construction gives a pleasantly protected and enclosed feeling to the room, setting off the obvious items of comfort – bed and wing armchair. More spartan in feeling is this traditional Canadian bedroom, although the four-poster and the portraits on the wall suggest that this room was highly regarded within the household (*above right*).

Now preserved in a folk-museum, the interior of the Quebec trapper's cabin nevertheless expresses the fundamental human need for comfort, protection and warmth that its constructors would have felt in the midst of the Canadian winter. A sturdy stove occupies the central position among the simple furniture, while tiny windows are intended to minimize heat loss. The rest of the furniture is of rustic simplicity, and yet its very ordinariness lends it a kind of dignity and modernity.

These two Scandinavian interiors, very different in their degrees of finish, are both in a way expressive of the same traditions. A painter's studio, reconstructed at Skansen (*top left*), is filled with the artefacts of a culture that has a high regard for the materials it uses in design and production: simple yet peculiarly sophisticated wooden furniture and objects, flat-weave hangings and rugs, all within a construction in the material most immediately to hand.

A similar sense of respect for materials is evident in the house (*below left*) designed by Eliel Saarinen at Hvittsträsk, Finland, during the first decade of the twentieth century. There is an integrated quality about the relationship of the furniture and decorative elements of this sitting-room, reflecting the architect's own interpretation of the Arts and Crafts ideal of the family house as a total work of art.

Wood in the house, especially in the form of exposed beams, seems to draw out pleasurable feelings for most people. Is it a sense of being in contact with the structural fundamentals of the building that protects us? In the attic floors of old houses, especially, there is the sense of living with what, literally, keeps the roof over our heads. There is also a secretive, hideaway quality about the cavity just below the roof, wonderfully expressed in these two bedrooms in French houses, one near Grenoble (*top right*) and the other in the central *département* of Allier (*below right*).

These four interiors (*this page* and *opposite*) show how a sense of comfort is built up within a small space by the intense concentration of pattern, texture, small objects and articles of furniture. In this Normandy interior (*above left*), rendered warm and comfortable by the wooden panelling, even a hanging hat and coat take on ornamental value. The decoration of a trailer home presents exceptional problems of space. Yet this home to a family of Parisian performance artists (*above right*) manages to produce effects of comfort and opulence. Everything has been planned so that the majority of the space can be given over to extending the illusion that this is a conventional sitting-room, with rugs, chairs, tables, and chests of drawers.

In the same trailer, the bedroom (*above left*) is a veritable nest of knick-knacks, of soft furnishings and even toys. It is separated from the living space by a heavy velvet curtain that can be drawn back during the day to create extra seating. In some ways, the heavy ornamental effects within the trailer recall the Victorians' taste for intensely patterned schemes in their interiors. This classic example of a nineteenth-century room (*above right*) reflects the standard European styles which were exported to Canada during that period, with a profusion of interlocking motifs on curtains and carpets, here preserved in an old Quebec house.

The effect of books lining a room is welcoming and pleasant in all these interiors (*this page* and *opposite*), yet the overall impression is of book-rooms less finished than those previously illustrated in this book. In the Chiapas region of Mexico, at San Cristobal de Las Casas, lies an institute devoted to safeguarding the interests of the local population. Originally founded in the 1940s, the institute was established in an old seminary and now welcomes volunteers to its pleasantly relaxed rooms; this sitting-room is made remarkable by a fireplace faced in local brick (*above*).

This study (*below left*) is yet another example of the Swedish restraint in interior decoration we have already noted in the many rooms conserved at Skansen. This example, though, makes much more of small ornament and wall display, yet all with a touching humility; as though the user of the desk and books here must have been a worthy but not a grand member of society.

From this photograph (*opposite*) it is easy to see how the arrangement of highly personal objects, furniture and the apparently casual lining-up of the books on the shelves makes this book-room in a Paris fashion stylist's apartment such a success as a comfortable working place.

If ever any recognized style of interior decoration suggested comfort, then it is the English Style. It invokes thoughts of massive, maybe slightly worn, armchairs and sofas, club fenders, and a general atmosphere of *usé* opulence. In fact, this interior (*top left*) – however much it may suggest these characteristics – is part of a converted north London warehouse in which the owners both live and carry on their antique furniture business. A nineteenth-century lamp casts a sympathetic light through a silk shade on to two massive armchairs, a pile of books on architecture distributed between the floor and a nineteenth-century console table; beneath lies a litter of plaster dogs. This space – a study – is separated from a kitchen by Neoclassical columns.

A similar feeling of comfort coupled with tradition is exhaled by this book-lined study in an old Quebec house (*below left*). Again, there is a sense that time is standing still somewhere in the late Victorian or Edwardian era. And how dark wood contributes to this effect!

Although far removed from England, this well-furnished study in a Chilean house has the same well-cared-for feeling that characterizes the other interiors illustrated on these pages. The furniture, however, is conspicuously ornate, while the addition of a guitar hints at the decor's Iberian origins.

Very English is the study at Charleston, the farmhouse in Sussex made famous by the occupancy of prominent members of the Bloomsbury circle. The painting around the fireplace and the design of the fabric of the armchairs are the work of the Omega Workshops, founded in 1913 by the art critic Roger Fry and which promoted the work of young Bloomsbury artists like Vanessa Bell and Duncan Grant.

Though lacking the ostentatiously comfortable accoutrements of the English Style – large armchairs and sofas – this room in a Paris apartment (*above*) manages to convey a very sympathetic, lived-in feeling. The articles of furniture are spare and elegant, but the accumula- tions of paintings, drawings, books and a well-filled pinboard make for a very agreeable study-type bedroom. There is also an air about the arrangement of objects and furniture that suggests everything came together in an unplanned, accidental fashion.

Comfort, Mitteleuropa style, does have a certain formality about it: chairs, based on eighteenth-century French models, arranged in a formal conversation grouping around a small table; the very deliberate distribution and arrangement of pictures and other objects; the polished wooden floor left bare. Yet, the room is obviously intended as a place where people can meet and converse in a pleasant, welcoming atmosphere, where books and the more treasured collections of the owners of this Budapest apartment can be displayed (*above*).

If the two opposing principles of interior decoration could be described as, first, a search for pure unadorned line and form, and second, a glorying in elaboration and decoration, there can be no doubt where the sympathies of the owner of this Brussels apartment (*these pages*) would lie. Every surface, horizontal and vertical, is filled with additional elements to create a vivid environment in which the world beyond the apartment has little part to play. Dark walls and bookcases create a sense of enclosure, while providing a wonderful counterpoint to the lighter coloured spines of the books. Everything within the rooms has been called into service as ornament; and in addition to the more orthodox embellishments of paintings, screens, urns and vases, there is a remarkable wall display of the corner sections of antique picture frames.

Dark colours and a flamboyant use of heavily patterned surfaces were two dominant features of the late Victorian interior – or, at least, of its middle-class version (*above left* and *above right*). Heavy woods, notably mahogany, lavish ornament, and Persian carpets would denote the prosperity of a family of standing in town or city. Interestingly, though, there are recollections in this Quebec house of what the Victorian bourgeoisie no doubt considered to have been the decorative indulgences of the gentry – a trophy head, a library atmosphere, and the ostentatious display of costly objects.

In this Victorian setting (*above left*) the taste of that era for pattern has been heavily indulged: every conceivable surface, including the ceiling, bears a heavy weight of decoration in the causes of comfort and homeliness. Yet, there is a simple Arts and Crafts feel to the furniture, an indication that the latter part of the nineteenth century would engage seriously with issues of design and fitness for purpose. And in contrast to the Victorian decorators, how simply and elegantly this late-eighteenth-century Scottish interior (*above right*) achieves a sense of pleasant warmth; how attractive paintings and furniture look against the green-painted panels.

INDIVIDUAL TOUCHES

Many of the interiors illustrated on the following pages make extensive use of very personal possessions to create highly individual environments. Others derive their uniqueness from a deliberate avoidance of finished decoration. One suspects that the distressed knee-hole desk (*above left*) in this

Paris apartment is rarely used as anything but as a support for other decorative elements in the room. Much more workmanlike, albeit in a very decorative corner against an exposed stud wall, is this finely polished writing table, also in a Paris apartment (*above right*).

Sometimes a working desk can form an interesting focal point within a larger room, a kind of alternative to the main seating area. This can be an especially effective arrangement if the desk or table carries a still-life of unusual objects or small works of art, as in these two very different examples in Paris apartments (*above left* and *above right*).

Accumulation of intrinsically interesting objects is one certain way of building a distinctive atmosphere in any room. This Neapolitan interior (*top left*), for instance, derives much of its charm from the display of examples from the owner's collection of nineteenth-century fabrics, whose rich patterns dominate the decoration of the walls. Other, subsidiary arrangements make this room a veritable cabinet of curiosities: a clutter of books on the table, small pieces of statuary which may once have adorned a cemetery, even dolls' heads among the other *objets trouvés*. A similar sense of casually decorative effects through clutter pervades this Paris apartment (*below left*). Here, the main concentration of disparate objects is on a fine Neoclassical table, in keeping with a general sobriety in the furniture.

The effect of the Paris apartment (*opposite*) that belonged to Coco Chanel might be justly characterized as one of carefully finished opulence. Overall, there is a sense of luxury, but it is not arrived at accidentally. Everything here has its place, from the classical statuary on the mantelpiece to the positioning of the Louis-Quinze chairs; the scale of the objects is as important as their provenance. And everything is still exactly as it was when Coco worked here.

Ease, comfort and privacy: these are the qualities supremely expressed in the form of the traditional wing chair. Usually deeply upholstered, with padded arms, its high back rises to form two protruding rounded 'wings' which protect the occupant's head from draughts or unwanted intrusions. Quite when this form first developed is hard to ascertain, but certainly examples were being made in the late seventeenth century; the basic design retained its popularity through the eighteenth and nineteenth centuries and well into the Edwardian era, when it seems to have acquired its status, along with the Chesterfield, of being the classic seating for clubland. This particular example (*left*), at the farmhouse of Charleston in Sussex, does however retain some feeling of lightness, perhaps because the legs remain exposed and the covering fabric is light in colour. It is much more usual to see distinctly 'heavier' examples, with upholstery, often in thick velvets or leathers, reaching down to short, balled feet. Some interesting attempts have been made in the last hundred years to give a modernist look to the form, notably by Charles Eames in his rosewood and leather 'No. 670' of 1956 and by Arne Jacobsen in his 'Egg' chair of the following year.

In contrast to the relative sobriety of the English example, this Corsican wing chair (*right*) is distinctly flamboyant. All the features of the traditional form – the high back and wings – have been exaggerated to create a fitting piece for an elegant *salon*. Note, too, the cabriole legs, clearly intended to be left exposed.

SEE MORE

WING-BACK CHAIRS   239   249   297   304

Decorative eclecticism is the key principle in the arrangement of this New York apartment. Every room in the house has a different theme, expressed both in the furniture and in the wall decoration. The main bedroom (*top left*) is devoted to the culture of the Navajos; the rugs on the floor, the bed cover and the wall-hanging all have the distinctive strong patterning of their traditional weaving. A frieze around the room represents examples of Navajo pottery. The bed itself is in woven osier. Another bedroom (*below left*) is imbued with the spirit of eighteenth-century Europe, with distinct New World touches, like the rug. The large cushions, bed cover and the armchair are all in twill.

All the bedrooms illustrated here have one purpose – to render any time spent in them as comfortable as possible. Yet, they do have their differences, partly explicable by their locations. In a traditional Parisian apartment (*top right*), the exposed beams of the old structure lend a pleasantly warm note in an urban environment. A bedroom in a Neapolitan house (*top far right*) is yet another display area for the owner's eclectic tastes. A small votive shrine stands on a tripod in the corner; the wall decoration includes an angel's head in *papier mâché* fixed in an abstract metal structure. This Swedish bedroom (*below right*) is the epitome of Scandinavian Neoclassical restraint; note the palette of pale blues and yellows. In a Provençal house (*below far right*) the head and foot boards of the beds pick up the traditional colours and patterns of the region – those warm yellows and floral designs so often reproduced on the textiles and crockery of southern France.

There is an entirely seductive quality about the informality of these two sitting-rooms in a house in the Lot region of south-west France (*top left* and *below left*). They are warm, welcoming and clearly very lived-in. Each of them recognizes the primacy of the fireplace as a main point of focus, around which the collections of the owners' paintings and objects can be arranged. Both of them rely on colour to set the mood of the place – vibrant rugs and furniture coverings and a faded but nevertheless warm background.

SEE MORE

FIREPLACES   234   255   338   340

The fireplaces in these two interiors play a formal role in the overall planning of the rooms. Objects and paintings are arranged around them in an orderly fashion, though with different effects in mind. The exposed brick and distressed wood in a New York house (*top right*) give the whole room a 'country' air, reinforced by the rustic furniture and the 'naïve' paintings on the walls. Again, in a holiday home on the Île de Ré (*below right*), the arrangement of books, paintings and nautical models around the fireplace is carefully ordered, turning the whole wall into an area devoted to the owner's personal interests

Strong, earthy colours are the very stuff of Provence, to be found in textiles, crockery and, here, on the walls of a traditional house (*opposite* and *right*). Yellow, in warm tones, is especially associated with the pottery of the region; how appropriate, then, that the simple kitchen of the house should be painted in that colour. The ochrous red of the dining-room is also very much a local colour, used both inside and outside houses; it makes a marvellous background for a Cézanne-like still-life on the table. The paints used on the walls have an intensity that is quite unexpected.

Accumulations of objects, personal possessions, clutter, can be turned to good decorative use, making a virtue of creative mess. In a house just outside Paris (*above left*), the owner – a painter and stylist – has marshalled personal effects to create an atmosphere of light and charm. A work-bench and drawing equipment sit happily with old and new furniture, hanging garments and paintings. Other kinds of object make their presence felt by their unusualness in a domestic setting, like these tree sculptures in a Belgian fashion studio (*above right*).

Another Belgian interior (*above left*), part of an apartment right in the centre of Brussels, is much enlivened by the apparently random clutter which fills it. Books lie untidily, while a sense of the surreal is imparted by dummies for clothes display. More orderly is this dining area in a sculptor's studio in Stockholm (*above right*), but again the display of apparently unrelated objects and works of art makes for a space full of interest.

Private rooms – bedrooms and studies – often encapsulate the personal histories of their owners. It is there that we may keep the artefacts and records of the past in the form of possessions no longer used, forgotten toys and playthings. A pleasantly intimate air, for instance, pervades this bedroom in a Paris flat (*above*), as though the occupant had just vacated it.

Decorative licence, the freedom to juxtapose unlikely objects of a personal nature, seems so much more appropriate in a study than in a principal reception room. This private hideaway in a Santiago house (*above*) is full of references to the equestrian interests of the owner.

INHERITED TEXTURES

Homestyle, northern Pennsylvania: this minimally restored interior of a cottage (*right*) near the Delaware river is the weekend retreat of a New York couple, a dress designer and a conceptual artist. The cottage forms part of a larger estate of farm buildings that the present owners use very much in the original spirit of the place. There has been no major restoration, no attempt to prettify – just the effort to carry on life on the farm as it had been lived there for a hundred years before.

What goes around comes around; what was consigned to the rubbish skip twenty years ago is this year's retro style. One notable aspect of this form of interior decorators' nostalgia is a preference for artefacts of the pre-plastics age and a fascination with the modest and the ordinary of the past. In the Tenement Museum on New York's Lower East Side, several apartments have now been reconstituted to reflect life in a tenement between the mid nineteenth century and the pre-World War II period (*opposite* and *below right*). These are the conditions in which the urban immigrants who flocked to the city during that period would have struggled to find some dignity in life. The other kitchens illustrated here – in London (*top right*), in Tuscany (*top far right*) and in Paris (*below far right*) – all make extensive use of fixtures and utensils recycled from a bygone age. What was simple and basic has become chic.

A similar kind of nostalgia to that which makes us value our old pots and pans seems to haunt those owners of old houses who believe that a distressed look is, in some manner, more authentic than carefully finished decoration. The general effect, as in this Belgian house (*above*), is one of constant becoming, of an arrangement of these elements that might finally come together to form the completed environment. The lack of finish does, indeed, allow the display of variegated wall textures and colours; irregular, unsmoothed surfaces are a perfectly legitimate setting for articles of furniture.

The Dominican nuns who founded the beautiful convent of Santa Catalina in Oaxaca, Mexico, almost certainly had no thoughts of deliberately achieving a distressed look in its rooms (*above*). No doubt the interiors owe their simple rough walls to the lack of ostentation appropriate to the nuns' calling. Now transformed into a hotel, the convent offers rooms full of elaborately carved Iberian-style furniture that looks quite magnificent against the roughness of those walls.

The fascination of old, untreated wall surfaces and the random pattern effects they often display is part of a whole new way of looking at the question of 'finish' in decoration. It no longer seems essential to have solid, evenly applied colour on walls; ragging, dragging, marbling, colour washing all produce a variety of pleasingly irregular effects. The ravages of time, though, cannot be easily reproduced, and the owners of both these interiors – in France (*above left*) and in Belgium (*above right*) – have achieved a dramatic and pleasing effect by simply leaving things alone and letting the echoes of the past tell their own story.

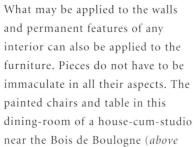

What may be applied to the walls and permanent features of any interior can also be applied to the furniture. Pieces do not have to be immaculate in all their aspects. The painted chairs and table in this dining-room of a house-cum-studio near the Bois de Boulogne (*above* *left*) wear their visible age with dignity and would lose much of their charm if stripped or given a fresh coat of paint. And rough rustic wood (*above right*), here in a Paris kitchen, does not necessarily need the attentions of varnish or wax.

The principle of minimum intervention has been applied throughout
this remarkably beautiful house in
south-west France (*these pages*). All
the exposed surfaces – walls, floors,
ceilings – have been left in the state
they were probably in at the end of
the nineteenth century. Surprisingly,
perhaps, the elaborate forms of
period furniture take on an
additional allure against the sombre
colours of untreated plaster and
boards. Fixed features, too, like the
fireplaces, stand out unexpectedly.

This graceful seventeenth-century house in Provence is furnished throughout in a supremely eclectic fashion; whatever pleases the owners is included in a brilliant and imaginative way. The bedrooms (*above*) are no exception; this one is made notable by the presence of the oddly shaped *baldaquin* and an array of vigorously patterned flat-weave rugs. In keeping with the untouched quality of the rest of a house in south-west France (*pp. 280-281*), this bedroom (*opposite*) relies entirely on furniture for any decorative effects, created mainly by the voluminous drapes attached to the central tester of one of the beds.

No furniture of contemporary manufacture has even been allowed through the doors of this rough-stone house in Connemara, Ireland. The building itself exhales the savage, mysterious quality of this part of the Irish coast, the very edge of Europe. In all the rooms the basic fabric of construction is exposed; and against the rugged walls and floor is arranged the furniture, all of which unashamedly displays the wear and tear of time and its origins as architectural salvage. Even the doors have been taken from other buildings, like the cast-iron fireplace in the dining-room (*top left*) and the features and furniture of the bathroom (*below left*). The cabinet above the bath was the upper part of a Victorian fireplace, but its cupboards and mirror now make it an ideal bathroom accoutrement. An assortment of furniture of all ages, including a Lloyd Loom table, completes a room of surprises.

The dining-room of a house in south-west France (*pp. 280-281, 283*) continues the theme of other rooms there: arrangements of decorative furniture in a setting of unrestored simplicity (*top right*). Here, though, there is an added feature of interest: the original stone floor. The accidental, random quality of untreated walls is spectacularly evident in this Paris apartment (*below right*), mainly because all the other features in the room have a certain formality in appearance and arrangement, making the wall surface all the more striking. The placing of the large mirror above the fireplace is a strictly classical juxta-position. And the very shapes of the Louis-Seize *fauteuils* bespeak formal elegance, which contrasts with the folding table.

The patina of the past is everywhere in the rooms of this seventeenth-century Provençal house (*p. 205*), originally home to several generations of lawyers. Its latest owner, a Parisian florist, has very clearly decided to let the unique charms of the place reveal themselves gradually, avoiding any over-hasty, comprehensive restoration that could easily destroy the spirit of the place. On the ground floor lies the *grand salon* (*right*) which, at some point in the past, has been stripped of the panelling and mirrors which would certainly have lined its walls. The accidental result is an amazing space in which colour, texture and light combine to create an entirely individual dining-room during the summer months. In winter, the proximity to the garden makes the room an ideal makeshift orangery for the potted plants that need protection from the cold.

Russet reds are everywhere in Roussillon, Provence: every wall, inside and outside, made of locally quarried stone, is tinted by the powder from the amazing ochre cliffs on which the village stands. Even its name is derived from the ochre; the Romans called the place Viscus Russulus ('red hill'). In this dining-room (*top left*) in one of the village houses the presence of the ochre is only too evident. There is also an array of other traditional Provençal colours – yellows and blues – in the form of the pots on the side table.

What is it about warmer climates that makes rough, untreated surfaces so much more pleasant than those where cold, wet conditions prevail? Something, perhaps, to do with keeping interiors simple in the knowledge that much of one's living can be done outside. Simplicity is certainly the keynote of this Mallorcan farmhouse, well inland and far from the tourist crowds of the island's coast. The bathroom (*below left* and *opposite*) is illuminated by small windows let into the thick walls and made of slightly opaque glass that filters the strong sunlight.

In this Provençal kitchen (*top left*), the symmetrical sets of shelves are framed in willow branches cut during country excursions. The materials of the units, too, have a humble origin; they are in fact made of simple rough planks of wood, nailed together. The attractive utensils, crockery and bottles were all found at bric-à-brac stalls in local markets.

Much more obviously finished are these elegant kitchen cabinets in a Paris apartment (*below left*), permitting an almost museum-like display of the owner's crockery. Kitchens, too, can extend the decorative possibilities of any home.

Although the jugs, utensils, baskets in this composition have very different shapes and purposes, the owner of this French kitchen (*right*) has imposed a carefully worked-out symmetry on the whole storage space. On the top shelf, decorative pottery provides pattern in interesting shapes, but even the more practical features, such as the basket and scales, are displayed as though they too were part of an overall design.

Vestiges of the former decoration of this Provençal house remain in the tidily arranged kitchen (*above left*) in the form of wall mouldings and the old cupboards. The whole space makes a pleasant breakfast area and supplementary dining-room.

In more rustic style, the kitchen of a farmhouse in the Cévennes is similarly equipped for communal eating (*above right*). All the pots and pans clearly have their designated place – essential in a kitchen that is also to be used for dining.

Order on a grand scale pervades the restored kitchens of two magnificent houses – one the château of Cormatin in Burgundy (*above left*) and the other the summer *palazzo* of the Chigi family near Rome (*above right*). All the original implements in the Burgundian kitchen are present and intact, including firedogs and the chimney hooks for hanging cooking pots and kettles, known as *crémaillères*. Such displays provide invaluable inspiration for the owners and decorators of more modest properties.

A NEW ECLECTICISM

Clarity in all forms seem to have been the guiding principle for the decoration of this New York apartment (*above*). The soft white of the walls and ceilings and the wood used for the floor maximize the daylight flooding into the room. There are relatively few articles of furniture in a large space and what is there forms a very balanced arrangement. Overall, a kind of modern classicism, emphasized by the pillars, sets the tone. But the classicism is far from strict: the pillars are non-structural and the paintings remain unframed.

Many of the objects in this house near the extraordinary village of Les Baux-de-Provence (*above*) have diverse and exotic origins, yet they have all been marshalled here to form a harmonious and perfectly balanced whole. A magnificent African shield above the fireplace acts as a point of focus. The proportions of the room, too, are such that a normally intrusive element like a staircase is easily accommodated and even forms a stylish additional feature in itself.

Nothing could be more straightforward than the positioning of the
furniture in an artist's Paris
apartment – central table and ostentatiously comfortable armchairs and
sofa around the walls, and large
classical looking-glass above the
fireplace. Yet there are other levels
here that render the place much
more interesting: a personal
statement in the painting and
numbering of certain pieces. Note,
too, that the furniture itself has
interestingly distressed surfaces.

All the traditional qualities of French interior decoration are on display in a Parisian sitting-room: beautifully proportioned Louis-Quinze furniture in a relatively simple setting. But clearly there are some gestures towards comfort in the form of the strange wing sofa and a 'duchesse' day-bed. Any feeling of formality is dissipated by the presence of loose covers, wooden kitchen stools and other seemingly incongruous objects.

Although this magnificently proportioned sitting-room is in a house in
the Cévennes (*above*), there is
certainly nothing rustic in the
careful balancing of individual
elements within it. The defining
note is struck by the formal

Neoclassical elegance of the Louis-
Seize *bergères* ranged in such a way
that all attention is directed towards
the imposing fireplace. Classical
urns and a pair of plaster
medallions complete the impression
of sophisticated moderation.

In the same way that a successful still-life is created by the pleasing juxtaposition of apparently disparate things, so this Brussels interior (*above*) succeeds in the very deliberate arrangement of varied articles of furniture and decorative objects. The whole room, in an apartment belonging to a film designer, looks like a complete surrealist composition, in which apparent differences are reconciled: a rustic table with vase and formal chairs of various periods.

Leaving the structural elements of a house or apartment still visible within the interior often creates bold decorative effects by contrasting natural textures with smoothly finished surfaces. Exposing the venerable beams in this Paris apartment (*top left*) also achieves an effective counterbalance to the formality of the furniture arrangement, with its focus on the imposing round table.

In shape, the round table is a versatile article of furniture. Sitting around it induces feelings of conviviality, of being part of a group – in this New York dining space, for instance (*below left*). It can also easily stand alone as a central point in transitional spaces, such as the hall in this private Paris house (*opposite*). In such positions, lit from above, it also serves as a very useful surface for the display of smaller decorative elements.

Both of these interiors show a similar measured and thoughtful approach to decoration on the part of their owners, although in very different contexts. In both cases, though, a monochromatic colour scheme acts as a unifying element. A light, airy sitting-room in a house in Saint-Rémy-de-Provence (*top left*) makes its effect through a relatively small number of pieces of furniture carefully arranged around a low table. There is more detailing in the combination of objects and furniture in this Paris *salon* (*below left*), but a similar sense of order prevails. Most of the sculptures, paintings, engravings and articles of furniture are small, apart from a work-table in wood and wrought-iron. The sofa is in fact a well-disguised folding metal camp bed. Two long mirrors with lead frames mounted on the wall give an extra illusion of spaciousness.

Proper measure in all things clearly guided the fashion-designer owner of this Paris apartment (*top right* and *below right*). Nothing is too much and nothing is too little. There is a sense of comfort, admittedly, yet this is counterbalanced by the undoubted elegance of the interiors, derived from fine traditional furniture and a balanced number of other objects. The whole ensemble feels light and airy, due to the large windows and the looking-glass above the fireplace. The effect of hard uncovered floors is softened by the folds of fabric which, like the walls, are of neutral tones.

Overleaf
There is an eclectic spirit at work in this *salon* in the château of Outrelaise in Normandy, yet the overall effect is one of careful composition. The furniture is a mix of styles – hybrid Louis-Quinze and Louis-Seize, Second Empire in the manner of Louis-Treize, with characteristic turned legs and back, nineteenth-century ease in the form of two capacious wing armchairs and small occasional articles of various dates. The floor is strewn with large Anatolian kilims. Yet, because of the presence of so many unlikely companions, the room has an entirely composed modern feeling, underscored by the choice of colour for the wall panelling, whose vertical and horizontal lines effectively define the space.

The magnificent proportions of this first-floor apartment in a seventeenth-century house in Versailles (*above*) are revealed and enhanced by the careful choice of furniture and the reticence of the decoration. Almost monochrome, the background colour allows the forms of the furniture to assume their true importance. Mixed with the lovingly assembled collection of fine pieces – the owner is an interior decorator of international repute – are objects of rougher texture. For instance, the wood for fuel is prominently arranged as much for its look as its function in a niche that housed a faïence stove.

Cool, pale colours set the tone for a dining-room in a Corsican house (*above*). No jarring element intrudes upon this scene of peace and quiet; even the angles of the high-backed dining chairs are subdued by loose linen covers, discreetly bordered in yellow. All the more dramatic in effect, then, is the interior designer owner's collection of mounted entomological specimens.

BRUSSELS

PARIS

PARIS

PARIS

PARIS

PARIS

The desire to achieve carefully composed interiors, illustrated on the preceding pages, can of course be applied to the less obviously public parts of any house or apartment. Corners of bedrooms, distribution of kitchen units, small transitional spaces (*opposite*) can all demand the attention of the ordering impulse, especially when large numbers of small objects are on display. These may not always be of intrinsic value or even have immediately recognizable decorative qualities. Yet, this corner of the kitchen in a Cévennes farmhouse (*right*) does make a pleasing composition, albeit of Neapolitan coffee-makers, assorted saucepans and two gas cylinders! All these arrangements appear the more powerfully decorative for being positioned against unifying colour schemes.

It isn't always the presence of furniture and artefacts in the same, formal styles that give an interior space a feeling of cohesion. There is considerable variety in the contents of this Belgium painter's studio: covered sofas, Lloyd Loom chairs, books, paintings, busts (*top left*). Yet, somehow, perhaps partly because of the generous proportions of the loft-like space, there is no sense of chaos or even of clutter.

Again, in this New York loft (*below left*) diverse artefacts – painting, Rococo mirror, rustic chair, dining chairs and tables – almost form a complete installation in themselves in the centre of a huge former industrial space.

The owner of this Milan apartment (*top right*) obviously wanted something dramatically visual as a main focal point when she chose an ornamental *pomme de pin*, a much loved object in the decoration of the Louis-Seize period, to stand in such a prominent position in this attic room. Beyond it lies another point of focus, further defining the main axis of the arrangement here: a handsome fireplace surmounted by a grouping of lighted candles. The colour of the walls and the greyish-blue Moroccan tiles cast a soft light over the whole room.

Even in kitchen areas, overall care in how the various elements – fixed units and movable furniture – relate to each other is well worth taking. In this Parisian interior (*below right*), how attractive the table looks as a place to sit, work or eat, placed at a distance from the more workaday installation of cooker and sink. The complexity of the rest of the room – pipes, columns and internal walls – is subdued by the overall white colour scheme.

Beauty and the beast in the bedroom of a Cévennes farmhouse (*opposite*); a decidedly gentle and feminine bed faces a brutal-looking stove across a wide expanse of tiled floor. The balancing effect of the two strong vertical forms is peculiarly satisfying.

As our major urban centres have become increasingly crowded and cramped, so too space and light have acquired a rarity value in the contemporary domestic environment. The pursuit of both is the stuff of completely new lifestyle choices for many people. One solution is to search out larger properties originally intended for entirely different uses – industrial premises, for example – and to convert them to personalized space. One New York couple found this abandoned brick factory in woods in New Jersey (*top right* and *below right*), where their conversion has taken full advantage of the original features of the building – huge windows, rough brick walls – to create a flexible environment for an idiosyncratic mix of furniture.

NEW YORK

NEW YORK

NEW YORK

ARGENTEUIL

We have already noted how effective attention to detailed arrangement can be in the rooms of traditional living quarters, whether applied to an overall plan or to the creation of 'vignettes' in odd corners or in transitional spaces. In these examples (*this page*), it is the opportunities presented by conversion that have exercised the talents of owners and decorators; basically, these are exercises in how to make areas of comfort and welcome in buildings never intended to engender such qualities: a conversation corner here, a reading area there, and skilful placing of chairs and sofas.

The further one strays from accepted conventions in furniture, the more domestic interiors tend to take on the appearance and presence of complete installations. As a centrepiece for this anthology of hard surfaces, the owner of one loft apartment in a converted railway engine shed in Argenteuil has chosen a former dentist's chair, used here as a rest for a small television set. This environment goes well beyond what used to be described as Hi-Tech, in that it deliberately poses questions about the function of furniture and our own preconceptions about comfort in the home.

Continuing the examination of the effect of careful arrangement of various areas of any interior, these compositions in a number of the converted Argenteuil lofts (*this page*), now homes for a group of artists, further demonstrate how the satisfactory effects of detailing can be observed in every part of house or apartment. A low table stands perfectly aligned with the main window of a sitting-room; the pots and pans arranged above the work surfaces of a kitchen seem to be in exactly the right place; a work-station and studio make a compositional virtue out of practical equipment.

In another part of the apartment in Argenteuil (*p. 315*) the sense of a very deliberate installation still prevails, although the overall effect of hardness is mitigated by the simple form of an African chair, underscoring the boundary-crossing nature of the whole assembly – industrial, domestic and ethnic.

AN EYE FOR DETAIL

The finishing touches

TRANSITIONAL SPACES

FEATURES OF FOCUS

TEXTURE, PATTERN AND COLOUR

ORNAMENT AND DISPLAY

'IT'S ALL IN THE DETAIL' is a maxim that holds more true in interior decoration and design than in most other fields of human activity. The finishing touches truly make the broader picture more convincing. The evidence of the following pages is that those touches are many and may not always be obvious. It would be easy to conclude, for instance, that the effectiveness of a decorative scheme could be extended simply by the addition of chosen objects, pictures and general ornament, arranged to complement furniture and furnishings against an appropriate background of walls, ceiling and floor.

But there are many more factors to consider: the treatment of transitional spaces, for instance, those awkward not-quite-certain places, like halls, landings, staircases, mezzanine floors, even doorways, which demand careful attention from the home-maker, since they are not necessarily susceptible to the grand, ordered decorative gestures appropriate to a *salon*. Certain fixtures also act as points of focus within a room; the fireplace is an obvious case in point, although it may be replaced by the stove or the television in certain cultures. Then there are those deviations from the basic foursquare room – alcoves, niches, arches, portals – which can be emphasized and made special by paint and pattern. Texture and colour can be added to the latter on the list of demands on the home-maker's attentions; wall and ceilings, obviously, but also other decorated surfaces dictate mood and feeling in any interior. Then there are the real details, the personal bits and pieces, collections and possessions, free-standing or displayed in cabinets, which are the final extension of that proud urge to create an environment that is a successful reflection of ourselves and in which we find true comfort. And display does not always end with the four walls of the home: it is equally important on patio, terrace and veranda, and in the garden.

Because of its complexity of form, the staircase presents unique opportunities for decorative dramatization. If it is grand, then it should be treated as such, and hung with items of display – paintings, rugs, tapestries – to complement massive carved banisters and newels. While no one in the contemporary world would expect elaborate effects on the scale of the Rococo splendours of the Palazzo Biscari in Sicily, staircases should be taken seriously and not just considered as a convenient way of moving from one level to another. Many of those illustrated on these pages have been made into design features in themselves by the apt choice of paint, the form of the handrail or even the complete absence of the latter. This is especially important for staircases that descend directly into living-rooms, where they must be accommodated as a dominant item.

As areas for the display of pictures and wall-hangings, the walls of the stairwell often offer surfaces larger than those available in the main reception rooms. This aspect has been put to good use in several of the examples which follow, either by using the extended height of the wall surface to display a particularly large artwork or to accommodate a mass of detail such as formal groups of

PARIS

smaller paintings, trophies or other three-dimensional ornament. Even if the staircase is narrow and enclosed and bereft of natural light, it is still an important component in the home and the application of bright, light hues helps to render it a place we enjoy passing through rather than one of gloom and neglect.

Staircases are one obvious feature of access and movement within the home; but there are other important ways of relating living spaces to each other that cry out for the decorator's attention. Corridors and passages are obvious examples where the visual excitements and decorative motifs of other rooms can be continued or find contrast. Let us not forget those glimpses through open doors of rooms and spaces and make sure that the vignette – an arrangement of furniture or wall decoration – framed

by the doorway is itself pleasing to the eye and yet another source of enjoyment as we move about our home.

As a practical way of heating the home, the open fire has long had its day, although most people would agree that the sight of soaring flames still strikes an atavistic chord of welcome, comfort and safety. Even if the widespread use of central heating has meant the demise of the open fire as a realistic daily source of heating, it still survives as an important decorative feature in many homes. Memories of its former importance make it the virtually automatic focal point towards which any arrangement of chairs and tables can be directed. Its traditional form makes it ideal for the display of ornamental objects: the mantelpiece can accommodate all manner of arrangements and even clutter; the chimney-breast is the obvious place to hang an important picture or large mirror. On either side of the fireplace the recesses created by its projecting form can be utilized easily for further wall display or for the fitting of bookcases and cabinets. Let us remember, too, those other features that break up simple foursquare spaces either by projecting into them or leading from them; those secretive corners and alcoves where quiet, secluded activities may occur outside the main areas of the larger room, or the more modest niches and archways of many contemporary

IRELAND

dwellings: all of them are fitting subjects for individualized applications of pattern and colour and, most important, light.

While walls and ceilings are surfaces where the effects of painting, wallpaper and other forms of decoration will be most obviously noticed, less fixed elements can also be used to achieve dramatic effects through the interplay of colour and fabric and the imaginative display of movable objects. Doors – those focal points of interiors and exteriors alike – may be carved, painted to make them blend into the overall decorative scheme or to contrast with it, or left as natural wood or metal to acquire the patinas of age. Movable objects, by sheer variety, offer an infinity of extensions and elaborations to effects of colour and pattern. Small, brightly coloured objects can illuminate and enliven a monochromatic setting: a bowl of *papier mâché* fruit on the kitchen table; a heavily textured and boldly patterned ethnic wall-hanging; a wall covered with paintings in heavy gilt frames.

PARIS

And individual items of furniture, especially if they are large and elaborate, can in themselves provide everything that a decor needs in terms of pattern and colour. In Scandinavia, for instance, where the decoration of whole rooms tends to be characterized by reserve and restraint, there is a long tradition of applying bold forms in bright colour to particularly prized articles of furniture. Large cabinets may assert their presence through elaborate carving, and such pieces demand that they be given plenty of space so that the full effects of the variations of surface in old wood can be appreciated.

Collecting and the display of collections is perhaps the ultimate refinement of all the urges and drives towards the creation and embellishment of a pleasing habitat that have formed thus far the subject-matter of this book. These are the finishing touches: cabinets of ceramics; display cases of glass; the still-life of a kitchen cupboard; a votive table-top arrangement; a close, orderly grouping of engravings; metal

moulds on a kitchen wall. Such arrangements of objects, so important in rendering any interior distinctive and individual, are the new cabinets of curiosities, those collections in the great houses of gentleman-scholars of the seventeenth and eighteenth centuries, which can still serve as an inspiration for contemporary design. Some of the cabinets of artefacts illustrated here are effectively the descendants of those lovingly arranged assemblies of *naturalia* – coral, shells, minerals, gems, plants – and the trophies of travel and trade – antiquities, clocks, fans, boxes, automata and miniatures – which delighted and amazed men of insatiable curiosity three centuries ago. Although such objects have great effect when displayed as groups – rows of baseball masks on a bedroom wall, for instance – sometimes positioned alone they add the final, decisive detail to a table-top, a window embrasure, a mantelpiece. Sometimes, too, the final, telling point is made by the sheer appropriateness of a practical feature: a door handle, a folded towel.

PARIS

Floral display is instantly gratifying: colour, form, texture and an overwhelming sense of refreshment and renewal; little surprise, then, that garlands, flower-heads and leaf forms should so often have inspired fabric design and painted wall decoration. In their natural state, even within the ordered confines of the cultivated garden, flowers provide that final burst of joyful exuberance that completes the building and decoration of the place we call home. And beyond this garden of delights lie the doorways and arches that promise a world full of possibilities, of new inspirations and cultural challenges.

NAPLES

NAPLES

SICILY

SICILY

MAURITIUS

SALZBURG

TRANSITIONAL SPACES

Staircases, landings, passages, corridors, mezzanine floors: these are the spaces of transition within the home. In their comparative awkwardness, they can prove a great challenge for the decorator. Staircases, in particular, capture the imagination; if they are wide, sweeping and monumental, then they do present a marvellous opportunity for the grand gesture (*these pages*). This can be in the form of display – of paintings or trophies – or in sculpted and carved newels and banisters.

NAPLES

A staircase, if light and open, can bring a wonderful sense of spaciousness to the very heart of a building. These two very different examples do exactly that. The open-work of the painted handrail of the staircase in the Musée des Beaux-Arts in Saigon allows light to stream down through the stairwell (*left*). In the Rococo Palazzo Biscari in Catania, Sicily, the staircase which leads to the orchestra gallery (*opposite*) has turned the narrow passage that separates the Salone da Ballo from the windows of the façade into a major decorative feature. Its vaulted ceiling is decorated with frescoes by Lo Monaco, while the exquisite stuccowork of the ceiling and of the staircase itself show the influence of French *rocaille* decoration.

In less grand domestic environments, staircases that lead directly into living-rooms have to be treated very carefully to avoid their becoming an intrusive element in an otherwise integrated scheme of decoration. Both these examples – one in Devon, England (*above left*) and one in Quebec (*above right*) – make their entrances unobtrusively and look very much part of the room itself.

These two staircases have the virtue of turning the spaces they occupy into places of additional design and architectural interest. Both of them are decorative features in their own right. One, in a traditional house in Mallorca (*above left*), brings a sense of sculptural scale to a low-ceilinged room. In a seventeenth-century Provençal house (*above right*), the main staircase adds a note of grandeur to a simple entry hall.

LONDON

BRUSSELS

PROVENCE

ROME

NEW YORK

LONDON

Staircases can influence the whole mood or feeling of a place by their very forms (*these pages*). Straight staircases fit reassuringly into the spaces to which they lead. Curving staircases and ones that disappear from view and then reappear inevitably excite an atmosphere of mystery or even of the sinister. This example, for instance, built as part of a film-set in the Cinecittà studio complex, Rome, looks like some visionary nightmare construction from Piranesi's *Carceri*, or 'Prisons' (*top right*).

ROME

NAPLES

TUSCANY

GRENOBLE

PROVENCE

CHILOË

PARIS

NEW YORK

PARIS

IRELAND

PROVENCE

BUDAPEST

NAPLES

BURGUNDY

All the staircases illustrated here (*opposite*) have been made into central decorative features in houses which vary from the modest to the grand. All of them, however, have the advantage of being interesting forms in themselves, twisting and turning their way from one level to another. And many of them have been used by their owners as additional display areas, of paintings or three-dimensional objects.

Of an entirely different order is the staircase that stands foursquare in a main living-room, like this example in a Belgian house (*right*). In spite of its central position, the staircase is somehow still just part of the overall scheme of things, benefiting from the height and extent of the room.

A supreme example of the use of the stairwell and related landings as areas for display is this modern metal staircase in a converted cheese factory in Milan (*left*). The generous proportions of the whole stairwell, enhanced by open treads and thin steel ribs, make it an ideal place for positioning furniture as an extra surface for the display of ornaments.

Less useful as display galleries are the very simple staircases illustrated here (*opposite*). It should be noted, however, that all of them succeed in looking attractive, mainly because the colours of the walls transform a dark and narrow transitional space into one of light and neatness, yet all of them present a slightly different solution to the simple act of getting upstairs.

CHILE

PROVENCE

SICILY

PARIS

PARIS

LONDON

DEVON

CHILE

GRANADA

PROVENCE

STOCKHOLM

CHILE

We tend to forget that it is the transition from one living area to another, from room to room, from exterior to interior, which creates the visual drama in any home. It is of fundamental importance to successful decoration schemes that the half or fully open door should reveal an enticing setting beyond.

A deliberately unfinished doorway in a Cévennes farmhouse leads the eye to another interior and a window on the outside world (*above left*). The bold colours of the upholstered furniture in this Paris apartment (*above right*) are clearly picked up and continued in the next room.

Open doors in a Burgundy château (*above left*) reveal a succession of elaborate panel decorations, each forming a visual set-piece when viewed in the frame of the doorway. Seemingly inspired by the colours of *commedia dell'arte* costumes, the passages in this Paris apartment (*above right*) are decorative items in their own right.

Overleaf
Looking to something beyond: in all these examples from around the world, the photographer's eye has picked out the promise of the next space, the next room, in vignettes framed by door-posts and lintels.

IBIZA

ÎLE DE RÉ

PARIS

PROVENCE

PARIS

IRELAND

IRELAND

UMBRIA

UMBRIA

IRELAND

UMBRIA

NAPLES

VERSAILLES

PARIS

PARIS

PARIS

STOCKHOLM

BUENOS AIRES

PARIS

BALI

GOA

PROVENCE

BRUSSELS

ROME

337

BRUSSELS

WALES

SCOTLAND

FEATURES OF FOCUS

In any interior, there are certain permanent features that merit the decorator's special attention, in colour, material and position. These include doorways and windows and that supreme point of focus, the source of heat. In these examples (*left*), it is towards the fireplace that the whole arrangement of the room has been directed. It is the feature – in both cool and warm climates – which is often the most elaborately worked in terms of shape and additional decoration. Even real estate agents inevitably identify a surviving original fireplace in a property as a major attraction.

IRELAND

MOROCCO

CANADA

PARIS

PARIS

PARIS

The mantelpiece is the obvious display surface for the most precious objects of a household and the chimney-breast the obvious place to hang a work of art or large looking-glass. In a Paris apartment (*top right*) the classic French fireplace exerts a strong individual presence amid the Louis-Quinze furniture, with which it is however entirely in keeping, almost as an additional important piece itself.

Very different is this cottage fireplace in Connemara, Ireland, although it too is clearly the most dominant feature in the simple sitting-room (*below right*). Its bright colours provide the occupants of the house with a very different palette from that of the greys, greens and browns of the surrounding countryside.

PARIS

TUSCANY

All these fireplaces (*left*), through their sober classical shape, impose a sense of order and formality in the rooms where they stand. They are relatively high in terms of overall ceiling height and the eye is constantly lcd to focus on them by the addition of other elements: a painting, two pots, a large looking-glass and a shrine-like arrangement of objects and pictures.

NEW YORK

PARIS

The light colours of these fireplaces (*right*), in rooms with white or near-white walls, make them initially less of a presence. However, in all these cases, their form and importance has been re-emphasized by the number of objects and wall decorations that surround them. Even the hearth and the spaces created by the side pillars have become areas for decorative display.

ÎLE DE RÉ

ÎLE DE RÉ

PARIS

IRELAND

Part of the importance of the open fireplace – at least when in use – is due to the visible flames. In countries where the closed stove is the traditional form of heating, notably in Scandinavia, the stoves themselves became room features in their own right (*these pages*). They were designed in shapes which reflected the stylistic preoccupations of the time and were usually clad in highly decorative faïence. Their height, too, made them a dominant presence in any room, although it was customary to position them in a corner rather than before a central chimney-breast.

BUDAPEST

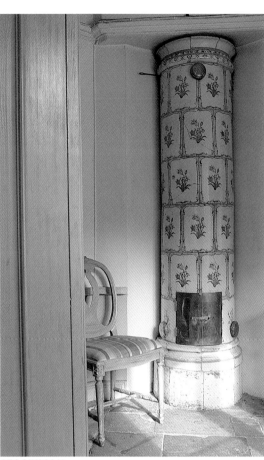

STOCKHOLM

STOCKHOLM

STOCKHOLM

STOCKHOLM

STOCKHOLM

343

MOROCCO

MOROCCO

In an earlier chapter, we saw how important an entry door can be in the overall external architecture of a building – a focal point to be elaborately decorated and embellished. Similarly, internal doorways, niches, arches and alcoves, any original features that add to the charm and complexity of an interior, can themselves become the focus of special decorative effects or arrangements of objects and furniture (*these pages*). Doors can be painted or carved; their surrounds can be decorated in colour or plaster relief; niches and alcoves can be filled with pots, baskets and books; varying levels of wall created by pilasters and arches can be picked out by special painted treatments; and articles of furniture and statuary can be given greater prominence by being placed in a recess or beneath a vaulted part of the ceiling.

VERSAILLES

NEPAL

STOCKHOLM

STOCKHOLM

ROME

AMALFI

MOROCCO

ROME

345

TEXTURE, PATTERN AND COLOUR

The impulse to decorate and elaborate our immediate environment is common to many cultures, and embraces both grand and humble settings. Both these examples of sumptuous wall embellishment are clearly extremely grand, yet there are differences in intention and purpose. The owners of Louhisaari, a 'Baltic Renaissance' house, north of Turku in Finland, were originally inspired by the styles of the great Italian Baroque palaces and decorated their own externally austere mansion with elaborate fabrics and tapestries (*left*). Simple beams were augmented with carvings and then painted, another feature of an interior that certainly does not mirror its exterior.

Italianate, but on home territory, are the great rooms of the summer *palazzo* of the Chigi family at Ariccia. In the larger reception room, great panels of Cordovan leather, embossed and coloured, give the walls a sumptuousness that threatens at times to overwhelm paintings and furniture alike (*opposite*).

Much more than their successors – even more than the practitioners of Rococo – the decorators of the great Renaissance and Baroque houses regarded the interior wall as a surface to be elaborated and embellished by every possible means. Sculptured, painted and gilded, the rooms of the great French châteaux of the early seventeenth century scarcely needed furniture to complete their decorative schemes.

The panelling of such splendid living quarters was generally one of two types: *de hauteur*, which treated the whole wall as a unified decorative surface; and *d'appui*, where the wall was divided into two distinct levels, sometimes by a cornice or by recessing. In one of the great rooms of the château of Cormatin in Burgundy (*top left*) the differentiation between upper and lower parts of the wall is quite startling, but carried off successfully by the sheer magnificence of the painted and gilded decor. Equally elaborate in its own way, and again divided in two, this panelled room in Salzburg makes its effect through ornamental carving and the patina and texture of wood rather than through colour (*below left*).

Built during the first decade of the seventeenth century, later associated with the literary circle of Madame de Sévigné and her cousin Roger de Bussy-Rabutin, the château of Cormatin is one of the gems of the reign of Louis XIII (*top right*). The walls of the great rooms combine meticulously carved wood with paintings of exceptional quality, which include landscapes and architectural subjects. Beams have been left exposed and painted. Non-decorated walls were hung with tapestries. But how strangely superfluous the furniture looks (*below right*)!

SEE MORE

PANELLED WALLS   216   255   304   335

Objects, furniture and features always derive some of their presence and effectiveness from the texture and colour of the walls against which they are arranged. The sheer eccentricity and quirkiness of this assembly (*above left*) – a makeshift counterbalanced lamp resting on a stool – suffers no competition from the rough monochrome of the wall. Lines, wherever applied, usually suggest simplicity and order. Here, their neurotic twitching (*above*) conveys very deliberate decorative intent, especially seen in combination with a heavy gilded frame and 'chair'.

How much dignity there is in this ensemble (*above left*)! The most rudimentary rustic chair can be a strong sculptural presence on occasions. And, clearly, in this very simple interior, someone has taken the trouble to think carefully about the effects of applied pattern.

Wall-hangings are an immediate way of introducing colour, texture and pattern to otherwise monochromatic interiors (*above right*). Rugs, kilims, bag-faces, weavings of various kinds, are effective bringers of history and culture to washed walls.

The importance of doors, exterior and interior, has been comprehensively illustrated in previous chapters. As focal points, they receive a fair share of the decorator's attention in pretty well all countries and cultures. Sometimes, a central motif is the device that fixes the door's importance. This ancient Moroccan door in carved wood is dominated by the rose form, above other polychrome panels (*above left*). Similarly, a wrought-iron panel at head-height is the major decorative element in this Art Deco door in Budapest (*above right*).

Touchingly, decoration and the bringing of pleasing effects into the home, affects us all, humble and grand alike. This door, straightforward in construction, now preserved in one of the houses at Skansen, Stockholm, has clearly inspired someone to make a decorative effort – to extend the large-scale marbling effects from the walls and to add a frame where no moulding exists (*above left*). In contrast, the overwhelming presence of a door (*above right*) in the manor house of Plas Newydd, Wales, leaves no doubt about the importance accorded to this particular entrance by the original builders.

Overleaf
In the present age, the ceiling seems to have become neutral territory in decoration. Since Victorian times it has not attracted the attentions of plasterers and painters in any significant way. These examples show just how effective this feature could be.

UMBRIA

UMBRIA

ROME

UMBRIA

KENYA

MOROCCO

MANILA

MEXICO

SICILY

MANILA

ROME

FLORIDA

ROME

BURGUNDY

SWEDEN

PROVENCE

KENYA

GUATEMALA

NAPLES

BALI

PARIS

CANADA

BURGUNDY

MANILA

NAPLES

UMBRIA

LUXOR

CAIRO

MOROCCO

COMOROS

MARSEILLES

SUSSEX

COPENHAGEN

SANTIAGO

GUATEMALA

GUATEMALA

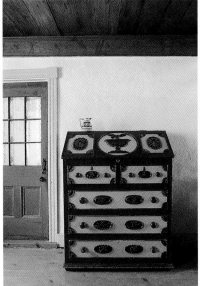

CANADA

SWEDEN

FINLAND

MALLORCA

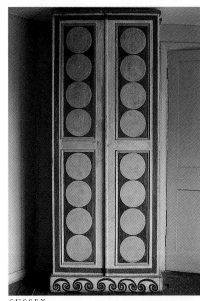

SUSSEX

BANGKOK

MAURITIUS

SWEDEN

SALZBURG

Preceding pages
There are so many ways to harness colour and texture to decorative effect. Attention to the minutiae of interior arrangement is one of them: juxtapositions of small objects, of hangings, of paintings, of furniture, even of foodstuffs, real and imitation. And inspiration for such 'vignetttes' can be found on our travels or in other parts of the home.

What can be applied to the fixtures of the home as colour and pattern also has a clear function in the embellishment of the movable items. Painted and carved free-standing furniture, especially cabinets and cupboards, enjoys a long and honourable tradition in many cultures (*left*). In all cases, such powerful pieces do need careful positioning in terms of background colour and light to achieve their full effect. Sometimes it is more effective to allow the colours and textures to assert their presence through arrangements on the furniture rather than by application to the piece itself, like this beguiling collection of shells in a small Mauritian museum (*opposite*).

MASSACHUSETTS

NEW YORK

FRANCE

KENYA

FRANCE

FRANCE

FRANCE

MANILA

FRANCE

NAPLES

FRANCE

NEW YORK

ORNAMENT AND DISPLAY

The urge to collect may take many forms and be directed in countless ways, but it is undoubtedly a very powerful one. The members of the scholarly European gentry who filled their cabinets of curiosities in the seventeenth century with a diversity of artefacts, or the English aristocrats who assembled their collections of classical antiquities and Renaissance paintings during the Grand Tour, probably had something in common with a more modest, contemporary spirit of acquisition. And with the urge to collect – not always, but usually – goes the urge to display. And with display comes a whole range of engaging decorative effects: glass-fronted cabinets full to overflowing with personal memorabilia or with carefully ordered ceramics; table tops covered with contrasting forms and materials; walls brought to life by paintings, drawings or heavily textured hangings. In their own different ways, all the arrangements illustrated here (*opposite* and *right*) are, effectively, individual 'cabinets of curiosities'.

PARIS

PROVENCE

PARIS

WALES

CHILE

FLORIDA

PARIS

PARIS

PARIS

IBIZA

IBIZA

As a means of creating pleasant environments, display should certainly not be confined to the principal living areas of the home. Kitchens, bedrooms, staircases and landings all have their claim to this aspect of the home-maker's art. Kitchens, because they are usually so full of interesting shapes and intriguing objects, present marvellous opportunities for display, and usually look the better for it when it is done with sensitivity to colour and form (*left*). Crockery – if attractive in shape and design – looks wonderful on open shelves. Other types of utensil, including bowls, wooden trays, implements of the pre-plastics age, can adorn work surfaces or dresser shelves. Humble metal moulds make intriguing wall arrangements.

STOCKHOLM

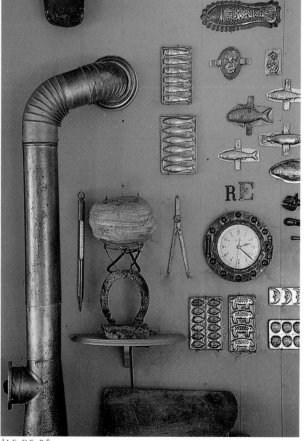

ÎLE DE RÉ

Around the kitchen, there are always certain specific areas that invite special attention. The dresser, or dresser-like work surfaces and shelves were designed for display, nowadays combining the expected accoutrements of the kitchen with more conventional ornamental elements (*top right* and *top far right*). But even the more obviously utilitarian features, like the kitchen sink, make a much more positive contribution to any overall design if everything around them is ordered for colour and form (*below right* and *below far right*).

MOROCCO

IRELAND

MASSACHUSETTS

FRANCE

BRAZIL

PARIS

IRELAND

BELGIUM

CORSICA

PARIS

PARIS

KENYA

BELGIUM

KENYA

SUMBAWA

PROVENCE

Sometimes it is the telling detail that makes the strongest decorative point in a room. All the objects illustrated here (*opposite*) look intriguing because of their form and inventive wit, yet none of them necessarily impress by being significant works of fine or decorative art. Indeed, many quite humble objects and utensils can make an effective contribution to our visual pleasure through careful placing or juxtaposition. The entirely original wall display in this New York bedroom (*right*) is composed of baseball masks from years gone by – a theme echoed by a bed and table made partly of baseball bats and balls.

Most immediate, most colourful of all decorative displays, of course, are flowers, bringing the colours and scents of the garden to interior and exterior alike (*above left* and *above right*), or inspiring a cornucopia of delights in the form of a mural (*opposite*). Around the home, they can bring vibrancy to any corner of the most uninspiring room; outside, they are the life of our own private enclosures, courtyard or walled garden (*overleaf*), from which doorways lead us to the vibrant life of the streets beyond (*pp. 370-71*).

THAILAND

BALI

SHANGHAI

MOROCCO

CUBA

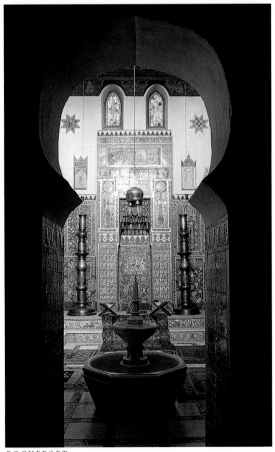

ROCHEFORT

SHANGHAI

ROME

POMPEII

SICILY

CHILE

GOA

THE WAY WE LIVE | *CHAPTER FIVE*

JUST LIVING

Outside the home

AROUND THE HOUSE

ON THE STREET

THE MARKET-PLACE

CELEBRATING PEOPLE

THE SEARCH FOR A SATISFACTORY LIFESTYLE, expressed in the arrangements of interiors to assure our warmth and shelter, comfort, and ultimately aesthetic satisfaction, is a powerful driving force. Yet, we also belong to a wider world, local, regional, national, and ultimately international. In the pages of this book we have looked at styles and expressions of taste from around the world; we have seen many differences, but we have also discovered an amazing number of similarities and connections, extending the usefulness of this book as a compendium of possibilities.

Thus, the richness of Oriental furniture may render it stunningly decorative when arranged in an all-white western modernist interior; an African chair has a humanizing effect on a grouping of heavy-duty, metallic 'furniture'. We begin to inhabit this world of multiple choices as soon as we move beyond the confines of our immediate domestic context, first to the extensions of our home, and then to the streets and markets beyond, whose own detailing, vibrancy, colours and shapes are yet more sources of visual inspiration and refreshment.

First, however, we impose ourselves on the areas immediately around the home – extended and open if in a warm and benevolent climate, or confined and closed if, say, a roof terrace in a northern city. In either case, such spaces can be truly an immediate extension of the rooms themselves. Furniture and ornament, too large or unwieldy for indoors, may be effectively disposed there. Even a modest roof terrace can become the 'room outside' with the addition of a couple of formal potted plants, a table and four chairs. The choice of furniture in such spaces, though, does need careful thought and attention; certain pieces, too finished and elaborate, can easily strike an incongruous note. Simpler forms and materials – cane, canvas and unpolished hardwoods – are often more appropriate. These are the places for alfresco dining, conveniently situated close to the kitchen, but also open to garden or even urban skyline. City terraces especially can evoke the entirely satisfactory feeling of being small corners of peace and tranquillity far from the sounds of traffic and the overwhelming presence of towering masonry.

Again, a special boon during warmer months, or in those climates with the good fortune to enjoy year-round fine weather, is the backyard or loosely delineated patio. Less architecturally structured than the formal veranda or terrace, it permits outdoor dining and relaxation simply

MARRAKESH

with the aid of a few chairs and perhaps an ad hoc awning.

Such arrangements are clearly a far cry from the formal courtyard or enclosed garden, although they share the essential quality of being places of transition. In Islamic and, to a large degree, Mediterranean culture in general, the court is an integral part of the domestic structure; by way of the shade cast by arcades the rooms of the interior are seamlessly connected with the fragrant plants of the central open area and, traditionally, with the soothing sound of gently bubbling water. Few of us are fortunate enough to enjoy the use of courtyards on the scale of the Moorish and Hispanic examples illustrated here, but they give us every reason to reflect on how we can make use of confined external spaces for the display of formal planting, large-scale ceramics and even statuary.

Living compound-style seems to strike a chord in all cultures – is there some buried recollection here of groups drawing together in a defensive circle to guarantee their warmth and security? Certainly, Balinese courtyard architecture, a practical expression of lives spent in constant movement between the inside and outside, has proved one of that island's durable cultural exports, influencing design and architectural practices throughout south-east Asia and the Pacific region. Again, open space around the house allows the architectural arrangement of large potted plants and even cultural and religious icons and, evitably, some water feature. Sometimes, however, our decorative ingenuity in relating our homes to the land around need not extend further than the simple setting-down of table and chairs in a pleasant and secluded spot and the preparation of a colourful and enticing spread. Even the impromptu, however, calls for a conscious attention to detail – perhaps in the choice of table cloth or crockery – for the full potential of the situation to be realized.

And so to our engagement with the community at large. Beyond our gardens and patios are the streets and squares, the buildings, which define the architectural and physical character of where we live, unless of course we have decided a rural isolation will be our dominant lifestyle. For most of

CHILE

us, however, as town and city dwellers, the shops, bars and restaurants are the places where we experience the world at large, where we find ourselves as part of the wider human network of styles, relationships, endeavours and cultures. In the Western world, the bar or pub is a universal institution, dispensing solace and camaraderie to the gregarious and to the lonely. In other cultures, the tea-house may serve the same purpose, and indeed the sight of a group of men in explosively animated conversation over glasses of green tea in any Islamic town or city is instantly memorable.

The more formal cousins of the bar, restaurants, are as varied as the cultures to which they belong and as full of inspiration; they are exportable, however – Chinese restaurants in Latvia, Greek restaurants in Melbourne. But in terms of the authentic, vibrant life of the street, there is little to better the experience of eating and conversing in restaurants or cafés that are a direct expression of the surrounding cultural fabric. Nowhere, except in south-east

TUNISIA

Asia, would a hawkers' market or Chinese tea-house seem entirely convincing; and how utterly natural it seems to eat, feet dangling in a river beneath the tables, at a popular open-air restaurant in Manila.

Good restaurants the world over use produce that is immediately and freshly available for the majority of their dishes, which argues a close relationship with that other concentration of human exchange, colours, scents and general vitality – the market. Is there any place more seductive than a group of stalls groaning under piles of fresh and colourful fruit and vegetables, or alive with the blooms of the season, or with the shallow trays of the day's catch? How fastidious are the displays in the best markets, usually arranged by the producers themselves, and how fastidious and conscientious are the buyers in any truly great market – touching, smelling, before finally committing to the all-important purchase. It was Elizabeth David who once remarked that the tourists who spend so

much time in art galleries, museums and cathedrals might also consider the local food markets as part of a city's cultural heritage.

A similar visual excitement to that of the brilliantly colourful market stall is exhaled by the traditional open-fronted shop, especially if the merchandise is of all shapes and sizes and, most important, in abundance. In these days of supermarket and shopping mall, what relief the small shop, still retaining its original façade, offers. In any street such shops, cluttered and crammed with goods, give us the sense of changing pace, of moving in a slower, more considered way. Something of the same quality is attached to the small workshop, especially if the activity is artisanal. We know there is no going back to a William Morris-like vision of a craft utopia, but it is important to value those places where human endeavour and skills still have a direct relationship to the quality of the finished article. These are the splashes of colour as the world becomes more monochrome.

SUMBAWA

At the end of this chapter appear some of the people who inhabit those places illustrated in quite remarkable profusion and variety on the foregoing pages; they go about their business in street or market, eat and drink in their local restaurants and bars. The cycle continues: we return to our homes with ideas and acquisitions, with the colours, life and energy which inspired us. Each in his or her own way continues to contribute to the whole human endeavour: to create satisfactory living spaces in whatever circumstances and make them one's own.

AROUND THE HOUSE

Somewhere halfway between the private and the public world, verandas, terraces, backyards, patios and, eventually, gardens provide places for eating and drinking, conversation, reflection and contemplation. In warm climates a loggia/veranda may very well serve almost as an additional room or gallery. In the Bragança Palace in Goa (*left*), this gallery provides enough shelter for a significant extension of the collection of furniture and objects in the main rooms within.

Open to the garden but still well sheltered, the loggia of a Guatemalan house (*opposite*) still provides space for furniture; most importantly, there is seating, making it a real area of transition from the interior rooms to the world without.

Overleaf
The uses to which verandas and loggias can be put are many and varied. If wide enough to accommodate tables and chairs, they are clearly ideal extra dining areas; in any case, they are wonderful places for simply sitting. They are useful places, too, for keeping objects whose material and size make them unsuitable for interior display, like large earthenware pots, or outsize baskets, or caged birds. Formal indoor furniture can look out of place here; more successful schemes are achieved with cane, twig or rustic chairs and tables.

MAURITIUS

MAURITIUS

MAURITIUS

SICILY

MAURITIUS

SAIGON

SICILY

BUENOS AIRES

SANTIAGO

NAIROBI

MEXICO

BURUNDI

This wide and accommodating loggia (*right*) runs along one side of a magnificent private house in Mauritius. It is clearly wide enough to provide a conversation area behind the woven blinds which unroll to filter the strong sunlight. Part of the house, yet at the same time an extension of the garden, this is a transitional space between two experiences. It also complements the dining-room, just visible at its far end (*p. 177*).

BALI

SAIGON

MAURITIUS

FINLAND

CANADA

MANILA

All the seating areas illustrated here (*opposite* and *overleaf*) show the flexibility that the veranda can have as a place accommodating the activities of the home – eating, drinking and conversation – while introducing the delights of the garden to its interiors. The form of verandas and terraces varies, of course, according to climate and topography. In sunny, sub-tropical regions there is an obvious concern with shade, protection and alleviation of the effects of heat. In alpine conditions, a veranda like one in a chalet near Grenoble (*right*), can take full advantage of whatever light and warmth there is, and offer the fullest possible view of mountains beyond.

MOROCCO

BORA-BORA

CAIRO

BALI

SAIGON

SRI LANKA

385

PROVENCE

NORMANDY

ÎLE DE RÉ

PROVENCE

TUNISIA

ÎLE DE RÉ

Verandas and terraces are of very deliberate construction, very distinctly part of the houses to which they are attached, though they usually present an opportunity to partake of the pleasures of surrounding garden or plantation. On the upper floors or roof, though, they can be entirely secluded. Less enclosed but equally attractive and useful is the variously named backyard or patio, an ambiguous area sometimes only defined by paving, walls or perhaps an awning. These examples (*opposite*) make the point that a pleasant outside dining area need not depend on an elaborate construction; all of them make use of a space immediately adjoining the home, but in an engagingly informal way. In some cases, it has only been necessary to introduce chairs and a table to an area within easy reach of the kitchen to create an atmosphere of warmth and conviviality, perhaps embellished by formally trained vegetation and some shade from open sunlight. All of these elements are brought together in a peculiarly satisfying way in this brick-paved area outside a house in Hammamet, Tunisia (*right*).

Enclosures, courtyards, walled gardens are of a very different order to the verandas and terraces illustrated on preceding pages. For one thing, they do not offer any *aperçus* of the world outside, the surrounding garden or landscape. In effect, they are additional rooms in the home, though open to the sky and even filled with formal vegetation and water features. Grand courtyards, like this one in Naples (*top left*), are ideal spaces for the display of monumental works in stone, often combined with ornamental planting. More modest, more informal, a Paris garden (*below left*) reinforces a feeling of privacy by a profusion of plants and trees around its borders. Such an area, within a heavily built-up city, inevitably assumes a secret, hidden air. The planting is formal, but not oppressively so; and the central area is defined by clipped trees and four large terracotta pots in a traditional Tuscan design.

SEE MORE
FOLDING TABLES   285   334   407

The enclosed garden, with its central axial pool, symbol of paradise, of the house yet not of the house, is one of the most refined expressions of Islamic art and architecture. Porticoes lead from the dwelling to the scented, watered space at its heart, making the transition from indoors to outdoors scarcely noticeable. Planting is usually minimal – box hedges, potted orange and lemon trees, myrtle bushes. Water is all-important, befitting its status as the differentiating element between survival in a civilized environment and the desert. Among the greatest achievements of the Islamic architects of Moorish Spain are the gardens of the Alhambra and the Generalife in Granada (*top right*) and (*below right*). They are also an expression of that quintessential Mediterranean feature, the patio or court, which can be created or imagined whenever there is an enclosed space: a few terracotta pots on a paved area, the sound of a gently bubbling fountain, the shade of vines trained around a pergola or of an olive tree.

Although this Marrakesh house dates, in fact, from the seventeenth century, its central area interprets the time-honoured Islamic court in an entirely contemporary way (*right*), yet with a sufficient number of antique features to underscore its authenticity; all the finely worked doors, for instance, are taken from an older building, as is the sculpted ogival arch that surmounts the entry to the court. The floor tiles pick up the motifs of Berber weaving. And the whole space is additionally defined by four orange trees around a low bubble fountain and – in the evening – four illuminated lanterns of traditional Moroccan design.

The gardens and courtyards of the West use water in a concealed way; even the traditional fountain is based on the sudden energetic appearance of water and then its disappearance for recycling. In Islamic courts (*above left*) and (*above right*) the bubble fountain, often scented with strewn petals, ensures that water is a constant presence, refreshing just by being heard. Both these Marrakesh courts are arranged around the central water feature, then further defined by carefully placed minimal vegetation.

The Moorish courtyard, understandably, became part of the Spanish vernacular in architecture. In this form it was exported to the Spanish colonial empire to grace the great houses of the capitals of Latin America – here, in Havana (*above left*). In an Andalucian courtyard (*above right*), another important feature appears: since the space is open to several storeys, it is usual for it to have one or more galleries, leading to the upper rooms.

Defined by high building, the courtyard provides an especially sympathetic frame for sculpture, both figurative and abstract, and for other large objects whose very size may preclude their proper display in an interior room. Any of the oppressive effects of enclosure can be softened by the judicious placing of vegetation and by arcading. A Rome courtyard (*top left*) is entirely dominated by classical statuary, bringing a strongly formal air to it. But in this gloriously untidy space in a Granada house (*below left*), plants are positioned haphazardly among the varied shapes of terracotta pots and bowls.

The acquisitive eclecticism behind the varied assembly of textiles and objects inside a Neapolitan house has evidently spilled over into this intriguing courtyard (*top right*). Large potted plants, placed on different levels, increase the feeling of mystery around unusual table and wall decorations.

Almost on too grand a scale for its immediate surroundings, this fountain in the courtyard of a Guatemalan house is indeed monumental (*below right*). Everything about its form looks overblown and exaggerated, an impression deepened by the placing of additional potted plants around the rim of the basin.

Size in courtyards really does matter, at least in terms of the effect they produce within the building. Neither of these two examples – one in a public garden in Delhi (*top left*) and the other in Granada (*below left*) – induces quite the same sense of secretive enclosure as those illustrated on the previous pages. Both have an openness derived from their size relative to the enclosing building, giving them a feel half-way between a court and a square. One expects that any significant human activity will not take place in the central area, but in the shade of the surrounding arcades.

The arched and vaulted arcade is one of the most important architectural attributes of the traditional courtyard. It acts as an area of transition from interior to exterior, from shade into light. It also provides scope for additional decorative forms: varieties of arch, sculpted columns and capitals, tiled floors and even wall-painting. In a house in Hammamet, Tunisia, the space and volume of a small courtyard are divided and articulated by a simple arrangement of vaults and arches, enclosing a fountain (*top right*).

Still showing the Moorish influence, but in Westernized fashion, this courtyard in a magnificent Seville house (*below right*) provides space for eating and conversation beneath its formal arches. The central area is given up entirely to a very deliberate arrangement of potted plants around a fountain.

It would be hard to imagine more pleasant environments than these two Islamic courtyards, one grand and spacious, the other secretive and intimate. An imposing arcade – so large that it can easily accommodate rows of potted plants – surrounds a vast courtyard in a Granada house (*top left*). The variety of architectural features creates an ever-changing play of light and shade.

In a Cairo garden (*below left*) the atmosphere is almost impossibly idyllic. Everything in the design vocabulary of the Islamic garden has been brought together to create a unique place of deep peace, yet also of visual excitement. A central fountain surrounded by a ceramic basin in tiles of traditional design provides the main focal point; a recessed alcove has become a kind of day-bed; and the whole is completed by a varied array of potted plants, to make the perfect secret garden.

The same intricacy and detailing that characterizes Islamic filigree-work also informs the long tradition of woodworking in north Africa, notably in Egypt. Beginning with the Fatimid dynasty – responsible for the founding of Cairo in the Middle Ages – a magnificent line of craftsmanship in wood stretches to the present day. This skill and artistry can be seen in doors, panelling, but especially in the kind of open-work so appropriate for the low-level screens which line the galleries around the central well of the traditional domestic courtyard. This example (*top right*) is in a house in Marrakesh.

More subtle, and more finely worked are the screens and friezes defining a Cairo courtyard (*below right*). Texts from the Koran create a fascinating play in elegant Arabic script against the background repeat pattern of the woodwork.

SEE MORE

OPEN-WORK SCREENS   78   155   167   179   447

It is often said of traditional Balinese building that it is an architecture of courtyards. Even modern houses on the island still consist of a series of pavilion-like structures arranged compound fashion around a number of courts. A central area serves as a place for communal living; a court within a court, to the north-east, is the site of the house temple where the gods of the island's unique mixture of Hinduism and animism are celebrated.

A large house in Ubud (*right*) enshrines all the traditional Balinese architectural virtues, yet in an entirely contemporary way, creating independent spacious interiors that nevertheless relate to each other within an overall plan. This flexibility in form has made the Balinese style a much imitated model in vernacular architecture throughout south-east Asia and the Pacific region, and even Australia.

Enjoying life around the house and the joys of eating alfresco does not necessarily demand a specially constructed courtyard or deck. Sometimes it is simply a matter of setting up a table within reasonable proximity to the source of food and in agreeable surroundings. Visual effects are still important; a vibrantly coloured table cloth in a meadow near Bordeaux (*top left*); a seaside spread at Arcachon on the French coast of the Bay of Biscay (*below left*).

All manner of elements can be combined to elaborate and extend the function of the 'outside room'. In a Corsican house belonging to an internationally known interior decorator (*right*), the rooms flow seamlessly into a terrace located next to a 'natural' swimming pool.

The terrace, or formal area for relaxation, can also effectively be located away from the immediate vicinity of the home. Because of the spectacular views available from this particular spot in a Balinese garden (*top left*), the owners decided to create a paved area to accommodate day-beds and a parasol, making a vantage point to look out over the dramatic hill scenery of the island.

In a French garden (*below left*) an impromptu dining area has been set up in a place made wonderfully attractive by trees and borders in combination with old iron gates and well-weathered masonry.

This spot near a Tuscan house does not look at first sight the most obvious place to set out a group of chairs, presumably for social purposes (*top right*). Yet, look closer, and there in the background is the classic Tuscan landscape beloved of poets and painters, of hills whose forms are punctuated by the tall fingers of cypress trees. The white sweeping forms of the chairs, too, offer an invitation to a sculptural gathering beneath the tree.

If one seeks shelter for the outside dining area, then this structural arrangement in the garden of a Mallorcan house (*below right*) would come pretty close to being the perfect solution. Hemmed in on all sides by lush vegetation, the area is sufficiently shaded to make the use of sunshades, awnings or parasols almost superfluous.

Overleaf
The combination of sunlight, terrace and planting, orderly or riotous, is universally irresistible as a setting for alfresco eating.

IBIZA

PROVENCE

ARGENTINA

TUSCANY

BELGIUM

CORSICA

SICILY

MOROCCO

MEXICO

RHODES

SWEDEN

IBIZA

SEVILLE

PROVENCE

PARIS

GUATEMALA

CORSICA

IBIZA

CORSICA

TUSCANY

CORSICA

IBIZA

FLORIDA

CUBA

BOMBAY

BUENOS AIRES

ATHENS

COPENHAGEN

ON THE STREET

Beyond the home, beyond its
immediate surrounding features, lie
the streets, the main arteries of
communication for the community
in village, town and city. And along
the streets lie the communal
meeting-places: bars, restaurants,
cafés, shops and markets. These are
the places of exchange: goods,
money and conversation, clearly an
important commodity in most of
the bars illustrated here (*opposite*).
And without conversation a bar can
seem a very doleful place indeed
(*right*). By and large, though, these
are the places where we seek a
certain atmosphere, where we spend
time in convivial company, and from
whose decor we may even derive
some inspiration.

DUBLIN

Bars across the world come in all shapes and sizes, from the cool and cosily intimate to great roaring beer-halls, where the last things on offer are peace and quiet. In general, though, they are content to declare themselves as places of varying degrees of sociability and conviviality, from Sri Lanka (*top left*) to Rome (*below left*). And even though the array of bottles behind this Marrakesh barman's head is sparse indeed (*opposite*), a smile confirms the café as a place of welcome and human warmth.

SAN FRANCISCO

NORWAY

ATHENS

MARSEILLES

PARIS

CAIRO

The difference between eating out in a restaurant of one's choice and eating at home is almost as great as that between theatre and real life. Attendance to the rituals of presentation and protocol bestow a special status on the food thus consumed. Restaurants themselves, of course, come in all shapes and sizes (*opposite*) and vary as much in atmosphere as domestic interiors. There is nothing quite as engaging as the Italian, French or Chinese family restaurant, where dishes have evolved over the years and the interior has remained untouched by the interior decorator. Sadly, we now have to travel further and further afield to find such places, although once there we will be forgiving of any culinary shortcomings.

Among the world's restaurants, the hawkers' markets of south-east Asia (*top right* and *below right*) offer the consumer an amazing array of food. Almost as amazing as the choice are the prodigious feats of memory by which stall-holders recall who has ordered what and from which table.

BALI

BANGKOK

SAIGON

BUDAPEST

Deserted, restaurants demand that we judge them as they are – temples to food that only fulfill their purpose when completed by the clientele they await. In their very different styles of decor (*left*), they are a kind of secular equivalent to those other places of escape from the pressures of urban life: the churches and temples. And how much we need such retreats: a strangely beatific expression in a tea-house in Saigon (*opposite*).

SALVADOR DI BAHIA

SAIGON

Carefully prepared food, attractively set out on a long table, is alluring in itself. Rice, crayfish, vegetable, chicken, with a traditional Vietnamese sauce, make an irresistible composition on the table of a French-owned private house in Saigon (*opposite*). The additional features required to make the experience of eating more entertaining are not always immediately predictable: in this restaurant in Manila (*left*) the feet of the diners are refreshed by the river that flows beneath the tables.

For those who take the preparation of food very seriously indeed, there is an almost religious intensity in the handling and preparation of the raw materials. Like the organized churches of the world, the kitchen is a place of hierarchy and ritual. Also, one hopes, of joy in this very vital activity; certainly that emotion seems evident on the faces of the kitchen staff in a popular Italian restaurant in Mexico City (*above*). The pared-down functionality of professional kitchens can be a style inspiration in itself, as witness the Hi-Tech movement of the 1970s.

Restaurants the world over are often family businesses, small units where everyone has a distinct idea of his or her position in the order of things. In a land of plenty, like Provence, a family restaurant – this one near Les Baux-de-Provence (*above*) – inevitably reflects the produce available at local markets in the dishes it offers. Thus is maintained an intimacy between the processes of cultivation and husbandry and that of consumption.

THE MARKET-PLACE

The fresh food market is the first step in the distribution of foodstuffs from kitchen garden, from farm and plantation, from field and orchard, from river and sea. Leaving aside the supply chains to supermarket and processed food plant, the market appeals to that deep human wish to acquire raw food in as fresh a condition as possible. And nowhere is this more true than in the fish and seafood stalls the world over (*this page*).

SALVADOR DI BAHIA

SALVADOR DI BAHIA

SANTORINI

COCHIN

Most markets impress by their colours and the simplicity of their presentation. In fish markets, especially those on the quayside illuminated by the intense light off the sea, the brilliance of the hues and the boldness of pattern make for delicious visual preliminaries to the pleasures of cooking and consumption. Pinks and reds combine with silvers to gleam and glow with phosphorescence in the fresh rays of a coastal dawn – here, in Tangier (*top right*). And all the colours of the ocean rainbow hang in a quayside fishmonger's in Valparaiso, Chile (*below right*).

MANILA

A market is a place of abundance and of richness of display: colours bright and fresh, whether arranged singly or in pyramids (*top left, below left* and *overleaf*). Thank goodness, what is on sale varies from place to place, country to country, but we recognize the authentic market the world over by its evocation of 'plenty', by the display of tomatoes, peppers, courgettes and aubergines in any Mediterranean town, or by the towering arrangements of guavas, papayas, pineapples and breadfruit in the tropics. The breadfruit – proudly displayed by a Balinese chef (*opposite*) – is native to the Pacific Islands. In 1793 it was introduced to Jamaica by Captain Bligh of *Bounty* fame in the belief that it could become the staple food of the slave population. The scheme was not a great success, but Jamaica does remain a major producer.

COCHIN

SRI LANKA

TUNISIA

BOMBAY

LUXOR

BANGKOK

MEXICO

LUXOR

SRI LANKA

NEPAL

SALVADOR DI BAHIA

BANGKOK

NAPLES

BANGKOK

MARSEILLES

BURUNDI

BANGKOK

MAURITIUS

MAURITIUS

The imagery of the market-stall, whether a boat in Bangkok or a food counter in Burundi, is among the most potent in our appreciation of the good things of life and as close as many people get to the wider natural world. The imagery is rich in colour, texture, form and pattern, brought to life by the presence of people, often producers, in the processes of exchange. This is a world of buyers and sellers meeting with immediacy impossible in more rigidly formal environments (*these pages*). Sometimes the two parties come together in unplanned, spontaneous ways; this roadside market in Burundi developed as an almost impromptu happening (*overleaf*). One man's meagre display is another's cornucopia; but however rich or spare the presentation, there is always the prospect – warm and reassuring – of acquisition and eventual consumption.

BURUNDI

BURUNDI

BALI

PROVENCE

MOROCCO

MAURITIUS

MAURITIUS

ROME

Whether a neighbourhood market in Paris, Rome or London or a village or country-town market in Morocco or Mauritius, the gathering together of people and produce is a real point of focus for a community, and any visitor. It is an opportunity for the exchange of views and gossip; and the feel-good fallout from the presence of so many good things is incalculable (*these pages*). Elizabeth David, surely the greatest English writer on food matters, found a unique joy in the sheer volume and variety on display in a good market: tomatoes, courgettes, peppers, melons, asparagus, strawberries, redcurrants, cherries, apricots, peaches, pears and plums. Her remarks were largely confined to descriptions of the markets of Provence and Italy, but her enthusiasm powerfully evoked the feelings aroused by food markets throughout the world.

GUATEMALA

SALVADOR DI BAHIA

NAPLES

NEPAL

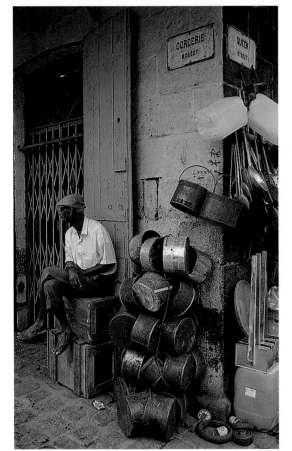

MAURITIUS

SHANGHAI

MOROCCO

If a market convinces by its displays of foodstuffs in abundance, the traditional open-fronted shop makes an initial impression by its stock. There are few sights more depressing than a retail outlet with just a few items for sale. Again, just as in the market, a rich and exciting display is all-important; unusual bric-à-brac and the utensils of the domestic environment, as well as foodstuffs, all tempt us, if their arrangement is sufficiently intriguing: baskets, cooking pots and pans, ewers and storage jars (*these pages*).

Overleaf
To be valued in the age of the shopping mall and supermarket, the small shop front has achieved the status of a folk-art form. Unlike the bland uniformity of the chain stores and retailing giants, here form, colour and individual ownership really count.

CAIRO

IRELAND

MAURITIUS

LUXOR

WALES

COCHIN

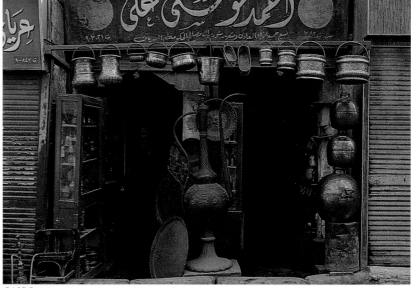

CAIRO

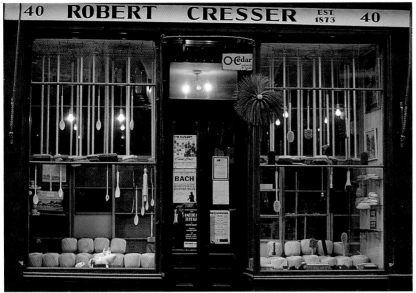

SCOTLAND

IRELAND

DELHI

MANHATTAN

TUNISIA

ATHENS

MEXICO

SHANGHAI

MANHATTAN

CAIRO

BANGKOK

IRELAND

Preceding pages
This general store in Chiloë,
southern Chile, has variety of stock
in profusion. The number of
different items, the cupboards and
shelves, even the counter, crammed
with goods for sale, make for a
peculiarly reassuring impression;
this is a place where shopping would
be a distinct pleasure and which
epitomizes everything we miss about
old-fashioned retailing.

In some of the domestic interiors
illustrated in previous chapters, we
noted that clutter and creative
untidiness could actually produce
living quarters just as pleasing in
general feel as immaculately planned
and furnished spaces. At a time
when retail outlets have become a
focus for fashionable contemporary
design, it is undoubtedly refreshing
to experience a change of pace by
wandering into some emporium
selling no matter what, but where
there is abundance, an absence of
planning, and entirely engaging
disorder (*these pages*).

SAIGON

SEE MORE
CHINESE FURNITURE   167   378

DELHI

MAURITIUS

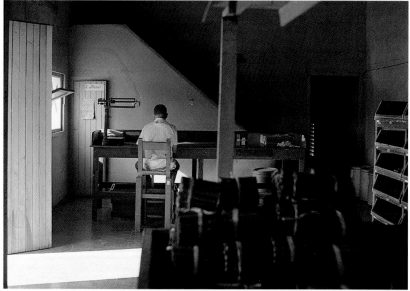

CUBA

MASSACHUSETTS

MARRAKESH

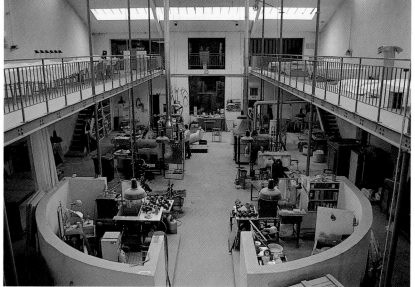

MARSEILLES

CELEBRATING PEOPLE

As an illustration and celebration of the way we all build, design and live, it seems appropriate that this final section of the last chapter should be devoted to people caught in various circumstances – some unaware – around the world. In virtually all cases, the response to the camera is marked by dignity and enjoyment of the human condition. And it is perhaps in a small atelier or workshop, beating pots or rolling cigars, that this enjoyment is most palpable among people at work (*these pages*).

DELHI

BALI

CHILE

ROMANIA

BANGKOK

ROMANIA

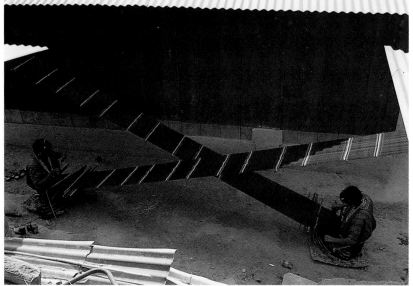

GUATEMALA

GUATEMALA

The photographs on these pages evoke the very essence of 'just living', whether in wedding feast preparations in Romania (*top right*) or the re-enactment of nineteenth-century rural life at a reconstituted village farm in New England (*below right*). All these people (*opposite*), wherever they may be, are in the process of defining their lifestyles, of simply living around the home or in that indispensable area – the garden or backyard – which is its immediate context; they are somewhere between doing something and just being there. Yet, in the apparent simplicity of these environments, the number of choices, of preferences expressed in matters of style and design, is quite limitless – colours, materials, textures and, most important, how they all fit around the particular human group.

SALVADOR DI BAHIA

NAIROBI

STOCKHOLM

CHILE

CHILE

ARGENTINA

TUSCANY

SANTIAGO

CHILE

MEXICO

GUATEMALA

SALVADOR DI BAHIA

Nothing quite engages feelings of sympathy for our fellow men as the single moments of vulnerability – sometimes posed, but usually not – caught by the camera. These vignettes are the stuff of life around the world (*opposite*), insights into other worlds, other lives, other pretensions, other preoccupations, but ones with which we can all identify. And if the subject is caught unawares, the effect of a fleeting moment increases tenfold (*right*).

SAIGON

Something of a lost art in television-obsessed Western society: serious conversation in an all-male group in Delhi, a city where vigorous debate is still a cherished activity.

Conversation, especially in public places (even in the shade of a stone elephant) is one of the most pleasant activities of the urban environment – being 'urbane'. All great cultures have been character- ized by the quality of public exchange, whether in formal debate or on the café terrace: Athens, Rome, Florence, the London of the coffee-house, the Paris of the *salon*, Hindu and Muslim cities everywhere. And when such meetings are rendered difficult by political pressures or the general deterioration of city life, so the whole culture suffers too.

Overleaf
This section is essentially a celebration of some of the many people who inhabit the villages, towns and cities illustrated in this book. These are the folk, some stopping for the camera, who follow their own traditions and create their own environments according to their needs and means and thus make their own important contribu- tion to the human collective.

SEE MORE
DECORATIVE STONEWORK   357   370   371   387

DELHI

CAIRO

MEXICO

CHILE

MAURITIUS

GUATEMALA

LUXOR

HAUTE-SAVOIE

ROMANIA

GUATEMALA

CANADA

CANADA

MEXICO

GUATEMALA

449

MEXICO

SICILY

NEPAL

NORMANDY

NEPAL

BELGIUM

NORMANDY

COMOROS

GUATEMALA

MEXICO

ROMANIA

COMOROS

Before designer labels and peer pressure, children can show as much individuality and joy in their dress as in their surroundings (*opposite*); pleasure is evident on the faces of these Mexican children (*right*) in all the finery and exuberant colours of traditional costumes.

Overleaf
These children create their own enjoyment without any special clothing or equipment in an almost timeless scene on the Brazilian coast at Salvador di Bahia.

Pages 454–55
The diversity of human life and experience throughout the world has been comprehensively illustrated in this book. Yet, touchingly, how similar we can all appear and how strong the bonds of the group, no matter what the size, when we are bound by a sense of community, a culture and a common goal.

ROMANIA

ROMANIA

MAURITIUS

CHILE

CHILE

MEXICO

INDIA

ROMANIA

MEXICO

BURUNDI

KENYA

SCOTLAND

IBIZA

IRELAND

BURUNDI

PARIS

NAPLES

NAIROBI

NORMANDY

JODHPUR

FRANCE

DELHI

FLORIDA

NORMANDY

CUBA

LONDON

MALLORCA

The environments we create
(*previous pages* and *left*), the
interiors we decorate and
personalize, from Ireland to Ibiza,
from Naples to Nairobi, from
Burundi to Brussels, are there to be
lived in and enjoyed. They should
serve and satisfy us and, at the same
time, stand as a contribution to the
greater world we have designed.
Contentment with what we have
created may be found in many
shapes and forms; here (*opposite*)
the nomadic hamlet (in Kenya) of
an internationally renowned wildlife
photographer is open house to
family and friends of all species.

BRUSSELS

CUBA

PARIS

PARIS

MALLORCA

MAURITIUS

A final note of pride and celebration in stunning colour: at harvest festival time, every household in the Filipino village of Lucban on the island of Luzon tries to outdo its neighbours in the opulence and brightness of its display of flowers, fruits and produce (*opposite, right* and *overleaf*). In some cases, frames are constructed before the façades to make them larger and more impressive. Whole streets are decorated end to end with columns and garlands of ravishing colours and textures – a truly individual art form. And the prize for the best display is a water buffalo!

THE INDEXES

A guide to
design and style
ideas

ACKNOWLEDGMENTS

Designed by Stafford Cliff
Text and captions Robert Adkinson
Production artwork Ian Hammond
Index compiled by Anna Bennett

First published in the United
Kingdom in 2003 by
Thames & Hudson Ltd,
181A High Holborn,
London WC1V 7QX

www.thamesandhudson.com

British Library Cataloguing-in-
Publication Data
A catalogue record for this book is
available from the British Library

ISBN 0-500-51137-3

Printed and bound in Singapore by
CS Graphics

Dedicated to
François de Chabaneix, Françoise Winter, Catherine, Martin & Simon de Chabaneix

Very special thanks are due to the many people who have contributed to the realization of this book, especially to Stafford Cliff who had the original idea. I also wish to thank Catherine Ardouin, Jean-Pascal Billaud, Catherine de Chabaneix, Daniel Rozensztroch & Francine Vormèse, who accompanied me on many of my travels, and Martine Albertin, Béatrice Amagat, Françoise Ayxandri, Anna Bini, Marion Bayle, Marie-Claire Blanckaert, Barbara Bourgois, Marie-France Boyer, Marianne Chedid, Alexandra D'Arnoux, Jean Demachy, Emmanuel de Toma, Geneviève Dortignac, Jérôme Dumoulin, Marie-Claude Dumoulin, Lydia Fiasoli, Jean-Noel Forestier, Marie Kalt, Françoise Labro, Anne Lefèvre, Hélène Lafforgue, Catherine Laroche, Nathalie Leffol, Blandine Leroy, Chris O'Byrne, Christine Puech, José Postic, Nello Renault, Elisabeth Selse, Caroline Tiné, Claude Vuillermet, Suzanne Walker and Rosaria Zucconi, who helped me to discover the world, and Mattias Bouazis, who helped me to classify all my photographs.

The following people and organizations were generous in allowing me access to their houses and apartments: Jérôme Abel Seguin, Jean-Marie Amat, Avril, Peter Beard, Bébèche, Luisa Becaria, Dominique Bernard, Dorothée Boissier, Carole Bracq, Susie and Mark Buell, Michel Camus, Laurence Clark, Anita Coppet and Jean-Jacques Driewir, Bertile Cornet, Jane Cumberbatch, Geneviève Cuvelier, Ricardo Dalasi, Anne and Pierre Damour, Catherine Dénoual, Dominique and Pierre Bénard Dépalle, Ann Dong, Patrice Doppelt, Philippe Duboy, Christian Duc, Jan Duclos Maïm, Bernard Dufour, Flemish Primitives, Michèle Fouks, Pierre Fuger, Massimiliano Fuksas, Teresa Fung and Teresa Roviras, His Majesty the Maharajah Gaj Sing Ji, Henriette Gaillard, Jean and Isabelle Garçon, John MacGlenaghan, Fiora Gondolfi, Annick Goutal and Alain Meunier, Murielle Grateau, Yves and Michèle Halard, Hotel Le Sénéchal, Hotel Samod Haveli, Anthony Hudson, Ann Huybens, Patrick T'Hoft, Igor and Lili, Michèle Iodice, Paul Jacquette, Hellson, Jolie Kelter and Michael Malcé, Dominique Kieffer, Kiwayu, Lawrence and William Kriegel, Philippe Labro, Karl Lagerfeld, François Lafanour, Nad Laroche, Rudolph Thomas Leimbacher, Philippe Lévèque and Claude Terrijn, Marion Lesage, Luna, Catherine Margaretis, Marongiu, Mathias, Valérie Mazerat and Bernard Ghèzy, Jean-Louis Mennesson, Ilaria Miani, Anna Moï, Leonardo Mondadori, Jacqueline Morabito, Christine Moussière, Paola Navone, Christine Nicaise, Christian Neirynck, Jean Oddes, Catherine Painvin, John Pawson, Christiane Perrochon, Phong Pfeufer, Françoise Pialoux les Terrasses, Alberto Pinto, Stéphane Plassier, Morgan Puett, Riad Dar Amane, Riad Dar Kawa, Yagura Rié, Guillaume Saalburg, Holly Salomon, Jocelyne and Jean-Louis Sibuet, Siegrid and her cousins, Valérie Solvi, Richard Texier, Jérôme Tisné, Doug Tomkins, Anna and Patrice Touron, Christian Tortu, Armand Ventilo, Barbara de Vries, Thomas Wegner, Quentin Wilbaux, Catherine Willis.

Thanks are also due to the following magazines for allowing me to include photographs originally published by them: *Architectural Digest* (French Edition), *Atmosphère, Elle, Elle à Table, Elle Décoration, Elle Décor Italie, Madame Figaro, Maison Française, Marie Claire, Marie Claire Idées, Marie Claire Maison, The World of Interiors.*

Gilles de Chabaneix

THE ILLUSTRATED HISTORY OF THE
TWENTIETH
CENTURY

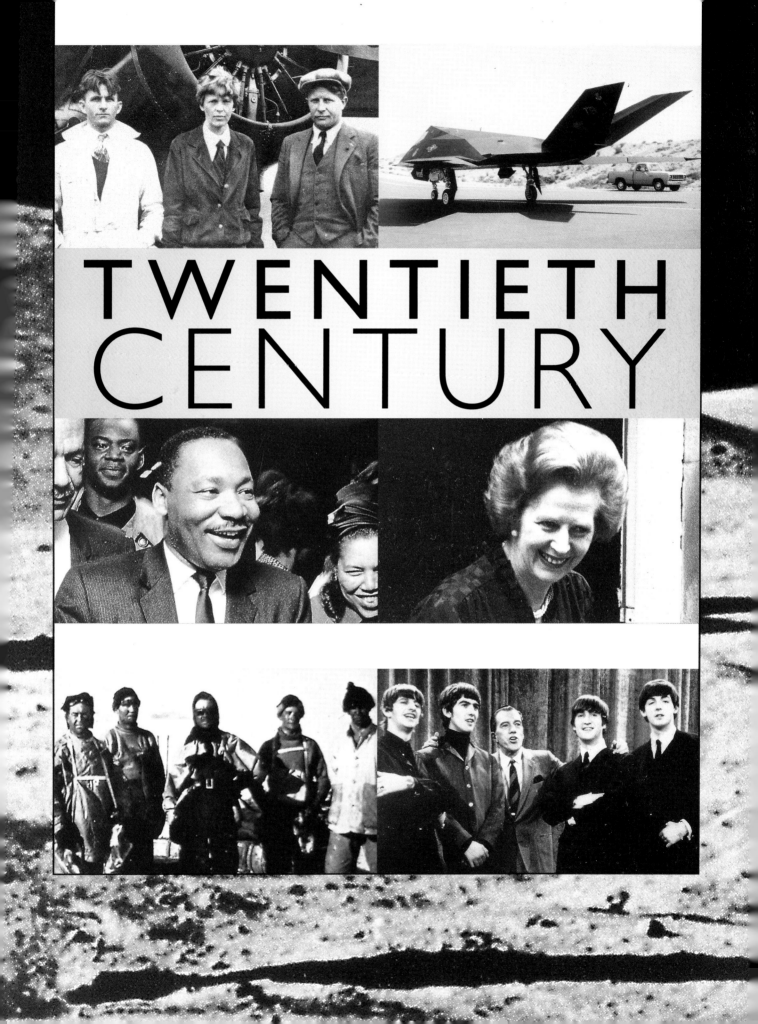

TWENTIETH CENTURY

This edition published by:
Grange Books
Kingsnorth Industrial Estate
Hoo, Nr. Rochester
Kent ME3 9ND

ISBN 1-84013-376-7

Editorial: Cover (to) Cover
Additional editorial assistance: Fiona Corbridge; Susan Wheatly

Text: Simon Adams
        Viv Croot
        Margaret Crowther
        Will Fowler
        Ann Kramer
        Dan McCausland
        ATH Rowland-Entwistle
        Helen Varley
        Philip Wilkinson

Index: Ingrid Lock

Design and typesetting: Casebourne Rose Design Associates,
Studio assistant: Mat Rose
Additional millennium design: Chuck Goodwin

Project co-ordinator: Tami Rex for Book Creation Illustrated Ltd

Picture research and photography by Anne Hobart Lang and Rolf
Lang at AHL Archives, Washington, USA. Additional research by
Heritage Picture Collection, London, Mirco De Cet.

CONTENTS

INTRODUCTION

THE TWENTIETH CENTURY has been called "the short century". Perhaps it may seem so but this century has been crowded with incident, fractured by global warfare and accelerated by technology and a communications revolution. We have been to the moon, stared nuclear destruction in the face, cured — and unleashed — killer diseases, and learned to cope on a planet whose population has more than doubled since 1900.

Significantly, the end of this astonishing century is also the end of the second millennium, giving the twentieth century a particular resonance and interest. Using dramatic pictures and accessible text, *The Illustrated History of the Twentieth Century* examines and describes the force of this resonance. The book begins with three introductory essays outlining the broad themes that have shaped the century — politics, culture and war. It then continues to tell the story of the century chronologically, moving through time decade-by-decade, and, within each decade, year-by-year. Each year, key events — from significant political occurrences, through to details of daily life — are presented in easy to access snippets. Striking black and white photographs, many of them contemporary, bring events to life in a startling and dramatic fashion.

At regular intervals feature spreads focus on topics of particular interest and significance, such as war, revolution, scientific developments and cultural highpoints. More than 100 major obituaries are also included, and *The Illustrated History of the Twentieth Century* finishes with wide ranging easy-to-access reference material on achievements in the fields of sport, cinema, science and the arts.

POLITICS AND IDEOLOGIES

TO MAKE SOME SENSE of the politics of our own century is to attempt to be objective about our own lives and the events we have lived through, perhaps even witnessed at first hand. Without the measure of distance, the politics of this century appear too personal, crowding together in a seeming confusion of the horrific and banal, the epic and the ordinary. Yet writing at the tail end of a century that is finishing, as it began, with wars in the Balkans, instability in Russia, poverty and exploitation in Africa, and the continuing dominance of the USA, it is possible to make some coherence out of events, to discern some abiding themes which make this century one of the most violent, and most changeable, of this millennium.

ABOVE: The Russian royal family before the Revolution of 1917 brought down the monarchy forever.

AN END TO EMPIRE

To begin the century in 1900 may make chronological sense, but there is nothing to distinguish that year from 1899 or 1901, or indeed 1910. The world order established in the second half of the nineteenth century lived on into the twentieth, an order based on European imperial dominance of trade, technology and colonial possession matched only by the aggressive frontier state of the USA, whose dynamic economy and growing population was fast providing a counterbalance to European hegemony. But while the imperial system of mighty empires was on proud display in Britain, France, Germany, Russia and Austria-Hungary, the edifice was not as strong as it looked. In 1911 the ancient Chinese Empire finally collapsed as a quasi-democratic and republican government took power in Beijing. In 1913 the Ottoman Empire had dwindled to a mere toehold in Europe, having already lost control of North Africa. And in 1914, in Sarajevo in the Balkans, the heir to the Austrian throne was assassinated, bringing the whole imperial system tumbling down. If the nineteenth century ended with the Chinese Revolution, the twentieth began with a gunshot in Sarajevo, the catalyst for the first war in history to be deemed a world war.

A NEW ORDER

The First World War changed the landscape of the world utterly and completely. A total war which mobilized entire populations in Europe and was fought out in colonies on every continent, it ended the certainties of the single world order of the previous century and redrew the map of the world. Gone were the German, Austro-Hungarian, Russian and Ottoman Empires; weakened were the French and British Empires. In their place were three dominant ideologies — the rampant Capitalism and liberal democracy of the United States, the totalitarian, state order of Fascism, and the equally totalitarian although supposed liberating system of Communism. The new order of the world was now disorder.

ABOVE: The image of the swastika dominated the 1930s and 1940s.

For the next 70 years, these rival ideologies strove for world dominance. With Communism confined to one country — Russia — the weakness of Capitalism when faced with the reconstruction of the European economies after the war led to Fascism gaining ground in Italy and then Germany, Spain, and a host of East European countries. Post-war political and economic instability and the collapse of the world economy after the slump of 1929 provided fertile ground for totalitarianism as both a resurgent Germany under the Nazis and an imperial Japan under military control used military might and economic muscle to address the unfinished business of the 1919 Treaty of Versailles which had supposedly ended the First World War. By 1939 the world had returned to war again, a three-sided conflict between rival ideologies that forced Capitalism and Communism together to fight the common foe, Fascism.

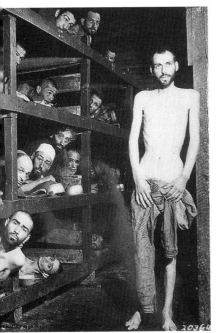

ABOVE: Pictures from Hitler's death camps shocked the world.

THE HORROR OF THE HOLOCAUST

To see the Second World War as an equally barbaric continuation of the First makes political sense, with much the same players on the same sides as before. One event, however, stands out as a unique disfigurement to this and indeed any century. Almost 60 years on, the world is still trying to come to terms with the Holocaust, the deliberate attempt by one nation to remove every member of another from the face of the world. The evil banality of the industry of genocide — the camps, the trains, the meticulous record-keeping — revealed the full and horrifying potential of human cruelty, and exposed Western civilization for the sham it really was.

RIVAL WORLD SYSTEMS

The defeat of Fascism by 1945 both simplified and intensified the ideological conflict. The new world order was now based on conflict between the two main victors — Soviet Russia and capitalist USA. This was the Cold War which was to dominate the world for the next 45 years. Despite the obvious flashpoints of Berlin, Poland, Hungary and Czechoslovakia, Europe was in many ways sidelined. Both superpowers, as they became known, poured in money and resources to rebuild their halves of Europe in their own image, while the major European colonial powers — Britain, France, the Netherlands, and later Spain and Portugal — retreated from international pretensions and gave up their colonies, ushering on to the world stage a host of new nations: some old countries such as India regaining their independence, most others new creations with unstable borders and little experience of self-rule. It was here, and in the rest of the so-called Third World, that the superpower conflict was fought out in a series of wars by proxy, with flashpoints in Korea, Vietnam and the rest of Southeast Asia, in Angola, the Horn of Africa, Afghanistan, Cuba and Nicaragua.

ABOVE: Berlin was divided and the wall guarded on both sides.

ABOVE: A US Pershing missile launch.

THE SUPREMACY OF THE SUPERPOWERS

Two responses were evident to superpower dominance. In South America, Africa and Asia, non-alignment became an act of political faith for many newly independent nations, based on the sound principle of a plague on both big houses. In Western Europe, the century-old rivalry between France and Germany was subsumed in an industrial and political partnership to rebuild Europe, which by the end of the century was to include fifteen countries in close political and economic union with a single currency and common institutions and laws. But, inescapably, the superpower rivalry cast a long shadow over the world. It was based on military might, with both sides developing nuclear weapons and space technology to achieve balances of terror in missiles and men. It was also based on ideological conviction, as both sides were convinced of the morality of their position. Oddly, despite protestations to the contrary, both sides soon came to resemble the imperial dinosaurs vanquished in 1914.

In the end it was money, not ideology, which counted. With its ability to generate wealth and develop new technology, the USA outperformed and outspent the USSR, bankrupting the country and causing it to collapse altogether in 1991. By then, however, new forces had emerged which made their conflict irrelevant. Across the world, a growing awareness of human rights and civil liberties led to the emergence of women's liberation and gay rights, of black consciousness movements, and demands for equality of both opportunity and outcome. Oil, and increasingly water, became resources to be fought over. And in the Arab world, the emergence of the state of Israel began a process which led to a fundamentalist renaissance similar to that experienced by Christendom 500 years before. In an increasingly secular age — both superpowers

ABOVE: Women marched for equal opportunity.

were, after all, based on an ideology of economics, not religion — the arrival of theocracies in Iran, Afghanistan and elsewhere placed in sharp relief the consumerism and commercialism of much of the rest of the world. Where once there were colonial powers, now there is Coca Cola and MTV, Microsoft and McDonalds. Stand in a shopping mall in Seoul or Jakarta and you could be in London or Los Angeles. Such material gains have their price, and just as the Islamic fundamentalists have turned their back on what they see as Western decadence, others have pointed out that such decadence is based on limited world resources and a planet highly susceptible to human maladministration. The world may be glad to turn its back on the horrors of this century, but can hardly face the next with any great comfort.

ABOVE: Ayatollah Khomeini brought fundamentalism to Iran.

THE ARTS AND POPULAR CULTURE

THE RAPID PACE OF CHANGE in the twentieth century affected the arts as much as any other field. Styles and movements followed each other in rapid succession as artists tried to extend their scope, inventing new forms, covering new subjects and using new technology. These trends were accelerated by improvements in communication, giving works of art wide exposure.

Changes in lifestyle, with more leisure for more people, and mass media supplying their needs, had profound effects on the arts. One result was the divergence of "popular" and "high" culture. New forms emerged, whose aims seemed far removed from those of "high" art. Yet, by the end of the century, many artists working in conventional modes have absorbed influences from popular culture and multimedia has brought "high" and "low" culture together again.

LITERATURE AND DRAMA

The century began with some of the most vital, revolutionary literary movements of all time. In poetry, writers such as Frenchman Guillaume Apollinaire and American Ezra Pound invented new forms and transformed readers' ideas about what poetry could be like. Movements such as Dadaism and Surrealism opened up new worlds of experimentation with language and imagery. The scope of the novel was also extended greatly. While many novelists continued writing realist fiction in the tradition of their nineteenth-century forebears, they would eventually include virtually every facet of human life in their work. One writer, James Joyce, extended the scope of the novel further than any other. His masterpiece, *Ulysses*, has influenced countless later works of fiction.

ABOVE: Literary giants of the century — James Joyce, Ezra Pound, Ford Maddox Ford and John Quinn.

The idea of the "well-made play" reached its fruition in the nineteenth century. Some twentieth-century dramatists, such as George Bernard Shaw, continued to draw on this tradition but others wanted to take drama in new directions. The German Expressionist movement sought a new intensity of language and action; dramatist Bertolt Brecht and composer Kurt Weill brought social comment to musical theatre; the French theatre of the absurd created an elusive symbolism; writers such as Irishman Samuel Beckett pared down dramato into its most basic constituents; French theorist Antonin Artaud inspired the "theatre of cruelty" in which violence, spectacle and religious experience were blended together in a new and potent mix.

MUSIC

Music more than any other art form has shown how popular and "mainstream" culture have diverged during the twentieth century. Composers in the "serious" tradition continued to write for classical ensembles but many others abandoned the concepts of tonality and melody that made earlier classical music accessible to a wide audience.

ABOVE: Igor Stravinsky, one of the century's great musical innovators.

Meanwhile, a flourishing popular culture continued to provide accessible music. Jazz, the music of black America, set the trend. Other cultures soon picked up on its idioms and it began to influence a host of popular styles that sprang up in the second half of the century. Popular music also used the new technologies. It became above all a recorded medium, as successive formats — wax cylinders, 78s, vinyl discs, tapes, CDs — provided better reproduction. "Serious" composers too were fascinated with the new technology. In the 1940s and 1950s, Karlheinz Stockhausen in Germany and Pierre Henri in France pioneered electronic music; later Pierre Boulez founded IRCAM, his Paris centre for research into electronics and acoustics in music.

ABOVE: The first discs.

ARCHITECTURE

The architects of the twentieth century took the materials of the nineteenth, such as steel and reinforced concrete, and put them to wider use. The first result was the rise of the skyscraper. Architects such as Le Corbusier were also at the forefront of social thinking, designing new cities that would provide a better living environment than before. Sadly, few of these cities were built in the way that their architects wished.

And yet the century did produce buildings that have withstood the test of time — the skyscrapers of New York and Chicago, housing projects by JJP Oud, the houses of Frank Lloyd Wright in the USA. Architects in Germany developed a keynote style at the Bauhaus, the

ABOVE: The Seagram Building (1954–8), New York, by Mies van der Rohe and Philip Johnson.

design school started at Weimar in 1919. Driven from Nazi Germany, the Bauhaus designers took their brand of modernism to the USA, where it became known as the International Style.

VISUAL ARTS

With a range of forms from photography to classical portraiture, nineteenth-century artists had achieved some of the most realistic styles in art history. Movements such as Cubism gave a new take on realism, refracting the image and seeming to capture several viewpoints at once. Other artists embraced Surrealism, using realist techniques to portray images from fantasy and dream. Abstraction, the abandonment of the subject altogether, was the route followed in Russia and the Netherlands. Towards the end of the century, in the form of the Abstract Expressionist style, it was favoured by many of the most prominent North American artists.

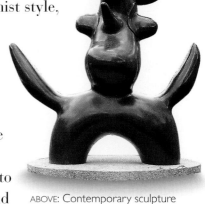

ABOVE: Contemporary sculpture

Another solution was to study the ideas inherent in images. From the "ready-mades" of French artist Marcel Duchamp to more recent conceptual works, many artists have tried to make their audience think, putting this aim before "pure" visual appeal. Artists have also been open to the influence of new media, making use of film and video in recent "installation" art.

Photography matured, developing its own language, techniques and technology. It became the democratic art form of the century, accessible to all and used for commerce as well as higher art forms.

FILM AND TELEVISION

The art of film grew with the century. Technological advances brought sound, then colour, then a seemingly endless range of special effects. The development of directing and acting techniques suited to film gave the medium its true power but the growth of sizeable film industries in Hollywood, India, and Australia provided finance, and the resources to screen films all over the world. Film became the art form most typical of the century. Television was born in the 1920s, and developed in a similar way to film, becoming the art form that found a place in every home. Television's power lay in its variety and its ability to provide information — documentaries, sports relays, and news broadcasts — that reported the century's events as they happened.

ABOVE: *The Empire Strikes Back*, part of the *Star Wars* trilogy, the pop culture phenomenon of the 1970s.

HOW WAR SHAPED THE CENTURY

IN THE FIRST 50 YEARS of the twentieth century war has directly and indirectly shaped not only the military, but also the diplomatic, social, scientific, technological and economic character of most of the world. Not all the side-effects of war are as grim as the event itself, and the twentieth century has benefited from medical and technological breakthroughs which may not have been made had research not been driven by the needs of the military. The damage that war causes to individuals and to a nation's psyche can last long after the last round has been fired and the peace treaties have been signed. The reparations demanded by the Prussians after the Franco Prussian War fuelled the French desire for revenge in World War I. After 1918 the Germans suffered as badly from French demands, and this in turn was a factor in the rise of Hitler and National Socialism and therefore the outbreak of World War II.

ABOVE: A soldier from World War I.

THE POSITIVE SIDE OF CONFLICT

However war also gives urgency to research and this included the areas of radar and radio. Penicillin and plastic surgery as well as the more questionable benefit of DDT were all developed or advanced as a result of research in World War II. Nylon — not merely as a substitute for silk in stockings and thus one of the weapons of the American GI's charm offensive in Britain between 1943 and 1945 — replaced silk and cotton webbing material in parachutes.

While war may inspire, finance and accelerate new research, it also creates the climate in which innovation prospers. The tank, developed to break through the barbed wire and trench systems of the Western Front in France and Belgium, would become a key weapon in land war for the rest of the century.

Even explosives — the destructive force of war — have their civil applications. The plastic explosives derived from gelignite, which had been developed by the British in the early 1940s and used for sabotage by resistance groups throughout Europe, is now used in the demolition of redundant industrial plants or high-rise apartments.

ABOVE: War brought women into factories.

The fire-retardant and bullet proof materials used in tank crew overalls and body armour, find applications in clothing for civilian firemen and even the sails and rigging of modern sailing ships.

ABOVE: World War II troops on Normandy Beach, 1941.

World War II accelerated the end of the colonial empires of Britain, France and The Netherlands and created new independent nations in Africa and Asia. As men were called up in huge numbers between 1914–18 to serve in the armed forces, so women went into the factories to take their places. Their work in areas that had previously been the preserve of men did much to accelerate emancipation after World War I. In World War II women again returned to the factories and in the post-war years job opportunities increased for women.

After World War I the first non-stop transatlantic flight was undertaken in an ex-RAF Vickers Vimy bomber. In four short years in World War I, aircraft had changed from fragile powered box kites, to robust machines capable of flying in poor weather. The jet engine that now powers most of the world's passenger aircraft, as well as combat aircraft, was developed in the United Kingdom and Germany during World War II.

THE ULTIMATE DETERRENT AND UNLIMITED POWER

The research that has had the greatest impact on the world, and received its impetus during World War II, was the development of the atomic bomb. While the Western Allies were developing the atomic bomb, in Germany rocket scientists produced the first ballistic missile, the V2.

The combination of missile and nuclear warhead has made the world since 1945 both a very dangerous and a safer place. As nuclear weapons proliferate beyond Russia, Europe and the USA the threat of global destruction in a "small" nuclear war increases. However in the past this threat kept the peace in Europe between the former Soviet Union and the West until the final collapse of the USSR and the end of the Cold War.

Nuclear power has vociferous critics, but harnessed for peaceful use it has provided electric

ABOVE: Atomic bomb on Nagasaki.

power and propulsion for major ships. The rocket technology that can deliver a nuclear warhead has been used to explore the outer limits of space. While part of the impetus for the drive has come from scientific curiosity the "Space Race" between the USSR and USA financed and drove the programme in its early years.

ABOVE: War in Vietnam.

Navigation and satellite technology, which was first intended for military reconnaissance use, has allowed cartographers to update maps in some of the remotest parts of the world and travellers to visit them using the remarkable accuracy of the Global Positioning System (GPS).

THE BENEFITS OF THE COLD WAR

It must be remembered that one of the remarkable aspects of this century has been the many years of peace — or at least lack of aggression on a global scale — which was the direct result of the East-West split at the end of World War II. With both sides equipped with more than enough fire-power to destroy a thousand Earths, the world basked in a kind of stand-off situation and a whole generation in the West has lived to middle age without experiencing the devastation known to their parents. Now that the Eastern bloc has imploded and been reborn as individual states, it seems we are going back to old-fashioned local incidents and skirmishes. What will happen after the millennium has yet to be seen.

ABOVE: Research into fusion power, a by-product of the arms race.

War in the twentieth century has been more destructive over shorter periods than any previous conflict. Humanity has harnessed science, technology and perverted medical knowledge in weapon design. War can be, and has been, a degrading, destructive, corrupting and corrosive activity. However it has also been the only option available to governments or liberation movements to defeat tyrants and liberate oppressed or enslaved nations.

A NEW CENTURY

CHANGE is in the air as the new century begins. In Europe, alliances change; in Asia, Japan emerges from isolation and China enters its last imperial phase. Russia experiences its first revolution; industry and technology grow apace in the United States. Women on both sides of the Atlantic opt for militancy in their quest for the vote. Science too is revolutionary: the first manned flight, wireless transmission, new plastics, psychoanalysis, relativity, and the arrival of mass-produced cars — society on the move.

OPPOSITE: World Exhibition opens on April 14 in Paris, France.

1900–1909

KEY EVENTS OF THE DECADE

- BOER WAR
- BOXER REBELLION
- FREUD DEVELOPS PSYCHOANALYSIS
- FIRST SUCCESSFUL MANNED FLIGHT
- RUSSO-JAPANESE WAR
- WOMEN FIGHT FOR THE VOTE
- REVOLUTION IN RUSSIA
- EINSTEIN PUBLISHES THEORY OF RELATIVITY
- HORMONES ARE DISCOVERED
- RADIOACTIVITY IS EXPLAINED

- BLERIOT FLIES THE CHANNEL
- FIRST NOBEL PRIZES AWARDED
- FIRST TRANSATLANTIC RADIO TRANSMISSION
- VACUUM CLEANER INVENTED
- FORD DEVELOPS MODEL-T MOTOR CAR
- PEARY REACHES NORTH POLE
- CUBISM IS BORN
- BALLETS RUSSES FOUNDED
- THE FIRST WESTERN IS SCREENED

WORLD POPULATION: 1,608 MILLION

BOER WAR AND BOXER REBELLION

As a new century opens, conflict remains a common theme. The Boer War continues in South Africa, where the establishment of concentration camps shocks the world, and in China the Boxer uprising gives violent expression to anti-Western sentiment. In the world of science, the findings of Sigmund Freud and Max Planck revolutionize psychology and physics, and in the visual world, Art Nouveau transforms the streets of Paris.

OPPOSITE: Chinese nationalist, member of the Boxer society "Fists of Righteous Harmony".

1 9 0 0

Jan	23	Battle of Spion Kop, South Africa. Boers force British retreat	July	1	Zeppelin, maiden flight, Germany
				19	Paris Métro opens
				29	Anarchist assassinates King Umberto of Italy
Feb	9	Dwight Davis creates Davis Cup tennis tournament			
	27	Labour Party founded, UK	Aug	13	*Deutschland* wins Blue Riband as the fastest transatlantic liner
Mar	19	Arthur Evans begins to unearth Knossos, Crete		14	Allied forces enter Peking, China
				25	Friedrich Nietzsche dies
Apr	14	World Exhibition opens, Paris, France	Sep	19	Alleged spy Alfred Dreyfus pardoned, France
May	17	British army relieves Mafeking, South Africa			
	20	Second Olympic Games begins, Paris, France	Oct	14	Sigmund Freud publishes *The Interpretation of Dreams*
	31	Boxer Rebellion breaks out, China		26	Britain annexes Transvaal, South Africa
June	19	Theodore Roosevelt is nominated for US vice-president	Nov	9	Russia completes annexation of Manchuria
	24	Boxers destroy foreign embassies, China		30	Writer Oscar Wilde dies in exile in France

THE BOER WAR

Following years of tension between Britain and the Boers in South Africa, British forces under General Buller attempt to break through Boer lines in January and relieve Ladysmith. After initial successes, the British are forced to withdraw, having suffered losses of 87 officers and 1,647 men.

In February, the diamond mining town of Kimberley, which has been beseiged by the Boers since October 1899 and under severe bombardment, is relieved by a British cavalry force numbering some 5,000.

The small town of Mafeking has been defended by a garrison of 700 irregulars and armed townsmen since October 1899. It is beseiged by 5,000 Boers under General Cronje. The town is bombarded continuously and on May 12, 300 Boers attack and break in, but are forced to surrender. On May 17, the town is relieved by a cavalry column commanded by Colonel Mahon.

ABOVE: Crowds outside the town hall, Cape Town, as the British decide to annexe the Boer Republics.

ABOVE: Descendants of Dutch colonists, the Boers fight bitterly for control of Transvaal and Orange Free State.

ABOVE: New South Wales troops leave Sydney for South Africa. Reinforcements from the Dominions aid British victory.

ABOVE: British forces cross the Tugela river on their way to Spion Kop, where Boers force a British retreat.

RIGHT: British prisoners of war at Nooitgedacht. In retaliation for Boer guerrilla attacks, the British set up concentration camps for Boer civilians.

BOXER REBELLION

Anti-Western sentiment explodes into revolt in China in May as the Fists of Righteous Harmony, or the Boxers, assassinate the German minister and besiege foreign legations. The Boxers, who have the support of the dowager empress, are campaigning to rid China of all foreign influences. European nations, led by Britain and Germany, relieve the legations later in the year and re-establish their authority in China.

DREAMS INTERPRETED

Sigmund Freud (1856–1939), a Moravian-born doctor working in Vienna, publishes his first major work, *The Interpretation of Dreams*. It promotes his theory, based on the study or "psychoanalysis" of his patients, that unconscious motives influence behaviour. He analyses the meaning of dreams, which are clues to unconscious memories. Freud's work will revolutionize thinking about the human psyche.

ANARCHIST ASSASSINATES ITALIAN KING

After 22 years on the throne, Umberto I of Italy is assassinated by an anarchist in July. It is thought that he was shot in revenge for using the army to crush a revolt in Milan in 1898. Umberto is succeeded by his son, Victor Emmanuel.

ABOVE: Allied forces prepare to enter the Forbidden City, Peking, China, breaking the Boxer siege.

POLITICAL PARTY FOR UK WORKERS

In Britain, representatives of the trade union movement, the Independent Labour Party (ILP), the neo-Marxist Social Democratic Federation, and the Fabian Society, a socialist think-tank, have come together to form the Labour Representation Committee (LRC) under its secretary Ramsay MacDonald, a member of the ILP. The LRC aims to increase the representation of working people in parliament and to reverse recent court judgements against trade unions.

FIRST BOX BROWNIE

George Eastman of the USA markets his first Box Brownie roll-film camera. It costs just $1 and brings photography to the mass market.

FIRST DAVIS CUP

American Dwight F Davis comes up with the idea of a tennis contest between nations. He donates a silver trophy and goes on to win the first match in the competition. Davis also leads the American team to victory over Great Britain in the first Davis Cup tie.

ABOVE: Count Zeppelin's mighty airship moored in its shed after making its successful flight.

ZEPPELIN TAKES TO THE AIR

Count Ferdinand von Zeppelin of Germany launches his first dirigible (steerable) airship, *LZ 1*, in July. Its flight lasts about 20 minutes.

SALOON BUSTER

In the United States, American temperance agitator Carry Nation campaigns for the closure of illicit saloons. Armed with a hatchet and accompanied by hymn-singing women, she goes on saloon-busting expeditions.

METRO TRANSFORMS PARIS

Art Nouveau architect Hector Guimard transforms the streets of Paris with his entrances to the new Paris Métro. He uses iron and glass in new ways, which are both beautiful in their use of whiplash curves, plant-like forms and distinctive typography, but also highly practical. The roof panels, for instance, are standardized for ease of manufacture.

PETER RABBIT IS BORN

This year sees the writing of *The Tale of Peter Rabbit*, the first of a series of children's stories by English author Beatrix Potter (1866–1943). First published privately, *Peter Rabbit* becomes a firm favourite and will be followed by many similar volumes, which remain popular throughout the century, overcoming fashion. The use of the author's own illustrations and a small format, perfectly suited for children's hands, make this a highly influential book.

TOSCA TAKES THE STAGE

Giacomo Puccini's opera *Tosca* is performed. The full-blooded melodies, violent action, tense emotions, and vivid characters of Puccini's work take traditional Italian opera just about as far as it can go. Puccini is also the chief exponent of the *verismo* or realism style; his plot is so dramatic that audiences can tell what is going on from the music and action, without understanding the language.

MINOAN DISCOVERY

British archaeologist Arthur Evans (1851–1941) uncovers Knossos, capital of the Bronze Age Minoan civilization on the Aegean island of Crete. His remarkable discoveries include the magnificent palace of the legendary King Minos and pottery fragments decorated with Minoan script.

LORD JIM

Author Joseph Conrad's first great novel *Lord Jim* launches the Polish exile on his path. His awareness of the power of evil and how idealism can be corrupted make him a major figure in fiction.

ABOVE: An imposing stairway leads to the Java Pavilion at the World Exhibition, Paris.

PAPER CLIP

The paper clip is patented in Germany by its Norwegian inventor, Johann Vaaler. Before its invention, papers are fastened together with pins.

PLUNGER SUBMERGES

American inventor John Holland has added further refinements to his submersible, the *Plunger*. The first streamlined submersible to be built, it is propelled by electricity when submerged (it was previously steam-driven on the surface). Now Holland has replaced the steam engine with a more efficient petrol engine.

The invaluable paper clip.

CONCENTRATION CAMPS

British troops conquer the Transvaal and Orange Free State in November and scatter the Boer armies. The British are beginning to intern Boer women and children in concentration camps to prevent them helping Boer soldiers. This move causes an international outrage.

ABOVE: Fashionable shooting outfit for sporting women.

PLAY CAUSES SCANDAL

Austrian writer Arthur Schnitzler publishes his play *Reigen*. It shows the relationships between ten people all connected to each other in a circle of sexual contact, and sums up the corruption and decadence of the last years of the Hapsburg empire. The play causes a scandal and will not be performed until 1920.

CAKEWALK

A strutting dance, the cakewalk, which originated among black American slaves, hits Europe's dance halls.

DARING SWIMSUIT

Annette Kellerman, American aquatic star, introduces the one-piece swimsuit.

SECOND OLYMPICS

The second of the modern Olympic Games is held in Paris, France, from May to October, to coincide with the World Exhibition. However, events are scattered over six months and across northern France, diluting public interest. In contrast to the all-male Games of 1896, women compete in a limited number of events.

THE QUANTUM THEORY

German physicist Max Planck (1858–1947) of Berlin University discovers that energy consists of basic units, each of which he calls quanta. This marks the beginning of quantum theory, revolutionizes the study of physics, and wins him a 1918 Nobel Prize.

RADIOACTIVE GAS

German physicist Friedrich Ernst Dorn discovers the dangerous radioactive gas radon, the sixth of the "noble gases". He finds it emanating from a sample of radium.

THE WORLD EXHIBITS IN PARIS

The world's most innovative technology goes on exhibition in Paris, France. The Palace of Electricity, illuminated at night, and escalators from the United States, show how the new century will transform daily life. The Rodin Pavilion, France's major exhibit, is a celebration of the great sculptor.

OSCAR WILDE
(1854–1900)

The once-flamboyant Irish writer and brilliant epigramist, Oscar Wilde dies in France aged 44. Author of *The Importance of Being Earnest* and *The Picture of Dorian Gray*, Wilde was imprisoned for homosexual offences in 1895. He served a two-year prison sentence, which he described in *The Ballad of Reading Gaol*.

YELLOW FEVER

An American army doctor, Walter Reed, discovers that the deadly disease yellow fever is transmitted by mosquitoes. He does this by studying the disease in Cuba with the help of human volunteers. Eliminating the mosquitoes in Panama later enables engineers to construct the Panama Canal.

GAMMA RAYS

French physicist Paul Ulrich Villard discovers that radium puts out a third kind of radiation, in addition to the alpha-rays and beta-rays already discovered. These new electromagnetic rays are later named gamma-rays.

ENTER ELECTRONS

French physicist Henri Becquerel (1852–1908) discovers that the radioactivity from the element radium consists of the subatomic particles, electrons. He also finds that radioactivity can cause one element to change into another.

SISTER CARRIE

The highly realistic novel, *Sister Carrie*, by American master Theodore Dreiser, is effectively suppressed by the publishers because of its alleged immorality — "sin" is not "punished". The book is published, but not publicized.

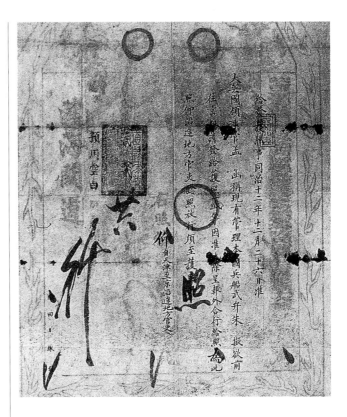

ABOVE: A Chinese passport signed by statesman Li-Hung-Chang. A pro-Westerner, Li-Hung-Chang promoted links with Europe, which were resented by the Boxers.

ABOVE: Severe flooding in Rome creates an unusual image of the Forum.

RADIO, TORPEDOES AND NOBEL PRIZES

European and Commonwealth countries mourn the death of Queen Victoria. She had reigned for 64 years, giving her name to a particular and remarkable period of history — the Victorian Age. As if to mark the start of a new era, the first-ever transatlantic radio signal is transmitted successfully and a black American is honoured at the White House for the first time.

OPPOSITE: British sailors prepare to draw Queen Victoria's coffin through the streets of London.

1 9 0 1

Jan	1	Commonwealth of Australia comes into being
	10	Oil discovered in Texas, USA
	22	Death of Queen Victoria, UK
Feb	26	Boxer leaders publicly executed, China
Mar	1	First monorail opened in Wuppertal, Germany
	13	First Mercedes built by Daimler, Germany
	17	Students riot in Russia
June	24	Unknown artist Pablo Picasso exhibits for the first time
Aug	4	Gold discovered in Rand, South Africa
Sep	6	President McKinley shot; Roosevelt becomes US President
	7	Peking Treaty ends Boxer Rising, China
	9	Artist Toulouse-Lautrec dies
Oct	16	Black American Booker T Washington dines at White House
Dec	10	First Nobel Prizes awarded
	12	Marconi sends first transatlantic wireless message

ABOVE: US President McKinley and his cabinet at the White House.

US PRESIDENT ASSASSINATED

President William McKinley is shot and killed in Buffalo, New York, by Polish anarchist Leon Czolgosz, in a September protest against the American government. Vice-president Theodore Roosevelt is on a climbing holiday when he hears the news and is sworn in as the 26th president at the age of 42.

FIRST TRANSATLANTIC RADIO

Worldwide radio communication becomes possible when the first transatlantic radio signal, the morse letter "S", is transmitted. A team working for the Italian pioneer of radio, Guglielmo Marconi (1874–1937), sends the signal from Poldhu, Cornwall, in the UK to St John's, Newfoundland, on December 12.

MEN IN THE MOON

Creator of science fiction, author HG Wells anticipates the future with his new novel *The First Men in the Moon*. The spirit of adventure, the explanation of technology, and the conquest of space are themes which will recur in science fiction of later decades.

EUROPEAN ELEMENT

French chemist Eugène Dumarçay discovers the rare earth element europium, which he names in honour of Europe.

BLACK AMERICAN AT THE WHITE HOUSE

President Theodore Roosevelt (1858–1919) entertains black American Booker T Washington to dinner at the White House, the first black man to be so honoured. Booker T Washington is a noted reformer and educator and president of the first university for blacks in the USA in Tuskegee, Alabama. Two weeks later, 34 people are killed in race riots which break out in the south of the USA in protest at the visit.

END OF AN ERA

Queen Victoria dies at the age of 82. She has ruled Britain since 1837 and seen it grow into the most powerful economic and military power in the world, with a vast empire on every continent. Through her children and grandchildren, she is related to every monarch in Europe and her funeral is attended by heads of state from around the world.

LEFT: Luxurious dining facilities for passengers on the Paris-Lyon-Mediterranean railway.

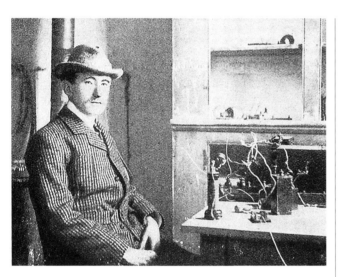

ABOVE: Marconi with his radio receiving set.

THREE SISTERS

Konstantin Stanislavsky directs Anton Chekhov's play, *The Three Sisters*, written especially for the Moscow Art Theatre, in a milestone production that brings him fame. His insistence on a permanent, high-quality company of actors, his enthusiasm for a realistic acting style, and his belief in the theatre as a means of educating people, later find expression in the Method style of acting, in which the actor draws on his or her past experiences in creating a role.

MORO WARS BREAK OUT

Violence breaks out in the Philippines when the US, in control of the Philippines since 1898, demands that the Moros, Muslim tribespeople, assimilate with Christian islanders.

BELOW: Loading an aerial torpedo — a new and deadly weapon.

ABOVE: Motor racing gains popularity; here a French contestant reaches Berlin.

BLOOD GROUPS

Viennese-born US immunologist Karl Landsteiner discovers that blood can be categorized into three groups, A, B and O, a method of sorting still used today. Landsteiner later discovers a fourth group, AB.

VACUUM CLEANER INVENTED

Herbert Cecil Booth, an English civil engineer, invents the vacuum cleaner. His first machine is mounted on a horse-drawn cart and powered by a petrol engine. Long tubes are passed into houses to clean them.

MUTATIONS

Dutch botanist Hugo de Vries, who in 1900 rediscovered Gregor Mendel's laws of heredity, discovers that new forms of plants can arise suddenly, and gives this process the name "mutation". He introduces the experimental method of studying plant evolution.

MERCURY LAMP

American electrical engineer Peter Coope-Hewitt markets the mercury-vapour electric arc lamp. It produces a light that is nearly shadow-free.

BUDDENBROOKS

German author Thomas Mann (1875–1955) publishes his first novel, *Buddenbrooks*. In it Mann portrays the decline of one German family, who lose their money, their creativity, and their very will to live, using this as a symbol for the decline of Germany itself.

WOMEN STUDENTS ENTER ROCHESTER

American feminist Susan B Antony persuades Rochester University, New York State, to accept women students. She raises nearly $100,000 to pay the tuition costs.

SHAVING TIME

The first safety razor with throwaway blades is made by King Camp Gillette of Boston, Massachusetts. For two years he has to give the razors away until he can find a backer to set him up with a factory. By 1908 he is selling 14 million blades a year.

KORFBALL INVENTED

Dutch schoolmaster Nico Broekhuysen invents the sport of Korfball. It is played by teams of twelve on a playing area with three zones. In the zone at each end stands a basket 3.5 metres (11.5 feet) off the ground in which goals are scored.

ANTARCTIC EXPEDITION

Robert Falcon Scott, commander of the British National Antarctic Expedition, sets sail in the *Discovery* from New Zealand. The expedition explores the Ross Sea area, sighting the Transantarctic Mountains, reaching the polar plateau and discovering Taylor Valley.

LEFT: Workmen strengthen wires on the Brooklyn bridge, which crosses the East River, New York.

LEFT: *Shamrock II*, challenger for the America's Cup.

RIGHT: Dunlop — the latest in pneumatic bicycle tyres.

ROCKEFELLER INSTITUTE FOUNDED

American philanthropist and oil magnate, John D Rockefeller, founds the Rockefeller Institute for Medical Research.

CHRISTMAS TREES ARE LIT UP

Christmas tree lights are among the ideas developed by the Edison General Electric Co. in the USA, founded by the inventor Thomas Edison in 1889.

FIRST NOBEL PRIZES

The first-ever Nobel Prizes for achievements in physics, chemistry, medicine or physiology, literature, and peace are awarded. They were endowed in 1895 by Alfred Nobel, the Swedish chemist and inventor of dynamite. Jacobus Henricus van't Hoff (Holland) is awarded the prize in chemistry for his work on thermodynamics and stereochemistry. Wilhelm Röntgen (Germany) receives the physics prize for his discovery of X-rays. Sully Prudhomme, of France, receives the literature prize, Jean-Henri Dunant (Switzerland), founder of the Red Cross, and Frédéric Passy (France) jointly receive the peace prize.

AUSTRALIAN COMMONWEALTH

The Commonwealth of Australia comes into being in January. The six former Australian colonies are now united within a single federal state, but there are already difficulties over non-white immigration and the growing demands of the trade union and labour movement for better working conditions.

ANTI-SEMITISM IN RUSSIA

Anti-Semitism drives many Russian Jews to Palestine to settle in farming colonies set up by Baron Rothschild.

BELOW: Excavation for the western channel of the massive Nile dam being built in Egypt.

TEDDY BEAR DEBUT

The Treaty of Vereeniging brings an end to the Boer War, the Japanese and British enter a formal alliance, and France and Italy sign an *entente*. Hormones are discovered and surgery makes a major advance when the technique of suturing is developed. Italian tenor Enrico Caruso becomes the world's first recording star and American president "Teddy" Roosevelt gives his name to what will become one of the world's favourite toys.

1902

Jan	7	Chinese imperial court returns to Peking after suppression of Boxer uprising
	30	Britain and Japan sign peace treaty
Feb	1	Footbinding outlawed, China
Mar	26	Cecil Rhodes, architect of imperialism, dies
May	31	Treaty of Vereeniging ends the Boer War
July	31	96 miners killed in a mining diaster at Port Kembla, Australia
Sep	29	French novelist Emile Zola (b. 1840) dies
Nov	1	Franco-Italian *entente*

ABOVE: Russian novelist and visionary Leo Tolstoy (1828–1910), famed for his novels and rejection of materialism.

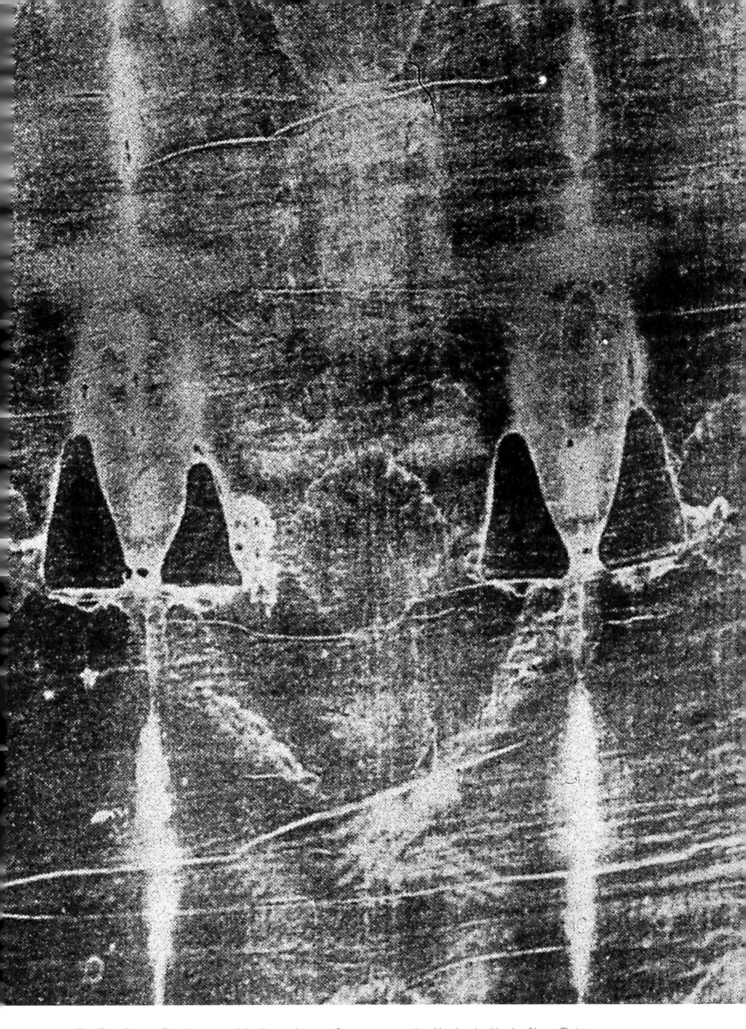

ABOVE: The Turin Shroud. Experimenters claim the marks came from vapours emitted by the dead body of Jesus Christ.

ABOVE: Despite appalling conditions in the camps, Boer prisoners maintain their spirits with amateur dramatics.

BOER WAR ENDS

At Vereeniging, South Africa, Britain and the Boer leaders finally sign a peace treaty in May that marks the end of the Boer War, which has lasted for nearly three years. The Boers are forced to accept British colonial rule, with a promise of self-government later, and a substantial grant of £3 million to help rebuild their shattered countries.

VOTES FOR ALL IN AUSTRALIA

Australia grants universal suffrage, allowing women aged 21 and over to vote in federal elections with the same rights as men. This follows New Zealand's example in granting universal suffrage, which is unknown throughout Europe and the United States.

JAPANESE-BRITISH ALLIANCE

Britain and Japan sign a treaty of alliance in January, by which both agree not to make a treaty with a third country without the other's consent. The agreement safeguards Britain's interests in China and Japan's interests in Korea, and is the first alliance Britain has signed for many years.

A TRIP TO THE MOON

Georges Méliès's latest film *A Voyage to the Moon* opens to acclaim. Using innovatory special effects and combining magic and fantasy, it consists of 30 scenes and will bring Méliès, a conjurer by training, international fame.

FIRST TEDDY BEAR

Russian-born Morris Michton, a New York candy store assistant, makes the world's first teddy bear. He was inspired by a Clifford Berryman cartoon in the *Washington Evening Star* which showed President "Teddy" Roosevelt on a hunting trip, refusing to shoot a mother bear.

STITCHES IN TIME

French surgeon Alexis Carrel develops the technique of suturing (sewing) blood vessels (arteries and veins) together end to end, a major development in surgery.

ABOVE: French novelist Emile Zola, author of *Germinal*, and defender
of Dreyfus. He dies this year.

TOP OF THE CHARTS

Italian tenor Enrico Caruso (1873–1921) becomes the first recording star when he makes ten records for the Victor company. They include "Vesti la giubba" from Pagliacci, which will eventually become the first classical record to sell one million copies.

FRANCO-ITALIAN ENTENTE

France and Italy sign an *entente* in which Italy assures France of its neutrality if France is attacked. The French government is increasingly concerned by the growing military and economic might of Germany and is thus ensuring the security of its border with Italy.

RIYADH RECAPTURED

Abdul Aziz ibn Abdul Rahman of the al Saud family recaptures Riyadh from the Turks following a series of campaigns against the Turks and other family groups.

EARLY MORNING TEA

Frank Clarke, a gunsmith from Birmingham, England, makes the first automatic tea-maker. It is powered by clockwork, strikes a match to light a spirit stove, and pours boiling water into a teapot. It then sets off a bedside alarm.

FLATIRON BUILDING

Daniel H Burnham's twenty-storey Flatiron Building in New York, with its slim lines tapering to almost nothing, shows for the first time how modern concrete-and-steel technology gives the architect scope to create new shapes and forms.

DISASTER IN AFRICA

On the French ruled island of Martinique, West Africa, the volcano Mount Pele erupts. Some 30,000 people are killed.

ABOVE: Franz Josef, Emperor of Austria. His attack on Serbia in 1914 precipitates World War I.

RIGHT: King Edward VII of Britain and Queen Alexandra on board the royal yacht *Victoria and Albert*.

PHOTO-SECESSION GROUP

This group of photographers, based in New York, is led by Alfred Stieglitz and Edward Steichen. They uphold the right of the photographer to be considered an artist, and publish the influential photographic journal, *Camera Work*, which will run until 1917.

CORONATION DAY

Rulers of Europe gather in London for the coronation of Edward VII on August 9. The coronation has been postponed from June when Edward was forced to undergo an emergency operation for appendicitis. The king, who is 60, has made a good recovery in time for the coronation and the many diplomatic and public events associated with it.

HORMONES DISCOVERED

British physicists Ernest Henry Starling and William Bayliss discover that secretin, produced in the duodenum, acts on another organ of the body, the pancreas. Three years later they name this and other substances "hormones".

FOOT BINDING BANNED

The binding of the feet of Han Chinese women is banned in China by imperial edict after petitions from reform groups. The first reform group was founded in Canton in 1894 and was followed by others in provincial capitals.

IONOSPHERE SUGGESTED

British physicist Oliver Heaviside suggests that a layer of electrical charges in the atmosphere might be reflecting wireless waves back to Earth. Simultaneously, Arthur Edwin Kennelly of the USA puts forward the same idea. It is proved twenty years later, and is now called the ionosphere.

ABOVE: Four years in the making, the now-completed Nile dam.

HEART OF DARKNESS

Joseph Conrad (1857–1924) publishes his novel *Heart of Darkness*. It portrays a journey into the interior of Africa, where Conrad himself had travelled. He brings to life the terrifying consequences of human corruptibility in a colonial setting.

PELLEAS ET MELISANDE

Creator of musical impressionism, Claude Debussy (1862–1918) premières his only completed opera, *Pelléas et Mélisande*. In this work Debussy evokes a nightmarish atmosphere influenced by the ghost stories of American writer Edgar Allan Poe.

MOWING MADE EASY

The first commercially successful motor-mower is made in Britain. It is driven by a petrol engine.

ELIZABETH CADY STANTON
(1815–1902)

The American feminist, Elizabeth Cady Stanton dies aged 87. In 1848, with the pacifist and anti-slavery campaigner Lucretia Mott, she launched the American women's rights movement at the Seneca Falls convention. She campaigned for sexual equality throughout her life, and in 1869, with Susan B Anthony, founded the National Woman Suffrage Association. She acted as president of the Association until 1892. In later life she completed three of the six volumes of *History of Woman Suffrage* (1881–86, with Lucretia Mott and Matilda Joslyn Gage), and her autobiography.

TROUBLE BREWS IN THE BALKANS

Trouble breaks out in the Balkans, where thousands of Bulgarians are massacred. In North America, the US/Canadian border is finally settled and in South America, Panama achieves independence. Women in Britain adopt militancy as the best means of achieving the vote, and Marie Curie becomes the first woman to receive a Nobel Prize. Colour photography is developed and France's first Tour de France bicycle race takes place.

1 9 0 3

Feb	24	British forces march against "Mad" Mullah Mohammed bin Abdullah
Apr	16	Jews massacred in Bessarabia
June	15	Cinema audiences flock to *The Great Train Robbery*
July	19	First Tour de France finishes
Aug	2	Uprising begins in Macedonia
Sep	8	Turks massacre Bulgarians
Oct	10	Women's Social and Political Union (WSPU) founded, UK
	13	Boston Pilgrims win first baseball World Series
	20	Alaskan boundary decided
Dec	17	Wright brothers make first successful flight

ABOVE: Scott's ship *Discovery* sails south from New Zealand on the Antarctic expedition. On board is a junior officer, Ernest Shackleton.

OPPOSITE: Macedonian revolutionaries dance around a campfire, while their priest looks on.

JEWISH POGROM

Many Jews are killed by local people in the town of Kishinev, Bessarabia, in southwest Russia. The police turn a blind eye to the pogrom, which started on Easter Sunday, as do the government, which has been persecuting Jews since Czar Nicholas came to the throne in 1894.

BOLSHEVIKS BREAK AWAY

At its congress in London, in August, the Russian Social Democratic Party splits between the moderate Mensheviks (minority), led by GV Plekhanov, and the more radical Bolsheviks (majority), led by VI Lenin. The split harms the effectiveness of the opposition to the government of Czar Nicholas II.

DEEDS NOT WORDS

Mrs Emmeline Pankhurst (1857–1928) and other women meet in Manchester, UK, to form a new women's suffrage society, the Women's Social and Political Union (WSPU). Their aim is the achievement of votes for women "by any means". In contrast to previous women suffragist groups, the WSPU determines a militant approach. Soon, they will be known as suffragettes.

FIRST SUCCESSFUL AEROPLANE FLIGHT

Two brothers Wilbur and Orville Wright, from Ohio USA, achieve the first successful heavier-than-air-flight in December at Kitty Hawk, North Carolina. Their machine, the *Flyer*, flies a distance of about 40m (120ft). Orville is at the controls while the plane makes its first flight.

FIRST WESTERN

Edwin S Porter's film *The Great Train Robbery* is the first US feature film and the first western. It marks the start of a major strand in American popular culture.

RADIUM PRIZE

French scientists Marie and Pierre Curie, with Henri Becquerel, share the Nobel Prize for Physics, for discovering the radioactive elements radium and polonium. Marie Curie (1867–1934) is the first woman to receive a Nobel award.

MEASURING THE HEART

The first electrocardiograph to measure heart beats is made by the Dutch physiologist Willem Einthoven at Leyden University. He uses a simple galvanometer.

BELOW: Scott's Antarctic expedition of 1901–4. The sledge party, photographed by Shackleton, sets out from winter quarters towards the South Pole.

BULGARIANS MASSACRED

In Macedonia, the Turkish army massacres more than 50,000 men, women and children in its continuing action against separatists in Macedonia. The victims, who are all Bulgarian, are killed by the Turks in their campaign to prevent Bulgaria expanding its territory into Turkish-held Macedonia.

BORDER DECISION

The commission set up to decide the frontier between the US state of Alaska and Canada finally agrees the borderline. The decision of the British representative to favour Alaska infuriates the Canadian government.

FIRST TOUR DE FRANCE

Maurice Garin becomes the winner on July 19 in the first ever Tour de France cycling race, which has lasted for sixteen days. The early years of the competition feature marathon stages, often completed in darkness.

SAFETY RAZOR

The safety razor is patented in Boston, Massachusetts, by King Camp Gillette in association with William Nickerson, a mechanic.

PANAMA DECLARES INDEPENDENCE

In November, the province of Panama declares its independence from Colombia in protest at delays by Colombia in agreeing the route for the proposed Panama Canal. In December, a treaty between Panama and the USA sets up the Canal Zone, which is handed over to the USA.

THE WAY OF ALL FLESH

This semi-autobiographical novel by Samuel Butler is published after his death. It shows the deadening influence of tradition and family on life, and forms part of the reaction against Victorian views and values that is currently taking place.

THE CALL OF THE WILD

This year sees the publication of *The Call of the Wild* by Jack London. The story of a dog, Buck, who leads a pack of wolves after his master dies, it becomes one of the most popular novels by this socialist writer.

HEADACHE REMEDY

The painkiller, aspirin, is launched by the German drug company AG Bayer.

ABOVE: Under construction — St Louis World's Fair of Industry and Technology. It will open in 1904.

EXPLAINING RADIOACTIVITY

British scientists Ernest Rutherford (1871–1937) and Frederick Soddy, working in Canada, discover that radioactivity is the result of the breakdown of atoms in a radioactive element, producing a new element. They publish this as *The Cause and Nature of Radioactivity*.

VIKING EXCAVATION

The Oseberg longship, found buried inside a peat mound overlooking a Norwegian fjord near Oslo, is excavated. Interred inside it are two women who may have been ninth-century Viking nobles. As well as the women, the longship contains magnificent sledges, carts, furniture, kitchen utensils and textiles.

PAUL GAUGUIN (1848–1903)

Paul Gauguin, the French Post-Impressionist painter, has died. In 1883 Gauguin abandoned his stockbroker career in Paris to become a painter in Brittany. His best-known work was inspired by the art and culture of the South Pacific, where he has lived since 1891. His primitive, exotic and dreamlike style (known as Synthesist) is seen in paintings such as *No Te Aha De Riri* (1896), and *Faa Iheihe, Decorated with Ornaments* (1898).

SALIVATING RESPONSE

Russian psychologist Ivan Pavlov (1849–1936) reports that ringing a bell will make a hungry dog salivate, if the bell has always been rung just before the dog's food arrives. Pavlov calls this a "conditioned reflex".

AMSTERDAM STOCK EXCHANGE

HP Berlage's reconstruction of the Amsterdam Stock Exchange, destroyed by fire in 1885, is completed. Based on a grid plan, the building is important for its use of red brick with a glass-and-metal roof.

FIRST CONES

The first ice-cream cone made of waffle pastry is patented by Italo Marcioni, an ice-cream salesman in New Jersey, USA. The cones will be introduced at the Louisiana Purchase Exposition in St Louis, Mo. in 1904.

COLOUR PHOTOGRAPHY

Louis and Auguste Lumière of France perfect the first single-plate process for colour photography. It will be marketed in 1907 as Autochrome.

PULITZER PRIZE

Joseph Pulitzer, a Hungarian-born American newspaper proprietor, once a journalist on the German-language *Westliche Post*, donates $2 million to found a school of journalism at Columbia University. He endows annual prizes for journalism. The first prizes will be awarded in 1917.

WORLD SERIES

The Boston Pilgrims win the first baseball World Series in the United States. Boston are champions of the American League, formed in 1901, and beat the Pittsburgh Pirates, the champions of the more established National League.

ABOVE: The splendour of the Raj — Indian princes, Bengal lancers and others process into Delhi to proclaim Edward VII Emperor of India.

HOMOSEXUAL SURVEY

Berlin's Scientific-Humanitarian Committee, the world's first organization for homosexual rights, founded in 1898, questions more than 6,000 students and factory workers and concludes that 2.2 per cent of the general population is homosexual.

TIME FLIES

French magazine *Temps* sends a telegram round the world in six hours.

ABOVE: Emigration often provided the only means of escape for persecuted Eastern Europeans.

BELOW: Ellis Island — first port of call for immigrants reaching the United States.

RUSSIA TAKES ON JAPAN

Japan, having emerged from centuries of isolation, and Russia, bent on eastward expansion, clash over conflicting ambitions in Manchuria and Korea, and go to war. By contrast, Britain and France bring to an end centuries of hostility when they sign an *entente cordiale*. In the United States, immigration figures soar as Eastern Europeans flood into the country, fleeing persecution. And the opening of Schlesinger-Meyer in Chicago heralds the arrival of the twentieth-century department store.

1904

Feb	8	Russo-Japanese War breaks out
Apr	8	Britain and France sign The Entente Cordiale
	13	Japanese torpedo boats sink the battleship *Petropavlovsk*
	30	World Exhibition opens in St Louis
May	1	Japanese army defeats Russians at Xinyizhou
	2	Japanese fleet block Port Arthur
	26	Russian forces land in Manchuria
July	1	Olympic Games open in St Louis, USA
	15	Russian author Anton Chekhov (b. 1860) dies
Sep	25	Trans-Siberian Railway is completed
Nov	8	President Theodore Roosevelt re-elected

THE RUSSO-JAPANESE WAR

In 1903 the Japanese had proposed that the Japanese and Russian governments should safeguard each other's special economic interests in Manchuria and Korea. Angered by the Russian lack of commitment, the Japanese ambassador broke off negotiations. In February 1904, sixteen Japanese warships under Admiral Togo attack a fleet of six Russian battleships and ten cruisers under Vice Admiral Stark, off Port Arthur. Japanese torpedo boats severely damage two battleships and a cruiser. Others are also damaged and the two countries are at war. In April Japanese torpedo boats sink the Russian battleship *Petropavlovsk*. In May Japanese ships penetrate Port Arthur and block the harbour.

In August the Russian fleet, trapped in Port Arthur and under fire from land batteries, fights to reach the open sea. The Japanese fleet under Togo blocks their exit and forces them back into the harbour.

RIGHT: The Chinese governor of SanSin being carried ashore.

FAR RIGHT: Japanese soldiers execute traitors.

LEFT: Russian troops keep a careful lookout for Japanese from a treetop vantage point.

After a year of fighting, Russia surrenders Port Arthur to the Japanese in January. Japanese losses are 58,000 killed or wounded, and 30,000 sick.

In May the Russian Baltic fleet, including seven battleships and six cruisers, meets a Japanese force of the same size but with greater fire-power and speed, in the battle of Tsu Shima. During the afternoon of May 27, the Japanese sink four Russian battleships and damage one, for no losses. The Russians attempt to escape to Vladivostok but the Japanese destroyers and torpedo boats attack in the night and sink three ships. The battle continues the following day until all but twelve of the Russian fleet are captured, driven aground or sunk.

In September, Russia and Japan finally sign a peace treaty ending the Russo-Japanese War. The treaty marks the first time a European power is defeated in war by an Asian nation.

ABOVE: Siege guns, captured by the Japanese in August, 1904, being moved by train before the battle of Liao-Yang.

RIGHT: Russian troops inflate a balloon at Mukdon in 1905. The Russians were completely routed.

ANTON CHEKOV
(1860–1904)

This year sees the death of the Russian writer Anton Chekov, whose dramatic voice was so quintessentially Russian and yet universal in its appeal. Also a doctor, he was the author of thirteen volumes of short stories, as well as the widely performed plays *The Seagull* (1896), *Uncle Vanya* (1900), *The Three Sisters* (1901), *The Cherry Orchard* (1904), and others. In 1897 he went to live in the Crimea suffering from tuberculosis and has died in Yalta.

ENTENTE CORDIALE

Britain and France sign the Anglo-French Entente Cordiale, ending centuries of hostility between the two countries. The Entente settles long-standing colonial disputes between the two countries in North America, Africa, and the Pacific, and continues the British policy of seeking alliances to secure its global interests.

INTERNATIONAL WOMEN'S SUFFRAGE

Veteran American feminist Susan B Antony (1820–1906), together with suffrage leader Carrie Catt, founds the International Woman Suffrage Alliance in Berlin.

FIRST LABOUR PM

John Watson becomes prime minister of Australia, the first time a Labour politician has led a government anywhere in the world. He holds power only until August, when his government falls and is replaced by a coalition.

IMMIGRATION SOARS

Competitive cuts in steerage rates by rival steamship companies stimulates Eastern European immigration into the USA. Slavs, Slovaks, Serbs, Croats, Bosnians, Herzegovinians, and many Jewish immigrants fleeing persecution begin to dominate the immigrant figures.

DIESEL-POWERED SUBMARINE

Maxim Laubeuf of France builds a diesel-powered submarine, the *Aigret*. Its lower flashpoint makes it safer than a petrol-powered submarine.

GIVE MY REGARDS TO BROADWAY

American musical *Little Johnny Jones* includes this song, which becomes a smash hit and sums up the importance of Broadway and its musicals in the national identity of the USA.

PAIN RELIEF

Organic chemist Albert Einhorn of Germany first produces procaine, also known as Novocaine, which acts as a local anaesthetic. It can be used instead of the more dangerous cocaine.

PETER PAN

Scottish dramatist JM Barrie's new play *Peter Pan*, with its forever-young hero, lost boys and Never Never Land, becomes an abiding success. Barrie follows it up with a story (1906) and a book (1911).

JEAN-CHRISTOPHE

French author Romain Rolland (1866–1944) publishes the first of his 10-volume novel, *Jean-Christophe*, a long study of a fictional musician. Socialist, idealist and pacifist, Rolland is important for bringing these values into fiction. He will later win the Nobel Prize in 1915.

CHICAGO DEPARTMENT STORE

One of the finest examples of an early twentieth-century department store is Louis Sullivan's Schlesinger-Meyer. Sullivan's style combines rich ornament on the lower floors with modern steel, glass and concrete construction. The building also includes public rooms such as an art gallery, restaurant and lounge.

NON-FLAMMABLE CELLULOID

French chemists produce a non-flammable version of celluloid by adding metallic salts during manufacture. This spoils the old joke about the readiness of celluloid to burn: "Please do not smoke as I am wearing a celluloid collar".

ELECTRIC EYE

The first practical photo-electric cell, also called the "electric eye", is invented by Johann Elster of Germany; in the same year German professor Arthur Korn uses one to transmit a picture over a telegraph wire.

ABOVE: The wrecked pleasure steamer *General Slocum* lies in New York harbour after a fire costing the lives of 1,000 passengers.

ABOVE: Pilgrims flood into Jerusalem to celebrate Christmas.

ABBEY THEATRE FOUNDED
Irish poet WB Yeats and Augusta, Lady Gregory (later joined by JM Synge as co-director) found the Abbey Theatre in Dublin. The theatre will be identified with a renaissance in Irish culture and many of the important twentieth-century Irish plays will be premièred there.

JUPITER SATELLITE
US astronomer Charles Dillon Perrine discovers Himalia, the sixth satellite of the planet Jupiter.

ST LOUIS OLYMPICS
The Olympic Games take place in St Louis at the same time as the World Exhibition. Crowds flock to the Exhibition but, as in 1900, the unfocused Games fail to attract large crowds. European involvement is limited because of the cost of travel. Only 680 athletes take part, 500 of whom are American or Canadian.

GIBSON GIRL
Charles Dana Gibson, a New York illustrator with a reputation for capturing aristocratic ideals, creates the Gibson Girl, an elegant beauty. His inspiration is his wife Irene Langhorne, whose fresh-faced image of perfect femininity is printed in society periodicals, such as *Life* and *Harper's*.

THERMIONIC DIODE VALVE
British electrical engineer John Ambrose Fleming patents the thermionic diode (two-electrode) valve (vacuum tube). It allows current to pass in one direction only and will be used for years as a key component in radio and TV receivers. After 1947 it will be replaced by transistors.

TEA IN A BAG
Teabags are unwittingly introduced by Thomas Sullivan, a New York wholesaler who sends samples of tea to his customers in small silk bags instead of tins.

RUSSIAN UPRISING AND RELATIVITY

Revolution breaks out in Russia when czarist troops fire on demonstrators outside the Winter Palace in St Petersburg. A mutiny follows and the Czar is forced to introduce reform. After bitter fighting, the Russo-Japanese War comes to an end, with Japan victorious. Norway declares independence from Sweden and Albert Einstein publishes his theory of relativity.

1 9 0 5

Jan	2	Russia surrenders Port Arthur to Japan
	22	Czar's troops massacre peaceful demonstrators in St Petersburg
Mar	24	French writer Jules Verne (b.1828) dies
May	27–8	Battle of Tsu Shima. Japanese devastate Russian Baltic fleet
June	7	*Die Brücke* exhibition in Dresden
	27	Mutiny on the battleship *Potemkin*
Aug	19	Duma (representative assembly) established in Russia
Sep	5	Russia and Japan sign peace treaty to end Russo-Japanese War
Oct	1	The Fauves exhibit in Paris
	14	English suffragettes Christobel Pankhurst and Annie Kenney imprisoned
	26	Norway separates from Sweden
Nov	28	Universal suffrage in Austria

BELOW: Cars for millionaires — a 4-cylinder Fiat on display.

OPPOSITE: Port Arthur, a strategic port in Manchurian China which falls to Japan this year.

RUSSIA ARISES

In January, strikers marching through the Russian capital of St Petersburg, to petition Czar Nicholas II for better conditions, are shot dead by troops defending the Winter Palace. More than 500 are killed and many more wounded. The massacre increases demands for reform in Russia.

In June, Russian sailors on the battleship *Potemkin* mutiny after complaints about conditions on board. Other ships in the port of Odessa join the mutiny, while the city is gripped by a general strike. The mutiny adds to the weakening of the czar's rule, following the St Petersburg massacre.

In October, Czar Nicholas II agrees a new constitution to turn Russia from an absolute autocracy into a semi-constitutional monarchy. The climbdown is forced on him by a general strike which has paralysed the country for months, as well as defeat in the war against Japan.

BELOW: *Potemkin* mutiny — a burnt-out railway shed left devastated after mutineers rampage through Odessa.

RIGHT: Battleship *Potemkin*, where the shooting of a sailor sparks off a serious mutiny.

THE KAISER IN AFRICA

The visit of the German Kaiser Wilhelm II (1859–1941) to Morocco leads to tension between Germany and France, who have traditionally claimed "a special standing" in Morocco. The Kaiser claims he is protecting German economic interests.

SALOME AND THE SEVEN VEILS

Based on Oscar Wilde's scandalous 1893 play, Richard Strauss's opera *Salome* opens in Dresden. Its striking harmonies and large orchestra (requiring singers of great power) establish Strauss (1864–1949) as the major German opera composer of the time. The famous Dance of the Seven Veils causes a scandal.

FREE NORWAY

The Norwegian parliament in Oslo declares independence from Sweden in June. The result is approved by the people in a plebiscite in August and Norway becomes an independent nation in October. Prince Charles of Denmark accepts the throne and rules as Haakon VII (1872–1957).

EINSTEIN, RELATIVITY AND OTHER THEORIES

German-born physicist Albert Einstein (1879–1955) publishes his Special Theory of Relativity, in which he revolutionizes thinking by proposing that time and motion are relative. He also publishes papers on Brownian motion and the photo-electric effect.

SOCIOLOGY RECOGNIZED

The American Sociological Society is formed in Chicago, Illinois, marking sociology's acceptance by the academic world. It follows the founding by the University of Chicago of the world's first sociology department, headed by Albion Small, and the publication of the first sociology journal.

DIE BRUCKE EXPRESS THEMSELVES

A group of German artists in Dresden mount their first exhibition in a lamp factory. They are the first Expressionists — the founding members are Fritz Bleyl, Erich Heckel, Ludwig Kirchner and Karl Schmidt-Rottluff (who gave the group its name, *Die Brücke*, meaning the bridge). Their bold outlines and strong planes of colour enliven European art for several years and have a lasting influence.

SPEED WARNINGS

The Automobile Association is founded in Britain to warn car drivers of police speed traps. The speed limit is 32km/h (20miph).

RADIOTHORIUM

German radio chemist Otto Hahn (1879–1968) discovers radiothorium, a radioactive isotope produced by the breakdown and decay of the radioactive chemical element thorium.

EARLY STRUGGLE FOR CIVIL RIGHTS

The militant Niagara Movement is founded in the US by 29 black intellectuals from fourteen states, led by Atlanta University professor, William Edward Burghardt Du Bois. They demand universal male suffrage and the abolition of discrimination based on race or colour.

WILD BEASTS IN PARIS

Work by the artists Matisse, Marquet, Derain, Vlaminck, Rouault and others is hung in the same room at the Salon d'Automne. The mass effect of bright colour and distorted patterns earns them the nickname Les Fauves (the wild beasts).

BELOW: Hussars charge striking workers in Warsaw.

ABOVE: Fishing for sturgeon through ice on the Ural River.

BELOW: Building the Panama Canal.

MAGNETIC NORTH TRACKED DOWN

Norwegian explorer Roald Amundsen (1872–1928) completes the passage from the Pacific to the Atlantic along the Arctic coast. On the way, he finds the current position of magnetic north.

NORDIC GAMES

The Scandinavian nations compete in the first Nordic Games. The event, which features cross-country skiing and ski jumping, is later overshadowed by the Winter Olympics.

FIRST SUFFRAGETTES IN PRISON

In the UK, Christabel Pankhurst (1880–1958) and Annie Kenney, of the militant women's suffrage movement, choose prison rather than fines. They have been convicted of assaulting policemen after having been forcibly ejected from a political meeting for demanding votes for women.

SILK FOR EVERYONE

Rayon, a new fabric dubbed "artificial silk", is to be produced by the British textile company Courtaulds. They have brought the UK manufacturing rights from its British inventor, CH Stearn, who patented it in 1898. It is ideal for underwear and stockings.

WASSERMAN TEST

German bacteriologist August Wasserman (1866–1925) develops a test for the disease syphilis.

PIZZA TO GO

The USA's first pizzeria, Lombardi's on Spring Street in Little Italy, New York, begins to sell pizza, a Neapolitan dish. It proves a popular fast food with busy New Yorkers.

ANYONE FOR TENNIS?

May Sutton becomes the first American to win a title at the Wimbledon Tennis Tournament; she becomes Ladies' Singles Champion.

TESTING FOR CHILDREN

Alfred Binet (1857–1911), Director of the Psychological Laboratory at the Sorbonne in Paris and his colleague, Theodore Simon, produce tests to classify children according to their mental ability. This is in response to the French government's request in 1904 for them to study children with special educational needs.

SPECIAL-NEEDS PIONEERS

The first special-needs schools for educationally disadvantaged children are introduced in the Netherlands and subsidized by the State.

RIGHT: New York's elevated railway before it plunged off the rails.

ABOVE: President Roosevelt watches submarine *Plunger* go through its paces.

EARTHQUAKES AND CORNFLAKES

Cubism is born with the work of Pablo Picasso, who introduces a revolutionary new way of painting the human form. In architecture too, Antonio Gaudí breaks with tradition, introducing startling new designs to the city of Barcelona. The eruption of Mt. Vesuvius in Italy and a major earthquake in San Francisco cause immense suffering and destruction.

OPPOSITE: Wreckage after Russian revolutionaries bomb Premier Stolypin's home.

1906

Feb	**10**	*HMS Dreadnought* launched
Apr	**7**	Mt. Vesuvius erupts, Italy
	8	Treaty of Algeciras ends Moroccan crisis
	18	San Francisco devastated by earthquake
May	**10**	First Duma meets in Russia
	23	Norwegian dramatist Henrik Ibsen dies
June	**26**	World's first Grand Prix, Le Mans, France
July	**12**	Alfred Dreyfus awarded Legion of Honour
Oct	**22**	Paul Cézanne dies
	23	Suffragettes imprisoned after demonstration at Houses of Parliament, UK

ABOVE: Christian Science temple, Boston, founded by Mary Baker Eddy.

VOTES FOR WOMEN

Women in Finland become the first women in Europe to gain the vote. The following year, nineteen women have seats in Finland's parliament. By contrast, in the UK, women's fight for the vote becomes increasingly militant as women throughout the country heckle political meetings in the lead-up to the general election. In June, a deputation representing some half a million women march on the Houses of Parliament to present a petition to the new Liberal government, demanding votes for women. Its rejection is followed by a huge rally in London's Trafalgar Square. In October, women disrupt the State Opening of Parliament and ten members of the WSPU are imprisoned rather than pay fines. This year, the militant tactics of WSPU members gain them the nickname "suffragettes", following an insult in the *Daily Mail* newspaper.

IBERIA

Spanish composer Isaac Albéniz begins the suite for piano that will become his most famous work. Inspired by the music and dance rhythms of Andalusia, Iberia shows Spanish composers how they can express national character in music.

SIMPLON TUNNEL

One of Europe's longest rail tunnels, the Simplon Tunnel connecting Brig in Switzerland with Iselle in Italy, is opened. It is about 20km (12mi) long.

CUBISM IS BORN

Pablo Picasso (1881–1973) produces *Les Demoiselles d'Avignon*, the pivotal painting of the early twentieth century. Its angular handling of human forms is so shocking that he is very selective about who sees the picture. From this painting derives Cubism and all the other art movements in which natural subjects are broken up into a new synthesis of form.

ELECTRIC WASHING MACHINE

Alva J Fisher of the USA patents the first electric washing machine, marking the beginning of a major reduction in household drudgery.

BELOW: City Hall is in ruins after an earthquake and three-day firestorm devastate San Francisco. Above, a policeman stands in the wreckage.

BREAKFAST CEREAL

Will Keith Kellogg and his partner Charles D Bolin
incorporate the Battle Creek Toasted Corn Flake Co. to
sell their breakfast cereals. Their new Sanitas cornflakes
are lighter and crisper than their first cornflakes,
produced in 1898.

NATURAL DISASTERS

Mt. Vesuvius erupts in April destroying the town of
Ottaiano and causing damage in nearby Naples. In the
USA that same month, a severe earthquake hits San
Francisco. The tremors and the following three-day
firestorm almost destroy the city.

HMS DREADNOUGHT

Britain launches the battleship HMS *Dreadnought*, the
fastest and most heavily armoured warship yet built.
As an "all big gun" ship, *Dreadnought* also carries the
heaviest fire-power with ten 30-cm (12-in) guns.

PAUL CEZANNE
(1839–1906)

Paul Cézanne, the French painter, has died. His work
increasingly concentrated on the underlying forms of
nature. It was not widely recognized until the last ten
years of his life but will widely influence the development
of abstract art. His best-known paintings include *The
Card Players* (1890–1892), *Aix: Paysage Rocheux* (1887)
and *The Gardener* (1906).

GANDHI, BALLOONS AND HELICOPTERS

Norwegian women gain the vote, following their Finnish sisters the previous year. Transport makes strides as the world's first "helicopter" makes a successful flight, the liner *Lusitania* crosses the Atlantic at record speed and French balloonists make the first-ever aerial crossing of the North Sea. Gandhi introduces the idea of non-violent civil disobedience. Home laundry becomes easier with new washing machines and washing powder.

OPPOSITE: The great nebula of Orion photographed at Yerkes Observatory, near Chicago, Illinois.

1907

Jan	14	Earthquake hits Jamaica
Mar	22	Gandhi begins civil disobedience campaign, South Africa
June	14	Norwegian women gain the vote
	16	Duma dissolved in Russia
July	29	Boy Scouts founded, UK
Aug	4	French fleet bombard Casablanca after anti-foreign riots
Sep	26	New Zealand becomes a dominion
Nov	13	Cornu makes first helicopter flight, France

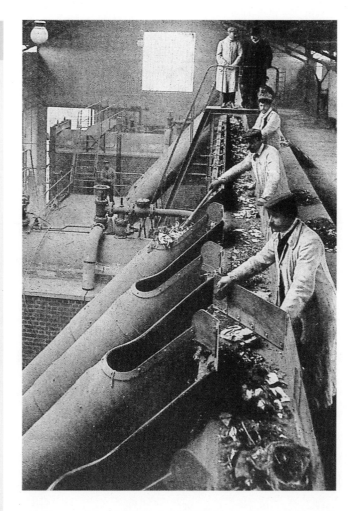

ABOVE: Paris rubbish is discharged through huge pipes to be treated and converted into electricity.

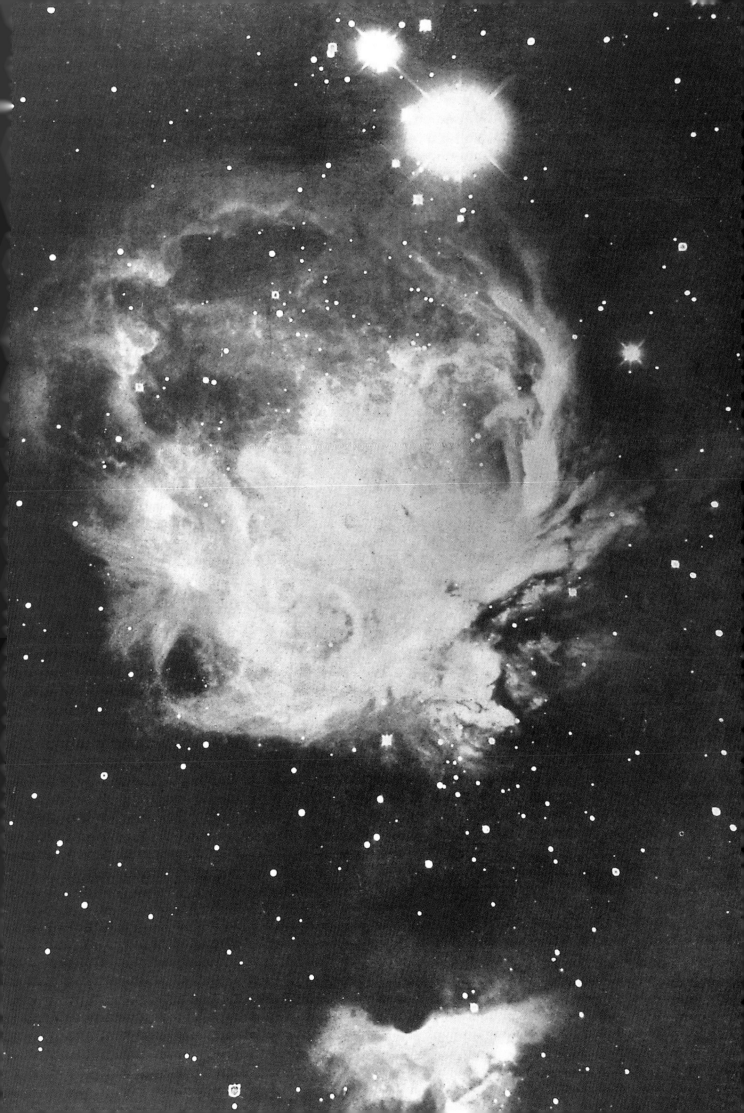

CIVIL DISOBEDIENCE
In South Africa, Mohandâs Gandhi (1869–1948) begins a campaign of civil disobedience, or *satyagraha*, against the state government in protest at its new law that requires all Indians to register their presence, submit to being fingerprinted, and carry a certificate of registration with them at all times. Gandhi declares that the new law discriminates against the Indian population in the Transvaal.

DISSOLUTION OF DUMA
In St Petersburg, the Russian Czar Nicholas II (1868–1918) dissolves the Duma, or parliament, when his prime minister, Peter Stolypin, accuses 55 socialist deputies of plotting against the czar. The czar had hoped that the Duma would contain deputies favourable to his conservative policies. Instead it contains liberals and socialists intent on radical reform.

NORWEGIAN WOMEN GAIN THE VOTE
The Norwegian parliament agrees to allow women to vote in elections on the same terms as men. It follows the decision of the Finnish parliament to grant women the vote last year, but since Finland is a province of Russia, Norway is the first independent European country to grant universal suffrage.

MOTHER
Russian novelist Maxim Gorky (1868–1936) publishes *Mother*, an influential novel about revolutionaries.

BELOW: Damming the waters of the Nile threatens the Temple of Isis on the island of Philae.

SUFFRAGETTES BATTLE WITH POLICE
In the UK, suffragettes demonstrate outside and "rush" the House of Commons. Their actions are met by considerable police brutality. Increasing numbers of women are imprisoned.

TRIPLE ALLIANCE RENEWED
Germany, Austria and Italy renew the Triple Alliance between their three countries for a further six years, despite Italian reservations. The alliance faces increasingly close links between France and Britain. The following month, Britain signs an understanding with Russia, which draws Russia into their alliance.

NEW ZEALAND
After 48 years as a British colony, New Zealand becomes an independent dominion in the British Empire, joining Australia and Canada.

DYING SWAN
Russian ballerina Anna Pavlova (1885–1931) dances the Dying Swan in *Swan Lake*. Choreographed by Mikhail Fokine, the dance becomes Pavlova's trademark. She will dance it, to Saint-Saëns' music, with the Ballets Russes in Paris, and later with her own company. It becomes an icon of classical ballet.

HENRI MATISSE
The painting *Blue Nude* by French artist Henri Matisse (1869–1954) causes offence to more conservative viewers. The artist painted it after a short visit to North Africa and combined a classical pose with a primitive treatment. It is the primitivism that distinguishes Matisse, and which has caused offence.

ABOVE: World leaders meet for a peace conference at The Hague. They discuss methods of resolving conflict.

RIOTS IN MOROCCO
The French fleet bombards the port of Casablanca and French troops occupy the city after Moroccans riot against foreign workers. More than 1,000 Moors are killed.

BOY SCOUTS FOUNDED
In the UK, Boer-War veteran Sir Robert Baden-Powell sets up a new organization for boys, based on his army experience. The organization is known as the "boy scouts".

PLAYBOY CAUSES RIOTS
Riots follow the première of playwright John Synge's *The Playboy of the Western World*. Performed at the Abbey Theatre, the play's portrayal of Irish life is too realistic for the audience. There are more riots as the play goes on tour, but it will ultimately be recognized as an Irish classic.

THE PRAYER
Constantin Brancusi (1876–1957), the Romanian sculptor, leads the way towards abstract sculpture with his work *The Prayer*. A funeral monument, the statue shows a young girl kneeling in prayer. Its simplified form will soon lead to complete abstraction.

FIRST VERTICAL TAKE-OFF
French bicycle dealer and inventor Pierre Cornu makes the world's first free flight by "helicopter". Cornu's machine has twin motor-driven rotors and a 24hp engine and lifts vertically off the ground.

LUSITANIA: WORLD'S FASTEST LINER
The Cunard liner *Lusitania*, built in 1906, captures the Blue Riband of the Atlantic, a notional trophy for the fastest crossing. She makes the crossing from Liverpool to New York at an average speed of 23.99 knots.

MOTORCYLE RACING
Motorcycle enthusiasts set up a racing festival on the Isle of Man, off the British coast, after racing is banned on mainland roads.

ABOVE: Irish suffragist Miss Maloney rings a handbell, successfully bringing to an end a speech by Liberal candidate Mr Winston Churchill, noted opponent of votes for women.

"JEWISH MARK TWAIN"

Author Sholem Aleichem has begun to publish his series of stories, *Mottel, or The Cantor's Son*. Written in Yiddish (later translated into English), they give expression to the experiences, and humour, of ordinary Jewish people in the United States. Publication continues until 1916 and Aleichem becomes known as the "Jewish Mark Twain".

A BETTER VALVE

American inventor Lee de Forest improves the diode valve invented by JA Fleming in 1904, by introducing a third electrode. This creates a triode valve. The third electrode, called a grid, has holes in it. By varying the electric charge on the grid, the flow of electrons can be varied.

CAUSE OF SCURVY

The British biochemist Frederick Gowland Hopkins suggests that lack of certain trace substances in the diet can cause diseases such as rickets and scurvy. The substances are later named vitamins.

SUICIDE COUNSELLING

A suicide counselling service is opened in New York by the Salvation Army.

OVER THE NORTH SEA

The first aerial crossing of the North Sea is made in the balloon *Mammoth* in October by three French aeronauts. The flight is from Crystal Palace, London, to the shores of Lake Vänern, Sweden, a distance of about 1,160km (725mi).

ELEMENT DISCOVERED

The French chemist Georges Urbain discovers the heaviest of the rare-earth elements, lutetium. A radioactive isotope of the element becomes useful in determining the age of meteorites.

ITALIAN WINS RACE

Entering the French capital two months ahead of the nearest competitor, Prince Scipione Borghese of Italy wins the Peking-to-Paris Automobile Race by a huge margin. Borghese and his mechanic covered 14,994km (9,317mi) in 62 days.

NATURAL DISASTERS

In January, a massive earthquake flattens Jamaica. Just one week later, a tidal wave sweeps the Dutch East Indies.

NURSING HONOUR

Florence Nightingale, now aged 87, blind, and an invalid, becomes the first woman to be awarded the British Order of Merit. The honour is conferred by King Edward VII for her services to the nursing profession.

LEFT: Hundreds of acres of tobacco are grown under cheesecloth in Puerto Rico — an American invention for increasing yield.

BELOW: The Cresta Run in Switzerland — the world's most famous toboggan run.

RECORD IMMIGRATION

1907 is a record year for immigration to the USA, with more than one million new American nationals admitted.

NEW WASHING POWDER

Persil, a washing powder produced by Henkel & Cie in Düsseldorf, Germany, is marketed in Britain for washing clothes.

AGITATED WASHING MACHINE

Thor, the first electric agitator washing machine, is marketed by the Hurley Machine Company in the USA. It was designed by US engineer John Hurley, who has used an electric motor to power a rotating dolly.

NEW ZOO

In Hamburg, Carl Hagenbeck creates a new kind of zoo. Animals live freely in their natural habitats.

DMITRI IVANOVICH MENDELEYEV
(1834–1907)

The Russian scientist Dmitri Mendeleyev dies this year. His work on the grouping of elements according to their atomic weight accurately predicted the properties of several elements which were waiting to be discovered. He also studied the aeronautics and behaviour of gases, and, in 1887, took a pioneering ascent in an air balloon.

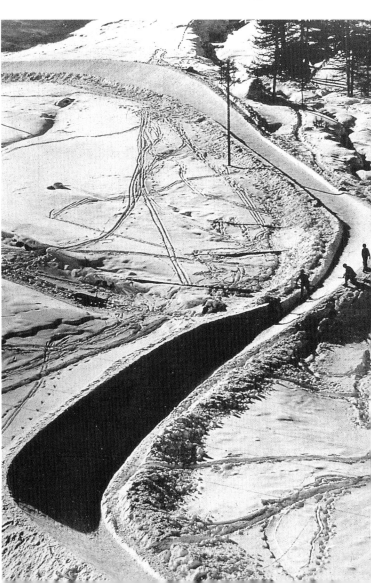

CARS FOR EVERYBODY

A two-year-old child becomes the last Manchu emperor of China. The first modern version of the Olympic Games is held and the first vacuum cleaner goes on sale in the USA. The largest earthquake ever recorded in Europe devastates the Italian town of Messina, and the dream of motoring for the masses becomes reality when the American car manufacturer, Henry Ford, begins production of the new Model-T motor car.

OPPOSITE: French can-can dancers wow audiences at London nightclubs.

1908

Feb	1	King Carlos and Prince Luiz of Portugal are assassinated
June	21	200,000 attend suffragette rally, UK, demanding that women be given the right to vote
July	13	Olympic Games begin, UK
Aug	12	Henry Ford's first assembly line Model-T appears
	20	Congo, Africa, becomes Belgian colony
Oct	5	Bulgaria declared independent
	6	Austria annexes Bosnia and Herzegovina
Nov	15	Two-year-old Pu-yi becomes Emperor of China
Dec	28	Earthquake devastates Messina, Sicily

ABOVE: Giant bamboo growing in the Botanical Gardens at Peradeniya, Ceylon. In the countryside, these densely packed trees are vulnerable to fire.

ABOVE: Orville Wright prepares for his flight.

BELGIAN CONGO

Leopold II, King of Belgium, hands over his vast private estate in central Africa to the control of the Belgian government. Belgium thus acquires its first colony, which is more than 90 times its own size.

EARTHQUAKE DEVASTATION

A massive earthquake, the biggest ever recorded in Europe, destroys the town of Messina in Sicily, southern Italy. Thousands of people are killed and made homeless.

THE BALKANS

In the Balkans King Ferdinand I (1861–1948) declares Bulgaria independent from Turkey and takes the title of czar. At the same time, Austria annexes the Turkish province of Bosnia-Herzegovina, and Crete proclaims its union with Greece. The Ottoman Empire continues to disintegrate.

MAKING AMMONIA

German chemist Fritz Haber (1868–1934) invents the Haber process for making ammonia artificially by combining nitrogen and hydrogen.

ABOVE: Orville Wright swoops over Fort Myer, Virginia. An accident during this military air trial kills Wright's companion, TE Selfridge.

CHILD EMPEROR

After the deaths of the Emperor Kuang-Hsu and the Dowager Empress Cixi, the two-year-old Pu-yi becomes emperor of China with the name Emperor Hsuan T'ung. Real power lies with the various warlords who control the Chinese throne.

MASS-PRODUCED MODEL-T

American car manufacturer Henry Ford (1863–1947) begins the mass production of his Model-T Ford car, using an innovatory assembly line method. He sells the new model for $850, but by 1925 has cut the price to $260. When production stops in 1927 he has made 15 million Model-Ts.

THE WAR IN THE AIR

In this prophetic novel, HG Wells describes the military use of aircraft, a form of warfare which will soon become all too well known. This prediction later helps to give Wells the status of modern prophet.

POWER AT LAST
After earlier failures, American inventor Thomas Alva Edison (1847–1931) perfects his alkaline storage battery. It stores more than twice as much power as a lead-acid battery.

DETECTING RADIATION
While working in Manchester, England, German physicist Hans Geiger (1882–1945) invents the Geiger counter, a device which detects radiation. It works by detecting and counting alpha particles emitted by a radioactive substance.

"THE EIGHT"
A group of American painters who have had work rejected from the National Academy of Design form "the Eight", part of what will later become known as the Ashcan School. They are ridiculed as "apostles of ugliness" and exhibit together only once.

MAGNETIC SUNSPOTS
American astronomer George Ellery Hale (1868–1938) discovers that sunspots have strong magnetic fields — the first magnetic fields detected outside the Earth. He also installs a 150cm (59in) reflecting telescope at Mount Wilson Observatory in California.

SPACE–TIME LINK-UP
Professor Hermann Minkowski, a Lithuanian mathematician, puts forward the view that space and time are interlinked as the "space-time continuum".

CELLOPHANE
Swiss chemist Dr Jacques Edwin Brandenburger patents a thin, transparent, flexible film made from wood cellulose. He calls it Cellophane.

EXPEDITION TO ANTARCTIC
Ernest Shackleton and Edward Wilson, with the National Antarctic Expedition, travel to latitude 88° 22' S, closer to the South Pole than any previous expeditions.

LIQUID HELIUM
Dutch physicist Heike Kamerlingh Onnes (1853–1926) discovers how to make the gas helium into a liquid. This strange liquid expands instead of contracting as it cools, and conducts heat well.

INTERNATIONAL PSYCHOLOGY CONGRESS
The first International Congress of Psychology is held in Salzburg in April. It is attended by the leading figures in this controversial new branch of medicine, including Sigmund Freud and his colleagues Alfred Adler and Karl Jung.

A NEW CHAMPION
Texan Jack Johnson becomes the first black heavyweight boxing champion of the world.

FIRST PSYCHOLOGY TEXTBOOK
The first social psychology textbook is published by William McDougall, a British psychologist who argues for a biological rather than a philosophical approach to psychology. He believes people inherit instincts and characteristics that direct them to unconscious goals.

MARATHON RUNNER DISQUALIFIED
London, England, steps in to host the Fourth Olympic Games after Rome, Italy, withdraws. Large crowds watch as the games are held as a self-contained event. The marathon ends in drama when Italian runner Dorando Pietri is helped across the finish line in first place. He is stripped of his gold medal as the help is against the rules, but wins public sympathy.

DISPOSABLE CUPS
Disposable paper cups are introduced into the USA by the International Paper Company, a conglomerate of American and Canadian paper companies.

CHAMPAGNE DISASTER
Champagne, in France, the last European wine region to be devastated by the vine-destroying phylloxera aphid, has its worst harvest failure this century. The year's total production equals little more than that normally produced by one vineyard.

VACUUM CLEANER
The first commercial vacuum cleaner is produced in the USA by William Hoover, a leather manufacturer.

ABOVE: Residues of pitchblende are stirred in these tanks to produce radioactive radium, first discovered by Pierre and Marie Curie.

BLERIOT AND BALLETS RUSSES

Louis Blériot makes headlines when he successfully flies the English Channel — the first man to do so. The Ballets Russes is formed, bringing dramatic innovation to the world of ballet, and the AEG Turbine Factory in Berlin proves that modern architecture can blend perfectly with the demands of industry. The world's first synthetic plastic is invented and the first newsreels appear in cinemas. Neon lights shine in the night. In Holland, the first organized eleven-city ice skating tour takes place. In Britain, imprisoned suffragettes go on hunger strike.

1 9 0 9

Jan	1	Old-age pensions introduced, UK
Mar	31	Pathé News shown in Paris
Apr	6	Robert Peary reaches the North Pole
	23	Armenians massacred in Turkey
	27	Young Turks depose Sultan Abdul Hamid
May	18	Ballets Russes performs in Paris
July	16	Twelve-year-old Soltan Ahmed Mirza becomes the Shah of Persia
	25	Blériot flies the Channel
Oct	26	Japan's first prime minister, Prince Ito Hirobumi, is assassinated
Dec	16	President Jose Zelaya resigns in Nicaragua

ABOVE: Royal England meets Imperial Russia — the Prince of Wales and the Czar with their sons.

ABOVE: Polar camp — from here, on April 6, Commander Robert Peary of the US reaches the North Pole, the first man to do so.

ARMENIAN MASSACRES

Thousands of Armenians are killed by Turks in the province of Cilicia in April. Sultan Abdul-Hamid (1842–1918) orders the killings after Armenian revolutionaries, demonstrating against oppressive Turkish rule, provoke the inhabitants and officials in Armenia. The USA and various European countries intervene to halt the killings. Following these events, Abdul Hamid is deposed by a unanimous vote in the two houses of parliament he was forced to set up last year. Opposition to the sultan is led by the Young Turks, who are pressing for reform in the vast and ramshackle Ottoman Empire. The sultan is replaced by his brother, Mahmud Reshad.

BLERIOT FLIES THE CHANNEL

The first man to fly across the English Channel is Louis Blériot (1872–1936) of France, flying a monoplane he has designed and built himself. His historic flight, from Calais to Dover, takes just 37 minutes.

MOROCCO

French and Spanish forces fight Rif tribesmen in Morocco as the Moroccan War continues.

NICARAGUAN CIVIL WAR

War begins in Nicaragua with a conservative revolt against liberal dictator President Jose Santos Zelaya. Dr Jose Madriz is elected to succeed him.

BALLETS RUSSES FOUNDED

Russian impresario Sergei Diaghilev (1872–1929) founds the company that will have the greatest influence over ballet in the twentieth century. Many of his dancers, choreographers and artists are Russian exiles, including Nijinsky, Pavlova, Karsavina, Fokine, and Stravinsky, but he also draws on the best of French talent. The company is notable for its new fusion of passion, fantasy, colour and sound with classical ballet.

HUNGER STRIKES

In the UK, imprisoned suffragettes begin to go on hunger strike. The British government orders them to be forcibly fed and there is a public outcry.

GLASGOW SCHOOL OF ART

Charles Rennie Macintosh brings Art Nouveau and Viennese Secession styles to Scotland in his own unique idiom. This building is one of the finest examples. It is famous because of its innovative use of space, unusual ornament, and inspired use of vertical elements. The library is finished in 1909 and is the best bit of all.

INDUSTRY MEETS ARCHITECTURE

Designed by pioneering German architect Peter Behrens (1868–1940), the AEG Turbine Factory in Berlin shows for the first time that the modern architectural idiom is well suited to industrial buildings — and that such buildings can in themselves be fine examples of architecture. Huge windows provide lots of light, metal uprights and roofing members give a broad roof span. No ornament is used but the structure itself has an austere elegance.

BAKELITE, FIRST SYNTHETIC PLASTIC

A Belgian-born American industrial chemist, Leo Hendrik Baekeland, markets the world's first heat-proof synthetic plastic. It is called phenolic resin but is better known under its trade name, Bakelite. It proves to be an excellent electrical insulator.

FIRST CINEMA NEWSREEL

French film pioneer Charles Pathé (1863–1957) begins making and showing the first cinema newsreel in Paris. He takes the idea to the United States in 1910.

DARING TO BE GAY

His novel, *Strait is the Gate*, launches Parisian writer André Gide (1869–1951) on a courageous career as a novelist. He defends his own right to be gay, but in this book pays tribute to his wife who appears as the character Madeleine.

LIGHTING UP WITH NEON

French scientist Georges Claude invents the neon tube, in which a glass tube containing a small quantity of neon gas glows red when a current is passed through it. Different colours are produced by adding other gases.

AUTOMATIC TOAST

The first electric toaster is sold in America by the General Electric Company. It toasts the bread on only one side at a time, and doesn't eject the toast.

PENSIONS FOR THE ELDERLY

In Britain, old-age pensions are introduced for people aged 70 and over. France introduced old-age insurance in 1850, followed by Germany, Denmark and New Zealand. Britain's is the first twentieth-century scheme, and the most comprehensive so far.

ABOVE: Louis Blériot stands in his monoplane before take-off. Later that day he becomes the first man to fly the Channel, flying from France to England in just 37 minutes.

ABOVE: Following his inauguration, President Taft and his wife drive to the White House. He succeeds former President Roosevelt.

RADIO SEA RESCUE

The first use of radio to save life at sea is made when the ship *Republic* collides with another vessel in the Atlantic and calls for help; rescuers arrive in time to save nearly all the passengers.

SIX PIECES FOR LARGE ORCHESTRA

This pivotal work of the Second Viennese School, composed by Anton Webern, is notable for his use of wind and percussion instruments to produce a unique orchestral colour and sense of space.

ORGANIZED ELFSTEDENTOCHT

This year sees the start of an organized eleven-city ice skating tour — Elfstedentocht. Skaters visit eleven cities in the Frisia area of the Netherlands in a loop beginning and ending in Leeuwarden. The first event is more of a tour than a race and the skaters start by heading north rather than south. Twenty-two skaters start and Minne Hoekstra is the first of the nine who finish 13 hours and 50 minutes later.

LILIOM: PLAY, MUSICAL AND FILM

Hungarian writer Ferenc Molnár publishes *Liliom*, his most famous play. Subsequently it is turned first into a musical (1945) and then the film *Carousel* (1956).

PEARY REACHES POLE

Robert E Peary, a US naval commander, is the first person to reach the North Pole (on his second attempt), having been accompanied during the final stages by his colleague, Matthew Henson, and four Inuit.

A NEW WORD

The National Conservation Commission, appointed by President Roosevelt, publishes the first inventory of the USA's natural resources. Advised by his chief forester, Gifford Pinchot, who has coined the term "conservation", Roosevelt has already introduced several legislative measures designed to preserve the natural environment.

GERONIMO
(1829–1909)

The Apache leader Geronimo, who led the Apache Indians in their struggle against Mexican, and later North American, usurpers, has died. After finally surrendering in 1886 he became a Christian and farmed in Oklahoma. His Native American name was Goyathlay which translates as "One who yawns".

THE WORLD
AT WAR

This is the decade that literally shakes the world. The war that breaks out in 1914 is the first, but sadly not last, incidence of global conflict that this century will endure. It will change lives and social customs forever and redraw the maps of the world. More than nine million people die and over twelve million are wounded. The Treaty of Versailles, which concludes the war, contains the seeds for conflict twenty years later. On a happier note, exploration has a good decade, with the rediscovery of Macchu Picchu and the pinning down of the South Pole.

OPPOSITE: The Palace of Peace in The Hague, Netherlands, brainchild of Andrew Carnegie.

1910–1919

KEY EVENTS OF THE DECADE

- UNION OF SOUTH AFRICA FORMED
- REVOLUTION IN CHINA
- BALKAN WARS
- MEXICAN REVOLUTION
- THE ARMORY SHOW, NEW YORK
- WORLD WAR I
- EASTER RISING IN DUBLIN
- EINSTEIN PUBLISHES HIS THEORY OF GENERAL RELATIVITY
- DADAISM INVENTED

- FIRST BIRTH CONTROL CLINIC IN USA
- REVOLUTION IN RUSSIA
- ATOM SPLIT
- WOMEN GET THE VOTE IN UK
- LEAGUE OF NATIONS FOUNDED
- BENVENETO MUSSOLINI STARTS FASCIST PARTY IN ITALY
- ALCOCK AND BROWN FLY THE ATLANTIC
- AMRITSAR MASSACRE

WORLD POPULATION: 1,712 MILLION

THE THRILL OF SPEED AND SOUND

The Union of South Africa is formed and Japan annexes Korea. Black Americans unite to campaign for an end to racial segregation, and slavery is abolished in China. International police work moves into a new dimension when radio is used for the first time to capture a criminal. The Dutch government introduces state pensions and a new, passionate dance, the tango, sweeps Europe. In Italy, a group of artists produce the Futurist Manifesto, an attempt to sweep away the past and welcome speed and power.

OPPOSITE: Fire at the Great Brussels Exhibition in Belgium leaves ruin and destruction in its wake.

1910

Feb	10	First woman pilot flies solo
Apr	21	US novelist Mark Twain dies aged 74
May	6	Death of King Edward VII of Britain; George V succeeds
	31	Union of South Africa formed
	31	Girl Guide movement established
June	19	Father's Day introduced in the USA by Mrs John B Dodd
	25	First performance of Igor Stravinsky's ballet *The Firebird*
July	1	Union of South Africa is proclaimed a dominion
	31	Dr Crippen arrested in Canada following a radio tip-off
Aug	20	Florence Nightingale, founder of modern nursing, dies aged 91
	24	Korea annexed
Sep	7	Marie Curie and André Debierne isolate pure radium
Oct	5	Portugal becomes a republic
	30	Red Cross founder Jean-Henri Dunant dies aged 82
Nov	11	Russian writer Leo Tolstoy dies aged 82
Dec	10	Dutch physicist Johannes Diderik van der Waals is awarded the Nobel Prize in physics

ABOVE: Infra-red photography, developed in the USA, shows scenes taken in the full sun as moonlit snowscapes. The technique will later be adapted for night espionage.

RACE RELATIONS

In New York, USA, African-American liberals form the National Association for the Advancement of Colored People (NAACP), with the goal of ending racial segregation and discrimination. The organization publishes a newspaper, *The Crisis*, edited by American writer and professor William Du Bois (1868–1963), which reports on race relations around the world.

SOUTH AFRICA UNION FOUNDED

The Union of South Africa is created out of the former British colonies of Cape Colony and Natal, and the former Boer states of Transvaal and the Orange Free State. The new country joins other former British colonies as independent dominions in the Empire.

US SUFFRAGE

In Washington, USA, women gain the right to vote.

COUNT LEO NIKOLAYEVICH TOLSTOY (1828–1910)

The great Russian writer Leo Tolstoy has died of pneumonia in a railway siding at Astapovo station, while in flight from his wife. After service in the Crimean War and a socialite life in St Petersburg and abroad, he married in 1862 and settled in his Volga estate. While his wife produced thirteen children, he wrote *War and Peace* (1863–69), *Anna Karenina* (1874–76) and *The Death of Ivan Ilyitch* (1886). From 1879 he espoused an extreme ascetic form of Christianity, condemned his own works as worthless, was excommunicated for his unorthodox views and irreconcilably alienated his wife.

KOREA ANNEXED

The Japanese government formally annexes the peninsula of Korea. Japan occupied Korea during the Russo-Japanese war of 1904–1905 and has exercised increasing control ever since.

REVOLUTION IN PORTUGAL

King Manuel of Portugal is deposed in a revolution and flees on his yacht to Gibraltar. The revolution comes after a decade of revolt against the monarchy. Portugal becomes a republic and adopts a liberal constitution the following year.

FIRST WOMAN PILOT

In February, Baronne Raymonde de Laroche, a French aviator, becomes the first woman to fly solo. She is the first woman ever to be granted a pilot's licence. The Baronne, born Elise Deroche, worked as a model and actress. She claims to be have been entitled by Czar Nicholas II of Russia.

SLAVERY ABOLISHED IN CHINA

The Chinese imperial government has abolished slavery. Until now, the Manchu ruling elite enslaved prisoners of war, and their servants kept slaves. Family members, usually women, were often made to be slaves.

BLACK MIGRATION

The founding of the NAACP marks the beginning of a great migration that brings some two million black people into the northern United States.

GASES INTO LIQUIDS

Dutch physicist Professor Johannes Diderik van der Waals (1837–1923) is awarded the Nobel Prize in physics for his work on the relationship between gases and liquids, which helps later scientists turn so-called "permanent" gases into liquids.

ABOVE: The Eiffel Tower stands witness to devastating floods in Paris when the Seine bursts its banks and almost drowns the city.

FIREBIRD

The Firebird by Russian composer Igor Stravinsky (1882–1971) is performed in Paris. Danced by the Ballets Russes, it is based on traditional Russian tales but displays strong rhythms, unusual harmonies and joy through the tone colours of individual instruments. This will mark the composer's later works.

CATCHING CRIPPEN

The first use of radio for catching criminals occurs in July when the captain of a New York-bound Atlantic liner radios Scotland Yard, in the UK, to say he thinks he has suspected murderer Dr Hawley Harvey Crippen on board. Crippen, an American born in Michigan, is later tried, found guilty of poisoning his wife, and executed.

MODERN HOUSING

The modern house makes its appearance with the Steiner House in Vienna. Designed by Austrian architect Adolf Loos (1870–1933), who is influenced by American industrial buildings, the house has no ornament, the pale exterior is symmetrically arranged, and there is a flat roof. Everything is highly functional.

MARY (MORSE) BAKER EDDY (1821–1910)

The founder of Christian Science, Mary Baker Eddy dies. Her work *Science and Health with Key to the Scriptures* (1875) expressed her belief that disease is illusory. With her third husband, Asa G. Eddy, she founded the Church of Christ, Scientist in Boston in 1879.

FUTURIST MANIFESTO

Italian artists Umberto Boccioni and Giacomo Balla produce the Technical Manifesto of the Futurist Painters. The artists aim to celebrate speed and movement, especially of machines such as cars and aeroplanes. The painters develop a particular style to do this, taking up the fragmented idiom of Cubism to suggest movement through space.

ELECTRIC FOOD MIXER

The first electrically-driven food mixer for domestic use is made by the Hamilton Beach Manufacturing Company of America.

ABOVE: Princess Hélène of Portugal goes hippo hunting in Portuguese West Africa, one of the last European colonies.

ABOVE: A skeleton of steel tubing supports the tandem biplane, designed by naval lieutenant JW Seddon to carry six passengers.

ISOLATING RADIUM

French scientists Marie Curie and André Debierne isolate the first sample of pure radium from the uranium ore pitchblende. They do so using an electrolytic process.

LET'S TANGO

A new dance, the tango, which originated in Argentina, has become a major dance craze in Europe and the United States, inspiring an ankle-length tango dress and tango shoe.

HALLEY'S COMET

In May the Earth passes through the tail of Halley's Comet, which returns every 76 years. Unwarranted fear of "poisonous gases" from the tail leads to brisk sale of a so-called antidote, "Comet Pills".

LEFT: Black Hussars, the paramilitary mounted police, use maces and revolvers on strikers in Philadelphia. The strike had started with tramway workers and escalated into a general strike.

MARK TWAIN
(1835–1910)

Born Samuel Langhorne Clemens, Mark Twain, the American author of *The Adventures of Tom Sawyer* (1876) and *The Adventures of Huckleberry Finn* (1884) has died. Journalist, humorist and lecturer, he incorporated his experiences as Mississippi boatman, Nevada gold-digger and foreign traveller into his writing.

PENSIONS

The Dutch government introduces pensions for people aged over 70, although they will not be implemented until the 1930s.

FIRST ABSTRACT WATERCOLOUR

This untitled new work by the Russian painter Wassily Kandinsky (1866–1944) signals the birth of abstract art as it is to become known in later decades.

ROBIE HOUSE

American architect Frank Lloyd Wright (1867–1959) designs a series of houses in which long, low, horizontal lines appear to ground the buildings, making them seem at one with the earth — an aspect of what Wright calls "organic architecture". Inside, the houses are notable for a flowing use of space. The Robie House in Chicago is one of the finest.

STANLEY CUP

The Stanley Cup, named after Governor General of Canada, Lord Stanley of Preston, is presented to the winner of the professional ice hockey play-offs. Until this year, it had been fought for by Canada's best amateur teams. Now it is the goal for the Canadian and American teams in the National Hockey League.

DEATH OF BRITISH MONARCH

Edward VII dies and is succeeded by his son, who becomes George V. Edward was a much-respected king whose love of foreign travel and public ceremony increased the popularity of the British monarchy.

POLAR TRIUMPH AND INCA CITY

Norwegian explorer Amundsen reaches the South Pole, one of the last of the great unexplored regions of the world. And in the Peruvian jungle, an American explorer uncovers the remains of a great Inca city. On the political stage, revolutions break out in Mexico and China, Germany announces her intention of achieving a "place in the sun" and Italian troops invade Tripoli. The first aircraft carrier is born and the first torpedo is tested.

OPPOSITE: Captain Robert F Scott, leader of the ill-fated expedition across the Antarctic.

1911

Jan	18	Eugene Ely lands aeroplane on battleship
	26	First performance of Richard Strauss's opera *Der Rosenkavalier*
Feb	3	Ulrich Salchow becomes world figure-skating champion for the tenth time
Apr	23	French and Algerian troops enter Morocco
May	18	Austrian composer Gustav Mahler dies aged 50
	25	Mexican dictator Porfirio Díaz resigns
	30	First Indy 500 motor race takes place in the USA
June	9	US temperance campaigner Carrie Nation dies aged 65

July	2	Germans send gunboat to Moroccan port of Agadir; leads to international incident
Aug	22	The painting *Mona Lisa* is stolen from the Louvre in Paris. It will be recovered in 1913
Sep	30	Italy attacks Ottoman Empire's port of Tripoli in Libya
Oct	9	Revolution begins in China
Nov	4	"Agadir Crisis" ends, Morocco
	14	First aeroplane take-off from a ship
Dec	14	Roald Amundsen's Norwegian expedition reaches the South Pole
	31	Marie Curie wins a second Nobel Prize

ABOVE: The inquiry into the sinking of the *Titanic* held in the USA.
MAIN PICTURE: The building of the *Titanic* at Shorts' shipyard in Belfast, Northern Ireland.

BALKAN WAR

War breaks out in the Balkans as Bulgaria, Serbia, Greece and Montenegro unite in an effort to take possession of the remaining Turkish territory in the Balkan peninsula, and invade the Ottoman province of Macedonia. Turkey has already lost Libya, Rhodes and the Dodecanese Islands to Italy in a separate dispute. In October, at the battle of Kirk-Kilissa, the Bulgarians throw back the Turks, inflicting heavy losses. In November, Serbs fighting at Monastir, assisted by Greek forces, drive back the Turks, causing 20,000 casualties.

TITANIC DISASTER

The mighty liner SS *Titanic* strikes an iceberg during her maiden voyage and sinks. Out of 2,224 passengers, more than 1,500 lose their lives, many freezing to death in the icy water of the Atlantic. The liner, which was the most luxurious in the world, had been declared unsinkable because of watertight compartments. In the event, these failed to prevent the disaster and lack of sufficient lifeboats exacerbated the tragedy.

MEASURING X-RAYS

Max von Laue, a German physicist, passes X-rays through a crystal and finds that this enables him to measure the wavelengths of the rays.

CIVIL WAR THREATENED IN IRELAND

In Britain, the House of Commons passes the Home Rule Bill, which promises home rule for Ireland. Unionists in the north of Ireland refuse to recognize the new parliament if it is set up and threaten civil war.

NEW US PRESIDENT

Woodrow Wilson (1856–1924), governor of New Jersey, USA, wins the presidential election for the Democratic Party and is elected 28th president of the USA. He is the first Democrat to be elected since Grover Cleveland in 1892.

MOROCCAN CRISIS ENDS

In Morocco, the sultan signs the Treaty of Fez, making Morocco a joint protectorate with France and Spain. This averts the threat of a European war over Morocco, following the arrival of the German gunboat *Panther* to the region.

US SUPPRESSES REVOLT IN NICARAGUA

In Nicaragua, liberals rise up against conservatism and US influence, under the slogan "Down with Yankee imperialism". President Díaz is forced to ask for US help, which comes in the form of 2,500 US marines. The rebellion is quelled within two months.

AUTOBIOGRAPHY OF AN EX-COLORED MAN

The first black barrister in Florida and consul to Venezuela and Nicaragua, James Weldon Johnson (1871–1938) publishes *Autobiography of an Ex-Colored Man*. Johnson does more than anyone in the early twentieth century to make Americans aware of the richness of black American culture.

WALKING

Ukranian-born American sculptor Alexander Archipenko bores holes into otherwise solid figures, to convey the notion of inner space. His sculpture, *Walking*, marks the first time that holes have been made in solid sculpture in this way.

QUO VADIS

The big, silent, Italian film *Quo Vadis*, by director Enrico Guazzoni, is the longest film yet produced. It is the first of several film versions of the novel by Henryk Sienkiewicz and is an influential cinematic epic.

PILTDOWN MAN

A fossilized skull and jawbone are found in Sussex in the UK. The remains, nicknamed "Piltdown Man" are hailed as the missing link in human ancestry. Many years later Piltdown Man is proved to be a hoax.

PARACHUTE ESCAPE

Albert Berry, an American stuntman, makes the first parachute jump from a moving biplane over St Louis, Missouri in March. He falls some 122m (397ft) before his parachute opens and his exploit proves that it is possible to save life in this way.

KEYSTONE KOPS

The Kops make their riotous appearance in the first of scores of films made by Mack Sennett (1880–1960), an uneducated Irish-Canadian who began as the apprentice of DW Griffith. His films with the Kops are made in his own studio, however, which will be highly successful until the arrival of sound.

NAMING VITAMINS

Polish-born American biochemist Casimir Funk (1884–1967) coins the name "vitamines" (later shortened to vitamins) for the substances discovered by Frederick Hopkins in 1907.

ADVERTISING LIGHTS

The first neon advertising sign — for the aperitif Cinzano — lights up in Paris. A red neon tube light was first demonstrated in Paris by French physicist Georges Claude in 1910.

ABOVE: The revived Olympic Games attract a great deal of publicity. This detail from a multilingual poster is the first attempt at international marketing.

LEFT: Five sisters working as "pit-brow" lasses in a coal mine in the north of England.

RIGHT: Still no vote, but women work the same shifts as men digging and sorting coal in mines all over Europe.

NUDE DESCENDING A STAIRCASE

This landmark painting by French artist Marcel Duchamp (1887–1968) uses the Futurist technique of breaking up the image to suggest movement. It causes a scandal, but becomes one of the most influential works of modern art.

POST OFFICE SAVINGS BANK

Otto Wagner's Savings Bank in Vienna becomes famous for exposing its structure to view — even the rivets are left visible. The whole form of the building follows the structure, with much use of metal and glass. Glass bricks in the floor allow light to enter the basement.

MONTESSORI SCHOOLS

Italian educationalist Maria Montessori (1870–1952) founds schools in Europe and New York following the success she achieved in the school for neglected children which she opened in Rome in 1907. The Montessori method involves stimulating children's natural desire to learn by using toys and puzzles.

ELECTRIC COOKER

The electric cooker invented by British engineer Charles Belling is the most successful of a number of attempts to apply electricity to the kitchen. However, as yet electric cookers do not have temperature control.

ABOVE: The national Republican convention in Chicago. The election of William Howard Taft as presidential nominee forces Theodore Roosevelt to quit the party in order to oppose him.

ABOVE: Russian peasants in the Novgorod area. This decade will see a revolution in their lives.

CONTINENTS DRIFT

German scientist Alfred Wegener (1880–1930) suggests that Africa and South America were once one mass, and have broken apart by a process that he calls continental drift. Because he is a meteorologist, not a geologist, geologists mock his theory.

PIERROT LUNAIRE

This work, by Austro-Hungarian composer Arnold Schoenberg (1874–1951), shocks its first audiences but will become a classic of modern music. It is a "melodrama" in which a female performer (dressed as a male pierrot figure with a whitened, mask-like face) half-sings, half-speaks the words of the text. The half-singing, half-speaking technique is known in German as *Sprechstimme*. Although the form was not invented by Schoenberg, *Pierrot* shows its potential for the first time.

GITANJALI

Indian poet Rabindranath Tagore (1861–1941) translates his collection of poems, *Gitanjali*, into English, bringing this mystical Indian poet fame in the West. Irish poet WB Yeats writes the introduction, helping to publicize Indian poetry in the Western world for the first time.

OLYMPIC GAMES

Athletes from five continents compete at the Fifth Olympic Games, held in Stockholm, Sweden. More women participate and the photo-finish and electric timing are introduced. American athlete Jim Thorpe wins two gold medals, but is stripped of them for previously having been paid to play baseball.

WOMEN'S SUFFRAGE

In the US, Arizona, Kansas and Oregon grant women the right to vote. In Britain, suffragettes raid the House of Commons and break shop windows in a co-ordinated campaign of protest. More than 200 women are arrested.

JUNG AND FREUD DISAGREE

Karl Gustav Jung (1875–1961), the pioneering Swiss psychologist who became President of the International Psychoanalytic Society in 1911, publishes *Psychology of the Unconscious*. This sets out his disagreements with his colleague Sigmund Freud on the sexual origins of unconscious motivations.

COMMERCIAL CELLOPHANE

Cellophane, invented by Jacques Brandenberger, a Swiss chemist, is produced commercially in Paris for use as a wrapping material.

JOHAN AUGUST STRINDBERG (1849–1912)

August Strindberg, the controversial Swedish writer, has died. His work has been a major influence on twentieth-century writing for the theatre. His novel *The Red Room* (1879) introduced naturalism to Sweden, and his plays and chamber plays such as *The Father* (1887), *Miss Julie* (1888) and *The Ghost Sonata* (1907) combine naturalism and psychological analysis.

WAR CLOUDS MASS IN THE BALKANS

Trouble continues in the Balkans as the world drifts towards war. Revolution intensifies in Mexico, where the first air-to-air combat takes place. Stravinsky's *Rite of Spring* causes a riot, and in New York the Armory Show gives Americans their first chance to view examples of European modern art. Also in New York, the new Woolworth Building is the world's tallest. Vitamins A and B are isolated and state-funded insurance is introduced into Britain.

1913

Feb	2	Grand Central Station, the world's largest train station, opens in New York
	23	Deposed president shot in Mexico
Mar	18	King George I of the Greeks is assassinated in Salonika
May	10	Bombs dropped on Mexican gunboats
	29	Igor Stravinsky's ballet *The Rite of Spring* performed in Paris to riots
	30	Treaty ends the First Balkan War
June	8	British suffragette Emily Davison killed by horse
July	31	Second Balkan War breaks out as Bulgaria attacks Serbia
Aug	10	Treaty of Bucharest ends the Second Balkan War
Sep	29	Rudolf Diesel, inventor of the diesel engine, dies aged 55
Oct	10	Last rock barrier on the Panama Canal is blasted away
Dec	10	Dutch scientist Heike Kamerlingh Onnes is awarded the Nobel Prize in physics

OPPOSITE: Suffragette Emily Davison lies fatally injured after falling under the king's horse, Anmer, during the annual Derby race.

ABOVE: One of Eadweard Muybridge's remarkable photographs capturing the body in movement. Muybridge's work has great influence on artists of the day.

PANAMA CANAL OPENS

The canal connecting the Pacific and Atlantic oceans is finally opened. The canal flows through a US-controlled zone and shortens the journey between the east and west coasts of America by many days.

GREEK KING ASSASSINATED

King George I of Greece is assassinated by a madman, Alexander Schinas, in Salonika, newly won from the Ottoman Turks. George had been king since 1863; he is succeeded by his son, Constantine I.

WOMEN'S SUFFRAGE

In the United States, Alice Paul and Lucy Burns lead a parade of 5,000 through Washington, demanding women's suffrage on the day before President Wilson's inauguration. In the UK, British suffragette, Emily Davison, dies after falling under the hooves of the king's horse in the Derby.

LES GRANDES MEAULNES

In his one completed novel, *Les Grandes Meaulnes*, French writer Alain-Fournier (1886–1914), who will die in the first weeks of World War I, evokes a dream world and a world of childhood, both of which are finally lost. It is one of the few successful novels to come from the Symbolist movement in art and literature.

THE FOURTH OF JULY

In this new work, American composer Charles Ives (1874–1954) creates a unique sound world, full of snatches of American tunes. Its technique and harmonies anticipate many later developments. Ives is an insurance executive who composes in his free time.

SPRING RITE CAUSES RIOTS

The *Rite of Spring*, a new work by Russian composer Igor Stravinsky (1882–1971) is premièred in Paris. Staged by the Ballets Russes, it portrays a fertility rite which ends in a ritual sacrifice, and it causes a riot in the theatre. With its strong rhythms and vibrant orchestral colours, the work will later become one of the most popular in twentieth-century music.

SWANN'S WAY

The first part of French writer Marcel Proust's great novel, *A la Recherche du Temps Perdu* (1913–1927) is published. Its evocation of memory and character over a large canvas make it one of the most important of literary works. Proust's literary goal is to release creative energies derived from past experience, from the hidden store of the unconscious.

ISOTOPES

British chemist Frederick Soddy (1877–1956) invents the term "isotope" to describe atoms of the same element that have different masses, for example, carbon-12, the most common form of that element, and carbon-14, which is radioactive.

BALKAN WARS

In March, Adrianople surrenders to the Bulgarians, who have been beseiging the city, and in May a peace treaty is signed with the Turks. However, war breaks out again and the Turks re-occupy Adrianople. After bitter fighting, in August peace is finally restored to the Balkans, after a year of war. The treaty limits the Ottoman Empire in Europe to Constantinople and its surrounds, creates the new state of Albania, doubles the size of Serbia and Montenegro, and confirms Greece as the most important power in the Aegean Sea. Both Bulgaria and Turkey bitterly resent the new settlement.

MEXICAN REVOLUTION

Right-wing general Victoriano Huerta seizes power from elected president Madero, who is murdered. Huerta's dictatorial regime leads to revolts led by General Alvaro Obregon, and revolutionaries Francisco "Pancho" Villa and Emiliano Zapata. In May, pilot Didier Masson, a supporter of the rebels, drops the first-ever bombs on to an enemy warship when he attacks Mexican gunships in Guayamas Bay. In November, the first air-to-air combat takes place when an aircraft piloted by Phillip Rader, in support of President Huerta, exchanges pistol shots with a rebel plane flown by Dean Ivan Lamb.

A BOY'S WILL

American poet Robert Frost (1874–1963) publishes his first volume of poetry and an authentically American voice is heard in modern poetry for the first time.

ARMORY SHOW
Some 1.600 works are exhibited at the Armory Show in New York. including around 400 modern European works. This gives Americans the chance to see many European modern works for the first time. and gives modern artists much publicity. Some of the paintings. such as Matisse's *Blue Nude* (which was burned in effigy) and Duchamp's *Nude Descending a Staircase*. cause controversy.

WORLD'S TALLEST BUILDING
The Woolworth Building in New York. architect Cass Gilbert's Gothic-style skyscraper is 241m (790ft) high. the tallest building in the world. It is so high that it influences the decision to introduce zoning. whereby tall buildings have to be set back to provide light and improve wind flow.

SOCIOLOGY PROFESSOR
Pioneering French sociologist Emile Durkheim (1858–1917) becomes the first professor of sociology at the Sorbonne. Paris. In *The Rules of Sociological Method* (1895) he advocated using the scientific method to study society. He believes that studying anthropology will throw light on the way society is organized.

PRIZE FOR ONNES
The Dutch scientist Heike Kamelingh Onnes is awarded the Nobel Prize in physics for liquefying helium.

BELOW: Members of the Scott expedition to the Antarctic, including Captain Scott (centre) and Captain Oates (second from the right). Five of the group died, including Scott himself.

STAINLESS STEEL
Metallurgists Henry Brearley (UK) and FM Becket (USA) produce stainless steel. an alloy of iron and chromium which resists rust.

GAS-FILLED BULBS
American chemist Irving Langmuir discovers that electric light bulbs last longer if they are filled with an inert gas such as nitrogen or argon.

NATIONAL INSURANCE
In Britain. payments are to be made to British workers under a new National Health Insurance Act. Under this. State and employers will give limited financial support during ill-health and unemployment. The state insurance scheme is based on pioneering schemes set up by Scandinavian governments in the late nineteenth century and the Dutch government in 1901.

OZONE LAYER FOUND
French physicist Charles Fabry discovers that there are quantities of ozone in the upper atmosphere. between 10 and 48km (6 and 26mi) above the Earth.

SCHWEITZER'S HOSPITAL
Albert Schweitzer's new hospital is opened in Lambarene. French Equatorial Africa. It will treat thousands of people suffering from tropical diseases.

VITAMINS A AND B
American biochemist Elmer Verner McCollum discovers fat-soluble vitamins A and B.

DEN NORWEGERN

BEHAVIOURISM

In *Behaviourism*, John Broadus Watson (1878–1958), an American psychology professor, argues that psychology is the study of observable behaviour, which is a response to physiological stimulus. His approach to psychology is well received by psychologists who question the value of studying the unconscious.

ARTIFICIAL KIDNEY

Medical theories come close to reality when American pharmacologist John James Abel and his colleages make the first artificial kidney. However, it is not completely practicable.

LEFT: An impressive present from the German Kaiser to the people of Norway, the colossal statue of Frijthof.

BELOW: Diamond hunters race to peg their claim at Killarney, dubbed the new "Eldorado" of South Africa.

DOMESTIC FRIDGE ON SALE

The first domestic electric refrigerator goes on sale in Chicago, USA. Called the Domelre, its compressor (which compresses air to reduce the temperature) is driven by an electric motor instead of the steam engine used on earlier refrigerators.

HARRIET TUBMAN
(1821–1913)

American former slave, Harriet Tubman, has died at her home in Auburn, New York. A courageous woman, known as the "Moses of her people", she smuggled more than 300 slaves to freedom via the so-called Underground Railway after her own escape from slavery.

THE END OF THE GOLDEN SUMMER

Archduke Ferdinand is assassinated in Sarajevo. The rival European powers mobilize and by August, France, Britain and Russia are at war with Germany and Austria-Hungary — the world's first global conflict is under way. Elsewhere, the Panama Canal opens and Mother's Day is invented.

OPPOSITE: Soldiers struggle to manoeuvre in the muddy trenches characteristic of World War I.

1914

June	28	Serbian student Gavrilo Princip assassinates Archduke Franz Ferdinand of Austria at Sarajevo
July	28	Austria-Hungary declares war on Serbia
	29	Russia mobilizes its army
	30	In Britain the Irish Home Rule Bill is shelved
Aug	1	Germany declares war on Russia because of Russian mobilization
	3	Germany declares war on Russia's ally, France
	4	Germany invades Belgium in order to reach France; Britain declares war on Germany
	5	First traffic lights are introduced in the USA
	6	Austria-Hungary declares war on Russia
	14	Official opening of the Panama Canal
	23	Battle of Mons: British army sent to help Belgium begins to retreat
	26–30	Battle of Tannenberg: massive German victory against Russians
Sep	5	Germans capture Reims, France
	6–8	Battle of the Marne: German advance halted
	19	South African troops invade German West Africa (Namibia)
	23	Germans sink British cruisers off the Netherlands
Oct	13	The Ottoman Empire (Turkey) joins the war on Germany's side
	14–Nov11	Battle of Ypres
	23–24	Battle of Mons
Nov	11	Trench warfare fully established on the Western Front in France
Dec	11	Battle of the Falklands: four German cruisers sunk
	25	Christmas Day truce on the Western Front: German and Allied troops play football

WORLD WAR I BREAKS OUT

In Sarajevo, Bosnia, Archduke Franz Ferdinand, heir to the Austrian throne, is assassinated by a Serb, Gavrilo Princip, in June. The Austrian government suspects Serbia of complicity in the killing and threatens reprisals. As a result of the assassination in Sarajevo, the rival European powers mobilize their armies. Austria declares war on Serbia, which is supported by Russia, and invades. Germany declares its support for Austria and declares war on Russia. France supports Russia and prepares for war. In August, Germany invades Belgium on its way to invade France. As a result, Britain declares war on Germany to protect Belgian neutrality. Italy, the Netherlands, Spain, Portugal, and the Scandinavian countries stay out of the war, which engulfs the whole of the rest of Europe. In September, the war spreads to the Pacific and Africa as British and Empire troops invade and seize the German colonies of Togo, Cameroon, German East Africa, German Southwest Africa, New Guinea, and the Caroline Islands. Fighting is now taking place around the world.

BELOW: Aircraft soon join the conflict on both sides.

ABOVE: HMS *Iron Duke* battles through the North Sea.

ABOVE: Dropping bombs from an aeroplane.

ABOVE: American artillery plays a crucial role in the final year of the war. This is a 41cm (16-in) pack gun which can be mounted on a railway carriage for ease of manoeuvring and firing.

ABOVE: German submarine crew in the North Sea.

LEFT: German high command plan tactics and strategy in the field.

RIGHT: Going over the top. As soldiers emerged from the trenches, they were only too often mown down.

OPPOSITE BELOW: Austrian troops shoot blindfolded Serbian prisoners.

FIRST SCREEN GODDESS

American actress Mary Pickford (1893–1979) stars in Edward S Porter's film, *Tess of the Storm Country*. This is her first famous movie, and one of the hits that launches her as the "first screen goddess".

FIRST TARZAN

Written by Edgar Rice Burroughs, *Tarzan of the Apes* is published. It is the first of a series of books featuring Tarzan, a British aristocrat who is abandoned in the jungle and brought up by apes.

PANAMA CANAL OPENS

The Panama Canal is officially opened to traffic in August, having taken ten years to build at a cost of $380 million; it shortens a voyage from New York to San Francisco by about 12,500km (7,750mi).

A PORTRAIT OF THE ARTIST AS A YOUNG MAN

The seminal autobiographical novel, *A Portrait of the Artist as a Young Man*, by Irish writer James Joyce (1882–1941) begins serial publication in *The Egoist*. It is the archetypal *Bildungsroman*, and inspires other writers. *Dubliners*, Joyce's volume of short stories, also appears this year.

FIRST TRAFFIC LIGHTS

As motor vehicles increase in number, the first two-colour electric traffic lights, red and green, are installed in Cleveland, Ohio, at the junction of Euclid Avenue and 105th Street.

SUFFRAGETTES SIGN FOR WAR

After fighting the British government for many years, suffragettes Emmeline and Christabel Pankhurst urge women to join the war effort. Many respond to the call; some join an international women's peace movement.

HORMONE ISOLATED

American biochemist Edward Calvin Kendall (1886–1972) isolates the hormone thyroxin, in crystalline form. This hormone is essential for physical growth and mental development.

A BLUE NOTE

Black composer WC Handy (1873–1958) becomes known as "the father of the blues" with numbers such as *St Louis Blues*. He integrates ragtime and jazz styles, and produces a characteristic effect with a "blue note" — a slightly flattened seventh note of the scale, which comes from traditional black music.

MOTHER'S DAY

Mother's Day is introduced in the United States. This follows lobbying by Anna Jarvis of West Virginia, who marks May 10, the day her mother died, with prayers. Congress signs a resolution that the second Sunday in May is to be a national holiday.

EARTH'S CORE

By studying earthquake waves, American geologist Beno Gutenberg decides that the Earth has a central core, a theory now generally accepted.

EARLY BRASSIERE

The first brassière is marketed, based on a design by Mary Phelps Jacob, a New York socialite; her first model is made from two handkerchiefs and some elastic.

FOOTBALL IN THE TRENCHES

During a Christmas Day truce, German and British soldiers fighting in France play football together in the no-man's land between their trenches. The following day, they return to killing one other.

GAS, GALLIPOLI AND ZEPPELIN RAIDS

Far from ending by Christmas, the Great War intensifies. Improved technology makes the machine gun a terrible weapon of war and both sides make use of poison gas, with awful results. Zeppelins bomb British cities. Italy enters the war. The *Lusitania* is sunk by a German submarine. And while men make war, some women travel to The Hague to discuss possible ways of achieving peace. Radio waves are sent across the Atlantic and in the USA the white racist organization the Ku Klux Klan is revived.

OPPOSITE: Turkish troops at Gallipoli, the campaign that lasted for almost a year.

1915

Jan	9	German zeppelins bomb English towns	Aug	30	Germans capture the Russian fortress of Brest-Litovsk
Feb	2	Germany begins U-boat blockade of the British Isles	Sep	5	Czar takes command of the Russian army
	19	British ships shell Turkish forts guarding the Dardanelles Strait	Oct	12	British nurse Edith Cavell is shot in German-occupied Belgium
Apr 22–May 25		First use of poison gas by Germans at Ypres	Nov	5	An aeroplane is catapulted from a US warship, the first such launch
	25	British, Australian and New Zealand troops land at Gallipoli, in the Dardanelles	Dec	10	The 100th car rolls off the Ford assembly line
May	7	German U-boat sinks the British liner *Lusitania*		20	The Gallipoli campaign is abandoned
	23	Italy declares war on Austria-Hungary			
June	1	Zeppelins bomb London			

ITALY ENTERS THE WAR

After renouncing the Triple Alliance with Germany and Austria, Italy enters the war and seizes Italian-speaking territory from Austria. Despite its early successes, the Italian army fights a series of inconclusive battles on the River Isonzo against the Austrians.

HOLLAND REMAINS NEUTRAL

Holland remains neutral during the course of World War I.

SINKING OF THE LUSITANIA

The liner *Lusitania* sinks off the coast of Ireland after it is torpedoed without warning by a German submarine. More than 1,100 of the 1,978 on board are drowned, including 128 American citizens. The sinking increases anti-German sentiment in the USA, which is trying to remain neutral in the war.

NURSE SHOT

In Belgium, the British nurse Edith Cavell (b. 1865) is shot by a German firing squad for sheltering Belgians fearful of conscription and helping young British and French soldiers escape to safety across the Dutch border. Her death causes an international outrage against the German action.

SYNCHRONIZED MACHINE GUN

Germany introduces a device that synchronizes a machine gun so that its bullets can be fired through an aircraft's rotating propeller without hitting the blades; it is fitted to a Fokker E-1 fighter plane.

POISON GAS

German armies use chlorine gas for the first time against the British at Ypres. Its effects are devastating and over the next four years, both sides develop phosgene and mustard gas, causing terrible injuries and deaths. English physicist, Hertha Ayrton (1854–1923), works on a fan for dispersing gas; it is later known as the Ayrton fan.

WOMEN AT THE HAGUE

In April, 2,000 women, delegates from many countries, meet at The Hague in Holland to discuss ways of ending the war. They set up the Women's International League for Peace and Freedom (WILPF) and agree to lobby governments for peace. By November women have formed peace groups in eleven European countries including Austria, Belgium, Britain, Germany, Italy, France and Hungary.

ABOVE: The ominous Ku Klux Klan regroup in Atlanta, Georgia.

LEFT: The passenger ship *Lusitania*, soon to be a victim of war.

KKK REVIVED
The Ku Klux Klan white supremacist movement, which arose after the Civil War in the southern USA, is revived in Atlanta, Georgia, by ex-preacher William J Simmons.

THE GOOD SOLDIER
The publication of *The Good Soldier* by English novelist Ford Madox Ford (1873–1939) brings him fame. The novel is valued for its subtle treatment of life's illusions and realities. Ford is also known for his championing of experiment in fiction and his support for important writers, such as DH Lawrence, at early stages in their careers.

HIGHER EDUCATION FOR CHINESE WOMEN
Ginling College, the first institution of higher education for women, opens in Nanking, China.

THE BIRTH OF A NATION
The most famous of American film director DW Griffith's great silent epics, *The Birth of a Nation*, is screened this year. It covers the US Civil War and is remarkable for its use of such cinematic techniques as close-ups, fade-outs and flashbacks. But Griffith (1875–1948) is criticized for the film's racial bias and glorification of the Ku Klux Klan.

HERLAND
Having written a famous short story *The Yellow Wallpaper* (1892), about a young Victorian woman's mental breakdown, American feminist Charlotte Perkins Gilman (1860–1935) publishes *Herland*, a feminist utopia.

CALLING LONG DISTANCE
In January the first North American transcontinental telephone service between New York and San Francisco is opened by the inventor of the telephone, the Scottish Alexander Graham Bell (1847–1922), and his former assistant Thomas Watson.

ABOVE: Sinking of the German cruiser *Bluecher* in the North Sea.   BELOW: German submarine in rough seas.

ABOVE: A Turkish field hospital at Gallipoli.

CATAPULTED INTO THE AIR
In November, a flying boat is catapulted from the deck of the US battleship *Carolina* in Pensacola Bay, Florida — the first aircraft launched at sea in this way.

BLACK SQUARE
Going further than the Cubists, Russian painter Kasimir Malevich (1878–1935) reaches abstraction by reducing his paintings to pure arrangements of flat geometrical shapes. He calls this style Suprematism.

TRANSATLANTIC SPEECH
Radio transmits speech across the Atlantic Ocean for the first time: it is sent from a US naval base in Virginia and received in Paris by a station on the Eiffel Tower.

HEAT-PROOF GLASS
By adding boric oxide to the mix, the Corning Glass Works in New York State make the heat-resistant glass known as ™Pyrex. Ideal for ovenware, the new substance is developed by technologists Eugene Sullivan and William Taylor.

PAUL EHRLICH
(1854–1915)

Chemist, bacteriologist, haematologist, German-born Paul Ehrlich has died. He pioneered the use of chemotherapy, formulated a successful treatment for syphilis, and in 1908 shared the Nobel Prize for medicine with Ilya Mechnikov, for their work in immunology.

NO QUIET ON THE WESTERN FRONT

War continues to engulf the globe. As always, war stimulates technology and a new weapon appears: the tank, first used on the Somme. Plastic surgery, too, develops as a result of terrible injuries and the term "shell shock" comes into use. The Easter Rising in Ireland is put down brutally. Rasputin the monk is murdered in Russia. The art movement Dadaism appears as a protest against the carnage of war.

OPPOSITE: Tanks first come into use in World War I. They are a British invention and first see service at Cambrai in France.

1916

Jan	6	British House of Commons votes to introduce military conscription
	16	Battle of Gallipoli ends after nine months, with Allied withdrawal
Feb	21	Battle of Verdun begins with German attack, ends Dec 18
Apr	25	The Easter Rising in Ireland begins; it is crushed within a week
May	21	Battle of Jutland begins; it continues until 1 June
June	6	Field Marshal Lord Kitchener, British War Minister, is drowned
	21	Arab leader Hussein, Sheik of Mecca, opens a rebellion against the Turks who control Arabia

July	1	First Battle of the Somme begins on the Western Front; it lasts until November 18. Losses on both sides amount to more than 1,260,000 killed or wounded
Sep	15	British first use tanks during the Battle of the Somme
Nov	21	Emperor Franz Joseph of Austria-Hungary dies aged 86
Dec	7	David Lloyd George becomes prime minister, UK
	30	Grigori Rasputin, self-styled "holy man" and adviser to the Czarina of Russia, is murdered by a group of noblemen

ABOVE: Armoured cruisers, or Dreadnoughts, steaming in formation.

MEXICAN REVOLUTION
In Mexico, soldiers of the rebel leader Pancho Villa cross into the USA and kill eighteen Americans working for a mining company. In response, US troops under General Pershing march into Mexico and attack Villa, killing 30 of his men and routing his army.

EASTER RISING
Rebel Irish republicans seize strategic buildings in central Dublin on Easter Sunday and declare an Irish Republic. The British bombard the city to end the rebellion, which spreads to other cities in Ireland, and execute the leaders. As a result, support for Irish independence increases throughout Ireland.

RASPUTIN
In Petrograd, a group of Russian nobles murder Rasputin, the Siberian monk and mystic who has held considerable power over the czar's wife and is blamed for exercising a malign control over affairs of state.

EASTER 1916
The Irish poet WB Yeats (1865–1939), who is already well known, writes the poem "Easter 1916" on the Dublin Easter Rising. The poem is well known for its celebration of Irish nationalist heroes and for its line "A terrible beauty is born". Later, in 1922, after the Anglo-Irish War, Yeats will become a senator in the Irish Free State.

ARAB REVOLT
Arabs rise in revolt against their Ottoman rulers in Hejaz, Saudi Arabia. The revolt is led by Emir Feisal and his son Hussein and is supported from December by Colonel TE Lawrence, a British soldier with close links to the Arab rebels.

BRITISH CONSCRIPTION
In the United Kingdom, the House of Commons agrees to introduce conscription to increase the size of the army. The government has been relying on single men to volunteer, but losses on the Western Front mean that volunteers can no longer be relied upon to ensure the army remains at full strength.

AUSTRO-HUNGARIAN EMPEROR DIES

Franz Josef, Emperor of Austria-Hungary, dies at the age of 86 after ruling his country since 1848. He is succeeded by his grand-nephew, Charles I.

BIRTH OF THE TANK

First trials of a military tank take place in Britain. It is first used in battle on the Somme. The name "tank" is used to confuse German spies. This new weapon of war is an armoured vehicle, which can cross the most difficult terrain and withstand powerful artillery.

PLASTIC SURGERY AND SHELL SHOCK

British surgeon Harold Gillies sets up a plastic surgery unit to deal with 2,000 cases of facial damage after the Battle of the Somme. This year too the term "shell shock" comes into use to describe the psychological disorder caused by battle fatigue and experiences in the trenches. It is often, mistakenly, regarded as a form of cowardice.

SCHEEPVARTHUIS

A striking new building, Scheepvarthuis, has appeared in Amsterdam, Holland. This office building, used by six shipping companies, is built using a concrete shell covered with bricks and reliefs depicting different aspects of sea trade. The nautical theme is continued in the interior and the stained glass. The building is notable for marrying a modern material (concrete) with a striking use of ornament.

DADAISM

In Zurich a group of young artists found the Dada movement, an anti-art movement that has its roots in their protest against the carnage of World War I. They start the Cabaret Voltaire, where they put on bizarre lectures and weird entertainments. They revel in nonsense and the irrational, and many of their number (who include Marcel Duchamp, Jean Arp, and the Romanian poet Tristan Tzara) will later become prominent Surrealists.

UNDER FIRE

French writer Henri Barbusse (1873–1935) publishes *Under Fire*. An anti-war novel, it is based on Barbusse's own experiences at the front. It portrays, unusually for these patriotic times, the squalid side of war and the lives of ordinary men in the trenches.

RELATIVITY

German theoretical physicist Albert Einstein publishes his General Theory of Relativity, which argues that the gravity of a mass (such as a heavenly body) distorts space.

DETERGENTS

German scientist Fritz Gunther develops the first synthetic detergents to replace soap; they prove too harsh for domestic use.

THE PLANETS

British composer Gustav Holst (1874–1934) writes this suite for large orchestra, inspired by his own studies of astrology. Despairing of the chances of such a large-scale work getting performed, he puts the score away. When friends discover the work and have it performed for Holst, the composer's handling of rhythm and orchestral colour will win over both audience and musicians alike.

FIRST GUIDE DOGS

In Austria and Germany the first guide dogs for the blind are trained to help soldiers blinded in battle.

BOEING TAKES OFF

US industrialist William E Boeing (1881–1954) founds the Pacific Aero Products Company, later the Boeing Company, one of the largest aircraft manufacturers.

NO OLYMPICS

The First World War forces the cancellation of the Olympic Games.

BIRTH CONTROL CLINIC

The USA's first birth-control clinic opens in New York, run by Margaret Sanger (1883–1966), a public health nurse. Like the pioneering clinic opened in 1878 in Amsterdam, the Brooklyn clinic is technically illegal. Mrs Sanger was jailed in 1914 for distributing birth-control literature.

FIRST CONGRESSWOMAN

Jeannette Rankin (1880–1975), a worker for women's rights, becomes the first woman to be elected to the US Congress. Her stance on the war in Europe is pacifist, and she will fight for independent citizenship for married women.

NATIONAL PARKS

The National Parks Service is set up by the US government. President Cleveland pioneered the creation of parks and preserves during the nineteenth century. Since 1872 the USA has protected over twenty areas of natural and scientific interest.

HORATIO HERBERT KITCHENER (1850–1916)

Lord Kitchener, the Irish-born British field marshal, has been lost at sea after his ship HMS *Hampshire* was mined off Orkney in June. He was veteran of the Sudan campaign (1883–1885), and commanded British forces in South Africa during the second Boer War (1900–1902) and in India (1902–1909). Appointed British secretary for war in 1914, he was responsible for a highly successful recruitment campaign.

WORLD WAR I

Sometimes called the Great War or "the war to end all wars", World War I is fought in Europe, Africa, the Middle and Far East. On one side are the Central European powers (Germany, Austria-Hungary and allies); on the other are the Triple Entente (Britain and Empire, France, Russia and allies) together with the United States of America, which enters the war in 1917. An estimated 10 million people die and twice that number are wounded.

❖ KEY DATES ❖
WESTERN FRONT 1914–18 FRANCE AND BELGIUM

- **NAMUR August 20–25, 1914.** German heavy artillery including 540 heavy guns batter Belgian fort into surrender, inflicting over 30,000 casualties.
- **MONS August 23–24, 1914.** The British 2nd Corps conducts a fighting withdrawal in the face of heavy German attacks. For losses of 1,600, British marksmen inflict 3,000 casualties on the Germans.
- **FIRST BATTLE OF THE MARNE September 6–8, 1914.** The battle that saves Paris, the Germans commit 44 infantry and 7 cavalry divisions, the Allies 56 infantry and 9 cavalry divisions. German casualties are 200,000, French 250,000 and British 1,071.
- **YPRES October 14–November 11, 1914.** The German offensive. It costs Germany 130,000 casualties, the French 50,000, the British 2,368 officers and 55,768 men, and the Belgians 32,000.
- **YPRES April 22–May 25, 1915.** Germans use poison gas against the British. Its use and subsequent fighting in the salient cause 60,000 Allied casualties and 35,000 German.
- **VERDUN February 21–December 18, 1916.** A grim battle of attrition. The Germans fire 40 million shells. Initially 1,000,000 Germans attack 500,000 French; at the close, the Germans have lost 434,000 and the French 543,000.
- **FIRST BATTLE OF THE SOMME July 1–Nov 18, 1916.** British lose 57,470 men on the first day. By November 18, the Allies have advanced 11km (7mi) over a 32km (20mi) front. The British lose 418,000, the French 195,000 and the Germans 650,000 (killed or wounded).
- **CAMBRAI November 20–December 4, 1917.** The first great tank battle in which 324 tanks are committed and made a 10km (6mi) gap in the German lines. The Germans counter attack and when the fighting is over the British have lost 43,000 including 6,000 prisoners, the Germans 41,000 including 11,000 prisoners.
- **YPRES July 21–November 6, 1917.** A British offensive designed in part to take the pressure off the French. German counter attacks and use of bunkers cause heavy casualties of 400,000 while the Germans suffer 65,000, including 9,000 prisoners.

- **VILLERS-BRETONNEUX April 24, 1918.** The first tank v tank action; three British Mark IV tanks fight a drawn engagement with three German heavy A7Vs.
- **SECOND BATTLE OF THE SOMME March 21–April 4, 1918.** A massive assault by 71 German divisions with 6,000 guns, the Germans advance 64km (40mi) but are halted by exhaustion and lack of supplies. The Allies lose 160,000 battle casualties and 70,000 prisoners, the Germans 150,000 killed or wounded.
- **SECOND BATTLE OF THE MARNE July 15–August 6, 1918.** A major German attack by 52 divisions which is stopped by 36 Allied divisions, French, American, British and Italian. The Germans lose 100,000 the Allies 60,000, including 20,000 dead.

❖ KEY DATES ❖
EASTERN FRONT 1914–17 RUSSIA POLAND, AUSTRIA, HUNGARY, ROMANIA

- **TANNENBERG August 26–30, 1914.** A massive German victory against the Russians. Russian losses 30,000 killed or wounded and 92,000 prisoners. The Germans lose 13,000 killed or wounded.
- **GORLICE-TARNOW April 28–August 5, 1915.** Germany and Austria advance through Poland and the Ukraine. Pounded by heavy artillery the Russians lose one million killed and wounded and one million prisoners as well as huge areas of valuable agricultural land.
- **LAKE NAROTCH March 18, 1916.** After initial successes the Russian infantry are counter attacked and lose more than 80,000 men.

❖ KEY DATES ❖
NAVAL WAR

- **CORONEL November 1, 1914.** Five German cruisers, the *Gneisenau*, *Scharnhorst*, *Nürnberg*, *Dresden* and *Leipzig*, meet and destroy HMS *Good Hope* and HMS *Monmouth*, the smaller faster HMS *Glasgow* is able to escape.
- **FALKANDS December 8, 1914.** HMS *Invincible*, *Inflexible*, *Kent*, *Cornwall*, *Glasgow*, *Bristol*, *Otranto* and *Macedonia* meet and destroy the German squadron that was victorious at the Coronel. Only *Dresden* escapes.
- **DARDANELLES February 19–March 18, 1915.** Abortive Franco-British attempt to force the narrows of the Dardanelles. A combination of mines and coastal batteries sinks three heavy ships and damages three.
- **JUTLAND May 21–June 1, 1916.** Germans lose four cruisers and five destroyers. They claim victory because British navy lose three battle cruisers, three light cruisers and eight destroyers. British claim victory because German fleet does not venture to sea again and the Allied naval blockade of Germany remains intact.

❖ KEY DATES ❖
AIR WAR IN THE WEST 1914–1918

- **August 14, 1914.** First bombing attack of World War I, undertaken by an aircraft of French Aviation Militaire against zeppelin sheds, at Metz-Frescaty.
- **August 30, 1914.** First bombing attack on a capital city, Paris. German Taube drops five bombs and a message; one person killed, two wounded.
- **October 5, 1914.** First aircraft is shot down in air to air combat.
- **April 15–26, 1916.** First aerial re-supply mission, Kut-el-Amara, Mesopotamia. Food, mail, currency, gold, silver and wireless parts are delivered by the RFC and RNAS.
- **April 5–6, 1917.** First British night bombing begins, hitting aircraft hangars at Douai airfield.
- **June 13, 1917.** German Gotha bombers make first and most costly mass bombing raid on London. Fourteen Gotha bombers drop 72 bombs killing 162 and injuring 432 people.

❖ KEY DATES ❖
MEDITERRANEAN AND MIDDLE EAST 1914–18 EGYPT, PALESTINE AND MESOPOTAMIA

- **GALLIPOLI April 25, 1915–January 16, 1916.** Amphibious landing on the Turkish coast which through British mismanagement fails to block the narrows of the Dardanelles. After heavy fighting the Allies are obliged to withdraw. Allied casualties: 252,000; Turkish casualties 251,000, including 66,000 deaths.
- **KUT-EL-AMARA December 8, 1915–April 29, 1916.** Initial British successes are followed by a decision to fortify and hold Kut, leading to a siege and British defeat. 10,000 starving and sick survivors surrender to the Turks.
- **ISONZO RIVER (Italian Front) June 23, 1915–October 1917.** Eleven battles in all. Italian troops launch attacks against Austrian positions on the Isonzo River. Four battles fought in 1915 cost the Italians 66,000 killed, 185,000 wounded, and 22,000 taken prisoner, for no real gains.
- **GAZA March 26–7, April 17–19, 1917.**
- **CAPORETTO October 24–November 12, 1917.** Seven German and eight Austrian divisions attack General Capello's mutinous 2nd Italian army. The Italians are driven back to the Brenta valley. At Caporetto, and subsequently, Italians lose 40,000 killed and wounded.
- **JERUSALEM December 11, 1917.** General Allenby enters Jerusalem following the defeat of the Turks at Nebi Samwil ridge. He guarantees religious toleration to all.
- **WADI FARA 1918.** First major fighter ground attack victory.
- **VITTORIO VENETO October 24–November 4, 1918.** Italians with 57 divisions and 7,700 guns attack the Austrians with 52 divisions and 6,000 guns. Italians, with British and French assistance, force crossings over the Piave and capture Vittorio Veneto. Victory leads to the collapse of the Austro-Hungarian empire. Austrians lose 5,000 guns and 300,000 prisoners; Italian casualties: 36,000.

WAR AND REVOLUTION

The United States enters the war on the Allied side. A revolution occurs in Russia that ends with the Bolsheviks victorious and the setting up of the world's first Communist state. Its effects will be felt for most of the century. In science too, a development occurs that will dominate the century: Rutherford splits the atom, paving the way for the nuclear age.

OPPOSITE TOP: French soldiers making a gas and flame attack on German trenches in Flanders.

OPPOSITE BELOW: Australian troops being treated at a dressing station near Ypres.

1917

Jan	10	William F Cody, better known as Buffalo Bill, dies
Feb	3	The USA severs diplomatic relations with Germany
Mar	8	Count Ferdinand von Zeppelin, airship designer, dies aged 78 Revolution breaks out in Russia
	14	Provisional government set up in Russia
	15	Russia's ruler Czar Nicholas II abdicates
	16–17	German U-boats sink three US ships
Apr	6	USA declares war on Germany
	16	With German help, Bolshevik revolutionary Vladimir Lenin returns to Russia after 10 years in exile
June	24	First American soldiers land in France

July	16	Alexander Kerensky becomes prime minister of Russia
	31	On the Western Front, Battle of Passchendaele begins in a sea of mud; it lasts until November 10
Sep	17	Germany captures Riga
Nov	2	Balfour Declaration: UK Foreign Secretary Arthur Balfour promises the Jews a homeland in Palestine
	7	"October Revolution" in Russia; Lenin and Bolsheviks seize power
	17	French sculptor Auguste Rodin dies aged 77
	20	Ukraine declares itself a republic
Dec	6	Finland declares independence from Russia
	15	Russia signs an armistice with Germany

UKRAINE AND FINLAND INDEPENDENT

As a result of the Russian Revolution, Ukraine declares itself a republic and breaks away from Russia. Finland follows the next month, and is recognized by the new Russian government as an independent state.

US ENTERS THE WAR

In April, the United States enters the war on the Allied side against Germany. President Wilson declares that "the world must be made safe for democracy". US resources, including shipbuilding and steel production, are put to work for the war effort as thousands of troops prepare to sail for Europe.

WOMEN'S WAR WORK

British and French women sign up for war work in munitions factories, agriculture, transport, and the auxiliary military units from 1915, and American women after April 1917. In the USA and Britain especially, their contribution softens attitudes to women's emancipation.

JEWISH HOMELAND

Arthur Balfour, British Foreign Secretary, issues a declaration promising the Jews a homeland of their own in Palestine. The British government hopes that the declaration will lead to Jewish support for the war effort.

DE STIJL

Dutch painter, poet, and architect Theo van Doesburg (1883–1931) founds the magazine De Stijl (the style). The De Stijl artists (including Mondrian and Gerrit Rietveld) embrace a theory of art that can also be applied to painting, architecture, and the decorative arts. They use primary colours and right angles, and reject art that takes its inspiration from nature.

RADIOACTIVE ELEMENT FOUND

Two teams of scientists independently discover the element protactinium, a radioactive metal; they are Otto Hahn (1879–1968) and Lise Meitner (1878–1968) of Germany, and Frederick Soddy and John Cranston of Britain.

MATA HARI SHOT

Mata Hari is executed in France as a spy. She was Netherlands-born Margaretha Geertruida Zelle, who, after divorcing her Scottish husband became a dancer in Paris. In 1907 she joined the German secret service and betrayed military secrets confided by unsuspecting Allied officers.

DETERGENT

The first artificial detergent, called Nekal, is produced commercially in Germany during World War I for washing clothes, to conserve soap for other purposes. Synthetic chemical detergents wash clothes cleaner than soap.

HILAIRE GERMAIN EDGAR DEGAS (1834–1917)

Edgar Degas, the French Impressionist painter and sculptor, dies at the age of 83. His paintings and pastel work portray the movement and line of horses and their riders, circus artists and ballet dancers. Among his best-known and best-loved works are Absinthe (1876–1877), Dancer Lacing her Shoe (1878) and Miss Lola at the Cirque Fernando (1879).

HUGE TELESCOPE

American astronomer George E Hale (1868–1938) instals a 2.54m (3yd) refracting telescope at Mount Wilson Observatory in California, of which he is director. Hale's telescope is the world's largest to date.

SPLITTING THE ATOM

British scientist Ernest Rutherford (1871–1937) bombards nitrogen atoms and breaks up the nucleus, thus becoming the first person to split the atom. He does not publish his results until 1919 but his achievement will have enormous and long-lasting implications.

SONAR BEGINS

French physicist Paul Langevin (1872–1946) invents a method of detecting sound under water; it is later developed as sonar (an acronym of Sound Navigation And Ranging) and used for locating submarines.

FIRST AIRMAIL STAMP

Italy issues the first airmail stamp in May by overprinting a 25 centime express letter stamp with ESPERIMENTO POSTA AEREA MAGGIO 1917 TORINO-ROMA-ROMA-TORINO.

BOBBED HAIR

A short haircut known as the bob, pioneered by Irene Castle, is adopted for safety by women workers in munitions factories and becomes the latest fashion in hairstyles.

DIXIELAND JAZZ

The Original Dixieland Jazz Band makes its first recording: The Darktown Strutters' Ball.

NAIL VARNISH

Transparent liquid nail varnish is first manufactured by Cutex.

RUSSIAN REVOLUTION

Czar Nicholas II (1868–1918) abdicates in March as revolution breaks out across Russia. Discontent with the unpopular war against Germany and Austria, high loss of life on the Eastern Front, and food shortages at home combine to weaken the czar's authority. A provisional government is set up after the czar's brother refuses to accept the throne. In July, the Bolshevik party, led by Vladimir Ilych Lenin (1870–1924), fails to take power in Russia after an abortive coup. Lenin flees in disgrace and Alexander Kerensky (1881–1970), a socialist member of the Duma and Minister of War in the provisional government, becomes prime minister. He promises to continue the war against Germany. In November (October in the Russian calendar) the Bolsheviks overthrow the provisional government of Alexander Kerensky and seize power in a bloodless coup. The Bolsheviks promise "Peace, land, bread, and all power to the Soviets". The new government, led by Lenin, opens peace negotiations with the Germans.

ABOVE: The luxurious lifestyle of the czars clashed with the deep poverty experienced by most Russians.

ABOVE: During the Revolution of 1917 important buildings were protected from damage and looting.

ABOVE: Crowds outside the Winter Palace, St Petersburg, scene of the revolution.

RIGHT: The ex-Czar Nicholas II, in exile under guard, the last of the Russian royals this century.

PEACE COMES AND EUROPE IS REDRAWN

Germany surrenders and World War I ends. Post-war peace settlements involve the break-up of the old Austro-Hungarian empire and redraw the map of Europe. In Russia, the Romanovs are shot and civil war breaks out as the Bolsheviks fight to protect the revolution. Women in Britain gain the vote. Airmail services begin in the US.

1918

Jan	**9**	US President Woodrow Wilson lists fourteen points for US war aims
Mar	**3**	Russia signs Treaty of Brest-Litovsk with Germany
	21	Germans begin series of three offensives on Western Front
Apr	**22**	German flying ace, the "Red Baron", is shot during the Second Battle of the Somme
July	**16**	In Russia, Bolsheviks execute Czar Nicholas and his family
Sep	**26**	Final Allied offensive begins on the Western Front
Nov	**3**	Austria signs an armistice with the Allies
	9	After riots in Germany, Kaiser Wilhelm II abdicates and Germany becomes a republic
	11	World War I ends Austria's Emperor Karl abdicates
	13	Austria and Hungary are declared republics

ABOVE: VAD nurses celebrate the end of the carnage.

OPPOSITE: The guns fall silent at last on the eleventh hour of the eleventh month, 1918.

126

WILSON'S 14 PEACE POINTS

In a speech to Congress, in January, US President Wilson sets out fourteen points for a peace settlement. Among them are the break-up of Austria-Hungary, the independence of Poland, and the establishment of an international organization to guarantee the independence and integrity of all nations.

RUSSIA OUT OF THE WAR

Germany and Russia sign a peace treaty at Brest-Litovsk in Poland, which takes Russia out of the war. Russia is forced to cede Poland and the Baltic states to Germany and large areas of the Caucasus to the Ottoman Empire, as well as recognize the independence of Ukraine. The treaty allows Germany to transfer its large armies to the Western Front.

CZAR SHOT

As Russia collapses into civil war, the former Russian czar, Nicholas II, and his family are shot by the Bolsheviks to prevent them falling into counter-revolutionary hands. The Bolsheviks organize a Red Army under Leon Trotsky (1879–1940), Commissar for War, to fight for the revolution.

WAR ENDS

As Germany collapses, Kaiser Wilhelm II flees into exile in the Netherlands. On November 11, Germany and the Allies finally sign a peace treaty. The Ottoman Empire and Austria also sue for peace. After more than four years of bitter fighting, World War I comes to an end. As an approximate estimate, more than ten million people have been killed.

NEW NATIONS

Following peace settlements, four new nations emerge out of the old multinational Austro-Hungarian empire. Austria and Hungary become independent republics, as does Czechoslovakia. The South Slavs form a new kingdom, later called Yugoslavia, which is ruled by King Peter of Serbia, who led his country to victory in the war.

WINNING THE VOTE

After a 67-year struggle, women in Britain finally gain the vote. New legislation gives the vote to women over the age of 30 and men over 21.

WILFRED OWEN
(1893–1918)

The young English poet Wilfred Owen is killed in action just one week before the end of World War I. His friend, the poet Siegfried Sassoon, will collect his unpublished work, for publication in 1920. Owen's famous poems "Dulce et Decorum Est" and "Anthem for Doomed Youth" are heartfelt appeals against war and its brutality.

ACHILLE-CLAUDE DEBUSSY
(1862–1918)

Claude Debussy has died after a long battle with cancer. The Parisian composer was responsible for the creation of musical Impressionism and has had a strong influence on contemporary composers. His works include the orchestral tone poem *Le Mer* (1905), chamber music, piano pieces, and many lovely song settings.

THE TWELVE

Set in St Petersburg during the Bolshevik revolution, "The Twelve", a poem by Russian poet Alexander Blok, describes a group of twelve Red Guards. A tribute to the revolution that uses techniques as diverse as folk songs and revolutionary slogans, the work portrays the revolutionaries as if they were the Apostles of Christ.

CALLIGRAMMES

The second of French writer Guillaume Apollinaire's two volumes of verse, *Calligrammes*, is published (the first was *Les Alcools*, 1913). It develops the technique of making the physical shape of the poems match their content. Thus rain is depicted in type that pours vertically down the page, and typography mirrors the shapes of field guns and cathedrals.

THREE-COLOUR LIGHTS

Three-colour traffic lights, with an amber phase between green and red, are introduced in England and in New York City.

SUPERHET RADIO

The superheterodyne (or "superhet") radio receiver is invented by US army major and electrical engineer Edwin Armstrong (1890–1954). It makes radios easier to tune. Subsequently, all radios will work on this principle.

AUSTRALIAN RADIO LINK

Using Morse code, the first-ever radio link is made between Britain and Australia.

FOOD MIXER

The universal food mixer and beater is invented by the Universal Company of America. It consists of a bowl and two beaters powered by electricity.

SUPREMATIST COMPOSITION

With his painting *White on White*, Russian artist Malevich takes his Suprematist style to its logical conclusion, painting white shapes on a white background. The work becomes the symbol of extreme modernism in painting.

RIGHT: Women take up heavy work in wartime.

ABOVE: Black American soldier getting ready for action. Over 116,000 US troops die.

RIGHT: The Red Baron, Manfred von Richthofen, the German air ace killed in action this year.

AFTERMATH OF WAR

ABOVE: Destroyed bridge over the River Meuse at Namur, Belgium.

ABOVE: Ruined fortifications near Liège, Belgium.

ABOVE: Paris, devastated by heavy artillery.

ABOVE: German POWs in a French camp.

BELOW: Passchendaele — a barren sea of mud.

PEACE OF PARIS AND THE WEIMAR REPUBLIC

The League of Nations is set up by a world temporarily sickened by the carnage of war. The Treaty of Versailles imposes reparations on Germany. In Germany, a new constitution establishes the Weimar Republic. In Italy, Mussolini founds the Fascist Party. British troops fire on Sikhs in the town of Amritsar and war breaks out between British India and Afghanistan. Aviators Alcock and Brown make the first transatlantic flight.

OPPOSITE: French tennis star Suzanne Lenglen wins the Ladies' Singles at Wimbledon.

1919

Jan	5	Spartacist uprising begins in Berlin; it is quickly suppressed
	6	Former US President Theodore Roosevelt dies aged 60
	18	Peace conference begins at Versailles, near Paris
	21	Sinn Fein MPs set up an unofficial "parliament" in Dublin
Feb	6	Bolsheviks capture Kiev, Ukraine
	14	The League of Nations is founded
	14	Bolsheviks invade Estonia
	20	Emir of Afghanistan murdered
Mar	23	Italian journalist Benito Mussolini founds the Fascist Party
Apr	13	British troops massacre 379 unarmed rioters at Amritsar, India
May	3	War begins between British India and Afghanistan
June	15	Aviators Alcock and Brown complete the first non-stop flight across the Atlantic Ocean
	28	Peace of Paris between Germany and the Allies is signed at Versailles
July	5	French tennis star Suzanne Lenglen wins the Ladies' Singles at Wimbledon
	13	British airship R-34 completes the first two-way Atlantic flight
	31	The Weimar Republic is founded in Germany
Aug	8	Afghanistan achieves independence
Oct	7	Dutch airline KLM is founded
Nov	3	French artist Pierre-Auguste Renoir dies aged 78
	15	Red Army captures Omsk

ABOVE: Captain John Alcock (left) and Lieutenant Arthur Brown (right) after their successful transatlantic flight. Alcock describes the historic journey as "terrible".

SPARTACIST UPRISING

A Communist uprising by Spartacist revolutionaries against the new German government is crushed. Its two main leaders, Karl Liebknecht and "Red" Rosa Luxemburg, are both shot.

SINN FEIN

The 73 members of parliament elected in the British general election of December 1918 to represent Sinn Féin, a republican party, set up their own Dáil Éireann, or parliament, in Dublin. The rebel parliament forms its own government in opposition to the British.

TREATY OF VERSAILLES

In June, Germany and the Allies sign a peace treaty in the Palace of Versailles, outside Paris. The treaty has 400 clauses and strips Germany of much of its territory. Germany is forced to pay reparations to the Allies, and to demilitarize the Rhineland. British prime minister, David Lloyd-George (1863–1945), considers the treaty too tough and predicts that it will cause another war within 25 years.

LEAGUE OF NATIONS

Allied nations meeting in Paris to agree a peace settlement in Europe hold the first meeting of the League of Nations. President Wilson of the USA presides. The peace conference later agrees the covenant which establishes this new international body.

FASCIST PARTY SET UP

An Italian journalist, Benito Mussolini (1883–1945), who broke with the Socialist Party at the outbreak of war, forms *Fasci di Combattimento*, a nationalistic party later described as fascist.

AMRITSAR MASSACRE

British troops, led by General Dyer, open fire on unarmed demonstrators in the holy Sikh city of Amritsar. The massacre follows several days of rioting caused by a business strike against new security laws and prompts widespread protests against British rule in India.

WEIMAR REPUBLIC

A new constitution is agreed in the German city of Weimar, establishing a republic and an all-powerful presidency. The new constitution is opposed by the extreme left and right parties.

THIRD AFGHAN WAR

Fighting breaks out between Britain and Afghanistan as Afghanistan, under Emir Amanullah Khan, objects to British intervention in Afghan affairs. After some skirmishes between British and Afghan troops, Afghanistan's sovereignty is recognized.

REDS AND WHITES

Civil war continues in Russia between the Bolshevik Red Army and the so-called Whites, or counter-revolutionaries. After nearly two years' fighting, by November the Red Army has taken Omsk and looks set to win the war.

SMALL-TOWN STORIES

American writer Sherwood Anderson (1876–1941) brings the lives, longings and frustrations of small-town Americans into the public gaze with his collection of linked stories, *Winesburg, Ohio*.

J'ACCUSE

This anti-war film is the first major work by French director Abel Gance (1889–1981). It is successful, and launches the director on a series of epics, perhaps the most famous of which will be *Napoléon vu par Abel Gance* (1927). Gance becomes known for his innovative use of wide- and split-screen techniques.

THE CABINET OF DR CALIGARI

Starring Conrad Veidt and Werner Krauss, *The Cabinet of Dr Caligari* by German director Robert Wiene (1881–1938), is a remarkable example of Expressionism. Narrated by a madman, the film portrays a series of murders carried out by a sleep-walker at the suggestions of a mad mountebank. Its use of projected light patterns gives the film a particular horror.

FLYING THE ATLANTIC

In May the US Navy flying boat NC-4, commanded by Lieutenant Commander AC Read, makes the first transatlantic flight from Rockaway, New York, to Plymouth, England. Read stops seven times — Chatham, Mass.; Halifax, Nova Scotia; Trepassy Bay, Newfoundland; Horta, Azores; Ponta Delgarda, Azores; Lisbon, Portugal; and Ferrol del Caudillo, Spain. The flight takes 23 days. One month later, two Britons, Captain John Alcock and Lieutenant Arthur Whitten-Brown, make the first non-stop Atlantic flight in a converted Vickers Vimy bomber, from St John's, Newfoundland to Clifden, Co. Galway, Ireland. Their time is 16 hours 12 minutes. And in July, the British airship R-34 makes the first lighter-than-air crossing of the Atlantic — twice: first from Scotland to New York, and second from New York to Norfolk, England. The distance totals 10,187km (6,316mi) and the time for this first-ever double crossing is 183 hours 8 minutes.

FIRST WOMAN MP

The first woman to take her seat in the British House of Commons is American-born Nancy Astor — sister of the ideal American woman, the Gibson Girl — now MP for the Plymouth constituency.

LITTERATURE

The French writer André Breton (1896–1966), with Louis Aragon and Phillippe Soupault, founds the influential magazine, *Littérature*. It will become an organ of the Surrealist movement, publishing the first example of "automatic writing" in 1920.

KLM FOUNDED

The Royal Dutch Airline, KLM, is founded in October.

PIERRE AUGUST RENOIR (1841–1919)

The French Impressionist painter, Pierre Renoir, who pioneered painting outdoors to capture the effects of light, has died. His Impressionist works *Moulin de la Galette* (1876) and *The Umbrellas* (1883) are typical of his style from 1874–1884, although in later years his work becomes more formal.

ABOVE: The Vickers Vimy plane, which had carried Alcock and Brown safely across the Atlantic, grounded in a bog in Ireland.

TENNIS FASHION

Frenchwoman Suzanne Lenglen (1899–1938) ushers in a new era for women's tennis with the first of her six Wimbledon singles titles. The "Empress of the Courts" wears loose one-piece dresses when heavy outfits with collars and cuffs, and petticoats were the normal attire.

CURE FOR SLEEPING SICKNESS

American scientist Louise Pearce discovers tryparsamide, a compound that cures sleeping sickness.

WEBER DISAGREES WITH MARX

Max Weber (1864–1920), German social scientist and author of *The Protestant Ethic* and the *Spirit of Capitalism*, becomes Professor of Sociology at Munich University. He supports a scientific approach to social science, but disagrees with Marx that economics alone determines social action — he emphasizes the effects of cultural factors, such as religion, on economic development.

PROTO-RADAR

British physicist Robert Watson-Watt (1892–1973) patents his "radiolocator", a device for locating aircraft or ships. Later it develops into radar.

POETIC JUSTICE

Italian poet and airman Gabriele D'Annunzio (1863–1938) seizes the small city of Fiume (modern Trieste) in Dalmatia on behalf of Italy. Supported by a force of 300 volunteers, he drives out the Allied government representatives and sets himself up as a dictator.

THE JAZZ AGE

The decade of the twenties reaps the whirlwind of World War I. People seem determined to live faster and more furiously. Fashions, hair, music and the arts become thoroughly modern, the change particularly affecting women. Travel becomes easier as ships and aeroplanes make the globe a smaller place. The economic consequences of war are felt at the end of the decade when financial depression engendered in Wall Street sweeps across the USA and then the rest of the world, making the ground fertile for unrest and further conflict.

OPPOSITE: The Wall Street Crash triggers panic and global economic depression.

1920–1929

KEY EVENTS OF THE DECADE

- PROHIBITION IN USA
- CHINESE COMMUNIST PARTY ESTABLISHED
- IRISH FREE STATE ESTABLISHED
- MUSSOLINI SEIZES POWER
- RUSSIA BECOMES THE USSR
- FIRST NAZI RALLY IN GERMANY
- SURREALIST MANIFESTO PUBLISHED
- STALIN RISES TO POWER
- SCOPES TRIAL IN USA

- SAUDI ARABIA ESTABLISHED
- BAUHAUS BUILT
- LINDBERGH FLIES THE ATLANTIC
- *THE JAZZ SINGER* HITS THE SCREEN
- MICKEY MOUSE IS BORN
- PENICILLIN DISCOVERED
- WALL STREET CRASH
- ZEPPELIN FLIES ROUND WORLD

WORLD POPULATION: 1,834 MILLION

THE TWENTIES START ROARING

The twenties kick off with prohibition in the USA. Banning the manufacture and sale of alcohol leads to an unprecedented crimewave. The Treaty of Trianon redraws the map of Europe and the former Ottoman Empire is split into protectorates policed by France and Britain. The Netherlands begins a literal expansion plan, reclaiming land from the Zuider Zee. Marcus Garvey raises black consciousness in the USA, establishing the Universal Negro Improvement Association. In Czechoslovakia, the robot is born.

OPPOSITE: Civic guards take a break during street demonstrations in Berlin.

1920

Jan	16	Prohibition (of alcohol) goes into force in the USA	July	9	Greek forces, with UK approval, capture Bursa in Asian Turkey
Feb	20	US polar explorer Robert Peary dies aged 63	Aug	10	Treaty of Sèvres robs Turkey of 80 per cent of the Ottoman Empire
				14	Olympic Games open in Belgium Little Entente between Czechoslovakia and Yugoslavia
Apr	7	French troops occupy Germany's Ruhr			
	25	League of Nations awards Middle East mandates to UK and France	Nov	16	Civil war in Russia ends after three years QANTAS airline set up in Australia
May	16	Pope Benedict declares Joan of Arc a saint		21	In Ireland the IRA kills fourteen British soldiers, the first "Bloody Sunday"
June	4	Treaty of Trianon redraws the map of Eastern Europe	Dec	10	Woodrow Wilson (1856–1924) is awarded the Nobel Prize for peace

MANDATES FOR FRANCE AND GREAT BRITAIN
In April, at San Remo, Italy, the League of Nations gives France a mandate over Syria and Lebanon, and Britain a mandate over Iraq and Palestine, all former Ottoman territories. Britain is thus free to abide by the Balfour Declaration of 1917 and allow Jews to settle in Palestine.

PEACE WITH TURKEY
In August, at Sèvres, France, a peace treaty is signed with the former Ottoman Empire, which cuts it back to one-fifth of its former size. The treaty is opposed by Turkey, which resents giving land to the Greeks.

END OF RUSSIAN CIVIL WAR
In November, the Red Army, under Trotsky, wins its final battle against counter-revolutionary forces in the Crimea, bringing an end to the three-year-old Russian civil war.

SOUND ON FILM
American scientist Lee de Forest invents a system of recording synchronized sound on a separate track on cinema film, to be "read" by a photo-electric cell.

THE TREATY OF TRIANON

In June, the Treaty of Trianon (Paris) is signed with Hungary, redrawing the map of Eastern Europe. Former Hungarian lands are divided between Czechoslovakia, Poland, Austria, Yugoslavia, and Italy, leaving Hungary a third of its former size. The treaty follows on from Versailles, St Germain and Neuilly, which together have settled the frontiers of Germany and Austria-Hungary.

THE LITTLE ENTENTE

In August, Yugoslavia and Czechoslovakia sign a treaty of friendship known as the Little Entente. Romania will join in April 1921. The countries are united in their desire to keep the current borders in Eastern Europe and not to allow any revival of the Hapsburg empire in either Austria or Hungary.

THE AGE OF INNOCENCE

The greatest book of the American writer Edith Wharton (1861–1937) is a study of American high society at the turn of the century, showing how human values such as love can be destroyed by the obligation to stick to outdated moral codes. In it Wharton condemns people "who dreaded scandal more than disease, who placed decency above courage".

BELOW: Prohibition starts and teams are sent to dismantle bars and drinking clubs all over America.

THE INKBLOT TEST

Swiss psychiatrist, Hermann Rorschach (1884–1922), develops a test by which the personality, intelligence and emotional stability of patients can be assessed by analysing their interpretations of random patterns made by inkblots.

BONJOUR CHERI

In the first of her mature novels, the French writer Colette (Sidonie Gabrielle Colette, 1873–1954) describes a liaison between a young man and an older woman. *Chéri* will be followed by many other books, remarkable for their vivid evocations of sights, sounds, and smells, and for their frank depictions of the lives of women in the France of her time.

QANTAS TAKES TO THE AIR

Queensland and Northern Territory Aerial Service (QANTAS) is set up as Australia's commercial airline on November 16.

BLACK POWER

Marcus Garvey, Jamaican editor of *The Negro World* published in New York, leads the first meeting of the Universal Negro Improvement Association (UNIA) in August. On the agenda for discussion by 3,000 delegates from across the USA is a bill of rights for Negroes.

BABE RUTH SOLD

In January, the Boston Red Sox sell Babe Ruth to the New York Yankees for $125,000 in the most infamous transaction in American sports history. After the sale the Red Sox will never win baseball's World Series — attributed to the "Curse of the Bambino" — while the Yankees will become the most successful team ever.

HUGH SELWYN MAUBERLEY

Mauberley, a collection of linked poems by the American poet Ezra Pound (1885–1972), describes the literary life of London just after World War I. For its classical, ironical style, its compression of language, and its use of allusion, it quickly becomes one of the most influential works of the modern movement in literature.

THE SEVENTH OLYMPIC GAMES

In August, the Seventh Olympiad is staged in Antwerp, Belgium. It is the sixth actually held, as there were no Games in 1916. The Olympic flag of five linked rings, symbolizing the continents, is used for the first time. American diver Aileen Riggin became the youngest winner at fourteen.

LAND FROM THE SEA

The Wieringen Polder, the greatest-ever land reclamation scheme, begins in the Netherlands. Embankments built from over 32,000 cu m (1,000,000 cu ft) of earth taken from the Zuider Zee will join north Holland to the Island of Wieringen, and that to Friesland.

THE TATLIN MONUMENT

Soviet artist Vladimir Tatlin (1885–1953) designs this great project, a construction which evokes technology and social progress in an upward-spiralling form containing cylinders and a glass pyramid. Although the monument is never built, and is known only in the form of a model, it is a lasting symbol of the kind of art embraced by the Soviet Union in its early years.

RUR: THE BIRTH OF THE ROBOT

Karel Capek's play (the initials stand for Rossum's Universal Robots) introduces the word "robot" into the vocabulary. The robots are part of an anti-utopia, in which people try to use machines to improve their lot, but the machines are so effective that they take over and dominate their creators.

RADIO CONTACT

The first US commercial broadcasting station, Pittsburgh KDKA, begins regular weekly broadcasts in November by announcing the Harding-Cox presidential election results. The new station, run by the Westinghouse Co., is also opening in France, Germany and Argentina.

ENTER THE TOMMY-GUN

US gunsmith John T Thompson patents a sub-machine gun, which later becomes known as the tommy-gun.

OLIVE SCHREINER
(1855–1920)

The writer, pacifist and feminist Olive Schreiner whose husband was persuaded to take her name when they married (in 1894), has died. Born of a German father and English mother in South Africa, where she spent most of her life, she published her first book *The Story of an African Farm* (1883) under the name Ralph Iron. Works under her own name include *Trooper Peter Halket* (1897) and *Woman and Labour* (1911).

NO MORE DRINKING

On January 16 it becomes illegal to manufacture, sell and transport intoxicating liquor in the USA when the Volstead Act, the Eighteenth Amendment to the US Constitution ratified on January 29, 1919, comes into effect.

LEGAL ABORTION

Abortion becomes legal for the first time in a modern European state, in legislation introduced in Russia. Since 1918 the new Bolshevik government has made marriage a civil ceremony, facilitated divorce, and introduced free maternity care. The new Czechoslovakia also legalizes abortion this year.

A NEW SAINT

Pope Benedict XV declares Joan of Arc a saint.

ROBERT EDWIN PEARY (1856–1920)

The American naval commander and explorer Robert Edwin Peary, believed to be the first man to reach the North Pole, in 1909, and veteran of eight Arctic expeditions, has died. The region of Greenland, Peary Land, is named in his honour.

BELOW: A nail bomb explodes outside the US Assay Office in Wall Street, under the gaze of George Washington. Over 300 people are injured and 35 killed, but no perpetrator is ever found.

THE RISE OF FASCISM AND COMMUNISM

There is mutiny and economic collapse in Russia. In China, the young Mao Zedong helps to establish Communism. The Irish Free State is ratified, dividing the island. Greece and Turkey are at war. Marie Stopes introduces birth control to the UK. In the USA, heavyweight Jack Dempsey knocks out Georges Carpentier and Band-aid is invented. The lie detector is introduced and the first woman priest ordained. In Italy, Mussolini becomes Il Duce and Enrico Caruso sings his last.

OPPOSITE: Crowds outside the Kremlin display religious icons as well as red flags.

1 9 2 1

Jan	6	Release of *The Kid*, Charlie Chaplin's first feature film
	21	Tanks patrol Dublin in search for IRA snipers
Mar	12	Lenin relaxes strict controls on Russia's economy
	17	Russia's Red Army crushes anti-Bolshevik rebellion at Kronstadt naval base
Apr	12	President Warren Harding says USA will not join the League
June	22	In Ireland King George V opens the first Ulster parliament
	30	First meeting of China's Communist Party is held
July	2	First $1 million "gate" at a boxing match
	10	Outer Mongolia gains independence from China
Aug	3	Italian tenor Enrico Caruso dies at 48
	5	Mustafa Kemal becomes virtual ruler of Turkey
Nov	5	Crown Prince Hirohito of Japan becomes regent for his father
	7	Benito Mussolini becomes head of Italy's National Fascist Party with the title of Il Duce, "the Leader"
Dec	7	Peace in Ireland: 26 southern counties become independent, six northern counties stay in the UK
	10	Albert Einstein wins Nobel Prize for physics
	16	French composer Camille Saint-Saëns dies at 86

MUTINY AND ECONOMIC COLLAPSE IN RUSSIA

In March, Russian sailors mutiny at the Kronstadt naval base (Petrograd, once St Petersburg) in protest at the new Communist government's policies. The sailors are demanding free elections and other reforms. The mutiny shakes the government, as the sailors were previously in the forefront of the revolution.

At the same time, in Moscow, Lenin announces to the Communist Party Congress that he is relaxing controls over the economy, ending state planning and encouraging private enterprise. The move is forced on Lenin because of the collapse in the economy as a result of the civil war.

CHINA TURNS RED

In July, the Chinese Communist Party holds its first meeting, electing Chen Duxiu, a Beijing university professor, as its first president. Among its founder members is Mao Zedong.

EINSTEIN TOWER, POTSDAM

Designed by German Erich Mendelsohn (1887–1953), this building houses an observatory and laboratory. It is designed in a wholly "plastic" form, consisting almost completely of curves, which owes nothing to previous styles. The original intention was for the building to be constructed from poured concrete, but it is actually built of brick covered with cement.

A FREE STATE FOR IRELAND

In December, Irish Republican negotiators finally agree a settlement with the British government, setting up an independent Free State in the south of Ireland. The British government decided in 1920 to divide Ireland, offering home rule to both the Catholic and Republican south and to the Protestant and Unionist north, but the south refused to accept limited home rule. The settlement comes after three years of vicious civil war in the south.

PROKOFIEV'S FIRST HIT

Russian composer Sergei Prokofiev (1891–1955) sees the première of his Piano Concerto No. 3, one of the most important (and most popular) of the works from his early Russian period. It helps establish him as a composer with his own distinctive style.

A MILLION-DOLLAR GATE

In July, Jack "The Idol" Dempsey knocks out Frenchman Georges "The Orchid Kid" Carpentier in front of 80,000 fans. The heavyweight championship bout is the first million-dollar gate in boxing and boosts boxing's popularity enormously.

FAST FIRST AID

Band-aid, the first stick-on bandage, is introduced in the USA by Johnson & Johnson.

LEFT: Mountaineer Captain Finch nears the summit of Mont Blanc, the giant of the French Alps.

ABOVE: President of the Irish Republic Eamonn de Valera, invited by Lloyd George to try to answer the Irish Question.

WAR IN THE AEGEAN

In January, war breaks out between Greece and Turkey with the Greeks invading western Anatolia, on the shores of the Aegean Sea. Fighting between the two countries continues in the region, which is home to many thousands of ethnic Greeks into 1922.

FIRST LIE DETECTOR

US medical student John Larson invents the world's first lie detector, which shows by means of heart rate, breathing rate and blood pressure if a subject is under stress when not telling the truth.

A HOUSEBOAT IN AMSTERDAM

Dutch architect Michel de Klerk, a member of the Amsterdam School, designs Het Scheep housing complex, notable for its decorative use of brickwork, tiling, and a variety of window shapes and glazing arrangements. Its nickname, meaning "the ship", derives from its wedge shape.

BIRTH CONTROL IN THE UK

In March Marie Stopes (1880–1958), opens the UK's first birth control clinic in London amid great opposition from the Establishment. In 1918 she published *Married Love*, the first sex education manual, and *Wise Parenthood*, which advocated birth control and sex education for women.

ABOVE: Georges Carpentier wilts under the onslaught of champion Jack Dempsey.

BELOW: Suzanne Lenglen and partner play to victory in the Wimbledon Mixed Doubles.

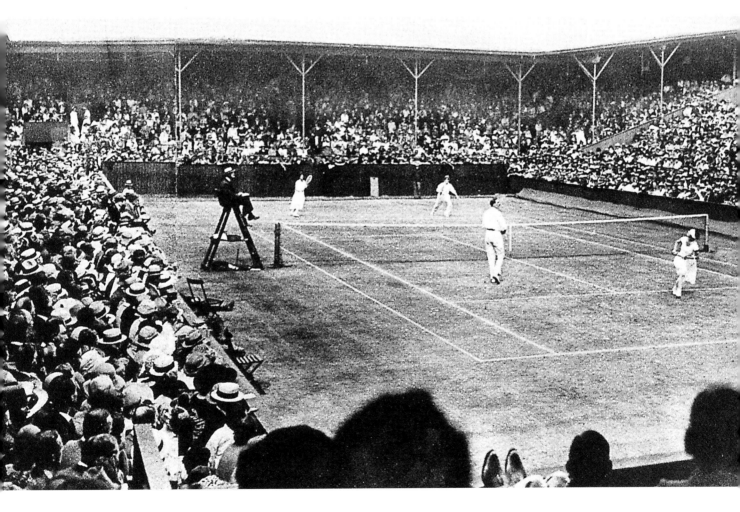

US COAST TO COAST
In February Lieutenant William D Coney of the US Air Service makes the first coast-to-coast flight across North America, from California to Florida.

FIRST EXPRESSWAY
The world's first express highway, the Avus Autobahn, is opened in Berlin, foreshadowing the Autobahn network to be built in the 1930s.

ENRICO CARUSO
(1873–1921)

The world-renowned Italian tenor Enrico Caruso has died in Naples. He leaves a wealth of gramophone recordings to ensure that his voice will be appreciated by future generations. His first performance was in Naples in 1895, and international fame came in 1902 when he sang in *La Bohème* with Dame Nelly Melba at Monte Carlo. He made over 600 appearances at the Met in New York, where he held his final performance on Christmas Eve 1920, and he sang some 40 roles.

ABOVE: Queen Wilhemina of the Netherlands, Prince Hendrik and Princess Juliana make an informal canal tour of their country.

FIRST WOMAN PRIEST
Rev. Antoinette Brown Blackwell becomes the first woman to be ordained in the Anglican Church in the USA.

LYSOZYME DISCOVERED
Scottish bacteriologist Alexander Fleming (1881–1955) discovers the existence of lysozyme, an enzyme present in saliva, tears, and nasal mucus, which helps to kill bacteria naturally, and so prevent infection.

SEXUAL REFORM
The World League for Sexual Reform is set up in Berlin by Magnus Hirschfeld, a homosexual doctor and founder, in 1919, of the Institute for Sex Research in Berlin.

GAMES FOR WOMEN
In Monte Carlo, the first Women's World Games are held in protest at women not being allowed to take part in Olympic track and field events.

ABOVE: The first glimpse into an Egyptian tomb unearthed near Thebes — excavation fever grips the decade.

SECRETS FROM AN EGYPTIAN TOMB

A year of alliance and excavation: Russia and its satellites become the mighty USSR, and Germany makes an alliance with the Soviets. Mussolini seizes power in Italy. The ancient city of Ur is unearthed in Iraq, and in Egypt the tomb of the young Tutankhamun yields its secrets. Retail therapy is introduced with the first shopping mall in the USA. Insulin is discovered and in Ireland Michael Collins is shot dead. French novelist Marcel Proust eats his last madeleine and Alexander Bell, inventor of the telephone, finally rings off.

OPPOSITE: Mask of Tutankhamun, whose tomb is discovered this year.

1922

Jan	5	British explorer Ernest Shackleton dies at 49
Feb	5	The first issue of *The Reader's Digest* is published in the USA
Apr	16	German and Soviet Russia sign a secret treaty
	21	Alessandro Moreschi, the last known castrato, dies
May	3	Four Canadian scientists announce the discovery of insulin
Aug	2	Telephone inventor Alexander Graham Bell dies at 75
	14	British newspaper owner Viscount Northcliffe dies aged 57
	22	In Ireland, Sinn Féin leader Michael Collins is shot dead, aged 32
Sep	4	US aviator James H Doolittle flies from Florida to California in one day
Oct	11	Treaty of Mudania ends the war between Greece and Turkey Benito Mussolini and the Fascists take power in Italy
Nov	15	British Broadcasting Company broadcasts its first wireless news bulletin
	26	The tomb of the Egyptian pharaoh Tutankhamun is found in Egypt
Dec	30	Soviet Russia changes its name to the Union of Soviet Socialist Republics (USSR)

ABOVE: A huge explosion rocks the Four Courts in Dublin, the result of a mine. Thirty Free State troopers are killed in the explosion and fighting continues for four hours afterwards.

GERMAN AND SOVIET ALLIANCE

In April, Germany and Soviet Russia sign a secret peace treaty at Rapallo, Italy, under which they re-establish full diplomatic and trading relations, agree to waive reparations payments, and commit to full co-operation between their armed forces. The treaty shocks Europe, as it allows Germany a way of rebuilding her army in defiance of the Versailles Treaty.

IL DUCE SEIZES POWER

In Rome, 24,000 members of the Italian Fascist Party march from Naples to Rome to seize power. Their leader, Benito Mussolini, waits in Milan, ready to flee to Switzerland if the coup fails. However, there is no opposition in Rome and King Victor Emmanuel asks Mussolini to form a government.

RUSSIA BECOMES USSR

Russia formally changes its name and becomes the Union of the Soviet Socialist Republics, a confederation with Belarus, Ukraine and the Transcaucasian Federation.

THE WASTE LAND

The major work of the American poet TS Eliot (1888–1965) uses imagery from myth and past literature to evoke the desolation of modern humanity and the breakdown of modern values and belief systems. Its mixture of styles, ranging from everyday Cockney speech to literary allusion and quotation, baffles but impresses its first readers.

COLLINS SHOT

The Irish prime minister, Michael Collins, is assassinated in County Cork by opponents of the treaty signed with Britain last December. Although the Irish parliament accepted the treaty in January, opponents have taken up arms against their former friends and civil war is now raging throughout the Free State.

TALES OF ULYSSES

Irish writer James Joyce's ground-breaking novel is published. It incorporates major innovations in the use of interior monologue, cinematic scene-setting, and use of language. It will be valued for these modernist features and also for its realistic portrayal of its main characters, for its humour, and for its vivid depiction of Dublin. Because of alleged obscenity, the book is printed in Dijon and published in Paris.

AIRCRAFT CARRIER

The USS *Langley* becomes the first US aircraft carrier; she is converted from a collier, the *Jupiter*.

DISCOVERY OF INSULIN

In February a group of Canadian scientists, Frederick Banting, Charles Best, James Collip, and Professor John Macleod, jointly announce the discovery of insulin, and its use in treating diabetes.

ABOVE: The New Lincoln Memorial is a huge but benign statue of Abraham Lincoln by American sculptor Daniel Chester French.

THE EARLIEST CITY

Ur, an ancient city on the River Euphrates in Iraq, is excavated by a British Museum and University of Pennsylvania expedition headed by Charles Leonard Woolley (1880–1960), the English archaeologist who has just excavated the ancient Egyptian site of Tel-el-Amarna. The discovery of a Sumerian temple proves that Ur flourished in Mesopotamia as early as 2600 BC.

IMPERIAL HOTEL, TOKYO

Asked to design a building that will withstand earthquakes, architect Frank Lloyd Wright (1869–1959) develops a system of concrete posts which support the structure while allowing it to "give" during an earthquake. About two years after completion, the building is shaken by a severe quake and remains standing — providing a refuge for those left homeless.

SAVING THE KOALA

The koala bear, a native marsupial found only in Australia, is now protected by rigidly strict legislation, because fur trappers have killed some eight million animals over the last four years alone.

IMMORTALIZING THE LIVING DEAD

Nosferatu, the first major vampire movie, is also the first major film directed by FW Murnau. It includes effects such as negative imagery (black appearing as white and vice versa) to intensify the atmosphere of strangeness and horror. Many imitators will follow in its wake.

PEACE BETWEEN TURKEY AND GREECE

The war between Greece and Turkey ends when they sign the Treaty of Mudania. Greece withdraws from Anatolia and the area around Constantinople. As a result, the British wartime leader, David Lloyd George, loses power as prime minister and is replaced by the Conservative leader, Andrew Bonar-Law.

SOUND-ON-FILM MOVIE

The first commercial sound-on-film motion picture is *Der Brandstifter* (*The Arsonist*) made in Germany. But it does not immediately lead to the end of silent films.

TUTANKHAMUN COMES TO LIGHT

The tomb containing the sarcophagus of the ancient Egyptian boy king, Tutankhamun, who reigned during the Eighteenth Dynasty (fourteenth century BC), is discovered in November by two British archaeologists, Howard Carter and his sponsor, the Earl of Carnarvon.

MARCEL PROUST
(1871–1922)

One of the most influential writers of modern times, the French novelist Marcel Proust has died. Born in Paris, where he spent his life, he was a semi-invalid, and spent his last seventeen years writing reclusively in his apartment. His thirteen-volume work *A la Recherche du Temps Perdu* (translated into English as *Remembrance of Times Past*) has won great acclaim. The second volume won the Prix Goncourt in 1919 and an international reputation followed. At the time of his death three final volumes are awaiting publication.

ALEXANDER GRAHAM BELL
(1847–1922)

Alexander Graham Bell, the inventor of the telephone and founder of the Bell Telephone Company (1877) has died. This American, of Scottish birth and education, established a training school in Boston for teachers of deaf people and later became Professor of Vocal Physiology. The telephone sprang from experiments with acoustical devices to aid deaf and dumb people. His other interest was aeronautics.

MR LINCOLN COMES TO WASHINGTON
The Lincoln Memorial, Washington DC, becomes a place of national pilgrimage with the completion of Daniel Chester French's memorial statue.

DAY TRIP
Lieutenant James H Doolittle makes the first one-day flight across the United States from Florida to California: time 22 hours 35 minutes, including a refuelling stop.

ABOVE: The largest telescope in the world at Mount Wilson in California. It incorporates an instrument for measuring the diameter of stars and is to be significant in the discovery of galaxies.

RETAIL THERAPY
The world's first shopping mall, the Country Club Plaza, opens in the USA in July.

DANISH SUCCESS
Danish scientist Niels Bohr wins Nobel Prize for physics.

FIRST GLIMPSES OF NAZISM AND HITLER

Nazism rears its head as the first rally is held in Munich. At the same time, French troops occupy the Ruhr, impatient at the slow delivery of war reparations. The German mark collapses. Turkey becomes a republic, signalling the death of the once mighty Ottoman Empire. Far from the troubled Earth, galaxies and nebulae are discovered. A Spanish engineer flies the first rotor-driven flight machine and French actress Sarah Bernhardt takes her final curtain.

1923

Jan	25	French troops march into Germany's Ruhr to collect war reparations
	27	The first National Socialist (Nazi) rally is held in Munich, Germany
Feb	10	German X-ray discoverer Wilhelm Roentgen dies aged 77
Mar	9	Russian leader VI Lenin suffers a stroke and there is speculation about who will be chosen to be his successor as leader of the Soviet Union
	29	Legendary French actress Sarah Bernhardt dies at 78
Apr	28	Wembley Stadium, London, hosts its first football cup final
Aug	2	US President Warren Harding dies aged 69; he is succeeded by Vice President Calvin Coolidge

	12	Italian Enrico Triboschi swims the English Channel in a record 16 hours 33 minutes
Sep	16	An earthquake destroys Tokyo and Yokohama in Japan. At least 300,000 people die and two million are left homeless
Oct	29	Mustafa Kemal proclaims a republic in Turkey, with himself as president
Nov	12	Adolf Hitler tries to seize power in Bavaria, Germany, and is arrested
	15	German mark collapses to 20,142 billion to the pound sterling; a loaf of bread costs 201 billion marks
Dec	7	British General Election results in a "hung" Parliament
	28	French Engineer Gustav Eiffel dies at 91

ABOVE: A violent earthquake devastates Tokyo, destroying most of the city centre and killing 59,000 people.

THE "SICK MAN OF EUROPE" DIES

In October the Ottoman Empire finally collapses when Mustafa Kemal, a leading Nationalist politician, proclaims Turkey a republic and himself as president. The new peace treaty with Greece and the allies, signed at Lausanne in July, restores much territory to Turkey.

THE FIRST FOOTBALL CUP FINAL

In April the English Football Association Cup Final at Wembley Stadium in London is won by Bolton Wanderers 2–0 over West Ham. "The White Horse Final" will be remembered, however, for the huge crowd which swarms to the first game to be played at the stadium. Spectators fill the stadium to the very edge of the playing surface and have to be marshalled by mounted police.

WILHELM KONRAD VON ROENTGEN
(1845–1923)

The German winner of the first Nobel Prize for physics in 1901, Wilhelm Roentgen has died. In 1895 he discovered X-rays or electromagnetic rays, and he also achieved important results in the study of heat in gases and crystals, and in dielectrics (substances that do not conduct electricity).

FRANCISCO (PANCHO) VILLA
(1877–1923)

The Mexican revolutionary Pancho Villa has been murdered in Parral. Born Doroteo Arango, son of a field labourer, he became a military commander during the Mexican Revolution, and continued as a guerrilla fighter after his defeat in 1915. He made a truce with the government in 1920.

THE COSTS OF WAR

In January, French and Belgian troops occupy the industrialized Ruhr region to seize coal, timber, steel and other reparations owed to them by Germany as part of the peace treaty which ended the war. The Germans respond with strikes, acts of sabotage, and street protests. French troops remain in the region until July 1925.

FIRST AUTOGIRO FLIGHTS

Spanish aero-engineer Juan de la Cierva makes the first successful flight in an autogiro, an aircraft with a free-wheeling rotor that acts as the wing.

BELOW: A member of archaeologist Lord Carnarvon's team on the trail of new treasures from Egypt.

LEFT: The Great Citroën Expedition across the Sahara encounters a desert warrior using more traditional transport. The desert terrain is a great test of the car's abilities.

LOUIS MARIE ANN COUPERUS
(1863–1923)

Louis Couperus, the Dutch poet and novelist has died. His first novel, *Eline Vere*, written in the new naturalistic style, was published in 1889 and this was followed by several others set in the Dutch East Indies, where he grew up, and a tetralogy (1901–1904), *Dr Adriaan* (translated into English as *The Books of Small Souls*), set in The Hague.

THE BEER HALL PUTSCH
The National Socialist Party, or Nazis, led by Adolf Hitler, attempts a coup in Munich against the German government by trying to seize control in Bavaria. It fails, and Hitler is sent to prison.

HEAT CONTROL
The thermostat begins a revolution in the efficiency of domestic appliances when it is fitted to a New World gas cooker in Britain. Commercial companies seek to exploit its potential for regulating electric cookers, electric irons, kettles and water heaters.

MONEY FOR NOTHING
In November, the German mark collapses, losing so much value that its exchange rate falls to 4,200,000 billion marks to the dollar. As prices soar, the German government issues a new currency, the Rentenmark, at a level of 4.2 to the dollar.

GALAXIES GALORE
US astronomer Edwin Powell Hubble (1889–1953) discovers that the Andromeda nebula lies outside the boundary of our own galaxy; this leads to the realisation that each nebula is a separate galaxy.

ELECTRONIC CAMERA TUBE
Russian-born electronics engineer Vladimir Zworykin (1889–1982) invents the iconoscope, the first electronic camera tube.

CONCRETE SPACE
Airship hangars at Orly, Paris, designed by French civil engineer and concrete expert Eugène Freyssinet, show how steel-and-concrete construction can be used to create enormous spaces. The great parabolic concrete vaults are 60m (197ft) high and 175m (574ft) long. The vaults get their strength from their ridged construction (similar to corrugated cardboard) on a vast scale.

THE GOOD SOLDIER SCHWEIK
This unfinished masterpiece by Jaroslav Hasek is based on the author's experiences in the Austro-Czech Army in 1915, and portrays an anarchic, anti-authoritarian, even antisocial "hero", a Czech who ridicules his Austrian masters. Schweik becomes a symbol of all those who struggle as individuals against oppressive political systems.

AN EARLY SUPERMARKET
A precursor of the supermarket opens in San Francisco. Called the Crystal Palace, it sells food, drugs, cigarettes and jewellery, and it has a barber's shop, a ladies' hair and beauty salon, and a dry-cleaner.

THEY SHOOT HORSES DON'T THEY?
In the wake of the Depression and huge unemployment, the craze for marathon dancing hits the USA. Couples dance until they drop, to win cash prizes.

SARAH-MARIE-HENRIETTE ROSINE BERNHARDT
(1844–1923)

The French actress Sarah Bernhardt, who was born Sarah-Marie-Henriette Rosine Bernard in Paris in 1844, has died. After fourteen years on the Paris stage she first became internationally known in 1876. Famous for her tragic roles, such as Phèdre in Racine's play of the same name, she founded her own theatre in 1899. Despite having a leg amputated in 1915 she continued to give stage performances in France, the United States, London and other European cities.

THE RISE AND RISE OF ADOLF HITLER

The Nazis begin their inexorable rise in Germany as members of the party are elected to the Reichstag. In Russia, Lenin dies. Perhaps in response to an increasingly complex world, the Surrealist Manifesto is declared by French artist and poet André Breton. On the domestic scene, spin-driers, frozen food and refrigerators are introduced. The first Winter Olympics takes place in the French Alps, and novelist Franz Kafka undergoes the final human metamorphosis.

1924

Jan	21	Russian leader Vladimir Lenin dies at 54
	22	Britain has its first Labour government, led by Ramsay MacDonald
		A council is appointed to succeed Lenin: Grigoriy Zinoviev, Leon Kamenev, Joseph Stalin
	24	First International Winter Sports Week is held at Chamonix, France; it is later called the Winter Olympics
Feb	12	US pianist George Gershwin gives the first performance of his *Rhapsody in Blue*
Apr	1	Adolf Hitler is jailed for five years for high treason
May	4	The first Nazis are elected to the German Reichstag (Parliament)

June	2	First wireless conversation between Britain and Australia takes place
	3	Czech author Franz Kafka dies at 40
July	5	The Eighth Olympic Games open in Paris
Aug	3	Author Joseph Conrad dies aged 66
	16	London conference adopts the Dawes Plan to help Germany pay its war reparations
	24	British liner *Mauretania* sets a new Blue Riband record for crossing the Atlantic: 5 days 1 hour 35 minutes
Nov	4	French composer Gabriel Fauré dies aged 79
	29	Italian composer Giacomo Puccini dies aged 65
Dec	20	Adolf Hitler is released from jail on parole

ABOVE: Adolf Hitler is jailed then released and begins his rise to power in Germany.

THOMAS WOODROW WILSON (1856–1924)

Woodrow Wilson, the 28th American president (1913–1921), and winner of the Nobel Prize for peace in 1919, has died. President Wilson reluctantly led the US into World War I in 1917 and helped to bring the War to an end. A Democrat, he was instrumental in forming the League of Nations, which the Senate prevented the US itself from joining.

DEATH OF LENIN

Vladimir Ilyich Lenin, the founder of the USSR, dies in Moscow aged 54. He had suffered the first of three strokes in May 1922 and control of the government had been passed to other people, notably Joseph Stalin, General Secretary of the Communist Party.

FIRST BRITISH LABOUR GOVERNMENT

A Labour government takes power in Britain for the first time ever. Led by Ramsay MacDonald, the Labour government is supported in power by the Liberals, but soon collapses and loses in the general election called in October.

NAZIS BECOME ESTABLISHMENT

In May, the Nazis enter the Reichstag, the German Parliament, for the first time, taking 32 seats in the general election. The Social Democrats remain the largest party, but both the Nationalists and Communists gain ground.

SURREALISTS SHOW THEMSELVES

French writer André Breton (1896–1966) publishes his Manifesto to mark the official beginning of the Surrealist movement, which aims to break down the distinctions between dream and reality, madness and rationality, in art of all forms.

A PASSAGE TO INDIA

English writer EM Forster (1879–1970) publishes what is probably his greatest book, the last of his novels to be published in his lifetime. A picture of life in India under British rule, the book lays bare the prejudices that both Britons and Indians have about each other and the clashes that result.

LIVING IN STIJL

With its white walls, clean lines, and primary-colour details, the Schröder-Schräder house, Utrecht, designed by Gerrit Rietveld, is a classic example of De Stijl design. The right-angle is everywhere in this building. Even the windows can only be opened so that they are at 90 degrees to the façade.

GOODBYE TO WASHDAY BLUES

The spin-drier, consisting of a spinning drum built into a washing machine, which extracts water by centrifugal force, is produced by the Savage Arms Corporation in the USA and used to dry wet clothes.

GERMANY SETTLES HER DEBTS

Germany and the Allies accept the Dawes Report to settle the issue of reparations by establishing a plan for annual payments. As a result, the German Reichsbank introduces a new mark to stabilize the economy, which is supported by a foreign loan.

QUICK-FROZEN FOOD

Birds Eye Seafoods launches the first commercially produced fast-frozen food. US fur trader Clarence Birdseye (1886–1956) experimented with preserving perishable foods by freezing, after visiting Labrador in 1917 and eating palatable fish that had been preserved in ice. Now he sets up a company to produce quick-frozen food for the retail market.

CONTROVERSY ON STAGE

Paul Robeson and Mary Blair play an interracial couple in *All God's Chillun Got Wings* by American dramatist Eugene O'Neill (1888–1953). It is a controversial play attacking racism.

MY LIFE IN ART

Konstantin Stanislavsky (1865–1938), the great Russian director, looks back over his life and his experience in the theatre. In the book he outlines various theories which have influenced the way many modern theatre directors have approached their work. The Method becomes increasingly popular in the 1920s as the result of Stanislavsky's books.

PARTICLES = WAVES

French physicist Louis de Broglie discovers that electrons and other particles can behave as waves, as well as particles, thus becoming the founder of the science of wave mechanics.

JOSEPH CONRAD (JOZEF TEODOR KONRAD NALECZ KORZENIOWSKI) (1857–1924)

The Polish-born, naturalized British writer, Joseph Conrad has died. At the age of 21 he joined a British merchant ship, and six years later gained his master's certificate. He spent many years at sea but settled in Kent after his marriage in 1896. There he became a writer, using his experiences as inspiration. Among his best-known works are *Lord Jim* (1900), *Nostromo* (1904), *Heart of Darkness* (1902), and *Victory* (1919). He was working on a novel, *Suspense*, when he died.

RHAPSODY IN BLUE
American composer George Gershwin (1898–1937) writes this popular piece — originally for Paul Whiteman's jazz band. It will later become better known in the form of an arrangement for classical symphony orchestra. The work is the first distinctively American piece of concert music, although if Charles Ives had been better known the story would have been different.

THE SOUTHERN APE
Australian anthropologist Raymond Dart (1893–1988) discovers a skull in a South African quarry. It is a primitive hominid which Dart names Australopithecus (southern ape).

ELECTRIC REFRIGERATOR
Swedish engineers Balzer von Platen and Carl Munters patent the first refrigerator using an electric motor to drive the compressor; they call it the Electrolux.

WINTER OLYMPICS
In January, the International Winter Sports Week in Chamonix, France, is retrospectively declared the First Winter Olympics. The Scandinavians dominate the event, which is organized by the French Olympic Committee. The success of the event leads the International Olympic Committee to stage Winter Games in tandem with Summer Olympics.

ROUND-THE-WORLD FLIGHT
Two US Douglas DCW biplanes, *Chicago* (piloted by Lieutenant Lowell H Smith) and *New Orleans* (piloted by Lieutenant Erik Nelson), make the first round-the-world flight between April and September in 175 days; two others fail to make the full journey.

FRANZ KAFKA
(1883–1924)

The Czech writer of German-Jewish parentage, Franz Kafka has died of tuberculosis in Berlin after many years of ill-health. His novels, written in the German language, express the angst of the sensitive individual in a seemingly irrational society, and the adjective "Kafkaesque" will soon be familiar to those who have not even read his books. The books include the short story 'Metamorphosis' (1916) and the unfinished novels *The Trial*, *The Castle*, and *Amerika*, all to be published after his death.

ENTER KLEENEX
US firm Kimberley Clark introduces the first tissues, called Celluwipes — and now known as ™Kleenex.

THE EIGHTH OLYMPIAD
Finnish athlete Paavo Nurmi wins five golds as the Olympics returns to Paris, France, for the Eighth Olympic Games. The Olympic Village, where athletes live, makes a return, and events are broadcast on radio for the first time. Eric Liddell and Harold Abrahams, later to be immortalized in the film *Chariots of Fire*, win sprint medals for Britain.

FREE EDUCATION
An educational experiment is launched with the founding of Summerhill, a self-governing co-educational boarding school, by a British schoolmaster, Alexander Sutherland Neil. Pupils are allowed to develop in their own way without the constraints of discipline, direction, moral or religious instruction.

SWEDISH HEAT
The Aga, a cooker which uses solid fuel cleanly and has an efficient temperature control, is invented by Gustav Galen, a blind Swedish scientist.

HIGHWAY NETWORK
Italian companies begin building a 500-km (310-mi) network of *autostrada*, toll highways; the first opens in September.

LEFT: Artists and writers in exile — James Joyce, Ezra Pound, Ford Maddox Ford and John Quinn gather in Ezra Pound's Paris studio.

STALIN GETS A TIGHTER GRIP

Three men who will dominate the world are active this year. In the USSR, Stalin seizes power. In Germany, Hitler publishes *Mein Kampf*. And in China, Chiang Kai-shek succeeds as leader of the People's Party. In the USA, the Scopes trial focuses on fundamentalism and evolution, and the Ku Klux Klan march is unopposed by the Establishment. Charlie Chaplin films *The Gold Rush* and Sergei Eisenstein films *Battleship Potemkin*. The first frisbee is thrown.

OPPOSITE: The Murrumbidgee River hits the Burrin Jack Dam during Australia's May floods.

1925

Jan	16	In Russia, Stalin sacks Leon Trotsky as Commissar for War		21	Biology teacher John Scopes is fined $100 in Tennessee for teaching evolution
Mar	12	Dr Sun Yat-sen, leader of the Kuomintang, China's People's Party, dies aged 69; he is succeeded by General Chiang Kai-shek	**Aug**	16	Première of Charlie Chaplin's film *The Gold Rush*
	23	State of Tennessee bans the teaching of evolution theory	**Oct**	16	Belgium, Britain, France, Germany and Italy sign the Locarno Pact, promising to keep peace with one another
Apr	25	Field Marshal Paul von Hindenburg is elected president of Germany			
May	1	Cyprus becomes a British colony	**Nov**	14	First Surrealist art exhibition in Paris includes work from Picasso and Klee
July	18	Adolf Hitler's book *Mein Kampf* (*My Struggle*) is published	**Dec**	10	George Bernard Shaw is awarded the Nobel Prize for literature

THE LOCARNO PEACE

A major peace conference between Germany and the Allies agrees a security pact for western and central Europe, guaranteeing frontiers and settling outstanding disputes. The treaty appears to guarantee peace between Germany and her former enemies.

NICARAGUAN CIVIL WAR

1925 sees the start of the civil war in Nicaragua. It will last until 1933. President Calles is opposed by three separate guerrilla groups led by Generals Moncada, Díaz and Sandino. Díaz and Moncada eventually become allies, but Sandino remains independent. The United States backs the president and sends in the marines. General Sandino escapes to Guatemala, but returns when the marines leave. The war is eventually won by the presidential forces, but the rebel Sandinistas (named for General Sandino) keep up guerrilla warfare.

TROTSKY DISMISSED

Leon Trotsky is dismissed as Commissar for War by Joseph Stalin and placed under house arrest. Many of his supporters are imprisoned or exiled to Siberia. The moves consolidate Stalin's grip on power in the USSR after the death of Lenin.

THE GREAT GATSBY

F Scott Fitzgerald (1896–1940) was already famous as a writer and representative of the "jazz age" when he published this, his greatest novel. It portrays the doomed passion of rich Jay Gatsby for Daisy Buchanan, and evokes the sophistication and squalor of New York. The book is remarkable for describing the glamour and the dream of Gatsby, showing the hollowness of this vision as it turns to dust, and yet convincing us that the dream does have some value after all.

GERMANY ELECTS A PRESIDENT

In April, Field Marshal Paul von Hindenburg becomes the first directly elected German president. Hindenburg is supported by right wing and nationalist parties, many of which want to see the German monarchy restored.

COSMIC RAYS

US physicist Robert Millikan (1868–1953) coins the term "cosmic rays" for radiation from outer space.

RUDOLF STEINER
(1861–1925)

The founder of the Anthroposophical Society (in 1912), the Croatian-born Austrian, Rudolf Steiner has died. Influenced by theosophy, he believed that our spiritual development has been blocked by modern materialism. Many Steiner schools have developed since his founding of the first one in 1919.

ERIK ALFRED LESLIE SATIE
(1866–1925)

The French composer Erik Satie (whose mother was Scottish) has died in Paris. After training at the Paris Conservatoire he at first earned his living as a pianist in a Montmartre cabaret. His compositions for the piano, such as *Gymnopédies* (1888) and *Three Pear-shaped Pieces* (1903), were eccentric and avant-garde. He composed the music for the Diaghilev ballet *Parade* in 1917, and was part of the circle of Surrealists and Dadaists.

DRINKING IN STIJL

Designed by JJP Oud, the Café De Unie in Rotterdam is a De Stijl building that makes a bold statement. In a city street flanked by two old, traditional-style buildings, its brightly coloured façade and bold sans-serif signage shine out as symbolic of the modern era.

THE FIRST FRISBEE

The frisbee is improvised by Yale University students using tin plates meant to hold pies baked by the Frisbie Baking Company of Bridgeport, Connecticut. An aerodynamically designed version is later marketed as a game.

THE TRIAL

Franz Kafka's novel is published a year after his death. It is the story of Josef K, caught in a labyrinth of law and officialdom, and powerless to escape or control his fate. More than any other of Kafka's books, it has given us the term "Kafkaesque" for this situation.

THE BATTLESHIP POTEMKIN

The brutalities of the czarist regime are dramatized in Sergei Eisenstein's landmark film about a mutiny during the 1905 revolution. Eisenstein's most famous work shows the effectiveness of his technique of montage, a method of editing that boldly exploits visual metaphor.

BETTER VACUUM PACKS

Thermos vacuum flasks covered in plastic go on sale. They are lighter, longer-lasting and cheaper than their predecessors, patented in 1902 by a German, Reinhold Burger. These were large, cumbersome, fragile and rather expensive because they were covered in nickel.

THE RISE OF THE KLAN

The Ku Klux Klan suffers a setback when its Kentucky leader, DC Stephenson, is imprisoned for assault, rape and kidnapping. The Klan's political power and membership have grown in recent years — over 40,000 members attend its first national congress on August 8, complete with a parade through Washington.

SCOPES TRIAL

Science teacher John T Scopes faces trial in July for violating a state law in Tennessee, USA, forbidding the teaching of evolutionary theory; he is convicted and fined $100, but cleared on appeal. The state law will be repealed in 1967.

ELECTRICITY METER

US electrical engineer Vannevar Bush devises the first induction watt-hour meter for measuring electricity. Such meters are now found in homes all over the world.

ALL FALL DOWN

Engineers report that the famous leaning tower of Pisa will eventually fall down, but give no date for this.

THE GOLDRUSH

Charles Chaplin writes produces, directs, and acts (playing the Tramp) in this film, one of many features he makes with United Artists. The unique combination of humour, pathos and resilience of his tramp character makes his films popular.

MEIN KAMPF PUBLISHED

Hitler publishes *Mein Kampf* (*My Struggle*), written while he was in jail and containing the main tenets of his Nationalist-Socialist philosophy, including the idea of *Lebensraum*, the expansion of German territory.

BELOW: A new design of parachute, the seat-pack, designed in America and favoured by the air stunt artists who perform in shows all over the USA and Europe.

A YEAR OF STRIKE AND DISCONTENT

In England, the General Strike paralyses and polarizes the country. The North Pole receives two flying visits: one by plane and one by airship. Saudi Arabia is established as a country. Germany joins the League of Nations and at Dessau, Walter Gropius erects the first Bauhaus, the seminal school of art and architecture. Hearts are broken as Rudolph Valentino dies young, and art appreciates as Claude Monet comes to the end of a long and prolific career at the easel.

OPPOSITE: Mussolini addresses a crowd in Rome hours after a failed assassination attempt.

1926

Jan	**6**	German airline Lufthansa is founded
	8	Ibn Saud is proclaimed King of the Hejaz, in Arabia
	27	Scot John Logie Baird gives the first demonstration of television
Mar	**6**	Robert A Goddard launches the first liquid-fuel rocket
Apr	**30**	In Britain, coal miners go on strike; the strike lasts until November
May	**5**	Britain's first General Strike begins in support of the miners
	9	Richard Byrd and Floyd Bennett fly over the North Pole in an aeroplane
	12	General Strike in Britain ends, but the miners stay out
	13	Umberto Nobile, Roald Amundsen, and Lincoln Ellsworth fly over the North Pole in an airship

June	**10**	Spanish architect Antonio Gaudí is run over by a bus and killed
Aug	**23**	Screen heart-throb Rudolf Valentino dies at 31
Sep	**8**	League of Nations votes to admit Germany
Oct	**14**	AA Milne's *Winnie-the-Pooh* is published
	23	In Russsia, Stalin expels Leon Trotsky and Grigori Zinoviev from the Politburo, the central committee of the Communist Party
Nov	**20**	Canada, Australia, South Africa, and Newfoundland to become self-governing dominions with Great Britain as head of the newly formed Commonwealth
Dec	**5**	French artist Claude Monet dies at 86

ABOVE: Armoured cars in London guard the food lorries driven by strike breakers during the General Strike that grips the country.

THE BIRTH OF SAUDI ARABIA
Ibn Saud is proclaimed King of the Hejaz at Mecca. This marks the end of a long struggle by the Saud family to control the Arabian peninsula. Further conquest will result in the kingdom of Saudi Arabia in 1932.

BRITAIN'S STRIKING MINERS
A General Strike is called by the Trades Union Congress to support the miners in the struggle with the coal owners over pay and conditions. The strike lasts for just over a week, but the miners continue to stay on strike until November, when they are forced to accept a longer working day and local rather than national bargaining in pay and conditions.

GERMANY JOINS THE LEAGUE
The League of Nations votes unanimously to admit Germany. However, both Russia and the USA remain outside the League, reducing its importance in international affairs.

DE VALERA AND THE FIANNA FAIL
The Republican leader, Éamon de Valera, who opposed the treaty setting up the Irish Free State, breaks with his hardline allies and forms Fianna Fáil, the "Soldiers of Destiny", to fight for power in Ireland. They enter the Dáil, the Irish parliament, for the first time in August 1927, ending a lengthy boycott by anti-treaty Republicans.

TROTSKY AND ZINOVIEV EXPELLED
Leon Trotsky and Grigori Zinoviev, chairman of Comintern, the Communist International Committee, are both expelled from the Politburo, the ruling committee of the Communist Party. Stalin now holds supreme power in the USSR.

IS IT A BIRD?
Romanian sculptor Constantin Brancusi (1876–1957) exhibits his sculpture, *Bird in Space*. The degree of abstraction that sculpture has reached becomes a public talking point when the authorities in New York refuse to admit Brancusi's sculpture is a work of art and try to tax it as a piece of metal. There is a court case, and the court finally accepts that it is art after all.

A NEW BAUHAUS, DESSAU

Walter Gropius (1883–1969) designs this landmark building for a landmark institution, which moves to Dessau after political pressure forces it to leave Weimar. The elegant but austere building, like the institution it houses, seems to unite art and industry. Inside, some of Europe's greatest artists and designers (such as Kandinsky, Moholy-Nagy, and Gropius himself) teach the arts of design and architecture, and spread the ideals of modernism.

THE NEW DUTCH SCHOOL

The Vondelschool is built in Hilversum. Impressive for its sober, elegant use of brickwork and its strong horizontal lines, this is one of many such buildings by Dudok in the new town to the southeast of Amsterdam.

PIAGET'S THEORY

A pioneering study of children's mental development is published by Jean Piaget (a Swiss psychologist who studied under Jung and worked with Alfred Binet on children's intelligence tests). He theorizes that the development of mental processes is determined genetically and always occurs in four stages.

MEXICAN INSURRECTIONS 1926–29

In this year, anti-clerical provisions in the Mexican 1917 Constitution are implemented. Clerical land is seized, church property is nationalized, and bishops are exiled. A guerrilla group calling themselves the Cristoferos, fight on the side of the clergy. There are no major outbreaks but many skirmishes. In 1929, agreement will be reached between the two parties.

CLAUDE MONET
(1840–1926)

The French Impressionist painter, Claude Monet, whose painting *Impression, Soleil Levant*, exhibited in 1874, initiated the term Impressionism, has died. His technique was to build up a painting from patches of pure colour, and his paintings often consist of a series examining the same subject again and again in different lights, as in his *Argenteuil* series (1872–75), *Views of London* (1902), *Rouen Cathedral* (1892–95), and the countless *Water-lilies* (1899–1926).

RUDOLF VALENTINO (RODOLPHO ALPHONSO GUGLIELMI DI VALENTINA D'ANTONGUOLLA) (1895–1926)

The Italian-born actor and heart-throb has died unexpectedly of peritonitis in New York. He emigrated to the US in 1913, and worked first as a stage dancer, then as a Hollywood extra. With his flashing eyes, handsome and athletic bearing, and dramatic talent, he soon became the leading man in a series of silent films of the 1920s. His funeral caused hysterical public displays of grief.

FIRST TV DEMONSTRATED

In January Scottish inventor John Logie Baird (1888–1946) demonstrates the first true television transmission to 50 scientists at the Royal Institution in London, using a mechanical scanner.

NORGE OVER THE NORTH POLE

Italian aviator Umberto Nobile flies across the North Pole in his airship *Norge*, accompanied by explorers Roald Amundsen (Norway) and Lincoln Ellsworth (US).

WATERPROOF WATCH

The first waterproof watch is made by the Rolex Company of Switzerland, and marketed as the Oyster.

METROPOLIS

This important film by Austrian director Fritz Lang (1890–1976) uses the genre of science fiction to create a vision of a nightmare urban landscape, which influences many other movie-makers. Set in a mechanized, slave-served society in the year 2000, the film uses expressionistic sets and techniques to depict the horrors of the city — and of the class warfare that breaks out.

ROCKET LAUNCH

In March US physicist Robert Goddard (1882–1945) launches the first liquid-fuel propelled rocket near Auburn, Massachusetts; it flies 56m (184ft).

NATIONAL PARKS INVENTED IN THE US

The US Forest Service identifies 55 million acres of American wilderness area in the initiative to preserve regions of natural beauty and geological and ecological importance.

THIAMINE ISOLATED

Thiamine (vitamin B1) is the first vitamin to be isolated in its pure form. This is achieved by American scientist Robert Runnels Williams (1886–1965).

LEFT: The Gothic-style Woolworth Building, at 264m (792ft) high, one of the distinctive New York skyscrapers. It will soon be dwarfed by even more upwardly reaching buildings.

ABOVE: The Italian airship *Norge*, which successfully flew over the North Pole this year, carrying an international crew.

ZIP UP
Zip fasteners, invented in Chicago in 1891 by Whitcomb L Judson, redesigned in 1913 by Gideon Sundback, and used by the US military from 1914, are being used to fasten jeans.

CHANNEL CROSSING
American Gertrude Ederle is the first woman to swim the English Channel from France to England. She takes 14 hours 31 minutes, knocking two hours off the record.

POWER TO THE WOMEN OF INDIA
Indian women are permitted to stand for public office.

MAYAN CIVILIZATION REDISCOVERED
Archaeologists guided by descriptions in books by the nineteenth-century American travel writer, John L Stephens, rediscover five ancient Mayan cities in the Yucatan, Mexico, and prepare to excavate the largest sites, the cities of Chichen Itzá, Uxmal and Coba.

BIGGER AND BETTER
Safeway Stores becomes the USA's largest chain store when Marion B. Skaggs unites the Safeway chain of grocery stores he founded in Maryland in 1923, with a Californian company, to create a chain of 466 stores.

FLYING OVER THE NORTH POLE
On May 9 US aviators Richard Byrd and Floyd Bennett are the first to fly over the North Pole. They make the round trip in fifteen hours from Spitsbergen, Norway, in a Fokker tri-motor aircraft piloted by Bennett, with Byrd as navigator.

A NEW EMPEROR
Hirohito is crowned Emperor of Japan. He became regent for his ailing father, Yoshihito, in 1921 and succeeded him to the throne on his death in December.

HARRY HOUDINI (ERICH WEISS) (1874–1926)

The American escape artist and president of the American Society of Magicians, Harry Houdini, has died. Famous for his ability to withstand any blow, sadly he developed peritonitis after being punched by a member of his audience when unprepared. Houdini, who was born Erich Weiss in Budapest, Hungary, could extricate himself from any form of restraint and frequently escaped from imprisonment in underwater boxes or when suspended in mid-air. He was a vigorous campaigner against charlatanry.

THE MOVIES SWITCH TO SOUND

Civil war rages in China but it is also a year of American triumphs: aviator Charles Lindbergh flies the Atlantic solo and sound is introduced to the movies. In the USSR, Stalin rises to supreme power by exiling, imprisoning, or executing his opponents. Swiss architect Le Corbusier establishes the canons of modern architecture.

ABOVE: A "flapper" with bobbed hair, short skirt and a new attitude.

OPPOSITE: General Chiang Kai-shek, bracketed by his guards, visits the Ming Tombs at Nanking.

1927

Feb	9	Revolution in Portugal is crushed after heavy fighting
Mar	21	In China, the Nationalists capture Shanghai
May	20–21	US aviator Charles Lindbergh makes the first solo aeroplane flight across the Atlantic
July	15	In Austria, troops crush a riot in Vienna
Sep	14	Dancer Isadora Duncan dies in an accident aged 49
	30	Baseball player Babe Ruth hits 60 home runs in one season
Oct	6	Première of *The Jazz Singer*, first film to contain live dialogue
Nov	3	Lt-General A Montgomery-Massingberd forecasts war with Germany within twenty years
Dec	19	In China, Nationalists execute 600 alleged Communists

ABOVE: American aviator Charles A Lindbergh lands safely at Le Bourget near Paris after his pioneering non-stop flight from New York.

ABOVE: The single-engine *Spirit of St Louis*, Lindbergh's record-breaking plane. It was funded by the citizens of St Louis, Missouri.

STORMY WEATHER
Freezing blizzards in Britain end a year of disastrous weather, devastation, and casualties. Floods hit Britain in February, devastate the USA's Mississippi Valley in May, Galicia in Poland in September, and in November, the northern USA and even Algeria.

CIVIL WAR IN CHINA
Kuomintang Nationalist forces capture the port of Shanghai from northern warlords and continue their campaigns to unite the country under the leadership of Chiang Kai-shek. The Kuomintang soon remove Communists from the party, leading to increasing tension between the two sides and eventual civil war.

TROUBLE IN VIENNA
Riots and a general strike break out in the Austrian capital after three anti-Socialists were acquitted of the murder of two Communists. Troops loyal to the government crush the strike, but the Austrian government is now seriously weakened.

STALIN TRIUMPHS
Stalin finally wins total control of the Communist Party when he expels Trotsky and Zinoviev from the party. The following year, Trotsky is sent into internal exile near the Chinese frontier, while other opponents are imprisoned.

CLOSER SHAVES
The first commercially successful electric shaver, with a cutting surface that moves backward and forward, is patented by Colonel Jacob Schick in the USA.

ABOVE: Manchurian warlord Chang Tso Lin being received at the American HQ in Tientsin, China. America supports Manchuria in the Chinese civil war.

CBS ABD BBC
CBS (Columbia Broadcasting System) is formed in the USA when William S Paley buys a small radio network. In January, the BBC (British Broadcasting Corporation), founded in 1922 from a consortium of radio manufacturers and now incorporated under royal charter, makes its first broadcasts.

LE CORBUSIER SETS THE STYLE
Villa Les Terrasses, Garches, near Paris, is one of a group of Le Corbusier's great houses, and shows all the features associated with this important modernist architect at this point in his career: white walls, long bands of windows, roof terrace; no load-bearing walls and thus large open interior spaces.

DEATH COMES FOR THE ARCHBISHOP
American writer Willa Cather (1876–1947) writes most movingly about pioneers and missionaries — the difficulties they have in adjusting to their new surroundings, their relationships with the local people, and so on. This novel is remarkable for her understanding of the outlook of both missionary Roman Catholics and of native Americans.

PEKING MAN
Canadian anthropologist Davidson Black discovers fossilized prehistoric human remains near Beijing (Peking), which he names "Peking Man"; they prove to be an example of *Homo erectus*.

YOU AIN'T HEARD NOTHING YET
The sound era in the movies is inaugurated with *The Jazz Singer*, the first major sound picture, starring the Jewish minstrel singer Al Jolson.

FLESH AND THE DEVIL
Greta Garbo's first Hollywood film is also said to be the best of her silent dramas. She is already creating the air of mystery that surrounds her in her later sound films.

ISADORA DUNCAN
(ANGELA DUNCAN) (1878–1927)

The American-born dancer and choreographer Isadora Duncan (born Angela) has died in a tragic motoring accident. The pioneer of contemporary dance, which incorporates the fluid movements of birds and animals, as well as walking, running and skipping, and classical poses, she founded schools of dance in Berlin, Salzburg, and Vienna. Internationally known, and with an ardent following, she has led an unconventional life. In 1922 she married the young Russian poet Sergei Yesenin, who died by committing suicide in 1925. Shortly before her untimely death she published her autobiography, *My Life*.

ABOVE: The Utitsky Palace in Leningrad inscribed with the Soviet hammer and sickle.

RIGHT: Manhattan Island, New York from the air — 777 sq km (300 sq mi).

COUNTING THE WORLD
First international World Population Conference is organized by US feminist Margaret Sanger.

RECORD RUTH
Babe Ruth hits a record 60 home runs in a single season for the New York Yankees. Ruth's achievement and more home runs around the game, due to a livelier ball, rekindle America's enthusiasm for baseball.

UNDERWATER COLOUR
In January *National Geographic Magazine* publishes the first natural colour photographs taken beneath the surface of the sea, following months of experiment by ichthyologist WH Longley and photographer Charles Martin.

ATLANTIC SOLO FLIGHT
On May 20–21, US aviator Charles A Lindbergh (1902–74) makes the first solo non-stop flight across the Atlantic in his plane *Spirit of St Louis*, covering 5,790km (3,590mi) in 33.5 hours.

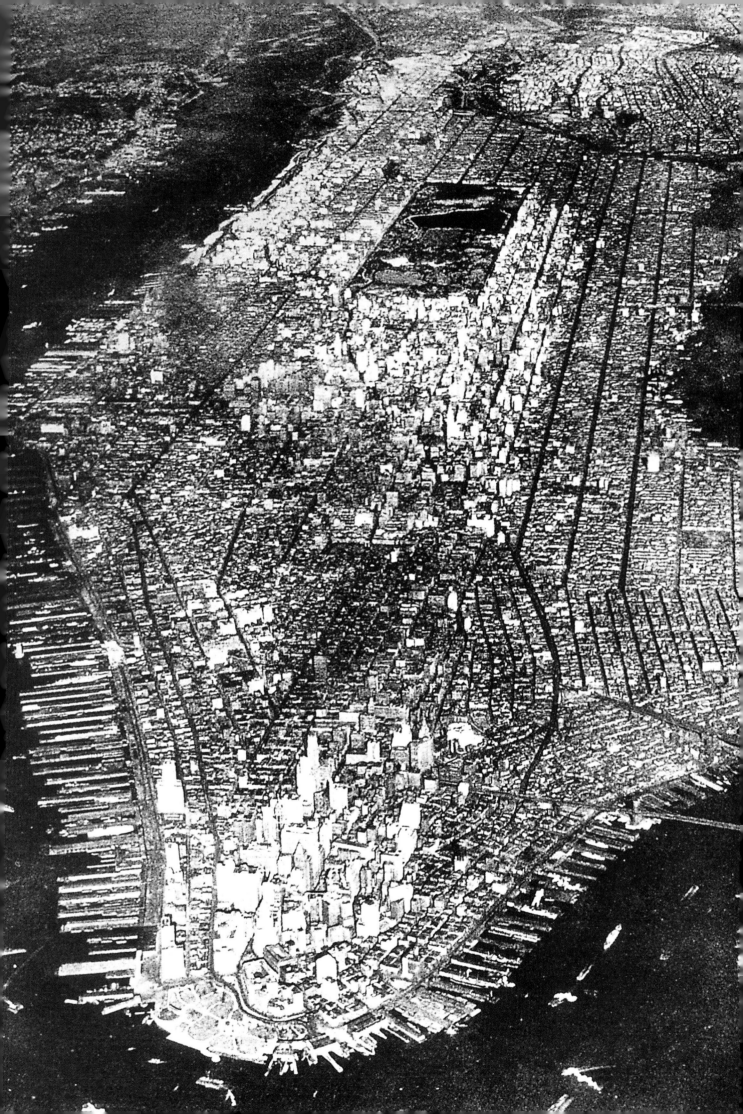

THE DEVELOPMENT OF THE CAR

LEFT: President William Taft riding in the White Model touring car that formed part of the presidential motor fleet. The steam-powered, seven-seater car was built around 1910 and cost $4,000 to buy.

ABOVE: Henry Ford driving his "999" racing car at the Grosse Pointe horse-racing track in 1903. Racing with him is Harry Harkness in a Simplex.

Since Henry Ford rolled his Model Ts off the production line in 1908, the car has become part of American life. Early models are driven by steam power, petrol and even electricity, although "gas" will eventually be the fuel of choice. Women take up driving enthusiastically and a roadster suits the fast-living flapper style very well.

RIGHT: The Model T is the first car to go into mass production, pouring off the line in his Highland Park factory.
ABOVE: Mr Ford publicizes the arrival of the fifteen-millionth model.

ABOVE: The first electric car, built between 1917 and 1919 — the Detroit Electric coupé — recharging its batteries. On a full charge it could travel over 336km (210mi) on a test run, but 128km (80mi) was an average distance.

LEFT: Amanda Preuss at the wheel of the 1915 Oldsmobile Model 44 eight-cylinder roadster which she has driven from San Francisco to New York City in 11 days 5 hours and 45 minutes.

BELOW: The stylish La Salle roadster, which was being produced in 1927.

FIVE-YEAR PLANS AND VOTES FOR WOMEN

British women get the vote in the same year that veteran suffragette Emmeline Pankhurst dies. Emperor Hirohito comes to power in Japan, and Japan and China go to war. Germany, Britain, France and 24 other countries sign the Kellogg-Briand Pact to outlaw war. Small pleasures include chewing gum and sticky tape. Mickey Mouse makes his first appearance. In Australia, the Flying Doctor service takes off.

OPPOSITE: Health and strength: a German swimming pool with wave effects and sunshine.

1928

Jan	14	British novelist Thomas Hardy dies, aged 87
	16	In Russia, Stalin sends all his political rivals into exile
Feb	11	The Second Winter Olympics open at St Moritz, Switzerland
Mar	29	In Britain, all women aged 21 or over are given the vote
May	11	In China, Japanese forces beat off a Chinese army which is trying to recapture Jinan, capital of Shandong province
	15	Australia's Flying Doctor service starts
June	14	British suffragette leader Emmeline Pankhurst dies, aged 69
	20	Roald Amundsen dies in a plane crash while going to rescue Umberto Nobile, who had crash-landed in the Arctic
July	12	Nobile and his crew are rescued by an icebreaker
	21	English actress Ellen Terry dies at 81
	30	George Eastman demonstrates moving colour pictures in the USA
Aug	12	The Eighth Olympic Games open in Amsterdam
	27	Twenty-three countries, including Germany, sign the Kellogg-Briand Pact for the Renunciation of War
Sep	19	First screening of the animated cartoon film *Steamboat Willie*, featuring Mickey Mouse
Oct	1	In Russia, Stalin begins a Five-Year Plan to boost industry
Nov	6	Democrat Herbert Hoover is elected President of the USA

NEW BROOM FOR PORTUGAL
António de Oliveira Salazar (1889–1970) becomes minister of finance, with wide-ranging powers. He soon transforms the Portuguese economy, taking dictatorial powers for himself when he becomes prime minister in July 1932.

CHINA TAKES ON JAPAN
Nationalist forces clash with the Japanese army as they advance towards the old imperial capital of Beijing. Although the Nationalists capture the city in June, uniting China under one leader for the first time since the revolution of 1911, tension grows between China and Japan for control of northern China. The Kuomintang leader, Chiang Kai-shek, is elected president of China in October.

PEACE IN OUR TIME
Twenty-three nations, including the USA, France, Germany, and Britain sign a pact in Paris outlawing war. The pact is the work of the US secretary of state Frank Kellogg and the French foreign minister, Aristide Briand.

THE FIRST FIVE-YEAR PLAN
The first Five-Year Plan begins, designed to transform Russia into a major industrial power. In the countryside, smallholdings are being merged into vast state-owned collective farms, freeing up farmers to work in the new factories and towns.

THE NINTH OLYMPIAD
Established stars Paavo Nurmi and Johnny Weissmuller shine again but there are significant changes at the Ninth Olympiad in Amsterdam, Holland. The rise of a rival organization forces the International Olympic Committee to allow women to compete in track-and-field events. The ritual of lighting the Olympic flame is begun in the new Olympic stadium.

ABOVE: Japanese imperial banners are seen in China, but the struggle between the two countries goes on.

CIVIL WAR IN AFGHANISTAN
Amanullah Khan is still trying to introduce reform but is meeting opposition. He puts his brother on the throne, becomes a rebel himself, and leads a band of guerrillas to depose his brother. Khan's cousin, Nadir Khan, joins in the fight and kills Amanullah. The British support Nadir Khan's claims to the throne. He brings in modern practices, placates the rebels, and calms things down. By 1929, it is all over.

STEAMBOAT WILLIE
Walt Disney introduces Mickey Mouse in this animated film. It is also the first animated film with sound. The mouse is instantly popular, sequels appear, and eventually the character becomes the ubiquitous symbol of Disney and one of the best-known logos of the century.

BELOW: Fashions reflect a new freedom for women. These are beach and swimming costumes.

> ## EMMELINE PANKHURST (NEE GOULDEN) (1858–1928)
>
> The English campaigner for women's rights, Emmeline Pankhurst, has died. Married to a barrister, and advocate of women's suffrage and women's property rights, she was a vociferous campaigner for the cause. She founded the Women's Franchise League in 1889 and both she and her daughter Christabel suffered frequent imprisonment and ill-treatment in the cause. The Representation of the People Act, 1928, passed shortly before her death, was the end of her 40-year campaign and a just and fitting tribute to her.

THE WELL OF LONELINESS

With its treatment of lesbian relationships, Marguerite Radclyffe Hall's novel creates controversy and is banned in some countries, including Hall's native Britain, where its description of the relationship between a young girl and an older woman causes scandal. An American court, however, decides that the book should not be banned.

THE THREEPENNY OPERA

Bertolt Brecht and Kurt Weill create a form of musical that admits biting social comment. Weill's music combines memorable tunes and bitter harmonies, while Brecht's words embrace vivid characterization and social satire.

SOLO TO AUSTRALIA

In February the first solo flight from England to Australia is made by Squadron-Leader Bert Hinkler of the RAF, touching down sixteen times on the 17,711km (10,981mi) journey.

WOMAN PASSENGER

In April American pilot Amelia Earhart becomes the first woman to fly across the Atlantic — as a passenger; the journey is from Newfoundland to Wales.

STICKY TAPE

The first cellulose adhesive tape is invented by Richard Drew of the 3-M Corporation in America; it is marketed under the brand name of ™Scotch tape.

FLYING DOCTOR SERVICE

On May 15 the first flight of Australia's Flying Doctor Service, founded by Presbyterian minister John Flynn, takes place from Cloncurry, Queensland; the service provides medical help for people living in the remote outback.

PENICILLIN DISCOVERED

Scottish bacteriologist Alexander Fleming (1881–1955) accidentally discovers a mould which produces a substance that kills bacteria; he calls the substance penicillin, but does not study it further.

ABOVE: Swimming is a major event in the Ninth Olympics in Holland.

THE SECOND WINTER OLYMPIAD

The Second Winter Olympics in St Moritz, Switzerland, sees the return of German athletes banned after the war. Warm weather forces the cancellation of some events and while Norway again leads the medal table, the USA disrupts Nordic dominance by finishing second. Norway's Sonja Henie, though just fifteen, captures figure skating gold and spectators' hearts.

WALK AND CHEW GUM

Fleer's Dubble Bubble gum marketed in the USA.

LEAVING AFGHANISTAN

The RAF undertake first large-scale civilian evacuation by air: 568 people and 10,975kg (24,194lb) of baggage flown from Kabul December 23, 1928 to February 25, 1929. They are flown in eight Vickers Victoria transports of the RAF's No 70 Squadron, and a Handley Page Hinadi.

UN CHIEN ANDALOU

The quintessence of Surrealism is reached in this short film by Luis Buñuel and Salvador Dali. At a time when film-makers are trying to be as realistic as possible, this piece, with its often grotesque imagery, comes as a shock to artists and audiences alike.

BIG BAND VENUE

In New York, The Cotton Club is established. It quickly becomes a favourite venue for the new style of big band jazz, attracting artists such as Duke Ellington and many enthusiastic jazz fans.

FINANCIAL RUIN AS WALL STREET CRASHES

In the USA, Wall Street crashes and the world trembles. The Pope teams up with Mussolini and the Graf Zeppelin airship floats around the world in three weeks. Tintin and Snowy have their first adventure. The universe is proved to be expanding. Foam rubber enters the home. Doomed British dirigible, the R101, has its test run.

1929

Jan	13	Former US marshal Wyatt Earp dies in his sleep, aged 80
	30	Stalin orders Leon Trotsky to leave the USSR
Feb	1	Popeye the Sailor Man makes his debut
	11	In Italy, Mussolini and the Pope sign a treaty guaranteeing Vatican sovereignty
	13	Trotsky seeks refuge in Turkey
Aug	29	The Graf Zeppelin completes the first airship round-the-world flight
Sep	5	French Prime Minister Aristide Briand proposes a United States of Europe
Oct	24	Black Thursday: Wall Street stock market crashes, and 13 million shares are hurriedly sold
	29	Even heavier selling on Wall Street: 16,400,000 shares are sold
Nov 28–29		US aviator Richard Byrd makes the first aeroplane flight over the South Pole

POPE ALLIES WITH IL DUCE
Mussolini signs the Lateran Pact with the Pope, which guarantees the sovereignty of Vatican City. The Pact ends 59 years of tension between the Pope and the Italian state, since the Papal States were annexed by Italy in 1870. In July, Pope Pius X becomes the first pope to leave the Vatican since 1870.

WALL STREET CRASHES
The New York Stock Exchange on Wall Street crashes, with many shares losing up to half their value. The crash brings to an end a decade of rising share prices and prosperity in the USA, and sends the economy into depression.

FLYING OVER THE SOUTH POLE
Richard Byrd, US naval commander, makes the first flight over the South Pole as navigator of an aircraft piloted by Bert Balchen, in a nineteen-hour round trip from Little America, the expedition's base on the Ross ice shelf.

HOMOSEXUALITY DECRIMINALIZED
Homosexuality is decriminalized in the Weimar Republic. After lobbying by the Coalition for Reform of the Sexual Crimes Code, the German Reichstag committee approves a penal reform bill removing Clause 175 from the Penal Code, which made homosexuality illegal.

ROUND THE WORLD AIRSHIP
In August the German airship Graf Zeppelin makes the first round-the-world flight by an airship, starting and finishing at Lakehurst, New Jersey; the journey takes 21 days, 7 hours and 34 minutes.

OPPOSITE: Crowds wait in London's Trafalgar Square for the general election results. Vote numbers and the final result will be affected by newly enfranchised women.

GERMAN PAVILION, BARCELONA EXPOSITION
Ludwig Mies van der Rohe (1886–1969) is the German architect of this, one of the simplest of all modernist buildings. The large expanses of glass, simple form, and high-quality materials are all typical of the work of this architect in Europe and, later, in the USA.

VICEROY'S HOUSE, NEW DELHI
In total contrast to the modernist buildings being designed by people like Mies van der Rohe and Le Corbusier, Edwin Lutyens' Viceroy's House is a mixture of traditional styles and elements — domes, minarets and details influenced by the Renaissance.

OPPOSITE: A spectacular eruption from the crater of Mt. Vesuvius: its most powerful outpouring since 1906.

ABOVE: The Middle East is in turmoil. Arabs demonstrate against the Jewish population of Jerusalem, in what is currently Palestine.

THE SOUND AND THE FURY
American writer William Faulkner's novel depicts the decline of the American South through the eyes of a number of different characters, the "idiot" Benjy Compson, the mean Jason, and the sensitive Quentin. This is probably the most ambitious use of different narrative perspectives in fiction to date.

HUBBLE'S LAW
US astronomer Edwin Hubble confirms that the more distant a galaxy is from our own, the faster it is moving away; this discovery, known as Hubble's Law, proves that the universe is expanding.

GEORGES EUGENE BENJAMIN CLEMENCEAU (1841–1929)

The great French statesman, orator and journalist Clemenceau has died at the age of 88. First elected to the National Assembly in 1871, he took a principled stand on many issues, including, most famously, the Dreyfus case (as a Dreyfus supporter). He was prime minister of France during the years 1906–09 and 1917–20, and presided over the 1919 Paris Peace Conference, which negotiated the Treaty of Versailles at the end of World War I.

SERGEI PAVLOVITCH DIAGHILEV (1872–1929)

The legendary Russian dancer and impresario Sergei (Serge) Diaghilev, director of the Ballets Russes de Diaghilev, has died. Diaghilev first brought Russian dance to Paris in 1908 and established the Ballets Russes there in 1909. Under his spell the company has attracted the greatest dancers, choreographers, artists and composers of the century, including the dancer/choreographers Nijinsky and Massine, the artists Matisse and Picasso, and the progressive composers Ravel, Prokofiev, Poulenc, Satie and Stravinsky.

ABOVE: The doomed airship R101 on its test bed.

TROTSKY EXILED

Trotsky goes into exile in Constantinople after being expelled from the USSR at the end of January. Many of his supporters are exiled or imprisoned.

ALL QUIET ON THE WESTERN FRONT

German writer Erich Maria Remarque's novel of World War I, seen from the point of view of an ordinary soldier, is an enormous success, and it is said to speak for an entire generation. It shows war in its horrific and non-heroic aspects.

BIRTH OF TINTIN

The first appearance of Tintin, Snowy, Captain Haddock, Professor Calculus and the Thompson Twins as Hergé produces his first adventures. Although Belgian, he becomes an icon of French culture. Hergé will later be suspected of sympathizing with the Nazis.

FIRST IRON LUNG

American engineer Philip Drinker develops the first iron lung, a machine that helps people paralysed by poliomyelitis to breathe; it saves many lives.

FOAM RUBBER

Scientists at the Dunlop Rubber Company develop foam rubber, made by whipping air into latex, the white juice of the rubber tree.

ELECTROENCEPHALOGRAPH

German psychiatrist Hans Berger develops the electroencephalograph, a device that measures electrical voltages produced in the brain; a print-out of these voltages is called an electroencephalogram (ECG).

HAIR AND BEAUTY

Colorinse, the first commercial hair colourant for home use, is launched by Nestlé in the USA.

ALETTA JACOBS (1849–1929)

The Dutch doctor's daughter Aletta Jacobs who, as a result of petitioning the prime minister, became the first woman to study medicine in the Netherlands, has died. After qualifying she set up in practice with her father, offering free treatment for the poor. A committed feminist, she set up the first birth control clinic in Amsterdam in 1882 and was a vocal spokeswoman for women's health education, women's suffrage, and reform of legislation affecting women.

ABOVE: The German airship the Graf Zeppelin sitting on the tarmac at Los Angeles airport after its transatlantic trip.

THE GREAT DEPRESSION

A frightening decade of extreme ideologies, economic disaster and war. Communism, Fascism and Nazism confront each other, each led by fanatical leaders. Adolf Hitler's image, stage-managed rallies and swastika sign dominate these ten years. Gandhi takes the opposite path, advocating non-violent resistance. Financial depression leads to global poverty. In the USA, Roosevelt introduces the New Deal while in China Mao Zedong leads the Long March. Nothing can stay the inevitability of World War II, which brings the decade to an end.

OPPOSITE: Adolf Hitler and his followers at one of the many Nazi rallies of the decade.

1930–1939

KEY EVENTS OF THE DECADE

- CIVIL WAR IN CHINA
- THE RISE OF STALIN
- GANDHI AND CIVIL DISOBEDIENCE
- AIRSHIP DISASTERS
- NAZISM IN ASCENDANCY
- THE CULT OF HITLER
- PLASTIC AND NYLON
- JET AIRCRAFT
- SPANISH CIVIL WAR
- RADIO FROM SPACE

- FINANCIAL DEPRESSION
- THE NEW DEAL
- THE LONG MARCH
- THE OKLAHOMA DUSTBOWL
- WAR BETWEEN ITALY AND ETHIOPIA
- KEYNESIAN ECONOMIC THEORY
- WORLD WAR II BEGINS

WORLD POPULATION: 2,295 MILLION

PLASTICS, PLUTO AND THE RISE OF NAZISM

The new decade brings civil war in China and revolt in India as Gandhi shows civil disobedience to the British. The new material, plastic, is taken up with enthusiasm by designers working in the new Art Deco style. Haile Selassie is crowned Emperor of Ethiopia, and in Germany, the jackboot stamps into the Reichstag as Hitler's Nazi Party proves a vote-winner. In France, André Maginot takes the threat of German expansionism to heart and begins constructing the defensive Maginot Line. Triumph is in the air: Amy Johnson is the first woman to fly from Europe to Australia and the prototype jet engine is patented. A new planet swims into view: it is named Pluto, after the god of the underworld.

1930

Feb	18	American astronomer Clyde Tombaugh discovers the planet Pluto
Apr	6	Gandhi and his followers end their march to the sea in protest against the salt laws imposed by the British in India
	24	Amy Johnson lands in Australia after flying from Britain
July	1	In the USA, the first Greyhound bus pulls out of the garage
Nov	2	Haile Selassie crowned Emperor of Ethiopia

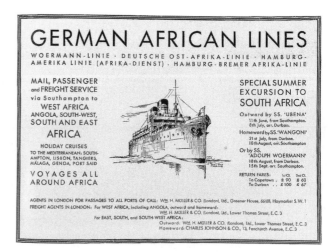

ABOVE: Europe and the great African continent are linked by fast, regular mail steamers offering every modern comfort and convenience for their passengers.

OPPOSITE: The British airship, the *R101*, crashes into a French hillside on its maiden voyage.

CIVIL WAR IN CHINA

This year sees the start of the war fought between the Kuomintang (KMT) (Nationalist) armies of Chiang Kai-shek and the Communists, which is to last until 1934. The KMT drive the Communists out of their bases in the southern mountains of China and force them on to the Long March to new bases. Mao Zedong is among the marchers.

COLLECTIVIZE OR DIE

Following the success of the Five-Year Plan in collectivizing all smallholdings, Stalin extends the programme to larger farms, ordering the kulaks, or rich peasants, to hand over their land. Millions of kulaks are subsequently killed as collectivization is ruthlessly enforced.

THE SALT MARCH

In India, Gandhi begins a campaign of civil disobedience against British rule by protesting against the government monopoly of salt production. He leads a march to the sea, to make a symbolic amount of salt from sea water. His arrest and imprisonment in April causes widespread rioting and strikes across India.

FIRST CYCLOTRON

An American team led by Ernest O Lawrence build the world's first experimental cyclotron, a device that accelerates atomic particles in a circle.

ABOVE: Children in a Russian collective are cared for in a kindergarten so that their mothers can work on the land. This was part of Stalin's first Five-Year Plan for the collectivization and industrialization of agriculture.

FIRST WORLD CUP

Only thirteen nations, of which just four are from Europe, compete in the first football World Cup in Uruguay on July 30. The USA is one of four seeded nations. The hosts win, beating neighbouring Argentina 4–2, starting a trend of victories by host nations. The competition is the brainchild of Frenchman Guerin and Dutchman Hirschman.

FLYING SOUTH

English pilot Amy Johnson (1903–41) arrives in Australia in her Gipsy Moth on May 24, the first woman to make a long-distance solo flight from London. She sets a world record of six days from London to India and reaches Darwin in nineteen days.

HAILE SELASSIE

In April, Ras Tafari, Regent of Ethiopia, becomes emperor on the death of the empress. He takes the name Haile Selassie, and will be crowned in November. Rastafarians in Jamaica, British West Indies, hail him as a living god, the fulfilment of a prophecy by American black nationalist leader Marcus Garvey.

PLUTO DISCOVERED

American astronomer Clyde W Tombaugh, working at the Lowell Observatory in the USA, discovers Pluto, the outermost planet. Its existence has been predicted by Percival Lowell; it proves to have an irregular orbit around the Sun.

WHITE VOTES IN SOUTH AFRICA

In May white South African women win the vote, but black men and women remain disenfranchized.

EXTREMISM COMES TO POWER

The Nazis make huge advances in the general election in September, gaining 107 seats, second only to the Socialists. The growing economic crisis in Germany after the Wall Street Crash causes many to support the party in the hope that it can provide strong government for Germany.

FIRST LARGE COMPUTER

A team led by American scientist Vannevar Bush develops the world's first big analogue computer, an electro-mechanical machine.

FANTASTIC PLASTIC

Solid, clear plastics made from acrylic acid (discovered by scientists in Britain, Canada and Germany in the 1920s). They will go on the market as Perspex in Britain, and as Lucite and Plexiglas in North America.

ABOVE: Mahatma Gandhi, marked by an arrow in the picture, watching as his followers scoop up sand and salt water at Dandi, defying the Indian government.

ABOVE: Amy Johnson, in her Gipsy Moth *Jason*, becomes the first woman to fly solo from England to Australia. A year later, she will make a record-breaking solo flight to Cape Town.

ABOVE: Adolf Hitler inspires the party faithful at a vast open-air rally held to celebrate the recent election success of the National Socialists (Nazis).

ABOVE: Plastic frames for glasses encasing lace and other fabrics become a fashionable designer accessory as makers experiment with this new acrylic material.

ART DECO REACHES NEW HEIGHTS

The Chrysler Building in New York, designed by William van Alen, is completed. Phantasmagoric Art Deco detailing (the steel-faced seven-storey spire, the curving lines of the top storeys, the interior decoration, the doorways) make this perhaps the most beautiful of all skyscrapers. Until the Empire State Building is completed, it will remain the highest building in the world at 319m (1,056ft).

THE BEST THING SINCE ...

Sliced bread is introduced in the USA under the Wonder Bread label by Continental Baking — in the year that the first successful automatic electric toaster is produced by the McGraw-Electric Co. of Elgin, Illinois.

BRIDGES IN SWITZERLAND

Swiss engineer Robert Maillart creates a series of elegant bridges in reinforced concrete, of which the Salginatobel Bridge, with its fine lines and dramatic gorge setting, is the most striking. Functional simplicity produces beauty in Maillart's work.

AMERICAN GOTHIC

This memorable painting of a Midwestern farmer and his wife seems to sum up rural America and becomes a lasting symbol of the rural way of life. Painted in Iowa by Grant Wood (1892–1942), it becomes the most famous painting of the American Regionalist group of artists (which also includes Thomas Hart Benton and John Steuart Curry).

THE FIRST JET ENGINE

British aero-engineer Frank Whittle (1907–96) patents a jet engine for aircraft use.

DISASTER IN THE AIR

The British airship R101 crashes into a French hillside on its maiden voyage, killing 47 people. The disaster signals the end of the British airship industry.

FRIDTJOF NANSEN
(1861–1930)

The Norwegian explorer, zoologist and oceanographer has died. His first Arctic adventure was in 1882 on board a sealer, and from 1893 to 1895 he tested his theory that he could reach the North Pole by drifting with an ice floe. He went further north by this method (86°14'N) than anyone had so far reached. After independence (1905) Nansen was Norwegian ambassador in London (1906–08). He was League of Nations commissioner for refugees from 1920 to 1922, devising the Nansen passport for stateless persons, and won the Nobel Peace Prize in 1922 for his Russian relief work.

TREE SICKNESS
Dutch elm disease, first seen in Holland in 1919, spreads to the USA and is attacking American trees.

MIND MATTERS
Karl Menninger, who in 1920 founded with his father the pioneering Menninger psychiatric clinic in Kansas, USA, publishes *The Human Mind*. Although written for medical students, it is widely read because it explains how psychiatry can help mentally disturbed people.

HAYS RULES
Motion Picture Production Code established in response to calls for censorship of motion pictures. It is spearheaded by Will H Hays, president of the Motion Pictures Producers and Distributors (known as the Hays Office). The code consists of a detailed list of what is and is not acceptable on screen.

FRENCH DEFENCE
French workmen begin building the Maginot Line, named after French war minister André Maginot; it is a series of forts built to protect France against possible German invasion.

COUP IN PERU
After an army coup in August, Colonel Luis Sánchez Cerro becomes president of Peru, overthrowing the elected government. A month later, an army revolt in Argentina overthrows the reformist president, Hipólito Irigoyen, and installs a military government under General José Uriburu

TICKET TO RIDE
The Greyhound Bus Company opens up bus routes all over the United States.

RIGHT: The two spans of the Sydney Harbour Bridge inch towards each other to form the world's largest arch bridge. It will enable pedestrians and road and rail passengers to cross 52m (170ft) above even the largest of the harbour's ocean liners.

WAR IN THE EAST, BUILDING IN THE WEST

Japan flexes its imperial muscle and poaches Manchuria from China, initiating the Sino-Japanese War, which will last until 1945. In Spain, a republic is declared, but this will not prevent eventual civil war. In America, despite the Depression, building is on the up and up and towers begin to scrape the sky. In France, Swiss architect Charles Jeanneret, better known as Le Corbusier, establishes the canon of modern architectural orthodoxy. Conquering the skies is still very much on the agenda: Swiss scientist Auguste Piccard reaches the stratosphere in a balloon. The disputed father of the light bulb, Thomas Alva Edison, dies.

1 9 3 1

Feb	5	British racer Malcolm Campbell sets a new world land speed record at Daytona: 392km/h (245miph)
Mar	3	"The Star-Spangled Banner" becomes the official national anthem of the USA
Apr	14	Spain becomes a republic
May	1	Empire State Building opens in New York
	28	Swiss scientist Auguste Piccard balloons to the stratosphere
Oct	17	Al Capone imprisoned for tax crime

ABOVE: Robert Frost (1874–1963) wins the Pulitzer Prize for the second time this year. He is one of America's most popular poets.

BIRTH OF THE SPANISH REPUBLIC

King Alfonso abdicates in April and goes into exile in London as Spain is declared a republic. The collapse of the monarchy follows huge gains made by the Republican Party in the local elections. The new government is headed by Alcalá Zamora. In the general election in June, the Socialists make huge gains.

AUSTRIA TRIGGERS EUROPEAN RUIN

In May, the collapse of Credit-Anstalt, a minor Austrian bank, leads to a major financial crisis throughout Central and Eastern Europe. The crisis spreads to Germany in July and to Britain in August, causing the minority Labour government to fall and a National government, under the leadership of the Labour prime minister, Ramsay MacDonald, to take office. Britain comes off the gold standard and devalues the pound in September, causing financial turmoil around the world. Unemployment soars across Europe.

A COMMONWEALTH CHARTER

The British Parliament passes the Statute of Westminster, which defines the independence of the five dominions within the British Empire. The Statute becomes the basic charter of the modern British Commonwealth as British colonies gain their independence.

NIGHT FLIGHT

French writer and aviator Antoine de Saint-Exupéry (1900–44), author of the well-known children's book, *The Little Prince* (1943), publishes *Night Flight*, probably his best book, about the outwardly hard nut, inwardly tender head, of a new South American airline and its chief pilot. The book contributes to the 1930s literary love affair with everything to do with the air and aviation.

EMPIRE STATE BUILDING

The latest of New York's skyscrapers is now the world's tallest building. It is famous for its great height of 381m (1,250ft), later increased by antennae to 449m (1,472ft), for the speed of construction, for its shimmering walls (many clad in metal alloy) and its fine foyer. It opens during the Depression, much of the office space remains unlet, but the owners reap revenue from sightseers.

MAIGRET STONEWALLED

Belgian writer Georges Simenon (1903–89) creates Inspector Jules Maigret in this novel (originally titled *M. Gallet décédé*), and elevates the *roman policier* to a psychological novel of some subtlety. Maigret is notable for being perhaps the first of the "caring" policemen in fiction, a man who solves crimes by understanding the criminals. The books are also famous for their depictions of the atmosphere and even the smells (Simenon had an extraordinary nose) of Paris.

ABOVE: New York City's George Washington Bridge, opened on October 24, spans a record-breaking 1,100m (3,609ft).

ANNA PAVLOVA
(1885–1931)

The Russian ballerina has died. She left Russia in 1909 to work with Diaghilev's Paris-based Ballets Russes, and later set up her own company, becoming internationally known for performing highlights from the classic ballets — perhaps the most celebrated being the dying swan. Pavlova cake is named in her honour.

VILLA SAVOIE

This house at Poissy, France, is one of the most famous by Swiss architect Le Corbusier, and is the physical manifestation of his famous *Five Points of Architecture*. It popularizes the use of concrete pillars (or *pilotis* as Le Corbusier calls them) to raise the living floor above the ground. Other typical features include ribbon-windows, white walls, a flat roof and large terraces.

THE WAVES

English novelist Virginia Woolf (1882–1941) publishes her most experimental work. In it she describes the lives of a group of friends, from childhood to middle age, through their own words and thoughts. Between the characters' thoughts come poetic mood-setting passages describing a seascape with the rising and setting sun, the shore and the waves breaking.

FRANKENSTEIN'S MONSTER COMES TO LIFE

English-born actor Boris Karloff (1887–1969) stars as the monster in *Frankenstein*, directed by James Whale, a film loosely based on Mary Shelley's novel of 1818. This is the most popular of many films based on the story.

IONIZATION

French modernist composer Edgard Varèse (1885–1965) writes the first piece of Western music solely for percussion. The piece relies on the contrast between the deep, rich sound of the tam-tam and the drier sound of the military drum.

POPULATION CONTROL

Contraception is forbidden to Roman Catholics by Pope Pius XII in his encyclical Casti Connubi, but approved for Anglicans by the Archbishop of Canterbury. As the world population approaches two billion, abortion is outlawed in Italy by Mussolini.

UP UP AND AWAY

Auguste Piccard (1884–1962), a Swiss physicist, and Charles Kipfew, his assistant, become the first people to reach the stratosphere. They ascend to 17,000m (55,000ft) in an enclosed, pressurized aluminium sphere carried by a balloon.

KNOW YOUR MARKET

The Starch Ratings are introduced by Daniel Starch, Director of the American Association of Advertising Agencies, to measure advertising readership and radio audiences.

FLASH BANG

Electronic flashguns for photographers are invented. This does away with expendable flashbulbs.

LEFT: Smog-bound Pittsburgh (top) gags for controls on air pollution, and sighs with relief at the result (bottom).

THOMAS ALVA EDISON
(1847–1931)

The Ohio-born inventor has died. He took out over 1,000 patents during his prolifically industrious life, his inventions ranging from a vote-recording machine and the stock exchange ticker tape, to the phonograph, the incandescent electric light bulb, the humble megaphone, the first electricity power plant and the "talking" movies.

BRIGHT LIGHTS, BIG CITY?

The first study of air pollution is carried out by the US Public Health Service. It estimates that one-fifth of the natural light of New York City is cut out by smoke pollution.

FASTER SHAVES

The electric razor, patented in 1923 by Colonel Jacob Schick, is produced and marketed by his own company, Schick Dry Shaver Inc.

RADIO FROM SPACE

US radio engineer Karl G Jansky discovers radio waves emanating from outside the solar system; this marks the beginning of radio astronomy.

SAFETY KETTLE

British manufacturer Walter Bulpitt invents an electric kettle that automatically ejects a resettable safety plug if the kettle overheats.

ENTER TELEX AND TWX

The American Telephone and Telegraph Company introduces two-way teleprinter services, called TWX in America and telex in Britain, which can be used by subscribers in their own offices.

THE MORNING AFTER

Alka Seltzer, a new painkiller produced as a tablet that effervesces when dissolved in water, is introduced by Miles Laboratories of Indiana, USA. It contains an antacid indigestion agent and is a popular treatment for hangovers.

SUSPENSION RECORD

The George Washington Bridge over the Hudson River, connecting New York City with New Jersey, is opened; its suspension span is 1,100m (3,609ft) — a record for the time.

ELECTRON MICROSCOPE

German scientists Ernst Ruska and Max Knoll construct the first electron microscope, which gives a much greater enlargement than ordinary microscopes.

ABOVE: Thomas A Edison dies. Physicist and world-famous inventor, he is shown outside the office of a mining plant seeking his famous "one per cent inspiration".

DAME NELLY MELBA (HELEN PORTER ARMSTRONG, née MITCHELL)
(1861–1931)

The renowned Australian soprano has died in Sydney. Born Helen Mitchell near Melbourne, she took her stage name from the city. Having been trained in Paris she performed in the world's great opera houses, and such was her reputation that she could command the casting. Among the many roles she made her own were Mimi in *La Bohème*, Gilda in *Rigoletto* and Desdemona in *Otello*, and like Caruso, with whom she sang, she was among the first opera singers to make recordings. Peach Melba and Melba toast are named in her honour. She was famous for her many "last" performances.

SINO-JAPANESE WAR

Japanese troops attack a Chinese garrison at Mukden, in the northern province of Manchuria, in September and speedily occupy the entire province. The following February, they set up the puppet state of Manchukuo, with the former Chinese Emperor Pu Yi as emperor.

In January of 1932, Japanese troops enter the city of Shanghai, starting an invasion of China. Although the Chinese drive them out of the city in March, the Japanese continue acts of aggression against Chinese territory for the next five years.

LEFT: Invading Japanese forces encounter stiff resistance and, backed by armoured vehicles, fire from the safety of a reinforced emplacement.

BELOW: Defending Chinese soldiers return rifle fire from behind a hastily constructed barricade on Paoshan Street.

ABOVE: Japanese soldiers place logs across a river for their tanks to cross.

RIGHT: An armed convoy of Japanese sailors races through the city.

BELOW: General Tsai, Commander of the 19th Route Army, observes the damaging effect of one of his howitzers.

THE WEST SINKS INTO DEPRESSION

Depression tightens its grip on the Western world in the continuous fall-out from the Wall Street Crash of 1929. In the USA, Franklin D Roosevelt comes to power on his promise of a New Deal to fight poverty; in Germany, Adolf Hitler's policies are equally attractive to a nation still recovering from World War I. The world of physics concentrates on detail: the development of particle accelerators allows scientists to observe what are at the time considered to be the smallest building blocks of the universe. Amelia Earhart becomes the first woman to fly the Atlantic.

1932

Jan	**31**	Japan captures Shanghai
Mar	**2**	The infant son of aviator Charles Lindbergh is kidnapped. Sadly he will be found dead two months later
May	**10**	President Paul Doumer of France assassinated
	21	Amelia Earhart flies from Canada to the UK
July	**5**	Antonio Salazar becomes dictator of Portugal
Aug	**6**	First Venice Film Festival
Nov	**8**	Franklin D Roosevelt elected president of the USA

ABOVE: Mies van der Rohe is director of the Bauhaus (1930–33). The Seagram Building (completed in 1958) epitomizes Bauhaus principles.

LAND FROM THE SEA

The drainage scheme of the Zuider Zee in the Netherlands is completed, vastly increasing the amount of available arable farmland and reducing the risk of flooding from the North Sea.

GRAN CHACO WAR

War breaks out between Bolivia and Paraguay over their disputed border, the Chaco Boreal or Gran Chaco, which is a potential shipping route to the sea for oil. Paraguay declares war, but Bolivia is better trained and equipped, and has successes. Paraguay then fully mobilizes and counter-attacks. The war drags on until June 1935. Both sides became war-weary and, at a peace treaty in 1938, Paraguay receives the Chaco region and Bolivia gains access to the Atlantic via two rivers.

DE VALERA LEADS IRELAND

Éamon de Valera wins the Irish general election and becomes prime minister the following month. He begins to loosen Irish ties with Britain, adopting a new constitution in 1937 which renames the Irish Free State as Eire.

THE INTERNATIONAL STYLE

This work on architecture, by Philip Johnson and Henry-Russell Hitchcock, publicizes the modernist style and influences a whole generation of architects. The book, together with the arrival of exiled scholars and architects from Nazi Germany, will influence the development of architecture, first in North America, then all over the world. The book describes a style in which form follows function.

FDR FOR PRESIDENT

Franklin D Roosevelt wins the presidential election by a landslide for the Democrats, defeating the sitting Republican president, Herbert Hoover. Roosevelt, who is in a wheelchair as a result of polio, wins all but six of the 48 states of the Union.

ANDRE LOUIS RENE MAGINOT (1877–1932)

The French politician André Maginot has died this year. During the 1920s, in preparation for a possible further war with Germany, he organized fortifications around the Franco-German border, known as the Maginot Line. When war came, the Germans invaded through Belgium, rendering these defences useless. Maginot's name is doomed to go down in history attached to a useless mega-project.

NEUTRON DISCOVERED . . .

English physicist James Chadwick discovers the neutron, a particle with no electrical charge found in the nuclei of all atoms except hydrogen.

. . . AND POSITRON DISCOVERED

US physicist Carl D Anderson discovers the positron (positive electron), the first subatomic particle of antimatter to be found.

HINDENBURG BEATS HITLER

President Hindenburg wins re-election in the German presidential election in a close-run contest with Adolf Hitler. In the general election in July, the Nazis become the biggest party, although they do not have a majority and so cannot form a government.

PARTICLE ACCELERATOR

Physicists John Cockroft of England and Ernest Walton of Ireland build the first linear atomic particle accelerator; with it they bombard lithium with protons and transform it into helium — the first artificial atomic transformation.

BELOW: Jobless Californians contemplate a bleak future as they wait in line for unemployment compensation.

ABOVE: Amelia Earhart, set to become the first woman to fly solo across the Atlantic — from Harbour Grace, Newfoundland, to Londonderry, Northern Ireland.

BROTHER CAN YOU SPARE A DIME?

This plangent tune, written by EY Harburg and Jay Gorney, is the archetypal song of the Depression. It will later become popular sung by Bing Crosby and Rudy Vallee.

WOMAN'S ATLANTIC SOLO

American aviator Amelia Earhart (1898–1937) becomes the first woman to fly the Atlantic solo, from Harbour Grace, Newfoundland, to Northern Ireland.

DOUBLE DUTCH

Flemish, a language almost identical to Dutch, becomes the official language of Belgium's Flemish provinces, which border on Holland. French becomes the official language of the Walloon provinces.

BRAVE NEW WORLD

Aldous Huxley's seminal dystopian novel is published. It depicts a society in which humans are "programmed" from birth to accept their social destiny, and are graded in a pseudo-scientific caste system (from intellectual to "semi-moron"). The novel describes what happens when a savage from a reservation confronts the World Controller, and plays out the debate between social stability and individual freedom.

AMERICAN OLYMPICS

In February, worldwide economic depression and warm weather leave competitors and snow thin on the ground at the Third Olympic Winter Games in Lake Placid, USA. Again, the North Americans (who make up half of the competitors) and the Scandinavians dominate. Nineteen-year-old Sonja Henie of Norway repeats her success in the women's figure skating.

In July, Los Angeles hosts a Tenth Olympic Games depleted by economic turmoil. Only 1,400 athletes, half the 1928 tally, travel to California. The International Olympic Committee block Olympic hero Paavo Nurmi from adding to his nine golds and three silvers, for breaking rules on his amateur status. With two golds and a silver, American Mildred "Babe" Didrikson is the star of the Games.

LEFT AND BELOW: Los Angeles is home to the Tenth Olympic Games and, despite the world's money worries, thousands attend to cheer the athletes to ever greater feats.

THE NEW DEAL VERSUS NATIONAL SOCIALISM

In Germany the Reichstag burns, Adolf Hitler takes power and his secret police, the Gestapo, begin the process of what will become known as ethnic cleansing. In the USA, Roosevelt deals with financial collapse by putting his New Deal into practice. Everyone can celebrate as prohibition ends in this year. The League of Nations, formed after World War I to prevent any future global warfare, disintegrates. Cuba becomes a dictatorship. American aviator Wiley Post flies round the world in just over a week, and in the cinema, *King Kong* storms the box office.

1933

Jan	**30**	Hitler apppointed chancellor of Germany
Feb	**27**	Reichstag burns down
Mar	**20**	First concentration camp opened at Dachau near Munich
May	**27**	Japan leaves the League of Nations
June	**23**	Hitler dissolves all opposition parties
Oct	**14**	Germany leaves the League of Nations
Dec	**5**	Prohibition repealed in the USA

ABOVE: Thomas Mann speaks out against the increasing dangers of political extremism and, after 1933, moves from Germany to Switzerland. He settles in the USA in 1936.

NEW DEAL, NEW ENERGY

Franklin D Roosevelt takes power in the USA and begins to tackle the economic crisis. New Deal legislation is soon introduced to control industry and production, money is pumped into public works, farmers and banks are bailed out with public money and a vast scheme is introduced to revive the Tennessee Valley. Three million acres will be restored to cultivation, erosion halted and 42 dams and eight hydroelectric projects built. The energy of the new government does much to lift depression in the USA.

LEAVING THE LEAGUE

Japan withdraws from the League of Nations in May; Germany follows in October.

ABOVE: Prohibition sees millions of gallons of illegal alcohol go down the drain. The Eighteenth Amendment that brought it about is to last until December 1933.

ART DIASPORA

Nazi Germany drives out "degenerate" artists. They include composers Kurt Weill (1900–50) and Arnold Schoenberg (1874–1951), and writers Thomas Mann (1875–1955) and Bertolt Brecht (1898–1956).

BACK TO MOTHER

The dominion of Newfoundland, which received its independence from Britain in 1917, reverts to colonial status after complete financial collapse.

ABOVE: The New Deal offers encouragement to American farmers, and the summer's harvest is savoured by this young crop-picker.

THE REICHSTAG BURNS

In February, fire guts the Reichstag, the parliament building in Berlin. A young Dutchman is arrested but the new Nazi government blames the Communist Party, using the excuse to suspend civil liberties such as freedom of speech and of the press and to crack down on political opponents.

CUBAN DICTATOR

In Cuba, the army, led by Fulgencio Batista and supported by the USA, overthrows President Machado and takes power in a coup in August. Batista becomes increasingly dictatorial, and although he will go into voluntary exile in the Dominican Republic in 1944, he will return to power by another coup in 1952, hanging onto power until 1959.

PAINLESS CHILDBIRTH

Grantley Dick-Read publishes *Natural Childbirth in the USA*, a manual of exercises and procedures for childbirth without drugs.

POLYTHENE BY CHANCE

British chemists accidentally discover the plastic polythene (polyethylene) while doing experiments on high pressures. Its discovery is based on research by a Dutch chemist, AMJS Michels of Amsterdam. It is the first true plastic made by the polymerization of ethylene.

ABOVE: The Marx Brothers' anti-war satire *Duck Soup* stars the hapless team delivering their distinctive brand of irreverence.

DUCK SOUP

The Marx Brothers star in this anti-war satire. Their rapid-fire irreverent humour has a lasting influence on cinema comedy.

LEFT: "Tea, anyone?" The all-electric Teasmade is launched in Britain by Goblin.

TUBERCULOSIS SANATORIUM

Finnish architect Alvar Aalto (1889–1976) is the leading modern architect in Scandinavia. His Sanatorium Paimio, Finland, shows how the modernist style adapts well to buildings with a humanitarian purpose. The clean lines and sound planning of the building are praised by Le Corbusier, Mies van der Rohe and Walter Gropius.

MAN AT THE CROSSROADS

Eminent Mexican muralist Diego Rivera (1886–1957) completes this work for the Rockefeller Center's RCA Building. Because of its content (it includes a portrait of Lenin), its commissioners destroy the mural.

42ND STREET

Busby Berkeley (1895–1976) is the choreographer of the elaborate set-pieces in this musical, which immediately becomes a classic. It is the second of such films, and a number of other films follow in which Berkeley is given full rein to include similar set-pieces, in which special effects produce kaleidoscope-like patterns of precision dancers.

MORNING TEA

The Teasmade, the first all-electric automatic teamaker, invented in the UK by Brenner Thornton in 1932 and stylishly designed, is marketed by the British company, Goblin.

NOT CRICKET

During the "Bodyline" cricket tour of Australia, the tactics of the English team cause anger and draw diplomatic protests. A number of Australians are hit as England bowls at the bodies of the batsmen in the hope of catches as they fend the ball off or hook it in the air. The most demonic of the demon bowlers is Harold Larwood.

SOLO WORLD FLIGHT

Pioneer American aviator Wiley Post makes the first solo flight around the world, using a single-engined Lockheed aeroplane; the flight takes him 7 days 18 hours 49 minutes.

THE BIG BANG

Belgian astronomer and priest Georges Lemaître (1894–1956) publishes *Discussion on the Evolution of the Universe*, which first states the theory of the Big Bang. It is based on his 1927 theory of the cosmic egg, the beginning of all things.

GESTAPO CRACKDOWN

In Germany the Gestapo begin closing gay institutions, bars, clubs, journals and libraries, burning magazines and books, and hunting down and imprisoning homosexuals. They dissolve the Bund Deutsches Frauenverein and other women's organizations, remove women from the government and professions, and award "Aryan" women cash for producing children.

CONSERVATION WORK

The Civilian Conservation Corps is founded in the USA to create work, enlisting three million young men for environmental conservation work. They plant more than two billion trees, build small dams, aid wildlife restoration and tackle soil erosion.

TECHNICAL PROGRESS

The Chicago Exposition portrays technical progress since the city's foundation in 1833. Rocket cars carry millions of visitors along the elevated Skyride. General Motors shows off its fast vehicle assembly line, and soya products are displayed in the Ford Motor Company's Industrializes American Barn.

MONKEY BUSINESS

King Kong, a film directed by Merian Cooper and Ernest Schoedsack, breaks all box office records. It stars Fay Wray, Robert Armstrong, the Empire State Building and special effects by Willis H O' Brien.

RIGHT: Pretty in polythene, despite the weather.

THE LONG KNIVES AND THE LONG MARCH

Hitler consolidates his position by despatching the enemy within during the Night of the Long Knives. In China, the Long March begins as Chinese communists, including Mao Zedong, begin their epic walk to escape from Chiang Kai-shek's Nationalist troops. In the USSR, Stalin's purges continue unchecked. In the USA, the first stirrings of black Islam are heard. Tornadoes tear across the Dust Bowl of the Midwest, devastating already-depleted prairies. In Italy, Fascist dictator Mussolini hitches his star to the Italian football team's triumph in the second World Cup.

1934

May	23	Bonnie Parker and Clyde Barrow die in a hail of bullets
June	10	Italy wins football's second World Cup
	30	The Night of Long Knives among Germany's Nazis
July	2	Lázaro Cárdenas, revolutionary leader, becomes president of Mexico
	25	Chancellor Dollfuss assassinated in Austria
Sep	26	Liner *Queen Mary* launched
Oct	21	The Long March begins in China

STORMTROOPERS STORMED

German chancellor Hitler crushes the S.A. (Sturmabteilung), known and feared as the Brown Shirts, and kills their leaders in the Night of the Long Knives. The excuse for the killing is that the S.A. were plotting a coup, but as a result, Hitler now has complete control over his party. Other opponents of the regime are also killed.

PURGE AND PURGE AGAIN

Stalin begins a massive purge of his opponents following the assassination of the Communist Party leader in Leningrad, Sergei Kirov. It is possible that Stalin ordered Kirov's murder himself, but over the next four years more than seven million people are arrested and three million people killed through execution or forced labour. Those killed include more than half the generals in the Red Army, as well as many leading Communist Party members.

HEIL HITLER

Germany: President Hindenburg dies and Hitler takes absolute power, abolishing the presidency and making himself Führer and Reich chancellor. More than 90 per cent of voters approve of the action in a referendum held later in the month.

DOLLFUSS ASSASSINATED

Members of the Austrian Nazi Party attempt a coup by killing the chancellor, Engelbert Dollfuss. The unsuccessful coup follows the attempt by the Socialists to seize power in February, and further weakens Austrian independence. The Nazis keep up the pressure to unite Austria with Germany.

THE LONG MARCH

Chinese Communists begin the Long March to escape attacks from the Nationalist government. An estimated 100,000 people leave Jiangxi in southern China and march 9,600km (6,000mi) to safety in Yanan in the northern province of Shaanxi. They will arrive in October 1935.

CONNUBIAL RADIOACTIVITY

French husband and wife physicists Jean-Frédéric and Irène Joliot-Curie discover how to make radioactive elements artificially; they share a Nobel Prize in 1935.

DIONNE QUINS

Oliva Dionne gives birth to five girls in Callanda, Ontario. Canada's Dionne quins are the first recorded case of quintuplets to be born in one delivery and survive. They are taken away from their parents and raised in a nursery as a kind of public spectacle.

STREAMLINED CARS

Four manufacturers introduce streamlined cars at the International Car Exhibition in Berlin: the models are the Chrysler-Airflow, the Steyr 32 PS, the Tatra 77 and the 1-litre DKW.

CAT'S-EYE ROAD STUDS

English road engineer Percy Shaw patents cat's-eye road studs, invented for marking out roads to make them easier to see while driving in fog or at night. They will be in use in 1935.

FORZA ITALIA

Italy triumphs on home soil in the second football World Cup. Thirty-two countries take part but holders Uruguay do not participate. The Italians beat Czechoslovakia 2–1 in the final. This is a great propaganda coup for Mussolini and the Fascists and the Italian team gave the Fascist salute before kick-off.

BLACK ISLAM

Black Muslims at the Temple of Islam, a black sect organized in Detroit by Walli Farrad (WD Fard), are led by former Baptist teacher Elijah Poole (Elijah Muhammad), Farad's assistant until his disappearance in 1934, who styles himself the "Messenger of Allah" and advocates black separatism.

DUST DISASTER

Dust storms blow 272 million tonnes (300 million tons) of topsoil from the US Midwest into the Atlantic; some 122 million hectares (300 million acres) are damaged, the result of the ploughing of virgin lands when wheat prices were high during World War I.

DIVING FOR GRAVITY

Dutch Professor Felix Andries Vening Meinesz, who has been using submarines to investigate gravity, makes his longest, deepest and most widely reported dive so far in the submarine K18.

CULTURAL STUDIES

Ruth Benedict, a social anthropologist at Columbia University in the USA, publishes *Patterns of Culture*, a ground-breaking work which disseminates the concept of culture and, by describing Native American and contemporary European cultures, helps combat current racist attitudes.

DAWN OF THE PLASTIC AGE

Perspex, a colourful, transparent acrylic plastic, is produced commercially in the UK by ICI. The process, discovered in 1930 by ICI chemist Roland Hill, was improved in 1932–33 by John WC Crawford. It incorporates research carried out earlier in the century by German chemists.

COLLECT $200

Monopoly, the game that makes a capitalist of everyone, is launched in the USA. It will be translated to suit the property map of many other countries.

BELOW: Representatives of the German army honour their dead from World War I as they rearm for the next conflict.

SOMETHING FOR THE WEEKEND

Durex manufacture the first condoms for male contraception.

CHEESE PLEASE

The cheeseburger is the inspiration of a restaurateur in Louisville, Kentucky, USA, who places a slice of cheese on top of grilled meat inside a hamburger bun and lets it soften, before serving it in his restaurant.

THE BACHELORS

French novelist Henri de Montherlant publishes *The Bachelors*, a study of two ageing aristocrats. It combines humour with tenderness and comments on a society in which such people no longer fit. Probably his best work, the book is moving because it finds emotional accommodation for the senile and foolish.

WE ROB BANKS

Bonnie Parker and Clyde Barrow, lovers and thieves, die in a hail of machine-gun bullets in Louisiana. Their two-year crime spree has made them famous and they have become a regular feature in the local media. They will be immortalized by Faye Dunaway and Warren Beatty in Arthur Penn's film *Bonnie and Clyde* (1967).

DUCKS ON FILM

Irascible fowl Donald Duck joins the animated Disney menagerie.

ABOVE: Marie and Pierre Curie work together on the characteristics of magnetism and on radioactivity, a word Marie herself coined in 1898.

DEATH AND THE ARTIST

German graphic artist Käthe Kollwitz begins her series of lithographs (her last such series) which anticipates images from concentration camps. She combines her compassion with self-portraiture.

PENGUIN CLASSIC

Penguins at London Zoo move into a concrete rookery designed by internationally acclaimed Russian architect Berthold Lubetkin and his London-based group Tecton. One of Britain's best modern buildings, it uses dramatic curving concrete ramps to stunning effect — not only are they beautiful to look at, but they provide an ideal environment for the pool's inhabitants.

MARIE CURIE
(née MARIA SKLODOWSKA)
(1867–1934)

The Warsaw-born French physicist has died of leukaemia, having spent some 40 years working with radioactivity. In Warsaw she worked as a governess to save the money that would enable her to study physics in Paris. She and her husband Pierre Curie were awarded the Nobel Prize for Physics for work on the study of magnetism and radioactivity, with Antoine Becquerel, in 1903, and after Pierre's death she received the Nobel Prize for Chemistry in 1911 for isolating pure radium. She developed X-radiography during World War I and from 1918 until her death was director of the Radium Institute in Paris.

NAZI SUPREMACY

Adolf Hitler takes power after the German government collapses in January and street warfare breaks out between the Nazis and Communist Party members. Apart from Hitler, there are only two Nazis in the eleven-member cabinet; the rest are right-wing Nationalists who believe they can curb the excesses of the Nazi Party.

OPPOSITE ABOVE LEFT: Nazism looks to the glorious past when the Knights Templar were the military ideal.

OPPOSITE ABOVE RIGHT: Hitler's desire for a powerful empire is reflected in the legionary-style standards of his troops.

OPPOSITE BELOW: The Nazi ideology is forcefully directed at women and young people as well as to the military.

ABOVE: Hitler and his mistress Eva Braun. They will marry in a Berlin bunker on April 29, 1945.

BELOW: Hitler understands the power of public appearances and how crowds behave under a charismatic leader.

GERMANY REARMS AND ITALY GOES TO WAR

War clouds begin to drift together over Europe. France and Russia ally in unexpressed apprehension at German expansionism. Hitler makes his intentions clear by creating the German Air Force (Luftwaffe) and reintroducing conscription. He also proves himself to be a master media manipulator with a sound grip on the usefulness of propaganda. Spectacular rallies in Nuremberg, filmed by Leni Riefenstahl, bedazzle the world as anti-Semitism is enshrined in German law. Not to be outdone, Mussolini foments war in Ethiopia. As if anticipating the world-shattering events to come, Charles Richter devises the scale named after him for measuring the force of earthquakes.

1935

Feb	27	Shirley Temple is the youngest person ever to win an Oscar
Mar	16	Germany introduces conscription
	21	Persia renames itself Iran
Apr	11	Dust storms sweeps across the American Midwest
May	19	TE Lawrence dies after a motor-cycling accident five days earlier
	25	Jesse Owens breaks five world records in one day
June	28	Roosevelt orders the building of Fort Knox
Sep	8	Alexis Stakhanov, a prodigiously productive Russian coalminer, is established by Stalin as the heroic ideal of the Soviet Worker.
	10	US senator Huey Long dies after being shot two days earlier by Dr Carl Weiss
	15	Hitler introduces laws to exclude German Jews from public life
Oct	2	Italy invades Ethiopia

SAARLAND GOES HOME

Separated from Germany by the Treaty of Versailles, the coal-rich region of Saarland votes overwhelmingly to return to German control.

FRANCE AND RUSSIA ALLY

The USSR and France sign a mutual assistance pact pledging assistance if either is attacked. The pact reveals fears in both countries about the intentions of the Nazi government in Germany.

INDIA SCENTS FREEDOM

The British Parliament passes the Government of India Act, which creates a central legislature in Delhi, grants greater self-government to provincial governments, and separates Burma and Aden from India. The Act goes some way to granting India full self-government.

ABOVE: One of the many rallies held by Hitler and the Nazis. The Führer's emotional speeches were heard by thousands of Germans.

INSTITUTIONALIZED ANTI-SEMITISM

Hitler announces new anti-Jewish laws at a mass rally in Nuremberg. Marriage between Jews and non-Jews is banned, and Jews are excluded from working in public services. The new laws are the latest in a long line of anti-Jewish measures in Germany.

GERMANY CALLING UP

Hitler introduces the Luftwaffe (Air Force) and announces that he is reintroducing conscription, and plans an army of 50,000. Both acts make nonsense of the Treaty of Versailles, which was designed to curb German military expansion.

UNIVERSAL TURING MACHINE
British mathematician Alan Turing (1912–54) devises a theoretical machine — the Universal Turing Machine — for solving mathematical problems; it is never built, but leads to many aspects of modern computers.

PORGY AND BESS
George Gershwin (1898–1927) wanted to create an American opera, and this is the result, his last major work. Its use of a black American cast, its tunes, and its ability to close the gap between classical and popular music have kept it in the repertoire ever since.

ONE DAY AT A TIME
Alcoholics Anonymous is founded anonymously in New York by ex-alcoholics Bill Wilson and Dr Robert H Smith as a self-help and support group for alcoholics.

BERG'S VIOLIN CONCERTO
Alban Berg's concerto is famous for combining modern musical techniques (a twelve-note row) with quotations from a Lutheran chorale (*Es ist genug*), finally played in Bach's harmonization at the end of the piece. The work is a memorial to Manon Gropius, who died at the age of eighteen.

EARTHQUAKE SCALE
US seismologist Charles F Richter devises a scale — the Richter Scale — for measuring the magnitude of earthquakes. Each number on the scale equals ten times the force of the number below it.

FIRST SUCCESSFUL RADAR
In great secrecy Scottish physicist Robert Watson-Watt builds the first effective radar equipment for detecting aircraft; he is subsidized by the British government.

NYLON INVENTED
US chemist Wallace H Carothers, working for the Du Pont Company, invents nylon by polymerizing (making large molecules) of two substances called adipic acid and hexamethylene adipamide; large-scale production begins in 1938.

WAR BETWEEN ITALY AND ETHIOPIA
Italian forces under Fascist leader Benito Mussolini invade the independent African nation of Ethiopia using aircraft, chemical weapons and armour. The ill-equipped Ethiopians are forced back and Emperor Haile Selassie flees the capital Addis Ababa. League of Nations sanctions against Italy are ineffective, and Italy eventually leaves the League in 1937. The Italian king is proclaimed Emperor of Abyssinia, as the Italians call their new acquisition. Ethiopia remains under Italian control until 1941 when British, French and Ethiopian forces reinstate the emperor.

THE TRIUMPH OF THE WILL
Shot at the Nuremberg Nazi Party Conference the previous year, this film by Leni Riefenstahl is one of the most effective pieces of Nazi propaganda. She makes it after impressing Hitler with a short film of the previous rally. Her work is a key plank in Hitler's propaganda platform.

FAST WORK
In his car Bluebird, British driver Malcolm Campbell advances the land speed record past the 480km/h (300miph) barrier. He records a speed of 4884.955km/h (301.129miph) at the Bonneville Salt Flats in America.

FIRST WONDER DRUGS
The first sulphonamide drugs are introduced when German bacteriologist Gerhard Domagk discovers that the red dye prontosil rubra is an active antibacterial agent. Prontosil itself is no longer used.

OPINION POLLS
George Gallup, an Iowa statistician, is asked to gauge reader reaction to newspaper features and founds the American Institute of Public Opinion to carry out market and political research.

CENTRAL PARK
The first Dutch national park, De Hoge Veluwe, is founded in central Holland. It is the gift of Anthony George Kroller.

WORKING LIGHT
The Anglepoise lamp, a pivoting desk lamp with a jointed arm designed by a British designer, George Carwardine, is produced in the UK.

BEER TO GO
Beer in easy-carry, throwaway metal cans is marketed by Kreuger in New Jersey, USA, and launched in New York.

PAYING TO PARK
The first parking meters appear in the streets of Oklahoma City, USA. They were designed and patented in 1932 by the editor of the town's newspaper, Charles Magee.

CAN YOU HEAR ME?
The first wearable hearing aid, with an electric valve and a battery-operated amplifier weighing 1kg (2.25lb) is introduced by its British inventor, A Edwin Stevens, who founds a company, Amplivox, to market it.

COLOUR PICTURES
The Kodak Company introduces Kodachrome film, for taking colour transparencies.

ABOVE: An early type of mobile radar detector. Radar, first developed in the UK, will be an important defensive advantage in World War II.

ALFRED DREYFUS
(c.1859–1935)

The French army officer and subject of a *cause célèbre* has died. Dreyfus, born c.1859 of Jewish family, was falsely accused of treason in 1893–94 and sent for life imprisonment to Devil's Island. France was strongly divided over the case, and through the active support of many people in political and intellectual life, including the writer Emile Zola and the statesman Clemenceau, he was eventually reinstated in 1906. He went on to fight in World War I and was awarded the Légion d'honneur.

THOMAS EDWARD (TE) LAWRENCE
(LAWRENCE OF ARABIA)
(1888–1935)

The author of *Seven Pillars of Wisdom*, Col. TE Lawrence (Lawrence of Arabia) has been killed in a motor-cycling accident near his home in Dorset. Born in 1888 of Anglo-Irish stock, he encountered the Bedouin people when working on an archaeological dig on the Euphrates as a young man, and became a fervent admirer of their character and way of life. He was an Arab guerrilla leader in the Arab struggle against the Turks (1916) and was a delegate at the Paris Peace Conference in 1919. Later, to escape his own fame, he enlisted in the Royal Air Force under the name JH Ross.

WAR IN SPAIN AND THE BIRTH OF THE AXIS POWERS

Spain becomes the theatre of European war as General Franco, supported by Nazi Germany and Fascist Italy, fights against Republican Spain (supported by Communists and Socialists from all over Europe and Russia). In Germany, Jesse Owens, the black American super-athlete, confounds Hitler by sweeping the board at the Olympic Games in Berlin. Germany, Italy and Japan join up to become the Axis Powers. In Britain, the prototype of the Spitfire, the fighter plane that will win the Battle of Britain, takes a test flight. The British Broadcasting Corporation transmits the first television programmes.

1936

Feb	**26**	Volkswagen factory opens in Germany
Mar	**7**	German troops march into the Rhineland in defiance of the Treaty of Versailles
July	**19**	Spanish Civil War breaks out
Oct	**5**	In England, unemployed workers march from Jarrow to London in protest at unemployment
Dec	**11**	Edward VIII abdicates the British throne

ABOVE: The British film actor and director Charlie Chaplin charms cinema audiences with his comedic but endearing performances.

SPEND, SPEND, SPEND

The British economist John Maynard Keynes (1883–1946) publishes *The General Theory of Employment, Interest and Money*, which advocates public spending to cure unemployment. Keynesian economic theories become widely accepted within a few years, and form the basis of the post-war economic boom.

FALSE DAWN IN SPAIN

The Popular Front of left-wing parties wins the general election in Spain. Manuel Azaña becomes prime minister and restores the 1931 Republican constitution. Anti-clerical and anti-landlord sentiments explode throughout Spain, and churches are attacked and land seized.

UNEASE OVER GERMANY

German troops occupy the Rhineland, demilitarized since 1919. The move alarms France, but Britain makes no protest.

BRITAIN IN THE MIDDLE IN PALESTINE

A revolt against British rule in Palestine breaks out among the Arab population. Jews are murdered and Jewish property is attacked. The revolt leads to the intervention of the British army, which is attacked by both Arabs and Jews.

BRITAIN AND EGYPT

Britain ends its protectorate over Egypt, with the exception the Suez Canal Zone, entering into an alliance with Egypt which lasts for twenty years.

JARROW MARCHERS

Two hundred unemployed men march from Jarrow in northeast England to London, to focus attention on unemployment in the town; 68 per cent of all working men in Jarrow are unemployed after the collapse of the shipbuilding and iron and steel industries in the region.

ANYTHING FOR LOVE

King Edward VIII abdicates because he wishes to marry a divorcee, the American Wallis Simpson. He is succeeded by his younger brother, George VI. Edward goes into exile, marrying Wallis in France the following June.

IVAN PETROVICH PAVLOV
(1849–1936)

The Russian physiologist whose laboratory experiments with dogs established the theory of conditioned reflex or conditioned response (applicable also to human beings) has died. He won the Nobel Prize for his work in 1904.

ABOVE: A shot by photographer Leni Riefenstahl of a gymnast taken at the 1936 Olympic Games held in Berlin.

GREAT SHADES

Polaroid lens anti-glare sunglasses, developed by US physicist Edwin Land, are introduced by Land-Wheelwight Laboratories.

AXIS POWERS LINE UP

The Italian and German governments sign the anti-Communist Axis Pact; later in the month, Germany signs the Anti-Comintern Pact with Japan.

MODERN TIMES

One of a number of (virtually) silent feature-length films that Charlie Chaplin (1889–1977) produces with his company United Artists, this example brings his brand of serious clowning (tramp as everyman) to bear on a satire of the mechanization of modern life and work. Chaplin is writer, director, producer, and actor (with Paulette Goddard).

OL' MAN RIVER

Black actor and singer Paul Robeson (1898–1976) plays Joe in the film version of *Show Boat*, and turns this song into a personal signature tune and symbol of a black American artist's success and role as social conscience.

MIGRANT MOTHER

Working, like several other great American photographers, for the Farm Security Administration, Dorothea Lange (1895–1965) documents rural America during the Depression — the poverty of the people, the erosion of the land. Lange's photograph, "Migrant Mother", sticks in the public mind more than any other and helps win support for federal aid.

SAFETY IRON

The first electric hand iron with a thermostat goes on sale in the USA. Electric irons first appeared in 1920, but their temperature could not be controlled.

THE PEOPLE'S PORSCHE

The first prototypes of the Volkswagen "Beetle" are displayed at the Berlin Motor Show, designed by Ferdinand Porsche and praised by Adolf Hitler.

MAXIM GORKY (ALEKSEI MAKSIMOVICH PESHKOV) (1868–1936)

The Russian writer has died. A largely self-educated peasant who worked in many lowly occupations and described in his writings the life of peasants and outcasts, he was a valiant supporter of the Russian Revolution and had become a national hero.

FALLINGWATER (AKA THE KAUFMANN HOUSE)

Frank Lloyd Wright's most famous house is built over a waterfall at Bear Run, Pennsylvania. It is a daring design, both for the way it seems precariously balanced above the water and for the way it mixes old and new materials (concrete with stone and wood).

MUSIC FOR STRINGS, PERCUSSION AND CELESTA

One of the major works of Béla Bartók's fruitful period in the 1930s, this piece shows his flair for combining different instrumental colours and for handling rhythm.

SANITARY TOWELS

Kotex sanitary napkins are introduced by Kimberley & Clark Co. of Wisconsin, USA, using a wood-cellulose cotton substitute developed for World War battlefield dressings by German chemist Ernst Mahler. Tampax Inc. is founded in New Brunswick, New Jersey, to produce cotton tampons.

FIRST PUBLIC TV SERVICE

The first regular public electronic TV service is started in Britain by the British Broadcasting Corporation.

ACHTUNG! SPITFIRE!

The first prototype of the British Spitfire fighter plane, designed by Reginald J Mitchell, makes its test flight.

FLIGHT FROM HAWAII
The first solo flight by a woman from Hawaii to mainland America is made by Amelia Earhart in 18 hours 16 minutes.

SUCCESSFUL HELICOPTER
In June the world's first completely successful helicopter, the Focke-Wulf Fw 61, makes its maiden flight.

DESERT TREASURES
The Swedish explorer Sven Hedin returns (aged 80) from a nine-year trip to the Gobi Desert to investigate the shifting locations of the Lopnor salt lakes. He has discovered a major Stone Age culture between Manchuria and Sinkiang.

FEDERICO GARCIA LORCA (1899–1936)
The assassination at Granada (on the instructions of the Civil Governor) of the young Spanish poet and dramatist Federico García Lorca (known as Lorca) is one of the shameful incidents of the Spanish Civil War. His works, such as the poems *Gypsy Ballads* (1928) and *Lament for the Death of a Bullfighter* (1935), and the play *Blood Wedding* (1933), capture the intensity of the Spanish spirit.

BELOW: Frank Lloyd Wright, now 69, displays his genius for blending modernistic design into a natural setting.

SPANISH CIVIL WAR

❖ KEY DATES ❖

July 1936–March 31, 1939 SIEGE OF MADRID: A siege by the Nationalists which includes artillery and air attacks and civil war within the capital, when an anti-Communist revolt breaks out.

July 20–Sept 27, 1936 SIEGE OF TOLEDO: A Nationalist garrison of 1,300 holds the palace fortress of the Alcázar against 15,000 Republicans in a siege which is broken by two columns of Nationalist troops on September 26.

July 21, 1936 The world's first large-scale airlift begins when over six weeks German Junkers Ju 52/3m fly 7,350 Nationalist troops from Morocco to Spain.

March 8–17, 1937 BATTLE OF GUADALAJARA: Some 22,000 Nationalist troops with 30,000 Italians attack the Republicans who fall back but launch a counter-attack backed by Soviet tanks and aircraft. They rout the Italians, killing 2,000, wounding 4,000 and halting the Nationalists.

January 17, 1937 BATTLE OF MALAGA: The city, defended by 40,000 poorly organized militiamen, falls to three Nationalist columns and nine battalions of Italian mechanized infantry. As the Republicans withdraw they are ground strafed by Italian and German aircraft. They suffer 15,000 casualties.

April 26 BOMBING OF GUERNICA: German bombers attack Guernica, capital of the Basque region, ostensibly to support Franco. The city is of no strategic importance, but a third of the population are killed. The raid is a piece of psychological warfare and good practice for the Luftwaffe.

Dec 23, 1938–Feb 10, 1939 BATTLE OF BARCELONA: Six Nationalist armies with four Italian divisions attack northwards in December and push the Republicans back towards Barcelona, which was heavily bombed on January 26. A few days later the Nationalists occupy the city and about half a million Republican troops and dependants cross the border into France.

Civil war breaks out on July 17 as the Nationalist army, led by General Francisco Franco, rises against the Republican government. Led by Britain and France, many nations pledge non-interference in the war, although both Italy and Germany actively support the rebels. An International Brigade of left-wing activists from Europe and America is formed to support the government and sees action in many battles, notably the siege of Madrid, which begins in November and lasts until March 1939. Many new weapons and tactics are tested in Spain by the backers of both sides. The war will officially end on April 1, 1939, with Franco victorious.

ABOVE: Bombardment and mining are used to devastate historic buildings in cities such as Toledo, Barcelona and Madrid.

BELOW: Horses are used by both sides to carry pack guns over rough terrain and, if killed, to act as barricades for artillery.

ABOVE: Italy and Germany support Franco with men and equipment. The Republicans are aided by the USSR and the International Brigade.

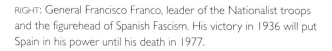

ABOVE: As ever, civil war means upheaval, dispossession and the movement of vast numbers of refugees around the country.

RIGHT: General Francisco Franco, leader of the Nationalist troops and the figurehead of Spanish Fascism. His victory in 1936 will put Spain in his power until his death in 1977.

HITLER'S OLYMPICS

The Eleventh Olympics and the Fourth Winter Olympics are held in Germany. They give Hitler a chance to showcase his ideology, and show off Germany's resurgence and the supposed superiority of the Aryan race through a broad propaganda campaign.

The Winter Games are held in Garmisch-Partenkirchen and see the first alpine event, a combined downhill and slalom competition. Sonja Henie retires after winning her third successive figure-skating gold for Norway, and Britain scores an upset win in ice hockey.

The Olympics proper take place in Berlin. For the first time a relay of runners, 3,075 in all, bring a torch from Olympia in Greece to light the Olympic flame in Berlin. Despite Nazi hopes, the undisputed star of the Games is not a German but Jesse Owens, a black American. Owens takes gold in the 100 metres, 200 metres, 4x100 metres relay and the long jump. Hitler leaves the stadium rather than present the medals to a black athlete. The most successful female competitor is swimmer Hendrika "Ria" Mastenbroek of Holland. She wins three golds and a silver.

ABOVE LEFT: The Aryan ideal, exemplified by classical statues. These are used to set the tone for the film record of the Games made by director Leni Riefenstahl: Hitler's choice to document what he hopes will be an Olympiad to fuel Nazi propaganda.

ABOVE: The Games are extremely well organized and well equipped with specially built pools and tracks. No expense is spared to show that Hitler's Germany sees itself as a player on the world's stage.

LEFT: A dramatic Leni Riefenstahl shot of a swimmer. Holland dominates the women's swimming events and Japan and the USA share the honours almost equally in the men's events.

ABOVE: Young German female athletes display the body beautiful. Germany takes gold for the discus and javelin events but does not manage to outpace the athletes from the USA on the track.

ABOVE: Riefenstahl's stylized images, such as this discus thrower, are very powerful. In the real world, the USA takes gold and silver in the discus event and Italy takes bronze.

LEFT: Star of the Olympics is the black American athlete Jesse Owens, who confounds Hitler's "Aryan" expectations, winning gold in four events.

ATROCITIES AND DISASTERS, SHOW TRIALS AND SNOW WHITE

Japan bombs Shanghai in China and Germany bombs Guernica, in the Basque region of Spain. Both atrocities shock the world. In the USSR, Stalin continues his horrific show trials, an excuse to eliminate his enemies. In the USA, the Golden Gate Bridge opens up California to all comers, but in New Jersey the airship *Hindenburg* explodes while trying to land. The principle of photocopying is established, but noone can think of how to apply it. Walt Disney cheers a gloomy world with the first full-length animated cartoon, *Snow White and the Seven Dwarfs*.

1937

Apr	**26**	Guernica bombed by Germany at the request of Franco
May	**6**	The airship *Hindenburg* explodes on landing
	27	Golden Gate Bridge opens in San Francisco
Aug	**13**	Japan invades China, attacking Shanghai
Sep	**28**	Hitler and Mussolini stage a joint "Peace Rally" in Berlin

ABOVE: German ground crew help to steady the *Hindenburg*.

ANSCHLUSS

German troops enter Austria and unite the country with Germany. The *Anschluss* (unification) between the two countries is forbidden by the Treaty of Versailles, and alarms the rest of Europe.

GERMANY TAKES SUDETENLAND

Sudeten Germans living on the border with Germany demand autonomy from Czechoslovakia. They are prompted by Hitler, who uses this as an excuse to increase pressure on the Czech government.

PEACE IN OUR TIME?

At a conference in Munich between Britain, France, Italy and Germany to end the Sudeten crisis, the four powers agree that Czechoslovakia must give up the Sudetenland to Germany. The following month, German troops occupy the territory while Poland seizes the Teschen region. Eduard Benes resigns as president of Czechoslovakia. In November, Hungary occupies southern Slovakia. Czechoslovakia is now effectively dismembered.

THE SOUND OF BREAKING GLASS

In a night of looting and violence, more than 7,000 Jewish shops are attacked and many Jews beaten up. Hundreds of synagogues are burned down. *Kristallnacht*, or the Night of Broken Glass, marks a major attack on the Jewish community in Germany.

HOOVER BUILDING, PERIVALE

Strong geometric forms and sparing use of striking colour and pattern mark Wallis Gilbert's factory for Hoover on the outskirts of London as one of the most notable Art Deco (or Moderne) buildings of its time.

WAR OF THE WORLDS

The power of the mass media is brought home dramatically when thousands panic during this broadcast version of HG Wells' science fiction novel *War of the Worlds*, which describes what happens when Martians land on earth. The actor Orson Welles of the Mercury Radio Theatre reads out the lines that scare so many listeners.

PICTURE POST

Not the first picture magazine, but one of the most influential, *Picture Post* brings the news and contemporary events to life with pictures and telling captions. *Picture Post* leads the way, inspiring the development of photojournalism (which is being made more viable as precision cameras get smaller) and influencing editors to explore the relationship between words and pictures.

ENTER THE BALLPOINT PEN

Ladislao Biró, a Hungarian journalist, patents the ballpoint pen; it will go into production in 1940 but he makes very little money from it.

ABOVE: Orson Welles' radio production of *War of the Worlds* convinces many of his audience that an alien invasion is taking place. His fascination with the power of radio continued throughout his life.

BILLY THE KID

Aaron Copland's music brings the hero to life in *Billy the Kid*, his American folk ballet version of an enduring legend, choreographed by Eugene Loring, who also dances the lead role. This is the first of several notable Copland ballet scores based on American folklore.

ROCKET DEVELOPMENT

A German team led by engineer Wernher von Braun (1912–27) builds a liquid-fuel rocket that travels about 18km (60ft), the longest flight yet.

SUZANNE LENGLEN
(1899–1938)

The French tennis idol, who was many times a Wimbledon champion, has died. She won her first major championship (women's world hard-court singles in Paris) at the age of fifteen. She retired in 1927, founded her own tennis school in Paris and wrote a book on tennis, *Lawn Tennis, the Game of Nations* and a novel, *The Love Game* (both in 1925).

GABRIELE D'ANNUNZIO
(1863–1938)

The Italian writer and patriot, World War I soldier, sailor and airman, has died. D'Annunzio collaborated with Friedrich Nietzsche on the trilogy *Romances of the Rose* (1889–1894); he became a parliamentary deputy in 1897. Later colourful achievements include an affair with the actress Eleonora Duse, for whom he wrote plays, and appointing himself dictator of Fiume (Rijeka). He became a supporter of Fascism in later years.

NUCLEAR FISSION DISCOVERED

German radio chemists Otto Hahn and Fritz Strassmann discover nuclear fission by bombarding uranium with neutrons, leading to the development of nuclear power and atomic bombs.

NO MORE BURNT SAUCEPANS

Du Pont engineer Roy Plunkett in the USA accidentally discovers polytetrafluroethylene, a plastic better known as ™Teflon or ™Fluon; it is used in astronauts' spacesuits and as a non-stick coating for saucepans.

LIVING FOSSIL

In December a South African fisherman hauls up a "living fossil": a coelacanth, a primitive type of fish that scientists hitherto knew only from fossils and believed to have been extinct for 70 million years.

NO MORE DRINKING AND DRIVING

The Drunkometer — the first breathalyzer to test for alcohol in drivers' breath, designed by RN Harger — is tested in Indiana, USA and finds that of 1,750 drivers tested, 250 are drunk.

ABOVE: A parade through Paris to mark the signing of the Entente Cordiale between France and Britain.

ABOVE: Nylon stockings bring smiles of sheer delight and prove popular throughout the world.

ENCORA ITALIA

The Italians repeat their World Cup victory in Paris, France, by beating Hungary 4-2 in the final.

MISS MOODY TAKES WIMBLEDON

American tennis star Helen Wills Moody collects her eighth and final Wimbledon singles crown. With ruthless efficiency, the wins were collected in just nine attempts between 1927 and 1938 and complemented seven US Open titles and six French triumphs.

SAVING THE WHALE

The International Convention for the Regulation of Whaling introduces voluntary quotas for whaling nations, but the Japanese, Russians and Norwegians ignore the agreement.

MUSTAFA KEMAL ATATURK
(born MUSTAFA KEMAL)
(1881–1938)

Mustafa Kemal, the Turkish leader later known as Atatürk (Father of the Turks), has died. He was a nationalist leader during and after the World War I. As the first president of modern Turkey, from 1923, he was responsible for many reforms, including the emancipation of women and the introduction of the Latin alphabet.

AN AWFUL LOT OF COFFEE

Instant coffee is marketed by Nestlé of Switzerland after a request from the Brazilian government to find a use for Brazil's coffee surpluses. Eight years' research have produced a freeze-dried coffee powder that is reconstituted by adding water.

AIR-CONDITIONED JEWELLERY

Tiffany & Co.'s new store on Fifth Avenue, New York, is the first fully air-conditioned store. Invented by WH Carrier in 1902, air-conditioning has up to now been used for cooling factories.

VICTORY AND FREEDOM

A "V for Victory" campaign is started by two Belgians working for the BBC in London, who realize that "V" stands for *vrijheid* (freedom) in Flemish and Dutch, and *victoire* (victory) in French. The first Vs appear on walls in German-occupied Belgium.

SILK STOCKINGS?

Nylon, invented in the USA by Wallace Hume Carothers, who patented it in 1934, is produced commercially by Du Pont in the USA and used to make women's stockings.

GAS IN CHINA

Lewisite poison gas is used by the Japanese against the Chinese during a series of incursions into China via Manchuria, as well as during amphibious landings to seize parts of the hinterland and major ports.

ABOVE: The Duke of Windsor and Wallis Simpson, for whom he gave up the throne.

BELOW: Street fighting in Manchuria as Japan invades the Chinese mainland.

WAR ENGULFS THE WORLD ONCE MORE

A war-torn decade ends with the greatest conflict of them all so far. By the end of the year, most of Europe is at war. Allies and Axis Powers line up on opposite sides and America stays out of the fight. On the silver screen, Dorothy and her three eccentric musketeers make a stand against evil in *The Wizard of Oz* and Scarlett O' Hara endures the American Civil War on the losing side in *Gone with the Wind*. Meanwhile, scientists are unlocking the secrets of nuclear fission that will lead to the atomic bomb.

1939

Apr	**7**	Italy invades Albania
May	**22**	Germany and Italy form alliance
July	**20**	New Dalai Lama is discovered in Tibet
Aug	**23**	Hitler and Stalin sign a non-aggression pact
Sep	**1**	Germany invades Poland
	3	Germany and England officially at war
Nov	**8**	Bomb wrecks Munich beer hall where Hitler has been speaking
Dec	**18**	German pocket battleship *Graf Spee* scuttled by her crew

ABOVE: Polish troops mobilize to face the might of the invading German war machine.

WAR AT LAST

German armies invade Poland from the west, with Russian armies later invading from the east. Britain and France declare war on Germany. British children are evacuated from the cities because of fears of air attacks and the British army lands in France to protect it against a possible German attack. A phoney war begins as both sides increase war production, but no fighting takes place.

FRANCO VICTORIOUS

The Spanish Civil War ends with victory for the Nationalist forces of General Franco. Britain and France recognize the new government, which represses all dissent and becomes increasingly Fascist in nature. In April, Spain joins Italy, Germany and Japan in the Anti-Comintern Pact.

SEPTEMBER 1, 1939

This is English poet Auden's poem mourning for a Europe slipping towards war. It confirms his role as leading poet of the pre-war period, and social commentator.

BELOW: The New York Giants and the Brooklyn Dodgers open the 1939 season at Ebbets Field, Brooklyn.

OVERTURES TO WAR

In January, Slovakia declares its independence from Czechoslovakia and becomes a German protectorate. Germany annexes the western Czech provinces of Bohemia and Moravia and the eastern province of Ruthenia is seized by Hungary. Hitler enters Prague in triumph. In the same month, Germany seizes the Baltic region of Memel from Lithuania.

In March, following the German take-over of Czechoslovakia, Hitler denounces the German non-aggression pact with Poland, signed in 1934, and demands the Free City of Danzig, on the Baltic, and routes to eastern Prussia through the Baltic corridor, which gives Poland access to the sea. Britain and France pledge to defend Poland from attack. In April, they extend this guarantee to Romania and Greece.

In April, the USSR proposes an alliance with Britain and France against Germany and Italy. Britain refuses, but takes urgent steps to rearm: conscription is introduced and arms production is stepped up. France steps up its war effort.

In August, Stalin and German foreign minister Joachim von Ribbentrop sign the Nazi-Soviet Non-Aggression Pact in Moscow, allowing Germany a free hand in western Poland.

ABOVE: German soldiers advance through the rubble-strewn streets of Warsaw.

ITALY EXPANDS
Italy invades and conquers the Adriatic state of Albania, increasing its empire in the Mediterranean.

FINNEGANS WAKE
James Joyce's *Ulysses* had explored the events of a single day; in *Finnegan's Wake*, Joyce turns to the upside-down inside-out world of night, sleep, and dreams. He creates his own language (involving multi-linguistic wordplay), to write a book which, because of its difficulty, becomes more talked about than read.

EASTER SUNDAY CONCERT
The Daughters of the American Revolution refuse black singer Marian Anderson's request to sing in Constitution Hall, Washington, because of her race. Eleanor Roosevelt sponsors an outdoor concert at the Lincoln Memorial instead, and around 100,000 people attend.

PHOTOCOMPOSITION
American inventor William C Hueber introduces the first photocomposition system, replacing metal type.

THE WIZARD OF OZ
The musical film of the novel by L Frank Baum stars Judy Garland. She wins a special Academy Award for singing "Somewhere over the Rainbow" and is launched on a series of starring roles in major American films.

GONE WITH THE WIND
The film of Margaret Mitchell's novel quickly becomes a worldwide success. Vivien Leigh stars as Scarlett O'Hara and Clark Gable does not give a damn as Rhett Butler.

STAGECOACH
John Ford's classic western stars the "cowboy's cowboy" John "The Duke" Wayne. This is the film that makes Ford's name synonymous with the western and with films looking back on America's past. It is also Wayne's first major role in a big film, and so establishes him as a major star.

FIRST JET AIRCRAFT
The German Heinkel He 178, the world's first jet-propelled aircraft, makes its test flight, with an engine designed by Dr Hans von Ohain; it reaches 500km/h (313miph).

SIKORSKY HELICOPTER
Russian-born US engineer Igor Sikorsky designs his first helicopter, the VS-300; it makes a tethered flight in September, but is not suitable for mass production.

NUCLEAR FISSION

Austrian-born physicists Otto Frisch and his aunt Lise Meitner continue the work started by Meitner and Otto Hahn. They realize that the production of barium atoms after the bombardment of uranium nuclei with neutrons means that the nucleus has been split, and call the process "nuclear fission"; this leads to atomic power.

DDT COMES INTO ITS OWN

Swiss chemist Paul Hermann Müller finds that dichlorodiphenyltrichloroethane — DDT, discovered in 1874 — is a powerful insecticide; it is successfully tested against the Colorado beetle, a potato pest.

THE HEAT OF THE SUN

The first solar-powered house is built as an experiment at the Massachusetts Institute of Technology in the USA. A solar panel on the roof heats water stored in a tank.

AN EARLY ANTIBIOTIC

French scientist René Dubos, working in New York, discovers the antibiotic tyrothricin, but it proves too poisonous for use on humans

LITTLE LEAGUE

Carl Stotz and George and Bert Bebble form Little League Baseball in Williamsport, Pennsylvania. The format for youth baseball has since spread across America and the world, and the Little League season now culminates in the Little League World Series between an American team and a foreign side.

THE WORLD'S FAIR

New York's World's Fair focuses on Trylon and Perisphere, a 218m (728ft) high pyramidal tower and a gigantic globe which exhibit futuristic films. Innovative exhibits from 60 nations include a pressure cooker, Electro, a robot who speaks, and Sparks, a dog who barks and wags his tail.

ABOVE: On April 26, 1939 Captain Wendel of the German Luftwaffe sets a world air speed record of 755km/h (468.9miph).

FINNS WRESTLE WITH THE BEAR

The USSR invades Finland in November, but the attack is thwarted by the Finnish army used to fighting in winter conditions. The Soviet Union has demanded that Finland demilitarize its border defences and cede islands and a base to the USSR. Finland has refused and in November the USSR sends in an estimated 1 million men against 300,000 Finnish troops. Defending the Mannerheim line and using their skills as ski troops they inflict heavy losses on the Soviets.

❖KEY DATES❖
IN THE RUSSO-FINNISH WAR

Dec 11, 1939–Jan 8, 1940 SUOMUSSALMI: Two Soviet divisions are annihilated in the woods of eastern Finland in a succession of ambushes and running battles.

Feb 1940 MANNERHEIM LINE: The defences across the Karelian Isthmus are subject to intense air and artillery bombardment and heavy attacks and in February, despite heavy losses, the Soviet forces break through. This forces the Finns, who had 25,000 killed and 44,000 wounded, to accept Soviet terms. Soviet casualties are estimated at 200,000 dead.

THE POWER OF THE MOVIES

ABOVE LEFT: Barbara Stanwyck, star of many a Hollywood *film noir* and always the most fatale of femmes.

ABOVE: Joan Crawford, undisputed queen of the 1930s genre known as women's pictures.

LEFT: Dashing screen hero Clark Gable will enlist and train as an aerial gunner when the USA enters the war.

ABOVE: Hollywood hoofer Fred Astaire swings a mean shoe on a wartime fundraising tour.

PENICILLIN IS DEVELOPED

Australian-born pathologist Howard Florey and German-born chemist Ernst Chain, working in Oxford, develop penicillin as an antibiotic; it goes into mass-production in the USA.

COELIAC DISEASE

Dutch doctors recognize that coeliac disease — in which the small intestine fails to absorb food, particularly fats — can be caused by sensitivity to gluten, the major protein of wheat and rye. This discovery comes about fortuitously when the occupying German forces requisition all supplies of wheat and rye flour, after which coeliac patients in Dutch hospitals begin to show improvement.

COLOUR TELEVISION

The first daily transmission of colour TV begins in the USA, with rotating colour filters in the cameras and in the receivers.

RH FACTOR DISCOVERED

American scientists Karl Landsteiner and Philip Levine discover the Rh factor in blood — an antigen which can cause harm to newborn babies.

WHO IS ADENOID HYNKEL?

This is the name given by Charlie Chaplin to the protagonist of his film *The Great Dictator*, mocking the activities of Hitler and Mussolini.

GAMES OFF

The Winter and Summer Olympics are cancelled because of the war.

ABOVE: Erwin Rommel, one of Hitler's leading commanders, successfully leads a panzer division during the invasion of France in 1940 and is later appointed commander of the Afrika Corps.

TWO MORE ELEMENTS

US physicists Edwin M McMillan and Philip H Abelson discover the element neptunium, with an atomic number of 93; McMillan, Glenn T Seaborg and others then discover plutonium, atomic number 94.

GPV SPELLS JEEP

The US Army test-runs a prototype all-terrain reconnaissance vehicle, the GPV or General Purpose Vehicle. Later this acronym will be shortened to jeep.

BIG MACS START SMALL

Movie theatre owners Richard and Maurice McDonald set up their first hamburger stand, a drive-in near Pasadena, California.

(ARTHUR) NEVILLE CHAMBERLAIN
(1869–1940)

The former British prime minister has died, six months after being replaced by Winston Churchill. He will go down in history waving the Munich Agreement of 1938 and saying "Peace in our time" as he returns having yielded to Hitler's claim for Sudetenland (in Czechoslovakia) in exchange for peace.

THE USA JOINS IN THE FIGHT

Franklin D Roosevelt introduces the Lend-Lease plan without which it is likely that the Allies would lose the war. This is not popular with isolationists in the USA, but tunes change when Japan strikes home, devastating the US Air Force stationed at Pearl Harbor, Hawaii. America enters the war in earnest. Hitler invades Russia. Civilian populations on both sides suffer from heavy bombing raids on cities and towns. Jet aircraft enter the fray on both sides and the world is introduced to Spam, the taste of wartime.

1941

May	27	*Bismarck* sinks
June	1	Greece falls to Germany
Aug	11	Churchill and Roosevelt meet to sign the Atlantic Charter
Sep	19	Germany takes Kiev, going back on the non-agression pact
Nov	1	Mt. Rushmore unveiled
Dec	7	Pearl Harbor bombed

LEND-LEASE

The Lend-Lease Bill becomes law, allowing the US president to sell, lend or lease material to countries whose defence is important to the USA. Britain benefits hugely from this, granting 99-year rent-free leases for naval bases in the Caribbean and Newfoundland to the USA in return for 50 destroyers.

USSR AND JAPAN MAKE A PACT

The USSR signs a neutrality pact with Japan, which lasts until the final days of the war in 1945. The pact ensures that both Japan and the USSR do not have to fight on two fronts. It frees up the USSR to fight Germany, and Japan to attack the USA and Southeast Asia.

LONDON DEVASTATED

The heaviest German bombing raid of the war hits London, with 550 bombers dropping 100,000 incendiaries and numerous bombs on the capital. The House of Commons is destroyed, and more than 1,400 people are killed. More than 20,000 people have been killed in London, and 25,000 injured, since German bombers began hitting the city.

SHELTER ART

English sculptor Henry Moore (1898–1986) produces a series of drawings of people in London's air-raid shelters. Images of ordinary people coping in a crisis, they are some of the most poignant pictures of the war. They are also highly sculptural, fine examples of how a sculptor can capture the mass and form of figures in a drawing.

ABOVE: The US base at Pearl Harbor is attacked unexpectedly at dawn by some 360 Japanese aircraft.

PEARL HARBOR

Following the Japanese attack on the US fleet in Pearl Harbor in the Pacific Ocean, the USA enters the war. The US economy is put on a war footing, with factories turned over to war production and thousands of women pressed into factory work.

YELLOW STAR

The infamous yellow Star of David is imposed on German Jews over the age of six, to make them easily recognizable. Jews in Poland already wear such a star.

AMY JOHNSON
(1903–1941)

The English pioneer aviator has been lost in a plane accident while on active service in the British Air Transport Auxiliary. She was the first woman to fly solo from England to Australia, in 1930, and made several record solo flights, as well as flying across the Atlantic with her husband, James Mollison, in 1933 and with him to India in 1934.

WORLD WAR II

The greatest conflict of the twentieth century, World War II touches every continent and devastates some. The best estimate for casualties is 15 million military dead and 25 million military wounded. Civilian deaths are about 38 million. Huge parts of the European and Russian infrastructure are destroyed and the populations of Eastern European states displaced as national borders are adjusted.

❖KEY DATES❖
WORLD WAR II

March 12, 1938 AUSTRIA ANNEXED German troops enter Austria to ensure *Anschluss* (union) with Germany.

March 15, 1939 CZECHOSLOVAKIA German troops enter Prague, Czechoslovakia dismantled.

Sept 1–Oct 7, 1939 POLAND Poland is crushed by armoured and mechanized forces backed by bombers and fighter ground attack aircraft. German casualties are 14,000 killed and 30,300 wounded, Polish casualties are believed to exceed 120,000 plus 450,000 prisoners.

Sept 3, 1939 BRITAIN Britain declares war on Germany.

April 9, 1940 DENMARK The tiny country is seized by the Germans to give them airfields for the attack on Norway.

April 8–9–June 8, 1940 NORWAY The German invasion of Norway, intended to protect supplies of iron ore from Sweden, cost the Germans 5,300 killed and wounded, three cruisers, ten destroyers, eight submarines, eleven transports and eleven other ships.

May 10–June 25, 1940 HOLLAND The Germans attack in the west, which draws British and French troops into Holland before the Germans break through at Sedan and in a drive to the Channel cut the British off from France. Holland falls on May 15 and Belgium on May 27, France capitulates on June 22 and hostilities end on June 25. On the ground, Germany suffers 27,000 killed, 110,000 wounded and 18,000 missing. France loses 90,000 dead and 200,000 wounded and 1,900,000 are either taken prisoner or missing. The Belgians have 23,000 casualties and the Dutch 10,000. Britain loses 68,000 casualties. In the air, the Luftwaffe lose 1,284 aircraft, the RAF 931 and the French 560.

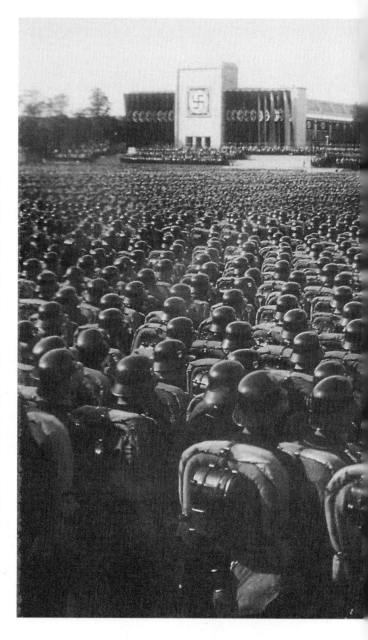

ABOVE: A mass roll-call of SA, SS and NSKK troops in Nuremberg. During the first year of the war, Germany has the manpower, equipment and will to win that gives her a great advantage.

DUNKIRK EVACUATION

German tank divisions trap British, French and Belgian troops around the port of Dunkirk on the north coast of France. Between May 26 and June 4, 1940, in one of the most dramatic events of the war, 338,000 soldiers are rescued by the Royal Navy with assistance from the French and many civilian vessels from England.

ABOVE: Nazis rally in Nuremberg.

BELOW: Hitler announces the annexation of Austria to an ecstatic Reichstag

RIGHT: A Czech woman's grief-stricken submission as Germany annexes Czechoslovakia, in one of many expansionist actions towards the east.

THEATRES OF WAR

NORTH AFRICA AND THE MEDITERRANEAN 1940–43

The campaign in North Africa fought by the British with United States' assistance in late 1942, against the Italians and Germans (Axis Powers), is unique in World War II. The theatre has few civilians so casualties are confined to the armies and the tactics developed for the desert are similar to those employed in naval warfare.

TOBRUK
Jan 22–Nov, 1941 and June 18–June 20, 1942
The former Italian port is held by British and Commonwealth forces behind German lines from January to November 1941. However, when it is again besieged by the Germans in June 1942, they press their attacks home and this time the port is captured with valuable stores and 33,000 prisoners.

EL ALAMEIN Oct 23–Nov 4, 1942
The British and Commonwealth attack the Axis forces, who are well dug in. The British losses are 2,350 killed and 8,950 wounded, with 2,260 missing. The Axis losses are 10,000 killed, 15,000 wounded and 30,000 captured.

TORCH LANDINGS
Nov 8, 1942
Some 36,000 British and American forces land in two locations in French Northwest Africa, in effect squeezing Axis forces from the west.

YUGOSLAVIA AND GREECE
April 6–April 23, 1941
After the Italian Army becomes embroiled in Greece and Yugoslavia launches a coup against its pro-Axis government, Hitler decides to invade Yugoslavia and Greece. German casualties in Yugoslavia are 558 while 345,000 Yugoslavian soldiers are captured. In Greece the Germans have 4,500 casualties. Greek losses are 70,000 killed or wounded and 270,000 captured. British forces assisting the Greeks suffer 12,000 casualties.

OPERATION "MERCURY" May 20, 1941
German airborne assault on Crete. The Luftwaffe lands 22,750 men using 493 Ju 52 transport aircraft and about 80 gliders. Though it is a German victory, 4,500 of their men are killed and 150 transport aircraft lost.

ABOVE: General Montgomery's determination overcame Field Marshal Rommel's Afrika Korps.

LEFT: Russians break through German defences outside Leningrad.

SOVIET UNION AND EASTERN FRONT 1941–44

Hitler boasts that the Soviet Union is so decrepit that "We have only to kick in the door and the whole rotten structure will come crashing down". Invading the USSR is the logical outcome of the Nazi doctrine.

SIEGE OF LENINGRAD
Sept 1, 1941–Jan 27, 1944

Besieged for almost the duration of the war, Leningrad withstands German attacks. By 1944 nearly one million of its inhabitants have been killed or starved to death.

MINSK June–July, 1941

A battle of encirclement in which fifteen Soviet divisions are destroyed.

SEVASTOPOL Nov 1941–July 3, 1942

The Black Sea port and Soviet naval base is besieged by ten German infantry divisions with 120 batteries of artillery. The Soviet forces number 106,000 men with 700 guns and mortars. Though the port is captured some defenders are evacuated by small boat.

KHARKOV Oct 24, 1941–Aug 22, 1943

The scene of heavy fighting in 1942 and 1943, Kharkov is the location for a major battle of encirclement in which 250,000 Soviet prisoners are taken in 1942.

STALINGRAD Aug 19, 1942–Jan 31, 1943

The attack on the Russian city is a disaster for Hitler, leading to the defeat of the German 6th Army and the loss of 1.5 million men, 3,500 tanks, 12,000 guns and mortars, 75,000 vehicles and 3,000 aircraft.

KURSK July 5–July 17, 1943

This is the German counter-offensive, of which the Russians are well aware through signals intelligence. In the fighting both sides lose over 1,500 tanks, but the Russians swing on to the offensive and the Germans lose the initiative for good.

BERLIN April 16–May 2, 1945

The final battle for the German capital costs the Russians 100,000 killed, while 136,000 prisoners are taken. It is estimated that 100,000 civilians are killed in the fighting.

WARSAW UPRISING

Between August 1 and October 2, 194 Polish patriots rise to liberate their city from German occupation as the Soviet army approaches. However, on Stalin's orders they halt until the Poles have been defeated.

ABOVE: A massive bombardment is launched at Monte Cassino.

SICILY AND ITALY 1943–45

Churchill proposes that Italy should be attacked since he describes it as "the soft underbelly" of the Axis. It proves to be a much tougher undertaking than imagined, involving amphibious operations and fighting in mountains in bitter winter weather.

SICILY July 10–Aug 18, 1943

Landings by British and American forces push the Axis towards the Strait of Messina. They are able to evacuate 40,000 Germans and 60,000 Italians but suffer 178,000 casualties and captured. Allied casualties are 31,158 including 11,923 Americans.

SALERNO Sept 9, 1943

The landing on the mainland of Italy by US and British forces is vigorously counter-attacked by the Germans. Only after reinforcements have been rushed in does it become secure, and on September 15 the Germans begin to pull back.

MONTE CASSINO Feb 15–May 18, 1944

This strong defensive position costs the Allies 21,000 casualties including 4,100 killed in action. When Cassino falls the Allies take 20,000 prisoners and open the road to Rome.

ANZIO Jan 22–May 25, 1944

An amphibious operation intended to outflank Cassino, the Anzio attack becomes in effect stuck on the beaches where the US forces suffer 21,000 casualties and the Germans about 11,000.

ROME June 5, 1944

Liberated by the Americans, the drive on the Italian capital city actually allows the German 10th Army to escape as a formed unit.

THE FIGHT FOR EUROPE

NORMANDY AND NORTHWEST EUROPE 1942–45

BRUNEVAL Feb 27–28, 1942

In a combined operation, a company of British paratroops launches a raid against a German radar station and an RAF technician removes key components before the force is evacuated by the Royal Navy.

DIEPPE Aug 19, 1942

A large-scale raid against the French port of Dieppe by 5,000 Canadians and 1,000 Commandos is almost a complete disaster. The Canadians lose 215 officers and 3,164 men, the Commandos 24 officers and 223 men, while German losses are 345 killed and 268 wounded.

COUTANCES
July 17, 1944

USAAF P-38 Lightnings are involved in the first napalm attack in Normandy launched against a fuel depot at Coutances.

BELOW: The Allied raid on Dieppe costs the lives of thousands of Canadian troops.

D-DAY JUNE 6, 1944

The Anglo-American landings on the Normandy coast turn the tide of the war in Europe. It involves 1,213 warships, 4,126 landing ships, 736 ancillary vessels and 864 merchant vessels. By midnight on June 6, 57,500 American and 75,000 British and Canadian forces are ashore. The Allied casualties are 2,500 killed and 8,500 wounded.

FALAISE POCKET
Aug 13–21, 1944

The German forces trapped by the US break out at St. Lo and are pounded from the air. When the pocket closes only 20,000 out of the 80,000 trapped Germans escape. They leave behind vast amounts of weapons and equipment.

ARNHEM
Sept 17–25, 1944

The Arnhem operation is part of an airborne attack to capture bridges across the lower Rhine. British forces from the 1st Airborne Division are forced to withdraw after heavy German attacks. British losses are 1,130 killed and 6,000 captured, of whom half are wounded.

ABOVE: Normandy, June 6, as American soldiers leave their landing craft and plunge towards the shore.

RIGHT: Arnhem's sky blossoms with British paratroopers as the disastrous Operation Market Garden begins.

ARDENNES
Dec 16,1944–Jan 16, 1945

The last great German offensive in the West has initial successes against the US Army but is halted and destroyed by US forces with some British help. Losses are 100,000 German casualties, 81,000 American and 1,400 British.

REMAGEN
March 7, 1945

The Ludendorf railway bridge across the Rhine is captured intact by men of the US 9th Armoured Division.

RHINE CROSSINGS
March 23, 1945

Full-scale amphibious crossings and airborne landings put British and US forces in a position to capture the industrial heartland of the Ruhr.

WAR IN THE EAST 1941–45

Although Japan has been involved in China, its war with the US and Britain does not begin until December 1941. The Japanese hope that through tactical success at Pearl Harbor they will be able to access oil, raw material supplies and territorial assets.

HONG KONG Dec 8–25, 1941
Despite being outnumbered and outgunned, the British put up a stout defence. Casualties are 2,000 with 11,000 prisoners; the Japanese lose 2,745 killed.

MALAYA AND SINGAPORE
Dec 8, 1941–Feb 15, 1942
The British fight a series of delaying actions down the Malay Peninsula, suffering 5,000 casualties following Japanese landings in three locations. The Japanese capture Singapore for 9,800 casualties. They take 32,000 Indian, 16,000 British and 14,000 Australian prisoners, more than 50 per cent of whom are to die in captivity.

PHILIPPINES Dec 10, 1941–May 6–7, 1942
Japanese troops land on the Philippines and push the American and Filipino soldiers back to the Bataan Peninsula, which they hold until April 9. Some 76,000 men surrender; however, at least 10,000 die during their march to prison. The last defences to fall are those of Corregidor, where the garrison suffers 2,000 casualties.

BELOW: Japanese forces land on the island fortress of Corregidor, overcoming a valiant stand by US and Filipino troops.

NEW GUINEA 1942–Aug 26, 1944
Following Japanese landings, Australian and US forces counter-attack and, over a long campaign, defeat Japan. The cost is 57,046 Australian casualties, of whom 12,161 are killed. US casualties are 19,000, while the Japanese lose 13,000 in Papua and 35,000 in New Guinea.

TARAWA Nov 20–23, 1943
Defended by 4,800 Japanese marines, Tarawa costs the US Marine Corps 1,500 killed or wounded.

KOHIMA/IMPHAL, BURMA April 4–18, 1944
About 13,000 Japanese are killed in the siege of Kohima and at Imphal 53,000 perish from a combination of disease and combat. These two victories are the turning point for the British in Burma.

SAIPAN June 15–July 9, 1944
Out of a garrison of 30,000 only 1,000 Japanese prisoners are taken. US casualties are 1,037 marines and 3,674 soldiers including 3,426 dead.

GUAM July 21–Aug 10, 1944
Defended by 20,000 men, the island falls for the loss of 6,716 marines, 839 soldiers and 245 sailors including 1,023 dead. Its capture gives the USAF a base for heavy bomber raids on Japan.

THE PHILIPPINE CAMPAIGN

This lasts from October 17, 1944 to July 4, 1945. The liberation of the Philippine Island group is a particular concern for the US commander in the Far East, General Douglas MacArthur, who has spent much of his career in the area.

LEYTE Oct 17–Dec 25, 1944

The American casualties are 15,584 including 3,584 killed, Japanese figures are not known but are believed to be 70,000 killed.

LUZON Dec 15–July 4, 1945

Heavy fighting leads to the liberation of the island which contains the capital of the Philippines, Manila. The Americans suffer 37,854 killed or wounded, in Manila alone. Japanese losses are 16,000 killed.

CORREGIDOR Feb 16–21, 1945

The Americans launch a combined sea and airborne attack on the fortified island, where at least 3,300 Japanese perish.

ABOVE: US soldiers cross Burma's Chindwin River.

IWO JIMA Feb 16–March 26, 1945

Fighting for a tiny island of 21km² (8mi².) defended by 21,000 troops, the Americans suffer 6,821 dead and 18,200 wounded. There are few Japanese survivors. Iwo Jima is strategically important: it had been used as an airstrip for Japanese fighter planes, making it easy for them to attack US bombers.

OKINAWA April 1–July 2,1945

The casualties in the fighting for this 2056 sq km (794 sq mi) island are 2,938 marines and 4,675 soldiers dead, 31,807 wounded. The Japanese lose 100,000 killed and 10,000 captured.

BELOW: US marines race for the beaches of Iwo Jima.

AIR WAR IN THE WEST

THE BATTLE OF BRITAIN July 10–Oct 12, 1940
With the fall of France, Britain has no allies left in Western Europe. Hitler's plan is to launch air attacks against Britain as a preliminary for an invasion by German ground forces. The Luftwaffe strength is 2,800 aircraft, the RAF has 700. Nearly 500 RAF pilots are killed and 400 are wounded. Even so, Britain holds off the Luftwaffe and prevents invasion.

BLITZKRIEG Sept 7 1940–May 10 1941
After failure in the Battle of Britain, Hermann Goering, commander of the Luftwaffe, turns to flying by night and dropping bombs on civilian targets. Ports and big cities get the worst of it. London is hit almost every night. On November 14/15, 1940, the Midlands city of Coventry is devastated when some 449 German bombers drop 503 tons of high explosive and 881 canisters of incendiaries, killing 550 and injuring 1,200.

FIRST FLIGHT OF TWIN-ENGINED JET AIRCRAFT April 2, 1941
The German He 280 goes into action. The maximum level speed is 820km/h (510miph).

THE DAMBUSTERS May 16–17 1943
Attacks by RAF bombers using specialized "bouncing" bombs against the Sorpe, Mohne and Eder dams are launched. Though the Mohne and Eder are breached the Sorpe is only damaged.

PEENEMUNDE 17–18 August, 1943
Following intelligence that Peenemunde on the Baltic is a rocket research centre, it is attacked by RAF Lancaster bombers.

JET FIGHTERS IN ACTION Oct, 1944
Me 262 jet fighters engage the USAAF and RAF. The first aerial victory is a B-17 shot down by a pilot of Kommando Nowotny.

V-WEAPON CAMPAIGN
June 13, 1944–March 29, 1945
The *Vergeltungswaffen* or vengeance weapons are the V-1 (the ZZG-76 flying bomb) and the V-2, (the A-4 ballistic missile). About 35,000 V-1s are produced, 9,521 are fired at the UK of which 4,621 are destroyed. About 5,000 V-2s are launched against London, Antwerp and Liège. On August 4, 1944, a Gloster Meteor jet fighter downs a V-1. The pilot, Flying Officer Dean, tips the missile into the ground with his wing.

OPPOSITE: The V-2 rocket, Hitler's vengeance weapon.

RAF AND USAAF BOMBING CAMPAIGN

The Royal Air Force (RAF) opens the war by dropping leaflets over Germany. By the close of the war the United States Army Air Force (USAAF) is attacking enemy targets by day while the RAF flies by night. Though military and economic targets are hit, the RAF also destroy huge areas of housing.

• On May 30–31, 1942, the RAF flies 1,046 bombers over Cologne where it dropps 1,455 tons of bombs killing 486 people, injuring 5,027 and destroying 18,440 buildings. Between 1943 and 1944, the Ruhr, Germany's industrial heartland, is attacked by the RAF and USAAF. By the end of 1943 the Allied Air Forces have dropped 200,000 tons of bombs on Germany and much of that on the Ruhr.

• On July 24, 27, 29 and August 2, 1943 incendiary attacks create a firestorm that destroys 22 sq km

(8.5 sq mi) of Hamburg and kills 44,600 civilians and 800 servicemen. Between August 23, 1943 and March 1944, a series of sixteen heavy raids by the RAF on Berlin damages the city, but does not prevent it working as a capital. Out of 9,111 sorties, the RAF loses 492 bombers.

• On August 17 and October 14, 1943, the USAAF stages raids on the German ball-bearing plants at Schweinfurt, which, though of considerable strategic value, are very costly: 36 bombers are lost in the first and 60 in the second raid.

• On February 13–14, 1945, RAF and USAAF bombers kill between 30,000 and 60,000 civilians in Dresden, many of them refugees, in day and night attacks.

AIR WAR IN THE EAST

PEARL HARBOR, HAWAII Dec 7, 1941

This is the event that brings the USA into the war. In a surprise early-morning attack by the Japanese, lasting no more than two hours, 135 Japanese dive bombers, 104 high-level bombers and 81 fighter aircraft flying from carriers, sink or damage 18 warships, destroy 187 aircraft and kill 2,400 US servicemen. The US carriers are at sea, escape and become the main warships in the Pacific. The Japanese lose 29 aircraft and five midget submarines.

DOOLITLE TOKYO RAID April 18, 1942

Sixteen North American B-25 Mitchells commanded by Lt. Col. James Doolittle, flying from the USS *Hornet*, attack Tokyo, Nagoya, Kobe and Yokohama and then fly on to China.

KAMIKAZE ATTACKS Oct 19, 1944–April 1945

Attacks by about 5,000 suicide aircraft sink or damage about six major Allied ships including an escort carrier at Leyte Gulf in the Philippines.

TOKYO FIRE RAIDS March 9–10, 1945

The first incendiary attack against the Japanese capital devastates the city centre and kills 100,000 people.

HIROSHIMA 08.15, Aug 6, 1945

Atomic bomb nicknamed "Little Boy" is dropped on the Japanese city by a B-29 piloted by Colonel Paul Tibbets, and initiates nuclear warfare. The bomb destroys 122 sq km (47 sq mi) and kills 70,000 people.

NAGASAKI Aug 9, 1945

Atomic bomb nicknamed "Fat Man" is dropped by a B-29 piloted by Major Charles Sweeney, killing 24,000 people.

LEFT: Lt. Col. James Doolittle with one of his B-25 Mitchell bombers that carried out the Tokyo raid. He is to become the commander of the 8th Air Force in 1944 and 1945.

NAVAL WAR IN THE WEST

THE ADMIRAL GRAF SPEE
Dec 13–17, 1939
After a running battle with three British cruisers, the German pocket battleship *Admiral Graf Spee* is scuttled by her captain in the River Plate, on orders from Berlin.

TARANTO Nov 11, 1940
In this naval–air action, 27 Swordfish torpedo bombers from the carrier HMS *Illustrious* attack the Italian fleet, safe in its base at Taranto. They cripple three battleships and two cruisers, and sink two other ships. The British lose two aircraft.

CAPE MATAPAN
Mar 27–28, 1941
Using signal intercepts, three British battleships are able to close with three Italian 8-inch cruisers, two smaller cruisers and two destroyers, and sink them as well as damaging a battleship. The British lose two naval aircraft.

ABOVE: The *Graf Spee*, severely damaged during the Battle of the River Plate, is scuttled by its captain.

HMS HOOD AND BISMARCK May 24–27, 1941
The *Bismarck* is one of the most powerful battleships of the war, used to attack Atlantic shipping. On May 24 1941 it sinks the British battle cruiser HMS *Hood* off the Greenland coast. Almost the entire British Navy sets out to hunt the *Bismarck* down and finally catches her off the coast of France on May 26. It takes the combined fire-power of five destroyers, two battleships and a cruiser to sink her.

OPERATION CERBERUS, THE "CHANNEL DASH" Feb 12, 1942
The German battle cruisers *Gneisenau* and *Scharnhorst* and heavy cruiser *Prinz Eugen* make a daylight run up the Channel from Brest, France, to Germany. Both battle cruisers are damaged by British mines.

NAVAL WAR IN THE EAST

THE BATTLE OF THE CORAL SEA
May 6–8, 1942
This is the first major naval action in the world fought entirely by aircraft. The US Navy loses the carrier *Lexington* and the Japanese the carrier *Shoho*. The victory prevents Japan from attacking shipping lanes to Australia.

MIDWAY June 3–6, 1942
This is the turning point of the naval war in the Pacific. The US Navy sinks the Japanese heavy carrier *Akagi*, the carriers *Kaga* and *Soryu*, and later the carrier *Hiryu*. The US loses 150 aircraft, 307 men, the destroyer *Hammann* and the carrier *Yorktown*. Victory for the US cripples Japanese air-power and prevents Japan from taking Midway to use as a base to attack Hawaii.

THE BATTLE OF THE PHILIPPINE SEA
June 19–20, 1944
US pilots down 330 Japanese aircraft for losses of 30, in an air action called "The Great Marianas Turkey Shoot". The US submarine *Albacore* sinks the carrier *Taiho* and the submarine *Cavalla* sinks the carrier *Shokaku*.

THE BATTLE FOR LEYTE GULF, PHILIPPINES
Oct 23–26, 1944
Losses are severe on both sides in a three-part naval action, the biggest ever in terms of tonnage. By the close, the US Navy has lost three carriers, two destroyers and a destroyer escort. The battle costs the Japanese three battleships, four carriers, ten cruisers and nine destroyers. The Japanese use kamikaze planes, but victory goes to the US.

ABOVE: British and Australian survivors are rescued by the USS *Sealion*.

MUSASHI AND THE YAMATO SUNK
Oct 24 and April 7, 1945
The *Musashi* and her sister ship the *Yamato* are the largest, most heavily protected and armed battleships in the world and constitute a threat to Allied forces. They are sunk by aircraft from US carriers.

ABOVE: The American navy enters Ulithi anchorage.

RIGHT: The USS *Pennsylvania* and three cruisers move into Lingayen Gulf.

CONFLICT GOES GLOBAL: AFRICA AND THE FAR EAST

The Japanese take Singapore and Europe has to face fighting in the East, at the same time as establishing a front in North Africa. America avenges Pearl Harbor with a victory over the Japanese at Midway in the Pacific. In France, the collaborationist Vichy government falls. In Berlin, Hitler openly discusses the "Final Solution" to what he considers to be the Jewish problem. The forerunner of the United Nations is established. The film *Casablanca* encapsulates the romance of resistance to tyranny.

1942

Jan	**1**	26 nations sign the Declaration of the United Nations
Feb	**15**	Singapore falls to Japan
June	**7**	Battle of Midway; US avenges Pearl Harbor
Oct	**23**	Allies win battle of El Alamein

RIGHT: Russian air ace Col. Tashin leaves one of the bombers supplied by the US.

ABOVE: An Allied convoy moving through Iran with supplies for Russia. The USA supplies weapons, equipment and aeroplanes to the USSR.

LEFT: US military aircraft in Alaska waiting to be ferried to Russia, as part of the Lend-Lease plan.

ABOVE: A welcome halt for this US supply convoy in the mountains of Iran.

THE NATIONS UNITE

The USA, USSR, Britain, China and 22 other allied nations, calling themselves the United Nations, pledge not to make separate peace treaties with Germany, Italy or Japan. The conference in Washington forms the basis of the United Nations Organization.

ANTI-BRITISH FEELING IN INDIA

The Congress Party of India calls upon the British to "quit India" immediately. Civil disorder follows in the autumn and several Congress leaders are interned.

MARTIAL MUSIC

American bandleader Glenn Miller heads up a band composed of US Army personnel.

BELOW: Irving Berlin's "God Bless America" becomes the unofficial US national anthem.

ABOVE: British premier Winston Churchill at a march-past of Russian troops during his visit to Moscow.

THE NAZI SOLUTION

Nazi leaders meeting in secret at Wannsee discuss the "Final Solution of the Jewish Question". Plans are drawn up to exterminate all Jews in Europe in six death camps established for the purpose.

LOSING SINGAPORE

The surrender of the island fortress of Singapore to Japan marks the end of British invincibility in the Far East. The Japanese encourage revolt among the British, French and Dutch colonies in the region and support Asian claims to independent government.

WAR IN AFRICA

As German forces continue to invade the USSR, pressure grows for a second front in Western Europe against Hitler, to relieve pressure on the Red Army. Britain and the USA consider invading North Africa.

MESSERSCHMITTS OUT OF THE SUN

The German Messerschmitt Me 262A-1a twin-engined fighter becomes the world's first jet aircraft to enter operational service.

ABOVE: In the film *Casablanca*, Humphrey Bogart and Ingrid Bergman play star-crossed lovers in a city riddled with wartime intrigue.

FIRST NUCLEAR REACTOR
Italian-born physicist Enrico Fermi (1901–1954) starts up the first nuclear reactor, built on the squash court of Chicago University; it demonstrates the first controlled chain reaction.

VICHY FALLS
German troops occupy Vichy France, ending the semi-independence of the country. The French fleet is scuttled in Toulon harbour to prevent it falling into German hands.

MILITARY CHOPPERS
The Sikorsky XR-2 becomes the first helicopter designed and built for military service, and is tested by the US Army.

FIRST V-2 ROCKET
On October 2 the Germans make the first successful launch of their V-2 rocket; it flies for about 19km (12mi); V-2s go into active service in 1944.

FAMINE RELIEF
The charity Oxfam is founded in the UK as the Oxford Committee for Famine Relief, to fight world famine.

THE WARSAW GHETTO
The Germans storm the Warsaw Ghetto in September, killing its 50,000 Jewish inhabitants. The population of Polish Jews, which numbered 2.5 million in 1939, is steadily reduced as the Germans kill or transport all Jews to death camps.

OF ALL THE BARS IN ALL THE TOWNS …
Humphrey Bogart stars as Rick, Ingrid Bergman as Ilsa, in *Casablanca*, the anti-Nazi film directed by Hungarian-born Michael Curtiz which becomes an instant classic and combines the tension of a thriller with the element of romance.

ABOVE: Bing Crosby (left) and Bob Hope (above) continue their popular road movies; this year Morocco is the destination.

THE OUTSIDER
French novelist Albert Camus' novel about a man who cannot respond to normal conventions and social rituals becomes emblematic of a modern dilemma — how to find our own values when we reject those of the society around us. This first novel puts its author at the forefront of modern debate. His book of essays *The Myth of Sisyphus*, introducing the idea of "the Absurd", also appears this year.

ANTIGONE: A MYTH FOR TODAY
French dramatist Jean Anouilh's updating of the Greek myth enacts the troubles of contemporary France. The oppressive Creon becomes symbolic of the Vichy compromise, the idealistic Antigone with the values of freedom.

CORE SET UP
The Congress of Racial Equality (CORE) is founded by University of Chicago students led by James Farmer, to end racial segregation and discrimination in the USA by non-violent means. John Harold Johnson begins publication of the *Negro Digest* in Chicago.

FIRST SIGHT OF A FASHION BASIC
The T-shirt appears as regulation US Navy outerwear, specified as a "T-type" knitted cotton vest, with a round neck and short sleeves set at right angles for maximum underarm sweat absorption. T-type shirts were formerly worn only as underwear.

HOT STUFF
The self-heating can is produced by Heinz to sustain hungry troops when cooking is impossible. When the cap is peeled back, a fuse ignites a heating mixture stored in a tube running through the centre of the can.

THE TIDE TURNS AS THE ALLIES FIGHT BACK

The Allies get a grip on their strategy and plan to knock Italy out of the war, then to turn their attention to Germany and finally Japan. Sicily is first to fall and Italy eventually surrenders. Meanwhile, the arrival of aircraft carriers in the North Atlantic decimates the German submarines that have been preying on the convoy ships, and so food and supplies get through once again. The first electro-mechanical computer grinds into action in the UK, decoding German messages. In a Swiss laboratory, Albert Hofmann stumbles into LSD. In New York, the young Francis Albert Sinatra croons his way to stardom.

1943

Jan	**3**	Siege of Leningrad comes to an end
May	**18**	The Dambusters raid
Apr	**18**	Uprising by the inhabitants of the Warsaw Ghetto
July	**10**	Allies invade Sicily
Sep	**8**	Axis Powers broken as Italy surrenders
Nov	**28**	Churchill, Roosevelt and Stalin meet in Tehran

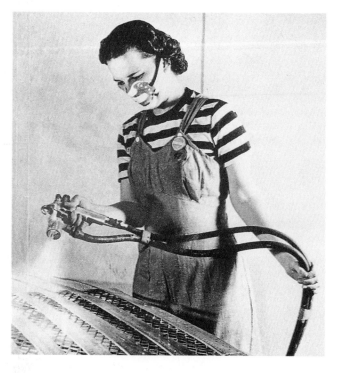

ABOVE: Increasing numbers of women go to work in factories to replace the men who have gone to war.

ASSASSINATION FOILED

A plot by senior German officers fails to kill Hitler in his eastern HQ at Rastenburg. The leader of the plot, Count Claus von Stauffenberg, is shot the same evening, with more than 5,000 people executed for complicity over the next few months.

REVOLT IN WARSAW

Citizens of Warsaw rise in revolt against their German occupiers as the Soviet Red Army approaches the city in August. The Russians, however, do nothing to assist the rising, which collapses with the destruction of the city in October by the German Army. Many Poles are killed or exiled, strengthening Russia's hand in Poland.

GAMES OFF AGAIN

The Olympics are again stopped by World War II.

ABOVE: The Eighth Air Force destroy the Focke Wulf plant in Marienburg in one of the first big air raids.

LIBERTY FOR PARIS

Paris is liberated by the Allies. General De Gaulle enters the city in triumph and brings back the Provisional Government from its exile in Algiers, North Africa. In November 1945 he is elected President of the Provisional Government.

WORLD BANK ESTABLISHED

An international monetary and financial conference is held at Bretton Woods, USA to establish a world economic order based on fixed exchange rates. The World Bank and the International Monetary Fund are set up to provide funds and loans to help the international economy.

(ALTON) GLENN MILLER
(1904–1944)

The American big-band leader is presumed dead, as he was travelling in a small plane that disappeared crossing the English Channel. He began his musical career in 1924 when he joined the Ben Pollack band, and has been a dance band leader since 1937. Hejoined up in 1943 and was stationed in Europe where his Glenn Miller Army Air Force Band entertained the troops.

DAME ETHEL MARY SMYTH
(1858–1944)

The English composer and feminist has died. Somewhat eccentric, she composed "The March for Women", the battle-song of the Women's Social and Political Union in 1911, and works such as *The Boatswain's Mate* (1916) and the opera *The Wreckers* (first performed in Germany in 1906). Her autobiographical works are *Female Pipings for Eden* (1933) and *What Happened Next* (1940).

LEFT: The liberation of Paris — Parisians run for cover as snipers fire from a building on the Place de la Concorde.

HUNGER WINTER
Cut off behind German lines and starved of food in the harsh winter, many people in the Netherlands die of hunger and cold during the winter months before they are liberated in March 1945.

STREPTOMYCIN
Russian-born US microbiologist Selman Waksman isolates the antibiotic streptomycin, which is used to treat tuberculosis.

ICELANDIC INDEPENDENCE
Iceland's parliament votes to become independent from Denmark. Iceland was occupied by British forces in 1940, when Denmark was invaded, to stop it being occupied by the Germans, and since July 1941 has been garrisoned by US forces.

PIET MONDRIAN
(PIETER CORNELIS MONDRIAAN)
(1872–1944)

The Dutch painter and founder of the influential De Stijl group has died. He set up the group in the 1920s, concerned with developing modernism in architecture, painting and design, and, apart from early figurative paintings, his work is determinedly abstract, using grid structures and primary colours. In the past six years he has lived in England, and then New York, and he has had a strong influence on modern art.

DOODLEBUGS OVER LONDON
Germany's secret weapon — the pilotless V-1 missile — is launched against the southeast of Britain. The doodlebug, as it is known, contains 1016kg (1 ton) of high explosives and travels at more than 644km/h (400miph). Its high impact causes British authorities to order a second mass exodus of more than a million children and their mothers out of the capital to safety in the countryside.

MAN-MADE FIBRE
The first yarn is made from polyester fibre, discovered in 1941 by British chemist John Rex Whinfield and marketed as Terylene in the UK and Dacron in the USA. It is resistant to heat and wear, and holds its colour well.

MORE BOMBS
Despite continuing air raids on Germany, the German Air Force retaliates in February by launching its heaviest raids on London since May 1941. The following month, US bombers begin daylight raids on Berlin.

PAPER CHROMATOGRAPHY
British biochemists Archer JP Porter and Richard Synge develop the process of paper chromatography, in which paper filters are used to separate the components of complex chemical mixtures.

SYNTHESIZED QUININE
A synthezised (laboratory-made) form of quinine is created in the USA in 1944, because supplies of quinine are cut off from Europe and North America by Japanese occupation of the East Indies.

LEFT: Soldiers of the US Women's Army Corps report for duty in Dutch New Guinea.

BELOW: The Dutch royal family pose in the garden of their temporary home near Ottawa.

ABOVE: General Eisenhower addresses his crack paratroopers prior to take-off.

A CHILD OF OUR TIME

English composer Michael Tippett (1905–98) writes the text to this oratorio (which also includes traditional spirituals) as well as the music. The subject concerns the real-life incident in which a German diplomat is killed by a young Polish Jew, in a protest on behalf of the thousands of Polish Jews stuck (without money, food or possessions) on the border of Poland and prevented from crossing.

MECHANICAL CALCULATOR

US data-processing pioneer Howard H Aiken leads a team to build the Harvard Mark I, the world's first automatic sequence controlled calculator: it is mainly mechanical, 15m (50ft) long and weighs 4 tons.

THREE STUDIES FOR FIGURES AT THE BASE OF A CRUCIFIXION

These paintings establish Irish painter Francis Bacon (1909–92) as a major artist. These three monstrous, freakish figures seem to reflect the suffering of the war and to say that the world had changed as a result. They will cause sensation and consternation when they are put on public show in 1945.

THE ARAB LEAGUE

Seven Arab governments, plus representatives of the Palestinians, set up the Arab League to promote inter-Arab links and minimize conflict between Arab nations. A Council is set up in Cairo, Egypt, the following year.

AFTERMATH AND ATOMIC BOMBS

After six years of bitter conflict, World War II finally comes to an end. The Allies liberate the death camps, revealing appalling horrors and evidence of the Holocaust. Two atom bombs are dropped on Japan, ushering in a new and terrifying nuclear age. The United Nations is founded with the aim of preventing future conflicts and maintaining global security. The first electronic computer is built.

1945

Jan	**17**	Soviet Army takes Warsaw, Poland	**May**	**2**	Berlin surrenders to Soviet army
	27	Soviet troops liberate Auschwitz death camp		**8**	VE (Victory in Europe) Day
			July	**16**	US tests first atomic bomb
			July 17–		Potsdam Conference
Feb 4–11		Yalta Conference. Roosevelt, Stalin and Churchill plan for Germany's surrender	**Aug 2**		
	13–14	Allies bomb Dresden, Germany	**Aug**	**6**	Atomic bomb dropped on Hiroshima, Japan, by US plane
				9	US plane drops atomic bomb on Nagasaki, Japan
Mar	**7**	American troops capture Ludendorf Bridge		**17**	Indonesia proclaims independence
	9	*Les Enfants du Paradis* premières in Paris	**Sep**	**2**	Japan surrenders. World War II is over
	23	Allied armies cross the Rhine			
Apr	**1–**	Battle of Okinawa. US forces capture	**Oct**	**11**	Fighting breaks out in China between Nationalists and Communists
	July 2	Okinawa with massive casualties		**24**	United Nations formally comes into being
	12	US President FD Roosevelt dies			
	28	Benito Mussolini is shot by partisans	**Nov**	**2**	Trial of Nazi leaders begins in Nuremberg, Germany
	30	Adolf Hitler commits suicide			

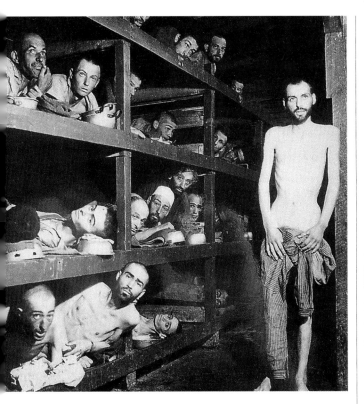

DEATH CAMPS LIBERATED

In January, Soviet troops are the first to liberate a death camp when they enter Auschwitz, in Poland, finding just 7,000 inmates alive. Over the next five months, Allied troops liberate all the death and concentration camps in occupied Europe, revealing thousands of badly malnourished and ill-treated inmates. US troops entering Dachau are so appalled at the state of the 33,000 survivors and the piled-up bodies of the dead that they shoot all 500 SS guards within the hour. The exact number who died in the camps is not known, but is thought to total more than six million. Most are Jews, although gypsies, gays and others defined by the Nazis as "undesirable" have also been killed.

ABOVE AND RIGHT: The horrors of Germany's "final solution" are slowly revealed as the concentration camps are opened up.

BELOW: One of the few survivors of Japan's bombing of Shanghai.

ABOVE: Churchill, Roosevelt and Stalin, allied in the fight against Germany, meet at Yalta to discuss the future.

ABOVE: Grand Admiral Karl Doenitz, Germany's new political leader, is arrested by Allied forces acting on Eisenhower's orders.

YALTA CONFERENCE

The three Allied leaders — US president Roosevelt, Soviet premier Joseph Stalin and British prime minister Winston Churchill — meet at Yalta in the Crimea to plan Germany's unconditional surrender and its division into four parts after the war. They also agree the fate of Berlin and Poland, and make arrangements for the first United Nations conference, to be held in San Francisco. Stalin also agrees to enter the war against Japan when the war in Europe is finished; in return the Soviet Union will gain control over the north of Korea.

DRESDEN BOMBED

In order to prevent supplies reaching the Eastern Front against Russia, British and US bombers reduce the industrial city of Dresden to ruins, killing between 30,000 and 60,000 civilians. The bombing causes widespread condemnation in Britain. Some attack it for humanitarian reasons, others because it diverts bombers from attacking vital communications and oil supplies.

TOKYO FIRE RAIDS

The first incendiary attack against the Japanese capital devastates the city centre and kills 100,000 people.

ABOVE: After Japan's surrender, Lt. Gen. Torashiro Kawabe boards a plane for a conference in Manila.

FIGHTING IN THE PHILIPPINES

The Americans launch a combined sea and air attack on the island of Corregidor to liberate Okinawa, Manila, and the tiny island of Iwo Jima. Casualties on both sides are enormous. The capture of the heavily fortified island of Iwo Jima in particular provides the Americans with a jumping-off point for bombing raids against Japan.

DEATH OF WAR LEADERS

Three war leaders die within days of each other: Franklin Roosevelt dies of a cerebral haemorrhage and is succeeded by Vice President Harry Truman (1884–1972), Benito Mussolini is shot by Italian partisans, and Adolf Hitler takes his own life.

UNITED NATIONS FOUNDED

The founding conference the United Nations (UN) begins in April in San Francisco, USA. In June, 51 member nations sign the United Nations Charter. Like the League of Nations, which it supersedes, the aim of the UN is to maintain international peace and security. An International Court of Justice is set up in The Hague, Netherlands.

BLACK BOY

In his autobiography, *Black Boy*, black American writer Richard Wright (1908–60) is eloquent about the plight of black people.

VE DAY

War in Europe comes to an end in May with the unconditional surrender of Germany. Throughout the continent, people celebrate Victory in Europe (VE) Day on May 8, even though many of its cities are in ruins and food is in scarce supply.

SIGNALLING THE MOON

American and Hungarian experts simultaneously reflect radar signals from the Moon back to Earth.

DAVID LLOYD GEORGE
(1863–1945)

The British Liberal prime minister, who presided over the coalition government during and immediately after World War I (1916–22), has died. He was in Parliament until the year of his death. Of Welsh parentage and upbringing, he was a fine and fiery orator. As chancellor of the exchequer, from 1908 to 1915, he was responsible for the radical "people's budget" of 1909, and introduced pensions, sick pay and the social insurance system.

ABOVE: Clement Attlee (second from left) becomes Britain's prime minister.

HIROSHIMA AND NAGASAKI

In August, US bombers drop atomic bombs on the Japanese cities of Hiroshima and Nagasaki, so initiating the age of nuclear warfare. The atomic bomb on Hiroshima is nicknamed "Little Boy". Dropped by a B-29, piloted by Col. Paul Tibbets, it destroys 122 sq km (47 sq mi) and kills 70,000 people. The one dropped on Nagasaki is nicknamed "Fat Man"; it kills 24,000 people.

CHINESE CIVIL WAR

Civil war resumes between the nationalists or Kuomintang, under Chiang Kai-shek (1887–1975), and the Communists, under Mao Zedong (1893–1976), for control of the former Japanese-run province of Manchuria. The war spreads throughout China the following year.

FRANKLIN D(ELANO) ROOSEVELT (1882–1945)

The American Democrat president Franklin D Roosevelt, who has seen the United States almost through to the end of World War II, has died. He had been president since 1932, winning four successive elections. He introduced the New Deal that helped the United States out of the Great Depression, devised the Lend-Lease deal of 1940–41, whereby the United States supplied arms to Britain, and was instrumental in sorting out post-war Europe at Yalta shortly before his death.

INDONESIA PROCLAIMS INDEPENDENCE

On the surrender of Japan, which was occupying the archipelago, the Indonesian Nationalist Party proclaims independence from the Netherlands, which refuses to recognize the new government. Fighting soon breaks out between the Nationalist Indonesian People's Army and British (and later Dutch) forces. A truce is declared in November 1946 and again in January 1948.

JAPAN SURRENDERS

The USSR declares war on Japan and invades Manchuria, occupying northern Korea and the northern islands of Japan. Japan surrenders unconditionally, ending the war in the Pacific.

FIRST ATOM BOMB TESTED

US scientists led by American nuclear physicist Professor Robert Oppenheimer (1904–67) test the first atomic bomb in the desert at Alamogordo, New Mexico; it produces a 1,220m (4,000ft) high mushroom cloud.

POTSDAM CONFERENCE

Stalin, Churchill and Truman meet in Potstdam, eastern Germany, to organize the occupation of Germany. German land east of the Oder-Neisse rivers is to be under Polish jurisdiction, with Austria under four-power control.

ABOVE: The Nuremberg trials hears evidence of the appalling war crimes ordered by Germany's leaders.

ABOVE: Sir Alexander Fleming, who discovered penicillin, explains some of its properties to a grateful former patient.

ABOVE: Frozen food becomes popular in the US, and many Americans freeze and pack their own at home.

VIETNAM DECLARES REPUBLIC

Nationalist and Communist Vietminh forces under Ho Chi Minh (1890–1969) enter Hanoi and force the emperor to abdicate. The following month they declare Vietnam a republic, which the former colonial ruler, France, refuses to recognize.

WAR CRIMES

The Allied International Military Tribunal opens the trial of former Nazi leaders at Nuremberg in Germany. At its conclusion in September 1946, twelve Nazis are sentenced to death, three to life imprisonment, four receive long sentences, and three are acquitted.

BUCHENWALD PHOTOGRAPHS

American photographer Margaret Bourke-White (1906–71) shows photographs of the concentration camp at Buchenwald, taken when the camp was liberated by the Allies. For the first time people see the truth about the Nazi atrocities.

ANIMAL SATIRE

English author George Orwell (1903–50) publishes his novel *Animal Farm*. A satire on revolutions, the novel describes how a new tyranny replaces the old when pigs drive out their human masters from the farm, only to turn into something like humans themselves.

HENRY V

British actor Laurence Olivier's film version of Shakespeare's play, *Henry V*, has a special resonance for its British audience. Portraying an England in the grip of a long war in Europe, it reflects Britain's contemporary position and inspires patriotism.

HUIS-CLOS

French existentialist Jean-Paul Sartre (1905–80) has written a new play, which will become his most famous. Entitled *Huis-Clos* (In Camera), it shows three people trapped in a room in hell.

ABSTRACT EXPRESSIONISM

American painter Jackson Pollock (1912–56) is one of the leaders of this rising art movement. His technique of drip-painting seems random, but enables him to create works of striking beauty and energy.

LES ENFANTS DU PARADIS

French actor Jean-Louis Barrault (1910–94) plays the mime Deburau in the film version of Marcel Carné's romantic theatre drama, *Les Enfants du Paradis*. The film becomes an instant classic.

ENTER ENIAC . . .

The first completely electronic computer, ENIAC (Electronic Numerical Integrator And Calculator) is built at the University of Pennsylvania: it weighs more than 27 tons and has 18,000 valves.

. . . AND THE COMPUTER BUG

Mathematician Grace Murray Hopper, working on a new computer, finds a moth has stopped a relay working. This is the first actual computer bug.

"MISSING" ELEMENT FOUND

Element 61, the rare-earth metal promethium, is found by three US chemists, Charles D.Coryell, Lawrence E. Glendenin and J. A. Marinsky; this fills the last gap in the table of the elements.

THE ATOMIC BOMB

ABOVE: The Enola Gay in a dispersal area after its mission against Hiroshima.

ABOVE: The plutonium "Fat Man" bomb is used against Nagasaki.

ABOVE: The Enola Gay's crew receive their final pre-flight instructions.

RIGHT: The awesome cloud billows above Nagasaki.

INSET: This victim's burns have etched her skin with the pattern of her kimono.

ABOVE AND BELOW: Evidence of the dreadful destructive power of the world's first atomic weapons.

THE IRON CURTAIN COMES DOWN

The United Nations holds its opening session but the first signs of the Cold War appear as former British prime minister, Winston Churchill, warns of an "Iron Curtain" dividing Communist countries from non-Communist countries in Europe. The word "bikini" enters the language, partly after American atomic testing at Bikini Atoll, and partly after a new and "explosive" swimsuit. Paris becomes a centre for bohemian writers and artists, and espresso coffee is the new craze from Italy.

1 9 4 6

Jan	10	First session of United Nations opens in London
	20	General de Gaulle resigns as president of France
Feb	1	Norwegian Trygve Lie is elected president of the UN
	4	Juan Perón is elected president of Argentina
Mar	5	Churchill makes "Iron Curtain" speech
	6	France recognizes the Democratic Republic of Vietnam
May		Civil war breaks out in Greece
June	2	Italy votes for a republic
July	4	Philippines becomes independent of US rule
	5	Bikini swimsuit displayed in Paris
Oct	3	United Nations General Assembly meets in New York
Nov	23	French troops bomb Haiphong, Vietnam, killing around 20,000. The French Indochinese War begins.
Dec	20	French troops occupy Hanoi, capital of Vietnam. Ho Chi Minh calls for resistance to the French

OPPOSITE: An atomic, or "mushroom" cloud, rising from Bikini Atoll in the Marshall Islands, the site of nuclear weapon testing by the United States in the 1940s and 1950s.

ABOVE: General Charles De Gaulle resigns as head of France's provisional post-war government after only two months in the post. More than ten years later he is once again elected president by the people of France, a position he holds for over a decade.

DE GAULLE RESIGNS

In France, General de Gaulle (1890–1970) resigns as French president because of continued Communist opposition to his rule.

PERON ELECTED PRESIDENT

Juan Perón (1895–1974) is elected president of Argentina. He first came to power as one of the leading officers who took over the government in 1943, and consolidated his power among both the army and the workers. In October 1945, he briefly lost power in a US-sponsored coup, but was quickly returned to power. Much of his popularity is due to his wife, Eva.

GREEK WAR

Civil war breaks out in Greece between the monarchist Democratic Army of Greece (DSE) backed by Britain, and the Communist National Popular Liberation Army (ELAS) backed by Albania, Bulgaria and Yugoslavia. In September, a plebiscite agrees to restore the monarchy. Fighting continues until the defeat of the Communists in October 1949.

IRON CURTAIN

Making a speech in Fulton, Missouri, British wartime leader Winston Churchill (1874–1964) warns that an "Iron Curtain" is descending in Europe from the Baltic to the Adriatic, as the USSR strengthens its grip on Eastern Europe. For many people, this speech marks the beginning of what becomes known as the Cold War.

FRENCH INDOCHINESE WAR

France recognizes the creation of the Democratic Republic of Vietnam, headed by the Communist leader Ho Chi Minh, as part of a French-led Indochinese Federation. Relations between France and Ho Chi Minh break down, and in November, the French bomb the northern port of Haiphong, killing around 20,000 people, as they seek to maintain control of Vietnam. This marks the start of a war which lasts until 1954.

ZORBA THE GREEK

The novel *Zorba the Greek* by Nikos Kazantzakis (1883–1957) is published. His portrayal of Zorba and his passionate love of life is a success in Greece and will soon be widely translated.

ITALIAN REPUBLIC

A referendum in Italy produces a huge majority for a republic. King Umberto II (1904–83) goes into exile; the prime minister, Alcide de Gasperi (1881–1954), becomes provisional head of state. The Allies agree to transfer the Italian-owned Dodecanese Islands to Greece, some lands to Yugoslavia, and parts of northern Italy to France.

ITALIAN WOMEN GAIN THE VOTE

In June, Italian women gain the right to vote in national elections for the first time.

RIOTS IN INDIA

More than 3,000 people die as Muslims and Hindus clash in Calcutta, India. The riots are the culmination of unrest caused by British proposals for Indian independence.

PHILIPPINES INDEPENDENT

In July, the Philippines become independent of US rule.

THE HOUSE OF BERNARDO ALBA

This year sees the publication of *The House of Bernardo Alba*, the last tragedy to have been written by Spanish poet Federico Garcia Lorca (1899–1936). Performed in 1945, nine years after the writer's death, it confirms his stature as Spain's greatest modern dramatist.

ATOMIC TESTING

Americans explode the first of several atomic bombs over Bikini Atoll in the Marshall Islands of the Pacific Ocean; the purpose is to test the effects on warships and animals.

JOHN MAYNARD KEYNES
(1883–1946)

The English economist and patron of the arts John Maynard Keynes has died. He was a Treasury advisor during both World War I and World War II, and put forward the theory of the planned economy. He greatly influenced Franklin D Roosevelt's New Deal and helped set up the International Monetary Fund. His two major works, *A Treatise on Money* (1930) and *General Theory of Employment, Interest and Money* (1936), were written in response to the unemployment crisis.

ABOVE: Renowned American art collector and politician Nelson A Rockefeller. He goes on to become the 41st Vice-President of the United States.

ESPRESSO COFFEE
The Gaggia coffee machine is invented in Italy; it uses steam to produce espresso coffee, which rapidly becomes popular.

EXPLOSIVE BIKINI
French fashion designer Louis Réard displays an abbreviated two-piece bathing costume for women in Paris; he calls it a "bikini" because he thinks its effect is as explosive as the bomb just tested.

PATERSON
American poet William Carlos Williams begins to publish his long poem, *Paterson*; he will add to it for the rest of his life. Using a collage of anecdotes, letters, reports, conversations and more traditional "poetic" passages, the poem attempts to create a typically American work of art by describing the everyday life of ordinary Americans.

EJECTOR SEAT
British aeronautical engineer James Martin, using dummies, makes the first tests of an ejector seat to enable pilots to escape from crashing aircraft.

MEMOIRS OF HECATE COUNTRY
American writer and critic Edmund Wilson (1895–1972) publishes this collection of short stories. It is accused of obscenity and banned in some jurisdictions, so becoming a bestseller in others.

ZOOM LENS
US scientist Frank Back of the Zoomar Corporation develops the first zoom lens for cameras.

BOHEMIAN QUARTIER
The Paris quarter of St. Germain-des-Prés becomes the focus of writers, artists and musicians, including the existentialist Jean-Paul Sartre, feminist Simone de Beauvoir and sculptor Alberto Giacometti.

BELOW: East meets West as Allies (pictured in 1945). This year rifts emerge and the alliance shows signs of disintegration.

NEW COUNTRIES AND A BABY BOOM

India is partitioned into two separate, independent countries: India and Pakistan. The partition causes conflict. The UN votes to divide Palestine, a decision that also leads to conflict. Marshall Aid is provided to rebuild Europe and a US pilot breaks the sound barrier. Women's fashion adopts a "New Look" and Method acting takes to the stage. This year too sees the start of the "baby boom" and a liberal approach to child-rearing.

1947

Jan	25	Chicago gangster Al "Scarface" Capone dies
Feb	12	French designer Christian Dior launches the "New Look"
Mar	12	US President Truman outlines "Truman Doctrine"
	19	Chinese Nationalists capture Communist capital, Yan'an
Apr	7	Automobile manufacturer Henry Ford dies
	15	Jackie Robinson is first black American in major league baseball
June	5	US Secretary of State George Marshall calls for aid for Europe
	15	Anne Frank's diary is published
Aug	15	India becomes independent
	15	Pakistan is created
Sep	18	USAAF becomes United States Air Force
Oct	14	US pilot Chuck Yeager breaks the sound barrier
	29	Benelux customs union is formed
Nov	29	United Nations announces plan for partition of Palestine

LEFT AND BELOW: Reclusive millionaire businessman Howard Hughes in the cockpit of his 18,500-kg (400,000-lb) "flying boat", the world's largest plane, at Long Beach, California. A record-breaking pilot, Hughes is set to take the eight-engined aircraft to speeds of 160km/h (100miph) .

TRUMAN DOCTRINE

In response to Britain's announcement that it can no longer afford to keep troops in Greece to fight the Communists in the civil war, President Truman of the USA plans to give aid to both the Greek and Turkish governments to protect them from Communism. This becomes the Truman Doctrine, under which the USA offers to support "free peoples who are resisting attempted subjugation by armed minorities or by outside pressures".

MARSHALL AID

US Secretary of State George Marshall (1880–1959) announces massive financial aid for European nations to enable them to rebuild their economies after the war. Marshall Aid, as it is known, is accepted in Western Europe but rejected by those Eastern European nations occupied by the USSR.

US AIR FORCE

USAAF becomes the United States Air Force in September. The Air Force was previously a branch of the Army, first established in August 1907. It is now a separate and independent force.

INDIA PARTITIONED

Britain partitions the Indian Empire, granting India and Pakistan independence, with Burma and Ceylon to follow the following year. Partition brings to an end more than 160 years of British rule. Fighting breaks out between India and Pakistan over the state of Kashmir, whose Muslim population riots in favour of joining Pakistan, but whose Hindu leader wishes to join India. Many millions die across the subcontinent in inter-communal fighting.

THE NEW LOOK

French fashion designer Christian Dior launches a sensational "New Look". After the austerity of the war years, Dior's look, with its generous use of material, nipped-in waist, soft shoulders and billowing skirts, is welcomed with enthusiasm by women.

FIGHTING IN PALESTINE

Britain hands back the mandate for Palestine to the UN because it is unable to control the country. The UN votes to partition Palestine with separate homelands for Jews and Palestinians. Both sides disagree, and fighting soon breaks out.

ABOVE: Record snowfalls hit New York in December 1947, making it necessary to shift as much of the snow as possible into the East River at Manhattan.

BELOW: American pilot Captain Charles "Chuck" Yeager becomes the first person to break the sound barrier, in his rocket-propelled Bell X-1 aircraft.

HIGHER EDUCATION BOOMS

Colleges and universities everywhere are swamped by applications for places. In the USA, where many colleges closed down or were almost bankrupted during the war, applications reach an all-time high of more than two million.

UFOS

Unidentified Flying Objects (UFOs) are reported in Washington State, USA, first by a pilot, Kenneth Arnold, and later by members of the public. The many reports of flying saucer-shaped objects illuminating the night sky are ridiculed by the United States Air Force.

BRANDO STARS IN STREETCAR

Tenessee Williams' play, *A Streetcar Named Desire*, opens with Marlon Brando (b. 1924) in the role of Stanley Kowalski. Brando uses the Stanislavski Method of acting, which emphasizes realism and an understanding of the psychology of the character, rather than a declamatory approach.

ACTOR'S STUDIO

Founded by Elia Kazan, Robert Lewis and Cheryl Crawford, the Actor's Studio in New York propounds and popularizes the Stanislavski Method in the USA. Many well-known American actors will be trained here, especially during the 1950s.

ABOVE: American Method actor Marlon Brando makes his stage breakthrough in the Tennessee Williams' play *A Streetcar Named Desire*. Brando goes on to star in the film version of the play and to become one of the most famous screen actors in the world.

ABOVE: The great baseball player Jackie Robinson becomes the first black player to play outside the Negro Leagues when he joins the Brooklyn Dodgers. Robinson's outstanding performances are a major step in overcoming racial bigotry in sport in the USA.

THE "HOLLYWOOD TEN"

Ten American directors and screenwriters refuse to testify before the House of Un-American Activities Committee, which is obsessed with hunting out alleged Communists. The "ten" are given one-year jail sentences, signalling the beginning of "witch hunting" in the cinema world and elsewhere.

ANNE FRANK'S DIARY

The diary of a young Jewish girl, Anne Frank, who died in 1945 in a concentration camp, is published, providing a remarkable insight into the Holocaust. The story of her family's concealment from, and eventual discovery by, the Nazis in Amsterdam becomes known all over the world.

BENELUX FORMED

A customs union is formed by Belgium, the Netherlands and Luxembourg. It is known as the Benelux customs union, an acronym of Belgium, Netherlands and Luxembourg.

SUPERSONIC FLIGHT

In October Charles "Chuck" Yeager, a US Army pilot, becomes the first man to fly faster than the speed of sound (about 343m/1,125ft per second), flying a Bell X1 rocket plane.

CHLORAMPHENICOL DISCOVERED

Scientists discover chloramphenicol, a broad-spectrum antibiotic; in some patients it causes damage to the bone marrow, so its use is confined to severe infections which safer drugs cannot touch.

CARBON-14 DATING

US chemist Willard F Libby (1908–80) and co-workers perfect carbon-14 dating, by which the amount of this decaying radioactive material left in organic remains shows how long they have been dead.

ALPHONSE (AL) CAPONE (1899–1947)

American gangster Al Capone, sometimes known as Scarface, has died. He joined a street gang as a boy and during the prohibition era amassed profits and notoriety. The infamous St. Valentine's Day Massacre of 1929 was fought between his and a rival gang. Sent to jail in 1931 on tax fraud charges, Capone was released early on health grounds and spent the remainder of his life in his Florida estate.

STRONG FORCE FOUND
British chemist Cecil F Powell discovers the pion, a sub-atomic particle that produces a "strong force" which holds an atom's nucleus together.

CRAB NEBULA
Australian radio astronomers discover that the Crab Nebula is a strong radio source; the nebula is the gaseous remains of a supernova, a star which exploded in 1054.

TRANSISTOR INVENTED
US physicists John Bardeen, Walter Brattain and William Schockley invent the transistor, a tiny electronic device that controls electric current; it revolutionizes all electronic apparatus.

POLAROID CAMERA
US scientist Edwin H Land (1909–91) invents and demonstrates the ™Polaroid Land Camera, which can produce a print seconds after a picture is taken.

HELLS ANGELS ARRIVE
The Hell's Angels — Harley-Davidson biker gangs — cause a riot when they converge on the town of Hollister, Northern California, USA. Dressed in leather, bikers in their thousands roam Califorinia breaking the law in a quest for thrills.

BABY BOOM
A baby boom begins, with 3,411,000 births recorded in the USA, and 20.5 births per 1,000 — one-fifth more than the 1939 figure — in the UK.

MICROWAVE OVENS
The first microwave ovens are sold in the USA. Invented in 1945 by Percy LeBaron Spencer after a factory radar power tube melted a chocolate bar in his pocket, they are bulky and designed for use in commercial food preparation.

FIRST BLACK BASEBALL MAJOR
Jackie Robinson becomes the first African-American to play baseball in the major leagues. He plays for the Brooklyn Dodgers and paves the way for the racial integration of the American pastime.

DEAD SEA SCROLLS
The Dead Sea Scrolls are discovered when a Bedouin boy, Muhammad ad-Dibh, explores a cave at Qumran in Jordan and finds an earthenware jar containing leather and parchment scrolls. They were written by the Essenes, a Jewish sect of the 1st century BC.

DOMESTIC ELECTRIC BLENDER
An electric blender is produced for home use in the USA. Invented in 1919, it was used only in commercial kitchens until Frederick J Ossius introduces the Waring Blender, named after band leader Fred Waring.

PERSONALITY DIMENSIONS
Hans Eysenck (1916–97), a British psychologist, publishes *Dimensions of Personality*, a study of neuroticism and extrovert behaviour. He argues that personality is biologically determined and criticizes psychoanalysis because it does not increase the likelihood of recovery from the disorder being treated.

LIBERAL CHILD CARE
American paediatrician Benjamin Spock (1903–98) publishes *The Common Sense Book of Baby and Child Care*, the first practical manual of childcare, which he wrote while serving in the army. He rejects authoritative child-raising methods and advocates a liberal upbringing.

HENRY FORD
(1863–1947)

American car manufacturer Henry Ford, who founded the Ford Motor Company in 1903, has died. He introduced the assembly line technique which allowed cars to be produced with great efficiency "on the line". While refusing to accept unionization, he paid unusually high wages, even when this was in opposition to government policy under the New Deal. He set up the Ford Foundation. Always eccentric, at the age of 82 shortly before his death, he attempted to regain control of the Ford Motor Company from his grandson.

OPPOSITE ABOVE: US Secretary of State George Catlett Marshall puts forward the European Recovery Programme, better known as the Marshall Plan, which helps to put post-war Europe back on its feet. About $13 million is spent on aid for Europe in the form of food and machinery. Here a US cargo ship fills its hold with supplies.

ABOVE: Not only Europe benefits from the Marshall Plan. Flour and rice are shipped to North Africa, which was also a battleground in World War II.

RIGHT: Equipment, vehicles and machinery are also part of the Plan. Although the driving motive is to contain the spread of Communism in Europe, the Marshall Plan certainly helps nations to recover as quickly as possible from the devastation of war.

BERLIN BLOCKADE AND A NEW ISRAEL

Indian leader Gandhi is assassinated and in South Africa, the incoming Nationalist government introduces apartheid, a policy of racial separation. The independent state of Israel comes into being, leading to an immediate Arab-Israeli conflict. Communist forces in China move to capture Beijing and the Berlin Airlift breaks the Soviet blockade of West Germany. The Olympic Games return to the sporting calendar and American sexologist, Alfred Kinsey, exposes the reality of male sexual behaviour.

1 9 4 8

Jan	**20**	Mahatma Gandhi is assassinated by extremist Hindu, Nathuram Godse
	30	Winter Games begin, St. Moritz
Feb	**11**	Soviet film director Sergei Eisenstein dies
	20	Communists seize power in Czechoslovakia
May	**14**	Independent State of Israel proclaimed
	15	Egypt, Jordan, Syria, Iraq and Lebanon invade Israel
	26	Jan Smuts ousted in election, South Africa
June	**16**	Malayan Communists begin campaign against British
	26	Berlin Airlift begins
	28	Yugoslavia is expelled from the Cominform
July	**5**	National Health Service introduced in Britain
	29	Olympic Games open in London
Aug	**14**	Australian cricketer Don Bradman bowled out
	16	US baseball star "Babe" Ruth dies
Sep	**4**	Queen Wilhelmina of Holland abdicates
	9	North Korea proclaimed a republic
Dec	**10**	UN Assembly adopts Declaration of Human Rights
	15	Dutch troops seize Jakarta, Indonesia

ABOVE: An American skier takes part in the women's downhill event in the Fifth Winter Olympics.

ABOVE: Czech figure-skating champion Aja Vrzanova practising her art before the 1948 Winter Olympics in St. Moritz. World War II led to the cancellation of the 1940 and 1944 Games.

RIGHT: The Norwegian bobsledding (or bobsleighing) team in action at the 1948 Games in St. Moritz. The sport's popularity began in the Swiss town in the previous century.

INDEPENDENT ISRAEL
On the day the British mandate ends, the Jewish National Council and the General Zionist Council proclaim an independent State of Israel, with David Ben-Gurion (1886–1973) as prime minister and Chaim Weizmann (1874–1952) as president. Both the USA and USSR recognize the new State.

ARAB-ISRAELI WAR
Six Arab armies from Egypt, Jordan, Syria, Iraq and Lebanon attack Israel, on the day after its independence. The Israelis hold the attacks and then counter-attack. Fighting continues until ceasefires are declared in1949. Borders are stabilized with Jerusalem divided but accessible by a narrow corridor of land. The Israelis suffer 8,000 casualties and the Arabs about 20,000.

HALE TELESCOPE
The Hale telescope, with a 500cm (16ft) glass mirror, the largest of its time, is officially dedicated at Mt. Palomar, California. It was designed by astrophysicist George E Hale (1868–1938).

THE NAKED AND THE DEAD
US journalist Norman Mailer (b. 1923) publishes his first novel, *The Naked and the Dead*, marking his emergence as a writer. A realistic novel based on his army experiences in the Pacific, it is considered one of the best American books about World War II.

ABOVE: A replica of the Brandenburg Gate is set up in Berlin to demonstrate against its post-war placement in the Soviet-occupied sector of the city. The slogan reads "Freedom Will Win" and the bear portrayed on the flags is the emblem of Berlin.

NATIONALISTS TAKE POWER

In South Africa, Jan Smuts is defeated in the general election by the extreme right-wing Afrikaaner Nationalist Party. Douglas Malan (1874–1959) becomes prime minister and introduces legislation for the apartheid system of racial separation, to ensure white supremacy in South Africa.

MALAYAN EMERGENCY

In June, the Malayan Races Liberation Army (MRLA), largely ethnic Chinese Communists, begins a violent campaign against the British government. The MRLA campaign includes sabotage, assassination and terrorism; the British respond with a variety of tactics including resettling populations and long-range patrols. The MLRA are defeated in 1957, although emergency regulations remain in place until 1960.

OAS

The Organization of American States (OAS) is formed to link together all the countries in the Americas.

CRY, THE BELOVED COUNTRY

South African writer Alan Paton (1903–88) publishes this novel describing the experiences of Revd Stephen Kumalo, who leaves his township for Johannesburg, where he discovers that tragedies have overtaken the lives of his sister and son. The book eloquently puts the case for understanding between the races.

CAMERA IN LONDON

Photographs by Bill Brandt (1904–83) show a peaceful London, in acknowledgement of the war's ending. He evokes a city lit by soft sunlight or the light of the moon. They are in contrast to Brandt's earlier, starker wartime series, such as *A Night in London*.

COMMUNIST COUP

The Communist Party stages a coup in Czechoslovakia and takes over the government. The following month, in March, the popular foreign secretary, Jan Masaryk, is found dead outside his flat; many suspect the Communists of murdering him. Throughout the year, Communist governments strengthen their hold on power throughout Eastern Europe.

YUGOSLAVIA EXPELLED

The USSR expels Yugoslavia from Cominform, the Communist Information Bureau designed to co-ordinate Communist Party activities throughout Europe, because of policy differences with Joseph Stalin. Over the next decade Yugoslav leader Tito, the name adopted by Joseph Broz (1892–1980), gains increasing support from Western Europe in his confrontation with the USSR.

TURANGALILA SYMPHONY

This huge ten-movement symphony, for large orchestra plus piano and ondes Martenot, is described by its French composer Olivier Messiaen (1908–92) as a love song or a hymn to joy. Its exotic sound-world makes it the composer's most popular work.

QUEEN WILHELMINA ABDICATES

In the Netherlands, Queen Wilhelmina abdicates due to ill-health. She has been queen for 50 years. She is succeeded by her daughter Juliana (b. 1909).

HUMAN RIGHTS

The United Nations adopts the Universal Declaration of Human Rights, recognizing the rights and freedom from oppression and slavery of all humans, regardless of race, sex, social status, language, religion and colour. Much of the work in drafting the charter is done by Eleanor Roosevelt (1884–1962), widow of the former US president and a delegate to the UN.

CHINESE CIVIL WAR

In China, the Communists have gained the upper hand, defeating the Nationalists and taking Manchuria. The Nationalists under Chiang Kai-shek retreat southwards. The Communists take Peking and declare a Communist state in northern China. By November, the Nationalists have retreated behind the Great Wall.

INDONESIA

Hostilities continue in Indonesia. Dutch airborne forces seize Jakarta, capturing Ahmed Sukarno's government.

THE PISAN CANTOS

US poet Ezra Pound (1885–1972) publishes The Pisan Cantos, an instalment of his epic poem, The Cantos. It was conceived while Pound was in an American prison camp during World War II, for alleged treacherous broadcasts, and completed when he was detained in a mental hospital.

MAHATMA ("GREAT SOUL") GANDHI (1869–1948)

Indian leader Mahatma Gandhi has been assassinated. Venerated as a great pacifist leader, patriot and social reformer, Gandhi trained as a lawyer. He gave up a lucrative practice to live in South Africa, where he spent 20 years opposing discrimination. In 1914, he returned to India and, although an ardent supporter of Britain, spearheaded the campaign for Indian independence. He was committed to non-violent civil disobedience but his various campaigns, including the salt march of the 1930s, brought him several terms of imprisonment. In 1946, he negotiated independence with the British Cabinet Mission. His last months were clouded by Muslim-Hindu strife.

CHRISTINA'S WORLD

US artist Andrew Wyeth paints his paralysed neighbour, Anna Christina Olson, against a background of an open horizon and a house. The painting, which becomes one of the artist's best known, shows Wyeth's ability to suggest the limited world of the disabled woman, as well as reflecting his love of the scenery around his Maine summer home.

NATIONAL HEALTH

In Britain, the National Health Service is formed. It is one of the first comprehensive health services in the world. The service provides free healthcare to all, "from the cradle to the grave".

LONG-PLAYING RECORDS

By using plastics instead of shellac, American record companies are able to introduce long-playing records, at two speeds, 33.5 rpm and 45 rpm.

MARTIAN ATMOSPHERE

Dutch-born US astronomer Gerard P Kuiper (1905–73) predicts that the atmosphere of Mars is mostly carbon dioxide, a fact later proved by space probes. He also discovers Miranda, the fifth moon of the planet Uranus.

FIRST ATOMIC CLOCK

The first atomic clock is built at the US National Bureau of Standards, in Washington DC; it is accurate to one second in 300 years. Later atomic clocks are accurate to one second in 200,000 years.

BATHYSCAPHE INVENTED

Swiss physicist Auguste Piccard (1884–1962) invents the bathyscaphe, a deep-sea diving craft, and tests it o a depth of 1,370m (4,495ft). Its development makes possible the exploration of the deepest parts of the oceans.

NUCLEAR STRUCTURE

Physicists Hans Jensen of Germany and German-born Maria Goeppert Mayer of the USA independently discover the structure of atomic nuclei.

DELVING INTO THE ATOM

US physicist Richard Feynman (1918–88) develops the theory of quantum electrodynamics, the interaction between the sub-atomic particles, electrons, photons, and positrons.

TUBELESS TYRES

The American Goodyear Company introduces the tubeless tyre for motor vehicles.

CYBERNETICS INVENTED

US statistician Norbert Wiener invents and names a new branch of science: cybernetics, the study of information control in animals and machines.

RECREATING EARLY NAVIGATION

Thor Heyerdahl (b. 1914), a Norwegian ethnographer, sails from Peru with a Scandinavian crew on a balsawood raft built using techniques known to the Incas. After sailing and drifting more than 8,046km (5,000mi), he has reached the Tuamotu archipelago, proving that Precolumbian people could have crossed the Pacific and colonized Polynesia.

FIRST SNEAKERS

Adidas of Germany, a sportswear manufacturer, develops sneakers from war-surplus canvas and fuel-tank rubber. Their first shoe, designed by Adolf Dassler, is decorated with three white stripes.

VELCRO DEVELOPED

Velcro fastening is invented by a Swiss engineer, George de Mestral, inspired by spiny burrs found sticking to his clothing and his dog's coat after a walk.

BRADMAN BOWLED OUT

Australian hero Don Bradman needed just four runs in his last innings in a cricket test match to score 7,000 test runs and record an incomparable average of 100. To the disbelief of all, he is out for nought but still cheered back to the pavilion.

GEORGE HERMAN (BABE) RUTH (1895–1948)

The American baseball player and coach "Babe" Ruth has died. He played in ten World Series and has set a record for home runs that will not be broken until 1974. During his career he played for the Boston Red Socks (1914–19), the New York Yankees (1920–34) and the Boston Braves (1935–38).

PLANNED PARENTHOOD

The International Planned Parenthood Federation is founded by American social reformer and founder of the birth control movement, Margaret Sanger.

ABORTION ON DEMAND

As the population of Japan approaches 80 million, and in response to increased foetal abnormalities resulting from the 1945 nuclear explosions, the Eugenic Protection Law authorizes abortion on demand.

WINTER GAMES

The Fifth Winter Games are held in St. Moritz, Switzerland, where the facilities have survived World War II unscathed. However, post-war shortages mean hardship for athletes and few visitors. Downhill races for men and women are added to the events, indicating the growing importance of alpine events.

AUSTERE OLYMPICS

The Olympic Games are held in London, England, which was the proposed site for the cancelled 1944 Games. Events are beset by scarcity and competitors live in army barracks, but crowds flock to Wembley for the Games. Athlete Fanny Blankers-Koen, a mother of two, and nicknamed the "flying housewife", takes four gold medals back to Holland.

SKYDIVING

Frenchman Leo Valentin develops the modern sport of skydiving by discovering that arching the back is the way to control free fall before opening the parachute.

ABOVE: US President Harry S Truman (rear left) enjoys a Welcome Home parade in Washington after his re-election to office in November. The dome of the Capitol is seen in the background.

ABOVE LEFT: American Flying Wing aircraft, notable for the absence of tails and fuselages, which shortens their overall length to about a third of other planes. These super-efficient new bombers are pictured at Hawthorne, California.

ABOVE RIGHT: The house of American architect and designer Charles Eames in Santa Monica, California. Eames is especially famous for his innovative chairs, which are set to become collectors' items.

LEFT: California has proved to be an important oil-producing area in the US, and this oilfield in Long Beach, with its many derricks, is typical of those found in the state. Oil has played an important part in the wealth of the US.

MAKING MOVIES

ABOVE LEFT: The British-born director and producer Alfred Hitchcock (centre) is one of early Hollywood's most important figures.

ABOVE RIGHT: Backstage in Hollywood; the romance of a film is created by unsung craftsmen.

RIGHT: The splendour of Hollywood, illuminated by searchlights as a new film is premièred.

ABOVE: The director surveys the scene from the platform of a movable crane. The use of the crane increases the number of angles from which a shot can be taken on a film set, and improves the overall fluidity of movement.

ABOVE: On location for the film version of Ernest Hemingway's novel *For Whom the Bell Tolls*. The director explains to the actors exactly what he has in mind.

RIGHT: The Austrian-born director Fritz Lang (centre) is seen explaining a scene of the film *Woman in the Window* to actress Joan Bennett (left). Lang is one of the many European film directors who went to Hollywood when the Nazis came to power.

BELOW: The western is the film genre that distinguishes American movies from those of other cultures. Irish-American John Ford is the maker of many seminal westerns, including *Stagecoach*.

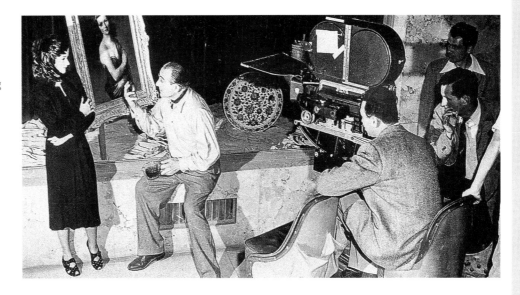

NATO AND THE PEOPLE'S REPUBLIC

Chinese Communists defeat the Kuomintang and set up the People's Republic of China, headed by Mao Zedong. NATO is formed to provide mutual support for Western nations and the division of the world into Communist and non-Communist blocs is emphasized by the separation of Germany into East and West. Architecture features glass and steel, a Soviet-US arms race begins and the novel *1984* warns of a bleak future.

1 9 4 9

Jan	1	Ceasefire ends India-Pakistan war over Kashmir	**July**	20	Ceasefire declared in Arab-Israeli war
	10	Communists capture Xuzhou, China			
			Sep	23	Soviet Union tests atomic bomb
Apr	4	North Atlantic Treaty Organization (NATO) is formed		30	Berlin Airlift ends
	16	Western Allies fly 1,398 sorties in 24 hours, delivering 13,147 tonnes (12,937 tons) of supplies to Berlin in the greatest number of sorties during the Berlin Airlift	**Oct**	1	Mao Zedong proclaims establishment of People's Republic of China
				7	Communist Democratic Republic established in East Germany
	24	Communist forces advance on Shanghai, China		16	Greek Civil War ends, with defeat of rebels
			Dec	8	Kuomintang (Chinese Nationalists) leave mainland China for Formosa (later Taiwan)
May	12	Berlin blockade ends			
	23	Federal Republic of Germany (West Germany) comes into being		27	Netherlands transfers sovereignty of Indonesia
	26	Shanghai falls to Communists, China			

LEFT: Delegates for the USA and the Netherlands add their signatures to the North Atlantic Treaty. The original twelve members include the Netherlands, Britain, France and the United States.

NATO AND COUNCIL OF EUROPE

Ten European nations, including the Netherlands and Britain, join with the USA and Canada to form the North Atlantic Treaty Organization (NATO), providing mutual support for each other against aggression. In May, ten Western European nations, including the formerly neutral nations of Sweden and Ireland, set up the Council of Europe to support freedom and the rule of law. The Council meets in Strasbourg and includes a European Court of Human Rights.

WEST AND EAST GERMANY

The USA, Britain and France merge their three zones in West Germany to create the Federal Republic, which comes into being in May with its capital in Bonn. In September, the Christian Democrat, Konrad Adenauer (1876–1967), becomes chancellor. The following month, the USSR establishes the German Democratic Republic in East Germany.

ARMS RACE BEGINS

The Soviet Union carries out its first atom bomb test, exploding it at a site in Kazakhstan. This marks the start of an arms race with the USA.

PEOPLE'S REPUBLIC OF CHINA

Following their victory in the civil war, the Chinese Communist Party establishes the People's Republic under the leadership of Mao Zedong (1893–1976). The Kuomintang Nationalists retreat to the offshore island of Taiwan under the leadership of Chang Kai-shek.

INDONESIA

After lengthy and complex UN-sponsored peace talks the Netherlands transfers sovereignty to Indonesia under the leadership of President Sukarno (1902–70). Indonesia therefore becomes independent of its former colonial masters, the Dutch. The costs of four years' war include some 25,000 Dutch and 75,000 Indonesian casualties.

THE THIRD MAN

US actor and director Orson Welles (1915–85) gives a brilliant performance as Harry Lime in Carol Reed's film *The Third Man*, with a screenplay by Graham Greene. The "Harry Lime Theme" by Anton Karas becomes almost as famous as the film itself.

DEATH OF A SALESMAN

One of the most successful American plays of all time, *Death of a Salesman* establishes Arthur Miller as a leading American dramatist. It tells the story of the salesman Willy Loman, who loses his grip and disintegrates because he relies too heavily on the hollow values of modern society.

1984

English author George Orwell's seminal dystopia, *1984*, is published and immediately engages the interest of readers in the English-speaking world and beyond. Many phrases from the book, such as "doublethink" and "Big Brother" find a permanent place in the language.

ABOVE: Chiang Kai-shek, who fought against the invading Japanese during World War II.

ABOVE: United Nations officials distribute clothing made from cotton supplied by the UN International Children's Emergency Fund to needy Japanese people at the Reikan Building in Tokyo.

THE SECOND SEX

French feminist Simone de Beauvoir (1908–86) publishes *The Second Sex*, which draws on art, literature and philosophy to describe how men have consistently denied the right of humanity to women, and calls for the abolition of the myth of "the eternal feminine". A significant and ground-breaking work, it will later become a key text of the Women's Liberation Movement and a global best-seller.

CONVENIENT CAKES

Cake mixes prepared by General Mills & Pillsbury in the USA increase the range of convenience foods available in the USA.

GLASS HOUSE

Philip Johnson's Glass House in New Canaan, Connecticut, essentially consists of a glass box with a steel frame, typical of a number of modernist houses currently being designed. Influenced strongly by US architect Mies van der Rohe, this house is the perfect example of the tenet "less is more".

NEPTUNE'S MOON

Dutch-born US astronomer Gerard P Kuiper (1905–73) discovers the second moon of the planet Neptune, now named Nereid.

ROCKET RECORD

Americans launch the WAC Corporal, a research rocket which reaches the record height of 402km (250mi); it is launched as a second stage from a V-2 rocket.

MORE ELEMENTS FOUND

American chemists headed by Glenn T Seaborg create and discover two more elements: numbers 97, berkelium, and 98, californium; they are radioactive rare earths.

SICKLE-CELL DISEASE

American biological chemist Linus C Pauling (1901–94) discovers that the inherited sickle-cell disease is caused by differences in the blood; people with this trait are also found to have immunity from malaria.

INDO-PAKISTAN WAR

Fighting between India and Pakistan ends and Indian troops control Kashmir.

US BASKETBALL ASSOCIATION

Rivals the National Basketball League and the Basketball Association of America merge to create the National Basketball Association in America.

RIGHT: A night-time game of baseball in the small American town of Mount Vernon.

ABOVE: The new transatlantic flights mean sleeping during the trip. Beds are made up for the passengers of this Constellation aircraft.

ABOVE: The world's oldest airline, KLM, introduces the "Flying Dutchman" which flies between New York and Amsterdam.

ABOVE: Front view of a mechanical calculator which is able to add numbers running into their billions in less than one-fifth of a second.

ABOVE: After the war, even neutral Switzerland finds the going tough. The US supplies aid in the form of food.

BERLIN AIRLIFT

Western Allies begin running an airlift to carry supplies into Berlin. Land access to the western sector of Berlin, which is administered by France, Berlin and the USA, has been blocked off by the Soviet Union. The airlift continues until May 1949, when the USSR relaxes its grip on the city, allowing convoys to use the autobahns across East Germany. A total of 277,264 flights are made, lifting 2,343,315 tons of cargo.

ABOVE: A West German policeman shouts instructions to waiting crowds of East Germans in Berlin as food parcels are distributed in the second joint American-West German food relief programme.

ABOVE: Mini-parachutes drop sweets and chewing gum for German children.

BELOW: C-54 Skymasters unload their cargoes at Templehof Air Force Base.

ABOVE: A C-74 Globemaster aeroplane arrives at Gatow airfield with a supply of flour to help the blockaded Berlin.

RIGHT: The baby's pram seems an ideal place to secrete tins of food received as part of the joint American-West German food relief programme.

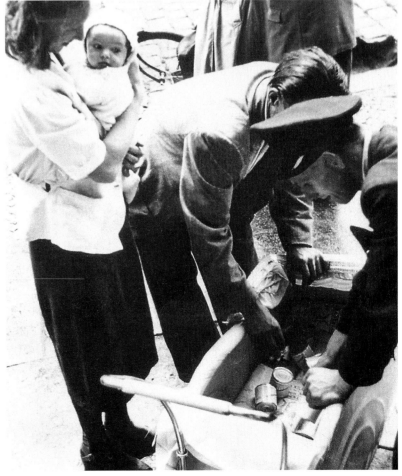

ABOVE: For these East Berliners the trip to West Berlin to collect their food parcels has been a tiring one.

THE NUCLEAR AGE

Post-war paranoia flavours the decade: espionage, Cold War and witch-hunts preoccupy the military and political classes. Unfinished business in the East leads to war in Korea and there are uprisings in Africa and Cuba. The babies who "boomed" in the 1940s grow up into a new phenomenon known as a teenager. Rock and roll is born: Elvis Presley thrusts his pelvis into the face of the Establishment and the Beat Generation try to articulate the joys of existential freedom. The space race begins, with the USSR launching the satellites *Sputnik I* and *II*.

BACKGROUND: The handwriting of Albert Einstein, describing his theory of relativity.

1950–1959

KEY EVENTS OF THE DECADE

- KOREAN WAR
- COMMUNIST WITCH-HUNTS
- CHINA INVADES TIBET
- ROCK AND ROLL
- CIVIL WAR IN CUBA
- MT. EVEREST CLIMBED
- DNA STRUCTURE DISCOVERED
- HYDROGEN BOMB
- BEAT
- THE WARSAW PACT

- POLIO VACCINE DEVELOPED
- HUNGARIAN UPRISING
- SUEZ CRISIS
- EEC SET UP
- RUSSIAN SPUTNIKS IN SPACE
- CND FOUNDED
- ELVIS PRESLEY
- CASTRO TAKES CUBA

WORLD POPULATION 2,516 MILLION

alls – wie dieselbe gegenwär[tig]
in ihrer Anwendung auf bewe[gte]
welche dem Phänomenen nicht
t. Man denke z. B. an die elektr[o]
schen einem Magneten und
rom hängt hier nur ab von
d Magnet, während nach
tölle, dass der eine oder der
sei; streng voneinander zu
iche der Magnet und ruht der
das Magneten ein elektrisches
welches an den Orten, wo sich
u erzeugt. Ruht aber der Magnet
ht in der Umgebung des Magnet
dertin eine elektromotorische
ie entspricht, die aber – Gleichheit
ins Auge gefassten Fällen vor

WAR AND WITCH-HUNTS

The Korean War breaks out when Communist North Korea invades South Korea. UN forces, headed by the USA, side with South Korea. Later in the year, China invades Tibet. The fight against Communism in the Western world becomes an obsession with a witch-hunt in the USA and a spate of notorious spy trials. European countries make plans for a common trading market and a Dutch-born astronomer measures the planet Pluto.

1950

Jan	9	US senator McCarthy alleges that Communists are working in the US State Department
Mar	1	Atomic scientist Klaus Fuchs sentenced to fourteen years' imprisonment for betraying secrets to the USSR
May	1	Marriage Law passed in China gives women full equality in marriage and divorce
	9	Schuman Plan proposed to create single European authority for German and French coal production
June	25	North Korean forces invade Republic of South Korea Korean War breaks out
	28	North Korean forces capture Seoul, South Korea

July	1	First UN forces, most from USA, arrive in Korea
	16	World Cup takes place in Brazil
Aug	1	King Leopold III of Belgium abdicates
Sep	11	South African statesman Jan Smuts dies
	16	US marines make amphibious landings at Inchon, Korea
	26	UN forces recapture Seoul, South Korea
Oct	1	South Korean and UN troops cross 38th parallel, border between North and South Korea
	21	Chinese forces occupy Tibet
Nov	24	UN forces launch offensive into North Korea
	26	Chinese forces enter Korean War

COMMUNIST WITCH-HUNT

US senator Joe McCarthy (1909–57) alleges that 57 Communists and 205 Communist sympathizers are working in the State Department. The Senate Foreign Relations Committee is given the job of investigating the charges, beginning an anti-Communist witch-hunt in the US which lasts, with McCarthy in the lead, until he attacks the US Army in October 1953, leading to his censure in October 1954 and rapid downfall.

SPY-FEVER

In Britain, atomic scientist Dr Klaus Fuchs (1911–88) is arrested and jailed for fourteen years for giving nuclear secrets to the Russians. The information he passed on enables Soviet scientists to advance their nuclear plans by many years. The following year, American Communists Julius and Ethel Rosenberg are tried and executed in the USA for similar crimes. In June 1951, two British diplomats, Guy Burgess and Donald MacLean, defect to the USSR. These and other cases lead to a spate of spy-fever in the Western world.

COMMON ECONOMIC POLICY

French foreign minister Robert Schuman (1886–1963) puts forward a plan for pooling the French and German coal and steel industries under a joint authority, to which other nations might join. The plan, worked out by French economist Jean Monnet, leads to the formation of the European Coal and Steel Community (ECSC), set up in Paris in April 1951 and joined by France, West Germany, Italy and the three Benelux countries. The ECSC starts functioning in July 1952.

PHILIPPINES HUK REBELLION

The Hukbalahap or People's Anti-Japanese Army, a Communist resistance group in Luzon, which has adopted guerrilla tactics against the newly independent Republic of the Philippines, attacks Manila. However, its secret HQ in the capital is raided and the attack is called off. With US military help and a programme of reforms initiated by President Magsaysay, the popularity of the Huks wanes and the surviving leader surrenders in 1954.

MILLIONS WATCH TELEVISION

More than 75 million people watch the first transcontinental American television broadcast, marking the growing popularity of commercial network services since 1946. Colour broadcasts are now transmitted by CBS. In the UK, almost half a million television sets now tune into one BBC channel.

FOURTH WORLD CUP

The winner of the fourth soccer World Cup, hosted by Brazil, is decided by matches in a final pool of four teams. Uruguay wins for the second time but the pool system is never used again. England, the nation which invented the game, plays in the World Cup for the first time, but is beaten 1–0 by the USA.

ABOVE: Television becomes one of the most sought-after consumer products in the early 1950s.

ABOVE: The Dalai Lama is forced into exile and flees to Dharamsala in Punjab, India where he is to set up an alternative government.

CHINESE INVADE TIBET

The Chinese invade Tibet and although the Tibetans appeal to the UN, their country is quickly overrun. The youthful Dalai Lama remains as a figurehead but finally escapes to India.

LEOPOLD ABDICATES

King Leopold III returns to Belgium after six years' exile, and abdicates in favour of his son, Baudouin.

ABOVE: Motion pictures enter a new golden age in the early 1950s. *All The King's Men*, based on a Pulitzer Prize-winning novel by Robert Penn Warren, stars Broderick Crawford, Jeanne Dru, John Ireland, John Derek and Mercedes McCambridge.

UNIVERSITY CITY
Modernist architects Mario Pani and Enrique del Moral design this Central American complex, the campus of the Autonomous National University of Mexico.

HOW BIG IS PLUTO?
In March Dutch-born US astronomer Gerard P Kuiper measures the planet Pluto, and finds it is tiny; its diameter is finally determined by the Hubble Space Telescope in the late 1990s as 2,324km (1,453mi).

THE OORT CLOUD
Dutch astrophysicist Jan Oort (1900–92) suggests that there is a huge reservoir of comets at a great distance from the Sun; it is later known as the Oort Cloud.

ENTER CYCLAMATES
Cyclamates, artificial sweeteners much used in food and drinks as an alternative to saccharin, are introduced; some countries ban them.

CHINESE WOMEN EQUAL
Mao Zedong's Communist government passes a new marriage law, which recognizes the role women played in the Communist victory. Chinese women now have full legal equality in marriage, divorce and the ownership of property. Forced arranged marriages, polygamy, child marriage and infanticide are forbidden.

INSIDE THE CELL
Using an electron microscope, Belgian cytologist (cell specialist) Albert Claude (1899–1983) discovers the endoplasmic reticulum, a network of space inside a living cell that holds things together.

KURT WEILL (1900–1950)
German-born American composer Kurt Weill has died. The composer of "Mack the Knife" and "September Song" worked with Bertolt Brecht on *The Rise and Fall of the City of Mahagonny* (1927–29) and the outstandingly successful *The Threepenny Opera* (1928). He left Nazi Germany in 1933 with his wife the singer Lotte Lenya, and settled in the United States in 1935, where he composed several Broadway musicals.

JAN CHRISTIAN SMUTS (1870–1950)
South African elder statesman and former prime minister Jan Christian Smuts has died. He helped to create the Union of South Africa (1910), was a member of the Imperial War Cabinet during World War l and acted as counsel to the British War Cabinet during World War ll.

DINER'S CREDIT CARD
Diner's Club is founded by Ralph Schneider, who issues the first charge card, a prototype credit card (it is paid off every month). Two hundred cardholders pay an annual fee for credit at 27 New York restaurants.

2,000-YEAR-OLD DEATH
Tollund Man, a 2,000-year-old corpse, is found preserved in a bog near Jutland, Denmark. Aged between 30 and 40, the man was killed by hanging or strangling — a leather rope is still around his neck.

OFF ON PACKAGE HOLIDAYS
Package holidays are launched by European entrepreneurs Gerard Blitz, a Belgian, and Vladimir Raitz, who advertise inexpensive campsite accommodation in "holiday villages" on the islands of Majorca and Corsica.

COMPUTER CHESS
US mathematician Claude E Shannon designs the first chess-playing computer.

VASLAV NIJINSKY (1890–1950)
The great Russian dancer and choreographer Vaslav Nijinsky has died. Trained at the Imperial Ballet School at St Petersburg, he became the leading dancer with Diaghilev's Ballets Russes. Sadly, after a period of internment in World War 1. he was diagnosed schizophrenic in 1917, and his life has been a struggle.

THE PLASTIC AGE

ABOVE: Newly invented nylon zippers are light enough for sheer fabrics and resistant to cleaning compounds or the heat of a pressing iron.

ABOVE: A tough, moisture-resistant plastic called Tenite covers this portable radio case.

ABOVE: A clock encased in transparent plastic, a popular ornament.

ABOVE: A telephone handset made of Bakelite, an early plastic.

ABOVE: Plastics are easily moulded, so can be used to make intricate shapes such as this record rack.

FIRST JET AIRLINER SERVICE

The first jet airliner service is inaugurated with a flight from London to Paris in the Vickers Viscount 630 four-engined turboprop aircraft.

YOUTH FASHION

Bobbysoxers, so called because of the knee-length socks they wear, emerge as a new youth group in the USA. They are teenage girl fans of the new singing sensation Frank Sinatra (1915–98), and they follow him wherever he performs.

RASHOMON

Japanese director Akira Kurosawa's film *Rashomon* is premièred, establishing his worldwide reputation. It is a study of a violent crime from four different points of view. Kurosawa will later become famous for the epic Samurai movie *The Seven Samurai* (1954).

STONE AGE NORTH POLE

The Danes complete a three-year expedition to Greenland in which they find traces of a Stone Age culture 750km (470mi) from the North Pole.

KOREAN WAR

North Korean forces invade South Korea, leading to three years of bitter conflict. United Nations troops, led by the USA, aid South Korea, while China joins in on the North Korean side in November. North Korean forces push South Korean and US forces down to a small perimeter at Pusan. In September 1950, US marines land at Inchon, the port serving Seoul, the South Korean capital, as part of the UN break-out operation from Pusan. The landings, which are a success, lead to a counter-offensive up to the Chinese border. With a combined strength of 485,000, Chinese and North Korean troops drive the 365,000-strong United Nations forces south. A UN counter-attack stabilizes the line; by June 1951 the two sides face each other across the 38th parallel. Negotiations and prisoner exchanges take place in 1953. By the end of the war, UN casualties are 118,515 killed, 264,591 wounded and 92,987 captured. The Communist armies suffer 1,600,000 battle casualties, with 171,000 taken prisoner.

The Korean War sees the first ever jet-versus-jet victory when in November 1950 an American USAF F-80C shoots down a Chinese MiG-15 fighter over Sinuiju on the Yalu River.

ABOVE: A soldier stands guard in a machine-gun nest.

ABOVE: US Navy Sky Raiders fire rockets at North Korean positions.

ABOVE: A US soldier comforts a fellow infantryman, while another writes casualty tags.

ABOVE: A 75mm recoilless rifle is fired in support of infantry units near Oetlook-tong.

LEFT: US marines use scaling ladders to storm ashore during the amphibious landings at Inchon.

RIGHT: A Korean delegate to the Kaesong Conference.

BELOW: Images from the conflict. Top left, US marines advancing under close air support. Top right, United Nations troops fighting in the streets of Seoul. Bottom left, bombardment of warehouses in Wonsan, North Korea. Bottom right, the USS *Missouri* fires a 16-in salvo to disrupt communications in the north of the peninsula.

SPIES, PACTS AND BEATNIKS

War continues in Korea and French Indochina. Libya gains independence. A new and most advanced digital computer — UNIVAC 1 — is developed. It uses magnetic tape to input and output information and will have a revolutionary impact on business. American author JD Salinger's novel *The Catcher in the Rye* creates a hero whose alienation is understood by adolescents everywhere. Italian-American composer Menotti creates an opera specifically for television.

1951

Jan	1	North Koreans and Chinese take Seoul
	26	UN launches counter-offensive against Chinese and Korean forces
Mar	30	Julius and Ethel Rosenberg found guilty of espionage
Apr	22	Battle of Imjin River, Korea. UN defensive action against Chinese and Korean troops
May	25	British diplomats Burgess and Maclean warned they are under suspicion of spying and leave Britain
Sep	1	USA, Australia and New Zealand sign Pacific Security Agreement.
	8	Peace treaty signed with Japan
Dec	13	French National Assembly ratifies Schuman Plan
	24	Libya becomes independent

ABOVE: President Harry S Truman addresses the American people. Television broadcasts are a common feature of the time.

OPPOSITE: Dramatic changes in aircraft design are represented by the 1912 "pusher" biplane, which can fly at 96km/h (60miph), and the North American F-86 Sabre jet, which holds the world speed record of 1,072km/h (670miph) in 1951.

ABOVE: In Saudi Arabia, American experts advise on the use of scientific farming techniques to help grow crops such as watermelons in the desert soil.

PEACE AT LAST

Representatives of 49 nations meet in San Francisco and sign the peace treaty with Japan, formally bringing World War II hostilities to an end.

LIBYA INDEPENDENT

The former Italian colony of Libya becomes independent. Occupied by the British during the war, Libya becomes the first independent state created by resolution of the UN, and the first former European colony in North Africa to gain independence.

FRENCH INDOCHINESE WAR

War continues in Indochina. The Vietminh establish a common front with Communist groups in Laos and Cambodia and move to conventional tactics.

PEST CONTROL

Biological pest control is tried out in Australia, when myxomatosis from Brazil is introduced by sheep farmers to kill rabbits, introduced by settlers in 1859 and now numbering about 500 million and consuming the grazing. In the USA, entomologist Edward F Knipling of the Department of Agriculture, introduces sterilization of female insects, which die without reproducing.

THE CATCHER IN THE RYE

American writer JD Salinger (b. 1919) publishes a short novel, *The Catcher in the Rye*. It portrays the adolescent Holden Caulfield, who runs away form boarding school. Holden's attacks on the "phoney" nature of adult attitudes make the novel an instant hit with teenagers.

THE DESTROYED CITY

This work by Russian sculptor Ossip Zadkine (1890–1967) is a memorial to the (predominantly civilian) victims of the Nazi bombing of Rotterdam in 1940. It is subsequently placed at the entrance to Rotterdam harbour.

AMAHL AND THE NIGHT VISITORS

US composer Gian Carlo Menotti composes this work specifically for the increasingly popular medium of television. A Christmas work, it is premièred on Christmas Eve and is his most famous work.

BILLY BUDD

The opera *Billy Budd* by English composer Benjamin Britten (1913–76) is performed. It is based on Herman Melville's novel *Billy Budd*. Novelist EM Forster collaborates with Eric Crozier on the libretto, and English tenor Peter Pears creates the lead role.

UNIVAC I ARRIVES

The first mass-produced computer goes into production; it is the UNIVAC 1 (Universal Automatic Computer). It is the first computer to store its data on magnetic tape.

STICKY SUBJECT

US scientist Fred Joyner accidentally discovers an adhesive that sticks to everything it touches; it turns out to be the first of the superglues, which harden in seconds in the absence of air.

FESTIVAL OF BRITAIN

The Festival of Britain opens in London around Robert Matthew's Royal Festival Hall and a Dome of Discovery. Exhibitions display new textiles, minimalist furniture of metal and plastic, and modern art and design. Telekinema, the star attraction, shows stereoscopic movies watched through polarizing spectacles.

ABOVE: The 35th annual Memorial Day 500-mile race at Indianapolis (the Indy 500) is won by Lee Wallard in a record time of 3 hours 57 minutes and 38 seconds, at an average speed of 201.99 km/h (126.25miph).

THE MILKY WAY
US astronomer William Morgan confirms that our own galaxy, the Milky Way, has a spiral structure: the solar system is on one arm of the spiral.

FLUORIDATION
Fluoride naturally present in some drinking water is discovered to prevent tooth decay: work begins to add fluoride to water supplies elsewhere.

LUDWIG JOSEF JOHANN WITTGENSTEIN (1899–1951)

Austrian-born British philosopher Ludwig Wittgenstein has died of cancer in Cambridge. His early work, *Tractatus Logico-Philosophicus* (1921), was highly influential among contemporary philosophers and he immediately had a great personal following when, in 1945, he finally took up a post at Cambridge, although nothing further was published. His second major work, *Philosophical Investigations* (1953), and other writings will be published after his death.

ROCK AND ROLL IS HERE TO STAY

The United States tests an H-bomb in the Pacific Ocean as the US–USSR rivalry steps up. Mau Mau disturbances break out in Kenya against British colonial rule and a state of emergency is declared. Transistors are applied to a variety uses from telephones to radios and rock and roll bursts on to the popular music scene. Cold War rivalry is reflected at the Olympic Games where Czech Zatopek runs off with three golds.

1952

Feb	6	The British king George VI dies Queen Elizabeth II succeeds him
	14	Winter Olympics open in Oslo, Norway
Mar	1	India holds first national elections Pandit Nehru's Congress Party wins 364 out of 489 seats in the National Assembly
July	19	Olympic Games open in Finland
	25	European Steel and Coal Community comes into being
	26	Eva ("Evita") Perón dies of cancer
	27	Emil Zatopek wins three gold medals for Czechoslovakia
Sep	11	Eritrea federated with Ethiopia, East Africa
Oct	20	Mau Mau disturbances begin. A state of emergency is declared in Kenya
Nov	1	US scientists test hydrogen bomb in the South Pacific
	5	Dwight D Einsenhower wins US presidential election
	9	Chaim Weizmann, first Israeli prime minister, dies

ABOVE: The California wine districts of Napa, Sonoma and Mendocino produce fine varieties of New World wines.

US TEST H-BOMB
American scientists test a hydrogen bomb at Eniwetk Atoll in the Marshall Islands of the Pacific. According to observers, a small island is completely obliterated in the blast. Radioactive dust rises some 40km (25mi) high and spreads some 126km (100mi). The hydrogen bomb is a thermonuclear weapon, which works by nuclear fission.

'IKE' WINS PRESIDENTIAL ELECTION
In November, former US general Dwight D Eisenhower (1890–1969) wins the presidential election for the Republicans with a landslide over his Democratic opponent, Adlai Stevenson. His vice-president is Richard Nixon.

MAU MAU CAMPAIGN
A revolt against British colonial rule in Kenya breaks out, headed largely by the Kikuyu and Meru tribes. The British declare a state of emergency and commit 50,000 troops. Trouble continues until 1960.

NEW BRITISH QUEEN
George VI dies and Princess Elizabeth (b. 1926) becomes queen as Elizabeth II. Many heads of state attend the state funeral in London.

ERITREA FEDERATED WITH ETHIOPIA
In East Africa, the former Italian colony Eritrea is federated by the UN with Ethiopia.

DEATH OF EVITA
Eva Perón (Evita), much-loved and popular wife of President Juan Perón, dies from cancer. Her death starts the gradual erosion of his appeal.

ROCK'N'ROLL ARRIVES
In the US rock and roll is launched with Alan Freed's Moondog's Rock'n'Roll Party on the WJW radio station in Cleveland, Ohio. The teen style movement has also reached the UK, where Teddy boys dress in updated Edwardian fashions.

THE COMET FLIES
The world's first all-jet airliner, Britain's De Havilland *DH 106 Comet 1*, inaugurates a regular passenger service between London and Johannesburg.

ELEMENTS DISCOVERED

Elements 99 and 100, einsteinium and fermium, are discovered — after a hydrogen bomb explosion — by US scientists working at the University of California and two national laboratories.

WAITING FOR GODOT

Irish writer Samuel Beckett's most famous play, *Waiting for Godot*, is performed and becomes a theatrical landmark. It portrays two tramps who wait for the mysterious Godot, who never comes. Their predicament seems to reflect the hopelessness of the modern world.

UNITE D'HABITATION,

French architect Le Corbusier (1887–1965) creates a remarkable housing development in Marseilles. It incorporates facilities such as shops, a swimming pool, a gym and a crèche, as well as many apartments, and meets the architect's aim of housing an entire community in a vast modernist block.

MULTIPLE-USE TRANSISTORS

In Japan the first pocket-sized transistor radio is produced by Masaru Ibuka, who improves the technology of the USA's Western Electric Co. division of AT&T and launches it under the Sony name. The first transistorized hearing aids are produced in the USA, and in the UK transistors are applied to central telephone dialling apparatus to provide automatic dialling.

WRECK INVESTIGATION BY SCUBA

The first archaeological investigation of a wreck using scuba-diving equipment is carried out by French diver and marine archaeologist Jacques Cousteau, who discovers an ancient Greek ship off the coast of Marseilles, which contains wine urns.

ANTABUSE

™Antabuse, a drug which helps alcoholics to stop drinking, is introduced; its generic name is disulphiram.

GAS CHROMATOGRAPHY

British biochemists Archer Martin and AT James invent gas chromatography, a method of separating chemical vapours.

4'33"

American composer John Cage (1912–92) has "written" a piano piece containing four minutes and 33 seconds of silence. The audience is encouraged to listen to the noises in the environment around them.

DREAMING SLEEP

Biologists studying sleep patterns discover a period in which a sleeper's eyes move rapidly; this is known as dreaming sleep or rapid eye movement (REM) sleep.

INSULIN ANALYSED

British biochemist Frederick Sanger (b. 1918) discovers that insulin is a protein and works out its structure.

MARIA MONTESSORI
(1870–1952)

Italian educational pioneer and physician Maria Montessori has died. Her teaching methods, which include learning through play, were developed from her early experiences in her school for children with learning disabilities, and Montessori schools have become established as a leading method of teaching nursery and primary school children throughout the world.

CHAIM AZRIEL WEIZMANN
(1874–1952)

Israel's first president, Dr Chaim Weizmann, has died. An eminent chemist of Russian birth, as a young man he worked in Switzerland where he became a leading Zionist. In Great Britain, where he lived from 1904 until 1934, he discovered the bacterium *Clostridium acetobutylium*, which is active in producing acetone from carbohydrate.

RIGHT: Television studios boom in response to the huge popularity of the new medium.

FLOAT GLASS

English glass-maker Arthur Pilkington invents float glass, in which liquid glass is floated on a bath of molten tin, producing a completely flat and shiny sheet.

AMNIOCENTESIS

Doctors develop amniocentesis, a procedure during pregnancy by which some of the amniotic fluid in a woman's womb can be examined to see if the baby she is carrying is healthy; it is used only in high-risk cases.

ACRYLIC GOES ON THE MARKET

New acrylic fibres such as Orlon, discovered by Du Pont, and Acrilan, produced by the Chemstrand Corporation, are marketed in the USA. They are soft and when spun into yarn can be knitted like wool.

ANTARCTIC MAPPED

The Antarctic is mapped by air and major glaciers are explored by a Norwegian-Swedish-British expedition organized by HV Sverdrup, former Director of the Scripps Institution in the USA, and Professor of Oceanography at the University of California.

AUSTRALIAN DISCOVERS ORE MOUNTAIN

An iron ore mountain is discovered in the Hammersley Range by Australian prospector Langley Hancock, who spots rust-coloured outcroppings when his aircraft is blown off course. He keeps it secret, awaiting a change in mining laws before staking his claim.

FIRST SUGARLESS SOFT DRINK

No-Cal Ginger Ale, the first sugar-free soft drink, uses the new cyclamate sweeteners instead of sugar. It is also salt-free, so suitable for people with obesity, diabetes and high blood pressure.

SCANDINAVIAN OLYMPICS

Mammoth crowds in Oslo, Norway, welcome the Winter Olympics to Scandinavia for the first time. Spectators on skis encourage cross-country competitors. 150,000 set an Olympic record to watch the ski jumping and home cheers ring out for speed skater Hjalmar "Hjallis" Andersen's three golds. Athletes from the USSR take part for the first time in the Summer Olympics held in Helsinki. Emil Zatopek (b. 1922), the "Czech Express", thrills Finnish spectators and takes golds in the 5,000m, 10,000m and marathon.

MARIA EVA (EVITA) DUARTE DE PERON (1919–1952)

Eva Perón, the immensely popular second wife of the Argentine populist right-wing president Juan Perón, has died from cancer at the age of 33. She had a strong influence on her husband and pursued the cause of women's suffrage and social and healthcare reform. Her death is greatly mourned by the Argentine people.

DOUBLE HELIX DECODED

Soviet ruler Joseph Stalin dies and is succeeded by Nikita Kruschev. The Korean War comes to an end. British scientists begin to unlock life's secrets by discovering the structure of DNA and the world's highest mountain — Mt. Everest — is finally climbed. The Netherlands experiences severe flooding and an American conservationist warns of the dangers of misusing the Earth's natural resources.

1953

Jan	**20**	Dwight Eisenhower inaugurated as 34th president of the USA
Feb	**10**	Common market for coal and steel begins among various European nations
Mar	**5**	Joseph Stalin, leader of the Soviet Union, dies (b. 1879)
Apr	**25**	British scientists discover the structure of DNA
May	**29**	Mountaineers Hillary and Tensing reach the peak of Mt. Everest; the news is received on June 1
June	**17**	Workers' strike turns into uprising against Communist government, East Germany
July	**5**	Imre Nagy becomes prime minister of Hungary
	26	Fidel Castro leads attempt to overthrow Batista government, Cuba
	27	Armistice is signed ending the Korean War
Sep	**12**	Nikita Kruschev appointed First Secretary of the Central Committee of the Communist Party, USSR
Nov	**23**	Hungarian football team beats the British at Wembley

STALIN DIES

Joseph Stalin, leader of the USSR for nearly 30 years, dies at the age of 73. He is succeeded by Georgi Malenkov as prime minister, but in September Nikita Khrushchev (1894–1971) becomes Communist Party First Secretary.

KOREAN WAR ENDS

An armistice is signed in Panmunjon, Korea, bringing to an end the three-year-old Korean War. Prisoners are exchanged and both sides withdraw from occupied areas. Under the agreement, Korea remains divided into North and South Korea.

UPRISING CRUSHED

In East Berlin, a workers' uprising against the partition of the city and the harsh Soviet rule is put down by Soviet tanks.

REGIME RELAXES IN HUNGARY

Imre Nagy (1895–1958) becomes the new prime minister of Hungary. He announces an end to enforced collectivization of agriculture and begins to relax Communist rule.

SHELLFISH POISONING

Environmental poisoning is identified as the cause of deaths from eating fish and shellfish caught in Minamata Bay in Kyushu and Niigata in Honshu, Japan. The waters are found to be contaminated with lead, a by-product of industrial processes.

ABOVE: Czech refugees make a dramatic escape to the West by crashing through the Czech-German border in a stolen tank.

BELOW: After the armistice is signed in July 1953, peace negotiations to end the Korean War continue and prisoner exchanges are completed in September.

ABOVE: A miniature weapon used by East German secret agents in the continuing conflict with the West. It is a standard cigarette case concealing cyanide-coated bullets.

ABOVE: East Germans burn and trample Soviet flags during riots in the divided city of Berlin.

CUBAN CIVIL WAR

Communist rebel leader Fidel Castro (b. 1927) leads an attack on army barracks in Cuba in an unsuccessful attempt to overthrow Cuban premier Batista. Some rebels are killed; Castro and others are imprisoned.

COMMON COAL AND STEEL

The countries involved in the European Coal and Steel Community — France, Italy, Luxembourg, Belgium, the Netherlands and West Germany — begin operating a common market for coal, iron ore and steel.

BACKGROUND: Atomic bomb tests are conducted at Bikini Atoll in the Pacific Ocean.

DOUBLE HELIX

British scientists Francis Crick, James Watson, Maurice Wilkins and Rosalind Franklin discover the structure of the complex molecule DNA (deoxyribonucleic acid), the chemical that forms the basis of genes, which pass on hereditary characteristics. The structure of DNA is made up of two strands that intertwine to form a double helix. With this discovery, scientists can now establish how living things reproduce themselves.

NETHERLANDS FLOODS

Hurricane winds and abnormally high tides cause heavy flooding in the Netherlands and hundreds of people are drowned. Work immediately begins on the 30-year Delta Project to build dams across coastal estuaries and inlets, a pioneering storm surge barrier across the Oosterschelde Estuary, and the world's longest bridge across the Scheldt River.

UNDER MILK WOOD

Welsh poet Dylan Thomas (1914–53) puts his vivid language and humour to use to create a play for voices. *Under Milk Wood* is set in a Welsh seaside town and deals with the daily lives, loves and dreams of the inhabitants. Thomas takes a lead role in the play, which is performed in New York, but dies later in the year.

EARTH'S LIMITS

American zoologist and conservationist Fairfield Osborne publishes *The Limits of Our Earth*, warning of the consequences of misusing available natural resources and the dangers of overpopulation. In *Our Plundered Planet*, published in 1948, he had explained the dangers of using DDT.

THE CRUCIBLE

American playwright Arthur Miller's play *The Crucible* is performed. It takes as its subject the 17th-century witchcraft trials in Salem, Massachusetts, using them as a metaphor for the McCarthyite hunting and trial of "communists" in contemporary America.

ABOVE: Methods of disposing of nuclear waste include burying it deep underground.

HEART-LUNG MACHINE

US surgeon John H. Gibbon develops a heart-lung machine and uses it to keep a patient alive while performing heart surgery.

GEODESIC DOME

Geodisic domes appear at Ford's HQ at Dearborn, Michigan. They are the invention of designer and writer Richard Buckminster Fuller (1895–1983), who developed them in the 1930s and 1940s. Based on polyhedra, geodisic domes are designed to allow the maximum space to be covered with the most lightweight structure. They are also cheap to make, and easy to prefabricate and assemble.

MICROWAVE OVEN

Percy L. Spencer, working for a firm in Massachusetts, USA, patents the microwave oven. Used initially for commercial catering, it is later manufactured for domestic use.

EVEREST CONQUERED

New Zealander Edmund Hillary, and Tibetan sherpa Tenzing Norgay, become the first climbers to reach the 8,840m (29,039ft) summit of Mt. Everest, the world's highest mountain.

STRANGENESS

US physicist Murray Gell-Mann introduces the term "strangeness" to classify subatomic particles.

RIGHT: Joseph Stalin, real name Iosif Vissarionovich Dzugashvili, dies. Expelled from a seminary in his youth for his Marxist evangelism, he rose through the ranks to lead the USSR.

MASER

US physicist Charles Townes invents a device for generating high-intensity microwaves; he calls it a maser, short for Microwave Amplification by Stimulated Emission of Radiation.

CREAM IN YOUR COFFEE?

Powdered cream for coffee, produced by M&R Dietetic Laboratories of Ohio, USA, in 1950 is followed by the production of dried milk by American dairy scientist David D. Peebles.

SCIENTOLOGY FOUNDED

The Church of Scientology is founded in Washington DC, USA, by a former seaman, Lafayette Ronald Hubbard. His science of Dianetics is a form of psychotherapy designed to eliminate neuroses and offer a spiritual alternative to personal problems.

GO TELL IT ON THE MOUNTAIN

US black American writer James Baldwin (1924–87) publishes his first novel, *Go Tell it on the Mountain*. Set in Harlem, and based on his own life, it establishes him on the literary scene as a writer who will portray the lives and plights of black Americans.

FOOTBALL SHOCK

The Hungarian football team, captained by Ferenc Puskas, defeats the English team by 6–3 at the English home ground at Wembley, so becoming the first overseas team to defeat England at home.

DISPOSABLE BIC

The Bic, a disposable ballpoint pen devised by Baron Bich, is sold in Paris.

JOSEPH STALIN
(1879–1953)

The Soviet ruler, Joseph Stalin, has died. Born in Georgia, the son of a shoemaker, Stalin became a Bolshevik and in 1922 was appointed General Secretary to the Central Committee. He began to build a power base and, after Lenin died in 1924, succeeded him as leader of the Soviet Union, ruthlessly crushing all opposition to his leadership. Through collectivization and a series of five-year plans, he transformed the Soviet economy and established it as a world power.

TROUBLE IN ALGERIA AND VIETNAM

Anti-French violence flares in Algeria as a war for independence begins. Vietnam, Laos and Cambodia gain independence and Vietnam is divided into two. The arrival of the nuclear age is underpinned by the launch of the world's first nuclear-powered submarine and the opening of the world's first nuclear reactor. An English athlete runs a mile in less than four minutes, Marlon Brando becomes a cult figure and the world's first successful kidney transplant is carried out.

1954

Jan	21	First nuclear-powered submarine launched, USA
Mar	1	USA tests H-bomb in the Marshall Islands, causing widespread concern
Apr	9	Comet jet airliner crashes north of Messina, Sicily
	24	Mau Mau rounded up in Kenya
May	6	Roger Bannister breaks the four-minute mile record
	7	French troops forced to surrender in Dien Bien Phu, Vietnam
	17	US Supreme Court rules that racial segregation in schools is unconstitutional
June	27	World's first nuclear power station opens, USSR
July	15	Boeing 707 makes maiden flight, Seattle, USA
	20	Armistice signed in Geneva ends French Indochinese War. Cambodia, Laos and Vietnam independent. Vietnam is divided along the 79th parallel
Sep	8	South-East Asia Treaty Organization (SEATO) established
Oct	8	Communist forces occupy Hanoi, North Vietnam
Nov	1	Violence breaks out in Algeria Algerian War of Independence begins
Dec	2	US Senate censures Senator Joseph McCarthy

ABOVE: Vietnamese civilians in Hanoi set up informal street markets while waiting to be evacuated to the south.

RIGHT: An anti-Communist former prisoner of war jubilantly waves the South Korean flag on reaching Seoul.

VIETMINH TAKE DIEN BIEN PHU

In Vietnam, some 10,000 French troops are surrounded at Dien Bien Phu by the 50,000-strong Vietminh Army led by General Giap and forced to surrender after a savage 56-day siege. This defeat leads to a series of agreements signed between France and other great powers. France recognizes the independence of Cambobia and Laos and agrees to the independence and partition of Vietnam: the Communist-led north under Ho Chi Minh (1890–1969) and the pro-Western south, a republic under Ngo Dinh Diem (1901–63).

FIRST NUCLEAR SUBMARINE

The world's first nuclear-powered submarine, the *Nautilus*, begins service with the US Navy; she is powered by two steam turbines, with the heat for the steam provided by a nuclear reactor.

LEFT: The opening ceremony of a stadium and sports complex in Bucharest, Romania.

ABOVE: The crashed remains of a Czech aeroplane flown across the Iron Curtain to West Germany by Karel Cihak.

SEGREGATION UNCONSTITUTIONAL

The US Supreme Court rules in the Brown v. Topeka Board of Education case that racial segregation in schools is unconstitutional. The judgement leads to considerable racial tension throughout the southern states of the USA.

BIKINI ATOLL

The USA tests its second H-bomb at Bikini Atoll in the Marshall Islands. It is more than 500 times as powerful as the A-bomb dropped on Hiroshima and its effects cause considerable concern. Nearby Japanese fishermen suffer radiation burns and sickness.

NUCLEAR POWER PLANT

The first nuclear power plant to produce electricity is built in the Soviet Union, near Moscow. It is capable of generating 5 megawatts of electricity, enough for a small town.

SEATO FORMED

Eight nations — the USA, Australia, New Zealand, Pakistan, Thailand, the Philippines, Britain and France — sign a defence treaty in Manila, establishing the South-East Asian Treaty Organization (SEATO) as a defence against Communist power in the region.

ROCKING AROUND THE CLOCK

Bill Haley and the Comets release their latest record "Rock Around the Clock". It rapidly sells a million copies and within a year has become a youth anthem, establishing the new sound of rock and roll. And in Memphis, Tennessee, Elvis Presley (1935–77) records "That's All Right Momma" for Sun Records.

SOLAR BATTERY

The solar battery is developed by Bell Laboratories of AT&T, making it possible to convert sunlight to electric power. The Association for Applied Solar Energy is founded and a periodical launched, *The Sun at Work*.

LEFT: On a state visit to Turkey, Marshal Tito of Yugoslavia, accompanied by President Bayar of Turkey, reviews a guard of honour on his arrival.

DUTCH AUTONOMY FOR TERRITORIES

The Dutch government grants full domestic autonomy to its territories in South America and the West Indies.

ALGERIAN WAR OF INDEPENDENCE

An insurrection breaks out against French rule in the North African colony of Algeria, which France regards not as a colony, but rather as mainland France. The rebels call themselves the Algerian National Liberation Front (FLN) and launch what is to be a long and bloody struggle for independence that continues until 1962. The French win the military campaign but lose the political battle in the UN. When General de Gaulle becomes president in 1958, he pulls out of Algeria.

LORD OF THE FLIES

English novelist William Golding (1911–93) publishes *Lord of the Flies*. The novel describes what happens when, after a plane crash on a desert island, a group of schoolboys try to create a democratic society. The social order rapidly degenerates and reverts to savagery.

LIJNBAAN, ROTTERDAM

This long pedestrian shopping way, stretching some 600m (656yd) from Rotterdam's commercial centre to the railway station, becomes highly influential in town planning. Many other pedestrian precincts will soon follow all over Europe.

LA STRADA

The poetic, tragicomic movie *La Strada* by Italian film director Federico Fellini (1920–93) is premièred. It portrays the lives of two wandering mountebanks, stars Fellini's wife, Giulietta Masina, and has a memorable score by Nino Rota.

BRANDO ON THE WATERFRONT

Starring Marlon Brando as an ex-prizefighter, *On the Waterfront* is the latest film directed by Elia Kazan. Brando's performance will gain him an Oscar, and follows his powerful performance as a leather-clad motorbike gang leader in *The Wild One*.

COMETS CRASH

Following a Comet airliner crash — one of a series — north of Messina, Sicily, all Comets are grounded and one is tested to destruction. Metal fatigue in the cabin is found to be the cause of the disasters.

GERMANY BEATS HUNGARY

The talented Hungarian side is beaten by Germany in the final of the 1954 World Cup in Switzerland. Hungarian star player Ferenc Puskas scores a goal but the final score is 3–2 to Germany.

RIGHT: Yugoslav troops parade in honour of the visit to Belgrade of President Bayar of Turkey, to sign the tripartite alliance between Yugoslavia, Turkey and Greece.

TABLE TENNIS CHAMPIONS

The Table Tennis World Championships take place in London, UK. China and Japan are confirmed as new powers in the sport when they displace previous leaders Hungary and Czechoslovakia.

MOONIES

The Unification Church is founded by Korean evangelist Reverend Sun Myung Moon. His acolytes are dubbed "Moonies". Moon becomes notorious for arranging mass marriages between members of the church who do not meet until the day of their wedding.

A MILE IN UNDER FOUR MINUTES

English athlete Roger Bannister achieves the holy grail of middle-distance running and runs a mile in under four minutes. Bannister, a 25-year-old medical student, breaks the four-minute barrier at the Oxford University running track, running the mile in 3 mins 59.4 seconds.

BIRTH PILL TESTED

The first oral contraceptive, a pill for women containing a synthetic hormone, is developed by US physiologist Gregory Pincus. It is successfully tested in Puerto Rico the following year.

EATING IN FRONT OF THE TV
TV dinners, a new convenience food, are introduced in the USA by Omaha's CA Swanson & Sons.

VTOL AIRCRAFT
The US Navy's Convair XFY-1 fighter aircraft makes its first test flight; it is a VTOL (Vertical Take-Off and Landing) aircraft, nicknamed the "flying pogo-stick".

SUCCESSFUL KIDNEY TRANSPLANT
US surgeons J Hartwell Harrison and Joseph Murray carry out the first successful kidney transplant, the donor being the recipient's identical twin brother.

PLASTIC LENSES
Contact lenses, known since 1887, are now available in plastic, and are lighter and more comfortable to wear.

ENRICO FERMI
(1901–1954)

The eminent nuclear physicist Enrico Fermi has died. Born in 1901 in Italy, where he was educated, and where he worked until 1938, he and his colleagues were the first to split uranium atoms by bombarding them with neutrons, contributing to the development of nuclear power and nuclear weapons. He was awarded the Nobel Prize for Physics in 1938, and left for the United States, where he became naturalized,, because of Italian anti-Semitism. He was responsible for the world's first nuclear reactor, built in Chicago in 1942.

ABOVE: Leaders of the three nations occupying West Germany — Pierre Mendes-France of France, Anthony Eden of Great Britain and John Foster Dulles of the United States — meet with Germany's Chancellor Konrad Adenauer in Paris to end post-war occupation.

HENRI EMILE BENOIT MATISSE
(1869–1954)

The great French painter, stained-glass artist and sculptor Henri Matisse has died in his eighties. Even as an old man he continued to work, most recently on making pictures from cut-out paper (*L'Escargot*, 1953). As a young man Matisse was one of the group known, from 1905, as the Fauves (wild ones). Although he was influenced by Cubism (and gave the movement its name) his painting was more representational; he is admired for his flow of line and use of pure colour.

ABOVE: The French Foreign Legion questions a Vietminh soldier in the Indochinese War.

TOP: The Dalai Lama and Chairman Mao Zedong at the First National People's Congress in Beijing.

RIGHT: Workers parade in Moscow's Red Square to celebrate the 37th anniversary of the Great October Revolution.

BELOW: Rocky Marciano delivers the winning punch that ends the challenge of Ez Charles.

AN END TO SEGREGATION

An amnesty in Kenya ends the Mau Mau rebellion. Countries in Africa and Asia join together to form a non-aligned bloc, separate from both superpowers. Eastern European nations form the Warsaw Pact as a counter to NATO. Polio vaccine goes on trial and a new vehicle — the hovercraft — is patented. The Beat Generation finds its voice. Jazzman Charlie Parker dies, as does the great scientist Albert Einstein.

1955

Jan	18	Amnesty declared in Kenya to calm Mau Mau rebellion
Mar	12	US jazzman Charlie Parker dies
Apr	18	Afro-Asian Conference is held in Bandung, Indonesia, to form "non-aligned" bloc. It lasts until April 24
	18	German-born scientist Albert Einstein dies
May	14	Warsaw Pact is set up
	15	Austria's independence is restored

June	11	More than 80 spectators and one driver are killed during the Le Mans car race
July	18	Disneyland theme park opens, California
Aug	30	Greek, Turkish and British foreign ministers meet in London to discuss Cyprus. The meeting lasts until September 7
Sep	30	US film star 23-year-old James Dean dies in car crash

ABOVE: Prime Minister Nehru of India discusses policy with Mr Richard Nixon on the latter's visit to India.

ABOVE RIGHT: Rosa Parks is arrested for violating the segregation laws in Montgomery, Alabama.

MAU MAU REBELLION ENDS

In Kenya, an amnesty by the British government calms the Mau Mau rebellion against British rule. The Mau Mau, a secret society of the Kikuyu tribe, was formed in 1948 and in 1952 began a campaign of arson and killings to drive whites off Kikuyu land and force the British to leave Kenya. Their leader, Jomo Kenyatta (1889–1978), was imprisoned, but the Mau Mau lost much ground after a massacre at Lari in the Rift Valley in March 1953 killed more than 80 people, mostly African. In total, more than 11,000 Mau Mau members have been killed in the uprising, mainly by fellow Africans.

WARSAW PACT

In response to West Germany joining NATO in October 1954, seven Eastern European nations — Albania, Bulgaria, Czechoslovakia, East Germany, Hungary, Poland and Romania — plus the USSR establish the Warsaw Pact. This provides for a unified military structure with its headquarters in Moscow and the stationing of Soviet armed forces in member countries.

MENDELEVIUM

Element 101 is produced artificially by a US team headed by Glenn T Seaborg. It is named mendelevium.

THE FAMILY OF MAN

Photographer Edward Steichen (1879–1973) mounts a notable exhibition at New York's Museum of Modern Art. A showcase of photography, it contains just over 500 photographs selected from more than two million.

ABOVE: President Ngo Dinh Diem of South Vietnam, in discussion with Buddhist priests.

BLACK WOMAN ARRESTED

In Montgomery, Alabama, USA, American civil rights campaigner Rosa Parks is arrested for sitting in the front of the bus in seats reserved for white people after the Interstate Commerce Commission orders the desegregation of transport. Her arrest leads to a mass boycott of all buses in Montgomery, led by Martin Luther King (1929–68).

ABOVE: Dizzy Gillespie, the originator of bebop jazz, hits a high note for New York Democrat Adam Powell.

NON-ALIGNED BLOC

Leaders of 29 African and Asian countries meet in Bandung, Indonesia, at the invitation of President Sukharno (1902–70) and form a "non-aligned bloc" of countries opposed to the "imperialism and colonialism" of the superpowers, the USA and USSR.

AUSTRIAN INDEPENDENCE RESTORED

The four occupying powers — USA, USSR, Britain and France — agree to restore Austrian independence within its 1937 frontiers in return for its neutrality, a ban on any *Anschluss* or unity with Germany, and a ban on any return of the Hapsburg monarchy. The treaty removes one of the major irritants in relations between East and West in Europe.

ABOVE: The jazz clarinetist Benny Goodman.

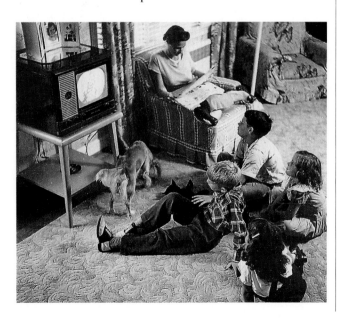

ABOVE: Television becomes the focal point of home entertainment for most Western families.

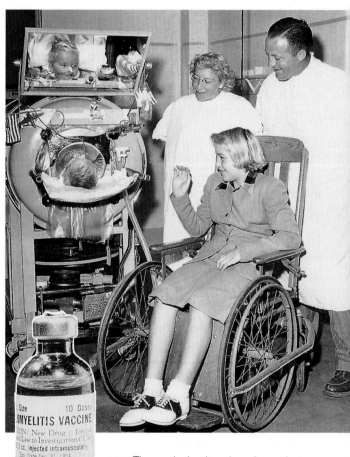

LEFT: The newly developed vaccine against poliomyelitis is expected to prevent death and disablement from the disease that causes infantile paralysis (above).

CYPRUS WAR OF INDEPENDENCE

Greek Cypriots begin a guerrilla war of independence against Britain. Their leading organization is the National Organization of Cypriot Combatants (EOKA) and their aim is unification or enosis with Greece. Their leaders include Cypriot Archbishop Makarios.

POLIO VACCINES

US physician and microbiologist Jonas Salk (1914–95) announces the development of a vaccine against poliomyelitis, which is rife in the USA. It is an injectible vaccine and is given a large clinical trial. US virologist Albert Sabin (1906–93) has also developed a vaccine against poliomyelitis. It is an oral vaccine, which can be taken on a sugar lump.

HOWL: ANTHEM OF THE BEAT GENERATION

American beat poet Allen Ginsberg (1926–97) has published *Howl*. A long poem, it is a rejection of material values and an elegy for the American dream. With its publication, a group of young writers known as the Beat Generation now become widely known.

ANTIPROTONS

Scientists detect antiprotons, short-lived subatomic particles identical to protons but with negative electrical charges.

MODERN-STYLE CHAPEL

French architect Le Corbusier completes his chapel of Notre Dame du Haut in Ronchamp, France. With its curved walls clad in white concrete and its great billowing roof, it brings a new, plastic language to modern architecture.

LOLITA

Russian-born US novelist Vladimir Nabokov (1899–1977) publishes *Lolita*. A novel about the infatuation of a middle-aged writer with a young girl, it provokes a storm of controversy — and increases Nabokov's reading audience.

ABOVE: Berlin students hold torches in the memory of the Germans who lost their lives in the uprising of June 17, 1953.

JAMES BYRON DEAN
(1931–1955)

The young American actor James Dean has been killed in a car crash. He made his name with the film *East of Eden* (1955), which was swiftly followed by *Rebel Without a Cause*. He began his acting career while studying at California University, and trained at the Actors' Studio. His last film *Giant* will be released next year.

ALBERT EINSTEIN
(1879–1955)

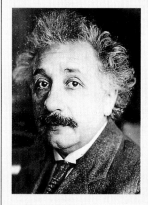

Almost certainly the greatest scientist of our age, Albert Einstein, has died. His work on the theory of relativity (published in 1905 and 1916) explained problems that had been waiting to be solved since Newton and gained him the Nobel Prize in 1921. German-born, he eventually became a citizen of the United States.

CHARLES "BIRD" PARKER
(1920–1955)

The great Kansas-born tenor and alto sax player, Charlie Parker, has died, partly as a result of lifelong addiction to heroin and alcohol. A much-admired improviser, he was one of the pioneers of the bebop style, and had a strong influence on the development of jazz in the 1940s. He played in quintets with musicians such as trumpeters Dizzy Gillespie and Miles Davis, and pianists Al Haig and Duke Jordan.

ABOVE: The USS *Nautilus* is the American Navy's first submarine to be driven by nuclear power.

HELP IN THE KITCHEN

French engineer Mark Grégoire begins producing and marketing non-stick frying pans coated with polytetrafluoroethylene (PTFE), a slippery plastic material discovered in 1938.

SYNTHETIC DIAMONDS

The General Electric Research Laboratory in the USA makes the first synthetic diamonds by treating carbon at very high temperature and pressure; the first products are small diamonds of industrial quality.

HOVERCRAFT PATENTED

English radio engineer and boat designer Christopher Cockerell (1910–99) patents the hovercraft, also known as an air-cushion vehicle or ACV.

KILLER SMOG

In the UK, a new Clean Air Act attempts to control city air pollution by banning the burning of soft, smog-producing coal. Smogs in London and other major British cities, as well as in the USA, have killed more than 9,000 people since 1950.

DISNEYLAND OPENS

US film director Walt Disney (1901–66) and creator of world-famous cartoon character Mickey Mouse, has opened a fantastic Disneyland amusement theme park at Anaheim, California. It features a whole host of rides and attractions based on the Disney cartoons.

BELOW: The ultra-modern St Louis Airport Terminal designed by the Missouri-based architects Hellmuth, Yamasaki and Leinweber.

FIFTIES FASHION

The Fifties see an explosion of new fashion ideas, celebrating Western women's growing independence and freedom of choice, as well as reflecting increasing affluence.

LEFT: Casual elegance is the of keynote of Fifties fashion.

ABOVE: Post-war women are entering the workforce and smart clothes for the office are in demand.

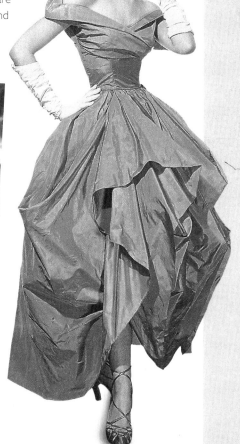

ABOVE AND RIGHT: After the war decade, fashion reflects the desire for luxury without sacrificing women's new-found independence.

ABOVE: Free and easy wear for the holidays more can now afford.

CRISIS IN SUEZ, REVOLT IN HUNGARY

Soviet tanks put down a pro-democracy uprising in Hungary, despite appeals by Hungary to the United Nations. World political tensions rise during the Suez Crisis and Israel attacks Egypt. Fidel Castro and his followers begin guerrilla warfare against the Batista regime in Cuba. In the field of medicine, kidney dialysis begins, and astronomers measure the surface temperature of the planet Venus. Popular music includes hits from *My Fair Lady* and Elvis Presley's "Heartbreak Hotel".

1 9 5 6

Jan	1	Sudan is declared an independent republic
	26	Winter Games televised, Italy
Feb	29	Soviet premier Nikita Kruschev denounces Stalin's policies
Mar	2	Morocco becomes independent from France
	9	Archbishop Makarios deported from Cyprus
	20	Tunisia becomes independent from France
July	26	President Nasser of Egypt nationalizes the Suez Canal
Aug	14	German playwright Bertolt Brecht dies

Oct	23	Demonstrations in Hungary call for democratic government
	24	Imre Nagy appointed Hungarian prime minister
	29	Israeli forces invade Sinai Peninsula
Nov	1	Emergency session of United Nations to discuss Suez Crisis
	2	Hungarian government appeals to UN for assistance against Soviet invasion
	5	British paratroopers land in Port Said, Egypt
	20	Castro and followers land in Cuba to begin guerrilla war against Batista
	22	Olympic Games open in Melbourne, Australia
Dec	5	British and French forces begin to withdraw from Egypt

ABOVE: Anti-government demonstrators in Salonika, Greece, use rolls of newsprint as roadblocks against the Army's armoured cars.

STALIN DENOUNCED

Nikita Khrushchev, now in firm control of the USSR, denounces Stalin at a closed session of the Communist Party Congress. The break with Stalinism leads to a relaxation of state control and terror in the USSR, and leads some Eastern European nations to loosen their ties with the USSR.

MAKARIOS DEPORTED

Britain deports Archbishop Makarios and other Greek Cypriot leaders to the Seychelles in the Indian Ocean on suspicion of involvement with EOKA terrorists fighting to unite Cyprus, a British colony, with Greece. Conflict between Greeks and Turks on the island has been growing for some years as the Greeks seek union with Greece and the Turks seek to protect their rights.

ARAB-ISRAELI WAR

In October, in a pre-arranged secret move with the British and French governments, the small but well-equipped and well-trained Israeli army attacks Egyptian forces in the Sinai who have been threatening Israel's access to the Red Sea from Eilat. In a lightning campaign they capture the Sinai Peninsula plus huge quantities of Egyptian military equipment and large numbers of prisoners. The Franco-British intervention at Suez was ostensibly a peacekeeping operation to separate the Israeli and Egyptian forces.

CUBAN REBELS

Having re-assembled, Fidel Castro and his followers, who include Castro's brother Raul and Che Guevara (1928–67), land in Cuba, from the yacht *Gramma*. They begin a campaign of guerrilla war to overthrow the dictatorial government of President Batista. As volunteers join Castro's group in the Sierra Maestra, he is able to go on the offensive.

FORMER COLONIES INDEPENDENT

The former Anglo-Egyptian colony of Sudan becomes independent from Britain in January. Morocco and Tunisia receive their independence from France in March.

KITCHEN SINK DRAMA

The play *Look Back in Anger* by British writer John Osborne (1929–94) is performed. It centres on an "angry young man", Jimmy Porter, who becomes the archetype of a generation. The play is typical of so-called British "kitchen sink dramas" which feature working-class or lower-middle-class domestic settings.

THE SEVENTH SEAL

Starring actor Max von Sydow, *The Seventh Seal* is the latest film by Swedish film director Ingmar Bergman (b. 1918). Including a game of chess between Death and a knight, who argues the goodness of humanity, the film establishes Bergman's reputation as a major force in the cinema.

HEARTBREAK HOTEL

Rock star Elvis Presley records best-selling "Heartbreak Hotel" and makes his film début in *Love Me Tender*. In the US, he appears live on TV on the Ed Sullivan Show. His fans adore him but some criticize his "provocative" movements.

MY FAIR LADY

Alan Jay Lerner and Frederick Loewe's musical *My Fair Lady* opens on Broadway. Based on George Bernard Shaw's play *Pygmalion*, it is a smash success.

SUEZ CRISIS

In July Egyptian President Nasser (1918–70) nationalizes the Anglo-French Suez Canal Company, which controls the vital waterway between the Mediterranean and Red Sea. The move is strongly opposed by Britain. Nasser makes the move after Britain and the US refused to provide funds to build the Aswan Dam across the Nile, which is designed to increase Egypt's cultivable land by more than half and to provide hydroelectricity. The dam is later built with Soviet aid. In November, in collusion with the Israelis, the British and French launch an airborne and amphibious attack to seize the Suez Canal. Operationally, the landings are a complete success, but politically they are a disaster. The UN votes for a ceasefire after international condemnation of the Anglo-French invasion, led by the USA. Britain and France are obliged to halt their attacks and withdraw in December. As a result of the débâcle, the British prime minister, Anthony Eden, resigns the following year, and both Britain and France lose considerable prestige.

LONG DAY'S JOURNEY

US playwright Eugene O'Neill's play *Long Day's Journey into Night* is performed. A family tragedy, partly based on the writer's own life, it depicts the disintegration of the relationships between the ex-actor James Tyrone, his drug-addict wife Mary and their two sons.

ABOVE: Demonstrators fill the streets of Polish cities, reflecting growing unrest that culminates in the Poznan riots.

TRANSATLANTIC PHONE CABLE
The first cable, called TAT 1, to carry telephone calls is laid across the Atlantic between Scotland and Newfoundland; it contains 51 repeaters along its 3,620km (2,263mi) length to boost the signal.

NEUTRINOS DETECTED
US physicists Frederick Reines and Clyde Lorrain detect the subatomic particles neutrinos and antineutrinos.

VIDEOTAPE BEGINS
The Ampex Company of California builds the first commercial videotape machine; it uses 5cm (2.5in) tape.

KIDNEY DIALYSIS BEGINS
The kidney dialysis machine, which was invented by Dutch physician Willem J Kolff (b. 1911) in 1943, comes into general use in America. The machine uses a membrane to filter out impurities from the blood.

VENUS IS HOT STUFF
American astronomers studying the microwaves emitted from the planet Venus discover its surface temperature is far above boiling point (in 1962, a space probe measures it at 500°C).

CELL MESSENGERS FOUND
Scientists studying cells discover messenger RNA (ribonucleic acid). This makes a reverse copy of the plans for making a protein from the DNA of that protein, and serves as a mould for making a new one.

INTERFERON
British virologist Alick Isaacs and a Swiss colleague, Jean Lindenmann, discover interferon, a protective substance produced in cells when they are infected by viruses.

TELEVISED GAMES
The first televised Winter Games sees action broadcast from Cortina d'Ampezzo in Italy. The Seventh Olympiad is rescued by heavy snow on the opening day. On the rink, the Soviets end Canadian domination of ice hockey.

BREASTFEEDING ENCOURAGED
The La Lèche League is founded at Franklin Park, Illinois in the USA, to encourage breastfeeding, since breast milk has been found to give babies additional protection against disease.

TIPPEX
Bette Nesmith, an American housewife, converts her cottage industry selling Mistake Out (a white paint preparation to blank out typing errors) to local typists, into a national corporation, Liquid Paper Inc.

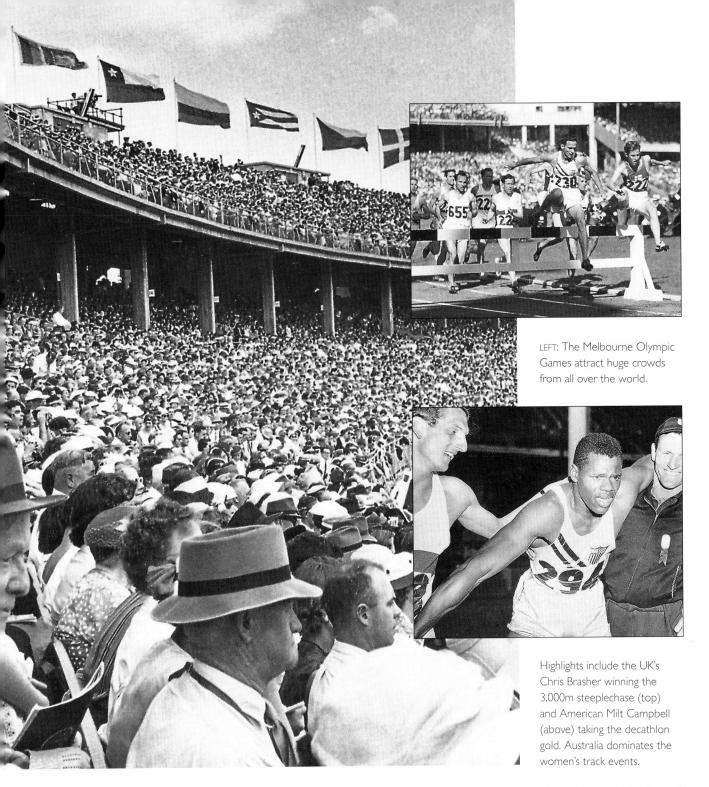

LEFT: The Melbourne Olympic Games attract huge crowds from all over the world.

Highlights include the UK's Chris Brasher winning the 3,000m steeplechase (top) and American Milt Campbell (above) taking the decathlon gold. Australia dominates the women's track events.

MELBOURNE GAMES

This year's Olympic Games are in Melbourne, Australia, the first to be held in southern hemisphere. They are affected by a series of political boycotts, in the wake of the Suez crisis and the Soviet invasion of Hungary. Soviet gymnast Larissa Latynina wins four golds, a silver and a bronze. The hosts sweep the board in the swimming events.

LEFT: Preparations for the American expedition to the South Pole, as the advance survey party leaves the supply ship anchored at McMurdo Sound.

BERTOLT EUGEN FRIEDRICH BRECHT (1898–1956)

The German-born playwright and theatre director Bertolt Brecht has died. Having settled in Hollywood after his retreat from Nazi Germany, he had returned to his native Germany to found the radical theatre company the Berliner Ensemble. Always mindful of his Marxist political beliefs, he introduced a revolutionary approach to theatre, which demanded the audience's detachment. His plays include *Mother Courage* (1941) and *The Resistible Rise of Arturo Ui* (1957). He also collaborated with the composer Kurt Weill on *The Threepenny Opera* (1928) and other musical works.

THE HUNGARIAN UPRISING

Demonstrations break out in Budapest against Soviet domination — Hungary has been part of the Communist bloc since 1946. The former Hungarian prime minister, Imre Nagy, who was forced out of office in February 1955, returns to power promising reform after demonstrators call for democratic government and the withdrawal of Soviet troops. However, demonstrations lead to a wider uprising against the Soviet Union. Nagy forms a government including non-Communists and takes Hungary out of the Warsaw Pact, appealing for Western aid against any Soviet invasion. However, in November, Moscow sends 2,500 tanks and armoured vehicles and 200,000 troops into Hungary. Street fighting erupts in Budapest but the Hungarians are crushed, suffering 12,000 killed. Nagy is deposed in favour of János Kádár, who changes sides to head the new government. Nagy is executed after a secret trial in June 1958.

ABOVE: Students pose in front of Budapest University with their machine guns during the October Revolution, having taken up arms against the threat of Soviet domination.

RIGHT: In Mexico, workers demonstrate in support of the Hungarian revolutionaries.

ABOVE: A huge statue of Stalin is pulled down and dragged through the streets of Budapest during the anti-Soviet riots.

ABOVE: The Hungarian flag is draped over the body of a freedom fighter.

RIGHT: A Hungarian resistance fighter explains how to use a Molotov cocktail.

SPUTNIKS ORBIT THE EARTH

The Space Race gets under way as the Russians launch the world's first artificial satellites: *Sputnik I* and *Sputnik II*. *Sputnik II* carries a little dog, Laika, and captures the imagination of the world. Free trade comes closer in Europe as various countries form the European Common Market. US troops are sent to Little Rock, Arkansas, to enforce racial integration in the schools. *West Side Story* opens on Broadway.

1957

Jan	21	Fashion designer Christian Dior dies (b. 1905)	**Aug**	4	Argentinian racing driver, Fangio, wins 24th Grand Prix
	22	Israeli forces make complete withdrawal from Sinai Peninsula but remain in Gaza Strip		31	Malaya gains independence from Britain
			Sep	25	Schools desegregate in Little Rock, Arkansas, after US troops are sent in
Feb	6	Gold Coast becomes independent as Ghana		26	The musical *West Side Story* opens on Broadway
Mar	25	Treaty of Rome sets up European Common Market	**Oct**	4	Russians launch the world's first artificial satellite, *Sputnik I*
	28	Britain releases Archbishop Makarios			
July	6	Althea Gibson, US tennis player, becomes first black player to win Wimbledon singles	**Nov**	3	Russians launch *Sputnik II*, carrying an animal
				25	Diego Rivera dies (b. 1884)

ABOVE: Althea Gibson receives a rapturous welcome on her return from winning the Women's Tennis Championship at Wimbledon.

EUROPEAN COMMON MARKET

Rome, France, West Germany, Netherlands, Belgium, Luxembourg and Italy sign the Treaty of Rome, setting up the European Common Market, later the European Economic Union (EEC). Its aim is the free movement of goods, money and people through its member nations. The Treaty also sets up the European Atomic Energy Authority (Euratom).

FIRST SPUTNIKS

Sputnik I, the world's first artifical Earth satellite, is successfully launched by the Soviet Union on the 50th anniversary of the Russian Revolution. A month later they launch *Sputnik II*, which carries the first animal to go into space, a female dog called Laika. This is in preparation for sending humans into space.

LITTLE ROCK

US federal paratroopers are sent in to enforce integration in local schools in Little Rock, Arkansas, after black pupils are refused admission to the Central High School and the Arkansas governor, Orval Faubus, uses the state militia to bar their entry. The action causes outrage in the southern states against the federal government.

MALAYA INDEPENDENT

The Federation of Malaya gains its independence from Britain, the last major British Asian colonies so to do.

GOLD COAST INDEPENDENT

The British colony of the Gold Coast becomes the first black African state to win its independence from European rule as Ghana, under the charismatic leadership of Kwame Nkrumah (1909–72).

DOCTOR ZHIVAGO

Russian author Boris Pasternak (1890–1960) publishes his novel *Doctor Zhivago* — in Italy because it will not be published in his native USSR. An account of Russia and its intelligentsia during the revolutionary period, the novel is a rapid success. The following year, Pasternak is awarded the Nobel Prize for Literature.

ON THE ROAD

American author Jack Kerouac (1922–69) publishes his partly autobiographical novel *On the Road*. Fast-moving and loosely structured, the style of the novel reflects the travels and life of the central character, writer Sal Paradise. It puts Kerouac on the literary map and makes him, together with writers Alan Ginsberg and William Burroughs, a leading figure of the Beat Generation. Followers of Beat Generation philosophy reject social and artistic conventions, favour progressive jazz and explore mystical experiences offered by Eastern religions.

PALAZETTO DEL SPORT

Italian architect Pier Luigi Nervi (1891–1979) designs the Palazetto del Sport for the 1960 Olympic Games to be held in Rome. The stadium is made of prefabricated parts (including striking concrete Y-frames) enabling construction of the main dome 61m (200ft) in diameter to be completed in a staggering 40 days.

WEST SIDE STORY

American conductor and composer Leonard Bernstein's musical *West Side Story* has opened on Broadway. An adaptation of *Romeo and Juliet*, the exciting musical is set among the street gangs of New York. US composer Stephen Sondheim has written the lyrics, including popular favourites "America" and "Maria".

VOSS

The Australian novelist Patrick White (1912–90) publishes *Voss*, a novel about a German explorer's bid to lead an expedition across Australia. It brings him international recognition.

VELCRO PATENTED

Swiss inventor Georges de Mestral patents ™Velcro, the cling fabric fastener based on the cocklebur principle; he has taken seventeen years to perfect it.

RADIO TELESCOPE

A radio telescope with a steerable dish 76m (249ft) across comes into operation at Jodrell Bank, Cheshire, England, for use by astronomers at the University of Manchester.

ABOVE: Screen icons Elizabeth Taylor and James Dean in *Giant*, a story of lust and oil in Texas, released the year after Dean's death.

ABOVE: In the People's Republic of China, the Cultural Revolution means that everyone does hard physical work.

PACEMAKER

US physician Clarence Lillehei devises a pacemaker small enough to be inserted in a patient's body and control a heart that is beating irregularly.

NUCLEAR ACCIDENTS

Two nuclear accidents release radioactivity into the atmosphere. One occurs at Windscale nuclear power plant in the UK; the other in a Russian nuclear waste store in the Ural Mountains.

PSYCHOLINGUISTICS

The psychology of language, or psycholinguistics, is galvanized by the publication of *Syntactic Structures* by Noam Chomsky (b. 1928). He theorizes that language began — and begins in children — not with sounds but with rudimentary sentences whose structure follows rules common to all languages.

GRAND PRIX WINNER

At the age of 46, Juan Manuel Fangio (1911–95) wins a record fifth Grand Prix World Championship with a stunning victory in the German Grand Prix. The Argentinian, driving a Maserati, smashes the lap record ten times during the race.

FATS CAUSE HEART DISEASE

A paper by University of Minnesota nutritionist Ancel Keys, published in the *Journal of the American Medical Association*, establishes a connection between diets high in animal fats and heart disease.

WOLFENDEN REPORT

In the UK, the Report of the Home Office Committee on Homosexual Offences and Prostitution by Sir John Wolfenden, Chancellor of Reading University, unexpectedly recommends an end to punitive laws against homosexual acts between consenting adults.

DODGERS TO MOVE

Walter O'Malley, president of the Brooklyn Dodgers, announces the team is moving from New York to Los Angeles. The news outrages Dodgers fans but is the first of many such transfers as baseball expands.

OPPOSITE: Archaeologists in Iraq unearth one of the biggest finds of inscribed Sumerian clay tablets ever discovered.

CHRISTIAN DIOR
(1905–1957)

Christian Dior, the French couturier who launched the post-war "New Look" on the Paris catwalks in 1947, has died. The House of Dior also introduced the A-line and the sack dress, and created several well-known perfumes, including "Miss Dior".

JOSEPH RAYMOND McCARTHY
(1909–1957)

The fanatical anti-Communist American Republican, Senator Joseph (Joe) McCarthy, has died. Since 1950 he had been conducting a witch-hunt among citizens and officials, becoming chairman of the so-called House Committee on Un-American Activities in 1953. Many prominent intellectuals and actors have been among those accused of being Communists. In 1954, McCarthy was censured by the Senate for his methods but he remained rabidly anti-Communist to the end.

ABOVE: US President Eisenhower, re-elected in 1956 is pictured here talking to Lyndon Johnson.

ABOVE: Future astronaut John H Glenn celebrates a non-stop flight round the world in a B52 bomber.

MARCHING AGAINST THE BOMB

The USA launches *Explorer I* into space, the first of a series of science satellites. Anti-nuclear feeling finds a voice as the Campaign for Nuclear Disarmament is formed. In the face of continuing Algerian problems, Charles de Gaulle becomes president of France. The new contraceptive pill goes on sale in the USA with the potential for transforming women's lives. The Netherlands hosts a conference on sexual equality and Barbie is born.

1 9 5 8

Jan	3	New Zealand expedition reaches the South Pole
	20	British expedition reaches the South Pole
	31	USA launches *Explorer I*
Feb	3	Benelux economic union formed.
	6	Manchester United footballers killed in major air crash
	17	CND formed in London, UK with the slogan "Ban the Bomb"
Mar	24	Elvis Presley begins two years' military service, USA
Apr	7	CND holds first "Aldermaston March" from London to Aldermaston nuclear research station
May	29	Algerian crisis forces recall of Charles de Gaulle
June	29	Brazil wins football's World Cup
July	14	Army mounts coup against King Faisal II of Iraq
	14	King Hussein of Jordan assumes power as head of Arab Federation
	15	USA sends troops to Lebanon
Sep	9	Race riots flare in Notting Hill district, London, UK
Oct	2	Guinea declared an independent republic
Dec	21	Charles de Gaulle is elected president of France

CND FORMED

Anti-nuclear protesters form the Campaign for Nuclear Disarmament (CND) at a rally in London, UK, addressed by the philosopher Bertrand Russell (1872–1970). They march from London to the nuclear research establishment at Aldermaston to protest against Britain's nuclear capacity. Other CND-type organizations are formed elsewhere in Europe.

BENELUX ESTABLISHED

Belgium, the Netherlands and Luxembourg meet at The Hague in the Netherlands and establish the Benelux economic union, which provides for the free movement of capital, goods and people between the three states.

DE GAULLE COMES TO POWER

Trouble continues in Algeria. After a revolt by French settlers in Algeria against moves by the French government to negotiate with the Algerian Nationalist forces, the French government falls and Charles de Gaulle (1890–1970) takes power. He takes emergency powers for six months and draws up a new constitution, which ends the unstable Fourth Republic and establishes the Fifth Republic with strong presidential powers. In December, de Gaulle becomes president of France, and promises talks with the Algerian rebels.

KING FAISAL OVERTHROWN

In Iraq, the army overthrows the pro-Western monarchy of King Faisal, destabilizing the region. In response, US troops land in Lebanon and British troops land in Jordan to support these governments against possible coup attempts.

ABOVE LEFT: Jerry Lee Lewis, a charismatic singer and pianist who outrages the Establishment.

ABOVE: Teenagers, with their own music, style, crazes and language, are the phenomenon of the 1950s in America and all over Europe.

ABOVE: Charles de Gaulle is elected first president of the Fifth Republic this year. He will remain in power until his resignation in 1969.

ABOVE: Marian Anderson, American contralto, is accompanied by the Bombay City Orchestra, in a scene from *The Lady from Philadelphia*.

ABOVE: Composer and conductor Leonard Bernstein conducting a rehearsal of the New York Philharmonic Symphony Orchestra.

GUINEA INDEPENDENT
Prime Minister Sekou Toure (1922–84) declares Guinea an independent republic in the French West African colony and leaves the new French community. Other French colonies remain tied to France.

THE LEOPARD
The only novel by Sicilian prince Giuseppe di Lampedusa (1896–1957) is published posthumously. Entitled *The Leopard*, it describes how a noble family in Sicily respond to changes after Italy annexes the island in 1860.

THE FIRE RAISERS
A play, *The Fire Raisers*, by architect and writer Max Frisch, is performed. It targets the complacency of the middle classes in the person of a man who will tolerate even the burning down of his own home.

NOBELIUM PRODUCED
Element 102, nobelium, is artificially created by American scientists. It is the ninth and last with which Glenn T Seaborg is involved.

LYCRA LAUNCHED
In the USA, Du Pont launches Lycra, the first of the Spandex fibres or man-made elastics.

ABOVE AND RIGHT: The Vanguard satellite (above) was sent into orbit successfully by the Vanguard rocket, at 22m (72ft) the largest of its kind at the time.

SEAGRAM BUILDING
A new office block, the Seagram Building in New York, is the ultimate modern tower — restrained in its details, well proportioned, based on a glass-and-metal structure. Designed by Mies van der Rohe (1886–1969) and Philip Johnson (b. 1906) the building's detail and high-quality material make it extremely distinctive.

EXPLORER I
The USA follows the Soviet Union and sends its first artificial satellite, *Explorer 1*, into space. The launch rocket has been developed by Werner von Braun, previously head of Germany's V-2 programme. *Explorer 1* is the first in a series of US scientific satellites.

VAN ALLEN BELTS
At the suggestion of physicist James Van Allen (b. 1914), US satellite *Explorer 4* carries radiation counters heavily shielded with lead. They register cosmic rays, showing that there are belts of very high radiation, later called the Van Allen Belts.

SUB UNDER ARCTIC OCEAN
US nuclear submarine *Nautilus*, launched in 1955, sails under the Arctic Ocean ice-cap, the first-ever underwater voyage from the Pacific to the Atlantic beneath the North Polar ice-cap.

NEW ZEALAND ARRIVES FIRST
Edmund Hillary's New Zealand team beats Vivian Fuchs's British team overland to the South Pole. Hillary's party sets out from McMurdo Sound and the British from the Vansee Sea. As a contribution to the International Geophysical Year, Britain's team goes on to make the first transantarctic crossing.

BIRTH PILL
The Pill, the first oral contraceptive for women, is marketed in the USA. Containing artificial hormones oestrogen and progesterone, it prevents conception by simulating pregnancy. The pill has been developed by Gregory Pincus, who in 1951 was visited by the feminist Margaret Sanger. Pincus produced the Pill in association with Hudson Hoagland and Min-Cheh Chang in 1954.

SEXUAL EQUALITY
The Netherlands COC (Cultuur-en-Ontspannings Centrum) sponsors the fifth International Conference on Sexual Equality; the first was in 1951. The Conference offers a beacon of rational support for lesbian and gay organizations elsewhere in Europe, where they are suppressed and persecuted.

BARBIE IS BORN
The Barbie doll is created in the USA by Mattel. A madeover version of an earlier doll, she is given a teenage fashion model look and a complete, up-to-date wardrobe is designed for her 1959 launch.

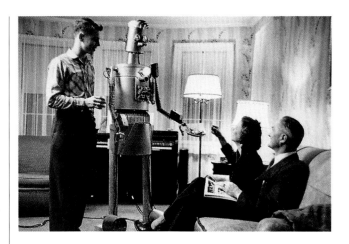

ABOVE: Robots seize the imagination: American Sherwood Fuehrer, age fourteen, invents a person-sized robot called Gizmo, which he can manoeuvre from a remote-control box.

AMERICAN EXPRESS
The Bank of America launches American Express, the first ever credit card. By December, it is being used by some 500,000 people.

HULA HOOP AND SKATEBOARD CRAZE
New crazes sweep the USA when the hula hoop, launched by Arthur Melin and Richard Knerr, and the skateboard, invented by Bill and Mark Richards, appear in California.

XEROX GOES COMMERCIAL
The first commercial Xerox copier goes on sale. Invented in 1947, it makes dry copies of documents.

STEREO RECORDING
Record companies in the USA and Britain issue the first stereophonic records.

UNDERSTANDING SOCIAL BEHAVIOUR
Claude Levi-Strauss, Belgian-born anthropologist and professor of ethnology at the University of Paris, publishes *Structural Anthropology*. He theorizes that societies have a similar structure that reflects the way myths are created, and these, when accurately understood, will enable us to understand their behaviour.

BRILLIANT BRAZIL
The World Cup takes place in Sweden and marks the arrival of Brazilian player Pelé, the world's greatest exponent of the beautiful game. He scores six goals in the tournament and Brazil takes home the title, beating the hosts 5–2 in the final.

POLYGAMY RESTRICTED
The government of newly independent Morocco liberalizes the law in favour of women, granting women the right to choose their own husbands and restricting polygamy.

CASTRO TAKES CONTROL IN CUBA

In Cuba Fidel Castro succeeds in toppling Batista to take over the Cuban government. The Dalai Lama, Tibet's spiritual leader, flees Chinese-occupied Tibet. The oldest known hominid remains are found in Africa. The new Guggenheim Museum in New York is opened but its brilliant architect, Frank Lloyd Wright, dies just before completion. Soviet spacecraft crash-land on the Moon and send back the first photographs of its dark side.

1959

Jan	1	Batista resigns and then flees Cuba, following guerrilla campaign
	3	Castro enters Havana and sets up provisional government
Mar	17	Tibetan uprising against Chinese. Dalai Lama is smuggled out of Tibet
Apr	3	Dalai Lama reaches India from Chinese-occupied Tibet
	9	Frank Lloyd Wright dies (b. 1867)
June	26	St Lawrence Seaway opens
July	17	British anthropologists discover *Homo habilis*
Aug	7	Chinese forces enter northeast India
Oct	26	Soviet spacecraft films dark side of the Moon

Nov	10	United Nations condemns apartheid in South Africa
	20	The "Seven" set up European Free Trade Agreement (EFTA)
Dec	1	Antarctic Treaty signed by twelve nations keeps Antarctic free of territorial or military claims

ABOVE: Emperor penguins and the USS *Glacier* in Antarctica.

BELOW: Astronaut monkeys provide important information about the biomedical factors affecting manned space flight.

ABOVE: Self-propelled anti-aircraft guns pass the reviewing stand at the May Day parade in East Berlin.

ABOVE: An East German bread vendor stands beside a poster of Soviet premier Nikita Khrushchev shaking hands with East Germany's Communist leader Walter Ulbricht.

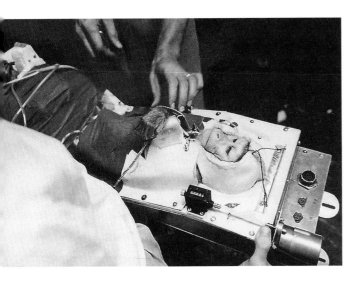

LEFT: A new type of radio telescope built by Australian astronomer Dr Ronald Bracewell.

ABOVE: The bows of the cruiser USS Long Beach, the US Navy's first nuclear-powered surface ship, stand tall in the naval shipyard at Quincy, Massachusetts.

BUDDY (CHARLES HARDIN) HOLLY (1936–1959)

Charles Hardin, the singer better known as Buddy Holly, has died in a plane crash. The fans of the American rock-and-roller will be devastated. He and his band the Crickets set up the new standard line-up of two guitars, bass and drums, and were innovatory in their recording techniques. A body of recordings is the legacy of Buddy Holly's brief career.

JOHN FOSTER DULLES (1888–1959)

American Republican politician John Foster Dulles has died of cancer. As Secretary of State in the 1950s, he devoted his energies to alerting the world to the threat of Communism, and at the same time contributing to the rise of Cold War tension.

CASTRO IN POWER

Fidel Castro takes power in Cuba after Batista flees into exile in the Dominican Republic. The takeover comes at the end of an insurrection that has lasted for more than two years. Dr Manuel Urratia is proclaimed provisional president of Cuba with Castro as prime minister.

DALAI LAMA FLEES

A rising against Chinese rule is repressed by the Chinese army and the Dalai Lama, Tibet's Buddhist spiritual leader, is smuggled out of Tibet and flees into exile in India, where he appeals for UN intervention to secure the independence of Tibet.

RWANDAN CIVIL WAR

Civil war breaks out in Rwanda, which has recently been granted self-government by Belgium, the colonial power. The ruling Tutsi people, who make up only a small percentage of the population, have been attacked by the Hutu, who make up 85 per cent of the population. A Hutu-dominated republic is proclaimed following a UN-supervised vote but when armed Tutsi *emigrés* attack the new nation they are driven off and many Tutsi are massacred in reprisal.

DISPUTE OVER INDIA/CHINA BORDER

A border dispute breaks out in the Himalayas between India and China, prompted by China's belief that the British-designated border is no longer valid.

ABOVE: India's Prime Minister Jawaharlal Nehru at the inauguration of the Hirakud Dam, one of several projects designed to boost food production through irrigation and to provide hydroelectric power for India's developing industry.

RIGHT: Dog models in Soviet rocket chambers designed to carry real canines on short space flights. Two dogs do in fact make the trip and return safely to earth.

EFTA

Seven European countries — Sweden, Norway, Denmark, Britain, Portugal, Austria and Switzerland — set up the European Free Trade Area (EFTA) to rival the EEC.

FIRST TRIP TO THE MOON

Lunar II, an uncrewed Soviet spacecraft, becomes the first space probe to crash-land on the Moon. On the way it confirms the existence of the solar wind, a flow of gases from the Sun. Later this year, *Lunar III* orbits the Moon and transmits pictures of its dark side — the side never seen from Earth.

GUGGENHEIM MUSEUM

With its unique spiral design, the new Guggenheim Museum in New York is one of the most striking modern buildings. The paintings are hung beside a continuous spiral ramp; visitors take the elevator to the top and walk down, thereby, in theory at least, minimizing "museum fatigue".

RHINOCEROS

Romanian-born dramatist Eugène Ionesco (1912–94) creates "anti-plays", in which a world of nightmare fuses with farce. His latest is *Rhinoceros*, in which the cast turn one by one into rhinoceroses, interpreted by most critics as the image of a totalitarian takeover.

HANDY MAN FOUND

British anthropologists Louis and Mary Leakey discover in Olduvai Gorge, Tanzania, fossils of the earliest human species. The species is named *Homo habilis*, "Handy Man", and lived two million years ago. Stone tools found on the site are the earliest so far discovered.

THE TIN DRUM

German novelist Günter Grass (b. 1927) publishes *The Tin Drum*. The novel, which features the hunchback Oskar who decides to stop growing in infancy, becomes a bestseller in Germany. Its narrative seems to sum up the history of Germany during the twentieth century.

SYNTHESIZER

The Radio Corporation of America invent the synthesizer, an electronic instrument which can imitate the sounds of many traditional instruments and also make new sounds.

SWISS WOMEN REJECTED

The Swiss electorate votes to reject a proposed amendment to the constitution to permit women to vote in national elections and run for national office.

SOME LIKE IT HOT

US film actress Marilyn Monroe (1926–62) stars as singer Sugar Kane in a new Billy Wilder film, *Some Like it Hot*. The film, which is a lively comedy, confirms her status as an international star.

BILLIE (ELEANOR FAGANA) HOLIDAY (1915–1959)

American jazz singer Billie Holiday, also known as Lady Day, has died. She sang with leading jazz artists such as Benny Goodman, Lester Young, Count Basie and Louis Armstrong, and leaves the world recordings of songs such as "Easy Living" (1937) which are bound to endure.

NOUVELLE VAGUE

French film director Alain Resnais (b. 1922) premières his first full-length film, *Hiroshima Mon Amour*. Set in Hiroshima it establishes Resnais as a leading member of the *Nouvelle Vague* (New Wave). This year too, French film director Jean Luc Godard (b. 1930) releases his first full-length film, *A Bout de Souffle*. The film is shot without a script, indicating Godard's emphasis on improvisatory techniques.

ANTARCTICA

The Antarctic Treaty signed by twelve nations, including the US, Britain and the USSR, suspends all territorial and military claims, restricts exploration of the Antarctic to peaceful purposes only, and establishes the continent south of 60° as a preserve for scientific research. The treaty lasts until 1989, then is renewed.

STOCK CAR RACING

The most prestigious race in American stock car racing is born at Daytona International Speedway in Florida. Lee Petty wins the first Daytona 500 in an Oldsmobile.

ST LAWRENCE SEAWAY

The St Lawrence Seaway, a system of rivers, lakes and canals that enables ocean-going ships to carry cargoes to and from the Great Lakes of North America, opens.

BULGING EARTH

The US satellite *Vanguard 1* makes thousands of orbits of the Earth and shows that the planet is about 7.6m (25ft) fatter in the south than in the north.

FRANK LLOYD WRIGHT (1867–1959)

The outstanding modern architect, the American Frank Lloyd Wright, has died in his 90s. He had been designing arresting buildings during the whole of this century, including domestic works such as the Prairie-style Robie House (1908) and the international modernist-style Fallingwater (1937), and offices such as the Johnson Wax Office Building (1936). He has almost completed the Guggenheim Museum in New York when he dies.

THE SWINGING SIXTIES

The Sixties witness a creative explosion of popular culture, a major shift in attitudes to personal and public morality. In the USA, there is a new Camelot with President Kennedy in the royal role. For a decade in pursuit of peace love and understanding, there is a remarkable amount of violence: revolutions, assassinations, riots, protests and demonstrations abound. In America and Africa, black people assert their rights. Energy and optimism are directed upwards as the USSR and the USA race each other to conquer space.

OPPOSITE: Civil rights protests and demonstrations characterize the decade.

1960–1969

KEY EVENTS OF THE DECADE

SHARPEVILLE MASSACRE	BLACK POWER
JOHN F KENNEDY ASSASSINATED	UDI IN RHODESIA
CONTRACEPTIVE PILL	POLIO VACCINE
HUMANITY IN SPACE	PRAGUE SPRING
THE CUBAN CRISIS	SUMMER OF LOVE
THE BERLIN WALL	THE SIX-DAY WAR
BLACK CIVIL RIGHTS	STUDENT PROTEST
VIETNAM WAR	MEN ON THE MOON
THE BEATLES	
MINISKIRTS	WORLD POPULATION 3,109 MILLION

WINDS OF CHANGE START TO BLOW

The decade starts as it means to go on, as liberation of all kinds scents the breeze. In Africa, European colonial power evaporates as more countries gain independence. Only South Africa bucks the trend, with white minority rule cracking down on the black populace. In the USA, a dynamic young president is elected. Italian director Federico Fellini anticipates the sexual revolution with his film *La Dolce Vita*, while in Britain, DH Lawrence's *Lady Chatterley's Lover* is declared a good (and legal) read.

1960

Jan	**4**	French author Albert Camus dies in car crash, aged 46
	8	Kenneth Kaunda freed from jail in Northern Rhodesia (Zambia); he later becomes president
	23	Bathyscaphe *Trieste* makes record dive of 10,910m (some 30,000ft) in Marianas Trench
Feb	**18**	Eighth Winter Olympics open at Squaw Valley, California
Mar	**21**	Sharpeville Massacre: South African police panic and kill 56 black protesters
Apr	**1**	First weather satellite, *Tiros 1*, is launched
May	**1**	Soviets shoot down US U-2 spy plane over the Ural Mountains
	30	Russian author Boris Pasternak dies

June	**30**	Belgian Congo becomes independent as Congo Republic
Aug	**16**	British colony of Cyprus becomes an independent republic
Nov	**8**	John F Kennedy is elected 35th US president

ABOVE: Democratic Senator John F Kennedy is president elect.

ABOVE: Wreckage from the alleged US U-2 spy plane shot down in Russian airspace goes on display in Moscow.

AN END TO WHITE RULE IN AFRICA
Cameroon gains its independence from France. Over the next eleven months, thirteen former French colonies, Somalia (combining former British and Italian colonies) and Nigeria all gain their independence. In June, the Belgian colony of the Congo becomes independent as the Congo Republic with Patrice Lumumba as prime minister. Visiting South Africa, British prime minister Harold Macmillan states that a "wind of change" is blowing through the continent, with black African states gaining independence and white rule ending.

MASSACRE IN THE TOWNSHIP
Police open fire against demonstrators in the black township of Sharpeville, south of Johannesburg, killing 56 Africans and injuring 162. The demonstrators were protesting against the new pass laws requiring all Africans to carry an identity pass at all times. As a result of the massacre, the African National Congress (ANC) and the Pan-African Congress (PAC) are banned. International protests force South Africa to leave the British Commonwealth and become an independent republic in May 1961, increasing the international isolation of the apartheid government.

EICHMANN FOUND
Israeli intelligence officers kidnap Adolf Eichmann, the SS officer who master-minded the Final Solution in Nazi Germany during the war, from Argentina and take him back to Israel. He is put on trial in Jerusalem in 1961 and hanged for crimes against the Jewish people in May 1962.

JFK RULES
John F Kennedy, aged 43, narrowly wins the presidential election against the Republican Richard Nixon and becomes the 35th US president.

SPY IN THE SKY
A US U-2 spy plane flown by Gary Powers is shot down over Russia. The four-power summit taking place in Paris, called to reduce tension in Europe, collapses with no agreement as the US refuses to apologize for flying over Soviet airspace.

BRASILIA BUILDINGS
Lúcio Costa and Oscar Niemeyer are the architects of the parliament buildings in Brasilia, Brazil's new capital city. The striking modernist forms of the buildings bring Latin American architecture to international prominence.

DIVIDED BUT INDEPENDENT
After five years of conflict, the island of Cyprus becomes an independent republic in the Commonwealth with the Greek Cypriot Archbishop Makarios as president and the Turkish Cypriot Dr Fazil Kütchük as vice-president.

THE BIRTH OF OPEC
In Baghdad, five oil-exporting nations — Iraq, Iran, Kuwait, Saudi Arabia and Venezuela — agree to set up the Organization of Petroleum Exporting Countries (OPEC) to protect their interests.

LA DOLCE VITA
Federico Fellini's film, starring Marcello Mastroianni, depicts and criticizes the decadent, pleasure-seeking society of Rome's "beautiful people".

ABOVE: The Voice of America broadcasts to West Berlin, offering a forum for defectors.

BELOW: Ghanaian troops form part of the UN presence in the troubled Congo.

BORIS LEONIDOVICH PASTERNAK (1890–1960)

Russian writer and poet Boris Pasternak has died. He is best known in the West for his novel *Dr Zhivago* (1957), which portrays the disillusion that displaced the idealistic visions of the revolution, a book banned in his own country. It is perhaps less well known that he was for many years Russia's official translator of works by Shakespeare, Goethe, the French poet Verlaine and other writers.

THE CARETAKER

The play *The Caretaker* establishes Harold Pinter as one of Britain's leading young dramatists. He is renowned for his powerful dialogue (realistic in its use of everyday language and telling pauses) and for his ability to evoke menace, stressed relationships and mental disintegration.

THE FIRST LASER

US physicist Theodore H Maiman builds the first laser. The name comes from the initial letters of Light Amplification by Stimulated Emission of Radiation. He uses an artificial ruby cylinder to produce a beam of light that hardly spreads at all. Laser light will go on to become essential in many applications, from surgery to nightclubs.

RABBIT, RUN

This is the first of American novelist John Updike's series of novels featuring the life of ex-basketball champion Harry Angstrom. The novel, with its vivid prose, establishes Updike as a major writer.

TO KILL A MOCKINGBIRD

Harper Lee's southern tale is told from the viewpoint of the two children of a white lawyer who is defending a black man accused (unjustly) of rape. The book will become a best-seller.

INTEGRATED CIRCUITS

Transistors become so small that they can be etched on to thin chips of silicon, producing integrated circuits; each chip can do the work of many transistors.

ROUND THE WORLD UNDER THE SEA

USS *Triton*, a nuclear submarine, becomes the first vessel to circumnavigate the Earth without ever surfacing. It completes the journey in 84 days.

DEALING WITH DELINQUENCY

In *Growing Up Absurd* American writer and psychologist Paul Goodman draws on literature, political theory and psychology to argue for an anti-authoritarian approach to dealing with delinquents and young offenders.

ALBERT CAMUS (1913–1960)

Algerian-born French existentialist novelist and former Resistance worker Albert Camus has died in a car crash, with an unfinished autobiographical novel at his side. His first novel, *The Outsider* (1942), gained him instant fame, and was quickly followed by *The Myth of Sisyphus* (also 1942). Other work includes *The Plague* (1947) and *The Fall* (1956), political writings such as *Chronicles of Today* (1950–53), and a number of plays. He was also editor, with Jean-Paul Sartre, of the left-wing newspaper *Combat* in the years immediately following the liberation.

THE CHATTERLEY TRIAL

Penguin Books Limited are prosecuted for publishing "an obscene book entitled *Lady Chatterley's Lover*", the notorious book written by English novelist DH Lawrence, first published privately in Florence in 1928. The defence calls numerous eminent literary people who testify as to the novel's literary merit, and the publishers are cleared; the book is made legally available.

SEA-FLOOR SPREADING

Harry Hammond Hess, professor of geophysics at Princeton University in the USA, puts forward the idea that the sea-floor is spreading outward from the volcanic mid-ocean ridges, thus causing continental drift.

WEATHER SATELLITES

Tiros I, the first weather satellite, is launched by the USA on April 1, followed by *Tiros II* in November. What they detect greatly helps weather forecasting, especially the early detection of tornadoes and hurricanes.

MORE ACCURATE METRE

The metre, originally set by Napoleon's advisors as one ten-millionth of the distance from the Equator to the North Pole, is more accurately defined as 1,650,763.73 wavelengths of orange-red light from the isotype krypton-86.

ARTIFICIAL HIPS

English surgeon John Charnley fits patients with the first artificial hip joints.

RECORD DEEP-SEA DIVE

The bathyscaphe *Trieste* descends nearly 11km (7mi) into the Marianas Trench in the Pacific, the greatest known ocean depth. It is piloted by US naval lieutenant Don Walsh and French engineer Jacques Piccard, son of its inventor, Swiss-born Belgian physicist Auguste. Piccard piloted his first bathyscaphe, an observation capsule suspended beneath a flotation tank, in 1948.

SRI LANKA'S FIRST LADY

Sirimavo Bandaranaike, widow of the assassinated prime minister of Ceylon and leader of the Sri Lanka Freedom Party, becomes the world's first woman prime minister, vowing to continue her husband's socialist policies.

ARRIVAL OF THE PILL

The first oral contraceptive, an oestrogen-progesterone compound, becomes commercially available in the USA. Its producer, GD Searle of Illinois, is carrying out a trial on 50 women in Birmingham, UK, preparatory to introducing "the Pill" in Britain in 1961.

RIGHT: May Day celebrations in Moscow, a tradition established to display the military might and muscle of the USSR.

ABOVE: The US Army's new Pershing missile, a two-stage ballistic weapon, on a test launch from a portable transporter-erector.

ABOVE: The shambles left by the worst of a series of earthquakes to hit Chile this year.

BELOW: US athlete Wilma Rudolph takes Olympic gold in the women's 100m sprint.

ABOVE: The USS *Triton*, the largest submarine in the world, gets ready for the first underwater circumnavigation of the globe.

RIGHT: Rafer Johnson wins gold for the USA in the decathlon at Rome.

WINTER OLYMPICS

The Eighth Winter Games in California take place in a resort built from scratch for them at Squaw Valley. Hosts America win the ice hockey gold against expectations and the Scandinavian hold on the Nordic events is broken by two German winners.

FOOTBALL RECORD

Spanish team Real Madrid take football's European Cup for the fifth consecutive time with a thrilling 7–3 triumph over Eintracht Frankfurt in the final. Ferenc Puskas scores four goals and Alfredo Di Stefano adds a hat-trick.

OLYMPICS AT ROME

The Soviets head foes America in the medal table at the seventeenth Olympiad in Rome, Italy. At his sixth Games, Hungarian Aladar Gerevich ends his career at age 50 by adding a fencing gold to his collection of six golds, a silver and a bronze. Cassius Clay (later Muhammad Ali) takes the gold medal for light-heavyweight boxing.

LIFE WITH THE LIONS

Born Free, an account of her work with lions in Kenya, by German-born writer Joy Adamson, is widely influential in publicizing the increasing threat to the world's wild animals.

DEPLETING THE SEAS

The world fisheries catch for 1960 reaches 40 million tons, double that of 1950, but Soviet trawlers and purse seiners reduce herring populations along US Atlantic coast by 90 per cent and virtually wipe out haddock.

A NEW PEN

The first felt-tip pen, the August Pentel, is introduced by the Tokyo Stationery Co.

RUNNING THE SPACE RACE

There is crisis in Cuba after a botched US-backed invasion. The US sends an unlikely number of military observers to Vietnam, taking the first step on a path paved with good intentions that will lead to all-out conflict. The big story of the year is the race to put a man in space, which is won by the Russians as cosmonaut Yuri Gagarin orbits the Earth in triumph. Alan B Shepard, for the USA, gets there second in a spacecraft that can be controlled by its pilot.

BELOW: The Moon becomes the focus for the rivalry between the USA and the USSR.

1961

Jan	20	John F Kennedy is inaugurated as US president
	14	South Africa introduces new decimal currency
Apr	12	Soviet cosmonaut Yuri Gagarin becomes the first man in space
	17	Cuban exiles land at Bay of Pigs, Cuba, but are routed
May	5	US astronaut Alan B Shepard becomes the second man in space
	31	South Africa leaves the Commonwealth as an independent republic
Aug	17	East Germans build Berlin Wall to separate East and West Berlin
Sep	17	UN Secretary-General Dag Hammarskjöld is killed in plane crash over Congo

BAY OF PIGS INCIDENT

In April, 1,500 Cuban exiles, trained by US military instructors, land in the Bay of Pigs (Bahia de Cochinos) in Cuba. The expected revolt against Fidel Castro fails to materialize and the invaders are killed or captured. The US government faces considerable criticism for its action.

ALGERIAN COUP FAILS

The French Army revolts against de Gaulle's government over its policy for independence in Algeria. De Gaulle declares a state of emergency and the coup collapses. The rebel leaders are tried for treason and eight are sentenced to death.

TOP LEFT AND RIGHT: Cars begin to eat the world; production rises and road systems become more complicated.

ABOVE: Cuban leader Fidel Castro plans battle strategy on the hoof during the Bay of Pigs invasion by the USA.

RIGHT: Cuban troops launch a counter-attack at Playa Larga.

INDEPENDENCE IN AFRICA

Sierra Leone (in May) and Tanganyika (in December) both gain independence from British rule.

THE WALL GOES UP

The East German authorities seal off West Berlin and erect a wall across the city, thus preventing the escape of East Germans to the West.

BABI YAR

The poem by Russian poet Yevgeny Yevtushenko (b. 1933) commemorates Jews massacred at Babi Yar, near Kiev, during World War II. His stand is against Soviet as well as Nazi anti-Semitism.

TRAGEDY FOR UN

UN Secretary-General, Dag Hammarskjöld is killed in a plane crash while trying to obtain peace in the Congo. His successor at the helm of the UN is a Burmese diplomat, U Thant.

A DANCER DEFECTS

Touring with the Kirov Ballet, Russian dancer Rudolf Nureyev (1938–93) leaps to freedom over an airport barrier while the company is in Paris. His defection brings a new star to Western ballet, and brings dance into the news. From 1962 on, he will regularly and memorably partner Margot Fonteyn.

MORE MILITARY HELP

The US increases the number of military advisers in South Vietnam to defend the government against Communist incursions from the north.

CATCH-22

American writer Joseph Heller's huge first novel, about life in the American Air Force during World War II, enjoys great commercial success. The title, *Catch 22*, adds a new phrase to the language. The book hits out at bureaucracy as well as war.

A NEW CONTRACEPTIVE

The loop, an IUD (intra-uterine device) contraceptive, is introduced by an American, Jack Lippes. Made of inert plastic, it is less likely to irritate the body or to be rejected than Ernest Grafenburg's simple silver ring, introduced in the 1930s.

FIRST MAN IN SPACE

The USSR beats the USA to win the space race. On April 12, cosmonaut Yuri Gagarin (1934–68) of the Soviet Union becomes the first man to orbit the Earth in a spacecraft launched from aboard *Vostok 1* from Kazakhstan. He completes a single orbit of the Earth at a maximum altitude of 327km (204mi) and a maximum speed of 28,096km/h (1,746miph). His craft parachutes down safely after 88 minutes near the village of Smelovka in the Saratov region of the USSR.

FIRST AMERICAN IN SPACE

On May 5, astronaut Alan Bartlett Shepard Jr. of the USA makes the world's second space flight, a "hop" of just fifteen minutes in the *Freedom 7* capsule.

SECOND RUSSIAN IN SPACE

On August 6, cosmonaut Gherman Titov of the Soviet Union makes seventeen orbits of the Earth, a day-long space flight.

MOON PLEDGE

On May 25 US president John F Kennedy says the USA will aim to put the first man on the Moon.

THE HUNTING OF THE QUARK

American theoretical physicist Murray Gell-Mann introduces the quark theory to account for the strange behaviour of particles. It will win him the Nobel Prize for Physics in 1969.

MEGA-CITY

In December, Tokyo becomes the world's first city to have a population of ten million.

ERNEST MILLAR HEMINGWAY
(1899–1961)

The American writer and Nobel Prize-winner has died by his own hand at his home in Idaho from a bullet in the mouth. After World War I (in which he worked as an ambulance driver for the Red Cross) he returned to journalism as a roving correspondent in Paris and began his career as a hard-living, hard-drinking, and later bull-fighting, writer. He was four times married and lived in Europe and Florida before settling in Cuba. Among his best-known works are *The Sun Also Rises* (1926), *A Farewell to Arms* (1929), *Death In the Afternoon* (1932), *For Whom the Bell Tolls* (1940, about the Spanish Civil War) and *The Old Man and the Sea* (1952).

ATMOSPHERES

Hungarian composer György Ligeti creates *Atmosphères*, a shimmering orchestral work in which every musician plays a separate part, the whole weaving together to create a floating, atmospheric texture. Ligeti himself describes it as one of his most radical works.

BEATING THE BABE

Roger Maris passes the supposedly unbreakable record of fellow Yankee, Babe Ruth, by hitting his 61st home run of the year. Maris has the advantage of a longer baseball season but the media attention is intense and the stress is so great that his hair starts to fall out.

BATTLE OF THE BULGE

Weight Watchers is founded by American housewife Jean Nidetch. Her weight-loss programme combines a high-protein diet (devised by Norman Joliffe of the New York Department of Health) with the proscription of certain foods and the use of group therapy methods.

LAWRENCIUM CREATED

The artificially created element 103, lawrencium, is synthesized by four US scientists, Albert Ghiorso, Torbjørn Sikkeland, Almon E Larsh and Robert M Latimer. It is named after Ernest Lawrence, the American inventor of the cyclotron.

BELOW: Oil derricks at Baytown, Texas. The oil from these rigs is used to make petroleum fuel for the growing number of cars.

GOLFBALL TYPEWRITER

International Business Machines of the USA introduces the "golfball" typewriter. The characters are mounted on a rotating sphere instead of on separate type bars. The typeface can be changed by changing the golfball.

STREET FIGHTING MEN

In the Netherlands, youth groups, the *nozems* (rowdies) clash with police on the streets of The Hague, marking the beginning of the 1960s youth protest movements in Europe.

EXPANDING CAMPUSES

Three new universities are to be built in Britain, marking the start of a huge worldwide expansion in university education, designed to accommodate the post-war baby boom.

FREEDOM FIGHTERS

Amnesty International, a non-political organization to help prisoners of conscience anywhere in the world, is founded in Britain.

TIME TO CHANGE

Electronic watches are introduced to the market. Winding becomes a thing of the past as the watches are battery driven.

BELOW: Missiles being transported to Cuba soon trigger the Cuban missile crisis.

SAVING THE ANIMALS

The World Wildlife Fund, an international organization to raise funds for wildlife conservation by public appeal, is founded. Its headquarters are in Switzerland. It will later become the World Wide Fund for Nature.

THE END OF COLONIALISM IN INDIA

Indian forces invade Portuguese Goa and other enclaves in India, removing the last European colonies.

ABOVE: Number 57 comes to grief spectacularly after losing a wheel in the Daytona 500 race held at Daytona International Speedway, Daytona Beach, Florida. Note the rocket in the background; the Kennedy Space Center is a close neighbour.

PATRICE LUMUMBA
(1925–1961)

Patrice Lumumba (born Katako Kombe), who became the first prime minister of the Democratic Republic of the Congo when the country gained independence from Belgium last year, has been arrested by his own army and murdered by the Katangese.

CARL GUSTAV JUNG
(1875–1961)

Carl Jung, the Swiss psychiatrist who has given us the concepts of the collective unconscious, introvert and extrovert, and the school of analytical psychology, has died. Early in the century Jung worked in Vienna with Sigmund Freud, but they parted company over the latter's over-insistence (in Jung's view) on the psycho-sexual nature of neurosis. Among Jung's works are *The Psychology of the Unconscious* (1911–12), *Psychology and Religion* (1937) and *The Undiscovered Self* (1957). He had just completed his autobiography, *Memories, Dreams, Reflections*, to be published in 1962.

FIRST AMERICAN IN SPACE

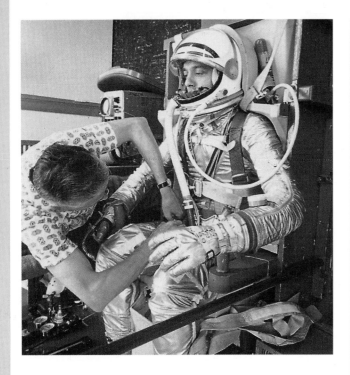

ABOVE: Astronaut Alan Shepard suits up for his space trip.

BELOW: Safe splashdown and rescue from the Atlantic.

BELOW: The president congratulates America's first space hero.

ABOVE: *Freedom 7* blasts off from Cape Canaveral.

THE WORLD ON THE BRINK

The USSR and the USA confront each other in Cuba and the world holds its breath as nuclear war seems to be imminent. Diplomacy saves the day. The space race continues. US astronaut John Glenn orbits the Earth three times and *Telstar*, the first communications satellite, is launched into permanent orbit and so catches the public imagination that a song is written for it. An unmanned space probe, complete with camera, is despatched to photograph the planet Venus. James Bond, superspy, makes his first appearance on the world's cinema screen and beautiful Marilyn Monroe is dead.

1962

Jan	1	Western Samoa becomes the first independent Pacific state
Feb	20	Astronaut John Glenn makes the first true US space flight with three orbits of the Earth
July	3	Algeria wins independence from France
	10	*Telstar*, first telecommunications satellite, is launched
Aug	5	Marilyn Monroe, American glamour star, is found dead
Oct	9	Uganda becomes independent within the Commonwealth
	22	US president John F Kennedy announces that the USSR has established missile bases in Cuba
Nov	28	Wilhelmina, Queen of the Netherlands from 1890 to 1948, dies aged 82
Dec	14	Space probe *Mariner 2* makes the first flight to another planet, passing close to Venus

ABOVE LEFT: A US sentry keeps watch during the Cuban crisis.

ABOVE: Anti-tank crew play pinochle as they wait in Cuba.

MORE INDEPENDENCE

Western Samoa becomes the first Pacific island state to gain its independence from Britain. During the year, Jamaica, Trinidad and Tobago, and Uganda all become independent from Britain, and Burundi and Rwanda gain their independence from Belgium.

LAWRENCE OF ARABIA

British director David Lean's sprawling epic brings together all the elements of film — camerawork, acting, settings, music, and so on — to make a notable whole, one of the masterpieces of British cinema. The film also makes Peter O'Toole an international star and introduces Omar Sharif to the anglophone world.

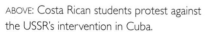

ABOVE: Costa Rican students protest against the USSR's intervention in Cuba.

LEFT: Marilyn Monroe, who dies this year, entertaining the troops.

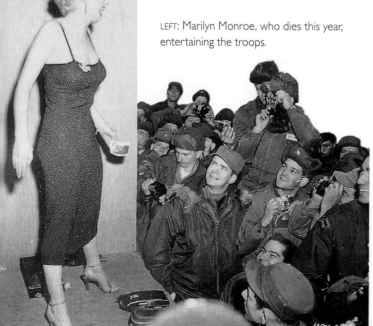

MARILYN MONROE (NORMA JEAN MORTENSON) (1926–1962)

American movie star Marilyn Monroe is found dead, apparently after taking an overdose of sleeping pills. After working as a model and bit-part Hollywood actress, she made her name with *How to Marry a Millionaire* and *Gentlemen Prefer Blondes* (both 1953) and went on to make the comedies *The Seven-Year Itch* (1955) and *Some Like it Hot* (1959). She then took acting lessons at the Actors' Studio and married playwright Arthur Miller, who wrote *The Misfits* (1961) for her, and from whom she was divorced last year. Her name has been linked with those of both the president of the United States, John F Kennedy, and his brother Robert.

ABOVE: *Telstar* is assembled in Bell Telephone Laboratories. The signals it sends from space will be picked up by the tracker, right.

TWA BUILDING, KENNEDY AIRPORT

Finnish-born architect Eero Saarinen (1910–61) designed the dramatic shell-concrete roof of the terminal, which is completed this year. It reminds many observers of a soaring bird. Although the architect denied that this was what he had in mind, the building shows that, for many, modern architecture can hold symbolic meanings.

TELSTAR LAUNCHED

America launches the first telecommunications satellite, *Telstar 1*. It makes possible transatlantic TV pictures, but only in twenty-minute sessions. This marks the beginning of global telecommunications.

CUBAN CRISIS

After the USSR places nuclear missiles on Cuba, the USA blockades the island. The USA and USSR confront each other, bringing the world to the brink of nuclear warfare, before the Soviet missiles are removed.

FIRST TRUE US SPACE FLIGHT

US astronaut John Glenn Jr makes America's first true space flight, three orbits of the Earth in the spacecraft *Friendship 7*. He remains in space for five hours.

TWO CHEESEBURGERS WITH EVERYTHING

American sculptor Claes Oldenburg, one of the leaders of the Pop Art movement, is famed for his off-beat, surreal interpretations of everyday items (plaster models magnified many times). Now he turns to soft sculpture, in which a subject is modelled in soft materials and stuffed with kapok. *Soft Typewriter* (1963) and *Soft Toilet* (1966) will follow.

DR NO

The first of the perennial series of movies featuring British agent James Bond, based on the creation of novelist Ian Fleming, is made. This one stars Scottish actor Sean Connery, who becomes identified with the part and will star in six further Bond films.

TAPE CASSETTES

Dutch electronics firm Philips introduces the compact tape recorder cassette. These can be played on portable tape machines. This will lead to music cassettes and talking newspapers for the blind.

ONE DAY IN THE LIFE OF IVAN DENISOVICH

Russian novelist Alexander Solzhenitsyn's novel of the Soviet Gulag describes the prisoner's world in the most vivid terms. For many in the West, it is the first such account to reach them.

THALIDOMIDE TRAGEDY

Thalidomide, introduced in 1958 as a safe sleeping tablet and remedy for morning sickness during pregnancy, is withdrawn after it is found that some women who take it give birth to children with serious abnormalities.

MARINER 2 LAUNCHED

US space probe *Mariner 2* sets out on a voyage to inspect Venus, the first such trip to another planet. It measures the planet's temperature and confirms the existence of solar wind.

VIVE ALGERIE

After eight years of warfare, Algeria wins its independence from France. Ben Bella becomes president of the new republic.

EQUAL EDUCATION

Black student and Air Force veteran James Howard Meredith enrols at the University of Mississippi, which is ordered to admit him by a court order upheld by the Supreme Court. Rioting breaks out on campus when he makes his first attempt to enter on September 30, and he is escorted by federal marshals and troops.

SILENT SPRING

American marine biologist Rachel Carson writes this chastening book warning of the indiscriminate use of pesticides. Her success in alarming the public begins a new era in environmental awareness.

BEER IN CANS

Beer is marketed in aluminium cans that open with pull-off tabs by the Aluminum Corporation of America. First produced in 1958, aluminium cans replace the traditional steel can plated with tin.

WORLD BEATERS

Brazil retains the football World Cup in a bad-tempered competition in Chile.

ABOVE: Crossing point in the "Bamboo Curtain" which divides the People's Republic of China from the city of Hong Kong.

LEFT: The *NS Savannah*, the first nuclear-powered merchant ship, sails the Panama Canal.

ABOVE: The launch of the nuclear-powered US polaris submarine *Alexander Hamilton*.

THE BERLIN WALL GOES UP

LEFT: East Berliners carry red flags on the first May Day parade after the Wall goes up.

BELOW LEFT: Willy Brandt, the mayor of West Berlin, and his sons look at the Soviet sector.

BELOW: East Berlin troops display military might and weaponry, although a number of soldiers defect to the West.

BOTTOM: President Kennedy visits the Berlin Wall.

A DREAM AND AN ASSASSINATION

Valentina Tereshkova scores a first for Russia and for women as she becomes the first female astronaut. A hotline telephone link is established between the White House and the Kremlin. President de Gaulle keeps the UK out of the EEC, Indonesia and Malaya seize independence and African nations unite under the umbrella of the Organization of African Unity. Black civil rights leader Martin Luther King leads a march on Washington and delivers a speech that will become famous. The year ends in tragedy and shock as President Kennedy is assassinated.

1 9 6 3

Jan	28	American poet Robert Frost dies aged 89
	29	The European Economic Community rejects Britain's request to join
June	3	Pope John XXIII dies after four years in office
	16	First woman in space, USSR's Valentina Tereshkova, begins her three-day flight
	20	The USA and USSR agree to set up a "hotline" between the White House in Washington DC, and the Kremlin in Moscow
July	31	In Britain, the Peerage Act allows hereditary peers to disclaim their titles; Viscount Stansgate (Tony Benn) is the first
Aug	5	The USA, USSR and UK sign a Nuclear Test-Ban Treaty
	28	Black leader Martin Luther King makes his "I have a dream" speech in Washington DC
Oct	18	UK premier Harold Macmillan resigns; he is succeeded by the Earl of Home (who will later renounce his title)
Sep	15	Confrontation begins between Malaysia and Indonesia
Nov	22	President John F Kennedy is assassinated at Dallas, Texas; he is succeeded by Vice-President Lyndon B Johnson
	24	Jack Ruby kills Lee Harvey Oswald, who had been accused of Kennedy's murder

ABOVE: The Texas School Book Depository, allegedly the place from which President Kennedy was shot. Possible positions for the killer are marked.

RIGHT: Alleged killer Lee Harvey Oswald in custody for the murder of the president. Before he can stand trial he is shot dead by Jack Ruby.

INDEPENDENCE FOR THE EAST INDIES

The final Dutch East Indies colony, West Irian, becomes part of Indonesia. In September, the British colonies of Singapore, Sarawak and Sabah join Malaya in the Federation of Malaysia. Conflict begins as Indonesian forces infiltrate Malaysia in an attempt to gain control over the whole of Borneo. British, Commonwealth and Malaysian forces counter-attack. The Commonwealth military and civilian services suffered 150 dead and 234 wounded, with four captured; the Indonesians count 590 dead, 222 wounded and 771 captured. Conflict continues until a peace agreement is finally signed in August 1966.

AFRICA UNITES

The Organization of African Unity (OAU) is formed in Addis Ababa, the Ethiopian capital, by African leaders to increase co-operation and remove colonialism from the continent.

KENNEDY IN BERLIN

President Kennedy visits West Berlin to support freedom, stating that "Ich bin ein Berliner" (I am a Berliner). In the same month, a "hotline" telephone link is established between Washington and Moscow.

BANNING THE BOMB

Britain, the USA and the USSR sign the Nuclear Test-Ban Treaty, prohibiting weapon tests in outer space, the atmosphere and under water. Many other nations sign the treaty later.

I HAVE A DREAM

More than 200,000 civil rights protesters, led by Martin Luther King, march on Washington DC, USA. In his "I have a dream" speech, King states that one day African-Americans will gain true equality.

DEATH IN TEXAS

President Kennedy is assassinated in Dallas, apparently by a lone gunman. Vice-President Lyndon Johnson takes over. A loner called Lee Harvey Oswald is quickly arrested but is himself assassinated before he gets to trial. The Kennedy assassination will engender countless conspiracy theories for the rest of the century.

FIRST WOMAN IN SPACE

Russian cosmonaut Valentina Tereshkova becomes the first woman in space when she makes 45 orbits of the Earth piloting *Vostok 6*.

QUASARS IDENTIFIED

Quasars — Quasi-Stellar Objects — are identified by American astronomer Allan Rex Sandage and the Australian astronomer Cyril Hazard. Quasars are objects in deep space, possibly galaxies, that may be as far as 16 billion light years away.

ENTER THE MOUSE

US scientist Douglas Engelbart invents the computer mouse, a device for controlling an on-screen pointer.

DUTCH PROTEST

In the Netherlands the Provos (young "provocateurs") agitate vigorously for the liberation of repressed minority groups such as homosexuals, for the introduction of anti-pollution laws and for the preservation of inner-city areas from property development.

SCORPIO RISING

Kenneth Anger, doyen of underground, independent film-making, makes *Scorpio Rising*, a documentary about motorcyclists in New York. Although made outside the normal film creation and distribution channels, it will be seen by millions of viewers over the years.

NEW ALLIANCES IN AFRICA

Kenya and Zanzibar become independent nations in the British Commonwealth. Zanzibar joins with Tanganyika to form the new nation of Tanzania in April 1964.

LEDS INVENTED

US scientist Nick Holonyak invents the Light-Emitting Diode (LED), a semiconductor device that glows when a current passes through it; they are used for clocks, calculators and other display lights.

CARBON FIBRE

Engineers at England's Royal Aircraft Establishment invent carbon fibre, a thin, tough fibre of nearly pure carbon combined with plastics. It is used in spacecraft because it is light yet strong.

FIRST HOLOGRAPHS

US scientists Emmett Leith and Juris Upatnieks give the first demonstration of holography, using the recently invented laser to project light to form three-dimensional images.

DE GAULLE A DIT NON

General de Gaulle forcefully vetoes Great Britain's attempt to join the Common Market.

THE FEMININE MYSTIQUE

Betty Friedan publishes *The Feminine Mystique*, a study of the social conditioning that shapes women's lives. She argues that women are victimized by false values and delusions that lead them to find fulfilment in husbands and children.

BUNKER MENTALITY

Nuclear bomb shelters are built in the cellars of houses and other private buildings across the USA and stocked with the necessities of life by citizens fearful of a nuclear war.

FLOATING BLADES

The Hover lawnmower is produced by Flymo, a UK company. It works on the same principle as the hovercraft, which floats on a cushion of air just above the ground, so is easy to push across grassy gardens.

DEATHS IN THE FRENCH ARTS

Poet and writer Jean Cocteau, composer François Poulenc and artist Georges Braque all die this year.

EDITH PIAF (EDITH GIOVANNA GASSION) (1915–1963)

French chanteuse Edith Piaf has died after a long period of ill-health. The "little sparrow", whose father was a well-known acrobat and who began her career singing in the streets of Paris, became famous for songs such as "La Vie en Rose" and "Non, je ne regrette rien".

ABOVE: Refugees from Cuba adrift off the coast of Miami.

ABOVE: Engineers work on a Mariner spacecraft at Cape Canaveral, fixing solar panels to harness the power of the Sun.

BLACK CIVIL RIGHTS MOVEMENT

ABOVE: The charismatic Martin Luther King leads the march.

ABOVE: Many black celebrities such as actor Sidney Poiter and singer Harry Belafonte join the protest.

BELOW: What started as a peaceful demonstration turns to violence as protestors make the strength of their feelings known.

BELOW: Entertainer Sammy Davis Jnr joins the cause.

OPPOSITE: The 20,000 marchers reach the end of the road at Washington DC.

ABOVE: Tension between white and black youths can be felt on the streets.

THE SIXTIES START TO SWING

Tension rises in southern Africa as Nelson Mandela, leader of the African National Congress, is jailed for life in South Africa and Ian Smith plans a unilateral declaration of independence on behalf of the whites in Southern Rhodesia. Things are looking better in the US, when Martin Luther King receives the Nobel Peace Prize and the Bill of Civil Rights becomes law. Three Russian cosmonauts orbit the Earth together and the US probe *Ranger* takes the first photographs of the Moon's hidden dark side.

1964

Jan	**29**	Ninth Winter Olympics open at Innsbruck, Austria
Apr	**5**	US General MacArthur dies aged 84
May	**27**	India's Prime Minister Jawaharlal Nehru dies aged 74
June	**11**	In South Africa, African National Congress leader Nelson Mandela is jailed for life for trying to overthrow the government
July	**6**	British territory Nyasaland becomes independent as Malawi
	31	Space probe *Ranger* photographs the Moon
Oct	**10**	Eighteenth Olympic Games open in Tokyo
	12–13	First three-man space flight by USSR crew
	14	Martin Luther King is awarded the Nobel Peace Prize
	15	USSR leader Nikita Kruschev is deposed. He is replaced by Leonid Brezhnev and Alexei Kosygin
	16	Harold Wilson forms Labour government in UK
	24	Northern Rhodesia becomes independent as Zambia

LEFT: British pop combo the Beatles take America by storm. Their fans (above) display all the symptoms of Beatlemania.

MANDELA JAILED
Nelson Mandela, leader of the African National Congress, is sentenced to life imprisonment for sabotage and attempting to overthrow the government after the Rivona trial. He is sent to Robben Island in Table Bay, Cape Town.

MORE FREEDOM FOR AFRICA
Malawi gains its independence from Britain, followed by Northern Rhodesia, to be known as Zambia, in October, thus ending the British attempt to construct a Central African Federation. Only white-dominated southern Africa, plus a few small British, Spanish and Portuguese colonies in West Africa, still remain in European hands.

CIVIL RIGHTS IN USA
The Civil Rights Act becomes law in the USA. It prohibits racial discrimination in employment, public accommodation, union membership and federally funded programmes. The act is the biggest single civil rights law in US history.

KHRUSCHEV OUSTED
Russian premier Nikita Khruschev is deposed while on holiday at his country *dacha* and replaced by Leonid Brezhnev as Communist Party leader and Alexei Kosygin as prime minister.

HOUSE FOR VANNA VENTURI
American architect Robert Venturi designs a proto-post-modern house for his mother at Chestnut Hill in Pennsylvania. Some of the features of the building (for example, the broken line of the entrance façade) look forward to the post-modern style, reflecting the fact that Venturi was writing his book *Complexity and Contradiction in Architecture* while the house was being built. This and other of his writings argue for the importance both of historical links and the inspiration of popular culture in architecture.

MARAT/SADE
The Persecution and Assassination of Marat as Performed by the Inmates of the Asylum of Charenton under the Direction of the Marquis de Sade (aka *Marat/Sade*) will be Peter Weiss's most famous play. It becomes the archetype of the Theatre of Cruelty. In it, Sade directs his play depicting the murder of Marat while lunatics murmur in the background.

FOR THE UNION DEAD
In this and other volumes, American poet Robert Lowell stands up against the deadening, depersonalizing influence of war and violence. His concern for America and its traditions sets him apart from his contemporary "confessional" poets and marks him out as perhaps America's most powerful poet.

ABOVE: Black voters exercise their rights in Baton Rouge.

BELOW: Brazilians celebrate a successful revolution in Rio.

JAWAHARLAL (PANDIT) NEHRU
(1889–1964)

The Harrow- and Cambridge-educated Indian leader and statesman Jawaharlal Nehru, known as Pandit or "teacher", has died. He spent a total of eighteen years in prison under British rule, during which time he was elected president of the Indian National Congress (1928). He became his country's first prime minister on the gaining of independence in 1947, and was responsible for India's non-alignment policy and the development of an industrial base.

MR SMITH TAKES CHARGE

Ian Smith becomes prime minister of Southern Rhodesia. He disagrees with the British plan to give democratic rights to the African majority and plans to go for unilateral independence.

DEATHS IN THE ENTERTAINMENT WORLD

Silent brother Adolph "Harpo" Marx (b. 1884) dies, as does writer Ian Fleming (b. 1908), the creator of James Bond. Irish playwirights Brendan Behan (b. 1925) and Sean O'Casey (b. 1884) also die.

DR STRANGELOVE, OR HOW I LEARNED TO STOP WORRYING AND LOVE THE BOMB

Stanley Kubrick (1928–99) directs this anti-war comedy, which stars Peter Sellers in three roles. It becomes popular all over a world sensitized to the nuclear question by the recent Cuban missile crisis .

REQUIEM

Russian poet Anna Akhmatova's elegiac tribute to those who perished under Stalin is published, after being suppressed since Akhmatova wrote it in the 1940s. Its appearance confirms her status as Russia's greatest and most courageous twentieth-century poet.

FAB FOUR IN USA

English pop group the Beatles, already legends in their own land, conquer the USA. Beatlemania grips American teenagers.

SHOT RED MARILYN

Andy Warhol produces one of his most famous Pop Art images, in which subject-matter from popular culture is depicted, and the modern reproduction methods (using the silkscreen technique, which Warhol was one of the first to exploit) is utilized.

DOUGLAS MACARTHUR
(1880–1964)

Douglas MacArthur, the American general and larger-than-life character, has died in his 80s. The much decorated veteran of World War I became commanding general of US forces in the Far East in 1941, and later supreme commander of the Pacific Area. As supreme commander of the Allied forces he took control of the Allied occupation of Japan after the Japanese surrender (1945–51). In 1950 he was appointed United Nations Commander in Chief in Korea, but was relieved of his duties by President Truman when they differed over the handling of the Chinese intervention.

IN C
American composer Terry Riley is one of the originators of minimalism, and this work brings the movement fame. The work consists of a repeated high C on the piano, which forms a backdrop to a series of 53 short fragments, which the players may repeat any number of times (but they have to do all 53 in a set order). There can be any number of players.

BULLET TRAIN
Japan's "Bullet Train" service between Tokyo and Osaka opens, with speeds up to 200km/h (125miph).

MULTI-PERSON SPACE FLIGHT
In October the Soviet spacecraft *Voshkod 1* carries three cosmonauts on a sixteen-orbit mission, the first multi-person spaceflight.

BELOW: Finnish troops serving with the UN force help to keep the peace during unrest on the island of Cyprus.

ABOVE: Funded by the US AID programme, the first stages of the Sharavathi Hydroelectric Project near Mysore, India, approach completion.

BELOW: The Cleveland Browns battle with the Baltimore Colts for the 1964 NFL title game. Jim Brown helps Cleveland to win the championship.

ABOVE: The cameras used on board the unmanned *Ranger II* spacecraft. They send back over 4,000 pictures of the cosmos.

ABOVE: Brigitte Bardot, international sex symbol and actress is later to champion animal welfare rights and the cause of endangered species.

ELEMENT 104

Scientists in Russia and the USA both claim to have artificially created element 104; the names kurchatovium, rutherfordium and unnilquadium are all proposed for it.

BOYS' TOYS

Action Man (in the UK and Europe) and GI Joe (in the USA) — a toy soldier doll aimed at boys — is launched by Hasbro and is as big a hit as Barbie has been with girls. Combat accessories and a wardrobe of uniforms are also provided.

BELOW: The Warren Commission, set up to investigate the Kennedy assassination. Its findings will not satisfy everybody.

ENGLAND SWINGS

Time magazine announces Swinging London, where a consumer boom rages, clothes designed to outrage are sold in diminutive boutiques instead of department stores or couture houses, discothèques are new-style nightclubs with lights flashing in time to amplified pop music, and homes will be transformed by designer Terence Conran's style ideas at Habitat, his furniture and interiors shop.

DISASTER IN ALASKA

An earthquake in Alaska measuring 8.4 on the Richter scale (later upgraded to 9.2) kills 110 people and sets off a 67-m (220-ft) *tsunami* (tidal wave), the largest ever recorded.

ABOVE: The Unisphere, symbol of the New York World's Fair. Over 200,000 people visit on the first Sunday of its opening.

BACKGROUND RADIATION

American scientists Arno Allen Prenzias and Robert Woodrow Wilson discover background microwave radiation coming from all directions in space: it is thought to be an "echo" of the Big Bang with which it is believed that the universe started.

DARK GLASSES

Photochromic spectacles are invented by Dr Stookey at the Corning Glass Works, New York. They are made from silica glass embedded with silver compound crystals. These absorb light, so the glasses darken rapidly when exposed to the sun, clearing again when light levels fall.

WINTER OLYMPICS

Thousands of tons of snow are moved to Innsbruck by the Austrian Army to permit the Ninth Winter Games to take place. Eleven hundred competitors take part in 34 events: both figures are records. Soviet Lidia Skoblikova wins all four speed-skating golds and Sjoukje Dijkstra wins the figure-skating for Holland. Lugeing, in which athletes slide down an ice course on their backs on a toboggan, makes its Olympic début.

MOON SHOTS

US Ranger spacecraft takes the first close-up television pictures of the Moon.

HE'S THE GREATEST

Cassius Clay beats champion Sonny Liston to take the heavyweight boxing championship at age 22. Clay had embraced the Black Muslim faith in 1962 and as champion uses his position to challenge racism in America. He changes his name to Muhammad Ali and refuses to be drafted for the Vietnam War. For that he is stripped of his title. He does not fight between June 1967 and February 1970 but will return to win the heavyweight crown twice more.

SOUTH AFRICAN SPORT BOYCOTT

The International Olympic Committee bans South Africa over apartheid. The international community later institutes a ban on all sporting links with South Africa.

JAPANESE OLYMPICS

The Eighteenth Games in Tokyo, 24 years after war robbed the city of the Olympics, are the first in Asia and see many world records set. Judo and volleyball are added and athletes from a record 93 nations take part.

RIGHT: Cassius Clay, soon to be Muhammad Ali, dances like a butterfly and stings like a bee.

RACE RIOTS AND THE LITTLE RED BOOK

In the USA, Black Muslim leader Malcolm X is assassinated, Nobel Prize-winner Martin Luther King is arrested marching in Alabama and riots flare in Watts, Los Angeles. Meanwhile in China the Cultural Revolution is under way, instigated by Mao Zedong and codified in his *Little Red Book*. In space, the first space walks take place and *Mariner 4* sends back pictures of the craters on Mars. War breaks out between India and Pakistan. Britain declares Rhodesia's UDI illegal and the country plunges into conflict.

1 9 6 5

Jan	24	Britain's wartime leader Sir Winston Churchill dies aged 90
Feb	1	Martin Luther King arrested after leading civil rights march in Alabama
	21	US black leader Malcolm X is assassinated in New York
Mar	18	Soviet cosmonaut Alexei Leonov performs the first space walk
Apr	6	*Early Bird*, the first geostationary telecommunications satellite, is launched
	9	Conflict breaks out between India and Pakistan
July	14	US space probe *Mariner 4* photographs Mars
Aug	15	Race riots break out in the Watts area of Los Angeles

Sep	1	War breaks out between India and Pakistan over Kashmir
	4	Franco-German missionary Albert Schweitzer dies in Africa aged 90
Nov	11	White government of Rhodesia makes illegal unilateral declaration of independence

LEFT: Malcolm X, the black American civil rights leader, is assassinated in New York.

MALCOLM X KILLED

Malcolm X, a prominent Black Muslim, is assassinated by his former colleagues in New York. Malcolm X had opposed the non-violent civil rights movement of Martin Luther King and supported black separatism, but in recent years had favoured co-operation rather than confrontation between the races.

MARCHING IN ALABAMA

Martin Luther King leads a march from Selma to Montgomery in Alabama to protest against the lack of civil rights in the southern state. In August, race riots break out in the Watts district of Los Angeles as racial tension rises throughout the USA.

WAR BETWEEN INDIA AND PAKISTAN

Border clashes break out between India and Pakistan on the Kutch–Sind border in April. In September Pakistani forces cross the cease-fire line in Kashmir, leading to war. India moves 900,000 troops into West Pakistan. In fighting near Lahore the Pakistanis lose 450 tanks. Indian casualties are 2,212 dead, 7,636 wounded and 1,500 missing. Pakistan estimates over 5,800 dead. Peace is agreed at talks in Tashkent in the USSR in January 1966.

CRATERS ON MARS

The US space probe *Mariner 4* photographs Mars from only 9,700km (6,063mi) away, and transmits 21 pictures showing that the surface is pitted with craters like the Moon but revealing no signs of life.

THE TERRACOTTA ARMY

The tomb of a Chinese Han Dynasty king, Liu Sheng, King of Zhongshan (near Beijing) 154–112 BC, is found to contain 3,000 miniature representations of cavalry and foot soldiers. The king is covered with 2,156 jade wafers sewn together with gold thread.

ABOVE: Eero Saarinen's eagle-shaped terminal for TWA at Kennedy Airport, New York.

CULTURAL REVOLUTION IN CHINA

Chinese leader Lin Piao urges a Cultural Revolution to renew revolutionary zeal and root out those opposed to the revolution. The Red Guards, who are leading the new revolution, target intellectuals and party officials, and many schools are shut down. The Cultural Revolution introduces the cult of Mao Zedong, and continues until the dismissal of the president, Liu Shaoqi, in October 1968.

IN THE HEAT OF THE NIGHT

Rioting erupts in Watts, a district of Los Angeles, USA, after a black man is arrested for drunken driving.

ARIEL

American poet Sylvia Plath's most famous book of poems impresses readers with a voice in which tight verbal and poetic control is used to describe extreme situations and unstable mental states.

ALBERT SCHWEITZER
(1875–1965)

Alsace-born Franco-German missionary, musicologist and theologian, Dr Albert Schweitzer, has died. In 1913, having qualified as a doctor, he went with his wife to set up a medical mission in French Equatorial Africa, where leprosy and sleeping sickness were rife. He was known in Europe for the organ recitals he gave to fund his missionary project, and for his many writings on religion, culture and music. In 1952 he was awarded the Nobel Peace Prize.

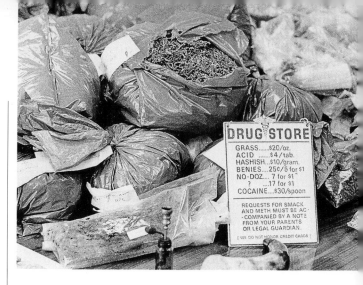

UDI IN RHODESIA
The minority white government of Southern Rhodesia, led by Ian Smith, makes a unilateral declaration of independence (UDI) from Britain. Britain declares the regime illegal and imposes sanctions. In December 1972 the black independence movements ZANU and ZAPU will launch a concerted campaign against Rhodesia with Soviet and Chinese support. The war will end with ZANU, under Robert Mugabe, gaining power. Rhodesia will become Zimbabwe.

WAR IN THE DESERT
War breaks out in Dhofar and Oman between the Sultan's armed forces, with British assistance, and the Communist Dhofar Liberation Front which later becomes part of the People's Front for the Liberation of the Occupied Arabian Gulf (PFLOAG). Between 1971 and 1975 the Sultan of Oman's forces will lose 187 killed and 559 wounded

CLOSELY OBSERVED TRAINS
Czech writer Bohumil Hrabal becomes famous for this short novel, about Milos Hrma, a railway worker who watches as the Nazis transport troops through Czechoslovakia to the Eastern Front. It will be made into a film directed by Jiri Menzel in 1966.

SALK INSTITUTE LABORATORIES
The handling of concrete masses marks this building in La Jolla, California, as one of American architect Louis Kahn's major achievements. The planning, with mechanical services on their own lower floors to give uninterrupted floor space in the labs, is also important.

OLD MAP OF A NEW CONTINENT
A parchment map drawn in 1440 — 52 years before Columbus reached America — is found, showing a large island west of Greenland called "Vinland". This is Newfoundland, the land discovered by Norse explorers Bjarni and Leif Eriksson, who crossed the Western Ocean in the eleventh century.

ABOVE: Drugs of all kinds become available, although illegal in the decade that turns on, tunes in and drops out.

FIRST SPACE WALKS
On March 18, Soviet cosmonaut Aleksei Leonov makes the first "space walk", floating free while tethered to his spaceship *Voskhod II*. He stays outside the spaceship for ten minutes. US astronaut follows up Edward H White makes a space walk on June 3 which lasts four minutes longer.

EARLY BIRD FLIES
On April 6, *Early Bird* (later called *Intelsat 1*), the first geostationary communications satellite, is launched from the USA. It provides a constant communications link between Europe and North America.

COMPUTERS SHRINK
The first so-called "mini-computer" is introduced in the USA; it has 4k of memory and costs a mere $18,000.

TURN ON, TUNE IN ....
Timothy Leary, former Professor of Psychology at Harvard University, USA, publishes *The Psychedelic Reader*, urging readers to "turn on"— to narcotic and psychedelic drugs — "tune in and drop out". He had been dismissed in 1963 for experimenting with the hallucinogen LSD.

ABOVE: Julie Andrews stars in the blockbuster *The Sound of Music*.

CHARLES-EDOUARD JEANNERET (LE CORBUSIER) (1887–1965)

Swiss-born French architect and town planner Charles-Edouard Jeanneret, better known as Le Corbusier, has died. He was one of the most influential architects of the modern movement, dedicated to developing architectural forms for the machine age, and deviser of the modular system (which uses standard units in building). His buildings include the Unité d'Habitation at Marseilles (1945–50), and he worked on the town plan and the Law Court and Secretariat buildings at Chandigarh, India (1951–56). His writings include *Towards a New Architecture* (1923).

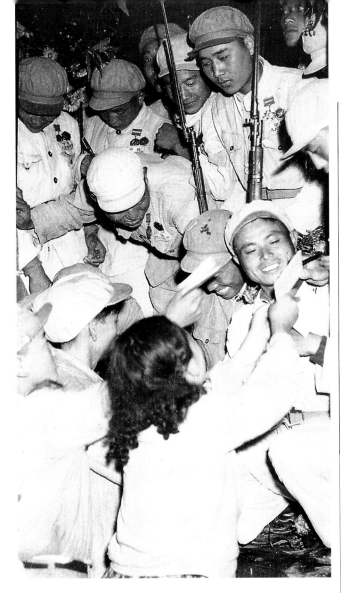

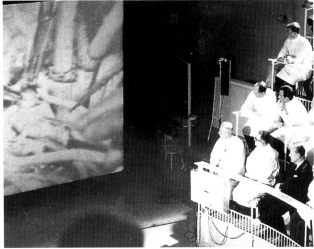

ABOVE: Open-heart surgery being performed in Houston, Texas, can be seen live in Geneva, Switzerland, thanks to transmission via the US Early Bird communications satellite.

LEFT: During the Cultural Revolution in China the population suffers intimidation at the hands of the Red Guard under the direction of Chairman Mao.

SURFING THE SLOPES

An engineer in Michigan, America, takes his daughter's sled and add "footstops" to create a sled you can stand on. He christens it the "Snurfer". Unwittingly, Sherman Poppen has created the snowboard, which now challenges traditional skis on slopes around the world.

HARE KRISHNA

The International Society of Krishna Consciousness is founded in New York by AC Bhaktivedanta, a Sanskrit scholar and chemist who arrived from Calcutta with $50 in rupees and a pair of cymbals to spread Lord Krishna's word. His young followers shave their heads, wear saffron-coloured robes and chant.

BABY RACERS

The lightweight, collapsible McLaren baby buggy appears.

SOFT FOCUS

Soft contact lenses are added to improvements in vision correction recently introduced. They include the omnifocal lens, developed in 1963, which allows close-up and distant vision without disruption.

ASTROTURF

Baseball's Houston Astros become the first team to play on Astroturf. Their ground, the Astrodome in Houston, USA, is enclosed. Clear glass panels in the roof are supposed to allow natural grass to grow. Fielders, however, are blinded by the glare of the sun when trying to catch high balls and so the panels have to be painted, killing the grass. A new artificial surface, named after the building and team, is used instead.

WINSTON LEONARD SPENCER CHURCHILL (1874–1965)

The venerable English statesman and wartime leader Sir Winston Leonard Spencer Churchill has died. Crowds line the streets to witness his funeral procession. He began his parliamentary career in 1900, was Conservative chancellor of the exchequer in 1924–29, and on the stepping-down of Neville Chamberlain, formed the wartime Coalition Government. As British prime minister from 1940–45, he used his powers of oratory to make morale-boosting broadcasts to the nation. He served again as prime minister during the days of post-war recovery, from 1951 until 1955.

FLOODS AND HAPPENINGS

Indira Gandhi takes the helm of the Indian government and Prime Minister Hendrik Verwoerd of South Africa is assassinated. Civil war breaks out in the Dominican Republic and the Marines are sent in. Priceless Italian art treasures are lost or damaged in floods which devastate Venice and Florence. Russian and American unmanned space probes land on the Moon at last. Back on earth, an H- bomb is lost at sea (but recovered), fibre optics are introduced and the art world unveils the Happening.

1966

Jan	11	Indira Gandhi becomes India's prime minister following the death of Lal Bahandra Shastri
Feb	3	Soviet space probe makes a soft landing on the Moon
	14	Australia adopts decimal currency
Mar	10	Princess Beatrix of the Netherlands marries Claus von Amsberg, a German diplomat
	31	Labour wins decisive victory in UK general election with majority of 96
Apr	24	Civil war breaks out in the Dominican Republic
May	26	British Guiana becomes independent as Guyana
June	3	US space probe makes a soft landing on the Moon
July	30	England wins football World Cup
Sep	6	South African prime minister Hendrik Verwoerd is assassinated in parliament
	13	BJ Vorster becomes South African prime minister
Dec	15	Cartoon king Walt Disney dies aged 65

GANDHI BECOMES PRIME MINISTER
Indira Gandhi, daughter of Nehru, becomes prime minister of India after the unexpected death of Lal Shastri.

INDEPENDENCE IN AFRICA AND THE CARIBBEAN
Guyana gains its independence from Britain, followed by Botswana, Lesotho and Barbados. Seven other Caribbean islands, plus Belize, will gain their independence from Britain by 1983.

DOMINICAN REPUBLIC CIVIL WAR
Some 20,000 US forces intervene in the civil war to restore peace following a coup that overthrows President Juan Bosch. In the fighting more than 2,000 Dominicans are killed but by October 1966 new elections will bring stability and US forces withdraw.

VERWOERD ASSASSINATED
South African prime minister Hendrik Verwoerd, a firm supporter of apartheid, is stabbed to death in Cape Town's parliament by a lone assassin. He is succeeded by Balthasar Johannes Vorster.

MOON PICTURES
Within months of each other, Soviet and US space probes make soft landings on the Moon. Both take photographs of the surface, enabling both sides of the Moon to be mapped for the first time.

YAMANASHI CENTRE
Japanese architect Kenzo Tange designs this centre in Kofu, Japan, for press and broadcasting. It uses an innovative structure in which office spaces are supported by sixteen massive concrete tubes, each some 5m (16ft) wide. The structure gives the building a unique appearance and character.

DOCKING IN SPACE
Aboard the *Gemini 8*, US astronauts Neil Armstrong and David Scott dock with the final stage of their rocket, but a technical error means the docking is not entirely successful. The ability to dock in orbit is essential to any attempt to land on the Moon.

THE BASSARIDS
German composer Hans Werner Henze reworks Euripides' ancient drama *The Bacchae* in what he feels to be his finest opera. Rational, disciplined King Pentheus (possibly an emblem of Nazism) is overcome by irrational Dionysus.

COOKING ON CHINA
The ceramic hob, a flat surface consisting of hotplates and cool surrounding areas, is introduced by an American glassworks. It is patterned to indicate the position of the hotplates, and heated by electric elements beneath.

ABOVE: A cable-controlled underwater research vehicle (top) and *Alvin* the midget sub find and recover an H bomb lost at sea.

AGAINST INTERPRETATION
In this, the first of several influential books of essays, US writer Susan Sontag ranges over many subjects — art, film, music, politics — and confirms her stature as one of America's new intellectuals.

PHONING BY GLASS
British scientists Charles Kao and George Hockham invent telephone cables made of glass optical fibres. Fibre optics make it possible for many more calls to be transmitted along one cable than before.

FLOODS IN ITALY
Venice is flooded when high waters affecting the Adriatic cause the Venetian Lagoon to rise above its normal level. Storms in northern Italy cause the Arno River to burst its banks, flooding the city of Florence. Ancient buildings, frescoes, paintings, sculptures and books are damaged.

IT'S ALL HAPPENING

The "Happening", a form of performance art, is introduced by American painter Robert Rauschenberg at the New York Armory Show. It is the first of many.

LOST H-BOMB FOUND

A hydrogen bomb inadvertently falls off a US bomber in February. Fortunately for all concerned, it is found intact on the Atlantic sea-bed two months later, and is carefully recovered.

DEATHS IN THE PERFORMING ARTS

American comic genius of the silent screen Buster Keaton (b. 1886) dies, as does poet André Breton (also born in 1886), founder of the Surrealist movement.

ON AGGRESSION

Austrian biologist Konrad Lorenz publishes this controversial book. His pioneering studies in ethology (animals in their environment) lead him to conclude that some aspects of animal and human aggression are innate. In *King Solomon's Ring*, published in 1963, he had argued controversially that Darwinian natural selection determines behavioural characteristics of animals.

WALTER ELIAS (WALT) DISNEY (1901–1966)

The death of Walt Disney is announced. The American cartoon film-maker has given us such characters as Donald Duck and Mickey Mouse, and the first colour animated film, *Snow White and the Seven Dwarfs* (1937). This was followed by *Pinocchio* (1940) and *Bambi* (1943), and later *The Lady and the Tramp* (1956), and many more. He opened his theme park, Disneyland, in California in 1955.

LEFT: Walt Disney dies aged 65. In addition to his well-known cartoon characters, he also produced coloured nature and adventure films.

BELOW: A model of Boeing's version of a supersonic aircraft. It does not take off from the drawing board.

LEFT: At work in *Sealab II*. The fish find it fascinating.

ABOVE: *Sealab II*, the US Navy's underwater research station.

CLEAN AND GREEN
Biodegradable liquid detergents are introduced. They are considered to be better for the environment.

THEY THINK IT'S ALL OVER
England uses home advantage to win the football World Cup for the first time. A thrilling final goes into extra time before England beats the Germans 4–2, thanks to a hat-trick from Geoff Hurst.

FOOD CRISIS
A world food crisis has resulted from prolonged drought in Asia and the Sahel, harvest failures in the USSR and rapid world population growth. High-yielding dwarf indica rice is introduced into Asian countries where there is widespread starvation.

BELOW: Cuban refugees are picked up off the coast of Florida.

THE SUMMER OF LOVE

The Monterey Pop Festival inaugurates the summer of love. In the USA and Europe the air is alive with the scent of flowers and the tinkle of bells. Civil war tears Nigeria apart and Israel fights and wins the Six-Day War. America's Vietnam involvement attracts escalating protest in the US and elsewhere, and there are marches and demonstrations. The military takes over Greece and both competitors in the space race suffer their first tragedies. Handsome, charismatic revolutionary Che Guevara is killed and his image becomes a poster icon for the age.

1967

Jan	**27**	Three US astronauts die when their spacecraft catches fire during test
Apr	**19**	Former German chancellor Konrad Adenauer dies aged 91
	21	Junta of colonels takes over Greece following a military coup
	24	Soviet cosmonaut Vladimir Komorov dies when his spacecraft's parachute fails on landing
May	**26**	Civil war starts in Nigeria after Biafra breaks away
	28	UK yachtsman Francis Chichester completes the first solo round-the-world voyage
June	**5–10**	Six-Day War: Israel defeats coalition of five Arab states
July	**1**	EEC, European Coal and Steel Community, and Euratom merge to form the European Community (EC)
	24	President Charles de Gaulle of France angers Canada during visit by supporting independence for Quebec
Oct	**9**	Revolutionary guerrilla leader Che Guevara is killed in Bolivia
Dec	**3**	First human heart transplant performed in South Africa; patient lives only eighteen days
	31	To celebrate Canada's centenary, Expo 67 opens in Montreal

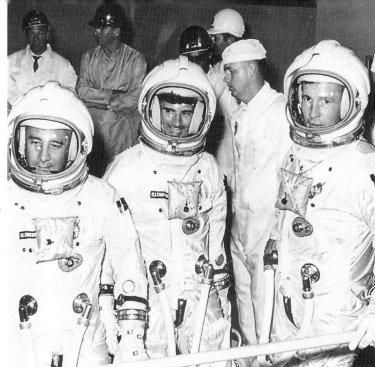

SPACE TEST-BAN

The treaty banning nuclear weapons from outer space is signed by the USA, USSR and 60 other nations.

GREECE UNDER MILITARY RULE

A junta of right-wing colonels, led by Colonel Georges Papadopoulos, takes military power in Greece and overthrows the civilian government.

CIVIL WAR IN NIGERIA

Following a military coup and tribal discord, the predominantly Ibo eastern region of Nigeria declares unilateral independence as the Republic of Biafra, under Lieutenant-Colonel Odemegu Ojukwu. The Nigerian Federal government launches ground and air attacks. Many refugees flee the fighting, and starvation causes many deaths, until the rebellion collapses in January 1970 with the fall of Owerri and the victory of the Nigerian Army. Biafra loses 200,000 dead from starvation and fighting, and Nigerian casualties are estimated at 10,000 dead.

THE SIX-DAY WAR

In a pre-emptive strike against its Arab neighbours, which had been threatening its borders, Israel invades Egypt, Jordan and Syria in a rapid six-day war, establishing new borders on the Suez Canal and in Jordan, gaining the strategic Golan Heights, and re-uniting the city of Jerusalem. The Israelis lose 679 killed; the Arabs lose 3,000 dead, 6,000 wounded and 12,000 prisoners. The refugees from the West Bank territories of Jordan form the basis for the Palestine Liberation Organization (PLO) which becomes the umbrella organization for attacks on Israel.

EUROPE UNITES

The European Community (EC) is formed out of the European Economic Community (EEC), the European Coal and Steel Community (ECSC) and Euratom. In December, France vetoes the second application for membership by Britain.

ANTI-VIETNAM RALLY

In Washington, anti-war protesters, novelist Norman Mailer and poet Robert Lowell among them, surround the Pentagon. Soldiers and police drive them back with night-sticks and rifle butts and 250 people are arrested. Anti-Vietnam marches and rallies will proliferate all over America and Europe until the war ends.

QUEBEC LIBRE

French president Charles de Gaulle stirs up Quebec nationalism on a visit to Canada by supporting a free Quebec.

CHE KILLED

Argentinian-born Marxist and co-architect of the Cuban Revolution, Ernesto "Che" Guevara is killed in Bolivia, trying to start a revolution against the government. He becomes an icon of student revolutionaries everywhere.

LOST LEADER

Australian prime minister Harold Holt is missing, presumed drowned, after swimming off the coast at Portsea in Victoria.

ONE HUNDRED YEARS OF SOLITUDE

Colombian writer Gabriel García Márquez's novel depicts a decaying village from the viewpoint of seven generations of one family. In the novel, the magical and fantastic can happen alongside real, everyday events, and every detail glows with significance. This makes the book the key text in the style known as "magic realism".

BLUEBIRD OF TRAGEDY

British racer Donald Campbell is killed on Coniston Water in the Lake District in an attempt to break the world water speed record in his jet-powered vehicle.

HOMOSEXUALITY LEGALIZED
Homosexuality is decriminalized in Britain by the Sexual Offences Act, which legalizes sex between consenting adult men aged 21 or over.

DEATH OF A PHYSICIST
J Robert Oppenheimer (b. 1904) dies. A nuclear physicist, he was part of the team that developed and built the atom bomb, but resigned in 1945 protesting against its use on Hiroshima and Nagasaki.

THE MEDIUM IS THE MESSAGE
In his sociological-philosophical tract, *The Medium is the Message*, Canadians Marshall McLuhan and Quentin Fiore analyse popular culture, media and the impact of printing on civilization. The work has a strong influence on thinking about everything from advertizing to literature. The book's title introduces a new buzzword into the language. McLuhan is also responsible for the concept of the "global village", referring to the proliferation of communication methods.

ROSENCRANTZ AND GUILDENSTERN ARE DEAD
Czech-born playwright Tom Stoppard's second play brings him fame and critical attention. Centred on the off-stage lives of two minor characters in Shakespeare's *Hamlet*, it shows the writer's talent for taking an idea and running with it, as well as his resourcefulness with language.

ABOVE: Psychedelic rockers Jim Morrison and The Doors release their seminal album, *Light my Fire*.

SPACE TRAGEDIES
Three US astronauts — Roger B. Chaffee, Virgil I. Grissom and Edward H. White — are killed during a ground test of an Apollo spacecraft, which catches fire. The Soviet spacecraft *Soyuz I* crashes to the ground when its parachute tangles on re-entry. Cosmonaut Vladimir M Komarov is killed.

ANOTHER NEW ELEMENT
The artificial radioactive element 105 is produced by Russian scientists; they propose the name nielsbohrium for it; American scientists also produce it and call it hahnium. Neither name has been accepted.

DEATHS IN THE ARTS
British actress Vivien Leigh (b. 1913), American jazzman John Coltrane (b. 1926), writer and critic Dorothy Parker (b. 1893), actress Jayne Mansfield (b. 1932), actor Spencer Tracy (b. 1900) and French writer André Maurois (b. 1885) all die in this year.

THE FASHION FOR JOGGING
The book *Jogging*, by University of Oregon athletics coach Bill Bowerman, helps create the jogging and running craze. Bowerman had observed jogging programmes for health and fitness in New Zealand and uses the ideas in his book.

PULSARS DISCOVERED

British astronomer Jocelyn Bell Burnell discovers pulsating stars (later called pulsars), using a multi-dish radio telescope she helped to build at Cambridge University, England.

NOVEMBER STEPS

Japanese composer Toru Takemitsu's *November Steps* is performed for the first time. Written for a Western orchestra and two Japanese instruments, the *biwa* and *shakuhachi*, it brings together Japanese and Western classical musical traditions and is regarded as his most important work.

EXPO 67

Expo 67 opens in Montreal to celebrate Canada's centenary on December 31, 1966. The Canadian pavilion is an inverted pyramid named Katimavik, the Inuit word for "meeting place". America displays contemporary art in a geodesic dome. Israeli-born Canadian architect Moshe Safde celebrates "a sense of house" in an imaginative apartment block with private outdoor space. This apartment block is made up of hundreds of prefabricated containers, held together by steel cables. The design allows other containers to be added at later dates. The block shows the scope of prefabrication.

ADEN INDEPENDENT

Britain grants independence to Aden, in Yemen, its last Middle East colony, after many years of local revolt.

FIRST HUMAN HEART TRANSPLANT

South African surgeon Christiaan Barnard performs the first human heart transplant at Grote Schuur hospital. However, the patient, Louis Washkansky, dies from pneumonia eighteen days later.

THE SUMMER OF LOVE

The Monterey Pop Festival in San Francisco, USA, marks the beginning of the hippy "Summer of Love", which spreads to London, where pop festivals are held in Hyde Park, and to Amsterdam, Europe's capital of alternative culture.

ABORTION REFORM

Abortion is legalized in Britain under medical supervision and subject to specified criteria. Sweden, Denmark and Iceland legalized abortion on several grounds before World War II, but Britain is the first Western European country to do so. The American state of Colorado also legalizes abortion this year.

THE NAKED APE

Published by British zoologist Desmond Morris, this book interprets aspects of human behaviour, such as hunting instincts, pair-bonding, mutual grooming and territoriality, with the behaviour of animals, especially that of apes.

KONRAD ADENAUER
(1876–1967)

German elder statesman Konrad Adenauer has died. Adenauer, whose political career began as Lord Mayor of Cologne in 1917, was dismissed from office and imprisoned by the Nazis, but reinstated by the Allies in 1945, when he founded the Christian Democratic Union. He was Chancellor of the Federal Republic of Germany from 1949 to 1963.

SUPERBOWL

The Green Bay Packers, of the National Football League, rout the Kansas City Chiefs, of the American Football League, 35–10 in Superbowl I. The Superbowl matches the champions of the two leagues after the merger of the bodies in 1966. The concept is not an immediate success and the game is not a sell-out.

COGNITIVE PSYCHOLOGY

In the theory put forward in this book, American psychologist Ulric Neisser focuses on analysing mental processes such as memory and perception, through which we acquire knowledge, rather than observing human behaviour. Neisser believes we use our experience to build models (called "schemas"), which we use to analyse impressions and anticipate what might happen.

ELEMENTS OF SEMIOLOGY

French philosopher Roland Barthes (1915–80) develops the idea that any product of culture, from language and literature to dress and children's toys, is a system of signs which together provide a means of interpreting and understanding the culture.

NUCLEAR FOOD

The US Department of Agriculture begins a test project of irradiating wheat and other foods to kill insects.

SAILING ROUND THE WORLD

British yachtsman Francis Chichester completes a solo circumnavigation of the world in *Gypsy Moth IV*.

RENE FRANÇOIS GHISLAIN MAGRITTE
(1898–1967)

Belgian Surrealist painter René Magritte has died. In 1924 he became a member of the newly founded Belgian Surrealist Group and then continued to produce bizarre but meticulously painted works depicting incongruously juxtaposed objects, such as the neat bowler-hatted men dripping from the sky in *Golconda* (1953).

VIETNAM WAR

With the exception of the American Civil War, the Vietnam War is the most divisive war ever fought by the United States. Under four presidents the United States is drawn into the war between North and South Vietnam and then struggles to withdraw with dignity. It began on July 8, 1959, when unprecedented numbers of "military observers" are sent into South Vietnam by the USA, and escalates into full-scale war in 1964. During the war the South Vietnamese suffer 150,000 killed and 400,000 wounded while the North Vietnamese and Vietcong suffer 100,000 killed and 300,000 wounded. Between January 1, 1961 and January 27, 1972 the United States suffers 45,941 killed and 300,635 wounded. The war lasts until April 30, 1975 and is very umpopular with the American people.

LEFT: American troops from a reconnaissance patrol discover part of the network of tunnels the Vietcong use as a strategic base.

❖ KEY DATES ❖
IN THE VIETNAM WAR

US ATTACKS 5 Aug, 1964
Aircraft from the USS Constellation and Ticonderoga attack North Vietnamese torpedo boat bases.

"ROLLING THUNDER" 2 March, 1965
This operation is the first of major USAF and USN air attacks on North Vietnam. On 8 March, 1965, the first US Marines arrive in South Vietnam.

KHE SANH 22 January – 14 April, 1968
Some 6,000 US Marines and South Vietnamese troops with 46 guns held a mountain base against 15,000 men in three North Vietnamese divisions.

TET OFFENSIVE 30–31 Jan, 1968
The attempt by the Vietcong and North Vietnamese to score a major victory over the United States and South Vietnam cost them 46,000 dead and 9,000 wounded, while South Vietnam suffer 2,788 killed and 8,886 wounded and the US forces 1,536 killed and 7,775 wounded. It is a military defeat for the North, but a political victory.

LAM SON 719 8 Feb – April 9, 1971
The South Vietnamese unsuccessfully thrust into Laos to disrupt supplies down the Ho Chi Minh Trail. US forces suffer 176 killed and 1,942 wounded. South Vietnam 1,483 killed, 5,420 wounded and 691 missing and North Vietnam 13,636 killed and 69 captured.

ABOVE: Fighting also takes place on the streets and is as dangerous as jungle warfare.

ABOVE: The chop of helicopter rotor blades is the defining soundtrack to the war in Vietnam.

ABOVE: South Vietnamese civilians run from the scene of a skirmish in which three Vietcong soldiers have been killed.

ABOVE: US Marines move cautiously through flooded rice paddies on a search and clear mission, Operation Deckhouse.

FIGHTING IN THE STREETS

A year of violence and confrontation as the Prague Spring in Czechoslovakia is stifled by Soviet tanks, Martin Luther King and Senator Robert Kennedy are gunned down, and student revolutionaries take to the streets of Paris. In Vietnam the Vietcong throw all their energy and fire power into the Tet Offensive. The American retaliation causes protest at home. In Northern Ireland, civil disobedience initiates what will be decades of troubles. The Olympic Games are held in Mexico and are memorable for the Black Power salute given defiantly by black athletes.

1 9 6 8

Jan	5	Reformer Alexander Dubcek becomes head of the Czech Commmunist Party
	30	Vietcong launch Tet Offensive on South Vietnam
Feb	6	The Tenth Winter Olympics open in Grenoble, France
Apr	4	US black leader Martin Luther King is assassinated in Memphis, Tennessee
May	2	Demonstrating students in Paris begin series of clashes with police
June	5	US senator Robert F Kennedy is shot in Los Angeles; he dies the next day

July	6	Sixty-one nations sign a treaty on the non-proliferation of nuclear weapons
	31	First regular cross-Channel hovercraft service begins
Aug	20	Soviet and allied troops invade Czechoslovakia to stop Dubcek's reforms
Oct	5–6	Civil rights demonstrators in Londonderry, Northern Ireland, clash with police
	12	The Nineteenth Olympic Games open in Mexico City
Nov	5	Republican Richard M Nixon is elected US president

LEEFT: Civil rights leader Martin Luther King is assassinated this year, provoking an outbreak of angry scenes and rioting (above).

SPRINGTIME IN PRAGUE

Alexander Dubcek becomes first secretary of the Czechoslovak Communist Party in January and begins the reforms known as the Prague Spring. Seven months later, Soviet and allied troops invade the country to stop reform. The reforms are abandoned, but Dubcek retains power until he is deposed in April 1969. He later becomes ambassador to Turkey.

DEATH OF A DREAM

Civil rights leader Martin Luther King is shot in a motel by an unknown gunman in Memphis, Tennessee. His death leads to major race riots across the USA.

ANOTHER KENNEDY SHOT

Leading Democratic politician, and brother of the former president, Robert Kennedy is shot and killed after winning the primary election in California. His death leads to widespread disillusionment in the USA, and results in the victory of the Republican candidate Richard Nixon in November's presidential election.

TET OFFENSIVE

The Vietcong use the lull of the Tet (New Year) holiday to launch an multi-targeted offensive on Saigon and other strategic ares of the country. They occupy the US embasssy in Saigon and capture Hue. The US and South Vietnam fight back and retake Hue in February, but the retaliation, which is televised and involves civilian executions, has a disastrous effect on US morale at home.

SINFONIA

Italian composer Luciano Berio writes *Sinfonia* for the virtuoso vocal group the Swingle Singers. Full of quotations, both musical and verbal, and references to recent events (the student unrest in Paris), the work finally comes to rest in a meditation on the life and death of Martin Luther King.

LEFT: "Earthrise", as seen and photographed by the US astronauts who orbit the Moon in *Apollo 8* in December of this year.

BELOW: Plastic research balloons are sent up into the stratosphere to collect data for the National Center for Atmospheric Research.

LEFT: Robert F Kennedy is assassinated this year by a Jordanian student, Sirhan Bissara Sirhan.

LES EVENEMENTS

French students protesting against the Vietnam War and other grievances occupy their universities and take their protests on to the streets. Barricades are erected in Paris, and the government almost falls. The protests are copied by students throughout Europe and the USA. Violent demonstrations take place against the autocratic structure of universities across Europe, from Britain to West Germany. The French universities close after demonstrations at the University of Nanterre spread to the Sorbonne in Paris. In the Netherlands, the Maris Report, calling for extensive centralization of university resources, leads to demonstrations in Utrecht, Delft, Wageningen, Groningen and, later, Amsterdam.

NON-PROLIFERATION PACT

In London, UK, 61 nations, including Britain, the USA and the USSR sign the Nuclear Non-Proliferation Treaty, which prohibits the spread of nuclear weapons.

TROUBLE IN IRELAND

Disturbances break out as civil rights demonstrators protesting against anti-Catholic discrimination by the Protestant majority government clash with police. In the next few months, civil rights demonstrators increase their agitation across the province. The minority Catholic population has not enjoyed full civil rights following the 1922 partition of Ireland. Rioting in Londonderry cannot be contained by the Royal Ulster Constabulary (RUC) and the British government sends in troops to regain control.

MILE-LONG DRAWING

Two parallel lines on the desert floor make up Walter de Maria's Mile-Long Drawing. It is an early work of conceptual art, and also an early example of making art on and out of the land.

POWER FROM THE TIDES

The first successful tidal power station goes into operation on the Rance River, in Brittany, France.

ASTRONAUTS ORBIT THE MOON

In December the US spacecraft *Apollo 8* orbits the Moon for twenty hours, carrying astronauts Frank Borman, James A Lovell and William A Anders, and returns safely to Earth.

ABOVE: Day-to-day images such as this wounded American soldier appear daily on television and help to bring an end to the war.

PULSARS IDENTIFIED

US astronomer Thomas Gold discovers that pulsars, first observed in 1967, are actually neutron stars. These are formed of closely packed neutrons and are the densest known stars.

MARCEL DUCHAMP
(1887–1968)

French-born American artist Marcel Duchamp, pioneer of Dadaism and Surrealism, has died. He moved to the United States in 1915 and shocked the art world with "ready-made" works such as his urinal, entitled *Fountain*, of 1917. His work includes *The Large Glass: The Bride Stripped Bare by Her Bachelors Even*, a construction of lead, wire and tinfoil on a large piece of sheet glass, which he abandoned as uncompleted in 1923 after eight years' work. After this he concentrated on playing chess.

REGULAR HOVERCRAFT SERVICE

The first regular hovercraft service across the English Channel, from Dover to Boulogne, begins. The N4 hovercraft carries 254 passengers and 30 cars.

OIL IN ALASKA

US petroleum companies discover a huge oilfield at Prudhoe Bay, on the Arctic Sea coast of north Alaska.

CLEANER WALLS

Washable wallpaper is manufactured by Du Pont in the USA. It is made from polythene and resists tearing. A flexible fabric version is used to make disposable underwear and uniforms.

WIMBLEDON OPENS TO PROFESSIONALS

Rod Laver takes the inaugural Open Wimbledon. After a long struggle in the face of rising professionalism, the tournament allows professional tennis players to participate for the first time.

ABOVE: Mrs Coretta King speaking in front of the Lincoln Memorial in Washington DC after the assassination of her husband.

WINTER OLYMPICS IN FRANCE

Events at the Tenth Winter Olympics centre on Grenoble in France, but events are spread over the surrounding area and seven "villages" host competitors. Drug tests after each event make an appearance. French skier Jean-Claude Killy makes home crowds happy with three skiing golds.

SUPERTANKERS

The first supertankers, giant ocean-going ships for carrying petroleum, come into general use.

BLACK POWER OLYMPICS

The Nineteenth Olympics in Mexico are filled with stunning performances and powerful protest. The altitude of Mexico City gives an advantage in sprint events and 34 world records and 38 Olympic records are set. American Bob Beamon smashes the long jump record by 55cm and his compatriot Jim Hines wins the 100m in 9.95 seconds. Fellow sprinters Tommie Smith and John Carlos create the image of the Games, however, when they raise gloved fists on the medal podium in a salute to black power. The US team sends the 200m medal winners home, but the world sees their protest. Dick Fosbury of America transforms the high jump with the technique that becomes known as the "Fosbury Flop."

LEFT: Led by his eldest son Joseph, the friends and family of Senator Robert F Kennedy carry his coffin to its burial site at Arlington National Cemetery, Virginia.

ABOVE: President Lyndon B Johnson is made to feel at home in El Salvador, where he has been on a goodwill mission.

ABOVE: Senator Richard M Nixon hits the campaign trail in Oregon hoping to take another step towards the presidency.

ABOVE: Neftali Temo wins gold for Kenya in the 10,000m men's event; it is the first gold medal of the Mexican Olympic Games.

MOON LANDING AND FLOWER POWER

The year is dominated by the successful US Moon landing and the world watches in awe as astronaut Neil Armstrong takes a giant step on our behalf. President Nixon initiates the long withdrawal of US troops from Vietnam but in South America, Honduras and El Salvador have a short, fierce war about football. Biafra starves as Nigeria blocks aid flights. The open-air rock festival at Woodstock, USA, three days of music, mud and love, stamps its image on the hearts and minds of a generation.

OPPOSITE: US astronaut Neil Armstrong fulfils President Kennedy's 1961 promise to put an American on the Moon.

1969

Feb	3	Yasser Arafat is appointed head of the Palestine Liberation Organization
	9	The American Boeing 747, the world's largest airliner, makes its first flight
Mar	2	Anglo-French Concorde, the first supersonic airliner, makes its trial flight
Apr	28	President Charles de Gaulle of France resigns
May	14	US president Richard Nixon proposes withdrawal of US, Allied, and North Vietnamese troops from South Vietnam

July	1	In Britain, Prince Charles is invested as Prince of Wales
	13	Row over football match leads to war between Honduras and El Salvador
	20	US astronaut Neil Armstrong becomes the first man to set foot on the Moon
Aug	19	British troops take over security duty in Northern Ireland
Sep	1	In Libya, Colonel Gaddaffi overthrows King Idris of Libya and becomes head of state
	3	President Ho Chi Minh of North Vietnam dies aged 79

ABOVE: President Nixon greets the press in the Socialist Rebublic of Romania. He is the first US president to visit the country.

TROOPS IN NORTHERN IRELAND
British troops patrol the streets to protect Catholics from attack by Protestant gangs. The troops are sent in as a temporary measure to keep the two communities apart, but are forced to remain for longer as the security situation deteriorates.

LIBYAN COUP
King Idris of Libya is toppled in a coup and replaced as head of state by Colonel Muammar Gaddafi, a follower of the political theories of Mao Zedong.

OSTPOLITIK IN GERMANY
The Social Democrats win the general election and Willy Brandt, former mayor of West Berlin, becomes chancellor, the first Social Democrat to lead West Germany. He begins a policy of *Ostpolitik*, or reconciliation with the Eastern bloc.

ISRAEL'S NEW LEADER
Seventy-year-old Golda Meir becomes the first woman prime minister of Israel.

MANSON FAMILY MURDERS
American actress Sharon Tate (wife of film director Roman Polanski) is found brutally murdered, along with four friends, at her Beverley Hills home. Another couple, Leno Lo Bianca and his wife are also found dead in the same fashionable district. Eventually Charles Manson, a charismatic ex-convict, and four members of his desert-dwelling hippie family are arrested, tried and found guilty of the crimes.

SLAUGHTERHOUSE FIVE
Set partly during the bombing of Dresden, American writer Kurt Vonnegut's cult novel cuts through genres. Part-science-fiction, part-anti-war tract, part-autobiography, its slangy, surreal approach makes it popular. It remains the best known of Vonnegut's many books.

PALACH'S PROTEST
Jan Palach, Czech philosophy student, sets light to himself and dies in protest against the Soviet occupation of his country.

THE GENERAL STEPS DOWN
General de Gaulle resigns as president of France after losing a constitutional referendum. The Gaullist Georges Pompidou wins the presidential election in June.

EIGHT SONGS FOR A MAD KING
A key work of "music theatre" (not quite opera, not quite concert music), the eight songs by British composer Peter Maxwell Davies are sung by the mad George III, or at least a character who thinks he is the mad George III. The range of musical references (Handel on the honky-tonk piano) and the violence of the emotions (and extremes of vocal technique needed to express them) makes the work notorious.

FLOWER POWER
The free music festival on a muddy farm in Woodstock, New York State, brings 400,000 people together for a three-day celebration of peace, love and understanding. Major music stars include Jimi Hendrix, The Who, The Band and Janis Joplin.

TRAGEDY IN BIAFRA
Following the Nigerian ban on aid planes, thousands of people in the breakaway province of Biafra are condemned to die of starvation. Television brings horrific pictures of skeletal children into the homes of the world.

OH, CALCUTTA!
English drama producer and critic Kenneth Tynan's famous musical begins its run in New York. The satirical work will run for years on Broadway. It contains nude scenes and the title is a pun on the racy French phrase "O, quel cul tu as" (oh, what a great butt you've got).

MONTY PYTHON'S FLYING CIRCUS

English comic John Cleese and company create a new brand of bizarre humour on television. Acting styles, linguistic wit and ground-breaking animation all push television humour in new, surreal directions and the Pythons gain popular following in Europe and America. The style will later be even more successful worldwide in a series of films.

ARCHITECTS TOP OUT

Influential German architects Ludwig Mies van der Rohe (b. 1886) and Walter Gropius (b. 1883) founder of the Bauhaus, die this year.

STONEWALL RIOTS

In New York, police raid the Stonewall Bar, popular with lesbians and homosexuals. They meet resistance. This marks the beginning of the fight for gay rights.

SUPERSONIC AIRLINERS

In March the world's first supersonic airliner, the *Anglo-French Concorde 001*, makes its first flight in France. Not to be outdone, Russia's supersonic airliner, the *TU-144* (called "Concordski" by the English-speaking press) makes its first flight two months later.

ANTIBIOTIC BAN

The British Ministry of Agriculture and the American Food and Drug Administration both ban the addition of penicillin and tetracycline antibiotics to livestock feed because of the danger of an increase in drug-resistant bacteria.

METEORITES FOUND IN ANTARCTICA

Japanese geologists find meteorites on the Antarctic ice cap.

OVER THE RAINBOW

Judy Garland (b. 1922), forever remembered as Dorothy in *The Wizard of Oz*, dies in London.

HO CHI MINH
(BORN NGUYEN THAT THANH)
(1890–1969)

Ho Chi Minh, the Vietnamese leader whose name is a household word around the world thanks to the Vietnam War, has died. The son of a mandarin, between 1912 and 1930 he spent much of his life in Britain, the United States, France and Moscow. Founder of the Indo-Chinese Communist Party (1930) and the Vietminh Independence League (1941), he led his country against the French (1946–54), and became prime minister of the newly established North Vietnam in 1954. He led the struggle against the US-aided South Vietnam which developed into war in 1964 and which still continues.

ABOVE: The King is back — Elvis Presley returns to the public stage this year, performing mainly in Las Vegas.

A GIANT STEP FOR MANKIND

US astronaut Neil A Armstrong becomes the first man to set foot on the Moon; he is followed by Edwin E "Buzz" Aldrin eighteen minutes later. They become the first people to photograph another planet, using modified Hasselblad cameras. The third astronaut, Michael Collins, orbits the Moon in *Apollo 11* ready to pick the others up and return them to Earth. The whole mission is televised and viewed across the world.

NORTHWEST PASSAGE VOYAGE

The American icebreaking supertanker *Manhattan* makes the first commercial voyage through the Northwest Passage, the seaway around Canada linking the Pacific and the Atlantic; it takes three months.

FOOTBALL CRAZY

El Salvador and Honduras go to war over a football game. Honduran citizens attack Salvadorians in Honduras after El Salvador wins a World Cup qualifying game in Mexico. The government of El Salvador retaliates. Fighting lasts a week.

AN ELEPHANT FLIES

The largest commercial jetliner, the Boeing 747, makes its first flight. Popularly known as a jumbo jet, it can carry 362 passengers.

NORTH SEA OIL FOUND

High-grade crude petroleum is found in the northern North Sea between Britain and Norway. The find will mean great prosperity for both countries.

WALKING ON WATER

The British Trans-Arctic Expedition led by Wally Herbert reaches Spitzbergen. Its members become the first people to cross the frozen Arctic Ocean on foot. They have travelled 5,760km (3,600mi) in 464 days from Point Barrow, Alaska.

OPEN SESAME

Sesame Street begins on American Public Service TV and revolutionizes children's attitudes to learning. Designed by Children's TV Workshop and funded by the Ford Foundation, Carnegie and the US Office of Education, it uses techniques of commercial television to teach letters and numbers in English and Spanish. Kermit the Frog and other "muppets" make their first appearance.

WORDS OF WARNING

Problems of the Human Environment, commissioned by the United Nations, reports that 500 million hectares (1,236 million acres) of arable land and two-thirds of the world's original forests have been lost, mainly through poor agricultural management and forest clearances.

OFF THE ROAD

American writer Jack Kerouac (b. 1922), the original "beatnik" and assiduous chronicler of the romance of the road, dies.

POLLUTION SPREADS

Alarm over pollution grows after millions of Rhine fish are killed by leakage from Thiodan 2 insecticide canisters that had been dropped into the river in 1967. In 1968 nerve gas from a US Army site in Utah escaped, killing 6,000 sheep, and now Japan reports cadmium-poisoning, Texas reports mercury-poisoning, and in Arizona DDT is found in mothers' milk.

SUPERBOWL SUCCESS

The upstart New York Jets of the junior American Football League beat the Baltimore Colts of the National Football League 16–7 to take the Superbowl, a win that had been confidently predicted by the Jets' brash quarterback Joe Namath. The Superbowl becomes America's top sporting occasion.

VOYAGE TO THE MOON

ABOVE: Lift-off for *Apollo 11* on its historic mission to the Moon.

LEFT: The command and service module of *Apollo 11* floats above the Sea of Tranquillity, photographed from the orbiting lunar module.

ABOVE: Safe splashdown for the crew of *Apollo 12*, the second team of US astronauts to walk on the Moon. They are (l to r) Charles Conrad Jnr, Richard F Gordon Jnr and Alan L Bean.

ABOVE: Aboard the USS *Hornet* President Nixon hails the *Apollo 11* crew on their safe return from the Moon.

MEN ON THE MOON

The Sixties see humans on the Moon. From the first short space-hops of 1961 to the full-scale multi-teamed expeditions that characterize this year, the whole Moon mission fits neatly into the decade. Using techniques learned on previous missions, *Apollo 11* at last lands the first men on the Moon as the world watches. The mission is followed up by the exploratory team from *Apollo 12* a few months later.

ABOVE LEFT: *Apollo 12* astronaut unpacks the Apollo lunar surface experiments package in the first EVA (extra-vehicular activity) period of the mission.

ABOVE RIGHT: The fragile-looking *Apollo 12* lunar module. Astronauts Alan Bean and Charles Conrad land on the Moon in this, while Richard Gordon remains with the command and service module in lunar orbit.

LEFT: *Apollo 11* commander Neil Armstrong, photographed by Edwin "Buzz" Aldrin, takes soil samples from the Moon as his first task, in case the expedition is cut short. Armstrong and Aldrin remain on the Moon for just over 21 hours.

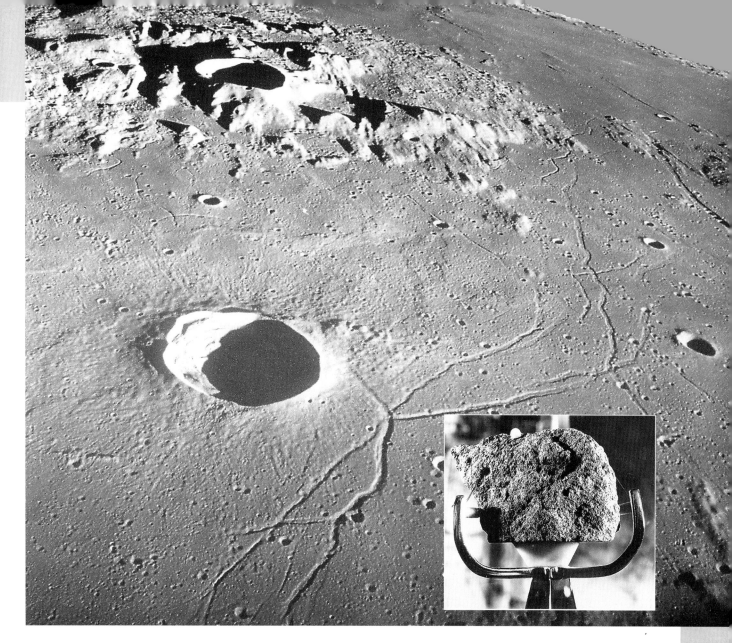

ABOVE: From close up, the Moon's surface appears pock-marked with craters and holes.

INSET: A piece of Moon rock brought back from the *Apollo 12* mission in November. This piece is a form of olivine basalt.

RIGHT: Humanity's first view of its own home, taken from the orbiting lunar module of *Apollo 10*. The blue and green beauty of Earth is a wonderful surprise to many of its inhabitants.

REVOLUTION AND LIBERATION

Against a background of civil war, coups and oppression, technology moves forward: commercial flight goes supersonic, computers invade everyday life and "test-tube" babies are born. Mars is found to be apparently barren; humanity loses interest in space and turns its attention to the pollution of the environment and the impact of technology on the ecological balance. Feminism becomes at once more militant and mainstream. The first signs of religious fundamentalism show themselves in the Middle East.

RIGHT: Demonstrators rally to protest about the war in Vietnam.

1970–1979

KEY EVENTS OF THE DECADE

- IDI AMIN SEIZES POWER IN UGANDA

- GREENPEACE BEGINS ITS PROTESTS

- TROUBLE IN NORTHERN IRELAND

- END OF VIETNAM WAR

- WATERGATE SCANDAL

- BLACK SEPTEMBER OLYMPICS

- PINOCHET COUP IN CHILE

- THE COD WAR

- POL POT REGIME IN CAMBODIA

- CIVIL WAR IN THE LEBANON

- THE STEVE BIKO INCIDENT

- ELVIS PRESLEY DIES

- FIRST TEST-TUBE BABY BORN

- CIVIL WAR IN NICARAGUA

- HOMOSEXUAL RIGHTS

- ISLAMIC REVOLUTION IN IRAN

- THREE MILE ISLAND

- RUSSIA INVADES AFGHANISTAN

WORLD POPULATION **3,693** MILLION

DÉTENTE IN THE EAST AND DEATH ON THE CAMPUS

The new decade sees continued protest over the American involvement in Vietnam, despite promises of withdrawal. Anti-war demonstrations continue and in the US four students are shot dead on the campus of Kent State University, Ohio, by the National Guard. West Germany's chancellor, Willy Brandt, initiates détente with East Germany. The Palestinian Black September movement is formed and attacks Jordan. *Apollo 13* proves as unlucky as its number and the astronauts in it get back to Earth on a wing and a prayer. Political heavyweights Charles de Gaulle and Gamal Nasser of Egypt leave the world stage.

1 9 7 0

Mar	**19**	First meeting of East and West German heads of state
Apr11	**(–13)**	US *Apollo 13* Moon mission aborted after explosion; crew return safely
Sep	**5**	In Chile, Marxist Salvador Allende is elected president
	16 (–27)	War in Jordan between Jordanian Army and Palestinian militia
	18	Jimi Hendrix (b. 1943), American guitar ace, dies

	28	In Egypt, President Nasser dies aged 52
	29	Anwar Sadat becomes president of Egypt
Nov	**9**	Former French president Charles de Gaulle dies aged 79
	17	Soviet space probe *Luna 17* lands on the Moon and deploys an unmanned exploration vehicle
Dec	**7**	West Germany and Poland sign treaty recognizing Poland's frontier

ABOVE: The staff at Houston Mission Control celebrate the safe return of the *Apollo 13* crew, whose mission went badly wrong.

GERMAN DETENTE

The first meeting between Willy Brandt of West Germany and Willi Stoph of East Germany, at Erfurt in East Germany, starts the process of détente in Europe.

DEATH ON THE CAMPUS

US National Guards shoot dead four anti-war demonstrators on Kent State University campus in Ohio, USA. Anti-war protests continue throughout the USA against US involvement in the Vietnam War.

ALLENDE WINS

Salvador Allende wins the presidential election. He becomes the first democratically elected Marxist head of state in the world, and begins a programme of reform, including the nationalization of copper mines owned by US subsidiaries.

BLACK SEPTEMBER

After militant Palestinians hijack three aircraft to Jordan, the Jordanian government evicts the Palestinians and regains control of the kingdom in a month of struggle which will be known as Black September.

TROUBLED INDEPENDENCE FOR ADEN

After four years, British troops withdraw from Aden as independence approaches. The withdrawal sees conflict with the National Liberation Front (NLF). The British suffer 57 dead and 651 wounded. Local civilian casualties are bad: 280 dead and 922 wounded.

POWER CHANGE IN EGYPT

Egyptian president Gamal Abdel Nasser (b. 1918) dies and is succeeded by Anwar Sadat.

RIGHT: Aquanauts replicate conditions in space, spending twenty days in *Tektite 11*, an underwater habitat designed and funded by NASA.

HIPPIES IN HOLLAND

Hippies are cleared from the Dutch National Monument in Dam Square, Amsterdam. The permissive Dutch capital has become the alternative capital of Europe for the young, called *asfaltjeugd*, or "asphalt youth", in Dutch, because they sleep in the city's parks and squares.

POLISH BORDER ASSURED

West Germany and Poland sign a treaty recognizing the current border between Poland and Germany, thus reassuring Poland about any possible German moves to re-acquire land lost after the war.

SPACE DRAMA

US spacecraft *Apollo 13*, on its way to the Moon, is crippled by an explosion. The astronauts on board, James Lovell, John Swigert and Fred Haise, guided by ground control in Houston and watched by the world, manage to swing the damaged craft round the Moon and return safely to Earth, using the lunar module Aquarius as a "lifeboat".

I KNOW WHY THE CAGED BIRD SINGS

American writer Maya Angelou's autobiography, including her account of sexual and racial oppression (raped at the age of eight, a period of muteness), marks her emergence as a major writer (although she has published poetry before). Further volumes of autobiography will follow.

LUNOKHOD EXPLORES THE MOON

Russian unmanned spacecraft *Luna 17* lands an eight-wheeled vehicle, *Lunokhod 1*, on the Moon; it travels more than 1km (2/3mi) exploring the surface by remote control.

M*A*S*H

Robert Altman makes moving comedy out of events in the Korean War. Two surgeons in a mobile army hospital try to keep themselves sane with joking, womanizing and subverting authority. Although set in Korea, the parallels with Vietnam are inescapable. The film forms the basis of a popular TV series.

ESCALATION IN IRELAND

In Belfast, the Provisional Irish Republican Army kills a British soldier on October 31. This signals war between the illegal army and the British government.

VENUS PROBE

The Russian space probe *Venera 7* drops a package of instruments on to the surface of the planet Venus; it sends back information for 23 minutes before the fierce heat destroys it.

THE FEMALE EUNUCH

Australian writer, academic and feminist Germaine Greer argues that characteristics in women traditionally valued by men (delicacy, passivity, etc.) show "castration" of the true female personality, something in which women have colluded. The book becomes a key feminist text.

RIGHT: Burt Bacharach wins an Oscar for his music score for the 1969 movie *Butch Cassidy and the Sundance Kid.*

ENVIRONMENTAL AWARENESS

The first Earth Day is celebrated by 20 million Americans, who attend teach-ins and rallies, and participate in schemes to clean up the environment.

CROW

This collection confirms Ted Hughes' early promise as the major English poet of his generation. The sinister figure of Crow, mythically memorable, surviving through hostility to humankind, is one of the most powerful creations in the literature of the time.

ACCIDENTAL DEATH OF AN ANARCHIST

In this play, Italian Marxist Dario Fo draws influence from traditional European forms (farce, *commedia dell'arte*) to bring a satirical sharpness to the theatre.

FLOPPY DISKS

US computer company IBM introduces floppy disks for storing computer information.

CROWDED SKIES

China and Japan launch their first space satellites.

COMPUTERIZED CATALOGUE

The Smithsonian Institution in Washington DC begins to compile a computerized catalogue of all US plants.

EXPLORING EARTH'S CRUST

Russian scientists begin drilling a deep well on the Kola Peninsula, north of the Arctic Circle, to examine the Earth's crust; they plan to drill down 15km (9mi).

CHARLES ANDRE JOSEPH MARIE DE GAULLE (1890–1970)

Former French president and founder in exile of the Free French Army (1940), Charles de Gaulle has died. The World War I army officer who headed post-war provisional governments and became President of the Fifth Republic in 1958 is credited with resolving the Algerian crisis and restoring stability to post-war France. His handling of the situation in May 1968 seemed at first to guarantee his continued popularity but he resigned last year after a disastrous referendum vote of no-confidence.

ABOVE: The film version of *One Day in the Life of Ivan Denisovich*, Solzhenitsyn's grim description of life in a Soviet prison gulag.

ECOWARRIORS AND BLACK HOLES

The Canadian pressure group for the environment, Greenpeace, carries out its first act of confrontation in Alaska. In Switzerland, women get the vote at last. East Pakistan declares itself independent and chooses a new name, Bangladesh, while in Uganda, Idi Amin seizes power. US astronauts visit the Moon again, and the USSR puts a space station into orbit. Homosexuals assert their rights and the term Gay Pride is coined. In space, black holes, the imprints of collapsed, gravity-sucking stars, are discovered.

1971

Jan	10	French fashion queen Coco Chanel dies aged 87
Feb	7	Swiss women get the vote
	15	UK introduces decimal currency
	20	Idi Amin seizes power in Uganda
Mar	26	Awami League declares East Pakistan independent as Bangladesh
Apr	6	Russo-American composer Igor Stravinsky dies aged 88
	19	Soviets put *Salyut 1*, the first space station, into orbit
	25	In the US, 200,000 people demonstrate against the Vietnam War in Washington DC
June	30	Three Soviet cosmonauts are found dead in their spacecraft after an apparently normal landing

July	1	West Indies cricketer and statesman Learie Constantine (Baron Constantine) dies aged 69
Aug	9	Internment without trial introduced in Northern Ireland
Sep	30	Canadian ecowarriors Greenpeace stage their first protest in Alaska
Nov	12	President Nixon ends the US offensive role in Vietnam
Dec	6	India recognizes Bangladesh's independence and goes to war with Pakistan
	17	End of the Indo-Pakistan War

ABOVE: Women demonstrate to legalize abortion and for the right to choose what to do with their own bodies.

ABOVE: Feminist writer Betty Friedan leads NOW, the National Organization of Women.

LEFT: Gloria Steinem, former Playboy Bunny, campaigns for women's rights.

ABOVE: Women demonstrate in support of the Equal Rights Amendment to the US Constitution.

ABOVE: Flags of 126 nations flutter outside the United Nations building in New York. China joins this year.

BELOW: The *Apollo 14* launch vehicle on the pad. Alan B Shepard, Stuart A Roose and Edgar D Mitchell are the astronauts on this mission.

THE HARDER HOUSE
Eccentric American architect Bruce Goff designs this house for a Minnesota turkey farmer. The building combines natural and "post-modern" materials (stone, wood and shingle on the one hand, orange roof covering and mirror mosaic on the other) to create a unique synthesis.

MADMEN AND SPECIALISTS
Nigerian writer Wole Soyinka's volume of verse and prose shows his versatility as a writer. His diverse writings stress the need for a distinctively African written culture, cross-fertilized by, but independent from, that of Europe.

UNDERNEATH THE ARCHES
London-based artists Gilbert and George impersonate English music-hall artists Bud Flanagan and Chesney Allen (one of whose best-known routines was a song and dance duet called "Underneath the Arches") to create the first "living sculpture". The work causes hilarity and controversy — which is presumably what the artists intend.

DIGITAL WATCH
US engineers George Theiss and Willy Crabtree develop the first digital watch, powered by a vibrating quartz crystal.

UAE FORMED
The United Arab Emirates is formed by six sheikhdoms as Britain leaves the Persian Gulf after 150 years. Bahrain and Qatar become independent in their own right.

GABRIELLE (COCO) CHANEL (1883–1971)

French couturier Coco Chanel has died. She founded her couture house in Paris in 1924 and created the classic chemise dress and the Chanel suit with its collarless jacket. She was also responsible for the "little black dress" that remains chic cocktail-party wear, and her own perfumes, especially Chanel No. 5. After a long period of retirement she took up her career again during the 1950s.

BANGLADESH GAINS INDEPENDENCE

Led by Sheikh Mujibur Rahman, the Awami League wins all the seats in East Pakistan in the general election in December 1970 and begins talks on a new constitution for the province. As talks break down, Rahman declares independence as Bangladesh, in protest against neglect of the province by West Pakistan, and establishes a government in exile in Calcutta in April. Tension rises during the year, until border clashes between India and East Pakistan lead to a brief war in December. Indian forces defeat the Pakistani Army; as a result, Pakistan is divided and Bangladesh gains its independence.

GAY LIBERATION GROWS

Gay liberation groups emerge in major American cities in North America, Australia and Western Europe, following the foundation of active American groups who led a successful campaign to challenge injustices perpetrated against homosexuals. Gay Pride marches raise public consciousness of the predicament of gay and lesbian people.

BLACK HOLES FOUND

Astronomers discover black holes in space. These have been predicted by English physicist Stephen Hawking. Black holes are collapsed stars whose gravity is so strong that not even light can escape from them, so they cannot be observed visually.

"POCKET" CALCULATORS

US company Texas Instruments introduces the first pocket calculator, the Pocketronic. It goes into mass production at once, weighing 1.134kg (2½lb) and costing $150.

ABOVE: Beat poet Alan Ginsberg meets his admirers.

BELOW: Dr Daniel Ellsberg, the whistleblower of Watergate.

ABOVE: British rockstar Rod Stewart performs in the USA.

ORBITING MARS

In November US space probe *Mariner 9* goes into orbit around Mars, the first planet to be explored in this way; *Mariner 9* sends back 7,329 photographs, allowing scientists to make accurate maps of the planet.

FIRST SPACE STATION

On April 19 the Russians put *Salyut 1*, the first space station, into orbit. The idea is to establish a kind of base camp in space so that teams of cosmonauts can work in shifts.

IGOR FYODOROVICH STRAVINSKY
(1882–1971)

Composer, pianist and conductor Igor Stravinsky has died in New York. Born in Russia in 1882, he left for France after the revolution and later became an American citizen, having moved to the United States in 1939. He first came to fame with his ballets for Diaghilev's Ballets Russes: *The Firebird* (1910), *Petrushka* (1911) and *The Rite of Spring* (1913). Other works include *Pulcinella* (1919–20) and *The Rake's Progress* (1951), and many orchestral, voice and chamber compositions. He incorporated such diverse influences as Russian folk music, American jazz, Verdi, Monteverdi, Baroque music and music of the Viennese school. His burial will be in Venice, in the cemetery of San Michele, close to Diaghilev.

ABOVE: The distinctive Smiley Face logo, icon of the LSD-taking classes and destined for a revival in the clubs of the 1980s.

COSMONAUT DEATHS

Three Russian cosmonauts are found dead in their spacecraft *Soyuz II* after an apparently normal landing: loss of air from the cabin is blamed for their deaths.

MOON ROCKS BROUGHT BACK

US spacecraft *Apollo 14* and *Apollo 15* bring back Moon rocks for analysis. Members of the *Apollo 15* crew, David Scott and James Irwin, gather theirs during a drive in a lunar roving vehicle or "Moon buggy".

INTERNMENT IN IRELAND

The British government introduces internment without trial in an attempt to prevent terrorism. It leads to riots and hunger strikes.

HOME VIDEO

Philips launches the first video cassette recorder (VCR) for home use. The 1-cm (1/2-in tape) plays for 1 hour.

CHINA IN THE UN

China takes its seat at the UN in place of Taiwan, which has held the seat since 1945.

BLOODY SUNDAY AND BLACK SEPTEMBER

Sunday January 30 in Londonderry, Northern Ireland, sees thirteen civilians killed, leading to decades of murders and bombings. President Nixon goes to China to make an alliance with the world's third superpower, while back in the US, burglars break into the Watergate Building to plant bugs. At the Munich Olympics, Palestinian activists murder eleven Israeli athletes. In Burundi, rival tribes Hutus and Tsutsis slaughter each other. FBI chief J Edgar Hoover dies and some very surprising secrets emerge from his closet.

1972

Jan	30	"Bloody Sunday" in Londonderry, Northern Ireland: British troops fire on demonstrators, killing thirteen
	30	Pakistan leaves the Commonwealth
Feb	2	Winter Olympics open in Tokyo, Japan
	21	US president Nixon begins visit to China
Mar	2	US launches *Pioneer 10* to photograph Jupiter
	30	Britain suspends Northern Ireland parliament and imposes direct rule
May	28	The Duke of Windsor (ex-King Edward VIII) dies aged 77
June	17	Intruders try to bug Democratic Party HQ in the Watergate Building in Washington DC
July	23	US launches *Landsat 1*, which orbits Earth taking strips of photographs
	31	Belgian statesman Paul Spaak dies aged 72
Aug	4	President Idi Amin of Uganda orders all Asian citizens to leave
	26	The Twentieth Olympic Games open in Munich, Germany
Sep	5	Arab terrorists murder eleven members of the Israeli Olympic team
Dec	2	Labour wins Australian general election
	7	Last Apollo mission to the Moon

ABOVE: Commander John W Young salutes the Stars and Stripes planted on the Moon during the *Apollo 16* mission.

BELOW: Commander Gene Cernan test-drives the Moon buggy on the *Apollo 17* mission.

ABOVE: *Apollo 16*'s lunar module, known as Orion.

ABOVE: President Nixon goes to China and meets Chou En-Lai, premier of the People's Republic.

WATERGATE
Burglars are arrested breaking into the Democratic Party headquarters in the Watergate Building. Over the next year, it is established that they were working for the US president, Richard Nixon, in his campaign to gain re-election in the 1972 presidential elections, which he wins easily against anti-war campaigner and Democratic candidate George McGovern.

ABOVE: Olga Korbut wins three Olympic golds in Munich.

BLOODY SUNDAY
In Londonderry, Northern Ireland, British paratroopers open fire on unarmed demonstrators protesting against the British policy of interning Irish Republican Army (IRA) members, and kill thirteen civilians. Bloody Sunday marks the low point of relations between the Catholic community and the British Army, and leads to a huge increase in violence across the province. In March, as a direct result of the violence, the Northern Irish parliament is suspended and direct rule is imposed from London.

NIXON IN CHINA
In a historic move, US president Richard Nixon visits China and meets the Communist leadership. The visit leads to a thaw in relations between the two superpowers, both of which have reason to work together against the USSR.

UGANDANS EXPELLED
President Idi Amin expels 50,000 Asians with British passports from Uganda, claiming that they are sabotaging the national economy. The Asians all leave within three months, causing economic ruin in Uganda as factories close and vital services stop.

AUSTRALIA TURNS TO THE PACIFIC
Gough Whitlam leads the Labour Party to victory in the general election in Australia. He radically changes Australian foreign policy away from the USA and towards Asia, recognizing China, giving Papua New Guinea its independence, pardoning Vietnam draft dodgers and ending national service.

GAY MINISTRY
A ministry to the gay community, founded in 1968 in Los Angeles by Troy Perry, an expelled Pentecostal preacher, is expanding across America, and the Evangelical Lutheran Church of the Netherlands declares that there is no obstacle to the appointment of gay ministers.

LASERVISION
The Dutch firm of Philips introduces a system of recording on plastic discs using lasers. The system is later marketed as LaserVision.

WINTER OLYMPICS IN JAPAN
Disputes over amateur status lead to the disqualification of a skier and the withdrawal of the Canadian ice hockey team from the Eleventh Winter Games in Sapporo, Japan. Revenue from TV rights climbs to $8.47 million, three times the 1968 sum.

SPEED OF LIGHT REMEASURED
US scientist Kenneth M Evenson produces a more accurate measurement of the speed of light than has been possible hitherto: 299,784km (186,282.3959mi) per second.

ABOVE: Writer Stokely Carmichael, a prominent activist in the black civil rights movement.

BLACK SEPTEMBER OLYMPICS

Palestinian terrorists hijack the Twentieth Olympiad in Munich, Germany. Their attack on the Israeli team in the Olympic Village leaves eleven athletes and a policeman dead. German authorities botch a rescue attempt as the terrorists and hostages transfer from helicopters to a plane at a military airfield. Five of the eight Palestinians are killed. The International Olympic Committee refuses to bow to violence and, with the backing of the Israeli government, the Games continue with flags at half-mast. In competition, US swimmer Mark Spitz claims an astounding seven golds. Soviet gymnast Olga Korbut is the crowd favourite and wins three golds.

IT'S A WRAP

Bulgarian-born French artist Christo wraps a section of the coastline of Australia. The enormous artwork uses some 930,000 sq m (1 million sq ft) of plastic sheeting and attracts publicity all over the world.

EQUIVALENT 8

US sculptor Carl André's *Equivalent 8* is a sculpture consisting of a pile of 120 bricks. It is bought by London's Tate Gallery, to derisive comments from press and public alike. (The sculptor explains his work in terms of making "cuts in space".)

ENDGAME

Maverick Bobby Fischer is crowned the first American chess world champion after defeating Russian Boris Spassky in Iceland.

THE UN AND THE ENVIRONMENT

A United Nations Conference on the Human Environment meets in Stockholm to discuss environmental issues.

LANDSAT 1 LAUNCHED

The USA launches *Landsat 1*, otherwise called the Earth Resources Test Satellite, which photographs the Earth's surface in a series of strips and covers all the globe, except the two Poles, every eighteen days. The photographs will yield vital information about crop growth, deforestation, floods and other data.

OFF TO JUPITER

NASA (America's National Aeronautics and Space Administration), launches *Pioneer 10*, a spaceprobe designed to take close-up photographs of the planet Jupiter. It is scheduled to fly past the giant planet in December 1973.

IN A FREE STATE

Trinidadian-born British writer VS Naipaul's novel explores identity through three linked narratives of people outside their native territory. Its bleak vision is typical of the author's later work.

CAT SCANNER

British engineer Godfrey Hounsfield and South African physicist Allan Cormack invent the Computerized Axial Tomography scanner (known as CAT). It uses computer technology to produce images of the brain and becomes an important diagnostic tool.

MASSACRES IN BURUNDI

Rebel Hutus massacre thousands of their compatriots from the minority Tsutsi tribe who are in government. The Tsutsis retaliate and much slaughter ensues.

POLLUTION AND WASTE

ABOVE: Pesticides and agribusiness dominate farming.

BELOW: Wrecked cars pile up, a symbol of Western waste.

ABOVE: Dallas, Texas, where the car and the road seem to cover the planet.

ABOVE: Atmospheric pollution from a steelworks.

ABOVE: Raw sewage discharging into a river.

PEACE IN VIETNAM, WAR IN THE MIDDLE EAST

Peace treaties are signed to end the wars in Vietnam and its neighbour Laos. The USA will take many years to recover from the war it did not win. In Chile, General Pinochet stages a coup and President Allende is murdered. Egypt and Syria attack Israel in the Yom Kippur War. In the North Atlantic, Icelandic fishing trawlers battle with the British fleet over disputed territories. CITES is established to monitor the trade in endangered species and the European Community admits Denmark, the UK and Ireland.

1973

Jan	1	Denmark, Ireland and the United Kingdom join the European Union
	22	Former US president Lyndon B Johnson dies aged 64
	27	Cease-fire in Vietnam signed by North and South Vietnam, the Vietcong guerrillas and the USA
Mar	8	US launches *Pioneer 11* to take close-ups of Jupiter and Saturn
Apr	8	Spanish painter Pablo Picasso dies aged 91
May	25	US launches *Skylab*, its first space station

Sep	11	Junta headed by General Augusto Pinochet seizes power in Chile; President Allende is killed
Oct	6	Arab countries attack Israel on Yom Kippur, the Jewish Day of Atonement
	10	US Vice-President Spiro T Agnew resigns after tax evasion scandal
	24	Yom Kippur War ends
Nov	3	US launches *Mariner 10* to photograph Venus and Mercury
Dec	1	David Ben-Gurion, former Israeli prime minister, dies aged 87
	6	Gerald Ford becomes new US vice-president

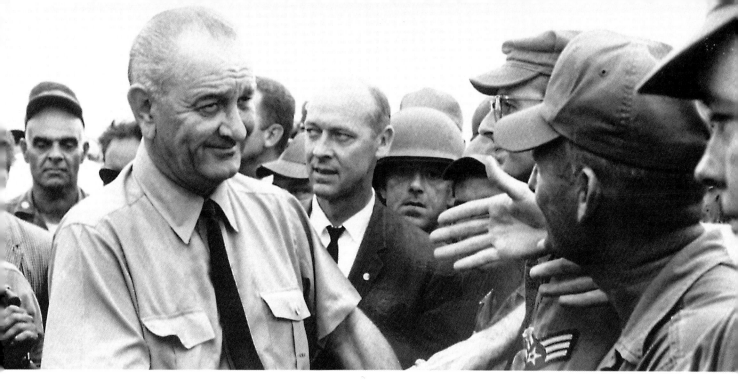

PEACE IN VIETNAM
A cease-fire is declared in Vietnam as a peace agreement is signed in Paris between the USA and North and South Vietnam. The US agrees to withdraw all its troops, and exchange prisoners of war.

COUP IN CHILE
President Allende of Chile is ousted and killed in a coup by General Pinochet. The new military government introduces martial law and imprisons its opponents, driving thousands into exile.

YOM KIPPUR WAR
Egypt and Syria attack Israel during the religious Yom Kippur holiday. Israel fights back, crossing the Suez Canal and threatening to cut off the invading Egyptian Army. A cease-fire is arranged by the UN, but oil-rich Arab nations raise the price of oil by 70 per cent in protest against US support for Israel. As a result, fuel shortages and inflation hit all the Western economies.

THE SECOND BATTLE OF WOUNDED KNEE
Members of the American Indian Movement seize Wounded Knee on the Sioux Reservation in South Dakota to protest against Indian treaties broken by the US government. Fighting to end the occupation results in two deaths and many injuries and arrests.

CEASE-FIRE IN LAOS
In this former French colony, the Pathet Lao, backed by the North Vietnamese, fight the Royalist Laotian government. Since the Ho Chi Minh trail passes through Laos the United States backs the Royalist forces against the 35,000 strong Pathet Lao. A cease-fire is agreed in 1973 when South Vietnam falls to the North. In 1975 Laos will come under complete Pathet Lao control.

INNER PLANETS
US space probe *Mariner 10* is launched, designed to observe Venus and Mercury, the two planets that orbit between Earth and the Sun.

ABOVE: Former president Lyndon Baines Johnson, seen here visiting troops in Vietnam, dies this year.

EC EXPANDS
The UK, Ireland and Denmark join the European Community (EC) after the new French government of Georges Pompidou relaxes its veto on British entry. Nine nations are now members of the EC.

OPEN STUDY
The first graduates of the Open University, founded in the UK in 1969 for mature students without formal qualifications to gain university-level education, receive their degrees.

CITES ESTABLISHED
A Convention on International Trade in Endangered Species (CITES) is drawn up at a conference to end the trade held in Washington, USA, and is signed by representatives of 80 countries.

RIDING ROUGH TERRAIN
A mountain bike is designed for riding the slopes of canyons in California, USA, by the Marin County Canyon cycling club.

PABLO CASALS
(1876–1973)

Spanish-born cellist Pablo Casals has died in Puerto Rico, where he has lived since 1956. He gave his first performances in Barcelona cafés, and ever since his first American tour in 1901 has been recognized as the world's leading cellist, playing as a soloist and with the pianist Alfred Cortot and violinist Jacques Thibaut. In exile from Franco's Spain, he founded the Prades Festival in France before settling in South America.

ABOVE: Richard M Nixon is sworn in for his second term in presidential office. It will only last for two years.

ABOVE: John Mitchell and his attorney at the Watergate trial.

ABOVE: Nixon's chief of staff Robert Haldeman testifies at the Watergate trial.

SYDNEY OPERA HOUSE

Jørn Utzon's opera house is finally completed. Its construction has been a saga of bumbles and U-turns; the authorities accepted Utzon's sketches before anyone had worked out how to build the roofs. They have to swap the roles of the two main auditoria and have to start a lottery to pay for it. But they get as great a civic symbol as any in the world.

A LITTLE NIGHT MUSIC

One of the most successful of US composer Stephen Sondheim's early musicals, *Night Music* has a tragi-comic plot based on Bergman's film *Smiles on a Summer Night*. The score is notable for its operatic vocal requirements and for being almost entirely in waltz time, and the lyrics demonstrate Sondheim's perennial wit. The whole thing cements Sondheim's reputation for creating grown-up musicals.

DAY FOR NIGHT

French director François Truffaut's film is about film-making. The loving depiction of both the pleasures and frustrations of the art explores all aspects from technical details and props to the relationship between actor and director — and between movie and reality.

GRAVITY'S RAINBOW

American writer Thomas Pynchon produces his largest book, set at the end of World War II. Its fantastic take on reality reminds some critics of Latin American magic realism.

MUSIC FOR PIECES OF WOOD

Steve Reich's work is a typical minimalist piece, scored for five tuned claves, which play separate repeated patterns of notes. This is one of the most extreme forms of minimalism.

THE COD WAR

Hostilities break out between Iceland and the UK when Icelandic territorial waters are expanded from 80km (50mi) to 320km (200mi) so encroaching on fishing grounds used by the British. British fishing boats are escorted into the zone by a super-tug and the situation rapidly escalates, involving the Royal Navy and Icelandic gunboats. There are riots outside the British embassy in Reyjkjavik.

ICELANDIC VOLCANO

A volcano erupts on the island of Heimaey and all 5,000 inhabitants have to leave their homes in the middle of the night.

SKYLAB

America's first space station, *Skylab*, is launched and goes into orbit 435km (270mi) above the Earth; three three-man crews are sent in turn to *Skylab* during the year. It delivers information about Earth's resources and the structure of the Sun.

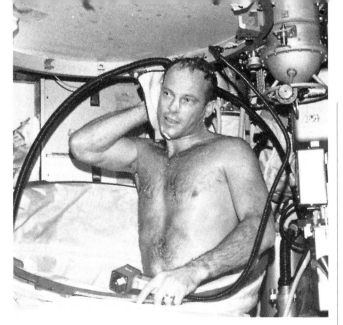

ABOVE: Almost-normal life is possible for the crew inside the space station *Skylab 3*.

RIGHT: Astronaut Jack Lousma works outside *Skylab 3*. He is one of a three-man team.

JUPITER AND SATURN TO BE EXPLORED

NASA launches *Pioneer 11*, a space probe designed to take close-up pictures of both Jupiter (in 1974) and Saturn (in 1979).

GENETIC ENGINEERING

US chemists Stanley H Cohen and Herbert W Boyer use the process of genetic engineering to make bacteria produce small quantities of insulin. This represents the beginning of genetic engineering.

DOLPHIN TRIUMPH

The Miami Dolphins cap a perfect seventeen-victory season by beating the Washington Redskins in Superbowl VII. The Dolphins are the only team in NFL history to win all their games in a season.

ABOVE: Redford and Newman in the Oscar-winning film *The Sting*.

DEATHS IN THE ARTS

Edward G Robinson (b. 1893), the screen gangster, US writer and Nobel Prize-winner Pearl S Buck (b. 1892), French painter Jacques Lipchitz (b. 1891), US Kung Fu star Bruce Lee (b. 1940), English playwright Noel Coward (b. 1899), film director John Ford (b. 1895), author JRR Tolkein (b. 1892) and poet WH Auden (b. 1907) all die this year.

POLITICAL DEATHS

Former US President Lyndon Baines Johnson (b. 1908), Jeanette Rankin, the first woman in Congress (b. 1880) and Fulgencio Batista, the Cuban dictator (b. 1901) all die this year.

SMALL IS BEAUTIFUL

American economist EF Schumacher introduces the idea of alternative technology in his best-seller *Small is Beautiful: a Study of Economics as if People Mattered*.

TELETEXT DEMONSTRATED

British TV companies demonstrate teletext, news and information pages in addition to normal programmes.

PABLO PICASSO
(1881–1973)

Pablo Picasso, the prolific painter, sculptor and ceramic artist, who was born in Spain in 1881 but who has for many years lived and worked in France, has died. Together with Georges Braque he developed Cubism and has had a hugely powerful influence on the direction of modern art. He designed costumes and sets for the Ballets Russes from 1917 onwards, and became a Communist during World War ll. His work *Guernica*, painted in 1937 during the Spanish Civil War, has become a byword for anti-war art.

RESIGNATION BEFORE IMPEACHMENT

The fall-out from the Watergate scandal forces President Nixon to resign before he is impeached. A military coup in the dictatorship of Portugal leads to democracy and independence for Portuguese colonies Goa, Mozambique and Portuguese Guinea. In Cyprus, President Makarios is overthrown and Turkey invades. Civilian rule reasserts itself in Greece. In Ethiopia Haile Selassie is deposed and exiled and the remains of humankind's oldest known ancestor are found. The propellant in aerosol cans, CFC, is unmasked as the agent that is blowing a hole in the ozone layer. From space, *Mariner 10* sends back images of Mercury and Venus.

1974

Feb	**8**	Three US astronauts return after a record 84 days aboard *Skylab*
Apr	**25**	General Antonio de Spinola seizes power in Portugal
July	**1**	Argentine president Juan Perón dies aged 78; succeeded by his wife Isabel
	15	In Cyprus, the National Guard overthrows President Makarios; former terrorist Nicos Sampson takes over
	20	Turkey invades Cyprus
	23	Greek military government resigns
	24	Constantine Karamanlis returns from exile to form civilian government in Greece
Aug	**9**	Because of Watergate scandal, Richard M Nixon becomes the first US president to resign; Vice-President Gerald Ford succeeds him
Sep	**12**	A military coup overthrows Emperor Haile Selassie of Ethiopia
Nov	**12**	"Lucy", ancient ancestor of humans, is found in Ethiopia

MOZAMBIQUE INDEPENDENT

Since 1962, the Front for the Liberation of Mozambique (FRELIMO) has been fighting the 40,000-strong Portuguese Colonial Army. In 350 actions, the Portuguese inflict 4,000 casualties on FRELIMO. However, under the Marxist Samora Machel, the 10,000 men of FRELIMO are able to profit from the 1974 military coup in Portugal and seize larger areas of Mozambique. Machel negotiates from strength with the Portuguese and is elected the first president of Mozambique in 1975. Instability will dog the early years of the new country as Rhodesian-backed members of the anti-Communist MNR (Mozambican National Resistance) sabotage oil supplies and communications and South African forces raid southern Mozambique attacking African National Congress (ANC) bases.

NIXON RESIGNS

President Nixon resigns rather than face impeachment for his role in the Watergate burglary. His is succeeded by Vice-President Gerald Ford, who promptly pardons Nixon for his misdemeanours. Several Nixon aides go to jail after their trial.

PERON DIES

On the death of President Juan Perón, his wife Isabel becomes president, the first woman to hold such a job anywhere in Latin America. She proves to be a weak leader and is toppled by a military coup in March 1976.

ABOVE: Joint USA and USSR space vehicles on exhibition.

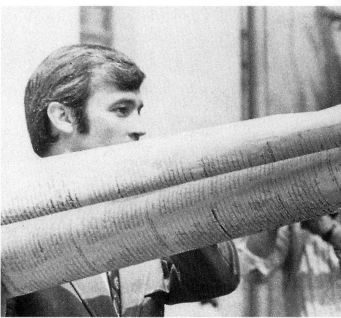

COUP IN PORTUGAL

A military coup led by General de Spinola overthrows the Portuguese government in the "Revolution of Flowers" and begins moves towards democracy. The Socialist leader, Mario Soares, returns from exile, leading his party to victory in the first democratic elections in April 1975. An attempted Communist coup by left-wing soldiers is defeated in November 1975, ensuring the survival of Portuguese democracy.

PARTITION IN CYPRUS

The National Guard overthrows President Makarios and installs former EOKA terrorist Nicos Sampson, who is in favour of union with Greece, in his place. Turkey promptly invades the north of the island and partitions it, setting up a separate state in February 1975.

SPACE MISSION RECORD

On February 8, three US astronauts return to Earth after having spent 84 days in *Skylab*, a space record; this is the last mission to the space station.

GERMAN TRIUMPH

The Dutch, playing free-flowing "total football" are everyone's choice to win the World Cup in West Germany, but the hosts take the title. Germany beats Holland 2–1 in the final.

GUINEA-BISSAU INDEPENDENT

Nationalists, the African Party for the Independence of Guinea and Cape Verde (PAIGC), have been fighting for independence from the colonial power Portugal since 1963. By 1973 PAIGC had gained control of two-thirds of Portuguese Guinea and the military coup in Lisbon in 1974 gives the country independence.

INCLUDE ME OUT

Sam Goldwyn, legendary film mogul, dies. Born Samuel Goldfish in Poland in 1882, he began life as a glove salesman. His films were always aimed at the family and he was famous for his "Goldwynisms" (such as "a verbal contract is not worth the paper it's written on"), not all of which he actually said.

HAILE SELASSIE DEPOSED

Emperor Haile Selassie is deposed in a left-wing military coup after a massive famine in 1973 weakens his rule. The new government introduces massive reforms, executes its enemies and kills Selassie in August 1975.

TOUR DE FORCE

Belgian cyclist Eddie Merckx crosses the line first in the Tour de France cycling race for the fifth time in six years. In the seven tours Merckx enters he wins 35 stages and wears the leader's yellow jersey for 96 days — both records.

EARLY FOOTPRINTS

At Laetoli, near Olduvai Gorge in Tanzania, fossils of hominids who lived three million years ago, the earliest known hominid footprints and the oldest human artefacts have been found by British archaeologist Richard Leakey and his team.

RUMBLING WITH THE GREATEST

Muhammad Ali regains the heavyweight boxing title in a fight against George Foreman in Kinshasa, Zaire. "The Rumble in The Jungle" goes eight rounds before Foreman is counted out.

ANOTHER MOON FOR JUPITER

US astronomer Charles T Kowall discovers another satellite of Jupiter, which is subsequently named Leda.

ABOVE: The tree-sized petition carrying signatures of people who believe that President Nixon should be impeached.

MARINER VISITS PLANETS
US space probe *Mariner 10* passes Venus and carries on to pass Mercury on March 29; it swings round the Sun to pass Mercury twice more, on September 21 and on March 16, 1975.

EASY SHAVES
Disposable lightweight plastic razors are developed by Gillette in Boston, USA.

ANCIENT AMERICAN
Anthropologists using new dating techniques discover that a human skull found in southern California is 48,000 years old, showing that people have lived in North America far longer than previously thought.

THE DUKE BOWS OUT
US jazz pianist Duke (Edward Kennedy) Ellington dies. One of the great men of big band jazz, his career lasted for 55 years.

AEROSOLS ACCUSED
US scientists Sherwood Rowland and Mario Molina point out that the chlorofluorocarbons (CFCs) used as propellants in aerosol cans could damage the ozone layer high above the Earth.

ANOTHER QUARK
US physicist Burton Richter discovers another quark (a sub-unit of protons and neutrons); this one is given the name of charmed quark.

RIGHT: The fearsome teeth of a shark loom out of the screen to terrify movie-goers in the blockbuster film *Jaws*.

GREEK CIVIL RULE RETURNS
As a result of the débâcle in Cyprus, the Greek military government resigns and civilian rule is restored in mainland Greece. The ex-premier, Constantine Karamanlis, returns from exile in Paris to form a new government, winning elections in November. In December, Greece votes to become a republic, ending any chance of a restoration of the monarchy.

"LUCY" DISCOVERED
US anthropologist Donald C Johanson discovers in Ethiopia the fossil skeleton of a female *Australopithecus afarensis*, an ape-like ancestor of humans. She is nicknamed "Lucy" after the Beatles song, "Lucy in the Sky with Diamonds".

POMPIDOU DIES
The president of France, Georges Pompidou, dies of an unnamed illness.

STANDING TALL IN CANADA
Toronto's stunning telecommunications tower, the CN tower, becomes the world's tallest free-standing structure. It is 553m (1,815ft) high.

SOLZHENITSYN EXPELLED
The first part of *The Gulag Archipelago* is published and its author Alexander Solzhenitsyn is expelled from the USSR. This marks the height of Solzhenitsyn's fame as Soviet dissident and prophet.

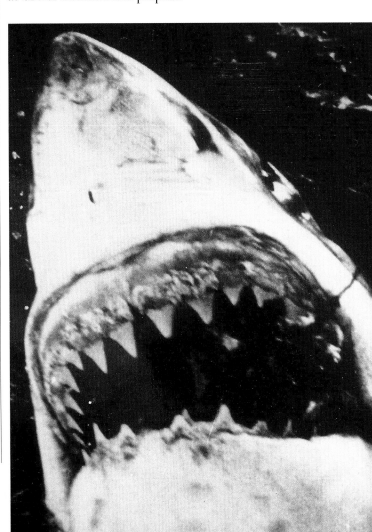

THE WATERGATE SCANDAL

ABOVE: Domestic Council Chief John D Ehrlichmann confers with his lawyer during his trial for his part in the Watergate affair.

ABOVE: John Ehrlichmann faces the press. Nixon's aides share the blame for the greatest political scandal of the 1970s.

LEFT: John Dean testifies at the trial of men implicated in the Watergate affair.

ABOVE: Senator Sam Erwin gives his testimony in what has become known as the Watergate trial.

ABOVE: Mountains of files and tapes, damning evidence on its way to the Watergate trial.

LEFT: President Nixon is left to face the music alone as even his lawyer testifies against him.

HANDSHAKE IN SPACE

The Vietnam War finally comes to an end. The Khmer Rouge, under Pol Pot, seizes Cambodia and embarks on a bloodbath. Indonesia invades East Timor. The US and Soviet Union link up in space when two of their spacecraft dock in Earth's orbit. The US sends out space probes in search of life on Mars while Soviet space probes send back the first-ever pictures from the planet Venus. General Franco dies and archaeologists find a 2,000-year old "army".

1975

Apr	5	President of Nationalist China, Chiang Kai-shek, dies aged 88
	17	Khmer Rouge takes control of Cambodia
	31	Vietnam War ends; Saigon surrenders to North Vietnam; mass evacuation of Americans
June	6	Israelis attack Lebanon
	12	Indian prime minister Indira Gandhi found guilty of corruption
	25	Mozambique gains independence
July	11	Archaeologists discover ancient terracotta "army" in China
	17	US astronauts and Soviet cosmonauts meet in space
Aug	1	Helsinki Conference on security and co-operation in Europe
Nov	10	Angola becomes independent of Portugal
	20	General Franco dies in Spain, aged 73
	22	Monarchy is restored to Spain
	24	Civil war begins in Angola
Dec	7	Indonesian troops invade East Timor

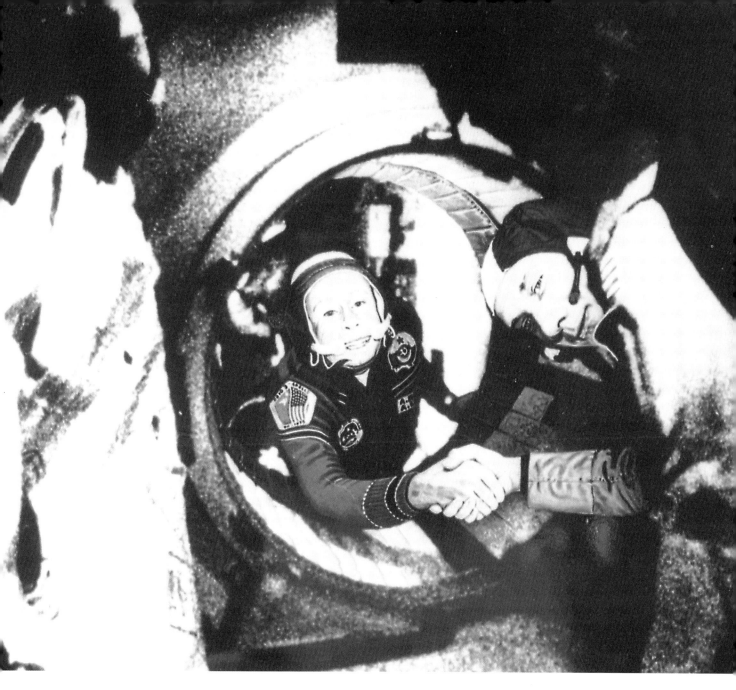

KHMER ROUGE SEIZE POWER

In Cambodia, Communist Khmer Rouge forces led by Pol Pot (1926–98) seize power in Cambodia and begin a four-year reign of terror. Within months, thousands of Cambodians are executed. The cities are emptied out and people forced to work on the land as the new government attempts to rebuild Cambodian society from Year Zero. More than 3.5 million people — half the total population — die during famine, fighting and political killings.

INDONESIA INVADES EAST TIMOR

Indonesian paratroopers invade the former Portuguese colony of East Timor, just before it gains independence. The country is engaged in a civil war between the Timorese Democratic Union (UDT), backed by the Timorese Democratic People's Union (APODETI), and the Communinist-backed Revolutionary Front for Independence (FREITLIN). The Indonesian move halts the fighting but is a land grab on the part of Indonesia. It provokes protests from the East Timorese and leads to violent repression and human rights abuses.

VIETNAM WAR ENDS

Communist North Vietnam finally takes over South Vietnam, ending the fifteen-year Vietnam War. The old southern capital of Saigon is renamed Ho Chi Minh City in honour of the Communist leader.

COLONIES INDEPENDENT

Mozambique gains its independence from Portugal, followed by the Cape Verde Islands, Angola and São Tomé and Príncipe. In South America, the former Dutch colony of Surinam gains its independence from the Netherlands.

MISSIONS TO MARS AND VENUS

The US launches two space probes — *Viking 1* and *Viking 2* — to look for signs of life on Mars. And in October, Russian space probes *Venera 9* and *Venera 10* send back the first pictures of the surface of Venus.

ABOVE: The USSR's *Soyuz* spacecraft and launch vehicle on their way to the launch pad.

ABOVE RIGHT: An artist's idea of what the *Soyuz* spacecraft will look like as it orbits the Earth.

CIVIL WAR IN ANGOLA

Within two weeks of gaining independence, civil war intensifies in Angola. Thousands die as rival groups struggle for control of the country. The Soviet Union and Cuba back the Marxist Popular Movement for the Liberation of Angola (MPLA); the US supports non-Marxist groups — the National Angolan Liberation Front (FNLA) and National Union for the Total Independence of Angola (UNITA).

INDIRA GANDHI FOUND GUILTY

Prime Minister Indira Gandhi (1917–84) is found guilty of electoral corruption. She declares a state of emergency, imposing censorship and imprisoning opposition leaders. The state of emergency lasts until January 1977, when she calls an election, losing heavily to the opposition Janata Party. However, she regains power in 1980.

TERRACOTTA ARMY

In China, archaeologists make a remarkable discovery when they uncover a vast army of 6,000 terracotta soldiers, near the ancient Chinese capital of Xian. The soldiers date back some 2,000 years and were probably made to guard the tomb of the first emperor in 206 BC. The terracotta soldiers stand in rows; each one is different from the other and was probably modelled on a real person.

NATIONS JOIN FOR HUMAN RIGHTS

In Helsinki, Finland, more than 30 European nations, plus the US and Canada, join together to sign the Final Act of the Conference on Security and Co-operation, promising to avoid the use of force in disputes and to respect human rights.

DEMOCRATIC SPAIN

General Franco dies and Spain becomes a monarchy once more as he is succeeded by King Juan Carlos. The new king begins moves to introduce democracy, granting an amnesty to all opponents of the previous government.

LEBANON CIVIL WAR

Seeking a pretext to attack the Palestine Liberation Organization (PLO) in southern Lebanon, the Israeli government launches operation "Peace for Galilee" in June. The attack takes them up to Beirut and costs the Israelis 368 killed and 2,388 wounded. Some 17,800 PLO, Syrians and civilians are killed and more than 30,000 wounded. By 1976, the PLO has evacuated Lebanon and abandoned heavy weapons.

MID-ATLANTIC DIVES

Three research submersibles make a total of 43 dives on the Mid-Atlantic Ridge, taking photographs and collecting rock samples.

BLACK TENNIS SUCCESS

At Wimbledon, Arthur Ashe (1943–93) beats fellow American Jimmy Connors to become the first black Wimbledon champion.

DISTANT GALAXIES

The enormity of space is emphasized when US astronomer Hyron Spinrad discovers that a faint galaxy he is studying is approximately eight billion light-years away from us. In Holland, Dutch astronomers at Leiden University map radio galaxy 3C236, the largest object in the universe, spanning eighteen million light years.

HANDSHAKE IN SPACE

US astronauts in an Apollo spacecraft link up with Soviet cosmonauts in a Soyuz spacecraft some 225km (140mi) above the Atlantic Ocean. One from each of their crew — US captain Tom Stafford and Soviet Alexei Leonov — shake hands through the hatches of their respective spacecraft. While linked together, the crews carry out joint scientific experiments and visit each other's crafts.

HEALTHY EATING

A healthy vegetarian diet becomes popular in the US and UK. It is influenced by the macrobiotic diet, based on brown rice, natural salt and green tea, which was fashionable in the 1960s. Its importance is also reinforced by a report from a British doctor indicating a link between bowel cancer and a low-fibre diet.

THE BOOK OF SAND

This collection of stories by Argentinian writer Jorge Luis Borges (1899–1986) confirms his international stature as a master of serious puzzles, play with truth and identity, and the role of time in fiction. His fiction is newly fashionable for its similarity to magic realism, but truly Borges is a one-off, belonging to no school.

NEW SHOPPING CENTRE

SITE Projects Inc have designed a stunning new shopping centre — the Almeda-Genoa — in Houston, Texas, which exemplifies their witty style. The façade seems to be crumbling, with holes, piles of bricks and jagged edges, a witty impersonation of a modern ruin.

RITUEL, IN MEMORIAM BRUNO MADERNA

French modernist composer Pierre Boulez (b. 1925) has created a work in memory of his Italian colleague, Bruno Maderna. The performing ensemble is divided into eight groups, dominated by a group of brass instruments, which play alternate sections. The work impresses with its manipulation of chords and rhythms.

FRANCISCO FRANCO
(1892–1975)

General Franco, leader of the Nationalists during the Spanish Civil War, and dictator of Spain since 1939, has died in Madrid. In 1969, he announced that the monarchy would be restored on his death.

ABOVE: Arthur Ashe, the first black male player to win the singles title at Wimbledon.

GAY ADVERTS

In the Netherlands, gays advertise openly as a result of a gay-recognition campaign conducted by COC (an organization for men) and MVM (Man-Vrouw Maatschappij or Man-Woman Society) for lesbians.

STREAKING

A new craze — streaking — has hit both sides of the Atlantic. In both the US and the UK, sports events are being interrupted by the arrival of naked people, both men and women, "streaking" across the playing areas.

PCS ON SALE

In the US, the Altair, the world's first personal computer (PC), is launched.

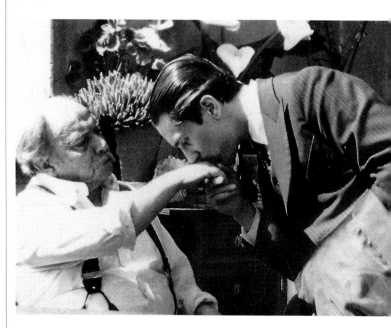

ABOVE: A scene from *The Godfather II*, winner of six Oscars.

APARTHEID VIOLENCE AND SUPERSONIC FLIGHT

Chairman Mao, Chinese cult figure and leader of the revolution, dies. Police fire on students in Soweto, South Africa, and African nations boycott the Olympic Games. Israeli commandos carry out a lightning rescue of hostages in Uganda. Concorde, the uniquely designed supersonic jet, begins regular passenger flights. Drug laws are liberalized in Holland.

1976

Jan	**21**	Concordes fly from Paris to Rio de Janeiro, and London to Bahrain, launching start of regular Concorde passenger flights
Feb	**4**	Winter Olympics open at Innsbruck, Austria
	27	Polisario Front declares independence of Western Sahara
Mar	**24**	Military coup in Argentina overthrows President Perón
Apr	**14**	Western Sahara partitioned between Morocco and Mauritania
June	**16**	South African police gun down students in Soweto and other black townships

July	**3**	Israeli commandos rescue hostages at Entebbe airport, Uganda
	20	US Viking space probe lands on Mars
	31	Olympic Games open, Montreal, Canada
Aug	**8**	Women launch peace movement in Northern Ireland
Sep	**9**	Chairman Mao Zedong dies in China aged 83
Oct	**23**	"Gang of Four", including Mao's widow, arrested in China
Nov	**2**	Democrat Jimmy Carter wins US presidential elections
	15	Parti Québécois wins large victory in Quebec elections, Canada
	27	Northern Irish women lead 30,000-strong peace march through London, UK

ABOVE: Operation Sail brings the tall ships from 28 nations to New York. This is the Portuguese ship *Sagres*.

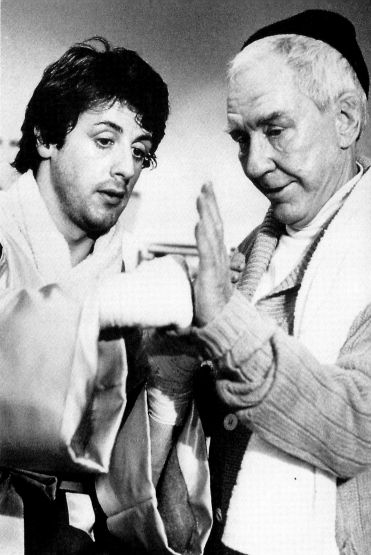

ABOVE: Surprise film hit of the year is *Rocky*, written by and starring Sylvester Stallone. It will be followed by a dynasty of *Rockies*.

WESTERN SAHARA DISPUTE

Following Franco's death, the Spanish colony of Western Sahara is divided between Morocco and Mauritania. However, a nationalist pro-independence movement known as Polisario, formed in 1973, rejects the partition and wages a guerrilla war. Mauritania later withdraws, leaving Morocco in sole control of the colony and fighting a lengthy campaign against Polisario, who fight for its independence.

KILLINGS IN SOWETO

Protest breaks out in the black township of Soweto, South Africa. This follows a government decision that secondary-school subjects must be taught in the Afrikaans language, which black South Africans see as the language of oppression. Police open fire; 76 students are killed and more than 1,000 are injured. Subsequently, the government drops its controversial education plans.

DUTCH LIBERALIZE DRUG LAWS

The drug laws are liberalized in the Netherlands with the revision of the Opium Act of 1928. Possession of soft drugs now has the lowest penalties in a new table of penalties for drug offences.

ENTEBBE RESCUE

Israeli commandos rescue 110 people held hostage in Entebbe airport, Uganda, after their Air France plane is hijacked by Palestinian guerrillas and flown to Entebbe. All seven hostage-takers and twenty Ugandan soldiers are killed in the raid, with the loss of only three hostages. Most of the Ugandan Air Force is destroyed on the ground by the Israelis.

SUPERSONIC BIRD

Air travel reaches supersonic speeds when two Anglo-French supersonic Concorde turbo jets, one taking off from Paris, one from London, begin a regular passenger service across the Atlantic. With its distinctive drooping nose and looking like a fantastic bird, Concorde cruises at 2,338km/h (1,461miph) and can cross the Atlantic in three hours.

QUEBEC VOTES

In Canada, the Parti Québécois, which is seeking an independent Quebec, wins a large majority in the state elections, led by René Levesque, and promises a referendum on independence from Canada. In May 1980 Quebec votes by a large majority to remain in Canada.

ABOVE: John Naber wins gold for the USA in the 100m men's backstroke event at the Montreal Olympics.

ARGENTINA "DIRTY WAR"

In Argentina, a military coup overthrows President Isabel Perón and a three-person junta led by Lt.-Gen. Jorge Videla is installed. The constitution is amended and the junta takes action against left-wing activists or those suspected of left-wing sympathies. Political and trade union activity is banned. Between 1976 and 1983, an estimated 10,000 to 15,000 people are murdered or "disappeared" during internal repression.

EINSTEIN ON THE BEACH

American composer Philip Glass (b. 1937) has produced a new opera, *Einstein on the Beach*. In typically minimalist mode, very little happens, although the opera has hypnotic qualities. It cements Glass's position as a major opera composer.

NO LIFE ON MARS

The US space probe *Viking 1* lands on Mars and sends close-up pictures of the surface of Mars back to Earth. These reveal a barren surface littered with rocks and no signs of life. But there are signs of dry river beds, showing that water once existed there. The space probes also scoop up soil samples and analyse them for the presence of micro-organisms.

ROOTS

American author Alex Haley (1921–92) has published a new book, *Roots*, the saga of a black African sold into slavery in the USA, and of his descendants. In this novel Haley, who has already published a biography of black American activist Malcolm X, depicts poverty and racial hatred as modern forms of enslavement for black people. It will be a phenomenal success.

WINTER OLYMPICS

The Winter Olympics are held at Innsbruck in Austria, using the facilities from 1968, after Denver, USA withdraws. Austrian hero Franz Klammer takes gold in the men's downhill event while Rosi Mittermaier wins the women's downhill and a further gold and silver for Germany.

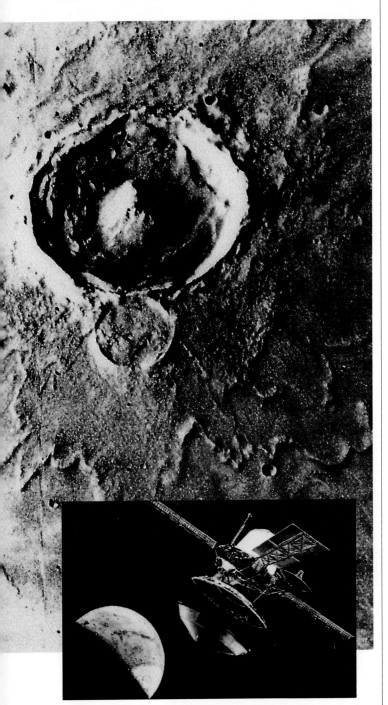

ABOVE: The surface of Mars photographed by *Viking 1*. The inset shows a model of the Viking spacecraft in orbit round the red planet.

WOMEN PRIESTS

The Episcopalian Church — the American wing of the Anglican church — approves the ordination of women Christian priests. Previously, in July 1974, four American Episcopalian bishops ordained eleven women priests in contravention of Church law.

IRISH WOMEN MARCH FOR PEACE

The women of Belfast, in Northern Ireland, launch a peace campaign. Subsequently, they organize a protest march against continued fighting in Northern Ireland, which is joined by 30,000 people. American folk singer Joan Baez (b. 1941) gives support.

SYMPHONY OF SORROWFUL SONGS

Polish composer Henryk Górecki produces a new symphony — *Symphony No 3* or *Symphony of Sorrowful Songs*. Its use of traditional form (canons) and a tonal idiom mark a turning-away from the harshly modernist style of the composer's earlier works.

GYMNAST SHINES AT BOYCOTTED GAMES

Amid strict security and unfinished building, the Olympic Games open in Montreal, Canada. African nations boycott the games in protest at New Zealand's rugby connection with South Africa. Romanian gymnast Nadia Comaneci, who is aged only fourteen, gives a dazzling display, winning five medals and the affection of the spectators.

HITE REPORT

US feminist Shere Hite (b. 1943) publishes *The Hite Report: A Nationwide Study of Female Sexuality*. The result of five years' research, it includes information from 3,000 women on all aspects of female sexuality. It challenges many traditional assumptions about women's sexuality and causes a sensation.

MAO ZEDONG (MAO TSE-TUNG) (1893–1976)

Chinese Marxist leader Mao Zedong has died. Mao was one of the founders of the Chinese Communist Party when it was founded in 1921, and a leader in the long struggle against the Japanese and then the Kuomintang Nationalists. In 1949, he became first chairman of the new People's Republic of China. In 1958, he launched the disastrous Great Leap Forward of agricultural reforms and resigned as head of state later that year. But he remained party chairman, and in 1962, his *Little Red Book*, containing his many sayings and thoughts, was fervently studied all over China. In 1966, now a cult figure, he set alight the Cultural Revolution with the aim of overthrowing the enemies of Socialism. At the end of this period, 1970, he became supreme commander of the nation.

ABOVE: Computer games make their début with this exciting game of virtual tennis. Over 200 such games are available.

LEGIONNAIRES' DISEASE

The first outbreak of a new type of pneumonia occurs at an American Legion convention in Philadelphia, USA; it is named Legionnaires' Disease.

MOUNTAIN BIKE RACE

The first official mountain bike race takes place on a 3.2km (2mi) course on Mount Tamalpais.

MOON ROCK DATED

Researchers discover that Moon rock sample 76535 is at least 4.54 billion years old.

ABOVE: The Washington Redskins battle with the New York Jets.

ABOVE: Rock fans chill out among the laid-back crowd.

ABOVE: Some fans find inspiration for their own musical efforts.

STADIUM ROCK CONCERTS

ABOVE: Rock legends Lynyrd Skynyrd electrify the audience at the RFK stadium open air concert.

STAR WARS AND MICROSOFT

Black South African activist Steve Biko is killed in police custody. African nations boycott the Olympic Games. Charter 77 calls for human rights in Czechoslovakia. Nineteen-year-old Bill Gates founds Microsoft. The inside-out Pompidou Centre is a dramatic new Paris landmark. A new film, *Star Wars*, opens to rapturous audiences. A new medical development — balloon angioplasty — offers new treatment for heart disease. Elvis Presley, "the King of Rock and Roll", dies.

1977

Jan	7	Charter 77 calls for human rights in Czechoslovakia
	17	Gary Gilmore is executed in US, the first execution for ten years
Feb	18	Archbishop of Uganda murdered by Idi Amin's forces
Mar	10	Astronomers discover rings of planet Uranus
	27	Jumbo jets collide in the Canary Islands, killing more than 500 people
June	15	First democratic elections in Spain since 1936 lead to victory for centre parties
Aug	16	King of Rock, Elvis Presley, dies in Memphis, US, aged 42
Sep	7	USA and Panama sign a treaty returning Canal Zone to Panama
	12	Black South African activist Steve Biko is killed in police custody
Nov	19	Egyptian President Sadat visits Israel on a peace mission

AIR DISASTER

Two jumbo jets collide at Tenerife airport, in the Canary Islands. More than 570 people are killed, most of them American holidaymakers. It is the worst disaster in the history of aviation.

CHARTER 77 CALLS FOR HUMAN RIGHTS

In Czechoslovakia, 240 intellectuals and dissidents sign Charter 77, calling for the Czech government to implement the human rights it agreed to support as part of the 1975 Helsinki Declaration. Several of the signatories are arrested, and the leader, Jan Potocka, dies after police interrogation.

POMPIDOU CENTRE

Italian Renzo Piano and Englishman Richard Rogers design a revolutionary new-style arts centre in Paris — the Pompidou Centre. It provokes considerable controversy. All the services (drains, wiring, elevators, heating ducts) are suspended on the outside of the building, making a striking decorative amalgam. This leaves the interior free for broad uninterrupted exhibition spaces.

STAR WARS

A new science-fiction film is released and is a smash success. Directed by US film maker, George Lucas (b. 1944), it is called *Star Wars*. It features the latest in special effects as well as starring a princess, dashing hero, and two robots — R2D2 and C-3PO. Two more films will follow, with more in the pipeline.

MICROSOFT FOUNDED

Paul Allen and Bill Gates (b. 1955) set up a new computer software company, Microsoft. Gates is only nineteen; be will be a millionare within ten years and Microsoft will be the world's largest producer of micro-computer software.

BIKO KILLED

Black consciousness leader Steve Biko is killed in custody by South African police. He was one of a number of black leaders who have been arrested under new security legislation. A post mortem reveals brain injuries. Some 15,000 people attend his funeral. Biko's death causes an international outcry, increasing international pressure on the apartheid National Party government, which wins a record majority in white-only elections in November.

EGYPT TALKS PEACE WITH ISRAEL

President Sadat (1918–81) of Egypt offers peace to Israel, alienating other Arab states. At the end of November, he visits Israel and addresses the Knesset, the Israeli parliament.

SIR CHARLES SPENCER (CHARLIE) CHAPLIN (1889–1977)

English comedian and film-maker Charlie Chaplin has died. After a tough childhood he became a member of the Fred Karno vaudeville company and went with them to Hollywood, where he was to make something like a film a fortnight between 1914 and 1916. He created the flat-footed, baggy-trousered, bowler-hatted tramp still regarded with affection today. His comic talent was at its best in the silent cinema, and he will be remembered for classics such as *The Kid* (1920), *The Gold Rush* (1925), and *City Lights* (1931).

TOP AND ABOVE: The Trans-Alaska oil pipeline under construction. It will be 1,280km (800mi) long.

RIGHT: An earth-moving machine helps to build the 576km (360mi) service road for the Alaska pipeline.

LIFE IN THE OCEAN DEEP

US scientists aboard the submersible *Alvin* discover worms, crabs and fish living in warm water from vents in the Galápagos Rift near Ecuador, far from sunlight and feeding on bacteria.

DEATH PENALTY BACK

The death penalty returns to the USA when convicted murderer Gary Gilmore is executed by firing squad. This is the first execution to take place for ten years and follows considerable protest and public debate.

CANAL BACK TO PANAMA

US president Jimmy Carter and General Omar Torrijos of Panama sign a treaty to return the Canal Zone to Panamanian control by 2000.

APPLE RIPENS

The Apple II, the first personal computer sold ready assembled, goes on the market.

ARCHBISHOP MURDERED

In Uganda, President Idi Amin's regime becomes increasingly repressive when Amin's forces murder the human-rights advocate, the Most Reverend Janani Luwum, Archbishop of Uganda.

DEMOCRATIC SPAIN

The first democratic elections since 1936 are held in Spain. They lead to victory for Adolfo Suárez (b. 1932) and the Democratic Centre Party.

BALLOON ANGIOPLASTY

Swiss doctor Andreas Grünzig devises balloon angioplasty. This involves inserting a tiny inflatable balloon into a blocked artery to clear it.

ABOVE: Rock music becomes an industry; vinyl is worth money.

BELOW: Greek-born opera diva Maria Callas dies this year.

MARIA MENEGHINI CALLAS
(1923–1977)

The great operatic soprano Maria Callas has died in Paris. Born in New York into a Greek family, she studied at the Athens National Conservatory from the age of about fifteen. Her début was in Athens in 1940. She sang many roles from Brunnhilde to Violetta, and her prima-donna status was secured by her first performance at La Scala in 1950 in *Aida*. She worked with conductors such as Giulini and Karajan, and with producers such as Visconti and Zeffirelli, drawing record-breaking audiences. Her last performance was in *Tosca* at Covent Garden in 1965 but she continued to make records and give occasional concerts. Her unsurpassed musicianship was accompanied by great dramatic talent. Her glamour made her the focus of attention in private as well as public life.

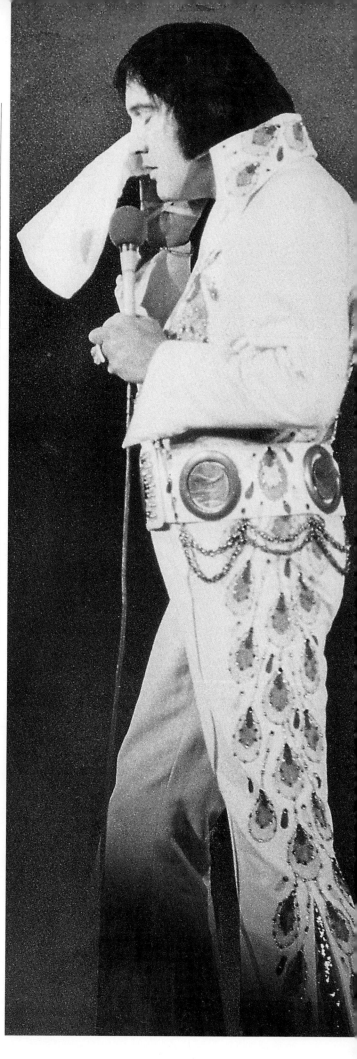

ELVIS AARON PRESLEY
(1935–1977)

Elvis Presley, the world's most popular pop star, has died suddenly at his home in Memphis of the accumulated effects of overweight and narcotics. Presley was born in Mississippi and first sang in his local Pentecostal church choir. He came to fame with his first single "That's All Right Mama" in 1954 and will always be remembered for his 1956–58 rock and roll classics such as "Heartbreak Hotel", "Hound Dog" and "Don't be Cruel", and the songs from the 1958 films of the same names, "Jailhouse Rock" and "King Creole". In the 1960s the King of Rock and Roll took to crooning and gave up live performances, but in the 1970s he had again been performing frequently, to huge audiences, in Las Vegas nightclubs.

URANUS RINGS FOUND
Astronomers discover the rings of the planet Uranus, confirmed and counted by *Voyager 2* in 1985.

GOSSAMER CONDOR FLIES
In California, cyclist Bryan Allen pedals a 36kg (81lb) aircraft, the Gossamer Condor, round a 1.9km (1.19mi) figure-of-eight course in 6 minutes 22.5 seconds to win an $87,000 prize for human-powered flight.

SMALLPOX ERADICATED
The world's last case of the disease smallpox occurs in Somalia, following a campaign by the World Health Organization to eradicate it. Formal eradication is announced in 1980.

RIGHT: Elvis Presley in the Vegas years that preceded his early death, apparently from an overdose of prescription drugs.

WERNHER VON BRAUN
(1912–1977)

German-born rocket expert Wernher von Braun has died. Having perfected the V-2 rockets used by Germany during World War ll, he and his team surrendered at the end of the war and took up residence in the USA, where he continued his work. An American citizen since 1955, he was responsible for the development of the satellite *Explorer l* (1958). As director of the Marshal Space Flight Center (1960–70), he developed the rocket used in the 1969 *Apollo S* Moon landing.

TEST-TUBE BABIES BORN

The world's first "test-tube" baby is born, following the development of *in-vitro* fertilization. Astronomers observe a new moon, that of the planet Pluto, and US space probes begin mapping the surface of Venus. Civil war breaks out in Nicaragua. Egypt and Israel make peace at Camp David. The world's worst oil spill to date occurs and environmentalists become increasingly concerned about the impact of CFCs on the ozone layer.

1 9 7 8

Mar	1	Communist support enables a new Italian government in "Historic Compromise"
	8	UN recognizes March 8 as International Women's Day
	16	World's worst oil spill occurs off coast of France
May	20	US launches space probe *Pioneer I*, which goes into orbit around Venus
June	22	Pluto's moon, Charon, is discovered
July	25	The world's first "test-tube" baby is born
Aug	17	First manned transatlantic crossing in a hot-air balloon
	22	Kenyan statesman Jomo Kenyatta dies aged about 89
	22	Sandinistas seize control of parliament building, Nicaragua
Sep	5	Peace summit at Camp David between US president Carter, President Sadat of Egypt, and Israeli prime minister Begin
	15	US boxer Muhammad Ali beats Leon Spinks
Oct	16	Archbishop of Cracow, Karol Wojtyla, becomes first non-Italian pope for more than 400 years
Nov	29	More than 900 people die in cult mass suicide, Guyana
Dec	25	Vietnam begins full-scale invasion of Cambodia

ABOVE: Women march in Washington to protest against the government's seven-year delay in ratifying the Equal Opportunities Amendment.

HISTORIC COMPROMISE

A "Historic Compromise" is agreed between Christian Democrats and Communists in Italy, allowing Prime Minister Andreotti (b. 1919) to take power with Communist Party support. The Italian Communist Party is the biggest in Western Europe and the deal gives it influence in government for the first time since the war.

CAMP DAVID PEACE SUMMIT

A summit held at the US presidential retreat at Camp David achieves peace between Egypt and Israel. In the deal, between President Anwar Sadat of Egypt and the Israeli prime minister, Menachem Begin, Israel agrees to give back the Sinai Peninsula to Egypt. The deal is heavily criticized in the Arab world.

POLISH POPE

Polish-born John Paul II (b. 1920) becomes the first non-Italian pope for 435 years after the deaths of both Paul VI and John Paul I. A conservative, John Paul II uses his office to attack Communist control of Eastern Europe and liberal tendencies inside the Church.

VIETNAM INVADES CAMBODIA

Vietnam invades to overthrow the Khmer Rouge government. The Vietnamese seize the capital, Phnom Penh, in January and install the rebel leader, Heng Samrin, in power. The discovery of the killing fields, where the Khmer Rouge disposed of their millions of victims, causes international outrage. Despite their fall from power, Khmer Rouge rebels keep up armed resistance until their leader Pol Pot dies, probably by suicide, in 1998.

NICARAGUAN CIVIL WAR

In August, guerrillas of the Sandinista National Liberation Front fight the government of President Anastasio Somoza in Nicaragua, taking over the parliament building in Managua. By September, the rebellion is suppressed at a cost of 5,000 killed and 10,000 wounded.

TEST-TUBE BABIES

Louise Brown, the world's first "test-tube" baby, is born in the UK. This follows work by physiologist Robert Edwards and gynaecologist Patrick Steptoe, who have devised a method of fertilizing an egg outside the human body. The new technique is known as *in-vitro* and involves fertilizing an ovum in a test-tube. The embryo is then replaced in the mother's uterus where it develops naturally. Some months later, in October, a second "test-tube" baby is born in Calcutta, India, to Bela and Pravat Agarwal.

PLUTO'S MOON OBSERVED

US astronomers James W Christy and Robert S Harrington of the US Naval Observatory, Washington, discover that the planet Pluto has a moon. It is named Charon. Earlier attempts to detect a moon have been unsuccessful because Pluto is so remote.

VENUS SPACE PROBES

The National Aeronautics and Space Administration (NASA) launches two space probes: *Pioneer 1* in May, and *Pioneer 2* in August. They go into orbit around the planet Venus in December, and map the surface using radar.

CFCS BANNED

The use of chlorofluorocarbons (CFCs) is banned in the USA and Sweden because they are thought to be harming the ozone layer. CFCs are synthetic chemicals used as propellants in aerosols, refrigerants in fridges and air conditioners and in the manufacture of foam boxes used for take-away foods.

GOLDA MEIR
(1898–1978)

Former Israeli prime minister Golda Meir has died. Born in Russia, she lived in the United States before settling in Palestine in 1921. Having been involved in the Labour Movement, she became Israeli ambassador to the Soviet Union on the founding of the new state. In 1949 she became a government minister and in 1969 was elected prime minister. She resigned after the fourth Arab-Israeli war in 1974.

VIRUS GENES EXAMINED

The genome (genetic structure) of Virus SV40 is worked out, the first organism to be examined and mapped in this way.

EVITA

A new musical, composed by Andrew Lloyd Webber with lyrics by Tim Rice, has opened. Called *Evita*, it is based on the life of Argentinian leader Eva Perón and achieves international success.

SUPERMAN THE MOVIE

Starring Christopher Reeve and directed by Richard Donner, a new movie, *Superman*, has opened. Featuring wonderful special effects, it is one of the most expensive films ever made.

MAJOR OIL SPILL

The Amoco Cadiz super-tanker runs aground in storms in the Atlantic off the Brittany coast and splits in two. Some 80,000 tons of crude oil devastate French beaches, wildlife habitats and fishing grounds. It is the worst oil spill to date.

TRANSATLANTIC BALLOON FLIGHT

Three US businessmen complete the first manned transatlantic balloon crossing from the US to France in 137 hours 18 minutes.

INTERNATIONAL WOMEN'S DAY

March 8 is officially International Women's Day. Seventy years ago, on March 8, 1908, hundreds of women clothing workers in New York demanded the vote, and in 1910 the Socialist Women's International led by German feminist Clara Zetkin (1857–1933), named the date International Women's Day. Now the United Nations has made it official.

TALES OF THE CITY

Armistead Maupin publishes *Tales of the City*. Stories of life in San Francisco, they began as a regular feature in the *San Francisco Chronicle*. Now they appear in book form for the first time, bringing Maupin widespread recognition.

MASS SUICIDE

More than 900 members of the People's Temple, a religious cult under the leadership of the Reverend Jim Jones, located in the rainforest of Guyana, commit mass suicide. The dead include adults and children, who have died by drinking cyanide, some under duress.

VERSATILE FOOD PROCESSOR

The Magimix electronic food processor comes on to the market. Designed in France, it combines several functions, such as blending, shredding, chopping and even kneading, in one operation.

DYSON CLEANER

Centrifugal force is harnessed by British inventor James Dyson to extract dust and dirt from the industrial or household environment. His Dual Cyclone is the only alternative to the vacuum cleaner since Hoover's first suction cleaner appeared in 1908.

SKATEBOARDING CRAZE

Teenagers have taken up a new craze — skateboarding. Sidewalks and parks in both the US and the UK are full of young people performing skateboarding stunts.

ARGENTINA BEATS HOLLAND

The Dutch again fall to the home country in the final game of the football World Cup. Argentina beats them 3–1 in front of an ecstatic crowd.

ALI VICTORIOUS

US boxing star Muhammad Ali beats Leon Spinks, who had taken the title from him, to regain the heavyweight boxing crown for an unprecedented third time.

IRONMAN RACE

The Ironman race in Hawaii begins when sports enthusiasts combine a 4km (2.4mi) swim, an 180km (112mi) bike race and a 42km (26mi) marathon to find the best all-round athlete. The race has grown from small beginnings to become a prestige event and has spawned other, shorter triathlons.

JOMO KENYATTA
(c.1889–1978)

Kenyan leader Jomo Kenyatta has died. The former herd boy, who eventually studied at London University, was president of the Pan-African Federation and, from 1946, president of the Kenyan African Union. He was the Kikuyu people's Mau Mau leader during the struggles for repossession of their lands and was imprisoned from 1952–59. He became prime minister in 1963 in the period up to independence and became president in 1964.

REVOLUTION IN IRAN

The Shah of Iran flees into exile. Fundamentalist spiritual leader Ayatollah Khomeini takes over and US hostages are seized. The Sandinistas gain victory in Nicaragua. The USSR invades Afghanistan. Idi Amin's rule comes to an end. A potentially catastrophic accident at Three Mile Island draws attention to the dangers of nuclear power. Space probes send back photographs of Venus and Saturn and a tiny personal stereo — the Sony Walkman — goes on sale.

1979

Jan	8	Vietnamese occupy Phnom Penh, Cambodia, overthrowing Khmer Rouge regime
	16	Shah of Iran flees into exile
Mar	26	Israel and Egypt sign peace treaty
	28	Major accident occurs at Three Mile Island nuclear plant, USA
Apr	2	Mass graves are discovered in north-east Cambodia, evidence of mass murders carried out by Khmer Rouge
	11	Tanzanian forces overthrow Ugandan dictator Idi Amin
May	4	Margaret Thatcher becomes the first British woman prime minister
June	18	USSR and US sign Strategic Arms Limitation Treaty (SALT 2)
July	17	General Somoza flees Nicaragua after Sandinista victory
Nov	4	Followers of Ayatollah Khomeini seize US embassy in Tehran and take hostages
Dec	4	First successful launch of European Space Agency's rocket, *Ariane*
	10	Mother Teresa wins Nobel Peace Prize
	27	USSR invades Afghanistan

ISLAMIC REVOLUTION IN IRAN

The Shah flees into exile in Egypt as supporters of the fundamentalist religious leader, Ayatollah Khomeini (1900–89), seize power. His flight follows months of demonstrations and unrest and is greeted with enormous celebration. The Ayatollah returns from exile in Paris and institutes an Islamic republic. In November, students seize the US embassy in Tehran and take its 63 US staff and 40 other people hostage, demanding the return of the Shah for trial. The crisis leads to a confrontation between Iran and the USA. The hostages are not released until January 1981, after 444 days in captivity.

SANDINISTA VICTORY

Fighting breaks out again in Nicaragua. This time the Marxist Sandinistas are better armed, and equipped by Cuba. By July, they have ousted Nicaraguan dictator General Anastastio Somoza, who flees to the USA. This brings to an end a cruel and corrupt dictatorship. The Sandinista rebels, named after a revolutionary leader killed in the 1930s, form a provisional government.

EL SALVADOR REBELS

A communist guerrilla movement, the Farabundo Marti Liberation Front (FMLN), is waging war against El Salvador's right-wing government.

THREE MILE ISLAND

A major accident occurs at Three Mile Island nuclear power station in Pennsylvania. Owing to a technical error, a nuclear reactor overheats, causing the release of some radioactive gas. The possibility of a total meltdown causes the evacuation of thousands of people. The crisis is averted but it is the worst nuclear accident in the USA and alerts people to the possible dangers of nuclear power.

THE CHINA SYNDROME

American actress Jane Fonda (b. 1937) stars as the journalist investigating the story of meltdown at a nuclear reactor in a new film, *The China Syndrome*. The title comes from the fire which, it is said, could theoretically burn through the Earth to China. The film gains new topicality after the accident at the power plant at Three Mile Island.

UGANDAN CIVIL WAR

Ugandan dictator Idi Amin (b. 1925) has annexed the Kagera area of northern Tanzania, near the Ugandan border. Tanzanian president Julius Neyere (b. 1922) sends troops to support the Uganda National Liberation Army (UNLA) which has been formed to fight the dictatorial and increasingly bloodthirsty Idi Amin. As they approach Kampala, Libyan troops, who have come to Amin's assistance, attack and halt them briefly, but UNLA takes the capital and Amin is forced to flee. A civilian government returns to power.

CHINA INVADES VIETNAM

Chinese forces invade the Cao Bang area of northern Vietnam to punish the country for its invasion of Cambodia. The Chinese are fought to a standstill and forced to withdraw after suffering 20,000 killed and wounded. Vietnamese casualties are estimated to be 27,000 killed and wounded.

APOCALYPSE NOW

Directed by Francis Ford Coppola (b. 1939), the film *Apocalypse Now* is a loose adaptation of Joseph Conrad's novel *Heart of Darkness*, set in the Vietnam War. The film stuns audiences with its images of helicopters and warfare, and its gripping tale of Captain Benjamin Willard's (Martin Sheen) quest for Kurtz (Marlon Brando).

ABOVE AND LEFT: Gays and lesbians march on Washington to demand human rights.

ABOVE: The mellow proprietor of a real drugstore in Washington DC. The shops sells marijuana and the equipment needed to use it.

THATCHER VICTORY

In the UK, Margaret Thatcher (b. 1925) becomes the first British woman prime minister when her Conservative Party wins the general election. She embarks on a right-wing, free-market policy of privatization of state assets and a tough anti-trade union policy.

SALT-2

US president Carter (b. 1924) and Soviet leader Leonid Brezhnev (1906–82) sign the SALT-2 (Strategic Arms Limitation Talks) Treaty, agreeing to restrict each side to 2,250 strategic nuclear missiles. The deal is never ratified by the US Senate and is abandoned as the arms race intensifies during the early 1980s.

POST-MODERNISM

Jean-François Lyotard publishes a new study summing up a distanced, ironic approach, which comes to be known as post-modernism, a term that will be widely used in the coming decade in fields as diverse as literature and architecture.

USSR INVADES AFGHANISTAN

Intending to make a quick change in government, Soviet president Leonid Brezhnev sends 55,000 troops into Afghanistan to oust President Amin and replace him with a new Afghan leader, Babrak Karmal. This leads to a long-drawn-out guerrilla war. The Communist coup is opposed by fundamentalist Muslim tribal groups, who are assisted by the USA.

PEDALLING OVER THE CHANNEL

In June the 34kg (77lb) aeroplane Gossamer Albatross flies across the English Channel powered by US biologist Bryan Allen, who drives the propeller using bicycle-type pedals.

THE DINNER PARTY

American feminist and artist Judy Chicago's multimedia creation, *The Dinner Party*, goes on show. A tribute to women's history, it takes the form of a triangular table with 39 symbolic place settings, each representing a key woman. The whole thing is positioned on a floor inscribed with the names of 999 other women of note.

PHOTOGRAPHS FROM SPACE

Photographs of Saturn are transmitted by US space probe *Pioneer 11*, launched in 1973. *Voyager 1*, launched in 1977 to take advantage of an alignment of Jupiter, Saturn, Uranus and Neptune, transmitted photographs of Jupiter's rings in March. Passing within 4,800km (3,000mi) of each planet's surface, *Voyager 1* and *2* discover Jupiter's powerful magnetic field, and its continuous thunderstorms. They also photograph the planet's moons.

AIR-CUSHIONED TRAINERS

The first air-cushioned trainer is developed by engineer Frank Rudy at Nike. The company was formed in 1967 to market track shoes with nylon uppers developed by William J Bowerman, the track-coach of the University of Oregon. Trainers will becomes the style statement for young people of the Eighties.

LEFT: Israeli leader Menachem Begin signing the Middle East peace agreement at Camp David. President Jimmy Carter, architect of the agreement, looks on.

RIGHT: The accident at Three Mile Island nuclear reactor polarizes opinion on the usefulness and safety of nuclear power. Thousands take to the streets to protest.

ABOVE: Cars in the USA line up for petrol during the politically inspired oil crisis that slows down the late Seventies.

LEFT: Smart shop owners stockpile cans of petrol in anticipation of panic buying by their customers.

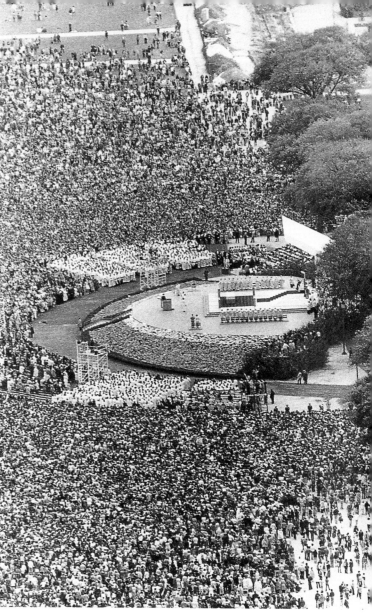

SKYLAB CRASHES

The US space station *Skylab I* falls back to Earth. It has travelled 140 million km (87 million mi) in orbit since its launch in 1973.

GLUONS DETECTED

US scientists detect the existence of subatomic particles that hold quarks together. They are called gluons.

PEACE PRIZE

Mother Teresa (1910–97), an Albanian Roman Catholic nun, founder of the Missionaries of Charity religious order who works among the poor in Calcutta, is awarded the Nobel Peace Prize.

WALKMANS

The Japanese company, Sony, has launched the Sony Walkman, a portable personal stereo cassette player with headphones. It is so small that you can listen to music anywhere, even when walking around the streets.

NEW DINOSAUR CLUE

US scientists Luis and Walter Alvarez discover traces of a huge meteorite impact some 65 million years ago. They propose that dust from it may have changed the climate and caused the extinction of the dinosaurs.

IRANIAN WOMEN PROTEST

March 8, International Women's Day, is marked by protests by Iranian women against strict Islamic laws introduced under Ayatollah Khomeini.

ROLLERBLADING

Brothers Scott and Brennan Olsen create the first popular Rollerblade or in-line skate in Minneapolis, USA. Keen ice skaters, they wanted to be able to practise in summer, when there is no ice.

OPPOSITE ABOVE: Disco fever still rages at the terminally hip New York night clubs.

OPPOSITE BELOW: Two years after *Saturday Night Fever*, young hopefuls still dance for prizes.

THE GLOBAL VILLAGE

The 1980s see countries of the world coming closer, largely through growing awareness of environmental destruction. Poverty and famine in Africa wake the world's conscience as the gap between rich and poor widens. However, discovery of a hole in the ozone layer and nuclear fallout from Chernobyl prove that pollution affects all equally. Politically, the decade sees monumental change as the INF Treaty is signed, the Berlin Wall comes down and the Cold War ends.

OPPOSITE: Live Aid, the one-off rock concert that raises over £50 million for famine relief.

1980–1989

KEY EVENTS OF THE DECADE

- IRAN–IRAQ WAR
- THE FALKLANDS CONFLICT
- CIVIL WARS IN CENTRAL AMERICA
- THREE MILE ISLAND AND CHERNOBYL
- LIVE AID AND FAMINE RELIEF
- INF TREATY
- IRANGATE
- SOVIET BLOC BREAKS UP
- COLD WAR ENDS

- ORGAN TRANSPLANTS
- AIDS EPIDEMIC
- SPACE SHUTTLE AND SPACE LAB LAUNCHED
- OZONE HOLE DISCOVERED
- COMPACT DISCS
- POST-MODERNISM

WORLD POPULATION: 4,450 MILLION

SOLIDARITY AND WAR

Independent trade unions are recognized in Poland and begin to change the country. Iraq invades neighbouring Iran, sparking off war between the two countries. Former film star Ronald Reagan wins the US presidential election for the Republican Party. Princess Beatrix becomes Queen of the Netherlands. US attempt to rescue hostages in Tehran fails. A new craze for health and fitness sweeps through the US and Europe. President Tito of Yugoslavia dies and John Lennon is assassinated by a crazed fan.

1980

Feb	**13**	Winter Olympics are held at Lake Placid, New York State
Apr	**18**	Rhodesia gains legal independence as Zimbabwe
	25	US attempt to rescue hostages in Tehran ends in disaster
	30	Crown Princess Beatrix becomes Queen of the Netherlands
May	**4**	President Tito of Yugoslavia dies aged 88
	18	Mount St. Helens volcano erupts, Washington State, US
July	**19**	The 22nd Olympic Games open in Moscow
Aug	**31**	Independent trade unions are recognized in Poland
Sep	**22**	Iraq invades Iran
Nov	**4**	Republican Ronald Reagan wins US presidential election
Dec	**8**	Former Beatle John Lennon is shot dead outside his home in New York, USA

ABOVE: Public grief after former Beatle John Lennon is shot dead in New York.

IRAN–IRAQ WAR

Profiting from disorder in Iran, Iraq invades neighbouring Iran in an attempt to gain the strategic Shatt al-Arab waterway to the Persian Gulf. During the eight-year war that follows, Iraq employs chemical weapons and both sides fire ballistic missiles at major cities. Iraq also launches anti-ship missile attacks against tankers shipping oil from Iran. In 1988, Iran accepts a UN-sponsored cease-fire.

FAILED RESCUE

In a rescue attempt, nicknamed "Operation Eagle Claw", the US sends men from Delta Force 322km (200mi) into Iran to rescue the hostages being held in the US embassy in Tehran. At a re-fuelling operation in the desert, there is an equipment failure. The Force withdraws but the aeroplane crashes into a tanker aircraft causing the death of eight Americans and injury to others.

ZIMBABWE

After the collapse of the rebel white-only government in Rhodesia, Britain agrees a new multiracial constitution for the country and grants its last African colony independence as Zimbabwe. Robert Mugabe (b. 1924) becomes prime minister of the new country.

TITO DIES

Yugoslav president Josip Tito dies. His death leads to an eight-man collective presidency. Tensions soon begin to emerge between Serbs and Croats in the country.

ABOVE: The coronation of Queen Beatrix of the Netherlands in Amsterdam's Nieuwe Kerk; her husband Prince Claus looks on.

BEATRIX BECOMES QUEEN

In the Netherlands, Queen Beatrix (b. 1938) takes the throne after her mother, Queen Juliana, abdicates.

HEALTH — THE NEW FASHION

Health clubs and gyms open all over the USA, the UK and Europe, offering electronic running machines, classes in aerobic exercise and dance-exercise, to cater for the desire for fitness. The trend influences fashions and cosmetic products.

POLISH SOLIDARITY

After two months of strikes and demonstrations against the government, independent trade unions are recognized in Poland in an agreement between Lech Walesa (b. 1943), strike leader in the Lenin shipyard in Gdansk, and the Polish government. The Solidarity union is formally registered in October.

REAGAN ELECTED PRESIDENT

Ronald Reagan (b. 1911) wins the US presidential election for the Republicans, defeating incumbent President Jimmy Carter. He reverses the consensus politics of his predecessor and begins an arms build-up against the USSR, working closely with the British government of Margaret Thatcher.

Rubik's cube.

DIFFICULT CUBE

Rubik's cube, a game consisting of 26 small coloured cubes rotating on a central axis, becomes Britain's Toy of the Year. It was invented by Erno Rubik, a Hungarian professor of design, who failed to patent his design so did not profit from it.

AMADEUS

A new play by English dramatist Peter Shaffer (b. 1926) has opened. *Amadeus* tells the story of Mozart and his alleged murder by "rival" composer Salieri. The play courts controversy with its frank portrayal of the earthy, scatological side of Mozart's character.

MOUNT ST. HELENS ERUPTS

The volcano Mount St. Helens in Washington State erupts, having been inactive since 1857. The explosion measures 4.1 on the Richter scale. It destroys all life in an area of 400 sq km (154 sq mi), and kills at least eight people.

MOSCOW OLYMPICS

Once again politics and sport mix at the Olympic Games. The United States leads a boycott, which includes West Germany and Kenya, in protest at the Soviet Union's invasion of Afghanistan. Competitive highlights include the achievements of British athletes Seb Coe and Steve Ovett on the track, and Soviet gymnast Alexander Ditiatin's perfect 10 in the vault.

SOLAR MAX IS LAUNCHED

Solar Max (the US Solar Maximum Mission Observatory) is launched to record events during a period of sunspot activity.

BYKER DEVELOPMENT

A ground-breaking housing development is created in Newcastle, England. Its importance lies in the fact that it involves the future residents in the design of the building. Members of Ralph Erskine's architectural practice live on site to ensure they are accessible to the future tenants.

SOLAR-POWERED FLIGHT

The *Gossamer Penguin* makes the first flight of a solar-powered aircraft in California. The power is obtained from panels of solar-electric cells.

WINTER OLYMPICS

The Thirteenth Winter Olympics in Lake Placid, USA, witness the first use of artificial snow. American skater Eric Heiden takes five speed-skating golds.

BELOW: The force is still with us when *The Empire Strikes Back*, crewed by the same heroes, is released three years after *Star Wars*.

ICELAND GAINS WOMAN PRESIDENT

Vigdís Finnbogadóttir (b. 1930) is elected president of Iceland. She wins a little over a third of the vote, defeating three male rivals to become the world's first democratically elected woman president.

BORG WINS FIFTH TITLE

Swedish tennis star Björn Borg (b. 1956) claims his fifth Wimbledon tennis title in a row, beating John McEnroe in the final.

JEAN-PAUL SARTRE
(1905–1980)

French existentialist philosopher and writer, Jean-Paul Sartre has died. During World War II, he was a member of the Resistance. A Marxist, he founded, with Simone de Beauvoir, the left-wing journal *Les Temps Modernes* and was known as one of the intellectuals of Left Bank Paris café society. His most important philosophical work is *Being and Nothingness* (1943) and his fictional writings include the trilogy *Roads to Freedom* (1945–49). During the events of May 1968 Sartre was once more out on the streets of Paris supporting student and worker rebellion, but of late he has suffered from ill-health and near-blindness.

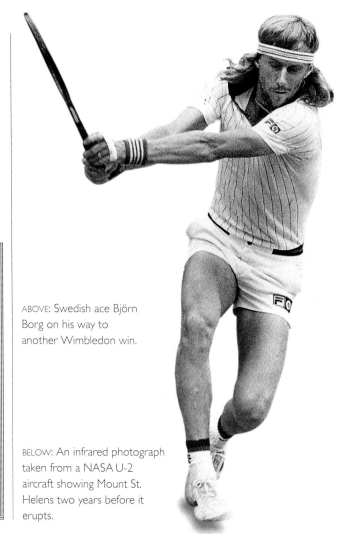

ABOVE: Swedish ace Björn Borg on his way to another Wimbledon win.

BELOW: An infrared photograph taken from a NASA U-2 aircraft showing Mount St. Helens two years before it erupts.

ABOVE: US golfer Jack Nicklaus (b. 1940), the "Golden Bear", confirms his position as one of golf's greats.

ABOVE: Ayatollah Khomeini, charismatic fundamentalist leader of Iran, has many supporters for his return to traditional values.

ABOVE: Josip Tito, president of Yugoslavia, and his wife.

JOSIP TITO (BORN JOSIP BROZ) (1892–1980)

President Tito of Yugoslavia, who became head of the Yugoslav Communist party in 1937 and has been the country's leader since the post-war establishment of the new Federal Republic in 1945, has died. Viewed by Stalin as a revisionist, he pursued a policy of liberalism, and although he has been president for life since 1974 he has established a rotating leadership during recent years. The country's future without his leadership is uncertain.

NEW DIRECTION IN THE MOVIES

The late Seventies and early Eighties see the rise of a new generation of young director-producers whose work helps the cinema to recover from the blow inflicted on it by television. Large-scale action films, blockbusters and science fiction sagas follow, and special effects almost take over as the stars of the films. Audiences flock back to the big screen.

ABOVE: Francis Ford Coppola, enigmatic director most famous for his Mafia-based *Godfather* series.

ABOVE: Michael Cimino directs Robert de Niro on the set of *The Deer Hunter* (1978), the film that makes his name.

ABOVE: Golden boy Steven Spielberg, creator of *Jaws, Close Encounters of the Third Kind, ET* and the *Indiana Jones* trilogy.

ABOVE: A scene from *Star Wars*, the film that launches George Lucas' career as a director.

ABOVE: Douglas Trumball, the special effects mastermind behind many science fiction films and the director of *Silent Running* (1972).

AIDS — A NEW KILLER

Iran releases the US hostages after 444 days in captivity. Unrest increases in Poland and martial law is declared. François Mitterand is elected the first socialist president of France. President Sadat of Egypt is assassinated. France's new high-speed train reaches speeds of more than 300km/h (186miph). A new disease — AIDS — is identified and the first successful heart-lung transplant takes place.

OPPOSITE: Prime Minister Margaret Thatcher meets socialist French president François Mitterand.

1981

Jan	10	Greece joins the European Union (EC)
	20	US hostages released from Tehran
Feb	3	Gro Harlem Brundtland becomes first woman prime minister of Norway
	23	Civil Guards storm Spanish Cortes (parliament) in abortive coup attempt
Apr	12	American re-usable space shuttle makes first flight
	30	Polish Communist government approves limited reforms
May	5	IRA activist Bobby Sands dies from hunger strike, Northern Ireland
	10	François Mitterand becomes first socialist president of France
July	29	Royal wedding of Prince Charles and Lady Diana Spencer, UK
Oct	6	President Sadat of Egypt is assassinated
Dec	13	Martial law declared in Poland

ABOVE: President Anwar Sadat of Egypt, who is assassinated this year.

ABOVE: American writer Susan Sontag, one of a group of Western intellectuals invited to tour Communist China.

ABOVE: Delegates from the US and USSR meet in Geneva to discuss the limitation of intermediate nuclear forces in Europe.

ABOVE: Oil rigs begin to reap the rich harvest of North Sea oil.

ABOVE: American composer Samuel Barber, best known for his *Adagio*, dies.

UNREST IN POLAND
In Poland, the Communist government hands over to the army, which takes power under General Jaruzelski (b. 1923) as prime minister. He introduces some reforms in April to placate the independent trade union Solidarity, which is leading a general strike. Following demonstrations against food shortages and unrest throughout the country, he introduces martial law in December after pressure from the USSR, curtailing all civil liberties and arresting Lech Walesa. Solidarity is banned in October 1982.

ATTEMPTED COUP
Right-wing members of the paramilitary Civil Guard storm the Cortes, the Spanish parliament, and attempt to overthrow the government. King Juan Carlos dons military uniform and instructs the army, which appears to support the coup, to rally behind the democratic government. The government quickly purges the army of former Franco supporters.

MITTERAND BECOMES PRESIDENT
François Mitterand (1916–96) becomes the first socialist president of France when he wins the presidential election, defeating the incumbent centrist Valéry Giscard d'Estaing. Mitterand's Socialist Party wins a landslide in the general election held in June; the new government includes three Communist ministers.

SADAT ASSASSINATED
Egyptian president Anwar Sadat is assassinated at a military parade by an Islamic extremist protesting against the peace deal with Israel. Sadat is succeeded by Vice-President Hosni Mubarak (b. 1928).

HOSTAGES RELEASED
The last 52 hostages are released from the US embassy in Tehran, where they have been held by followers of the Ayatollah.

GREECE JOINS EC
The newly democratic Greece becomes the tenth nation to be admitted to the European Union.

JAILED HUNGER STRIKER WINS ELECTION
IRA activist Bobby Sands wins the Fermanagh and South Tyrone by-election in Northern Ireland, defeating the Unionists by a clear majority. Bobby Sands, who is on hunger strike in prison, dies a month later.

HIGH-SPEED TRAIN
In February France's new TGV (*train à grande vitesse*, or high-speed train) begins a regular service between Paris and Lyon. It sets a world speed record of 380km/h (236miph). To reach such speeds, the TGV has specially-built tracks with steeply banked curves.

LEFT: April sees the launch of the first space shuttle, a re-usable vehicle that can orbit the Earth and return under its own steam.

ABOVE: Modern art in a modern setting. Alexander Calder's stabile *Flamingo* outside the Federal Center in Chicago, Illinois.

FIRST SPACE SHUTTLE FLIGHT
In April, America's first space shuttle *Columbia* makes its first flight, returning safely two days later. A second flight takes place in November.

AIDS IDENTIFIED
The US Center for Disease Control identifies the first cases of what appears to be a new disease — AIDS (Acquired Immune Deficiency Syndrome). The condition affects a person's natural disease-combatting immune system and the first cases are identified in gay men.

RAIDERS OF THE LOST ARK
A new film, *Raiders of the Lost Ark*, is a great hit. It stars US film actor Harrison Ford (b. 1942) who plays Indiana Jones, archaeologist and man of action, who overcomes a bunch of Nazis hunting for the lost Ark of the Covenant. The film is full of spectacular effects.

BOB MARLEY
(1945–1981)

Jamaican reggae artist Bob Marley (born Robert Nesta) has died of cancer. A Rastafarian, the singer and electric guitarist brought reggae to an international audience. Initially performing in a group of three known as the Wailers, Marley later went solo and gave performances worldwide. His latest album *Uprising* was produced last year. Among his best-known hits are *"No Woman No Cry"* and *"I Shot the Sheriff"*.

EXPLORING THE SOLAR SYSTEM

Since the beginning of space exploration in 1961, sophisticated probes have been sent to explore the solar system and bring back photographs of our nearest neighbours. More has been learnt about our home system in the last 30 years than over previous millennia.

ABOVE LEFT: Jupiter photographed from *Voyager I* in 1979.

ABOVE RIGHT: A thin coating of ice on Mars, recorded by *Viking Lander 2*.

RIGHT: Photomosaic of Mercury assembled from photographs taken by *Mariner 10*.

LEFT: The innermost of Jupiter's sixteen moons, seen from *Voyager I*.

BELOW LEFT: Venus, seen as a crescent, from *Pioneer Venus I*.

BELOW RIGHT: Saturn photographed by the probe *Voyager 2* in 1980.

ABOVE: Salman Rushdie, Bombay-born author of *Midnight's Children*, a novel about the partition of India. Later in the decade he will incur the wrath of Muslim leader Ayatollah Khomeini.

MIDNIGHT'S CHILDREN
British novelist Salman Rushdie (b. 1947) publishes an epic novel, *Midnight's Children*. Telling the stories of characters born at the moment of India's independence, the novel shows Rushdie to be one of Britain's foremost novelists.

HEART-LUNG TRANSPLANT IS SUCCESSFUL
In California Mary D Golkhe receives the first successful transplant of a heart and a pair of lungs. Three earlier recipients of heart-lung transplants lived only a few days.

ENTER THE PC
US firm IBM introduces its personal computer (the PC), using the Microsoft Disk Operating System (MS-DOS). It becomes a standard program throughout the computer industry.

REDS
US film actor Warren Beatty (b. 1937) stars in, co-writes and directs a new movie. *Reds* is the story of John Reed, journalist and founder-member of the American Communist Party. The film is criticized for its disorganized structure, but is beautifully shot by Vittorio Storaro.

ABOVE: Dacca, Bangladesh, where President Zia ur-Rahman, leader of the Bangladesh Nationalist Party, is assassinated in May.

NEW MICROSCOPE
Physicists Gerd Binnig (b. 1947) of West Germany and Heinrich Roher of Switzerland invent the scanning tunnelling microscope, which can identify individual atoms.

AUSTRIAN STATE RADIO REGIONAL STUDIO
In Austria, Gustav Peichl has designed a new radio studio that combines the economical use of prefabricated concrete sections with striking high-tech elements such as polished chromium heating pipes.

ANTI-APARTHEID PROTESTS
Serious anti-apartheid demonstrations disrupt the South African rugby tour of New Zealand, which has been nicknamed the "Barbed Wire Tour". Similar angry protests had met the South Africans' visit to Great Britain in 1969.

CIVIL WAR IN CENTRAL AMERICA

Britain and Argentina go to war over ownership of the Falkland Islands. Israel drives the PLO out of Beirut and Christian Phalangists massacre Palestinian refugees. A state of emergency is declared in Nicaragua. Helmut Kohl becomes chancellor of Germany. The UN warns of destruction of the world's rainforests. Architecture adopts post-modernism, compact discs (CDs) appear on the market, and the USSR puts a new space station into orbit.

1982

Mar	15	State of emergency declared in Nicaragua	Aug	30	Yasser Arafat and Palestinians leave Beirut
Apr	2	Argentinian troops invade Falkland Islands (Malvinas)	Sep	18	Palestinians massacred by Christian Phalangist militia
	4	British Royal Navy task force sets sail for Falklands			
	19	USSR puts new space station into orbit	Oct	1	Helmut Kohl becomes chancellor, West Germany
				28	Socialists win election in Spain
May	2	British submarine HMS *Conqueror* sinks Argentinian cruiser *General Belgrano*			
	4	Argentinian missiles sink British destroyer HMS *Sheffield*			
June	5	Israel invades Lebanon			
	14	Argentinian forces surrender; Falklands War ends			
July	23	International Whaling Commission votes for complete ban on whaling			

LEFT: Helmut Kohl, the chancellor of West Germany.

FALKLANDS WAR

War breaks out between Argentina and Britain over ownership of the Falkland Islands. In April, the Argentinian junta under General Galtieri launches Operation Rosario and invades the Falkland Islands. The UN passes a resolution calling for Argentina to withdraw. A British task force is dispatched and, after a fierce conflict, Argentinian troops surrender and the islands are returned to Britain in June. Throughout the campaign, the British lose four warships and a container ship, and suffer 237 killed, as well as 18 civilians and 759 military personnel wounded. Argentina loses the battleship *Belgrano* and suffer more than 1,000 killed, including the crew of the *Belgrano*.

ISRAEL INVADES LEBANON

After an air bombardment Israeli forces invade Lebanon, headquarters of the Palestinian Liberation Organization (PLO) since its formation in 1964. Israeli and Syrian forces clash in southern Lebanon and Israeli forces surround 6,000 PLO guerrillas in West Beirut and demand their surrender. In July, Palestinian leader Yasser Arafat (b. 1929) offers to accept a UN Security Resolution recognizing Israel's right to exist in exchange for US recognition of the PLO, but the US refuses. By the end of August, the PLO has been driven out of Beirut.

EL SALVADOR

Civil war continues in El Salvador where, in 1980, human rights champion Oscar Romero was killed. Elections take place, accompanied by considerable violence, with left-wing parties refusing to participate. The Christian Democratic Party, headed by José Duarte, who has been president since 1980, is returned but is blocked by a coalition of right-wing parties.

ABOVE: A British Vulcan bomber plays its part in the Falklands conflict between Britain and Argentina.

PALESTINIANS MASSACRED

Following the assassination of Lebanese president-elect Bashir Gemayel, Christian Phalangists enter Palestinian refugee camps in West Beirut and kill more than 800 Palestinians.

SHINING PATH

In Peru, the Maoist guerrillas Sendero Luminoso (Shining Path), led by Dr Renoso Guzman, become increasingly active, using terrorist tactics such as bombings and assassinations.

SOCIALISTS WIN IN SPAIN

In Spain, the Socialist Party of Felipe González (b. 1942) wins a landslide in the general election for the first time since the Civil War. He holds power until 1996.

INGRID BERGMAN
(1915–1982)

Swedish actress Ingrid Bergman has died. The English-speaking star (with Humphrey Bogart) of *Casablanca* (1942) had many other Hollywood successes during the1940s. After a period in Europe she returned to Hollywood in 1956 to make *Anastasia* and *The Inn of Sixth Happiness* (1958). More recently she appeared on stage and television, and in Ingmar Bergman's film *Autumn Sonata* (1978).

ABOVE: Henry Fonda (with daughter Jane and Katharine Hepburn) wins his first and only Oscar for the film *On Golden Pond*.

KOHL BECOMES CHANCELLOR

The Social Democratic government of Helmut Schmidt falls and he is replaced as chancellor by the Christian Democrat Helmut Kohl (b. 1930), who holds power until 1998. Kohl does much to increase European unity in the EC, and to bring France and Germany closer.

NEW SOVIET SPACE STATION

The Soviet Union puts a new space station into orbit. It is *Salyut 7*, which replaces an earlier space station that has been in orbit for four years.

NICARAGUA

President Daniel Ortega (b. 1945) declares a state of emergency in Nicaragua, following guerrilla attacks on bridges and petroleum installations. Relations with the USA have deteriorated since Reagan became US president, and US aid to the country has been frozen since 1981. This year, the US has begun actively attempting to destabilize the new Nicaraguan government by funding right-wing guerrillas known as Contras.

SOVIET LEADERS DIE

Soviet president Leonid Brezhnev dies, ushering in a period of weak leadership as two more leaders — Yuri Andropov and Konstantin Chernenko — both die within three years.

THE MARY ROSE IS RAISED

Archaeologists led by Margaret Rule raise the wreck of English king Henry VIII's warship *Mary Rose* to the surface off Portsmouth, England, after 437 years under water.

SHUTTLE LAUNCHES SATELLITE

The US space shuttle *Columbia* carries two communications satellites in its cargo bay and puts them into orbit. The shuttle carries two specialists, who are not astronauts, as additional crew members.

CDS ARRIVE

Compact discs (CDs), which store sound digitally as microscopic pits and play it back with a laser beam, and CD players, go on sale. They are introduced by the Dutch company Philips and CBS/Sony of the USA.

FIRST LASER PRINTERS

The first laser printers for computers go on the market, produced by IBM.

POST-MODERN BUILDINGS

Designed by US architect Michael Graves (b. 1934), the Portland Public Services Building in Oregon claims to the first post-modern building. The colourful treatment of the façade, the play of patterns on the outer walls, and the use of ornamental statuary set this building apart from any other recent architectural project. A building in New York, however, also claims to be post-modernism's "founding building". This is the AT & T Building designed by US architects Philip Johnson and John Burgee. A highly controversial building, the skyscraper attracts immediate attention because of its enormous broken pediment, a historical allusion typical of the new style. It is nicknamed the "Chippendale skyscraper".

LEFT: Jubilant members of the winning Italian team hold the Jules Rimet trophy aloft after beating Germany to win the World Cup.

THE COLOR PURPLE
American writer Alice Walker (b. 1944) has published her first novel, *The Color Purple*. Walker's story of the life of an African-American woman will win her the Pulitzer Prize and international recognition.

THE HOUSE OF THE SPIRITS
Chilean writer Isabel Allende (b. 1942) gains international fame following the publication of her first novel, *The House of the Spirits*. A mixture of mythical elements and realism, the novel arose out of Allende's flight from Chile following the assassination of her uncle, Salvador Allende.

DESTRUCTION OF THE RAINFOREST
Environmentalists are concerned about the state of the world's rainforests after a UN environment programme estimates that some eight million hectares (twenty million acres) of rainforest are being destroyed annually.

PAC-MAN FEVER
The Pac-Man computer game sweeps the USA and UK, becoming Time magazine's "Man of the Year".

ITALY WINS WORLD CUP
Italy wins the football World Cup for the third time at the final match staged in Spain. They beat Germany 3–1 in a disappointing final.

ABOVE: Russian premier Leonid Brezhnev dies and is buried in Moscow's Red Square. He is succeeded for a very short time by Yuri Andropov.

LEFT: Leader-in-waiting Mikhail Gorbachev; the death of Brezhnev begins the fall of the old guard and opens the way for liberalizers to come to power in the USSR.

WHALING MORATORIUM
The International Whaling Commission agrees to a four-year moratorium on commercial whaling to begin 1985–86. However, catches made for scientific research continue, and much commercial whaling is disguised as "scientific".

CASA ROTONDA
Swiss-born architect Mario Botta's Casa Rotonda shows the flair of European architects for creating original forms. It is a cylindrically shaped house that plays inventively with volume.

GREENHAM WOMEN AND GERMAN GREENS

Civil war begins in Sri Lanka. A Soviet fighter shoots down a South Korean Boeing 747. Anti-nuclear protests take place throughout Europe against the siting of Cruise and Pershing missiles in Europe. German Greens win seats in the Bundestag. US marines invade the island of Grenada. The AIDS virus is identified. A new device, the mouse, makes computer use easier. Steven Spielberg's film *ET*, starring a likeable extra-terrestrial, becomes a smash hit.

OPPOSITE: Fibre optics, glass tubes which will revolutionize the telecommunications industry.

1983

Mar	23	US president Reagan proposes new "Star Wars" defence system
July	27	Civil war in Sri Lanka between government and Tamil Tigers
Aug	21	Philippines opposition leader Benigno Aquino is assassinated
Sep	1	Soviet fighter shoots down South Korean Boeing 747
Oct	20	Speed of light redefined
	22	Anti-nuclear protests in Europe against siting of Cruise and Pershing missiles in Europe
	25	USA invades Grenada
Nov	28	European *Spacelab* goes into orbit
Dec	10	Raúl Alfonsín becomes president of Argentina

ABOVE: Boy George and his band Culture Club popularize gender-bending and cross-dressing across the westernized world.

USSR SHOOTS DOWN BOEING

A South Korean Boeing 747 civilian aircraft, flying over Sakhalin Island off the east coast of Siberia, is shot down by Soviet pilots. The 269 passengers all lose their lives; the USSR claims the plane was on a spying mission. The attack increases tension between the USSR and the West.

ANTI-NUCLEAR PROTESTS

Large anti-nuclear demonstrations take place in many European countries against the placing of US Cruise and Pershing II missiles in Europe. The missiles increase the number of nuclear warheads in Europe and add to the arms race between the USA and USSR. In Britain, women set up a permanent peace camp on Greenham Common, where 96 cruise missiles are to be located. The women established the camp in September 1981 and maintain a constant vigil for peace.

GERMAN GREENS

The Green Party (die Grünen) wins a 5.6% share of the vote in national elections to the Bundestag, so achieving its first representation in the German legislative chamber. Among those to win a seat is Petra Kelly (1947–92), environmentalist, anti-nuclear activist and co-founder of the Green Party. Since the European Green Party was formed in 1979, concerns about the environment and nuclear power have led to increasing support across Europe.

MILITARY RULE ENDS IN ARGENTINA

Raúl Alfonsín (b. 1927) becomes president of Argentina, ending eight years of military rule. The military's repressive measures affected all sections of society, but they have lost all authority since their defeat in the Falklands War in 1982.

US INVADES GRENADA

The presence of 1,000 US students and a left-wing unelected government that had requested Cuban help with the construction of an international airport prompts the US government to launch an invasion of the island of Grenada. Some 7,000 US serviceman take two days to subdue a relatively untrained, ill-equipped and unsophisticated enemy. The Americans suffer 18 killed, 45 wounded; the Cubans 24 killed and 40 wounded; and the Grenadans 60 killed and 184 wounded.

MICE HELP KEYBOARDS

Apple Computer, Inc. introduces the computer mouse, a device that moves a pointer on screen and sends commands to the computer by the pressing of a button.

AQUINO ASSASSINATED

The opposition leader Benigno Aquino is assassinated at Manila airport as he returns from a three-year exile to fight the forthcoming general election. His death is widely blamed on the government of President Marcos, and fuels the opposition to his rule.

ABOVE: The Hummer or Humvee, a high-mobility multipurpose vehicle, replaces the faithful Jeep in the US armed forces.

SRI LANKA

Civil war breaks out in Sri Lanka between government forces and northern Tamil separatists, the LiberationTigers of Tamil Eelam (LTTE), based in the Jaffna peninsula. It continues into the 1990s.

AIDS VIRUS IDENTIFIED

Researchers in France discover the virus that causes AIDS. It is labelled HIV-1, the Human Immune Deficiency Virus; US researchers confirm the finding the following year. There is some doubt about who is first to identify the virus but certainty that AIDS itself is likely to become an epidemic.

"IMPROVED" PETUNIAS

Scientists in Germany and the USA transfer genes from a bacterium into cells from petunias, producing plants that are resistant to antibiotics.

FURTHER INTO SPACE

The European-built space laboratory *Spacelab* is put into orbit by the US shuttle *Columbia*. In June *Pioneer 10*, launched in 1972, becomes the first space probe to pass through the asteroid belt and travel beyond the solar system.

ET

US film-maker Steven Spielberg (b. 1946) releases a new film, *ET*. A delightfully sentimental tale of an alien who visits Earth, it becomes a major box-office earner. Much of the film is cleverly shot from the eye-level of the ten-year-old boy who is the central character.

WORST EL NINO

Oceanographers report that the El Niño spell of extra-warm water along the coast of South America, which began in 1982, is the most intense ever recorded. It causes floods and droughts in many parts of the world.

ABOVE: US troops on the ground during the two-day invasion of the tiny island of Grenada.

LEFT: The 82nd Airborne Division poised to land.

BELOW: A combined Marine and Army patrol during Operation Urgent Fury, the US invasion of Grenada. The servicemen in the background are seated in a captured Soviet-built UAZ-469B light vehicle.

ADVANCES IN MEDICAL SCIENCE

Technological advances, partly developed for the space programme, are successfully applied to the field of medicine. Computers, lasers, electronics and nuclear science all take their place in diagnosis and surgical treatment.

RIGHT: Microsurgery uses powerful magnifying glasses, laser-guided instruments and video screens for complex work.

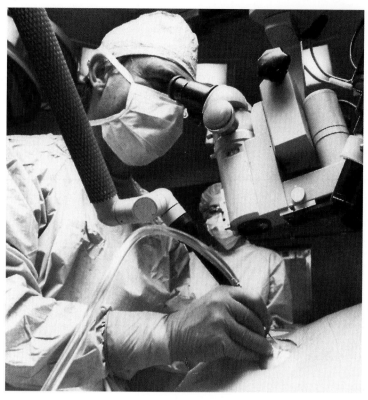

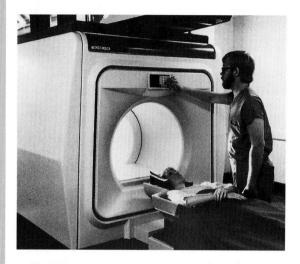

ABOVE: The Nuclear Magnetic Resonance Scanner is used to detect damage to, or cancers in, the bones and spine.

BELOW: Electrodes linked to a computer monitor the heart's rhythm and indicate any disruption to the patient's normal pattern.

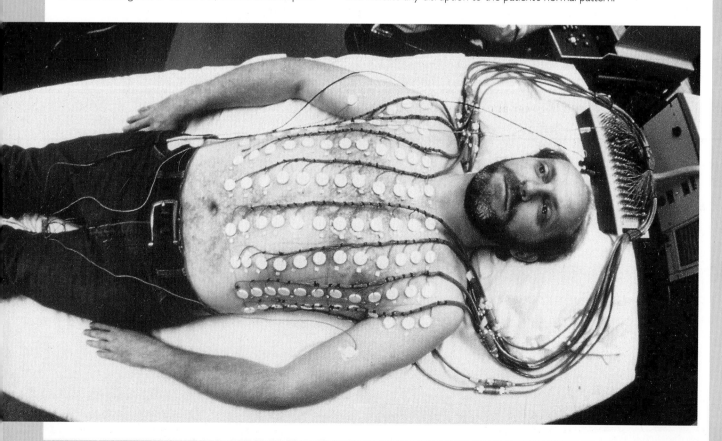

TALKING CAMERA

The Minolta Company introduces a 35mm camera which "talks" to the user, warning of problems before the next shot.

SPEED OF LIGHT REDEFINED

An international committee redefines the speed of light as exactly 299,792,458m (983,571,000ft) per second.

FASHIONABLE GENDER-BENDING

Gender-bending — sexually indeterminate dressing and lifestyle — becomes a fashionable youth subculture in the US and UK with the success of rock bands such as Culture Club, led by a gay singer Boy George.

ARTIFICIAL HEART

Retired dentist Barney B Clark, the first patient to be given an artificial Jarvik heart, dies after 112 days. The artificial heart does not fail but other organs do. The operation was carried out last year at the University of Utah. The artificial heart is made of plastic and metal and known as a Jarvik heart after its inventor, Robert Jarvik. It is to become useful as an interim measure while people wait for a suitable donor heart.

BALTHAZAR JOHANNES (JOHN) VORSTER
(1915–1983)

The Afrikaner Nationalist South African prime minister from 1966 to 1978, John Vorster, has died. He served as minister of justice during Hendrik Verwoerd's government (1961–66) and became prime minister after the former's assassination, continuing to enforce apartheid. He was forced to resign his position as state president in 1979 when found guilty of misappropriation of government funds.

ABOVE: The remains of the barracks at Beirut Airport, where 241 US Marines die in a terrorist bomb attack. The Marines are in Lebanon to help keep the peace between Israel and Palestine.

THE MASK OF ORPHEUS

British composer Harrison Birtwistle (b. 1934) retells the Orpheus myth in his new opera. As well as the traditional language of opera (voices and instruments), Birtwistle uses taped musical inserts of harp chords dissected, analysed and replayed by a computer to create rhythms faster and more complex than a human player could achieve.

AUSTRALIA WINS AMERICA'S CUP

Australia prises the America's Cup from the USA for the first time since 1851. John Betterand captained the Australian yachting challenge in *Australia II*, defeating Dennis Conner's *Liberty*.

RIGHT: Everybody's favourite alien, ET the extra-terrestrial, star of Spielberg's box office success, *ET*.

THE CHALLENGER ACHIEVEMENT

More than a decade after the first moon-shot, the USA launches the space shuttle, a two-component vehicle comprising a rocket and an orbiter which can return to Earth. The first of the orbiters is the *Challenger*, launched in 1981 and in service until 1986. The idea is to carry out commercial, military and scientific research. A major feature of the shuttle trips is the space walk, where astronauts leave the orbiter to carry carry out maintenance or construction work.

RIGHT: Astronauts F Story Musgrave and Donald H Peterson practise setting up a winch operation on the aft bulkhead.

BELOW: The astronauts spend almost four hours outside the *Challenger* as she orbits the Earth.

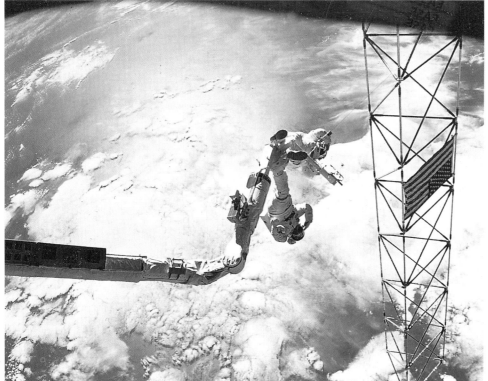

ABOVE: On a 1984 shuttle trip, astronaut Bruce McCandless II tests out the nitrogen-propelled, hand-controlled device called the Manned Maneuvering Unit (MMU), which allows great mobility. Previous space-walkers were restricted by tethers, tying them to the mother ship.

LEFT: On a 1985 mission astronauts Sherwood C Spring and Jerry L Ross practise the assembling of components outside the shuttle.

AMRITSAR, BHOPAL AND ACID RAIN

Sikh nationalists are massacred at the Golden Temple, Amritsar. Indian prime minister Indira Gandhi is assassinated in revenge. In the UK, the IRA bombs the Conservative Party Conference as part of a sustained campaign to get British troops out of Northern Ireland. Nations in Ottawa pledge to reduce carbon dioxide emissions, the source of acid rain, and toxic gas kills more than 2,000 in India. Women walk in space and Archbishop Tutu receives the Nobel Peace Prize.

1984

Feb	9	Soviet president Andropov dies. He is succeeded by Chernenko
	11	Iraq bombs non-military targets in Iran
Apr	20	Demonstrations in West Germany against deployment of US missiles in Europe
May	10	International Court of Justice at The Hague rules US should end blockade of Nicaraguan ports
	10	Danish parliament votes to suspend payments to NATO as protest against siting of Pershing II and Cruise missiles in Europe
	24	Iranian warplanes attack oil tankers off coast of Saudi Arabia
June	6	Sikh nationalists killed when Indian troops storm Golden Temple, Amritsar
July	28	The 23rd Olympic Games open in Los Angeles, USA
Aug	4	Tamils and Sinhalese clash in Sri Lanka
Sep	26	Britain agrees to hand over Hong Kong to China
Oct	12	IRA bombs Conservative Party Conference, Brighton, UK
	31	Indian prime minister Indira Gandhi is assassinated
Nov	4	Sandanista Front win Nicaraguan elections
Dec	3	Toxic gas leak in Bhopal, India, kills and injures thousands

ABOVE: Mourners and the dead in Bhopal, the Indian city devastated by the leak of poisonous gas from the Union Carbide factory.

ABOVE: Ronald Reagan in Congress. The ex-B movie actor has already served one term as president and this year is re-elected for a second term.

LEFT: Indira Gandhi, the prime minister of India, with the Sikh bodyguard who later assassinates her.

GOLDEN TEMPLE MASSACRE

In June members of the Sikh nationalist group the Akali Dal seize the Golden Temple, Amritsar, India, in an attempt to establish an independent Sikh state called Khalistan. The Golden Temple is one of the Sikhs' holiest places. The Indian government launches an attack and troops storm and seize the temple. Fighting is fierce: official figures give 493 nationalists and 83 soldiers killed. In October, the Indian prime minister Indira Gandhi is assassinated by her Sikh bodyguards, in revenge for the storming of the Golden Temple. Mrs Gandhi's son Rajiv (1944–91) succeeds her to the premiership. The assassination provokes a Hindu backlash in which some 3,000 Sikhs are massacred.

BRIGHTON BOMBING

The IRA bomb the Conservative Party Conference in Brighton, UK, narrowly avoiding killing prime minister Margaret Thatcher and her cabinet. Two people are killed and many injured in the blast, which wrecks the hotel they are staying in. The bomb is part of a sustained campaign by the IRA on the British mainland to force a British withdrawal from Northern Ireland.

FRANCOIS TRUFFAUT (1932–1984)

The *nouvelle vague* French film director and critic François Truffaut has died. His first full-length film *Les Quatre Cents Coups* (1959) immediately made his reputation, and he consolidated this in 1962 with *Jules et Jim*. Many of his films form a loosely connected series featuring the actor Jean-Pierre Leaud, the boy hero of *Les Quatre Cents Coups*.

POISON GAS LEAK IN BHOPAL

Some 2,500 people are killed and thousands more injured when toxic gas escapes from the American-owned Union Carbide plant outside Bhopal, Madhya Pradesh, India. The leak is caused by the failure of two safety systems. Bhopal is declared a disaster zone.

BELOW: The blasted façade of the Grand Hotel, Brighton, where the IRA nearly succeeds in destroying the Conservative Party.

ABOVE: The Anglo French supersonic aircraft Concorde continues to fly the Atlantic in spite of protests by environmental activists.

HONG KONG TO BE RETURNED

Britain agrees to hand back Hong Kong to China in 1997. The 99-year lease on the New Territories runs out in 1997, making the rest of the colony unviable when they are returned to China. In the agreement, Hong Kong will be allowed to keep its capitalist system for at least 50 years and have considerable internal autonomy.

WALK IN SPACE

In June Soviet cosmonaut Svetlana Savitskaya becomes the first woman to walk in space. She is followed in October by US astronaut Kathryn D Sullivan, who also walks in space.

FIRST CD-ROMS

Philips and Sony adapt the compact disc for computers, producing the first CD-ROMS (Compact Disc Read-Only Memory) for storing data.

OCEAN DRILLING

Eleven countries launch a ten-year programme of drilling to explore the continental shelves, parts of the continents that lie under the sea.

STAATSGALERIE EXTENSION

British architects James Stirling and Michael Wilford create their own muted version of post-modernism (with classical details and primary colours) for this art gallery extension in Stuttgart, Germany.

ACID RAIN PLEDGE

Ten nations meet in Ottawa and pledge to reduce sulphur dioxide emissions by 30 per cent to reduce acid rain, which has been found to be contaminating lakes and rivers and destroying forests in much of North America and Europe. Only in 1983 was it discovered to be caused by pollutants in the smoke from power stations and some factories.

JORDAN SELECTED

The Chicago Bulls select Brooklyn-born Michael Jordan (b. 1963) third in the basketball draft of college players.

LINDOW MAN FOUND

The remains of an Iron Age man are discovered preserved in a peat bog at Lindow Marsh, Cheshire, England; he appears to be the victim of a religious sacrifice.

OLYMPIC GAMES

The 23rd Olympics are held in Los Angeles. Many Communist countries boycott the Games, which are the first to be privately financed, in retaliation for US withdrawal in 1980. American sprinter Carl Lewis (b. 1961) achieves star status as he repeats Jesse Owens' haul of four golds. The women's marathon is an official Olympic event for the first time and is won by US athlete Joan Benoit. Windsurfing, won by Holland's Stephen van den Berg, and synchronized swimming also become Olympic sports.

TUTU WINS NOBEL PRIZE

South African Anglican bishop and campaigner against apartheid Bishop Desmond Tutu (b. 1931) is awarded the Nobel Peace Prize. In 1985 he becomes the first black bishop of Johannesburg.

INDIRA PRIYAD ARSHINI GANDHI (1917–1984)

Indian prime minister Indira Gandhi has been assassinated by one of her guards. The daughter of Jawaharlal Nehru, she was educated partly at Oxford and was always politically active in the Congress Party. She became prime minister in 1966 and lost her seat after a period of political upheaval in 1977. She was re-elected in 1980.

PERESTROIKA AND LIVE AID

Mikhail Gorbachev becomes the new leader of the Soviet Union. He promises reforms. Ethiopia suffers the worst-ever recorded famine. Millions contribute to famine aid through massive Live Aid rock concerts. Greenpeace ship *Rainbow Warrior* is sunk in New Zealand by French agents. The death of Rock Hudson stimulates awareness of the AIDS epidemic. Scientists discover a hole in the ozone layer. The wreck of the *Titanic* is found. English football clubs are banned from Europe competitions.

1985

Feb	8	ANC leader Nelson Mandela refuses offer of freedom, conditional on his renouncing violence
Mar	10	Soviet president Chernenko dies
	11	Mikhail Gorbachev becomes leader of the Soviet Union
	21	South African police fire on crowds on the 25th anniversary of the Sharpeville Massacre
Apr	11	Ramiz Alia becomes leader of Albania following death of Enver Hoxha
May	1	USA imposes trade sanctions on Nicaragua
	1	Solidarity supporters clash with police, Poland
	10	Sikh nationalists bomb Indian cities
July	11	Greenpeace ship *Rainbow Warrior* sunk in Auckland, New Zealand
	18	Organization of African Unity holds conference in Addis Ababa; it announces that most African countries are on verge of economic collapse
Sep	2	Pol Pot resigns as leader of Khmer Rouge
	17	More than 2,000 die after earthquake, Mexico City
Oct	1	Israel attacks PLO headquarters, Tunis
	2	US film star Rock Hudson dies of AIDS
Nov	15	Anglo-Irish Agreement signed giving Republic of Ireland consultative role in Northern Ireland
	29	Black union leaders form new trade union COSATU, South Africa

ABOVE: Tragedy in the Heysel Stadium, Brussels, as fans of football teams Liverpool and Juventus are crushed in a pre-match brawl.

GORBACHEV PROMISES REFORM

Following the death of Konstantin Chernenko, Mikhail Gorbachev (b. 1931) becomes leader of the USSR. He begins to reform the Communist system, promising glasnost (openness) and perestroika (restructuring).

ALBANIA OPENS UP

Enver Hoxha, leader of Albania since 1945, dies. His country had been isolated from the rest of Eastern Europe, taking its lead from China rather than the USSR, and is the poorest country in Europe. Slowly, the new government of Ramiz Alia (b. 1925) begins to end Albania's international isolation.

ANGLO-IRISH AGREEMENT

British prime minister Margaret Thatcher and Irish prime minister Garret Fitzgerald (b. 1926) sign the Anglo-Irish Agreement, which gives Ireland a consultative role in the running of Northern Ireland for the first time. The agreement is designed to counter the campaign of the IRA and to begin the process of finding a solution to the long-running troubles in Northern Ireland.

ABOVE: Ruins in Mexico City after the earthquake that hits the area in this year. Over 2,000 people are killed.

LIVE AID

Mass famine in Ethiopia leads Irish rock star Bob Geldof (b. 1954) to organize Live Aid, a massive rock concert held in London, UK, and Philadelphia, USA, to raise money for famine relief. Stars, who play for free, include Dire Straits, David Bowie, Queen and Mick Jagger. The concerts raise $60 million and do much to raise the world's consciousness about famine and poverty in Africa. The famine in Ethiopia, which began in 1981 after drought and prolonged civil war, is the world's worst as recorded last year by film cameramen.

GEORGE ORSON WELLES (1915–1985)

American film director and actor Orson Welles has died. His 1941 film *Citizen Kane*, in which he also starred, is greatly admired by film buffs, and his other work includes highly regarded films such as *The Magnificent Ambersons* (1942) and *Touch of Evil* (1958) (both cut and amended by the studio without his consent). As an actor Welles also leaves his famous performance as Harry Lime in *The Third Man* (1949). He will further be remembered for his panic-causing radio production of *War of the Worlds* in 1938.

KURDS ATTACK TURKEY

The Kurdistan Popular Liberation Army, formerly the Kurdish Worker's Party (KKK), begins military operations against the Turkish government.

RAINBOW WARRIOR SUNK

French secret agents sink the Greenpeace ship *Rainbow Warrior* in Auckland harbour, New Zealand. Environmental group Greenpeace sent the ship to the South Pacific to attempt to disrupt French nuclear tests on Mururoa Atoll, which are heavily criticized by all nations in the region.

OZONE HOLE DISCOVERED

Scientists of the British Antarctic Survey announce the discovery of a hole in the ozone layer over Antarctica. The discovery increases anxiety about global warming caused by carbon dioxide emissions.

AIDS EPIDEMIC

The World Health Organization (WHO) declares AIDS an epidemic. American film star Rock Hudson becomes the first celebrity to die of the disease, making people in the West more aware of its rapid spread.

BUCKYBALLS

US chemist Richard E Smalley makes new carbon molecules consisting of 60 atoms forming a hollow sphere. They are called buckminsterfullerenes, or buckyballs for short, after the inventor of the geodesic dome, R Buckminster Fuller.

TITANIC LOCATED

Video cameras aboard an underwater search vessel locate the wreck of the liner *Titanic*, sunk in 1912, on the floor of the North Atlantic Ocean. The wreck is discovered off the Newfoundland coast in 4,000m (13,200ft) of water.

GENETIC FINGERPRINTING

A team of British scientists led by Alec Jeffreys develops genetic fingerprinting, based on the fact that parts of the genetic code are unique to each person.

WOMEN'S RIGHTS

An international conference on women's rights takes place in Nairobi, Kenya; 10,000 women attend.

NATURAL DISASTERS

A massive earthquake hits Mexico City and kills 2,000. In Bangladesh, a cyclone and tidal wave kill 10,000.

YOUNG CHESS CHAMPION

The Russian Gary Kasparov (b. 1963) beats Anatoly Karpov (b. 1951), world champion and a fellow Russian, in one of the longest-running chess matches, to become the youngest-ever world chess champion.

RAN

Japanese film director Akira Kurosawa's *Ran* opens. A version of *King Lear*, set in sixteenth-century Japan, the film impresses audiences with its big set-piece battle scenes and strong characterization.

DEER FOR CHINA

Père David's deer, which became extinct in China in 1921, are sent to China from England, where they have been bred in captivity since 1894.

MARC CHAGALL
(1887–1985)

Little short of his centenary, the Russian-born Franco-Jewish painter Marc Chagall has died. He moved to France in 1922 and lived there for most of his life. He designed for the Ballets Russes and produced theatre posters, book illustrations and stained glass, as well as his many paintings. His style has been terms "fantastic art".

MAHABHARATA

English director Peter Brook (b. 1925) and French writer Jean-Claude Carrière (b. 1931) have produced a theatrical version of myths from the Hindu epic the *Mahabharata*. The production gains further recognition for Brook's Paris-based theatrical company, Les Bouffes du Nord.

ENGLISH FOOTBALL CLUBS BANNED

English football is devastated by two horrific events In the northern town of Bradford in the UK, 56 die when an old wooden stand burns to the ground. Then at the European Cup Final between Liverpool and Juventus in the Heysel Stadium in Brussels, Belgium, 39 supporters of Turin club Juventus are crushed to death trying to get away from attacking Liverpool fans. English clubs are banned from European competitions and the tragedies force the English authorities to tackle hooliganism and the dilapidated state of English stadiums.

BELOW: The sinking hulk of *Rainbow Warrior*, the Greenpeace protest ship sunk in New Zealand by the French secret service.

STAR WARS

"Star Wars" is the nickname given to the Strategic Defense Initiative launched by President Ronald Reagan in 1983 and lasting as a research and development project for a decade. The plan is to devise a missile that can seek, catch and destroy enemy missiles before they reach their target. Reagan sees it as the primary weapon in the battle against the Evil Empire, his description of the Communist world.

LEFT: An artist's impression of a space-based nuclear power source to fuel the Star Wars missile, seen with its launcher, above.

ABOVE: The tracker component of the project, which seeks and finds enemy intercontinental ballistic missiles.

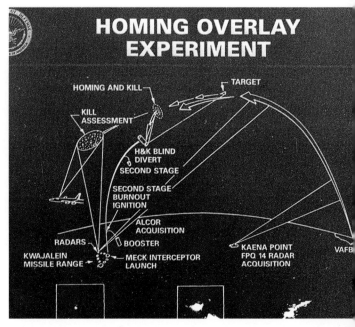

ABOVE: Diagram to show how the Star Wars missiles would intercept the enemy and what ground support would be needed.

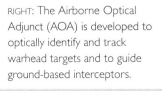
ABOVE: The Killl Mechanism of the Star Wars missile. A non-explosive "warhead", its metal ribs are wrapped around the neck of the defence missile during flight and unfurl seconds before impact. The force of the collision destroys the enemy missile.

RIGHT: The Airborne Optical Adjunct (AOA) is developed to optically identify and track warhead targets and to guide ground-based interceptors.

CHERNOBYL — NUCLEAR EXPLOSION

Amajor nuclear accident occurs at Chernobyl in the Soviet Union. Radioactive gas spreads across Europe. US space shuttle *Challenger* explodes seconds after take-off. Mrs Corazon Aquino topples Marcos in the Philippines. "Baby Doc" is overthrown in Haiti. The US launches air strikes against Libya. New architectural landmarks include the Hong Kong Bank and Lloyds Building. Canadian author Margaret Atwood publishes a chilling feminist dystopia. And Halley's Comet returns.

OPPOSITE: The space shuttle *Challenger* explodes on take-off, killing all aboard it.

1986

Jan	1	Spain and Portugal join the EC
	25	Gorbachev announces 25-year plan for elimination of nuclear weapons
	28	US space shuttle *Challenger* explodes
Feb	7	Haitian president Jean-Claude Duvalier flees to France
	9	Halley's Comet makes closest approach to the Sun
	24	Marcos flees Philippines; Corazon Aquino sworn in as president
	28	Olaf Palme, Sweden's prime minister, is assassinated
Apr	11	Brian Keenan, lecturer in Beirut, is taken hostage
	15	US bombers from British bases attack Libya
	17	John McCarthy, acting bureau chief for Worldwide Television, Beirut, is taken hostage
	26	Major nuclear accident occurs at Chernobyl, USSR
June	12	President Botha declares state of emergency in South Africa
	20	Conference in Paris of 120 nations calls for sanctions against South Africa because of its apartheid policies
July	29	Argentina wins World Cup in Mexico
Aug	21	Toxic gas kills 1,700 in northern Cameroon
Oct	19	President Machel of Mozambique and other government officials are killed in an air crash
	20	Israeli nuclear technician Mordechai Vanunu kidnapped in London after revealing nuclear secrets. He is held in Israel

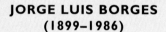

ABOVE: The map used by Caspar Weinberger, Secretary of Defense, at a White House briefing to the US Air Force during the Libyan action.

RIGHT: A Libyan patrol boat on guard in the Gulf of Sidra during the US raids on Libya in retaliation for terrorist attacks on their troops in mainland Europe.

JORGE LUIS BORGES
(1899–1986)

The highly regarded Argentine writer Jorge Luis Borges has died. His work consists mostly of essays or short narratives which engage the reader in the labyrinths of his complex metaphysical and multidimensional inventions. Because of increasing blindness he has dictated his ever-briefer essays since 1953. He was director of the Argentine National Library from 1955. The best-known collection of his works in Europe is *Labyrinths* (1962).

SIMONE DE BEAUVOIR
(1908–1986)

French writer and feminist Simone de Beauvoir, author of *The Second Sex*, has died. She was the fiercely independent companion of Jean-Paul Sartre and collaborated with him in producing the socialist paper *Les Temps Modernes* after the war. Her many published works include novels and autobiographical writings, and *Adieu: A Farewell to Sartre* (1984), about the last ten years of Sartre's life.

HAITIAN DICTATOR OVERTHROWN
The self-styled ruler for life of Haiti, Jean-Claude Duvalier, known as "Baby Doc", son of the dictator "Papa Doc", is toppled from power. Between them they have ruled the impoverished island since 1957, with the help of the dreaded Tonton Macoutes secret police. Duvalier flees to France, taking his considerable looted wealth with him. A military government takes over.

CHERNOBYL DISASTER
A nuclear power station at Chernobyl in Ukraine, Soviet Union, explodes causing a radioactive cloud to drift over northern Europe. Although a full melt-down and nuclear catastrophe are avoided, radioactive contamination in the area kills and maims many people. It is estimated that many thousands may die in the future.

STATE OF EMERGENCY IN SOUTH AFRICA
President Botha declares a state of emergency in South Africa as the government prepares for major anti-apartheid demonstrations on the tenth anniversary of the Soweto uprising. The move is criticized internationally and increases opposition to the white-only government among the black population.

EC MEMBERS
Spain and Portugal join the European Community as its eleventh and twelfth members.

US STRIKES LIBYA

Following the death of US servicemen in a bomb attack on Berlin, the USA name Libya as responsible for the act and launch an air strike against Libya, destroying military installations around Tripoli and Benghazi. Some of the US aircraft leave from British bases.

MACHEL KILLED

President Samora Machel of Mozambique and 28 government officials are killed in an air crash. South Africa is suspected, as part of its policy of destabilizing its black neighbours in order to weaken their opposition to the apartheid government.

CHALLENGER EXPLODES

The US space shuttle *Challenger* explodes at Cape Canaveral just 73 seconds after take-off. The explosion, which is seen by millions on television, kills all seven members of the crew and is the worst space disaster to date. Failure of rubber seals on a fuel line is blamed.

SPACE STATION MIR

The Soviet Union puts space station *Mir* into orbit around the Earth; it continues to function until the end of the century.

BELOW: Chernobyl power station, USSR, three days after the worst nuclear accident the world has yet seen.

US AND USSR END ARMS RACE

The US and USSR sign a treaty agreeing to eliminate intermediate-range nuclear weapons. British envoy Terry Waite is taken hostage in Beirut. Under the Montreal Protocol, 70 nations agree to limit the production of CFCs. Irangate causes a scandal in the US. The UN begins a peace mission to end the Iran–Iraq war. Work begins on an Anglo-French Channel Tunnel. Van Gogh's painting *Irises* fetches an all-time record price.

OPPOSITE: The particle beam fusion accelerator, capable of generating 100 trillion watts of power.

1987

Jan	20	Archbishop's envoy Terry Waite is taken hostage in Beirut	**Oct**	16	Hurricane sweeps across southeast England, the worst storm in Britain for 300 years
Feb	5	Iran launches missile attack on Baghdad, Iraq	**Nov**	2	Soviet leader Gorbachev criticizes Stalin in a speech marking the 70th anniversary of the Russian Revolution.
	26	Tower Commission reports on Iran-Contra scandal, USA		8	IRA bombs explode at Remembrance Day services, Enniskillen, Co. Fermanagh, Northern Ireland. Eleven killed
Mar	6	Cross-channel ferry capsizes off coast of Belgium			
Apr	17	Tamils ambush buses, Sri Lanka			
May	17	Iraqi Exocet missile hits USS *Stark* in Persian Gulf	**Dec**	7	INF Treaty: US president Reagan and Soviet leader Gorbachev agree to eliminate intermediate nuclear weapons
Sep	11	UN Secretary-General Pérez de Cuéllar begins peace mission to end Iran-Iraq war			

ABOVE: *Irises* by Vincent van Gogh (1853–90) sells for £30 million. Art has now become an investment commodity.

WAITE TAKEN HOSTAGE
Terry Waite (b. 1939), personal envoy of the Archbishop of Canterbury sent to Lebanon to negotiate the freedom of Western hostages in the country, is himself taken hostage by Hezbollah in Lebanon. Between 1983 and 1992, nearly 100 Westerners are grabbed off the streets of Beirut and held hostage for as long as seven years in guarded, underground cells throughout Lebanon.

IRANGATE
The profit from arms sent to Iran as part of a deal to free US hostages in the Lebanon is being used to support the right-wing Contra rebels fighting against the Nicaraguan government, contrary to the decision of US Congress to stop supporting the Contras. The full extent of the Irangate conspiracy is revealed in the report of the Tower Commission set up to investigate the affair. The Tower Commission finds that President Reagan did not deliberately mislead the American people but seems to be unaware of important aspects of the operation.

INF TREATY
The USSR and the USA sign an historic agreement to remove and dismantle all short- and intermediate-range nuclear weapons. The treaty requires the destruction of 1,752 Soviet and 859 US missiles with ranges from 482 to 5,471km (300 to 3,400mi).

THE LAST EMPEROR
A new film by Italian Bernardo Bertolucci (b. 1940) has opened. *The Last Emperor* tells the story of the last Manchu ruler. A roaring success with both audiences and critics, it wins nine Oscars in 1988.

SCHINKELPLATZ
Architect Rob Krier uses a muted style, combining classical and traditional details, to produce housing in Berlin on a human scale to blend in with older buildings nearby.

TOP PRICE FOR IRISES
The painting *Irises* by Van Gogh fetches £30 million, a world record for art of all types. It confirms that he is the artist most in demand by international collectors. Three years later, in 1990, Van Gogh tops even this price when his *Portrait of Dr Gachet* fetches £49.5 million.

ZEEBRUGGE DISASTER
On March 6 a cross-channel ferry capsizes off Zeebrugge, Belgium; 187 people die. It later transpires that the bow doors were left open.

COMPUTER COMPATABILITY
Apple Computer, Inc. announces new Macintosh machines that can use software designed for the rival IBM machines.

ENTER SMART CARDS
A new type of credit card, the Smart Card, is introduced. It contains electronic chips, a tiny keyboard and display, and can process and store data.

CFC BAN AGREED

Seventy nations sign a protocol in Montreal to maintain use of CFCs (chlorofluorocarbons) at 1986 levels and to reduce levels by half by 1999. CFCs are believed to have caused a 90 per cent thinning of the ozone layer over Antarctica. Ozone gas filters out harmful radiation from the Sun.

CHANNEL TUNNEL

Work on boring a tunnel under the English Channel between England and France begins on the English side. Work on the French side begins a year later.

A STAR EXPLODES

Astronomers in the southern hemisphere see a supernova (an exploding star) in a nearby galaxy.

USING GENETICS AGAINST CRIME

Genetic fingerprinting is first used in Britain to convict a criminal. The technique was developed in 1985 by Alec Jeffreys of the University of Leicester, who found that each person's core sequence of DNA is unique and can be used to determine family relationships.

DIGITAL TAPES

Digital audio tapes, which produce high-quality sound, go on sale. They are introduced by Aiwa in Japan.

RUGBY UNION

New Zealand wins the Webb Ellis Trophy in the inaugural Rugby Union World Cup, played in Australia and New Zealand. The All Blacks beat France 29–9 in the final of the sixteen-team event.

ABOVE: Fear and loathing in the New York Stock Exchange when the financial world collapses in the crash of 1987.

ANDY WARHOL
(1926–1987)

American artist and film-maker Andy Warhol has died. One of the leading exponents of Pop Art, his early days as a commercial designer may have influenced his silkscreen-produced repeated images of cans of soup and a photographic image of Marilyn Monroe. His avant-garde film factory in Greenwich Village produced works such as *Chelsea Girls* (1967). In 1968 his real life became much more eventful than his films when he was shot and seriously injured by the radical feminist Valerie Solanas.

FRED ASTAIRE
(1899–1987)

The inimitable American dancer, actor and singer Fred Astaire (real name Frederick Austerlitz) has died. After 1920s Broadway successes with his sister Adele, he moved on to Hollywood when she married Lord Charles Cavendish. He had several dancing partners but the best-known was Ginger Rogers. They danced together with apparently effortless grace in *The Gay Divorcee* (1934), *Top Hat* (1935), *Swing Time* (1936) and seven others. Despite his "retirement" in 1946 he continued to make musicals, and to act on screen until the late 1970s.

BUSH AND BHUTTO COME TO POWER

Ethnic and regional unrest begins in the Baltic states. Chilean dictator Pinochet steps down, clearing the way for democracy to return to Chile. A terrorist bomb explodes on a jumbo jet over Lockerbie, Scotland. The US shoots down an Iranian Airbus by accident. Drugs dominate the Seoul Olympics. Benazir Bhutto becomes the first Islamic woman prime minister. US climatologist warns that the "greenhouse effect" has begun.

OPPOSITE: Benazir Bhutto, the first woman prime minister of Pakistan.

1988

Jan	26	Australia celebrates 200th anniversary of arrival of white settlers. Aborigines hold protests and declare it a time of mourning
Feb	13	Winter Olympics in Calgary, Canada
Mar	13	Seikan Tunnel opens, linking islands of Honshu and Hokkaido, Japan
May	13	Soviet troops begin withdrawal from Afghanistan
July	3	USS *Vincennes* shoots down an Iranian Airbus
	6	Oil rig Piper Alpha explodes killing 290 people
	18	Nelson Mandela's 70th birthday; the event is marked by worldwide calls for his release
Aug	8	Iran-Iraq cease-fire ends eight years of war
Sep	17	Olympic Games open in Seoul, South Korea
Oct	3	Chad and Libya formally end war that has been going on since 1965
	6	Chilean dictator General Pinochet steps down after losing referendum
Nov	8	Republican George Bush wins US presidential elections
	16	Estonian parliament votes to give itself rights to veto laws from Moscow
Dec	2	Benazir Bhutto is sworn in as prime minister of Pakistan
	7	Soviet leader Mikhail Gorbachev announces plans to reduce Red Army
	21	Pan Am Flight 103 jumbo jet is blown up over Lockerbie, Scotland

UNREST IN BALTIC STATES

Ethnic and regional unrest grows in the Baltic states and Georgia as Gorbachev tries to reform the USSR without breaking it up. Discontent with economic failure and lack of civil liberties leads to growing unrest and demands for autonomy and even independence from the fifteen republics of the USSR. In December, Gorbachev announces huge unilateral cuts in the Red Army, including massive reductions in the armies kept in Eastern Europe.

PINOCHET STEPS DOWN

The Chilean military dictator General Pinochet (b. 1915) loses a referendum on democracy and steps down after fifteen years in power. During his presidency, 3,000 people have been assassinated, 1,000 "disappeared", 200,000 tortured, and a further 5,000–6,000 victims may have been buried in unmarked graves. In December 1989 Patricio Aylwin Azócar is elected president and democracy restored to Chile, with Pinochet gaining immunity for life.

BUSH BECOMES PRESIDENT

George Bush, vice-president for eight years, wins the US presidential election and continues Reaganite policies.

ABOVE: An earthquake devastates Armenia.

LOCKERBIE DISASTER

In December Pan Am Flight 103 crashes after a terrorist bomb detonates over Lockerbie, Scotland. All 259 passengers die when the 747 crashes and eleven inhabitants of Lockerbie are killed by wreckage. Evidence points to Libya and two intelligence officers are held to be guilty. Libya refuses to give them up and UN sanctions are imposed. In 1999 the two will be flown to Holland to be tried under Scottish law.

IRANIAN AIRBUS SHOT DOWN BY MISTAKE

The USS *Vincennes* shoots down an Iranian Airbus by mistake, killing all 290 passengers. Following the Iraqi Exocet air attack, directed at oil tankers en route to Iran which severely damaged the USS *Stark* in 1987, US Navy warships in the Gulf have been on high alert. The Aegis automatic air defence system on the *Vincennes* picked up an aircraft, identified it as hostile and shot it down. In fact, it was an Airbus.

GREENHOUSE EFFECT

US climatologist James E Hansen predicts that the "greenhouse effect" in which a build-up of carbon dioxide in the atmosphere traps heat at the Earth's surface, has begun.

HUMAN GENOME PROJECT

A research scheme called the Human Genome Project begins; it plans to map the complete sequence of nucleic acids in human DNA.

LEFT: Vice-President George Bush and his wife Barbara hit the campaign trail in California on their way to the White House.

ENVIRONMENTALIST MURDERED

Brazilian environmentalist and labour leader Chico Mendez is assassinated by a cattle rancher. Mendez had been actively campaigning against the destruction of the Brazilian rainforests and had unionized itinerant rubber tappers (rubber tapping being sustainable use of rainforest). In 1987 he was awarded a UN ecology prize but had received many death threats.

SEIKAN TUNNEL COMPLETED

The Seikan Rail Tunnel connecting the Japanese islands of Honshu and Hokkaido is opened after 24 years' work. At nearly 54km (34mi) long, it is the world's longest tunnel. It is also the final stage in the project to link Japan's four islands by train.

WOMAN MUSLIM LEADER

Benazir Bhutto (b. 1953), leader of the democratic Pakistan People's Party, is elected as Pakistan's prime minister. She is the first modern-day woman to be leader of a Muslim country.

MONTAG AUS LICHT

For years, German composer Karlheinz Stockhausen (b. 1928) has been engaged on a self-proclaimed masterpiece, a vast cycle of seven operas (one for each day of the week), known collectively as *Licht* ("light"). Now he has completed Monday.

WINTER OLYMPICS

Calgary in the Canadian Rockies is the venue for the Fifteenth Winter Olympics, which have been extended from twelve to sixteen days. Italian skier Alberto Tomba (b. 1966) wins two skiing golds and German ice skater Katarina Witt (b. 1965) becomes only the second woman to win back-to-back figure skating crowns.

ABOVE: Official investigators comb the wreckage of Pan Am Flight 103, which was blown up over the Scottish town of Lockerbie.

FIRST WOMAN BISHOP

Barbara Harris (b. 1930), a black woman priest, is elected the first woman bishop in the Anglican communion, to serve as suffragan bishop of Massachusetts, USA.

FOSSIL BIRD

Spanish scientists report the discovery of a previously unknown fossil of a bird which lived about 125 million years ago; it appears to be a link between the earliest known bird, *Archaeopteryx*, and modern birds.

FAKE SHROUD

A fragment of cloth from the Turin Shroud — believed to be the winding sheet of Jesus — is given a radiocarbon test that shows it was probably made no earlier than 1350.

FOOTBALL WIN FOR HOLLAND

Holland finally wins a major football competition. Ruud Gullit and Marco Van Basten lead the team to victory at the European Championships in West Germany.

SEOUL OLYMPICS

Drugs dominate the 24th Olympic Games in Seoul, South Korea. Ben Johnson claims the 100 metres gold in a world record 9.79 seconds, but the Canadian is stripped of both medal and record when he fails a test for banned drugs. Known for her fashion sense and painted nails, American sprinter Florence Griffith-Joyner (Flo-Jo) shows she is a true champion, winning three golds and a silver. She dies tragically young in 1998.

THE END OF COMMUNIST RULE

The Cold War finally comes to an end as the Berlin Wall comes down, uniting West and East Germany. Eastern European countries — Hungary, Poland, Romania and Czechoslovakia — move decisively away from Communist control. The last Soviet troops leave Afghanistan and the Angolan civil war comes to an end after fourteen years of fighting. In China, troops suppress the pro-democracy movement. US troops invade Panama. The Ayatollah issues a fatwa against author Salman Rushdie.

OPPOSITE: A Somalian refugee in Ethiopia waiting with her ration card for food.

1989

Jan	10	Cuban troops begin withdrawal from Angola
Feb	2	South African president Botha resigns; he is succeeded by FW de Klerk
	3	Military coup overthrows 35-year dictatorship of President Alfredo Stroessner, Paraguay
	14	Ayatollah Khomeini issues fatwa against author Salman Rushdie
	15	Last Soviet troops leave Afghanistan after ten years
Mar	24	Oil tanker *Exxon Valdez* runs aground, causing massive oil spill
Apr	17	In China, students call for democracy and march on Tiananmen Square
	20	Multi-party elections are held in Czechoslovakia, the first since 1946
June	4	Solidarity wins elections with landslide, Poland
	23	Angolan president dos Santos and UNITA leader Savimbi sign declaration ending civil war
Sep	10	Hungary opens borders for East Germans
	12	New Polish government is the first in Eastern Europe not under Communist rule since 1946
	26	Last of 50,000 Vietnamese forces leave Cambodia
Oct	19	Earthquake hits California
Nov	10	Berlin Wall demolished
Dec	19	US troops invade Panama to overthrow General Noriega
	30	Romanian dictator Nicolae Ceausescu executed

For the month of May 1989

SEX ....
FULL NAME .... REG. No. ....
COUNTRY ....
MARITAL STATUS ....
ACCOMPANYING DEPENDANTS ....
ZONE ....
DATE .... SUB-ZONE No. ....

PARAGUAYAN DICTATORSHIP ENDS

General Alfredo Stroessner, ruler of Paraguay, is overthrown in a coup after 35 years in power and replaced by General Andrés Rodríguez, who wins the presidential election held in May. The fall of Stroessner removes the longest-standing military dictatorship in South America.

AYATOLLAH ISSUES FATWA

In Iran Ayatollah Khomeini issues a fatwa or death threat against Salman Rushdie, the British author of *The Satanic Verses*, because of the book's supposed blasphemous content. Rushdie goes into hiding, only emerging cautiously when the threat is partly lifted in September 1998.

POLAND ADOPTS NON-COMMUNIST GOVERNMENT

Polish trade union Solidarity is legalized after talks between its leader, Lech Walesa, and the government. The Catholic Church is given a status unprecedented in Europe, and Poland begins to move towards multi-party democracy. In August the Solidarity candidate Tadeusz Mazowiecki is elected prime minister as the Communist General Jaruzelski (b. 1923) remains president. The new government is the first non-Communist government in Eastern Europe since the late 1940s.

HUNGARY OPENS BORDERS

The Hungarian Army dismantles the border fence with Austria as a symbol of the strengthening democratic reforms in the country. When the border posts are opened in September, many East Germans take the opportunity to flee to the West across Hungary's open borders.

COMMUNISM COLLAPSES

Hungary becomes a multi-party democracy as the Communist Party gives up power and changes its name and ideology. In the same month, the East German government collapses after mass demonstrations in the major cities led by the New Forum, a democratic pressure group calling for reform.

BERLIN WALL FALLS

In November, the government opens East Germany's borders and demolishes the wall separating East and West Berlin, uniting the city divided since 1945. In both Bulgaria and Czechoslovakia, the Communist Party renounces its monopoly on power as both governments fall. In December, the playwright Vaclav Havel (b. 1936) wins the election as the first non-Communist president of Czechoslovakia since 1948.

SAN FRANCISCO EARTHQUAKE

An earthquake caused by the San Andreas Fault strikes San Francisco and Oakland, California, killing 62 people and causing widespread damage and fires.

CEAUSESCU EXECUTED

Street fighting breaks out in Bucharest as the Committee for National Salvation, backed by the Army, attacks buildings held by the state secret police, the Securitate. Romanian dictator Nicolae Ceausescu and his wife flee Bucharest. They are swiftly recaptured and killed by a firing squad on Christmas Day for "crimes against the people". The Romanian Communist Party is abolished and the ruling National Salvation Front promises free elections as the country moves towards democracy.

OPERATION JUST CAUSE

Some 12,000 US troops invade Panama to oust General Manuel Noriega who has become implicated with Central American drug dealers as well as human rights abuses. In the fighting, 220 Panamanians and 314 soldiers are killed. The American forces suffer 23 dead and 324 wounded. Three civilians are killed.

STUDENTS KILLED IN TIANANMEN SQUARE

Students and other pro-democracy protesters occupying Tiananmen Square in Beijing, China, are fired on by the Red Army as it reoccupies the square. Many hundreds are killed and thousands later imprisoned as the pro-democracy movement is suppressed throughout China.

SOVIETS WITHDRAW FROM AFGHANISTAN

The last Soviet troops leave Afghanistan after a ten-year occupation. The long-drawn-out guerrilla war has cost the USSR more than 15,000 killed, 311 missing and 35,478 wounded. The Afghans lose over 100,000 killed.

THE PROTECTING VEIL

This new cello piece by British composer John Tavener (b. 1944) is hailed as a powerful example of the "new simplicity" in music. Its spiritual content makes it popular and it goes to the top of the CD charts.

CLOSE-UP OF NEPTUNE

Space probe *Voyager 2* passes within 5,000km (3,106mi) of Neptune after a journey of more than twelve years, sending back clear pictures and discovering a Great Dark Spot and fierce winds.

IVORY TRADE BANNED

The Convention on International Trade in Endangered Species agrees to a total ban on trading in ivory. In Kenya, 12 tons of elephant tusks are burnt as a sign of commitment to stamping out the trade.

ECSTASY FUELS RAVE SCENE

The development of the rave scene youth subculture is fuelled by the drug ecstasy and techno dance music. Tens of thousands of teenagers and people in their twenties are attracted to acid-house rave parties.

OPPOSITE: After almost 30 years, the Berlin Wall comes down as the Eastern bloc crumbles and the Cold War finally ends.

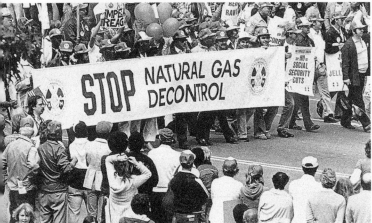

ABOVE: Batman, the caped crusader, in sombre mood amid props and sets reminiscent of the dystopian *Metropolis*.

LEFT: Unrest in Middle America as the downside of Reagonomics strikes home, just after their champion leaves office.

BELOW LEFT: Somalian refugees at the Hartisheik camp in Ethiopia make do with whatever is at hand to make a home.

BATMAN
American star Michael Keaton's portrayal of the caped do-gooder is more brooding than the light-hearted version of earlier cartoons and films; this is helped by the sets and props. This new version of Batman breaks box office records within months of opening.

HILLSBOROUGH FOOTBALL DISASTER
Overcrowding kills 95 Liverpool fans at an F.A. Cup semi-final at Hillsborough in Sheffield, UK. It is the highest death toll in British sports history and forces further reform of the game.

EXXON VALDEZ OIL DISASTER

The *Exxon Valdez* oil tanker runs aground in Prince William Sound, Alaska. Almost 50 million litres (11 million gallons) of crude oil spills into the sea and spreads over 2,300 sq km (900 sq mi) of coast, devastating marine life.

RIGHT: A boom is used to try and scrape surface oil off the water.

BELOW: The clean-up team move in to assess the damage to the coastline and plan a strategy to make good the damage.

ABOVE: A golden-eye duck, one of the innocent victims of the spill.

ABOVE: Aerial view of the huge extent of the damage.

INTO THE NEW MILLENNIUM

In the 1990s the political map is re-drawn. The Soviet Union crumbles, and more than 70 years of Soviet communism come to an end, leaving the United States as a solitary superpower. The collapse of Communism in Eastern Europe exposes ethnic tensions and war breaks out in the Balkans. However, in South Africa the oppressive apartheid system is finally dismantled. Peace also comes to war-torn Central America. In the world of science, distant planets such as Venus and Mercury are mapped.

OPPOSITE: Firefighters in the burning Kuwaiti oil fields during the Gulf War of 1991.

1990–1999

KEY EVENTS OF THE DECADE

- SOVIET UNION COLLAPSES
- GULF WAR
- APARTHEID ENDS
- YUGOSLAVIA BREAKS UP
- UN EARTH SUMMIT
- WAR IN BOSNIA
- RWANDAN CIVIL WAR
- DEATH OF PRINCESS DIANA
- COLLAPSE OF ASIAN ECONOMIES

- HALE-BOPP COMET
- HUBBLE SPACE TELESCOPE LAUNCHED
- PLANET VENUS IS MAPPED
- CLONING TAKES OFF
- ANIMATRONICS COME TO CINEMA
- CENTENARY OLYMPIC GAMES
- SINGLE EUROPEAN CURRENCY

WORLD POPULATION **5,295** MILLION

GERMANY UNITES, MANDELA IS FREED

ANC leader Nelson Mandela is released from prison after 27 years in captivity. Iraq invades Kuwait, prompting an immediate response from the United Nations and the USA. Tension rises as US forces mass on the Saudi Arabian border. East and West Germany are finally united. The Soviet Union begins to crumble as Lithuania declares independence. The Hubble Space Telescope is launched but proves to be defective. A new hand-held computer console goes on sale.

1990

Feb	2	President FW de Klerk ends twenty-year ban on ANC
	21	Namibia becomes an independent state
	25	US-backed Violeta Chamorro wins Nicaraguan elections
Mar	11	Lithuania declares independence from Soviet Union
Apr	24	Hubble Space Telescope is launched into orbit
May	29	Boris Yeltsin elected president of Russian Federation
June	8	Russian Federation declares itself a sovereign state
July	19	Iraqi troops mass on Kuwaiti border

Aug	2	Iraqi forces invade Kuwait. Emir flees to Saudi Arabia
	6	UN Security Council imposes sanctions against Iraq
	24	Hostage Brian Keenan, held in Lebanon since 1986, is released
Sep	28	Serbian parliament strips Kosovo of autonomy, Yugoslavia
Oct	2	East and West Germany are reunited
Dec	9	Slobodan Milosevic is elected president of Serbia in the country's first free elections for 50 years

MANDELA FREED

The South African government under President de Klerk (b. 1936) lifts the ban on the African National Congress (ANC) and other anti-apartheid parties and frees ANC leader Nelson Mandela after 27 years in prison. Talks begin on moving South Africa towards multiracial democracy.

NAMIBIA INDEPENDENT

The last white-run colony in Africa gains its independence as South Africa relinquishes its hold on South West Africa, renamed Namibia. The former German colony had been administered by South Africa since 1919 under League of Nations and UN mandates. Sam Nujoma (b. 1929), the leader of the SWAPO opposition, is elected president.

IRAQ INVADES KUWAIT

Iraq invades the neighbouring oil-rich sheikdom of Kuwait. The Emir flees to Saudi Arabia. Iraq's unprovoked invasion and potential threat to Saudi Arabia prompt an almost immediate reaction. The United Nations declares sanctions against Iraq and, in Operation Desert Shield, the United States airlifts 2,300 troops to Saudi Arabia, within 18 hours. Iraqi leader Saddam Hussein (b. 1937) makes a formal peace treaty with long-term enemy Iran.

GERMANY UNITED

East and West Germany are reunited after pro-unity parties in East Germany win a majority in elections held in March and open talks with West Germany. In July the government cedes sovereignty over economic, monetary and social policy to West Germany and the Deutschmark becomes the official currency. Elections held across Germany in December return Christian Democrat Helmut Kohl to power.

ABOVE: Free at last, ANC leader Nelson Mandela meets President George Bush in the White House.

THE EUROPEAN

A new concept in journalism, *The European* is founded as an English-language newspaper, dealing with news from a European perspective, on sale all over Europe.

POSSESSION

British writer AS Byatt (b. 1938) has published what is her best novel. Full of symbols and symmetries, it recreates the Victorian world (and writings) of the biographers' subject as well as their obsession with, and possession of, their quarry.

ABOVE: Hubble Space Telescope deployed from space shuttle *Discovery*.

ABOVE: Martina Navratilova takes the Pilkington Glass Ladies Singles Trophy at Eastbourne, UK, as an appetizer for her Wimbledon triumph a month later.

BURMESE ELECTIONS

The National League for Democracy wins multi-party elections in Burma but the army refuses to hand over power. The League's co-founder is Aung San Suu Kyi (b. 1945), who has been under house arrest since 1989 because of her opposition to the ruling military junta. She is awarded the Nobel Peace Prize in 1991.

NICARAGUAN ELECTIONS

Elections held in Nicaragua are won by US-backed Violeta Barrios de Chamorro. A month later the US lifts sanctions and by the end of June the Contras are disbanded. In 1991, US president Bush pledges economic support for Nicaragua. The cost to Nicaragua of economic sanctions and the Contra war is estimated at $15 billion, with some 30,000 people killed.

NEWS FROM NEPTUNE

US space probe *Voyager 2* flies within 4,800km (3,000mi) of Neptune, reporting four rings, six new moons and a stormy surface like that of Jupiter.

GAME BOY

Japanese computer manufacturer Nintendo launch Game Boy, the first programmable hand-held computer games console. It is an instant success.

BACK TO EARTH

Space shuttle *Columbia* returns to Earth after six years in orbit, bringing the Long Duration Exposure Facility, a railway truck-sized container of scientific experiments.

STRETCHABLE CERAMICS

Japanese researchers announce the development of ceramics that can be stretched at temperatures of about 1,600° C (2.912° F) during manufacture.

HUBBLE DEFECTIVE

The Hubble Space Telescope is launched by space shuttle *Discovery* from Kennedy Space Center, USA. Orbiting at an altitude of 600km (375mi) above the Earth, it is designed to see further into space than any Earthbound telescope. However, its main mirror is found to be flawed, distorting the images and limiting the telescope's usefulness.

SUCCESS FOR NAVRATILOVA

Czech-born American tennis star Martina Navratilova becomes queen of Wimbledon when she achieves her ninth singles title. She beats American player Zina Garrison in the final.

GERMANY WIN WORLD CUP

Defending champions Argentina scratch and fight to reach the final in Rome at the fourteenth football World Cup but lose a disappointing match to Germany.

RIGHT: American composer Aaron Copeland (b. 1900) dies. He is best known for his ballet *Appalachian Spring* (1944).

ABOVE: In the White House, the US and Russia agree to terms laying down the foundations for a future arms limitation agreement.

BELOW: A helicopter gunship covers the USS *Dwight D Eisenhower* as she sails through the Suez Canal to the Mediterranean.

THE SOVIET UNION COLLAPSES

The Warsaw Pact is dissolved. A Communist coup takes place in the Soviet Union. Boris Yeltsin comes to power. Mikhail Gorbachev resigns as leader of the Soviet Union. The USSR comes to an end, 74 years after the Russian Revolution. Operation Desert Storm launches the Gulf War and a US-led multinational operation liberates Kuwait from Iraqi occupation. Croatia and Slovenia declare independence and Yugoslavia begins to break up.

OPPOSITE: Iraqi forces set light to oil wells outside Kuwait City as they retreat from the region.

1991

Jan	15	Iraq fails to meet UN deadline for withdrawal from Kuwait
	16	Operation Desert Storm begins. US-led operation begins air offensive to liberate Kuwait
	18	Iraq sends Scud missiles against Israel
Feb	17	Serbia suspends provisional Kosovo constitution
	22	Retreating Iraqi forces torch Kuwaiti oil wells
	24	US-led troops begin ground offensive against Iraqi forces
	28	Gulf War ends
Apr	30	Kurdish refugees move into "safe havens"
May	28	Ethiopian People's Revolutionary Democratic Front captures Addis Ababa
	31	Civil war ends in Angola

June	17	Population Registration Act ends apartheid in South Africa
	25	Republics of Croatia and Slovenia declare independence
July	31	US president Bush and Soviet leader Gorbachev sign Strategic Arms Reduction Treaty (START) to reduce numbers of long-range nuclear weapons
Aug	19	Hard-line Communists stage coup against Soviet leader Mikhail Gorbachev
Sep	25	Peace accord ends civil war in El Salvador
Dec	25	Mikhail Gorbachev resigns; USSR comes to an end

USSR CRUMBLES

As Soviet control is removed from eastern Germany, the Warsaw Pact is formally dissolved. Inside the Soviet Union, Latvia and Estonia vote in referenda for independence, following the lead set by Lithuania. The USSR continues to fall apart as domestic, economic and political pressures mount. In August, hard-line Communists seize power while President Gorbachev is on holiday. The coup fails as Boris Yeltsin, president of Russia, leads popular resistance against it. As a result, Gorbachev's hold on power is seriously weakened and Ukraine and other states push for independence from the USSR. In December, Russia, Belarus and Ukraine set up the Commonwealth of Independent States (CIS). The USSR collapses and Gorbachev resigns on Christmas Day, bringing Communist Party rule and the Soviet Union to an end.

AIDS

The announcement that US sports star Magic Johnson is HIV positive, and the death from AIDS of UK rock singer Freddie Mercury, increase public awareness of the rapid worldwide spread of AIDS.

GULF WAR

In January, the US leads allied forces in an air attack, code-named Operation Desert Thunder, against Saddam Hussein's capital, Baghdad, Iraq. Following a month of intensive bombing, ground forces begin to liberate Kuwait in February, achieving their objective within four days and driving Iraqi forces out of Kuwait. During the retreat, oil wells are torched, causing serious pollution. At the end of the war, allied casualties are 95 killed and 370 wounded. The Iraqis suffered 30,000 killed in air attacks and the ground war and lost 20,000 prisoners with 270 tanks destroyed.

ASTEROID PHOTOGRAPHED

The *Galileo* space probe passes within 1,600km (995mi) of the asteroid Gaspra and photographs it. This is the first-ever asteroid photograph taken in space.

PREHISTORIC REMAINS

The preserved body of a man who died around 3300 BC is found in a glacier in the Austrian Alps. Probably a hunter, he is tattooed on his back, knees and ankles, and has a bow and a quiver of arrows.

ABOVE: A submarine bomb disposal expert attaches an explosive charge to an Iraqi mine in the Persian Gulf during the Gulf War.

ABOVE: An F-117A stealth fighter aircraft of the 37th Tactical Fighter Wing rolls towards the runway for the flight back home after Operation Desert Storm.

ABOVE: Demolished vehicles line Highway 8, the route that fleeing Iraqi forces took as they retreated from Kuwait.

ABOVE: Haitians, who had fled during the US invasion, are
repatriated and return home to their villages.

ABOVE: The UN Commissioner for Refugees, Sadako Ogata, visits refugees returning to Somalia after the civil war.

APARTHEID ENDS

In February President de Klerk announces plans to repeal all apartheid laws in South Africa. Legislation is passed to end racial controls on land ownership and in June all remaining discriminatory laws are repealed. The USA ends sanctions against South Africa, and the country is re-admitted into world sport.

ETHIOPIA AND SOMALIA

After a lengthy civil war, President Mengistu flees Ethiopia as seventeen years of Marxist rule are brought to an end. Neighbouring Somalia, meanwhile, collapses into anarchy as rival warlords fight for control following the overthrow of President Siyad Barrah in January.

JFK

A new film has been released about US president Kennedy and the conspiracy theory surrounding his assassination. Directed by US film director Oliver Stone (b. 1946), it stars American actor Kevin Costner (b. 1955) as the New Orleans district attorney.

MAPPING VENUS

While orbiting Venus, the US unmanned spacecraft *Magellan* compiles a map of the surface, using radar signals.

POWELL OVERTAKES BEAMON

US long jumper Mike Powell beats Bob Beamon's famous leap of 8.90 metres by five centimetres at the World Athletics Championships in Tokyo. The world record had stood since the 1968 Olympics.

NATURAL DISASTERS

In April a typhoon, travelling at 233km/h (145miph), strikes Bangladesh, killing more than 139,000 people and making ten million homeless. In June, Mt. Pinatubo, a Philippine volcano dormant for 600 years, erupts, killing more than 700 people.

CONFLICT IN YUGOSLAVIA

The delicate balance between Catholic, Muslim and Orthodox ethnic groups which held together under the tough rule of President Tito is now unravelling. Ethnic tensions between the different communities are rising and Yugoslavia is falling apart as Slovenia and Croatia declare their independence, exacerbated by newly elected Serbian leader Slobodan Milosevic (b. 1941) who is emphazising ethnic differences to consolidate his power base. The Serb-dominated Yugoslav National Army (JNA) tries to prevent the break-up of the country and attacks Croatia, starting a lengthy and bitter war between the two states.

THE SILENCE OF THE LAMBS

Welsh actor Anthony Hopkins (b. 1937) plays Hannibal Lecter, psychiatrist turned serial killer, in a new film, *The Silence of the Lambs*, which has opened this year. US film star Jodie Foster (b. 1962) plays the FBI agent. A chilling movie, the horror is tightly controlled by director Jonathan Demme.

YUGOSLAVIA CRUMBLES AND LOS ANGELES BURNS

Inter-racial war breaks out in former Yugoslavia, and the abhorrent term "ethnic cleansing" enters the language as evidence is televised of death camps in Bosnia. Race riots erupt in Los Angeles, after the savage beating of a young black motorist. The UN Earth Summit meets in Rio de Janeiro to discuss the future of planet Earth, Disneyland comes to Europe, and Expo 92 is held in Spain.

1992

Feb	1	UN-negotiated peace comes into effect in El Salvador
	8	Winter Olympics open
Mar	1	Bosnia-Herzegovina declares independence following referendum
	2	Violence breaks out in Sarajevo between Serbs, Croats and Muslims
	22	Communist rule ends in Albania after 45 years
Apr	8	Serb and federal army forces begin bombardment of Sarajevo as violence escalates in Bosnia Mujaheddin rebels take control in Afghanistan
	29	All-white jury acquits police of beating black American, precipitating riots, Los Angeles, USA
July	25	Olympic Games open in Barcelona
Aug	13	United Nations condemns Serbian policy of so-called "ethnic cleansing", describing it as a war crime
Sep	25	New canal links Maine and Danube rivers, Germany
Nov	3	Democrat Bill Clinton wins US presidential elections

ABOVE: General "Stormin" Norman Schwartzkopf, Commander in Chief, speaks to soldiers during Operation Desert Shield.

ABOVE: General Colin Powell consults the Pentagon while visiting troops during Operation Desert Shield.

WAR IN BOSNIA

After the former Yugoslav province of Bosnia votes for independence, a vicious war erupts as Croatia and Serbia attempt to carve up Bosnia along ethnic lines, threatening its multi-racial nature in a campaign known as "ethnic cleansing". Bosnian Serbs backed by the Yugoslav National Army attack the fledgling country which they wish to remain part of Greater Serbia. They overrun 70 per cent of the country and set up a Serb government in Pale. In August, evidence emerges of Serbian death camps where Bosnian prisoners are kept in appalling conditions.

MUJAHEDDIN VICTORIOUS

Mujaheddin rebels in Afghanistan take control after a lengthy civil war, overthrowing the Communist government of President Najibullah. The Mujaheddin led the resistance to the Soviet occupation of the country from 1979–89, and fought on to remove the Communist government.

LA RACE RIOTS

Race riots erupt in Los Angeles after police officers, who savagely beat a young black man, Rodney King, and are witnessed on video, are acquitted by an all-white jury. The verdict outrages the black community and reveals the extent of racial discrimination still experienced by many in the USA.

CLINTON WINS ELECTION

Bill Clinton (b. 1946) from Arkansas wins the presidential election for the Democrats, only the second time in 24 years that a Democrat has gained the White House. However, Clinton's record of draft-dodging and marital infidelity infuriates right-wing Republicans, who campaign incessantly against him and his government.

LAST EUROPEAN COMMUNIST GOVERNMENT

In Albania, the last Communist government in Europe ends after the opposition Democrat Party wins a majority in the general election.

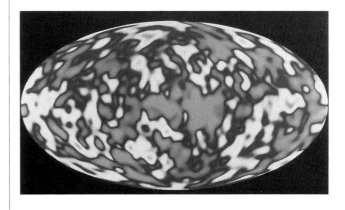

ABOVE: A microwave map of the whole sky compiled from a year's worth of data from NASA's Cosmic Background Explorer.

OPERATION RESTORE HOPE

In Somalia, United Nations military observers arrive in the capital Mogadishu to help distribute food aid. In what is code-named Operation Restore Hope, some 17,000 soldiers drawn from the United States and over ten other UN countries attempt to impose order to allow relief to be distributed. In a raid by US rangers to capture the Somali warlord Mohammad Farrah Aidid, in October 1993, eighteen soldiers are killed and 73 wounded.

EL SALVADOR

The United Nations finally brokers peace in El Salvador. The FMLN is granted the status of a political party. Peace talks began in 1990. It is estimated that about 100,000 people died in El Salvador between 1979 and 1990.

ABOVE: Riots and fires in Los Angeles follow after black motorist Rodney King was beaten up by the LAPD.

LEFT: Presidential candidate and Democrat Bill Clinton campaigns in Albuquerque, New Mexico. a key state in the election battle.

PERUVIAN GUERRILLA WAR

In Peru, Maoist leader Dr Renoso Guzman is captured by the Army and police special forces, bringing an end to the activities of the Shining Path. The campaign of bombings, assassination and terror has caused the deaths of more than 23,000 men and women since it began in 1982.

EXPO 92, SEVILLE

In April, Expo 92, the first Exposition Universelle for 22 years, opens in Seville, Spain. Nations from around the world display their innovations and achievements in industry, science and the arts. One of the lasting monuments will be Alamillo Bridge. Designed by Spanish architect and civil engineer Santiago Calatrava, it is one of the most beautiful of all modern bridges. Its harp-like cable-styled construction make it instantly.

GENETICALLY ENGINEERED WHEAT

US biologists report in June that they have developed the first genetically engineered wheat, which is proof against a powerful herbicide.

WATER LINK

In Germany, a new canal opens linking the Maine and Danube rivers. This completes a river and canal trade route from the Baltic Sea to the Black Sea.

DISNEYLAND COMES TO PARIS
Disneyland comes to Europe and the whole Disney culture — from the themed worlds to the cavalcades and wandering Disney characters brought to life — is transported to Paris, France.

SATELLITE CAPTURED
Three astronauts aboard the space shuttle *Endeavour* do a space walk to capture *Intelsat 6*, a communications satellite which has drifted into the wrong orbit. They put it back into the right orbit.

BIG BANG NEWS
NASA scientists announce that their Cosmic Background Explorer (COBE) satellite, launched in 1989, has detected 15-billion-year-old clouds of matter that relate to the Big Bang. American astrophysicist George Fitzgerald Smoot (b. 1945), who heads COBE's team of analysts, announces that the satellite had found fluctuations in the background radiation, preserved from about 300,000 years after the Big Bang. The variations gave rise to stars, galaxies and other cosmic structures.

ANTI-COLUMBUS DEMONSTRATIONS
Demonstrations against the celebrations of the 500th anniversary of the arrival of Christopher Columbus in the New World take place in many Latin American countries.

METHANE UNDER THE OCEAN
US scientists find deposits of methane hydrate off the coast of northern North America, which may prove to be a huge source of natural gas.

EARTH SUMMIT
In June representatives from 178 counties meet in an "Earth Summit" — the UN Conference on Environment and Development — in Rio de Janeiro, Brazil. Most agree to phase out CFC gases, which cause depletion of the ozone layer, to preserve forests and protect biodiversity.

WOMEN PRIESTS
The Church of England Synod votes to allow women to be ordained as priests. Ten women were ordained to the Anglican priesthood in Australia in 1992.

WINTER OLYMPICS
Twelve sites around Albertville in France are the venue for the sixteenth Winter Olympics. Short-track speed skating and freestyle moguls skiing become Olympic events. Sixteen-year-old Toni Nieminen takes ski-jumping gold on the big hill and in the team event and bronze on the small hill.

OLYMPIC GAMES
The emphasis returns to athletics at the 25th Olympic Games in Barcelona, Spain. In the long jump, US athlete Carl Lewis (b. 1961) wins a gold for the third successive Games, while Vitali Sherbo, of a post-Soviet Union team, dominates men's gymnastics and the American basketball "Dream Team" sweeps all before it.

ABOVE: Astronauts Hieb, Akers and Thuot reel in the *Intelsat 6* satellite as part of the nine-day STS-49 Mission.

ISRAEL AND PLO SIGN FOR PEACE

Israel and the PLO sign an historic peace accord. In Russia, the army crushes an attempted coup against Yeltsin's government. The European single market comes into force. Aborigines finally achieve recognition of their land rights in Australia. Explorers cross Antarctica on foot. New Zealander Jane Campion becomes the first woman film director to win the Palme d'Or and Spielberg's film *Schindler's List* opens to critical acclaim.

1 9 9 3

Jan	1	EC's single market comes into force
	1	Czechoslovakia divides
Feb	26	World Trade Center bombed, USA
Mar	17	Ballet star Rudolf Nureyev dies aged 55
May	24	Eritrea gains independence
Sep	13	PLO and Israel sign peace agreement
Oct	4	Army crushes potential coup, Moscow, Russia
	15	Nelson Mandela and President de Klerk jointly win Nobel Peace Prize
Nov	1	Maastricht Treaty comes into force, European Community
Dec	22	Aborigines win land rights, Australia

MIDDLE EAST PEACE ACCORD

In Washington, Prime Minister Rabin of Israel and the Palestine Liberation Organization (PLO) leader Yasser Arafat sign a treaty handing over control of the Gaza Strip and the West Bank city of Jericho to the Palestinians. Secret talks between the two sides in the Norwegian capital of Oslo have led to this historic agreement, which is designed to be the first stage in the gradual handing over of Israeli-occupied territory to the Palestinians in return for their recognition of the state of Israel.

SINGLE EUROPEAN MARKET

The European single market comes into force, removing all obstacles to the free movement of trade, services and people throughout the European Community. The Maastricht Treaty, establishing a single currency by 1999, comes into force and the European Community (EC) becomes the European Union (EU).

LANDMARK SPIELBERGS

US film director Steven Spielberg has released two remarkable but highly contrasting movies. His *Jurassic Park* involves genetically recreated dinosaurs that run amok in the theme park to end all theme parks and is a commercial coup. More sombre is *Schindler's List*. Based on Thomas Keneally's book *Schindler's Ark* and shot almost entirely in black and white, this moving film is concerned with the Holocaust and is Spielberg's account of Oskar Schindler, the German businessman who rescued Jews from the death camps by employing them in his factory. Liam Neeson (b. 1952) stars as Schindler. An epilogue shows actual survivors, and Schindler's widow, at Schindler's grave in Israel.

ABOVE: Rudolph Nureyev, probably the best-known ballet dancer of his generation, dies in Paris. He is seen here dancing in the USA.

CZECHOSLOVAKIA DIVIDES

Following the success of pro-independence parties in Slovakia, Czechoslovakia splits amicably in two, with both the Czech Republic and Slovakia becoming independent states.

COMMUNIST COUP FAILS

A hardline Communist coup against the Russian government of Boris Yeltsin is crushed when the army storms the White House, the parliament building in Moscow. The coup reveals levels of discontent in Russia caused by the failure of economic reforms.

ANOTHER SUPERNOVA

Spanish astronomer Francisco García announces that he has discovered another supernova (exploding star), some eleven million light years distant.

RUDOLF HAMETOVICH NUREYEV (1938–1993)

The great Russian ballet dancer Rudolf Nureyev has died in Paris of an AIDS-related disease. In 1961, Nureyev defected from the Kirov Ballet while visiting Paris, and in 1962 made his debut at Covent Garden with the great ballerina Margot Fonteyn. They formed a partnership that transformed ballet. From 1983 to 1989 Nureyev was artistic director to the Paris Opera. As a solo dancer he performed with the world's greatest companies.

ABOVE: US Marines take part in the multinational relief effort Operation Restore Hope in Mogadishu, Somalia.

WAR IN BOSNIA

UN forces are deployed as peacekeepers in war-torn Bosnia. However, Bosnian Serbs continue to shell the regional capital of Sarajevo. Croatian forces shell the town of Mostar.

FRANCIS VINCENT (FRANK) ZAPPA (1940–1993)

American rock musician Frank Zappa has died after a two-year battle with prostate cancer. Always at the forefront of experimental rock as guitarist, singer and music writer, Zappa founded the group Mothers of Invention in the 1960s. Their first album *Freak Out!* was released in 1966. Zappa's first solo album was *Lumpy Gravy* (1968) and his final album *Yellow Shark*, appeared this year.

FIRST WOMAN ATTORNEY-GENERAL

Janet Reno (b. 1938) becomes the first woman Attorney-General of the USA. The start of her new career is marred by a disaster during which more than 70 members of a cult religion die at Waco, Texas, while being besieged by the FBI.

"DONT ASK, DON'T TELL"

In the US, President Clinton reaches an agreement with the Department of Defense whereby gays can serve in the military provided that they neither openly declare their homosexuality nor engage in homosexual activity.

FERMAT'S LAST THEOREM

British mathematician Andrew Wiles claims to have proved Fermat's Last Theorem, a mathematical proposition put forward in 1627 Pierre de Fermat — who omitted to provide the proof.

8,000 KM TELESCOPE

In August the Very Long Baseline Array, huge radio telescope dishes at ten different sites scattered over 8,000km (5,000mi), begins operation.

ABOVE: President George Bush and Russian premier Boris Yeltsin who has just survived an attempted coup by Communist hardliners.

HUBBLE CORRECTED

During five spacewalks astronauts aboard the space shuttle *Endeavour* "capture" the Hubble Space Telescope, correct its faults and update it.

ROMANOVS FINGERPRINTED

Genetic material from the British relatives of the Romanovs, the last Russian Tsars, are compared with material taken from the supposed remains of Nicholas II and his family. Genetic fingerprinting methods prove that the remains are genuine.

SUPERMODEL STARS

Supermodels of the fashion industry, such as Cindy Crawford, Christy Turlington and Linda Evangelista, become stars, known internationally in their own right.

REICHSTAG

In probably the most important artistic aspect of German reunification, Alex Schultes wins the architectural competition to design the administrative district around the Reichstag.

PIANO WINS PALME D'OR

New Zealand film director Jane Campion (b. 1954) becomes the first woman to win the prestigious Palme d'Or at Cannes for her latest film *The Piano*. The film stars Holly Hunter (b. 1958), who also gets an award for her portrayal of the mute heroine who finds expression through her piano playing.

ERITREA INDEPENDENT

The former Italian colony of Eritrea, which has been joined to Ethiopia since 1952, wins its independence. This is in reward for its role in overthrowing the Mengistu government.

ABORIGINAL LAND RIGHTS

In Australia, the federal parliament passes the Native Title Act, recognizing Aboriginal rights to make claims on land taken away from them by early European settlers. The Act follows years of campaigning by Aboriginal rights groups.

FIRST WALK ACROSS ANTARCTICA

English explorer Ranulph Fiennes (b. 1945) and Mike Stroud become the first people to cross Antarctica on foot. After 95 days they are picked up 560km (350mi) from the sea, having walked 2,167km (1,347mi) pulling sleds loaded with supplies.

HOUSE

British sculptor Rachel Whiteread (b. 1963) inspires controversy with her sculpture *House*. It is a cast of a house in London's East End, made by pouring in concrete and then removing the walls and roof. Whiteread's work is shown in Paris, Chicago and Berlin.

MANDELA FOR PRESIDENT

South Africa holds multiracial elections and Mandela becomes the country's first black president. Violence breaks out in Rwanda. The IRA announces a ceasefire in Northern Ireland. Russian forces invade breakaway Chechnya. Dead animals pickled in formaldehyde are a talking point in the art world and the long-awaited Channel Tunnel is opened. Fossil remains in Ethiopia help to date human prehistory.

OPPOSITE: Displaced persons — internal refugees in Rwanda — seek safety in Kibeho Camp.

1994

Feb	**5**	Serb mortar bomb hits crowded market place, Sarajevo
	23	Ceasefire between Serbia and Croatia, Bosnia
Apr	**6**	The presidents of Burundi and Rwanda are killed in a plane crash; mass violence erupts in Rwanda
	26	First multiracial elections begin in South Africa, resulting in victory for the African National Congress (ANC)
May	**1**	Brazilian racing champion Ayrton Senna killed
	6	Channel Tunnel opens
	10	Nelson Mandela sworn in as first black president of South Africa
Aug	**14**	"Carlos the Jackal", most wanted terrorist, is arrested
	31	Irish Republican Army (IRA) declares ceasefire, Northern Ireland
Sep	**19**	US troops invade Haiti
Dec	**11**	Russian forces invade Chechnya, following its declaration of independence

PRESIDENT MANDELA

Nelson Mandela becomes the first black president of South African following the victory of the African National Congress (ANC) in the country's first multiracial democratic elections.

MASS SLAUGHTER IN RWANDA

Genocide breaks out in Rwanda as the Hutu-dominated army and Hutu extremists massacre 500,000 people from the Tutsi majority. The Tutsis establish control and two million Hutus flee for their lives into neighbouring Zaire. The genocide and mass exodus follow the death in a plane crash of the presidents of both Rwanda and neighbouring Burundi, which experiences similar massacres.

NORTHERN IRELAND CEASEFIRE

Following the Anglo–Irish Downing Street Declaration between the prime ministers of Britain and Ireland, John Major (b. 1943) and Albert Reynolds (b. 1932), to bring peace to Northern Ireland, the Irish Republican Army (IRA) declare a ceasefire. This allows Sinn Fein, their political representatives, to take part in the peace talks.

CHANNEL TUNNEL OPENS

The Channel Tunnel is open. Running under the sea between England and France, it provides a high-speed rail link.

RIGHT: The huge ozone hole over the Antarctic, mapped by the Russian *Meteor 3* satellite.

RUSSIANS INVADE CHECHNYA

Russian troops occupy the rebel Caucasian province of Chechnya after it unilaterally declared independence from Russia. The capital, Grozny, is levelled to the ground in the fighting, which continues until an agreement is reached which in effect grants the province de facto independence. The final Russian troops withdraw in January 1997. In May 1997, Russia and Chechnya sign a peace agreement formally ending the separatist war.

YEMEN CIVIL WAR

Tension, which has existed between the Northern and Southern Yemen elites since last year, explodes into war. This follows sporadic clashes when the southern leadership declares secession, formal unification having taken place in 1990. The fighting involves armour and artillery and in July the Northern forces capture Aden, which had been bombarded with SCUD missiles. In a frenzy of religious zeal the northerners destroyed the only brewery in the Arabian peninsula.

FINNISH DIAMONDS

Diamond deposits are discovered in northern Finland, leading to hopes that there are very large deposits in the region.

PEACE IN COLOMBIA

In Colombia, the government reaches peace with four left-wing guerrilla groups.

SARAJEVO BOMBED

In February a Serb 120-mm mortar bomb hits a crowded market place in Sarajevo, killing 68 people and seriously wounding 200 more. Subsequently, Serb forces bombard safe areas in Goradze and Srebrenica. NATO authorizes air strikes on Serbian posts, galvanizing the Contact Group of USA, UK, Russia and Germany.

AWAY FROM THE FLOCK SHOCKS

British artist Damien Hirst (b. 1965) provokes controversy and debate in the media with his work. This year sees *Away from the Flock*, featuring a dead lamb preserved in a glass tank of formaldehyde. Last year he used a similar technique to display *Mother and Child Divided*, a cow and calf sliced in half.

US INTO HAITI

The US army lands on the island of Haiti to restore civilian rule after a military coup deposed Jean-Bertrand Aristide, the democratically elected president, in September 1991. Presidential elections held in August 1995 result in victory for René Préval, a close associate of Aristide.

PULP FICTION

American director Quentin Tarantino (b. 1963), of *Reservoir Dogs* fame, produces a new film — *Pulp Fiction*. It stars John Travolta and Harvey Keitel, and is inspired by thrillers of the 1950s and 1960s.

KANSAI AIRPORT

One of the largest civil engineering projects of recent years, Japan's new airport has opened. The buildings are designed by Renzo Piano and are sited on a specially created artificial island.

COMET HITS JUPITER

Chunks of Comet Shoemaker-Levy 9 collide with the planet Jupiter in July, producing fiery plumes of gas; the comet had broken up in Jupiter's magnetic field.

MISSING LINK

The uncertainty surrounding human origins becomes a little clearer when anthropologists announce the discovery in Ethiopia of fossils of *Australopithecus ramidus*, the earliest direct ancestors of humans. The fossils are 4.4 million years old.

MASS SUICIDE

Members of an international religious cult, Order of the Solar Temple, commit mass suicide in Switzerland and Canada. It is one of a number of mass suicides and other events by members of religious cults heralding the end of the millennium.

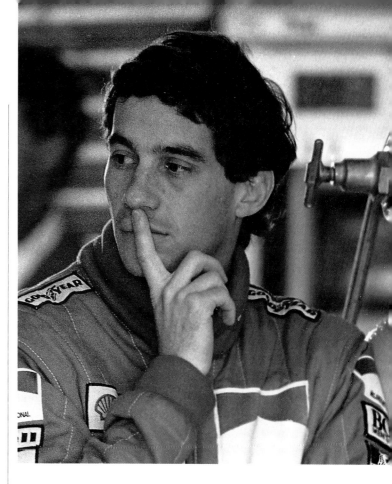

ABOVE: Brazilian racing champion Ayrton Senna is killed when his car crashes in the Grand Prix race at Monza, Italy.

EUTHANASIA PERMITTED

In the US, Oregon voters support Measure 16 permitting euthanasia in regulated circumstances.

WINTER OLYMPICS

The seventeenth Winter Olympics take place in the Norwegian town of Lillehammer just two years after the previous Winter Games. Television revenues are the reason for splitting the Winter and Summer games.

LARA BREAKS RECORD

West Indian cricketer Brian Lara (b. 1969) smashes the England cricket team for a world record 375 runs in the test match in Antigua.

BRAZIL WINS WORLD CUP

Brazil wins a record fourth football World Cup. The controversial decision to stage the World Cup in the USA, not a football power, is a success and leads to the formation of Major League Soccer in that country.

AYRTON SENNA
(1960–1994)

Brazilian motor racing legend Ayrton Senna has died after an 119km/h (190miph) crash in the San Marino Grand Prix at Monza in Italy. In his tragically short career he won 41 Grand Prix races and was three times Formula One world racing champion, in 1988, 1990 and 1992.

PEACE IN BOSNIA

The Dayton Peace Accord ends three years' fighting in Bosnia. A terrorist bomb explodes in Oklahoma. Israeli prime minister Yitzhak Rabin is assassinated. Worldwide outrage follows renewed nuclear testing and the execution of writer and human rights campaigner Ken Saro-Wiwa. An earthquake devastates the port of Kobe, Japan. Astronomers discover a brown dwarf and a talking pig becomes an unlikely film star.

OPPOSITE: The US space shuttle *Atlantis* photographed from the Russian *Mir* space station.

1995

Jan	1	Austria, Finland and Sweden join EU
	6	Tamils sign ceasefire in Sri Lanka but fighting resumes
	17	Earthquake devastates Kobe, Japan
Mar	20	Turkish forces launch attack against Kurds
Apr	19	Bomb in Oklahoma City, USA
July	11	Serbs capture UN-designated safe area of Srebrenica, Bosnia
	20	Serbs attack UN safe haven, Bihac, Bosnia
Aug	4	Croatian forces invade Serb-inhabited region of Krajina, Croatia
	30	NATO begins attacks on Serb positions, Bosnia
Nov	1	Peace accord signed in Dayton, Ohio, between Bosnia, Serbia and Croatia
	4	Israeli prime minister Yitzhak Rabin is assassinated
	11	Nigerian writer and human rights campaigner Ken Saro-Wiwa executed
Dec	28	International protests following French nuclear tests

ABOVE: Yitzhak Rabin, who is shot dead in Tel Aviv.

BOSNIAN CRISIS

In July the Serbs overrun the UN-protected zones of
Srebrenica and massacre the male population. They
also besiege Bihac. The following month Serbs bombard
Sarajevo, killing 37 people and leading NATO to
attack infrastructure targets in Serb-held Bosnia.
Following pressure on the Bosnian Serb leader Radovan
Karadzic by President Milosevic of Serbia, heavy
weapons are withdrawn from around Sarajevo. In
November, at Dayton, Ohio, a peace agreement is
signed, bringing an end to the Bosnian conflict: it splits
the state 51.49 between the Bosnian and Croat
Federation and the Republika Srpska (Bosnian Serbs).
The settlement creates a unified Bosnia but in fact
divides the country into two self-governing parts, a
Muslim-Croat federation and a Bosnian-Serb republic.

ABOVE: Ruins of the Alfred
Murrah Federal Building in
Oklahoma City after a bomb
has blown it up. A fanatical
right-winger, Timothy McVeigh,
will later be charged with
planting the bomb.

LEFT: Film-maker and comic
Woody Allen directs *Mighty
Aphrodite*, a comedy about
love, marriage and adopted
children, perhaps as an antidote
to the bad press he is receiving
about his relationship with his
adopted daughter.

ABOVE: A Bosnian Serb refugee from Krajina waits patiently in a government centre. The plan is to re-integrate refugees into society.

OKLAHOMA BOMBING
Federal government offices in Oklahoma City are blown up in a rare terrorist bombing in the USA. The blast kills 167 people. Two men are later indicted for the crime; both are associated with far-right militias active in the Midwest, which are fanatically opposed to the federal government.

SRI LANKA
Despite a temporary ceasefire, fighting resumes between the government and the Tamils. A state of emergency is re-introduced.

FRENCH NUCLEAR TESTING
In defiance of world opinion, France renews underground nuclear testing on Mururoa Atoll in the South Pacific. France carries out a series of tests before ending them in January 1996 and signing the Nuclear Test-Ban Treaty, which it had previously refused to do.

RABIN ASSASSINATED
Prime Minister Yitzhak Rabin is assassinated by a Hebrew fanatic in Tel Aviv, Israel, soon after leaving a peace rally. He is succeeded by Simon Peres. However Rabin's assassination jeopardizes the peace process with the Palestinians when Peres loses the general election in May 1996 to the right-winger Benyamin Netanyahu (b. 1949), who is opposed to the land for peace deal.

BROWN DWARF DISCOVERED
Astronomers discover a brown dwarf, a strange object smaller than a star but larger than a planet. The existence of brown dwarfs has long been suspected but never proved.

SARO-WIWA EXECUTED
In Nigeria the dissident writer and human rights campaigner Ken Saro-Wiwa (1941–95) and eight others are executed by the military government, prompting international outrage. Saro-Wiwa has led the protests by the Ogoni people of southern Nigeria against exploitation of their land by international oil companies; his death causes Nigeria to be suspended from the Commonwealth and sanctions imposed.

NEW EU MEMBERS
Austria, Sweden and Finland join the EU, bringing its members up to thirteen. Many other states, including the Czech Republic, Hungary, Poland, Estonia, Slovenia, and Cyprus, queue up to join.

POWDER HER FACE
British composer Thomas Adès attracts critical praise for his opera *Powder her Face*. It is based on the sometimes scandalous life of Margaret, Duchess of Argyll.

MILKY WAY BLACK HOLE
US astronomers report detecting signs of a black hole in our own galaxy, the Milky Way.

ANTIATOMS
A team of German, Italian and Swiss physicists make the first antiatoms. They last for only a fraction of a second before colliding with ordinary atoms and vanishing.

ORBITING JUPITER
In December the US spacecraft *Galileo*, launched in 1989, goes into orbit around Jupiter, and starts sending pictures and data back to Earth.

KOBE EARTHQUAKE
The Great Hanshin earthquake devastates Kobe in Japan. More than 2,700 lose their lives and more than 1,000 buildings are destroyed, as well as the region's roads and power supplies. The earthquake measured 7.2 on the Richter scale and is the worst earthquake to hit Japan since 1923.

ROAD PROTESTERS
In the UK environmentalists protest against the building of a new road through ancient British woodland. They tunnel into the forest floor and build tree houses to prevent the felling of 10,000 trees. The protesters are evicted but their cause attracts considerable publicity and sympathy.

BANNING LIVE ANIMAL EXPORTS
Animal rights activists achieve a temporary ban on exporting live animals from a British port. They claim that animals are carried in overcrowded conditions and deprived of food and water for long periods, and aim for an EU ban on such practices.

TALIBAN, HUTUS AND BROWN DWARFS

Taliban seizes Kabul in Afghanistan and imposes strict Islamic law. The Guatemalan civil war ends after 36 years of fighting. Tutsis attack Hutu refugees in Zaire. Prime minister Benazir Bhutto is dismissed from office. US president Bill Clinton is elected for a second term. The EU bans British beef after fears of BSE. A bomb blast mars the centenary Olympic Games.

1996

Feb	17	Space probe *NEAR* is launched
Mar	13	Sixteen schoolchildren and their teacher killed by gunman in Dunblane, Scotland
	25	EU ban export of British beef after BSE fears
Apr	29	UN war crimes tribunal opens in The Hague, Netherlands, to investigate alleged crimes against humanity in Yugoslav civil war
July	27	Bomb explodes at Olympic Games, Atlanta, USA
Aug	31	Iraqi aircraft violate UN no-fly zone
Sep	3	US launches cruise missiles against Iraq
	27	Taliban takes control of Kabul, Afghanistan
Oct	21	UN reports that 250,000 Hutu refugees have fled Zaire
Nov	5	Bill Clinton is elected US president for second term
	15	Tutsi rebels defeat extremest Hutu militiamen
Dec	17	Tupac guerrillas seize hostages, Lima, Peru
	29	Civil war ends in Guatemala

ABOVE: A US military engineeer directs traffic across the pontoon bridge built to link Croatia and Bosnia-Herzegovina.

BELOW: A US Howitzer at work during Operation Joint Endeavour, part of the response to the crisis in former Yugoslavia.

ABOVE: Animal rights activists demonstrate in London as BSE is discovered in cattle and is feared to affect human beings.

TALIBAN TAKE KABUL

The Islamic fundamentalist Taliban militia take control of Afghanistan's capital, Kabul, imposing strict Islamic law and forcing women to wear a full veil in public and all men to grow beards. Their control of the country is far from complete, but Taliban brings a measure of peace to Afghanistan not enjoyed since the Russian invasion in 1979.

RWANDAN REFUGEES

More than one million Hutu refugees from Rwanda living in refugee camps are attacked by Tutsis supported by the Rwandan government, driving them from their camps. Many die from cholera and other diseases, causing a major humanitarian crisis in Zaire and destabilizing the government of President Mobutu (b. 1930). During November, 400,000 of the Hutus return home to Rwanda after the extremists responsible for the 1994 genocide in Rwanda are driven out of the refugee camps.

BENAZIR BHUTTO DISMISSED

In Pakistan prime minister Benazir Bhutto (b. 1953) is again dismissed by the president for corruption for the second time in her career. Ms Bhutto, daughter of the former prime minister Zulfikar Ali Bhutto, who was overthrown and then executed by the military in 1978, first became prime minister in 1988 after the fall of the military government but was dismissed in 1990. She won re-election in 1993 but persistent charges of corruption against her, and in particular her husband, remove her from power once again.

CLINTON WINS SECOND TERM

US president Bill Clinton wins a second term in office against Republican Bob Dole, taking 49 per cent of the popular vote against 41 per cent for Dole. Democrats fail to win Congress, and face problems getting legislation through against Republican opposition.

KURDS CAPTURE SULAIMANIYA

The Kurdish Democratic Party (KDP), fighting with Iraqi assistance, capture the city of Sulaimaniya, stronghold of the umbrella anti-Iraqi organization the Patriotic Union of Kurdistan (PUK). The KDP shell a Kurdish refugee camp in Iran. Sulaimaniya is recaptured in October.

TUPAC GUERRILLAS SEIZE HOSTAGES

Movimiento Revolucionario Tupac Amaru (MRTA) guerrillas seize 460 hostages at the Japanese ambassador's residence in Lima, Peru. All but 72 hostages are released through negotiations. In April 1997, Peruvian special forces storm the residence, kill the fourteen members of MRTA and release the hostages.

HUGE DINOSAUR

Fossil bones of a huge carnivorous dinosaur are found in the Sahara. The dinosaur is larger than the famous *Tyrannosaurus rex*, but similar to another dinosaur found in South America eight months earlier.

ABOVE: The Spice Girls, living embodiment of "Girl Power" at the première of their film *Spice — the Movie*.

EUROPEAN ELECTIONS

In Britain Tony Blair (b. 1953) leads the Labour Party to a landslide victory after eighteen years of Conservative government. Victories for the French Socialists in June and the German Social Democrats in September 1998, removing Helmut Kohl after sixteen years in power, lead to Socialist or Social Democratic governments in almost every Western European nation.

HONG KONG

A British crown colony since 1841, Hong Kong reverts to Chinese rule. The Chinese agree to respect existing laws and economic structures, although democratic institutions are swiftly replaced by an assembly appointed by Beijing.

MOTHER TERESA OF CALCUTTA (born AGNES GONXHA BOJAXHIU) (1910–1997)

The Yugoslav-born Roman Catholic missionary Mother Teresa, whose work in Calcutta is known throughout the world, has died. In 1928 Mother Teresa joined the Sisters of Loretto in Calcutta and taught in their convent until 1948 when she left to work alone with the poor. In 1950 she founded her sisterhood, the Order of the Missionaries of Charity, which now has some 2,000 sisters, caring for the poor and sick.

DEATH OF DIANA

Diana, Princess of Wales is killed in a car crash in Paris, France. Her death causes an international outpouring of grief and leads to a sharp fall in the popularity of the British monarchy, whom many consider treated her poorly during her life. An estimated two billion people worldwide watch the funeral service on television. Her campaign to rid the world of landmines is successful in 1998, when an international treaty forbidding their use is signed in Ottawa.

FINANCIAL COLLAPSE

The collapse in value of the Thai baht leads to a financial crisis throughout South-East Asia as banks collapse and currencies lose their value. The crisis, caused by excessive national debt and poor financial controls, spreads to Japan, Indonesia and Russia, and then in 1999 to Brazil. Although the International Monetary Fund launches a rescue package for affected countries, the economic downturn creates chaos throughout the world's markets and leads to fears of a recession to match that of the 1930s.

MOBUTU DEFEATED

President Mobutu, leader and dictator of Zaire since 1965, loses power after rebels led by Laurent Kabilia overthrow his government. As leader, Mobutu treated Zaire as his personal bank account, bleeding the country dry and causing economic ruin.

FINANCIAL COLLAPSE IN ALBANIA

The small eastern European country of Albania descends into anarchy after the collapse of corrupt pyramid investment schemes. Albanians who have lost all their savings take to the streets, looting weapons from the army and attacking the government. Foreign nationals are evacuated and the government calls elections, which result in a landslide victory for the opposition Socialist Party in June.

UK/RUSSIAN AGREEMENT

In March the UK and Russian governments sign an agreement on joint military training and information exchange on new weapons.

SPICE POWER

Girl power in the form of the Spice Girls — Posh, Baby, Sporty, Scary and Ginger — is the latest success in the world of pop. The all-girl British band is achieving worldwide success with a string of best-selling numbers.

E. COLI MAPPED

An American team of geneticists led by Fred Blattner compile the complete genetic code of the bacterium *Escherichia coli*, which contains more than 4,200 genes. Some forms of *E. coli* cause food poisoning; this year an outbreak of *E. coli* bacteria derived from eating contaminated meat, has poisoned over 400 people in the UK, killing nineteen.

ABOVE: Dolly the sheep, the world's first adult animal clone, with Dr Ron James, head of PPL Therapeutics at Edinburgh's Roslin Institute.

ABOVE: Sarajevo, the Serbian capital, begins to rebuild as peace settles in the troubled countries of the former Yugoslavia.

THE FULL MONTY
A new British film is gaining unexpected success internationally. Directed by Peter Cattaneo, *The Full Monty* features a group of unemployed men in the north of England who turn to stripping to earn a living, extracting hilarious comedy from social deprivation.

DOLLY THE SHEEP
Scottish scientists announce that they have cloned a sheep from a cell taken from an adult animal; the sheep is nicknamed Dolly. This is the first successful cloning using non-reproductive cells. DNA from an adult cell was combined with an unfertilized egg that had had its DNA removed.

HALE-BOPP
Comet Hale-Bopp, a comet with three tails, nears the Sun in April. A mass of rock, dust and ice, the comet is named after the two American astronomers who first saw it: Alan Hale and Thomas Bopp. The comet will not return for 2,400 years.

CULT SUICIDE
As Comet Hale-Bopp appears, the brightest comet visible for 400 years, 39 members of the Heaven's Gate cult in San Diego, USA, commit mass suicide. The cult's members believed that they were to escape Earth's destruction by rendezvousing with a space vehicle obscured by the comet.

GUGGENHEIM MUSEUM
One of the most striking of recent buildings is the Guggenheim Museum in Bilbao. Designed by Frank O Gehry, the building has a striking metal-clad façade in which curved forms seem to invite the visitor into a mysterious space.

FLOODS CAUSE HOMELESSNESS
Flash floods make 70,000 homeless in the Czech Republic, Germany and Poland.

TIGER WOODS
US golfer Eldrick "Tiger" Woods wins the Masters golf tournament, aged 21, by a twelve-stroke victory at Augusta.

MCDONALD'S CLEARED
The longest trial in English history ends when fast food chain McDonald's is cleared of damaging the environment. McDonald's sued two protesters, David Morris and Helen Steel, for distributing leaflets criticizing the American chain's environmental record.

OFF TO SATURN
The spacecraft *Cassini/Huygens* is launched on a voyage to Saturn to arrive in 2004.

DIANA, PRINCESS OF WALES (1961–1997)

The world is shocked by the sudden and violent death of Diana, Princess of Wales, who has been killed in Paris during a car chase involving the press. The former wife of HRH the Prince of Wales (they divorced in 1996), she had been a constant focus of media attention since taking on her public role. She was actively involved in the work of many charities, but since 1994 had been working principally for the International Red Cross. Recently she had spear-headed the campaign against land mines. She was in the company of Dodi Fayed when she was killed.

SEX, TRUTH AND RECONCILIATION

In the US President Clinton avoids impeachment, following investigation into an alleged affair. In South Africa, the Truth and Reconciliation Committee publishes its report. Tension rises again in Serbia. Former Chilean dictator Pinochet is arrested. Terrorists bomb US embassies in Kenya and Tanzania. The Good Friday Peace Agreement brings peace to Northern Ireland. A hurricane devastates Central America. Viagra is the new wonder drug for impotence.

OPPOSITE: Bill Clinton, seen here with his wife and daughter, has a troubled year in office.

1998

Jan	21	Investigation launched into President Clinton's alleged affair with White House intern
Mar	5	NASA scientists announce evidence of water on Moon
Apr	10	Good Friday Peace Agreement brings peace settlement for Northern Ireland
May	6	Mudslides devastate towns in Italy
	20	Indonesian president Suharto resigns following riots
	28	Pakistan explodes five nuclear devices
Aug	7	Terrorists bomb US embassies in Nairobi, Kenya, and Dar-es-Salaam, Tanzania
Sep	24	Iran lifts fatwa on author Salman Rushdie
Oct	12	Nato threatens air strike against Serbia
	18	International observers arrive in Serbian province of Kosovo
	18	Former Chilean dictator General Augusto Pinochet arrested in London, UK
	24	Troops from South Africa and Botswana enter Lesotho
	29	Truth and Reconciliation Committee publishes report, South Africa
Dec	16	US and UK air strikes against Iraq

ABOVE: Frank Sinatra, "Ol' Blue Eyes", dies this year.

CLINTON SEX SCANDAL

President Clinton is accused of having an affair with a White House intern and asking her to lie about it. The allegations are investigated by a independent prosecutor, Kenneth Starr, and eventually lead to an attempt by the US Congress to impeach the president for perjury and other offences in November. The president gives evidence to the House of Representatives, which is televised, but despite pressure from Republicans, Clinton is not impeached.

GOOD FRIDAY AGREEMENT

In Northern Ireland political parties from Unionist and Nationalist communities sign the Good Friday Peace Agreement setting up an elected assembly and new institutions linking the North with the Republic. The agreement, which is overseen by Northern Secretary Mo Mowlam (b. 1949), also sets up a process to encourage paramilitary groups to decommission their weapons. The Unionist leader, David Trimble, and the Nationalist John Hume jointly receive the 1998 Nobel Peace Prize for their work in securing the agreement.

TITANIC

Starring Leonardo di Caprio and Kate Winslett, the disaster movie *Titanic* is the most expensive film ever made and a smash hit, taking eleven Academy Awards.

SUHARTO RESIGNS

In Indonesia, following economic collapse, demonstrators force the resignation of President Suharto, leader since 1967. He is succeeded by his deputy, Jusuf Habibie, who promises to end corruption and nepotism in government.

US EMBASSIES BOMBED

Islamic fundamentalists bomb the US embassies in Nairobi, Kenya and Dar-es-Salaam, Tanzania, killing 257 people and injuring hundreds more. In retaliation, US warships launch Tomahawk cruise missiles at targets in Afghanistan and Sudan in an attempt to kill Osama bin Laden, the Saudi millionaire who has been identified with terrorist bombings against US targets in Africa and the Middle East. The cruise missile attack does not kill him. US intelligence incorrectly identified a pharmaceuticals factory in Khartoum, Sudan, as a chemical warfare factory.

KOSOVO

International observers are sent to the Serbian province of Kosovo to police a ceasefire agreed between Kosovan freedom fighters and the Serbian army after NATO threatens air strikes against Serbia. The province, which is almost entirely Albanian in population, is fighting for independence from Serbia, which suspended the provincial constitution in March 1991 and introduced repressive measures against the Albanian population. The war is the latest chapter in the disintegration of the former Yugoslavia which began in 1991.

TRUTH AND RECONCILIATION

The report of the Truth and Reconciliation Commission, chaired by Nobel Peace Prize-winner Archbishop Desmond Tutu, is published. The Commission took evidence from many people in an attempt to reconcile the differences left by apartheid. The report condemns apartheid as a crime against humanity but finds the ruling African National Congress (ANC) as well as white-only parties to have been guilty of human rights violations.

PINOCHET ARRESTED

Former Chilean dictator Augusto Pinochet is arrested in London after Spanish judges apply for his extradition to Spain to face charges of murder and torture. Following legal debates over whether Pinochet has legal immunity, in 1999 the High Court decides that he does not have immunity and the British Home Secretary Jack Straw (b. 1946) orders his extradition.

LESOTHO

The Pretoria government, South Africa, sends troops into Lesotho to restore calm following civil unrest.

OPERATION DESERT FOX

The US and UK carry out air strikes against Iraqi targets following Saddam Hussein's non-compliance with UN weapons inspectors. The US Navy, US Air Force and RAF launch 650 attacks, the US Navy launches 325 Tomahawk cruise missiles and US Air Force B-52s 90 cruise missiles against 100 targets including Republican Guard barracks and chemical and biological warfare installations in Iraq.

BIRTHDAY LETTERS

Britain's Poet Laureate Ted Hughes (1930–98) publishes poems he has written about the suicide of his first wife, American poet Sylvia Plath. The book, which appears just before Hughes' death, wins critical acclaim and sells in large numbers.

NUCLEAR TESTING

India joins the nuclear club by testing nuclear devices in Rajasthan. Pakistan retaliates by testing five devices, although both pledge to sign the Nuclear Test-Ban Treaty at some stage.

FAST-SELLING VIAGRA

Viagra, a new treatment for impotence, has become the fastest-selling prescription drug.

ITALIAN EARTHQUAKE

Frescoes by Italian artist Giotto are destroyed after an earthquake in Assissi. There is controversy over whether the works of art could have been better protected.

CODE COMPLETED

For the first time, scientists compile the complete code of an invertebrate animal, a tiny worm.

FLYING GALAXIES

Astronomers discover that the galaxies in space are flying apart at ever-increasing speeds, against the force of gravity.

CIRCADIAN CLOCK

Research shows that nearly all living organisms, not just people, have a built-in mechanism, the "circadian clock", which uses light and temperature to keep track of night and day.

WINTER OLYMPICS

The Winter Olympics in Nagano, Japan, are a resounding success in front of huge crowds. The speed skating record book is rewritten with the use of the clap skate, invented in Holland. The new skates, named for the noise they make, have a spring-loaded hinge at the front which allows the racer's heel to rise without lifting the blade of the skate from the ice. Dutch skaters win five golds and six other medals and five world records are broken. The Czech Republic score a shock ice hockey win by beating the NHL professionals of Canada and America, and American Tara Lipinski captures figure skating gold.

FRANCE WINS WORLD CUP

France wins the football World Cup in Paris. The defeat of Brazil in the final was surrounded by intrigue over the poor performance of Brazilian star Ronaldo.

DRUGS DOMINATE TOUR DE FRANCE

The Tour de France is disrupted by revelations of drug use by cyclists and team support for the abuse. The discovery of a team masseur carrying banned drugs leads to a police investigation, arrests and then protests by racers, who complain of victimization. Cycling's top event is completed but the sport's image is tarnished.

BASEBALL

Mark McGwire, the first-baseman for the St. Louis Cardinals, hits his 62nd homer of the season to pass Roger Maris' tally. His race with Sammy Sosa of the Chicago Cubs to reach the record entrances baseball fans. McGwire finishes with 70 homers, Sosa with 66.

POL POT DEAD

The body of the former leader of the Khmer Rouge, Pol Pot, has been put on display in northern Cambodia. Due for trial, he may have committed suicide or have been murdered. During his rule over Cambodia (1975–79) he was responsible for some 1.7 million deaths.

DEVASTATING HURRICANE

Hurricane Mitch causes devastation in Honduras, Nicaragua, El Salvador and Guatemala before heading across Mexico into the Caribbean. More than 10,000 people are killed, and whole towns swept away.

BELOW: The "Agreement", the document produced as a result of the Northern Ireland peace talks, is torn up by a Unionist supporter.

BLOODY AND VIOLENT END TO THE CENTURY

War breaks out in the Balkans when Nato begins air strikes against the Serbian military targets in Yugoslavia. The action intensifies Serbian "cleansing" of ethnic Albanians and thousands flee Kosovo. The single European currency is introduced and the EU Commission resigns after evidence of fraud. King Hussein of Jordan dies. New research suggests flirting is good for you. A series of earthquakes in Turkey leaves thousands dead. Russian military battle in Grozny, Chechnya, as Christmas approaches.

OPPOSITE: Nelson Mandela bows out of South African politics.

1999

Jan	1	European single currency begins
	24	Cash-for-votes scandal hits International Olympic Committee (IOC); subsequently six members resign
Feb	4	Russians attempt to create artificial moon
	7	King Hussein of Jordan dies aged 64
	15	Abdullah Ocalan, leader of the Kurdish Workers Party, is captured in Nairobi by Turkish special forces
	23	Britain completes destruction of its stocks of anti-personnel mines
Mar	7	US threatens trade war against Europe for importing bananas from former US colonies in the Caribbean and Africa
	15	All members of the European Commission resign over fraud
	24	Nato begins air strikes against Serbia
	31	Serb forces capture three US soldiers
Apr	5	Two Libyans suspected of Lockerbie bombing in The Netherlands for trial
May	17	Ehud Barak elected prime minister of Israel in landslide victory
	26	Indian aircraft attack guerrillas in Indian part of Kashmir and lose two planes
Aug	17	Turkey rocked by first of a series of devastating earthquakes, thousands die
Sep	1	Anti-independence militia gangs rampage in East Timor
Nov	10	After many denials, Russia moves military forces against Chechnya
Dec	14	USA relinquishes control over Panama Canal
	31	Boris Yeltsin, Russian president, resigns

NEW NATO MEMBERS

Hungary, Poland and the Czech Republic join NATO, the first former Communist countries in Eastern Europe to do so. All three countries are also applying to join the EU.

SINGLE EUROPEAN CURRENCY

The European single currency begins in eleven EU nations, including France and Germany but not Britain. The Euro, which can only be used in paper transactions, will initially run alongside the different national currencies but will replace them in 2002, when the national currencies will be abolished and Euro notes and coins will circulate freely.

FRAUD IN EU

All twenty members of the EU Commission resign following a report into alleged fraud, which finds the executive guilty of mismanagement, corruption and nepotism. Former Italian prime minister Romano Prodi is appointed new president of the Commission.

NATO BOMBS YUGOSLAVIA

In March aircraft and cruise missiles from twelve Nato nations launch air attacks against more than 40 targets in Yugoslavia after Serbia refuses to accede to peace negotiations over Kosovo. Serb troops in Kosovo force ethnic Kosovan Albanians across neighbouring borders. By the end of March some 300,000 have been displaced. Three US soldiers from the 1st Infantry Division are captured at Kumanovo, Macedonia, by Serb forces who have crossed the border. US politician Jesse Jackson later negotiates their release.

INSTITUTIONAL RACISM

In the UK, the inquiry into the murder of a black teenager, Stephen Lawrence, finds that the police had mishandled the case and are guilty of institutional racism. In the US, a white supremacist is convicted of murdering a black man, James Byrd, in Texas.

BERLIN IS GERMANY'S CAPITAL

For the first time since the war, Berlin becomes the capital of Germany again as the government moves back from Bonn. Since the fall of the Berlin Wall in 1990 and the reunification of Germany, Berlin has been extensively rebuilt to accommodate the new government buildings.

CIVIL WAR IN SIERRA LEONE

Fighting intensifies in Sierra Leone when forces of the Revolutionary United Front (RUF) loot and burn Freetown. President Kabbah has criticized Liberia for supporting the rebels. Civil war began in 1991. In 1996, Ahmed Kabbah was democratically elected president but was overthrown nine months later by the RUF. In 1997, supported by 5,000 men from the Nigerian backed ECOMOG force, he returned to power, but the RUF continues its fight.

KURDISH LEADER CAPTURED

Turkish special forces in Nairobi capture the Kurdish leader Abdullah Öçalan. The capture precipitates protests throughout Europe as Kurds blame Greek diplomats for allowing their leader to be captured.

NEW ISRAELI PRIME MINISTER

Labour leader and Israel's most decorated soldier, Ehud Barak, is elected Israel's new prime minister, defeating right-winger Binyamin Netanyahu in a landslide victory. Barak's election will pave the way for a fresh start to Middle East peace talks.

SISTINE CHAPEL CEILING

The cleaning of Michelangelo's famous painted ceiling in the Vatican's Sistine Chapel is completed. It shows the familiar paintings in an unfamiliar light, much brighter in colour. Experts are divided over the result, some saying that the cleaning has brought the ceiling as close as possible to its original condition, others saying that the work has been too radical.

MIRROR FAILURE

A Russian attempt to create an artificial "moon" to light up dark areas of the country fails when a space mirror does not unfurl from space station *Mir*.

STARDUST TRIP

Space probe *Stardust* sets off on a 5 billion-km (3 billion-mi) journey to rendezvous with Comet Wild-2, carrying instruments to collect dust from the comet in order to learn more about it.

EXTRA-TERRESTRIAL CHAIR

The first academic chair for an astronomer to search for extra-terrestrial intelligence is founded at the University of California at Berkeley; first professor is William Welch.

GM FOODS DEBATE

In the UK, the safety of genetically modified foods comes under intense debate following a demand from pressure groups and some scientists for the UK government to impose a moratorium on new GM crops.

FLIRTING IS GOOD FOR YOU

Research published in the American magazine *Psychology Today* suggests that flirting may be designed to ensure that we attract the right mate. According to some research, flirting, far from being superficial party behaviour, may be a deeply ingrained means of exchanging vital information about the health and reproductive fitness of a potential partner.

THE WHOLE WOMAN

Australian feminist Germaine Greer publishes *The Whole Woman*, a sequel to *The Female Eunuch*, one of the landmark books of the Women's Liberation Movement. In her new book, Greer states that feminism has lost its way and women need to get angry again.

MICHAEL JORDAN RETIRES — AGAIN

Michael Jordan, on whose back professional basketball rose to international prominence, announces his second retirement. Jordan led the Chicago Bulls to six NBA titles; three before his first retirement and three after.

LOCKERBIE SUSPECTS

In April, the two Libyan intelligence officers believed to be responsible for the Lockerbie explosion in 1988, are flown to an air force base in Holland to be tried under Scottish law.

BANANA WAR

The US threatens a trade war with Europe, claiming that Europe favours bananas imported from former US colonies in the Caribbean and Africa. Caribbean-producing countries St Lucia and Dominica threaten to stall World Trade Organization talks.

KING HUSSEIN (IBN TALAL) OF JORDAN (1935–1999)

King Hussein of Jordan has died after a battle with cancer. Educated at Harrow and Sandhurst in England, he had ruled Jordan for 46 years and is widely accredited as an influential peace-maker in the troubled Middle East. More than 50 foreign leaders and 800,000 Jordanians gathered for his funeral.

ABOVE A family of Kosovan Albanians flee Serbian torture and executions.

BELOW: A distressed young Albanian demonstrates the misery of conflict.

WAR CRIME INDICTMENT

As diplomats work to reduce differences between the West and Russia over plans to end the Kosovo crisis, the International War-Crimes Tribunal announces that it plans to indict Serb leader Slobodan Milosevic, therefore reducing his incentive to compromise. Meanwhile, NATO announces that it is to increase to 50,000 the number of troops on standby in neighbouring Macedonia — though for what purpose is unclear. By June, Serbia announces agreement to a peace deal proposed by Russian, European and American envoys.

COLD WAR REVISITED

An American congressional committee reveals that China has stolen classified information on every deployed warhead in their missile system. The spying had gone on for more that 20 years at Los Alamos National Laboratory and appears to be continuing. The US government seems powerless to stop the information flow but promises to tighten security at government laboratories.

KASHMIR CONFLICT FLARES UP

Indian aircraft attacks guerrillas operating out of Kashmir on the Indian side, however, there is a price — two aircraft are lost. India accuses the Pakistani army of supplying military equipment to the guerrillas. Twice before the two countries have fought a war over this territory. By June tension reaches its highest level for 30 years. India's prime minister, Atal Behari Vajpayee, says the campaign will continue until the infiltrators are driven out.

BACK TO TIANANMEN SQUARE

Ten years after the killings in Tiananman Square, China prepares for the anniversary by closing foreign satellite TV channels and blocking the internet. In an unprecedented legal action, the relatives of some of the victims in the original demonstration submit evidence

BELOW: Izmit, Turkey is hit at 03.01 hours by an earthquake measuring 7.4 on the Richter scale. Rescue operations become a race against time as air runs out for survivors trapped under collapsed buildings.

to a Chinese court demanding a criminal investigation into the role played by officials and troops at the time.

ANC LANDSLIDE

The African National Congress wins almost two thirds of the vote in South Africa's second non-racial election, in June. It falls one seat short of a two-thirds majority in parliament. The ANC forms a coalition with the Inkatha Freedom Party giving a combined majority of more than three to one.

GREENPEACE FROZEN OUT

British Nuclear Fuels secure a Dutch court order to freeze Greenpeace's international bank account after arguing that the organisation's protests caused extensive delays in preparing two controversial shipments of reprocessed plutonium to be shipped from France back to Japan. Both Britain and France had banned Greenpeace vessels from their waters. Greenpeace argues that the 20 tons of plutonium is a dangerous shipment and a waste of money.

RELENTLESS RAINS AND FLOODING

Rivers in the Ganges, Brahmaputra and Meghna basins overflow displacing nearly one million people as seasonal rains fall relentlessly in Bangladesh. Meanwhile, in China emergency workers battle to contain the flow of water from the Yangtze river and its tributaries. The water has been rising since June and by August, fed by tropical storm Olga, an estimated 1.8 million people move from the flood plains in central and east China.

BLACK SKY

In south east Asia the sky was again painted black by smog from burning forests in Indonesia. Last year, the smog clouds reached Singapore and Malaysia causing sickness in the populations.

POPE OUT, THEN IN BY ANOTHER ROUTE

Pope John Paul is banned by China from visiting Hong Kong during his Asian tour because of the Vatican's ties with Taiwan. The pope still intends to visit the mainland via Macau.

A SOLAR ECLIPSE

Millions of onlookers are attracted to watch the path of a solar eclipse as it passes over Europe, the Middle East and Asia. Watching this natural phenomenon, many are anxious to dispel the idea that it is a precursor to an apocalypse as the century draws to an end. Others are concerned to avoid blindness while enjoying the view.

TURKEY EARTHQUAKE

The industrial north west of Turkey is struck by a massive earthquake. The town of Izmit is the focus of destruction. Over 13,000 people are missing, many buried in shoddily constructed apartment blocks. A hospital and a military base is destroyed. An oil refinery

ABOVE: Communications and freedom: by the end of the century laptop computers such as the iBook and mobile telephones afford a change of living style that is one life-style revolution for the coming decade.

is set alight. The government is criticized for contributing to a feeble rescue effort as international organisations dig for survivors and more than 200,000 people are made homeless. Three months later, in November, a second big earthquake hits a town 200 km west of Ankara, the capital. Over 500 people are killed.

DEATH WISH GRANTED

Plans to legalize euthanasia and doctor-assisted suicide are published by the Dutch government. This action formalizes practices already carried out and accepted in the country. Working to very strict guidelines children as young as 12 would be entitled to request death. If approved, The Netherlands will become the first country in the world to legalize mercy killings.

BLOOD MONEY

IG Farben was the world's largest chemical company during WWII, and one of its subsidiaries produced lethal gases used to kill camp inmates in Nazi Germany. In August, more than 50 years after the end of the war, the shareholders agree to establish a $1.6 million fund to compensate former slave labourers. The move fails to satisfy survivor groups who are demanding an estimated $15 million, liquidating the company's assets, to be distributed to its victims.

INDEPENDENCE FIGHT

In Dili, East Timor, as the August 30 referendum draws near, anti-independence thugs launch attacks on the UN and pro-independence groups. By September 1, these militias go on the rampage. Most East Timorese vote for independence, but the violence becomes overwhelming throughout September until it is eventually brought under control by a United Nations force led by Australia. More than 300,000 Timorese have been left homeless in an effort to escape attack by rampaging mobs. Indonesia cancels a four-year-old security agreement with Australia in protest at its attitude.

ABOVE: The newly constructed interior of the Reichstag building sees the first full session of the Bundestag in April as government power returns to Germany's historic capital.

RUSSIA DEFENDS ITS SOVEREIGNTY

In September, after more than three weeks of Russian artillery and air strikes, the guerrillas who invaded Dagastan are forced back into Chechnya in southern Russia. 30,000 soldiers are sent to Russia's border with Chechnya whose Islamic militants are accused of recent civilian bombings. Air attacks start against what the Kremlin describes as terrorist targets. In November, it is estimated that over 180,000 Chechen civilians have fled their homes. By December, Russian ground forces in Chechnya enter Grozny, the capital, fighting a dirty war of retribution.

JAPAN'S WOMEN COME LAST

Women in Japan finally get access to the birth control pill four decades after their counterparts in other industrialized countries. In contrast, it took just six months for the male dominated Japanese society to approve the sale of Viagra, the popular anti-impotence drug.

BATTERED BY FLOYD

More than 3.5 million people move out of the path of Hurricane Floyd as it works its way up the east coast of America. States of emergency are declared in several states as the country's largest evacuation in history begins. Florida and Georgia are declared disaster areas.

HAPPY BIRTHDAY?

China celebrates 50 years of communism. An edition of the American based *Time* magazine containing articles on human rights in China is banned. The Chinese authorities crack down on the banned Falun Gong movement — said to have more adherents than China's Communist Party — accusing it of being 'superstitious, evil thinking' and an organisation that 'sabotages social stability'. Government agencies arrest unknown numbers of followers in security sweeps across Beijing after a silent protest in Tiananmen Square by supporters of the movement.

BELOW: Hurricane Floyd over the Americas. This weather satellite image helps predict the path of damage lying in wait. Flooding affects more than 200,000 in the USA and even more in Central America.

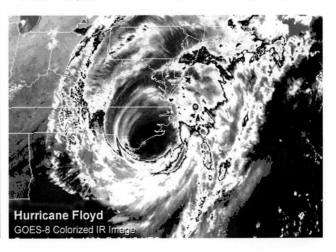

Hurricane Floyd
GOES-8 Colorized IR Image

ABOVE: By the end of 1999, use of the electronic World Wide Web and Internet leads to e-commerce becoming a household activity for communications and day-to-day activities such as shopping.

PAKISTAN COUP
In mid-October, Pakistan's army overthrows Nawaz Sharif's government after it tries to sack General Pervez Musharraf from the top military job. Troops seize Mr Sharif, airports and TV studio as the General promises to maintain stability. Governments all over the world condemn the coup. The Commonwealth suspends Pakistan as the country's constitution is suspended.

WALL REMEMBERED
Germans and other Europeans celebrate the 10th anniversary of the fall of the Berlin wall. At much the same time, prison sentences given to East Germany's 1989 head of state — Egon Krenz — and other top communists who oversaw the shooting of would-be escapers to the West are upheld on appeal.

WORLD CHAMPIONS AGAIN
Australia are the first national side to win the Rugby World Cup for a second time when they defeat France in the final at Cardiff's Millennium stadium in Wales. France were the rank outsider who against the odds defeated the New Zealand All Blacks in the semi-final to cause a major upset in the competition.

ASSASSINATION
Five men gun down Armenia's Prime Minister Vazgen Sarkisian and seven other officials in the parliamentary chamber. The attack is caught on television and stuns the nation. The gunmen take dozens of hostages but surrender after a 12 hour siege. Their leader accuses the government of letting the country disintegrate and of rampant corruption. The five are charged with terrorism.

FAT GET FATTER
The US-based Centres for Disease Control and Prevention publish a study which concludes that nearly 20 per cent of Americans are obese and that one in two adults are overweight.

CHINA ROCKET IN ORBIT
China successfully launches its first spacecraft becoming the third country after the former Soviet Union and America, to develop and launch a space vehicle capable of carrying a person into space.

BATTLE IN SEATTLE
World Trade Organization talks in Seattle, USA, face violent demonstrations not seen in America since the seventies. Protesters are dissatisfied with the industrialized countries manipulation of the markets in their favour at the expense of poorer countries. Many leaders appear on television looking shocked by the persistence and aggression of the mainly middle class demonstrators.

PANAMA CANAL HANDED OVER
Panama is soon to have full sovereignty over all its territory as the 51-mile-long canal cut through the mountains and policed by the Americans is handed back to its rightful owners. With 14,000 ships passing through the canal each year, the canal has huge earning potential said to be worth at least $5 billion. The project to build the canal was the most complex and expensive undertaken by the United States outside its borders. It was a project that became a source of American pride and international power for most of the century.

BERLIN AGREES COMPENSATION
Germany at last agrees to a $5 billion pay out to survivors forced by the Nazis to work in German factories. The German taxpayer bears the lions' share of the burden, only a minority of the companies that exploited the labour of enslaved citizens agree to contribute. About 12 million people were press-ganged to serve the Nazi war effort.

BRITISH-IRISH COUNCIL MEET
The momentum of the peace process in Northern Ireland is maintained in December at the first meeting of the British-Irish Council held in London set up as a result of the Good Friday Agreement.

YELTSIN RESIGNS
In a typically dramatic gesture, Boris Yeltsin resigns as Russia's president on New Year's eve amid speculation that he has secured a deal to suppress corruption allegations concerning his years in power.

PARTY TIMES

From the International Date Line, in the Pacific Ocean, the midnight deadline spreads inexorably west. Millennium Island and Kiribati start the fireworks, and are followed by spectacular displays in Auckland and Sydney. In China, fires light the Great Wall from end to end. In the desert of Africa, Timbuktu celebrates in the same spirit as ice-bound Anchorage in Alaska. The world parties in expectation: at the start of the 20th century, the life expectancy for a woman was 40 years, 100 years later it has doubled and the population stands at six billion. In non-industrialized nations there remains over 2 billion people still without electricity and even more with no sanitation. Thus the 21st century begins.

BELOW: Midnight, the final moment of the second Millennium, over Southampton Water, England.

1999 ⟶ 2000

LEFT: Jan 1 2000, daybreak in Tongan waters in the Pacific Ocean. To the west, the rest of the world awaits the midnight hour to start celebrations, as these islanders begin their day.

BELOW: The London Eye: a giant ferris wheel that fails to make its deadline. Built to herald the new millennium it was bedevilled by safety problems. The Millennium Dome, however, also on the banks of the Thames, is completed just in time and is the focus of the capital's effort to welcome in the New Year. It stages exhibitions and performances designed to attract visitors.

Sydney's Harbour Bridge and Opera House: one million people watch 22 tonnes of fireworks light the midnight sky.

ABOVE: West Beijing: revellers at the newly built China Century Monument, designed in the style of the Temple of Heaven used by Chinese emperors to perform major ceremonial rites, express their joy as the century turns.

ABOVE: Jerusalem, fireworks
explode over the Church of
Nativity, the traditional birthplace
of Jesus, in Manger Square,
Bethlehem.

RIGHT: Cairo, a new millennium
concert in the shadow of the
4,500-year-old pyramids. A mix of
ancient civilization and 20th
century techno-wizardry combines
to start another 1,000 year period.

ABOVE RIGHT: Moscow, as their
president resigns, a boy gazes into
the future as he watches the new
century sky above Red Square.

LEFT: Berlin, the Brandenberg Gate during Germany's festivities. Over a million are estimated to join the all-night party in this historic district.

FAR LEFT: Sarajevo, Bosnians see in the New Year close to the National Theatre lit against a background of exploding fireworks after years of war in the 1990s.

BELOW LEFT: Dubrovnik, the ancient Croatian city draws thousands into the main square to celebrate. CNN, the American TV company, announces the city is in its top ten places in the world to celebrate the New Year 2000.

BELOW: The Vatican City, Pope John Paul II watches the fireworks from his balcony at the Vatican at the start of the Christian third millennium. His message to followers is one of joy and peace.

LEFT: Paris, by popular vote the most visually stunning event in Europe. Fireworks burst from the Eiffel Tower as millions party on the boulevards by night.

BELOW: London welcomes in the new millennium. The River Thames and the Houses of Parliament are reflected in the light of fireworks as the river is lit by a 'wall of fire'. Thousands pack the riverbanks to watch the display.

LEFT: Rio de Janeiro, Copacabana beach hosts 100,000s of partygoers spectacularly welcoming the New Year and the 500th anniversary of the founding of Brazil.

BELOW: Toronto, a beautiful waterfront fireworks show rises from barges moored on Lake Ontario as Canadians join the celebrations twelve hours after they started to the east.

RIGHT: New York, two million gather in the city to toast the New Year. Times Square is the traditional backdrop for the waving and cheering crowd as confetti rains down on them and fireworks explode.

WINNERS AND ACHIEVERS OF THE CENTURY

For instant reference, the lists below cover the century's achievers in the fields of the arts, science, sport and politics. You will find the Oscar-winning actors, directors and movies; Nobel laureates in literature, physics, chemistry and medicine as well as the world's acknowledged peacemakers; the world's greatest racing drivers and football teams; the hosts of the Olympic Games; and a hundred years' worth of presidents of the United States of America.

Jack Nicholson in One Flew Over the Cuckoo's Nest, which swept the board 1975, winning Best Film, Best Director and Best Actor.

ACADEMY AWARDS

The Academy of Motion Picture Arts and Sciences was founded in 1927 by the movie industry to honour its artists and craftsmen. Every year it gives awards, affectionately known as "Oscars". All categories of motion picture endeavour are honoured; the most significant are listed below.

BEST ACTOR

1927–8 Emil Jannings *The Way of All Flesh, The Last Command*
1928–9 Warner Baxter *In Old Arizona*
1929–30 George Arliss *Disraeli*
1930–1 Lionel Barrymore *A Free Soul*
1931–2 Fredric March *Dr Jekyll and Mr Hyde*, Wallace Beery *The Champ*
1932–3 Charles Laughton *The Private Life of Henry VIII*
1934 Clark Gable *It Happened One Night*
1935 Victor McLaglen *The Informer*
1936 Paul Muni *The Story of Louis Pasteur*
1937 Spencer Tracy *Captains Courageous*
1938 Spencer Tracy *Boys' Town*
1939 Robert Donat *Goodbye, Mr Chips*
1940 James Stewart *The Philadelphia Story*
1941 Gary Cooper *Sergeant York*
1942 James Cagney *Yankee Doodle Dandy*
1943 Paul Lukas *Watch on the Rhine*
1944 Bing Crosby *Going My Way*
1945 Ray Milland *The Lost Weekend*
1946 Fredric March *The Best Years of Our Lives*
1947 Ronald Colman *A Double Life*
1948 Laurence Olivier *Hamlet*
1949 Broderick Crawford *All the King's Men*
1950 José Ferrer *Cyrano de Bergerac*
1951 Humphrey Bogart *The African Queen*
1952 Gary Cooper *High Noon*
1953 William Holden *Stalag 17*
1954 Marlon Brando *On the Waterfront*
1955 Ernest Borgnine *Marty*
1956 Yul Brynner *The King and I*
1957 Alec Guinness *The Bridge on the River Kwai*
1958 David Niven *Separate Tables*
1959 Charlton Heston *Ben-Hur*
1960 Burt Lancaster *Elmer Gantry*
1961 Maximilian Schell *Judgment at Nuremberg*
1962 Gregory Peck *To Kill a Mockingbird*
1963 Sidney Poitier *Lilies of the Field*
1964 Rex Harrison *My Fair Lady*
1965 Lee Marvin *Cat Ballou*
1966 Paul Scofield *A Man for All Seasons*
1967 Rod Steiger *In the Heat of the Night*
1968 Cliff Robertson *Charly*
1969 John Wayne *True Grit*
1970 George C Scott *Patton*
1971 Gene Hackman *The French Connection*

1972 Marlon Brando *The Godfather*
1973 Jack Lemmon *Save the Tiger*
1974 Art Carney *Harry and Tonto*
1975 Jack Nicholson *One Flew Over the Cuckoo's Nest*
1976 Peter Finch *Network*
1977 Richard Dreyfuss *The Goodbye Girl*
1978 Jon Voight *Coming Home*
1979 Dustin Hoffman *Kramer vs. Kramer*
1980 Robert De Niro *Raging Bull*
1981 Henry Fonda *On Golden Pond*
1982 Ben Kingsley *Gandhi*
1983 Robert Duvall *Tender Mercies*
1984 F Murray Abraham *Amadeus*
1985 William Hurt *Kiss of the Spider Woman*
1986 Paul Newman *The Color of Money*
1987 Michael Douglas *Wall Street*
1988 Dustin Hoffman *Rain Man*
1989 Daniel Day-Lewis *My Left Foot*
1990 Jeremy Irons *Reversal of Fortune*
1991 Anthony Hopkins *The Silence of the Lambs*
1992 Al Pacino *Scent of a Woman*
1993 Tom Hanks *Philadelphia*
1994 Tom Hanks *Forrest Gump*
1995 Nicolas Cage *Leaving Las Vegas*
1996 Geoffrey Rush *Shine*
1997 Jack Nicholson *As Good As It Gets*
1998 Roberto Benigni *Life is Beautiful*

BEST ACTRESS

1927–8 Janet Gaynor *Seventh Heaven, Street Angel, Sunrise*
1928–9 Mary Pickford *Coquette*
1929–30 Norma Shearer *The Divorcee*
1930–1 Marie Dressler *Min and Bill*
1931–2 Helen Hayes *The Sin of Madelon Claudet*
1932–3 Katharine Hepburn *Morning Glory*
1934 Claudette Colbert *It Happened One Night*
1935 Bette Davis *Dangerous*
1936 Luise Rainer *The Great Ziegfeld*
1937 Luise Rainer *The Good Earth*
1938 Bette Davis *Jezebel*
1939 Vivien Leigh *Gone with the Wind*
1940 Ginger Rogers *Kitty Foyle*
1941 Joan Fontaine *Suspicion*
1942 Greer Garson *Mrs Miniver*
1943 Jennifer Jones *The Song of Bernadette*
1944 Ingrid Bergman *Gaslight*
1945 Joan Crawford *Mildred Pierce*
1946 Olivia de Havilland *To Each His Own*
1947 Loretta Young *The Farmer's Daughter*
1948 Jane Wyman *Johnny Belinda*
1949 Olivia de Havilland *The Heiress*
1950 Judy Holliday *Born Yesterday*
1951 Vivien Leigh *A Streetcar Named Desire*
1952 Shirley Booth *Come Back, Little Sheba*

1953 Audrey Hepburn *Roman Holiday*
1954 Grace Kelly *The Country Girl*
1955 Anna Magnani *The Rose Tattoo*
1956 Ingrid Bergman *Anastasia*
1957 Joanne Woodward *The Three Faces of Eve*
1958 Susan Hayward *I Want to Live!*
1959 Simone Signoret *Room at the Top*
1960 Elizabeth Taylor *Butterfield 8*
1961 Sophia Loren *Two Women*
1962 Anne Bancroft *The Miracle Worker*
1963 Patricia Neal *Hud*
1964 Julie Andrews *Mary Poppins*
1965 Julie Christie *Darling*
1966 Elizabeth Taylor *Who's Afraid of Virginia Woolf?*
1967 Katharine Hepburn *Guess Who's Coming to Dinner*
1968 Katharine Hepburn *The Lion in Winter*, Barbra Streisand *Funny Girl*
1969 Maggie Smith *The Prime of Miss Jean Brodie*
1970 Glenda Jackson *Women in Love*
1971 Jane Fonda *Klute*
1972 Liza Minnelli *Cabaret*
1973 Glenda Jackson *A Touch of Class*
1974 Ellen Burstyn *Alice Doesn't Live Here Anymore*
1975 Louise Fletcher *One Flew Over the Cuckoo's Nest*
1976 Faye Dunaway *Network*
1977 Diane Keaton *Annie Hall*
1978 Jane Fonda *Coming Home*
1979 Sally Field *Norma Rae*
1980 Sissy Spacek *Coal Miner's Daughter*
1981 Katharine Hepburn *On Golden Pond*
1982 Meryl Streep *Sophie's Choice*
1983 Shirley MacLaine *Terms of Endearment*
1984 Sally Field *Places in the Heart*
1985 Geraldine Page *The Trip to Bountiful*
1986 Marlee Matlin *Children of a Lesser God*
1987 Cher *Moonstruck*
1988 Jodie Foster *The Accused*
1989 Jessica Tandy *Driving Miss Daisy*
1990 Kathy Bates *Misery*
1991 Jodie Foster *The Silence of the Lambs*
1992 Emma Thompson *Howards End*
1993 Holly Hunter *The Piano*
1994 Jessica Lange *Blue Sky*
1995 Susan Sarandon *Dead Man Walking*
1996 Francis McDormand *Fargo*
1997 Helen Hunt *As Good As It Gets*
1998 Gwyneth Paltrow *Shakespeare in Love*

BEST DIRECTOR

1927–8 Frank Borzage *Seventh Heaven*, Lewis Milestone *Two Arabian Knights*
1928–9 Frank Lloyd *The Divine Lady*
1929–30 Lewis Milestone *All Quiet on the Western Front*
1930–1 Norman Taurog *Skippy*
1931–2 Frank Borzage *Bad Girl*
1932–3 Frank Lloyd *Cavalcade*
1934 Frank Capra *It Happened One Night*
1935 John Ford *The Informer*
1936 Frank Capra *Mr Deeds Goes to Town*
1937 Leo McCarey *The Awful Truth*
1938 Frank Capra *You Can't Take It with You*
1939 Victor Fleming *Gone with the Wind*
1940 John Ford *The Grapes of Wrath*
1941 John Ford *How Green Was My Valley*
1942 William Wyler *Mrs Miniver*
1943 Michael Curtiz *Casablanca*
1944 Leo McCarey *Going My Way*
1945 Billy Wilder *The Lost Weekend*
1946 William Wyler *The Best Years of Our Lives*
1947 Elia Kazan *Gentleman's Agreement*
1948 John Huston *The Treasure of the Sierra Madre*
1949 Joseph L. Mankiewicz *A Letter to Three Wives*
1950 Joseph L. Mankiewicz *All About Eve*
1951 George Stevens *A Place in the Sun*
1952 John Ford *The Quiet Man*
1953 Fred Zinnemann *From Here to Eternity*
1954 Elia Kazan *On the Waterfront*
1955 Delbert Mann *Marty*
1956 George Stevens *Giant*
1957 David Lean *The Bridge on the River Kwai*
1958 Vincente Minnelli *Gigi*
1959 William Wyler *Ben-Hur*
1960 Billy Wilder *The Apartment*
1961 Robert Wise and Jerome Robbins *West Side Story*
1962 David Lean *Lawrence of Arabia*
1963 Tony Richardson *Tom Jones*
1964 George Cukor *My Fair Lady*
1965 Robert Wise *The Sound of Music*
1966 Fred Zinnemann *A Man for All Seasons*
1967 Mike Nichols *The Graduate*
1968 Sir Carol Reed *Oliver!*
1969 John Schlesinger *Midnight Cowboy*
1970 Franklin J Schaffner *Patton*
1971 William Friedkin *The French Connection*

1972 Bob Fosse *Cabaret*
1973 George Roy Hill *The Sting*
1974 Francis Ford Coppola *The Godfather, Part II*
1975 Milos Forman *One Flew Over the Cuckoo's Nest*
1976 John Avildsen *Rocky*
1977 Woody Allen *Annie Hall*
1978 Michael Cimino *The Deer Hunter*
1979 Robert Benton *Kramer vs. Kramer*
1980 Robert Redford *Ordinary People*
1981 Warren Beatty *Reds*
1982 Sir Richard Attenborough *Gandhi*
1983 James L Brooks *Terms of Endearment*
1984 Milos Forman *Amadeus*
1985 Sydney Pollack *Out of Africa*
1986 Oliver Stone *Platoon*
1987 Bernardo Bertolucci *The Last Emperor*
1988 Barry Levinson *Rain Man*
1989 Oliver Stone *Born on the Fourth of July*
1990 Kevin Costner *Dances with Wolves*
1991 Jonathan Demme *The Silence of the Lambs*
1992 Clint Eastwood *Unforgiven*
1993 Steven Spielberg *Schindler's List*
1994 Robert Zemeckis *Forrest Gump*
1995 Mel Gibson *Braveheart*
1996 Anthony Minghella *The English Patient*
1997 James Cameron *Titanic*
1998 Steven Spielberg *Saving Private Ryan*

BEST PICTURE
1927–8 *Wings*
1928–9 *The Broadway Melody*
1929–30 *All Quiet on the Western Front*
1930–1 *Cimarron*
1931–2 *Grand Hotel*
1932–3 *Cavalcade*
1934 *It Happened One Night*
1935 *Mutiny on the Bounty*
1936 *The Great Ziegfeld*
1937 *The Life of Emile Zola*
1938 *You Can't Take It with You*
1939 *Gone with the Wind*
1940 *Rebecca*
1941 *How Green Was My Valley*
1942 *Mrs Miniver*
1943 *Casablanca*
1944 *Going My Way*
1945 *The Lost Weekend*

1946 *The Best Years of Our Lives*
1947 *Gentleman's Agreement*
1948 *Hamlet*
1949 *All the King's Men*
1950 *All About Eve*
1951 *An American in Paris*
1952 *The Greatest Show on Earth*
1953 *From Here to Eternity*
1954 *On the Waterfront*
1955 *Marty*
1956 *Around the World in 80 Days*
1957 *The Bridge on the River Kwai*
1958 *Gigi*
1959 *Ben-Hur*
1960 *The Apartment*
1961 *West Side Story*
1962 *Lawrence of Arabia*
1963 *Tom Jones*
1964 *My Fair Lady*
1965 *The Sound of Music*
1966 *A Man for All Seasons*
1967 *In the Heat of the Night*
1968 *Oliver!*
1969 *Midnight Cowboy*
1970 *Patton*
1971 *The French Connection*
1972 *The Godfather*
1973 *The Sting*
1974 *The Godfather, Part II*
1975 *One Flew Over the Cuckoo's Nest*
1976 *Rocky*
1977 *Annie Hall*
1978 *The Deer Hunter*
1979 *Kramer vs. Kramer*
1980 *Ordinary People*
1981 *Chariots of Fire*
1982 *Gandhi*
1983 *Terms of Endearment*
1984 *Amadeus*
1985 *Out of Africa*
1986 *Platoon*
1987 *The Last Emperor*
1988 *Rain Man*
1989 *Driving Miss Daisy*
1990 *Dances with Wolves*
1991 *The Silence of the Lambs*
1992 *Unforgiven*
1993 *Schindler's List*
1994 *Forrest Gump*
1995 *Braveheart*
1996 *The English Patient*
1997 *Titanic*
1998 *Shakespeare in Love*

Jon Voight and Dustin Hoffman in *Midnight Cowboy*, 1969.

NOBEL PRIZES
The Nobel Prizes are an international award granted in the fields of literature, physics, chemistry, physiology or medicine and peace. The first prizes were awarded in 1901, funded by the £2 million left in the will of the Swedish inventor Alfred Nobel (1833–96) who gave the world dynamite.

PRIZES FOR LITERATURE
1901 Rene Sully-Prudhomme (French) for poetry
1902 Theodor Mommsen (German) for historical narratives
1903 Bjornstjerne Bjornson (Norwegian) for fiction, poetry and drama
1904 Frederic Mistral (French) for poetry, and Jose Echegaray y Eizaguirre (Spanish) for drama
1905 Henryk Sienkiewicz (Polish) for fiction
1906 Giosue Carducci (Italian) for poetry
1907 Rudyard Kipling (British) for fiction and poetry
1908 Rudolf Eucken (German) for philosophic writings
1909 Selma Lagerlof (Swedish) for fiction and poetry
1910 Paul von Heyse (German) for poetry, fiction and drama
1911 Maurice Maeterlinck (Belgian) for drama
1912 Gerhart Hauptmann (German) for drama
1913 Rabindranath Tagore (Indian) for poetry
1914 No award
1915 Romain Rolland (French) for fiction
1916 Verner von Heidenstam (Swedish) for poetry
1917 Karl Gjellerup (Danish) for poetry and fiction, and Henrik Pontoppidan (Danish) for fiction
1918 No award
1919 Carl Spitteler (Swiss) for fiction
1920 Knut Hamsun (Norwegian) for fiction
1921 Anatole France (French) for fiction and essays
1922 Jacinto Benavente (Spanish) for drama
1923 William Butler Yeats (Irish) for poetry
1924 Wladyslaw Reymont (Polish) for fiction
1925 George Bernard Shaw (Irish-born) for drama
1926 Grazia Deledda (Italian) for fiction
1927 Henri Bergson (French) for philosophic writings
1928 Sigrid Undset (Norwegian) for fiction
1929 Thomas Mann (German) for fiction, particularly *Buddenbrooks*
1930 Sinclair Lewis (American) for fiction
1931 Erik Axel Karlfeldt (Swedish) for lyric poetry
1932 John Galsworthy (British) for fiction and drama
1933 Ivan Bunin (Soviet) for fiction, short stories and poetry
1934 Luigi Pirandello (Italian) for drama

Thomas Mann, winner of the 1929 Nobel Prize for Literature.

1935 No award
1936 Eugene O'Neill (American) for drama
1937 Roger Martin du Gard (French) for fiction
1938 Pearl S Buck (American) for fiction
1939 Frans Eemil Sillanpaa (Finnish) for fiction
1940–1943 No award
1944 Johannes Jensen (Danish) for poetry and fiction
1945 Gabriela Mistral (Chilean) for poetry
1946 Hermann Hesse (German) for fiction, poetry and essays
1947 André Gide (French) for fiction
1948 TS Eliot (British) for poetry, essays and drama
1949 William Faulkner (American) for fiction (Award delayed until 1950.)
1950 Bertrand Russell (British) for philosophic writing
1951 Par Fabian Lagerkvist (Swedish) for fiction, particularly *Barabbas*
1952 François Mauriac (French) for fiction, essays and poetry
1953 Sir Winston Churchill (British) for essays, speeches and historical writings
1954 Ernest Hemingway (American) for fiction
1955 Halldor Laxness (Icelandic) for fiction
1956 Juan Ramon Jimenez (Spanish) for poetry
1957 Albert Camus (French) for fiction
1958 Boris Pasternak (Soviet) for fiction, especially *Dr Zhivago* (award declined).
1959 Salvatore Quasimodo (Italian) for lyric poetry
1960 Saint-John Perse (French) for poetry
1961 Ivo Andric (Yugoslav) for fiction, especially *The Bridge on the Drina*.
1962 John Steinbeck (American) for fiction, especially *The Winter of Our Discontent*
1963 George Seferis (Greek) for lyric poetry
1964 Jean-Paul Sartre (French) for philosophical works (award declined)
1965 Mikhail Sholokhov (Soviet) for fiction
1966 Shmuel Yosef Agnon (Israeli) for stories of Eastern European Jewish life, and Nelly Sachs (German born) for drama and poetry about the Jewish people
1967 Miguel Angel Asturias (Guatemalan) for writings rooted in national individuality and Indian traditions

1968 Yasunari Kawabata (Japanese) for fiction

1969 Samuel Beckett (Irish born) for fiction and drama

1970 Alexander Solzhenitsyn (Soviet) for fiction

1971 Pablo Neruda (Chilean) for poetry

1972 Heinrich Böll (German) for fiction and drama

1973 Patrick White (Australian) for fiction

1974 Eyvind Johnson (Swedish) for fiction and Harry Edmund Martinson (Swedish) for essays, drama, fiction and poetry

1975 Eugenio Montale (Italian) for poetry

1976 Saul Bellow (American) for fiction

1977 Vicente Aleixandre (Spanish) for poetry

1978 Isaac Bashevis Singer (Polish-born) for fiction

1979 Odysseus Elytis (Greek) for poetry

1980 Czeslaw Milosz (Polish) for poetry

1981 Elias Canetti (Bulgarian-born) for fiction and non-fiction.

1982 Gabriel Garcia Marquez (Colombian) for fiction

1983 William Golding (British) for fiction

1984 Jaroslav Seifert (Czech) for poetry

1985 Claude Simon (French) for fiction

1986 Wole Soyinka (Nigerian) for drama, poetry and fiction

1987 Joseph Brodsky (Soviet-born) for poetry

1988 Najib Mahfuz (Egyptian) for fiction

1989 Camilo José Cela (Spanish) for fiction

1990 Octavio Paz (Mexican) for poetry and essays

1991 Nadine Gordimer (South African) for fiction

1992 Derek Walcott (St Lucian-born) for poetry

1993 Toni Morrison (American) for fiction

1994 Kenzaburo Oe (Japanese) for fiction

1995 Seamus Heaney (Irish) for poetry

1996 Wislawa Szymborska (Poland) for poetry

1997 Dario Fo (Italian) for drama

1998 José Saramago (Portuguese) for fiction

PRIZES FOR PEACE

1901 Jean Henri Dunant (Swiss) for founding the Red Cross and originating the Geneva Convention, and Frederic Passy (French) for founding a French peace society

1902 Elie Ducommun (Swiss) for work as honorary secretary of the International Peace Bureau, and Charles Albert Gobat (Swiss) for administrating the Inter-Parliamentary Union

1903 Sir William Cremer (British) for activities as founder and secretary of the International Arbitration League

1904 The Institute of International Law for studies on the laws of neutrality and other phases of international law

1905 Baroness Bertha von Suttner (Austrian) for promoting pacifism and founding an Austrian peace society

1906 Theodore Roosevelt (American) for negotiating peace in the Russo-Japanese War

1907 Ernesto Moneta (Italian) for work as president of the Lombard League for Peace, and Louis Renault (French) for work on peace conferences

1908 Klas Pontus Arnoldson (Swedish) for founding the Swedish Society for Arbitration and Peace, and Fredrik Bajer (Danish) for work on the International Peace Bureau

1909 Auguste Beernaert (Belgian) for work on the Permanent Court of Arbitration, and Paul d'Estournelles (French) for founding and directing the French Parliamentary Arbitration Committee and League of International Conciliation

1910 The International Peace Bureau for promoting international arbitration and organizing peace conferences

1911 Tobias Asser (Dutch) for organizing conferences on international law, and Alfred Fried (Austrian) for his writings on peace as editor of *Die Friedenswarte*

1912 Elihu Root (American) for settling the problem of Japanese immigration to California and organizing the Central American Peace Conference

1913 Henri Lafontaine (Belgian) for work as president of the International Peace Bureau

1914–1916 *No awards*

1917 The International Red Cross for doing relief work during World War I

1918 *No award*

1919 Woodrow Wilson (American) for attempting a just settlement of World War I and advocating the League of Nations. (Award delayed until 1920.)

1920 Leon Bourgeois (French) for contribution as president of the Council of the League of Nations

1921 Karl Hjalmar Branting (Swedish) for promoting social reforms in Sweden and serving as the Swedish delegate to the League of Nations, and Christian Louis Lange (Norwegian) for contribution as secretary-general of the Inter-Parliamentary Union

1922 Fridtjof Nansen (Norwegian) for doing relief work among Russian prisoners of war and in famine areas in Russia

1923–1924 *No awards*

1925 Austin Chamberlain (British) for helping to work out the Locarno Peace Pact, and Charles G Dawes (American) for originating a plan for payment of German reparations

1926 Aristide Briand (French) for the formation of the Locarno Peace Pact, and Gustav Stresemann (German) for persuading Germany to accept plans for reparations

1927 Ferdinand Buisson (French) for work as president of the League of Human Rights, and Ludwig Quidde (German) for writing on and working for peace

1928 *No award*

1929 Frank Billings Kellogg (American) for negotiating the Kellogg-Briand Peace Pact

1930 Nathan Soderblom (Swedish) for writing on and working for peace

1931 Jane Addams (American) for work with the Women's International League for Peace and Freedom, and Nicholas M Butler (American) for work with the Carnegie Endowment for International Peace

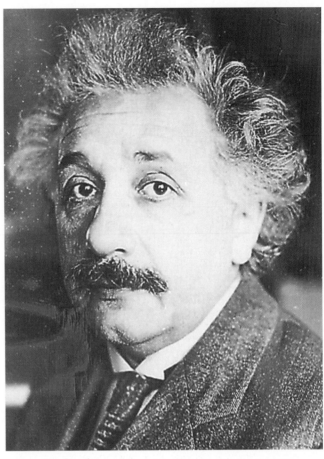

Albert Einstein, winner of the Nobel Prize for Physics in 1921.

1932 *No award*

1933 Norman Angell (British) for work with the Royal Institute of International Affairs, the League of Nations, and the National Peace Council

1934 Arthur Henderson (British) for work as president of the World Disarmament Conference

1935 Carl von Ossietzky (German) for promoting world disarmament (award delayed until 1936)

1936 Carlos Saavedra Lamas (Argentine) for negotiating a peace settlement between Bolivia and Paraguay in the Chaco War

1937 Edgar Algernon Robert Gascoyne Cecil (British) for promoting the League of Nations and working with peace movements

1938 The International Office for Refugees for directing relief work among refugees

1939–1943 *No awards*

1944 The International Red Cross for doing relief work during World War II

1945 Cordell Hull (American) for peace efforts as secretary of state

1946 John R Mott (American) for YMCA work and for aiding displaced persons, and Emily Greene Balch (American) for work with the Women's International League for Peace and Freedom

1947 The Friends Service Council and the American Friends Service Committee for humanitarian work

1948 *No award*

1949 John Boyd Orr (British) for directing the United Nations Food and Agriculture Organization

1950 Ralph J Bunche (American) for his work as UN mediator in Palestine in 1948 and 1949

1951 Leon Jouhaux (French) for work helping to organize national and international trade unions

1952 Albert Schweitzer (German-born) for humanitarian work in Africa (award delayed until 1953)

1953 George Marshall (American) for promoting peace through the European Recovery Program

1954 Office of the United Nations High Commissioner for Refugees for providing protection for millions of refugees and seeking permanent solutions to their problems (award delayed until 1955)

1955–1956 *No awards*

1957 Lester Pearson (Canadian) for organizing a UN force in Egypt

1958 Dominique Georges Pire (Belgian) for work in resettling displaced persons

1959 Lord Noel-Baker (British) for promoting peace and disarmament

1960 Albert John Luthuli (African) for peaceful campaigning against racial restrictions in South Africa

1961 Dag Hammarskjöld (Swedish) for efforts to bring peace to the Congo (awarded posthumously)

1962 Linus Pauling (American) for efforts to ban nuclear weapons, especially for campaigning against nuclear weapons testing

1963 International Committee of the Red Cross and League of Red Cross Societies for humanitarian work

1964 Martin Luther King, Jr (American), for leading the black struggle for equality in the United States through non-violent means

1965 United Nations Children's Fund (UNICEF) for its aid to children

1966–1967 No awards

1968 René Cassin (French) for promoting human rights

1969 International Labour Organization (ILO) for its efforts to improve working conditions

1970 Norman Borlaug (American) for developing high-yield grains to increase food in developing countries

1971 Willy Brandt (German) for efforts to improve relations between Communist and non-Communist nations

1972 No award

1973 Henry Kissinger (American) and Le Duc Tho (North Vietnamese) for work in negotiating the Vietnam War cease-fire agreement (Le Duc Tho declined)

1974 Sean MacBride (Irish) for working to guarantee human rights through international law, and Eisaku Sato (Japanese) for efforts to improve international relations and stop the spread of nuclear weapons

1975 Andrei Sakharov (Soviet) for work in promoting peace and opposing violence and brutality.

1976 Mairead Corrigan and Betty Williams (Irish) for organizing a movement to end Protestant-Catholic fighting in Northern Ireland (award delayed until 1977

1977 Amnesty International for helping political prisoners

1978 Menachem Begin (Israeli) and Anwar el-Sadat (Egyptian) for efforts to end the Arab-Israeli conflict.

1979 Mother Teresa (Rumanian born) for aiding India's poor.

1980 Adolfo Perez Esquivel (Argentine) for activities in Service for Peace and Justice in Latin America, a group promoting the cause of human rights

1981 Office of the United Nations High Commissioner for Refugees for the protection of millions of Vietnamese and other refugees

1982 Alva Myrdal (Swedish) and Alfonso Garcia Robles (Mexican) for contributions to United Nations disarmament negotiations

1983 Lech Walesa (Polish) for efforts to prevent violence while trying to gain workers' rights

1984 Desmond Tutu (South African) for leading a non-violent campaign against ethnic segregation in his country

1985 International Physicians for the Prevention of Nuclear War for educating the public on the effects of nuclear war

1986 Elie Wiesel (American) for efforts to help victims of oppression and racial discrimination

1987 Oscar Arias Sanchez (Costa Rican) for authoring a plan to end civil wars in Central America

1988 UN peacekeeping forces for controlling military conflict

1989 Dalai Lama (Tibetan) for non-violent struggle to end China's rule of Tibet.

1990 Mikhail Gorbachev (Soviet) for promoting world peace

1991 Aung San Suu Kyi (Burmese) for

non-violent struggle for democracy and human rights in Burma.

1992 Rigoberta Menchu (Guatemalan) for work to gain respect for the rights of Guatemala's Native Americans.

1993 Nelson Mandela and FW de Klerk (South African) for helping to integrate South Africa

1994 Yasser Arafat (Palestinian), Yitzhak Rabin (Israeli) and Shimon Peres (Israeli) for helping to promote Palestinian self-rule

1995 The organization known as the Pugwash Conference on Science and World Affairs and its president, Joseph Rotblat (British), for their efforts to eliminate nuclear weapons

1996 Carlos Ximenes Belo (Timorese) and Jose Ramos-Horta (Timorese) for their work on behalf of the people of East Timor

1997 Jody Williams (American) and the International Campaign to Ban Landmines for work campaigning to defuse landmines

1998 John Hume and David Trimble for efforts to find a peaceful solution to the conflict in Northern Ireland

PRIZES FOR PHYSICS

1901 Wilhelm Roentgen (German) for discovering X-rays

1902 Hendrik Antoon Lorentz and Pieter Zeeman (Dutch) for noting the Zeeman effect of magnetism on light

1903 Antoine Henri Becquerel and Pierre and Marie Curie (French) for discovering radioactivity and studying uranium

1904 Baron Rayleigh (British) for studying the density of gases and discovering argon

1905 Philipp Lenard (German) for studying the properties of cathode rays.

1906 Sir Joseph John Thomson (British) for studying electrical discharge through gases.

1907 Albert Michelson (American) for the design of precise optical instruments and for accurate measurements.

1908 Gabriel Lippman (French) for his

method of colour photography.

1909 Guglielmo Marconi (Italian) and Karl Ferdinand Braun (German) for developing the wireless telegraph

1910 Johannes van der Waals (Dutch) for studying the relationships of liquids and gases

1911 Wilhelm Wien (German) for discoveries on the heat radiated by black objects

1912 Nils Dalen (Swedish) for inventing automatic gas regulators for lighthouses

1913 Heike Kamerlingh Onnes (Dutch) for experimenting with low temperatures and liquefying helium

1914 Max von Laue (German) for using crystals to measure X-rays

1915 Sir William Henry Bragg and Sir William Lawrence Bragg (British) for using X-rays to study crystal structure

1916 No award

1917 Charles Barkla (British) for studying the diffusion of light and the radiation of X-rays from elements

1918 Max Planck (German) for stating the quantum theory of light

1919 Johannes Stark (German) for discovering the Stark effect of spectra in electrical fields

1920 Charles Guillaume (French) for discovering nickel-steel alloys with slight expansion, and the alloy invar

1921 Albert Einstein (German) for contributing to mathematical physics and stating the law of the photoelectric effect

1922 Niels Bohr (Danish) for studying the structure of atoms and their radiations

1923 Robert Millikan (American) for measuring the charge on electrons and working on the photoelectric effect

1924 Karl Siegbahn (Swedish) for working with the X-ray spectroscope

1925 James Franck and Gustav Hertz (German) for stating laws on the collision of an electron with an atom

1926 Jean-Baptiste Perrin (French) for studying the discontinuous structure of matter and measuring the sizes of atoms

1927 Arthur Compton (American) for

discovering the Compton effect on X-rays reflected from atoms, and Charles Wilson (British) for discovering a method for tracing the paths of ions

1928 Owen Richardson (British) for studying thermionic effect and electrons sent off by hot metals

1929 Louis Victor de Broglie (French) for discovering the wave character of electrons

1930 Sir Chandrasekhara Venkata Raman (Indian) for discovering a new effect in radiation from elements

1931 No award

1932 Werner Heisenberg (German) for founding quantum mechanics, which led to discoveries in hydrogen

1933 Paul Dirac (British) and Erwin Schrödinger (Austrian) for discovering new forms of atomic theory

1934 No award

1935 Sir James Chadwick (British) for discovering the neutron

1936 Carl David Anderson (American) for discovering the positron, and Victor Hess (Austrian) for cosmic rays

1937 Clinton Davisson (American) and George Thomson (British) for discovering the diffraction of electrons by crystals

1938 Enrico Fermi (Italian) for discovering new radioactive elements beyond uranium

1939 Ernest Lawrence (American) for inventing the cyclotron and working on artificial radioactivity

1940–42 No awards

1943 Otto Stern (American) for discovering the molecular beam method of studying the atom

1944 Isidor Isaac Rabi (American) for recording the magnetic properties of atomic nuclei

1945 Wolfgang Pauli (Austrian) for discovering the exclusion principle (Pauli principle) of electrons

1946 Percy William Bridgman (American) for his work in the field of very high pressures

1947 Sir Edward Appleton (British) for exploring the ionosphere.

1948 Patrick Blackett (British) for his discoveries in cosmic radiation

President Kennedy at a Nobel Prize Giving.

1949 Hideki Yukawa (Japanese) for predicting the existence of elementary particles called mesons

1950 Cecil Frank Powell (British) for the photographic method of studying atomic nuclei and discoveries concerning mesons

1951 Sir John Cockcroft (British) and Ernest Walton (Irish) for working on the transmutation of atomic nuclei by artificially accelerated atomic particles

1952 Felix Bloch and Edward Mills Purcell (American) for developing magnetic measurement methods for atomic nuclei

1953 Frits Zernike (Dutch) for inventing the phase contrast microscope for cancer research

1954 Max Born (German) for research in quantum mechanics, and Walter Bothe (German) for discoveries made with the coincidence method

1955 Willis E. Lamb, Jnr. (American) for discoveries on the structure of the hydrogen spectrum, and Polykarp Kusch (American) for determining the magnetic moment of the electron

1956 John Bardeen, Walter Brattain and William Schockley (American) for inventing the transistor

1957 Tsung Dao Lee and Chen Ning Yang (American) for disproving the law of conservation of parity

1958 Pavel Cherenkov, Ilya Frank and Igor Tamm (Soviet) for discovering and interpreting the Cherenkov effect in studying high-energy particles

1959 Emilio Segre and Owen Chamberlain (American) for work in demonstrating the existence of the antiproton

1960 Donald Glaser (American) for inventing the bubble chamber to study subatomic particles

1961 Robert Hofstadter (American) for studies of nucleons and Rudolf Mossbauer (German) for research on gamma rays

1962 Lev Davidovich Landau (Soviet) for research on liquid helium

1963 Eugene Paul Wigner (American) for contributions to the understanding of atomic nuclei and the elementary particles; and Maria Goeppert Mayer (American) and J Hans Jensen (German) for work on the structure of atomic nuclei

1964 Charles Townes (American) and Nikolai Basov and Alexander Prokhorov (Soviet) for developing masers and lasers

1965 Sin-itiro Tomonaga (Japanese) and Julian Schwinger and Richard Freyman (American) for basic work in quantum electrodynamics

1966 Alfred Kastler (French) for work on the energy levels of atoms

1967 Hans Albrecht Bethe (American) for contributions to the theory of nuclear reactions, especially discoveries on the energy production in stars

1968 Luis Alvarez (American) for contributions to the knowledge of subatomic particles

1969 Murray Gell-Man (American) for discoveries concerning the classification of nuclear particles and heir interactions

1970 Hannes Olof Goast Alfven (Swedish) for work in magneto-hydrodynamics, the study of electrical and magnetic effects in fluids that conduct electricity, and Louis Eugêne Felix Neel (French) for discoveries of magnetic properties that applied to computer memories

1971 Dennis Gabor (British) for work in holography

1972 John Bardeen, Leon Cooper, and John Robert Schrieffer (American) for work on superconductivity, the disappearance of electrical resistance

1973 Ivar Giaever (American), Leo Esaki (Japanese) and Brian Josephson (British) for work on the phenomena of electron "tunnelling" through semiconductor and superconductor materials

1974 Antony Hewish (British) for the discovery of pulsars, and Sir Martin Ryle (British) for the use of small radio telescopes to "see" into space with great accuracy

1975 L James Rainwater (American) and Aage Bohr and Ben Mottelson (Danish) for work on the structure of the atomic nucleus

1976 Burton Richter and Samuel Chao Chung Ting (American) for discovery of an elementary nuclear particle called the psi, or J particle

1977 Philip W Anderson and John Van Vleck (American) and Sir Nevill Mott (British) for helping develop semiconductor devices

1978 Pyotr Kapitsa (Soviet) for research in low-temperature physics, and Arno Penzias and Robert Wilson (American) for the discovery and study of cosmic microwave background radiation

1979 Sheldon Glashow and Steven Weinberg (American) and Abdus Salam (Pakistani) for developing a principle that unifies the weak nuclear force and the force of electromagnetism

1980 James Cronin and Val Fitch (American) for research on subatomic particles revealing that the fundamental laws of symmetry in nature could be violated

1981 Nicolaas Bloembergen and Arthur Schawlow (American) for contributions to the development of laser spectroscopy, and Kai Siegbahn (Swedish) for contributions to the development of high-resolution electron spectroscopy

1982 Kenneth Wilson (American) for the method of analysing the behaviour of matter when it changes form

1983 Subrahmanyan Chandrasekhar and William Fowler (American) for work on the evolution and death of stars

1984 Carlo Rubbia (Italian) and Simon van der Meer (Dutch) for contributions to the discovery of two subatomic particles — the W and the Z particles

1985 Klaus von Klitzing (West German) for developing a precise way of measuring electrical resistance

1986 Ernst Ruska (West German) for the invention of the electron microscope and Gerd Binnig (West German) and Heinrich Rohrer (Swiss) for the invention of the scanning tunnelling microscope

1987 J. George Bednorz (West German) and K. Alex Muller (Swiss) for the discovery of superconductivity in a ceramic material

1988 Leon Lederman, Melvin Schwartz and Jack Steinberger (American) for work on neutrinos

1989 Hans G Dehmelt (American) and Wolfgang Paul (German) for isolating and measuring single atoms, and Norman Ramsey (American) for work that led to the development of the atomic clock

1990 Jerome Friedman and Henry Kendall (American) and Richard Taylor (Canadian) for experiments proving the existence of subatomic particles called quarks

1991 Pierre-Gilles de Gennes (French) for analyses of alignments and other orderly arrangements of molecules in certain substances

1992 Georges Charpak (French) for the invention of devices that detect subatomic particles in particle accelerators

1993 Russell Hulse and Joseph Taylor, Jnr (American) for discovering dense pairs of stars called binary pulsars.

1994 Clifford Shull (American) and Bertram Brockhouse (Canadian) for developing neutron scattering as a technique for revealing the structure of matter

1995 Martin Perl (American) for research on a subatomic particle called the tau, and Frederick Reines (American) for the discovery of a subatomic particle called the neutrino.

1996 David M Lee, Robert C Richardson, and Douglas D Osheroff (American) for discovering that a type of helium called helium-3 becomes a superfluid, a rare form of matter, at an extremely low temperature

1997 Steven Chu and William Phillips (American) and Claude Cohen-Tannoudji (French) for methods of investigation using laser light to cool and trap atoms

1998 Robert B Laughlin (American) and Horst L Stormer (German-born) and David C Tsui (Chinese-born) for the discovery of a new form of quantum fluid with fractionally charged excitations

PRIZES FOR CHEMISTRY

1901 Jacobus Henricus Van't Hoff (Dutch) for discovering laws of chemical dynamics and osmotic pressure

1902 Emil Fischer (German) for synthesizing sugars, purine derivatives and peptides

1903 Svante August Arrhenius (Swedish) for the dissociation theory of ionization in electrolytes

1904 Sir William Ramsay (British) for discovering helium, neon, xenon and krypton and determining their place in the periodic system

1905 Adolph von Baeyer (German) for work on dyes and organic compounds and for synthesizing indigo and arsenicals

1906 Henri Moissan (French) for preparing pure fluorine and developing the electric furnace

1907 Eduard Buchner (German) forbiochemical researches and for discovering cell-less fermentation

1908 Ernest Rutherford (British) for discovering that radioactive elements change into other elements

1909 Wilhelm Ostwald (German) for work on catalysis, chemical equilibrium and the rate of chemical reactions

1910 Otto Wallach (German) for work in the field of alicyclic substances.

1911 Marie Curie (French) for the discovery of radium and polonium and for work in isolating radium and studying the compounds of radium

1912 François Grignard (French) for discovering the Grignard reagent to synthesize organic compounds, and Paul Sabatier (French) for the method of using nickel as a hydrogenation catalyst

1913 Alfred Werner (Swiss) for the coordination theory on the arrangement of atoms

1914 Theodore Richards (American) for determining the atomic weights of many elements

1915 Richard Willstatter (German) for research on chlorophyll and other colouring matter in plants

1916–17 No awards

1918 Fritz Haber (German) for the Haber-Bosch process of synthesizing ammonia from nitrogen and hydrogen

1919 No award

1920 Walther Nerst (German) for discoveries concerning heat changes in chemical reactions

1921 Frederick Soddy (British) for studying radioactive substances and isotopes

1922 Francis Aston (British) for the use of spectography to discover many isotopes and for discovering the whole number rule on the structure and weight of atoms

1923 Fritz Pregl (Austrian) for inventing a method of microanalysing organic substances

1924 No award

1925 Richard Zsigmondy (German) for a method of studying colloids

1926 Theodor Svedberg (Swedish) for work on dispersions and colloid chemistry

1927 Heinrich Wieland (German) for studying gall acids and related substances

1928 Adolf Windaus (German) for studying sterols and their connection with vitamins

1929 Sir Arthur Harden (British) and Hans August Simon von Euler-Chelpin (German) for research on sugar fermentation and enzymes

1930 Hans Fischer (German) for studying the colouring matter of blood and leaves and synthesizing hemin

1931 Carl Bosch and Friedrich Bergius (German) for inventing high-pressure methods of manufacturing ammonia and liquefying coal

1932 Irving Langmuir (American) for discoveries about molecular films absorbed on surfaces

1933 No award

1934 Harold Clayton Urey (American) for discovering deuterium (heavy hydrogen)

1935 Frederic and Irene Joliot-Curie (French) for synthesizing new radioactive elements

1936 Peter Debye (Dutch) for studies on molecules, dipole moments, electron diffraction and X-rays in gases.

1937 Walter Hayworth (British) for research on carbohydrates and vitamin

C, and Paul Karrer (Swiss) for studying carotenoids, flavins and vitamins A and B-2
1938 Richard Kuhn (German) for work on carotenoids and vitamins (declined)
1939 Adolph Butenandt (German) for studying sex hormones (declined), and Leopold Ruzicka (Swiss) for work on polymethylenes
1940–42 No awards
1943 Georg von Hevesy (Hungarian) for using isotopes as indicators in chemistry
1944 Otto Hahn (German) for discoveries in fission
1945 Artturi Virtanen (Finnish) for inventing new methods in agricultural biochemistry
1946 James B Sumner (American) for discovering that enzymes can be crystallized; and Wendell M Stanley and John H Northrop (American) for preparing pure enzymes and virus proteins
1947 Sir Robert Robinson (British) for research on biologically significant plant substances
1948 Arne Tiselius (Swedish) for discoveries on the nature of serum proteins
1949 William Francis Giauque (American) for studying reactions to extreme cold
1950 Otto Diels and Kurt Alder (German) for developing a method of synthesizing organic compounds of the diene group
1951 Edwin M McMillan and Glenn T Seaborg (American) for discovering plutonium and other elements
1952 Archer Martin and Richard Synge (British) for developing the partition chromatography process
1953 Hermann Staudinger (German) for discovering a way to synthesize fibre
1954 Linus Pauling (American) for work on the forces that hold matter together
1955 Vincent Du Vigneaud (American) for discovering a process for making synthetic hormones
1956 Sir Cyril Hinshelwood (British) and Nikolai Semenov (Soviet) for work on chemical chain reactions
1957 Lord Todd (British) for work on the protein composition of cells
1958 Frederick Sanger (British) for discovering the structure of the insulin molecule
1959 Jaroslav Heyrovsky (Czech) for developing the polarographic method of analysis
1960 Willard F Libby (American) for developing a method of radiocarbon dating
1961 Melvin Calvin (American) for research on photosynthesis
1962 Sir John Cowdery Kendrew and Max Ferdinand Perutz (British) for studies on globular proteins
1963 Giulio Natta (Italian) for contributions to the understanding of polymers; and Karl Ziegler (German) for the production of organometallic compounds
1964 Dorothy Hodgkin (British) for X-ray studies of compounds such as vitamin B-12 and penicillin
1965 Robert Burns Woodward (American) for contributions to organic synthesis

1966 Robert S Mulliken (American) for developing the molecular-orbital theory of chemical structure
1967 Manfred Eigen (German) and Ronald Norrish and George Porter (British) for developing techniques to measure rapid chemical reactions
1968 Lars Onsager (American) for developing the theory of reciprocal relations of thermodynamic activity
1969 Derek Barton (British) and Odd Hassel (Norwegian) for studies relating chemical reactions with the three-dimensional shape of molecules
1970 Luis Federico Leloir (Argentine) for the discovery of chemical compounds that affect the storage of chemical energy in living things
1971 Gerhard Herzberg (Canadian) for research on the structure of molecules, particularly on free radicals
1972 Christian B Anfinsen, Stanford Moore and William H Stein (American) for fundamental contributions to the chemistry of enzymes
1973 Geoffrey Wilkinson (British) and Ernst Fischer (German) for work on organometallic compounds
1974 Paul John Flory (American) for work in polymer chemistry
1975 John Warcup Cornforth (Australian-born) and Vladimir Prelog (Swiss) for work on the chemical synthesis of organic compounds
1976 William Lipscomb Jnr (American) for studies on the structure and bonding mechanisms of boranes, complex compounds of boron and hydrogen
1977 Ilya Prigogine (Belgian) for contributions to non equilibrium thermodynamics
1978 Peter Mitchell (British) for studies of cellular energy transfer
1979 Herbert Brown (American) and George Wittig (German) for developing compounds capable of producing chemical bonds
1980 Paul Berg and Walter Gilbert (American) and Frederick Sanger (British) for studies of the chemical structure of nucleic acids
1981 Kenichi Fukui (Japanese) and Roald Hoffman (American) for applying the theories of quantum mechanics to predict the course of chemical reactions
1982 Aaron Klug (South African-born) for work with the electron microscope and for research into the structure of nucleic acid-protein complexes
1983 Henry Taube (American) for research on electron transfer between molecules in chemical reactions
1984 R Bruce Merrifield (American) for developing a method to make peptides
1985 Herbert A Hauptman and Jerome Karle (American) for techniques to quickly determine the chemical structure of molecules vital to life
1986 Dudley Herschbach and Yuan Lee (American) and John Polanyi (Canadian) for work on chemical reactions
1987 Jean-Marie Lehn (French) and Donald Cram and Charles Pederson (American) for work on artificial molecules
1988 Johann Deisenhofer, Robert Huber and Hartmut Michel (West German)

for revealing the structure of proteins that are essential to photosynthesis
1989 Sidney Altman and Thomas Cech (American) for the discovery that RNA (ribonucleic acid) can aid chemical reactions in cells
1990 Elias James Corey (American) for artificially duplicating natural substances as compounds for use in drugs
1991 Richard Ernst (Swiss) for improvements in the use of nuclear magnetic resonance (NMR) to analyse chemicals
1992 Rudolph Marcus (American) for analysing the transfer of electrons between molecules
1993 Michael Smith (Canadian) and Kary Mullis (American) for devising methods that made possible gene therapy, detection of the AIDS virus and multiplication of fossil DNA
1994 George Olah (American) for work on hydrocarbon molecules
1995 Mario Molina and F Sherwood Rowland (American) and Paul Crutzen (Dutch) for work leading to the discovery of a "hole" in the earth's protective layer of ozone
1996 Richard E Smalley and Robert . Curl Jnr (American) and Sir Harold W. Kroto (British) for discovering carbon molecules called fullerenes
1997 Jens Skou (Danish) for showing that enzymes can promote the movement of substances through a cell membrane; and John Walker (British) and Paul Boyer (American) for discoveries about adenosine triphosphate (ATP), a molecule that living things use to store energy
1998 Walter Kohn for the development of the density-functional theory; and John A Pople (American) for the development of computational methods in quantum chemistry.

PRIZES FOR PHYSIOLOGY OR MEDICINE

1901 Emil von Behring (German) for discovering the diptheria antitoxin
1902 Sir Ronald Ross (British) for discovering how malaria is transmitted
1903 Niels Ryberg Finsen (Danish) for treating diseases, especially lupus vulgaris, with concentrated light rays
1904 Ivan Petrovich Pavlov (Russian) for work on the physiology of digestion.
1905 Robert Koch (German) for working on tuberculosis and discovering the tubercule bacillus and tuberculin
1906 Camillo Golgi (Italian) and Santiago Ramon y Cajal (Spanish) for studies of nerve tissue
1907 Charles Louis Alphonse Laveran (French) for studying diseases caused by protzoans
1908 Paul Ehrlich (German) and Elie Metchnikoff (Russian) for work on immunity
1909 Emil Theodor Kocher (Swiss) for work on the physiology, pathology and surgery of the thyroid gland
1910 Albrecht Kossel (German) for studying cell chemistry, proteins and nucleic substances
1911 Allvar Gullstrand (Swedish) for work on dioptrics, the refraction of light through the eye
1912 Alexis Carrel (French) for suturing

blood vessels and grafting organs
1913 Charles Robert Richet (French) for studying allergies caused by foreign substances, as in hay fever
1914 Robert Barany (Austrian) for work on function and diseases of equilibrium organs in the inner ear
1915–18 No awards
1919 Jules Bordet (Belgian) for discoveries on immunity
1920 August Krogh (Danish) for discovering the system of action of blood capillaries
1921 No award
1922 Archibald Hill (British) for the discovery of heat production in the muscles; and Otto Meyerhof (German) for work on lactic acid in the muscles
1923 Sir Frederick Banting (Canadian) and John Macleod (Scottish) for discovering insulin
1924 Willem Einthoven (Dutch) for discovering how electrocardiography works
1925 No award
1926 Johannes Fibiger (Danish) for discovering a parasite that causes cancer
1927 Julius Wagner von Jauregg (Austrian) for discovering the fever treatment for paralysis
1928 Charles Nicolle (French) for work on typhus
1929 Christian Eijkman (Dutch) for discovering vitamins that prevent beriberi; and Sir Frederick Hopkins (British) for discovering vitamins that help growth
1930 Karl Landsteiner (American) for identifying the four main human blood types
1931 Otto Warburg (German) for discovering that enzymes aid in respiration by tissues
1932 Edgar Adrian and Sir Charles Sherrington (British) for discoveries on the function of neurons
1933 Thomas Morgan (American) for studying the function of chromosomes in heredity
1934 George Minot, William Murphy and George Whipple (American) for discoveries on liver treatment for anaemia
1935 Hans Spemann (German) for discovering the organizer-effect in the growth on an embryo
1936 Sir Henry Dale (British) and Otto Loewi (Austrian) for discoveries on the chemical transmission of nerve impulses
1937 Albert Szent-Gyorgyi (Hungarian) for work on oxidation in tissues, vitamin C and fumaric acid
1938 Corneille Heymans (Belgian) for discoveries concerning the regulation of respiration
1939 Gerhard Domagk (German) for discovering Prontosil, the first sulpha drug (declined)
1940–2 No awards
1943 Henrik Dam (Danish) for discovering vitamin K and Edward Doisy (American) for synthesizing it
1944 Joseph Erlanger and Herbert Gasser (American) for work on single nerve fibres
1945 Alexander Fleming (British) for discovering penicillin, and Howard Florey and Ernst Chain (British) for

Ayrton Senna of Brazil, three times winner of the Grand Prix.

developing its use as an antibiotic
1946 Hermann Joseph Muller (American) for discovering that X-rays can produce mutations
1947 Carl and Gerty Cori (American) for their work on insulin; and Bernardo Houssay (Argentine) for studying the pancreas and the pituitary gland
1948 Paul Muller (Swiss) for discovering the insect-killing properties of DDT
1949 Walter Hess (Swiss) for discovering how certain parts of the brain control organs of the body; and Antonio Moniz (Portuguese) for originating prefrontal lobotomy
1950 Philip S Hench, Edward C Kendall (American) and Tadeus Reichstein (Swiss) for discoveries concerning cortisone and ACTH
1951 Max Theiler (South African-born) for developing the yellow fever vaccine known as 17-D
1952 Selman A Waksman (American) for work in the discovery of streptomycin
1953 Fritz Albert Lipmann (American) and Hans Adolf Krebs (British) for discoveries in biosynthesis and metabolism
1954 John F Enders, Thomas H Weller and Frederick C Robbins (American) for discovering a simple method of growing polio virus in test tubes
1955 Hugo Theorell (Swedish) for discoveries on the nature and action of oxidation enzymes
1956 Andre F Cournand, Dickinson W Richards, Jnr (American) and Werner Forssmann (German) for using a catheter to chart the interior of the heart
1957 Daniel Bovet (Italian) for discovering antihistamines
1958 George Wells Beadle and Edward Lawrie Tatum (American) for work in biochemical genetics, and Joshua Lederberg (American) for studies of genetics in bacteria

1959 Severo Ochoa and Arthur Kornberg (American) for producing nucleic acid by artificial means
1960 Macfarlane Burnet (Australian) and Peter Medawar (British) for research in transplanting organs
1961 Georg von Bekesy (American) for demonstrating how the ear distinguishes between various sounds
1962 James Watson (American) and Francis Crick and Maurice Wilkins (British) for their work on nucleic acid
1963 Sir John Carew Eccles (Australian) for his research on the transmission of nerve impulses, and Alan Lloyd Hodgkin (British) and Andrew Fielding Huxley (British) for their description of the behaviour of nerve impulses
1964 Konrad E Bloch (American) and Feodor Lynen (German) for work on cholesterol and fatty acid metabolism
1965 François Jacob, André Lwoff and Jacques Monod (French) for their discoveries concerning genetic control of enzyme and virus synthesis
1966 Francis Peyton Rous (American) for discovering a cancer-producing virus, and Charles B Huggins (American) for discovering uses of hormones in treating cancer
1967 Ragnar Granit (Swedish) and H Keffer Hartline and George Wald (American) for their work on chemical and physiological processes in the eye
1968 Robert W Holley, H Gobind Khorana and Marshall W Nirenberg (American) for explaining how genes determine the function of cells
1969 Max Delbruck, Alfred Hershey and Salvador Luria (American) for work with bacteriophages
1970 Julius Axelrod (American), Bernard Katz (British) and Ulf Svante von Euler (Swedish) for discoveries of the role played by certain chemicals in the transmission of nerve impulses
1971 Earl W Sutherland Jnr (American) for the discovery of the ways hormones act, including the discovery of cyclic AMP, a chemical that influences the actions of hormones on body processes

1972 Gerald M Edelman (American) and Rodney Porter (British) for discovering the chemical structure of antibodies
1973 Nikolaas Tinbergen (Dutch-born) and Konrad Lorenz and Karl von Frisch (Austrian) for their studies on animal behaviour
1974 Christian de Duve (Belgian) and Albert Claude and George E Palade (American) for pioneer work in cell biology
1975 David Baltimore, Renato Dulbecco and Howard M Temin (American) for research on how certain viruses affect the genes of cancer cells
1976 Baruch S Blumberg and D Carleton Gajdusek (American) for discoveries concerning the origin and spread of infectious diseases
1977 Roger Guillemin, Andrew Schally and Rosalyn Yalow (American) for research into hormones
1978 Werner Arber (Swiss) and Daniel Nathans and Hamilton O Smith (American) for discoveries in molecular genetics
1979 Allan Macleod Cormack (American) and Godfrey Newbold Hounsfield (British) for contributions to the development of the computerized tomographic (CT) scanner
1980 Baruj Benacerraf and George D Snell (American) and Jean Dausset (French) for discoveries about the genetic regulation of the body's immune system
1981 Roger W Sperry and David H Hubel (American) and Torsten Wiesel (Swedish) for research on the organization and functioning of the brain
1982 Sune Bergstrom and Bengt Samuelsson (Swedish) and John Vane (British) for discoveries regarding prostaglandins and related substances
1983 Barbara McClintock (American) for the discovery that genes sometimes behave unexpectedly inside cells.
1984 Niels Jerne (British), Georges Kohler (German) and Cesar Milstein (Argentine) for discoveries in immunology
1985 Michael S Brown and Joseph L

Goldstein (American) for explaining how high cholesterol levels in the blood cause heart disease
1986 Stanley Cohen (American) and Rita Levi-Montalcini (Italian-born) for research on cell and organ growth
1987 Susumu Tonegawa (Japanese) for discovering how genes produce antibodies against specific disease agents
1988 Gertrude B Elion and George H Hitchings (American) and Sir James Black (British) for discoveries of important principles of drug treatment
1989 J Michael Bishop and Harold E Varmus (American) for research on cancer-causing genes called oncogenes
1990 Joseph E Murray and E Donnall Thomas (American) for work in transplanting human organs and bone marrow
1991 Erwin Neher and Bert Sakmann (German) for discovering how cells communicate with one another
1992 Edmond Fischer and Edwin Krebs (American) for discovering a chemical process in cells that is linked to cancer and to rejection of transplanted organs
1993 Richard Roberts (British-born) and Phillip Sharp (American) for their discoveries about the structure and function of genes
1994 Alfred Gilman and Martin Rodbell (Americans) for discovering G-proteins
1995 Edward B Lewis and Eric Wieschaus (American) and Christiane Nuesslein-Volhard (German) for studies of how genes control early embryo development
1996 Peter C Doherty (Australian) and Rolf M Zinkernagel (Swiss) for discovering the signals that alert white blood cells to kill virus-infected cells
1997 Stanley Prusiner (American) for a theory on prions, a class of infectious proteins found in brain disorders
1998 Robert F Furchgott, Louis J Ignarro and Ferid Murad (American) for discoveries concerning nitric oxide as a signalling molecule in the cardiovascular system

Olympic Stadium in 1948 London.

Franklin Delano Roosevelt, president of the USA 1933–1945.

INTERNATIONAL SPORTS

Football, Grand Prix Racing and the Olympics are all truly international sports. The lists below show the countries and individuals that have been major players throughout the century.

WORLD CUP FINAL MATCHES

YEAR	LOCATION
1930	**Montevideo**

Uruguay 4/Argentina 2

1934	**Rome**

Italy 2/Czechoslovakia 1

1938	**Paris**

Italy 4/Hungary 2

1950	**Rio de Janeiro**

Uruguay 2/Brazil 1

1954	**Berne**

West Germany 3/Hungary 2

1958	**Stockholm**

Brazil 5/Sweden 2

1962	**Santiago**

Brazil 3/Czechoslovakia 1

1966	**London**

England 4/West Germany 2

1970	**Mexico City**

Brazil 4/Italy 1

1974	**Munich**

West Germany 2/Netherlands 1

1978	**Buenos Aires**

Argentina 3/Netherlands 1

1982	**Madrid**

Italy 3/West Germany 1

1986	**Mexico City**

Argentina 3/West Germany 2

1990	**Rome**

West Germany 1/Argentina 0

***1994**	**Pasadena**

Brazil 0/Italy 0

1998	**Paris**

France 3/Brazil 0

* Brazil won 3–2 on penalty kicks.

GRAND PRIX CHAMPIONS

YEAR	WORLD CHAMPION	NATIONALITY
1951	Juan Fangio	Argentina
1952	Alberto Ascari	Italy
1953	Alberto Ascar	Italy
1954	Juan Fangio	Argentina
1955	Juan Fangio	Argentina
1956	Juan Fangio	Argentina
1957	Juan Fangio	Argentina
1958	Mike Hawthorn	UK
1959	Jack Brabham	Australia
1960	Jack Brabham	Australia
1961	Phil Hill	USA
1962	Graham Hill	UK
1963	Jim Clark	UK
1964	John Surtees	UK
1965	Jim Clark	UK
1966	Jack Brabham	Australia
1967	Denis Hulme	NZ
1968	Graham Hill	UK
1969	Jackie Stewart	UK
1970	Jochen Rindt	Austria
1971	Jackie Stewart	UK
1972	Emerson Fittipaldi	Brazil
1973	Jackie Stewart	UK
1974	Emerson Fittipaldi	Brazil
1975	Niki Lauda	Austria
1976	James Hunt	UK
1977	Niki Lauda	Austria
1978	Mario Andretti	USA
1979	Jody Scheckter	South Africa
1980	Alan Jones	Australia
1981	Nelson Piquet	Brazil
1982	Keke Rosberg	Finland
1983	Nelson Piquet	Brazil
1984	Niki Lauda	Austria
1985	Alain Prost	France
1986	Alain Prost	France
1987	Nelson Piquet	Brazil
1988	Ayrton Senna	Brazil
1989	Alain Prost	France
1990	Ayrton Senna	Brazil
1991	Ayrton Senna	Brazil
1992	Nigel Mansell	UK
1993	Alain Prost	France
1994	Michael Schumacher	Germany
1995	Michael Schumacher	Germany
1996	Damon Hill	UK
1997	Jacques Villeneuve	Canada
1998	Mika Hakkinen	Finland

SITES OF THE OLYMPIC GAMES

1900 SUMMER Paris, France
WINTER *Not held*
1904 SUMMER St. Louis, USA
WINTER *Not held*
1908 SUMMER London, England
WINTER *Not held*
1912 SUMMER Stockholm, Sweden
WINTER *Not held*
1916 SUMMER *Not held*
WINTER *Not held*
1920 SUMMER Antwerp, Belgium
WINTER *Not held*
1924 SUMMER Paris, France
WINTER Chamonix, France
1928 SUMMER Amsterdam,
The Netherlands
WINTER St. Moritz, Switzerland
1932 SUMMER Los Angeles, USA
WINTER Lake Placid, USA
1936 SUMMER Berlin, Germany
WINTER Garmisch-Partenkirchen, Germany
1940 SUMMER *Not held*
WINTER *Not held*
1944 SUMMER *Not held*
WINTER *Not held*
1948 SUMMER London, England
WINTER St Moritz, Switzerland
1952 SUMMER Helsinki, Finland
WINTER Oslo, Norway
1956 SUMMER Melbourne, Australia
WINTER Cortina, Italy
1960 SUMMER Rome, Italy
WINTER Squaw Valley, USA
1964 SUMMER Tokyo, Japan
WINTER Innsbruck, Austria
1968 SUMMER Mexico City, Mexico
WINTER Grenoble, France
1972 SUMMER Munich, Germany
WINTER Sapporo, Japan
1976 SUMMER Montreal, Canada
WINTER Innsbruck, Austria
1980 SUMMER Moscow, Soviet Union
WINTER Lake Placid, USA
1984 SUMMER Los Angeles, USA
WINTER Sarajevo, Yugoslavia
1988 SUMMER Seoul, South Korea
WINTER Calgary, Canada
1992 SUMMER Barcelona, Spain
WINTER Albertville, France
1994 WINTER Lillehammer, Norway
1996 SUMMER Atlanta, USA
1998 WINTER Nagano, Japan
2000 SUMMER Sydney, Australia

LEADERS OF THE WEST

The president of the USA is not only leader of his own country but walks upon the world stage. Listed below are the men (and they have all been men so far) who have taken on the mantle of leadership of the Western world.

PRESIDENTS OF THE USA

1897–1901 President William McKinley *Republican*
1897–1899 Vice-President Garret A Hobart; 1901 Vice-President Theodore Roosevelt
1901–1909 President Theodore Roosevelt, *Republican*
1905–1909 Vice-President Charles W Fairbanks
1909–1913 President William Howard Taft, *Republican*
1909–1912 Vice-President James S Sherman
1913–1921 President Woodrow Wilson, *Democrat*
1913–1921 Vice-President Thomas R Marshall
1921–1923 President Warren Gamaliel Harding, *Republican*
1921–1923 Vice-President Calvin Coolidge
1923–1929 President Calvin Coolidge, *Republican*
1925–1929 Vice-President Charles G Dawes
1929–1933 President Herbert Clark Hoover, *Republican*
1929–1933 Vice-President Charles Curtis
1933–1945 President Franklin Delano Roosevelt, *Democrat*
1933–1941 Vice-President John N Garner; 1941–1945 Vice-President Henry A Wallace; 1945 Vice-President Harry S Truman
1945–1953 President Harry S Truman, *Democrat*
1949–1953 Vice-President Alben W Barkley
1953–1961 President Dwight David Eisenhower, *Republican*
1953–1961 Vice-President Richard M Nixon
1961–1963 President John Fitzgerald Kennedy, *Democrat*
1961–1963 Vice-President Lyndon Baines Johnson
1963–1969 President Lyndon Baines Johnson, *Democrat*
1965–1969 Vice-President Hubert H Humphrey
1969–1974 President Richard Milhous Nixon, *Republican*
1969–1973 Vice-President Spiro T Agnew; 1973–1974 Vice-President Gerald R Ford
1974–1977 President Gerald Rudolph Ford, *Republican*
1974–1977 Vice-President Nelson A Rockefeller
1977–1981 President Jimmy (James Earl) Carter, *Democrat*
1977–1981 Vice-President Walter F Mondale
1981–1989 President Ronald Reagan, *Republican*
1981–1989 Vice-President George Bush
1989–1993 President George Bush, *Republican*
1989–1993 Vice-President Dan Quayle
1993– President Bill Clinton, *Democrat*
1993– Vice-President Al Gore

Bill Clinton, elected for a second term in 1996, the president for the millennium.

ACKNOWLEDGEMENTS

The publishers would like to thank the following individuals and photographic organizations for their contributions:

Acme/The National Archives, Washington, DC
Allegheny Conference
Alyeska Pipeline Service Company
American Film Institute
American Telephone and Telegraph Company
Arabian American Oil Company
ARL Archive, USA
Bell Telephone Laboratory
Boeing Corporation
Brookhaven National Laboratory, USA
Bureau of Reclamation, USA
Carl Byoir and Associates
CBS
Centre of US-China Art Exchange
Communications Media US AID
Daytona International Speedway
Defense Advanced Research Project Agency, USA
Defense Department Photos (Marine Corps), USA
Department of Defense, USA
Department of Navy, USA
Du Pont Style News Service
Eastfoto
EPA Docuamerica/Charles O'Rear/Blair Pittman/Bob Smith/Bruce McAllister
Ezra Stroller Associates/TNA
Fairchild Camera and Instrument Corp
General Dynamics
George Bush Presidential Library

Heritage Picture Collection, UK
Hollywood Studios Photo
Howard Bingham
Howard Harrison
International News/TNA
IPS/TNA
J Baker Collection, UK
Jack M Judge
Laurence Lowry
Library of Congress, Washington DC, USA
Lick Observatory
Lockheed Corporation
Martin Luther King Memorial Library, Washington DC, USA
Maynard Lee/Cleveland Clinic Foundation
Metro Opera, Press Department
Mobile Oil Corporation
NASA
National Science Foundation, USA
NCAR Photo
New York Times Overseas Photo/TNA
Newsfeatures/TNA
North American Aviation Inc
Paramount Pictures
Pinto/TNA
Popperphoto/Reuter David Gray; Andrew Wong; Mark Baker; Dan Peled; Aladin Abdel Naby; Will Webster; Fabrizio Bensch; Danilo Krstanovic; Matko Biljak; HO/Vatican; Charles Platiau; Dylan Martinez; Paulo Whitaker; Andrew Wallace; Jim Bourg.
QA Photos/NMEC
Redwood Empire Association
Shell Oil

Smithsonian Institution
Sovfoto
Steven Spielberg/USIA
Tennessee Eastman Corp
Texas Highway Department
The Department of Energy, USA
The Domei News Photo Service
The Illustrated London News Picture Library
The National Archives (TNA), Washington DC, USA
Topham Picturepoint, UK
UNHCR/R Le Moyne; L Senigalliese; P Moumtzis; E Dagnino
United Nations
United States Army Photographic Agency
Universal Pictures
UPI/TNA
US Army Air Force
US Coast Guard
US Naval Photographic Center
US Navy
US Travel Service
USIA
USIS
USSR Academy of Science
Waldes-Kohinoor, Inc
Washington Star Photographic Collection, Washington Post by permission of the DC Public Library
White House, USA
Wide World/TNA
Woods Hole Oceanographic Institution
World Bank
World Health Organisation